...ysler ...l-size ...wheel drive ...tomotive ...pair ...nual

...y Warren
...nn H Haynes
...ild of Motoring Writers

Models covered:

All front wheel drive Chrysler LeBaron (1982 thru 1988), GTS, E Class, New Yorker (1982 thru 1988) Dodge 400, 600, Lancer and Plymouth Caravelle with 2.2, 2.5 and 2.6 liter engines (including fuel-injected and turbocharged models), 4-speed, 5-speed and automatic transaxles

1982 thru 1989

(5T4 – 1337)

ABCDE
FGHIJ

Haynes Publishing Group
Sparkford Nr Yeovil
Somerset BA22 7JJ England

Haynes North America, Inc
861 Lawrence Drive
Newbury Park
California 91320 USA

Acknowledgements
We are grateful for the help and cooperation of the Chrysler Corporation for their assistance with technical information, certain illustrations and vehicle photos, and the Champion Spark Plug Company who supplied the illustrations of various spark plug conditions.

A book in the **Haynes Automotive Repair Manual Series**

Printed in the USA

ISBN 1 85010 708 4

Library of Congress Catalog Card Number 90-82725

Contents

1986 Dodge Lancer

About this manual

Its purpose

The purpose of this manual is to help you get the best value from your vehicle. It can do so in several ways. It can help you decide what work must be done, even if you choose to have it done by a dealer service department or a repair shop; it provides information and procedures for routine maintenance and servicing; and it offers diagnostic and repair procedures to follow when trouble occurs.

It is hoped that you will use the manual to tackle the work yourself. For many simpler jobs, doing it yourself may be quicker than arranging an appointment to get the vehicle into a shop and making the trips to leave it and pick it up. More importantly, a lot of money can be saved by avoiding the expense the shop must pass on to you to cover its labor and overhead costs. An added benefit is the sense of satisfaction and accomplishment that you feel after having done the job yourself.

Using the manual

The manual is divided into Chapters. Each Chapter is divided into numbered Sections, which are headed in bold type between horizontal lines. Each Section consists of consecutively numbered paragraphs.

At the beginning of each numbered section you will be referred to any illustrations which apply to the procedures in that section. The reference numbers used in illustration captions pinpoint the pertinent Section and the Step within that section. That is, illustration 3.2 means the illustration refers to Section 3 and Step (or paragraph) 2 within that Section.

Procedures, once described in the text, are not normally repeated. When it is necessary to refer to another Chapter, the reference will be given as Chapter and Section number i.e. Chapter 1/16). Cross references given without use of the word ''Chapter'' apply to Sections and/or paragraphs in the same Chapter. For example, ''see Section 8'' means in the same Chapter.

Reference to the left or right side of the vehicle is based on the assumption that one is sitting in the driver's seat, facing forward.

Even though extreme care has been taken during the preparation of this manual, neither the publisher nor the author can accept responsibility for any errors in, or omissions from, the information given.

NOTE

A Note provides information necessary to properly complete a procedure or information which will make the steps to be followed easier to understand.

CAUTION

A Caution indicates a special procedure or special steps which must be taken in the course of completing the procedure in which the **Caution** is found which are necessary to avoid damage to the assembly being worked on.

WARNING

A Warning indicates a special procedure or special steps which must be taken in the course of completing the procedure in which the **Warning** is found which are necessary to avoid injury to the person performing the procedure.

Introduction to the Chrysler mid-size front wheel drive vehicles

The Chrysler mid-size front wheel drive vehicles, sold under Chrysler, Dodge and Plymouth nameplates, are based on the compact K-car chassis and drivetrain and share many components.

These models are available with transverse mounted, four-cylinder overhead cam engines made by Chrysler and Mitsubishi. These engines are available in three displacements — 2.2L, 2.5L (Chrysler) and 2.6L (Mitsubishi). The 2.2L engine is available in carbureted and fuel injected versions with turbocharging optional. The fuel injected 2.5L engine features counter-rotating balance shafts mounted below the crankshaft for smoother operation. The Mitsubishi engine is also equipped with balance shafts.

The engine drives the front wheels through either a four or five speed manual or a three speed automatic transaxle via equal length (turbocharged models only) or unequal length driveaxles. The rack and pinion steering gear is mounted behind the engine. The brakes are disc at the front and drum at the rear, with vacuum assist as standard equipment.

Available body styles include 2-door and 4-door sedans, station wagon, executive sedan (limousine) and convertible models.

Vehicle Identification Numbers

Modifications are a continuing and unpublicized process in vehicle manufacturing. Since spare parts manuals and lists are compiled on a numerical basis, the individual vehicle numbers are essential to correctly identify the component required.

Vehicle Identification Number (VIN)

This very important identification number is located on a plate attached to the top left corner of the dashboard of the vehicle. The VIN also appears on the Vehicle Certificate of Title and Registration. It contains valuable information such as where and when the vehicle was manufactured, the model year and the body style.

Body code plate

This metal plate is located on the left front inner fender, the wheel house or the top side of the radiator support. Like the VIN, it contains valuable information concerning the production of the vehicle as well as information about the way in which the vehicle is equipped. This plate is especially useful for matching the color and type of paint during repair work.

Engine Identification Number

The Engine Identification Number (EIN) on the 2.2 liter engine is stamped into the rear of the block, just above the bellhousing. On the 2.5 liter and 2.6 liter engines it is on the radiator side of the block, between the core plug and the rear of the block.

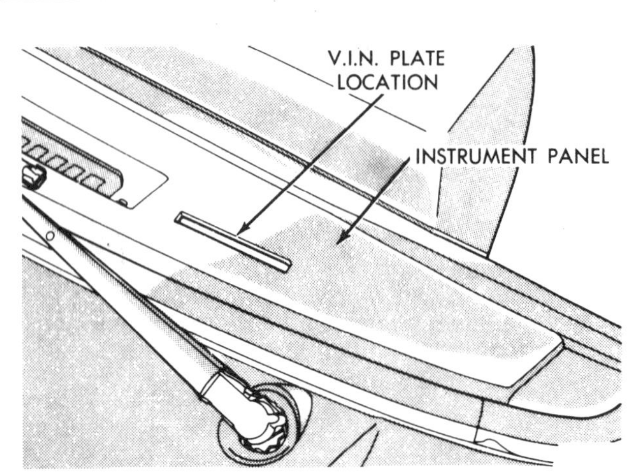

The Vehicle Identification Number (VIN) (arrow) is visible through the driver's side of the windshield

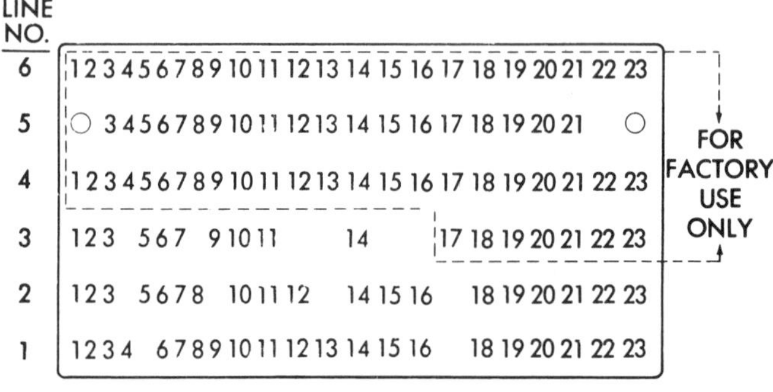

Typical body code plate

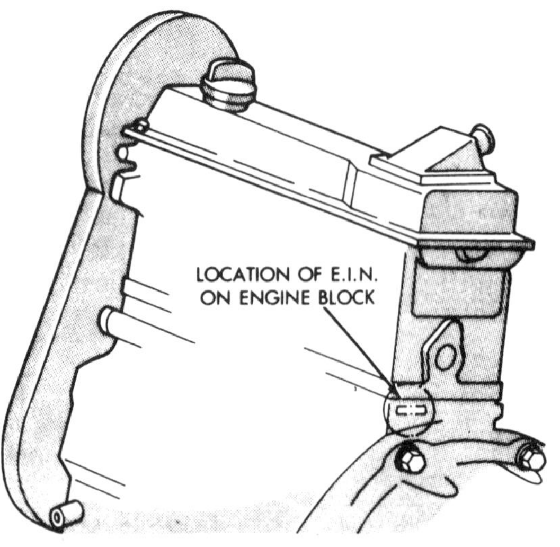

2.2L Engine Identification Number location

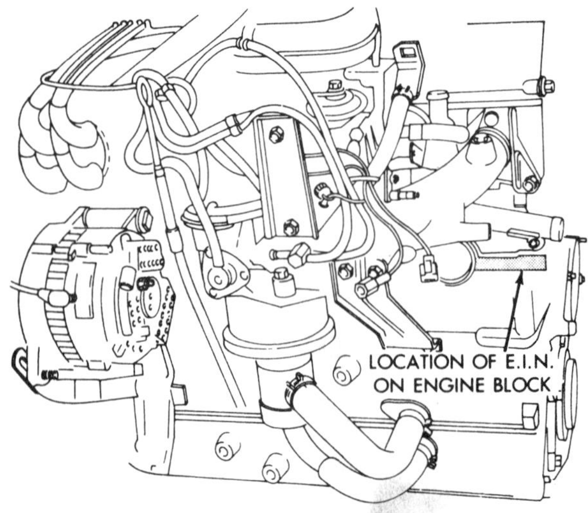

2.5L and 2.6L Engine Identification Number location

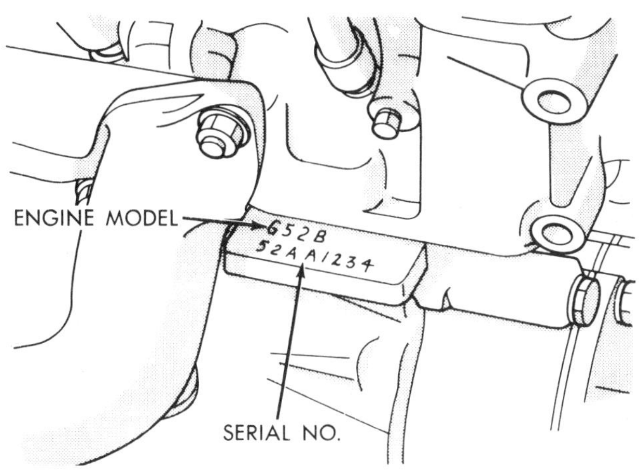

2.6L engine serial number location

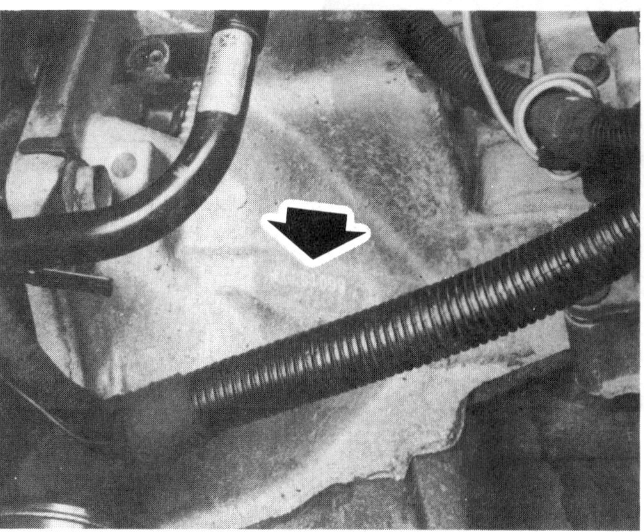

The transaxle identification number is stamped into the housing

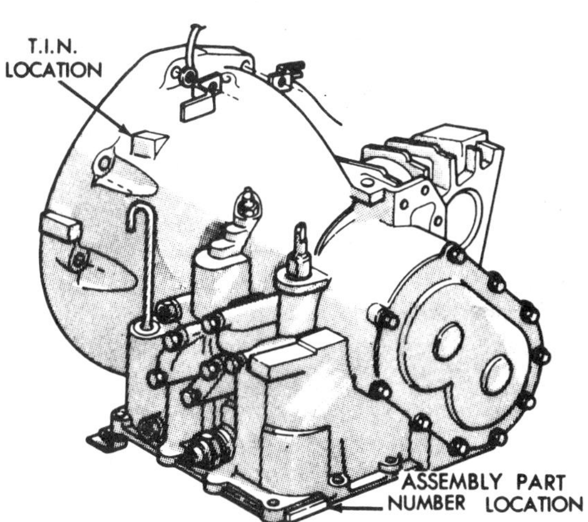

Automatic transaxle number locations

Engine serial number

In addition to the EIN, a serial number, which is required when buying replacement parts, is also used. On the 2.2 liter engine it is located just below the EIN on the block. On the 2.5 liter and 2.6 liter engines it is located on the right-front side of the engine block, adjacent to the exhaust manifold stud (dashboard side in vehicle).

Transaxle identification number

The transaxle identification number is stamped into the boss on the upper surface of the housing.

Transaxle serial number

The transaxle serial number, also called the assembly part number, is required when buying parts. On manual transaxles it is located on a metal tag attached to the front side of the transaxle. On automatics it is located on a pad just above the oil pan at the rear of the transaxle.

Vehicle Emissions Control Information label

The Emissions Control Information label is attached to the front edge of the hood, on the underside (see Chapter 6 for an illustration of the label and its location).

Buying parts

Replacement parts are available from many sources, which generally fall into one of two categories — authorized dealer parts departments and independent retail auto parts stores. Our advice concerning these parts is as follows:

Authorized dealer parts department: This is the best source for parts which are unique to your vehicle and not generally available elsewhere such as major engine parts, transaxle parts, trim pieces, etc. It is also the only place you should buy parts if your vehicle is still under warranty, as non-factory parts may invalidate the warranty. To be sure of obtaining the correct parts, have your engine and chassis numbers available and, if possible, take the old parts along for positive identification.

Retail auto parts stores: Good auto parts stores will stock frequently needed components which wear out relatively fast such as clutch components, exhaust systems, brake parts, tune-up parts, etc. These stores often supply new or reconditioned parts on an exchange basis, which can save a considerable amount of money. Discount auto parts stores are often very good places to buy materials and parts needed for general vehicle maintenance such as oil, grease, filters, spark plugs, belts, touch up paint, bulbs, etc. They also usually sell tools and general accessories, have convenient hours, charge lower prices, and can often be found not far from your home.

Maintenance techniques, tools and working facilities

Maintenance techniques

There are a number of techniques involved in maintenance and repair that will be referred to throughout this manual. Application of these techniques will enable the home mechanic to be more efficient, better organized and capable of performing the various tasks properly, which will ensure that the repair job is thorough and complete.

Fasteners

Fasteners are nuts, bolts, studs and screws used to hold two or more parts together. There are a few things to keep in mind when working with fasteners. Almost all of them use a locking device of some type, either a lockwasher, locknut, locking tab or thread adhesive. All threaded fasteners should be clean and straight, with undamaged threads and undamaged corners on the hex head where the wrench fits. Develop the habit of replacing all damaged nuts and bolts with new ones. Special locknuts with nylon or fiber inserts can only be used once. If they are removed, they lose their locking ability and must be replaced with new ones.

Rusted nuts and bolts should be treated with a penetrating fluid to ease removal and prevent breakage. Some mechanics use turpentine in a spout-type oil can, which works quite well. After applying the rust penetrant, let it work for a few minutes before trying to loosen the nut or bolt. Badly rusted fasteners may have to be chiseled or sawed off or removed with a special nut breaker, available at tool stores.

If a bolt or stud breaks off in an assembly, it can be drilled and removed with a special tool commonly available for this purpose. Most automotive machine shops can perform this task, as well as other repair procedures, such as the repair of threaded holes that have been stripped out.

Flat washers and lockwashers, when removed from an assembly, should always be replaced exactly as removed. Replace any damaged washers with new ones. Never use a lockwasher on any soft metal surface (such as aluminum), thin sheet metal or plastic.

Fastener sizes

For a number of reasons, automobile manufacturers are making wider and wider use of metric fasteners. Therefore, it is important to be able to tell the difference between standard (sometimes called U.S. or SAE) and metric hardware, since they cannot be interchanged.

All bolts, whether standard or metric, are sized according to diameter, thread pitch and length. For example, a standard 1/2 — 13 x 1 bolt is 1/2 inch in diameter, has 13 threads per inch and is 1 inch long. An M12 — 1.75 x 25 metric bolt is 12 mm in diameter, has a thread pitch of 1.75 mm (the distance between threads) and is 25 mm long. The two bolts are nearly identical, and easily confused, but they are not interchangeable.

In addition to the differences in diameter, thread pitch and length, metric and standard bolts can also be distinguished by examining the bolt heads. To begin with, the distance across the flats on a standard bolt head is measured in inches, while the same dimension on a metric bolt is sized in millimeters (the same is true for nuts). As a result, a standard wrench should not be used on a metric bolt and a metric wrench should not be used on a standard bolt. Also, most standard bolts have slashes radiating out from the center of the head to denote the grade or strength of the bolt, which is an indication of the amount of torque that can be applied to it. The greater the number of slashes, the greater the strength of the bolt. Grades 0 through 5 are commonly used on automobiles. Metric bolts have a property class (grade) number, rather than a slash, molded into their heads to indicate bolt strength. In this case, the higher the number, the stronger the bolt. Property class numbers 8.8, 9.8 and 10.9 are commonly used on automobiles.

Strength markings can also be used to distinguish standard hex nuts from metric hex nuts. Many standard nuts have dots stamped into one side, while metric nuts are marked with a number. The greater the number of dots, or the higher the number, the greater the strength of the nut.

Metric studs are also marked on their ends according to property class (grade). Larger studs are numbered (the same as metric bolts),

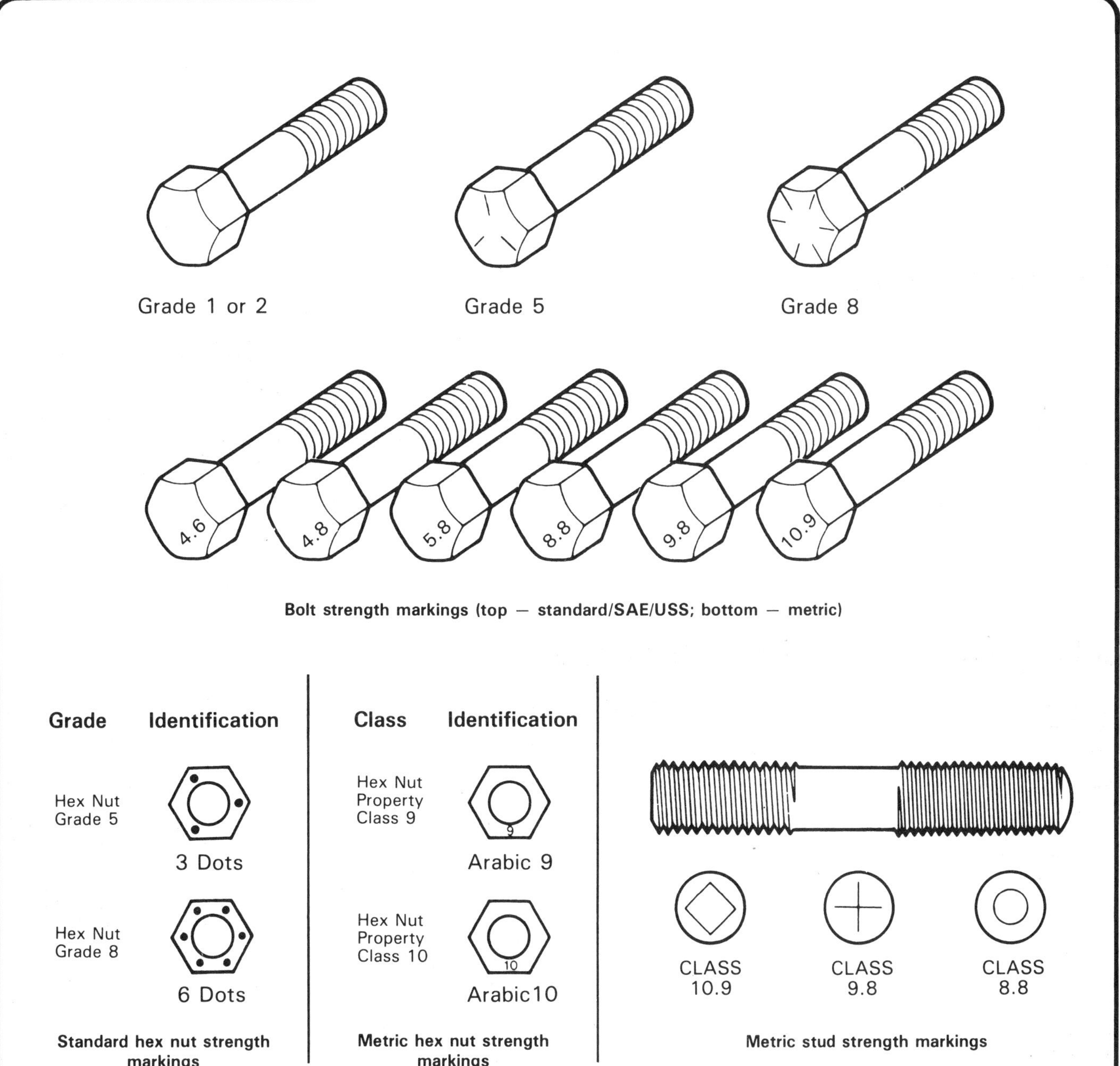

Bolt strength markings (top — standard/SAE/USS; bottom — metric)

Standard hex nut strength markings

Metric hex nut strength markings

Metric stud strength markings

while smaller studs carry a geometric code to denote grade.

It should be noted that many fasteners, especially Grades 0 through 2, have no distinguishing marks on them. When such is the case, the only way to determine whether it is standard or metric is to measure the thread pitch or compare it to a known fastener of the same size.

Standard fasteners are often referred to as SAE, as opposed to metric. However, it should be noted that SAE technically refers to a non-metric *fine thread* fastener only. Coarse thread non-metric fasteners are referred to as USS sizes.

Since fasteners of the same size (both standard and metric) may have different strength ratings, be sure to reinstall any bolts, studs or nuts removed from your vehicle in their original locations. Also, when replacing a fastener with a new one, make sure that the new one has a strength rating equal to or greater than the original.

Tightening sequences and procedures

Most threaded fasteners should be tightened to a specific torque value (torque is the twisting force applied to a threaded component such as a nut or bolt). Overtightening the fastener can weaken it and cause it to break, while undertightening can cause it to eventually come loose. Bolts, screws and studs, depending on the material they are made of and their thread diameters, have specific torque values, many of which are noted in the Specifications at the beginning of each Chapter. Be sure to follow the torque recommendations closely. For fasteners not assigned a specific torque, a general torque value chart is presented here as a guide. These torque values are for dry (unlubricated) fasteners threaded into steel or cast iron (not aluminum). As was previously mentioned, the size and grade of a fastener determine the amount of torque that can safely be applied to it. The figures listed here are approximate

Metric thread sizes	**Ft-lb**	**Nm/m**
M-6	6 to 9	9 to 12
M-8	14 to 21	19 to 28
M-10	28 to 40	38 to 54
M-12	50 to 71	68 to 96
M-14	80 to 140	109 to 154
Pipe thread sizes		
1/8	5 to 8	7 to 10
1/4	12 to 18	17 to 24
3/8	22 to 33	30 to 44
1/2	25 to 35	34 to 47
U.S. thread sizes		
1/4 – 20	6 to 9	9 to 12
5/16 – 18	12 to 18	17 to 24
5/16 – 24	14 to 20	19 to 27
3/8 – 16	22 to 32	30 to 43
3/8 – 24	27 to 38	37 to 51
7/16 – 14	40 to 55	55 to 74
7/16 – 20	40 to 60	55 to 81
1/2 – 13	55 to 80	75 to 108

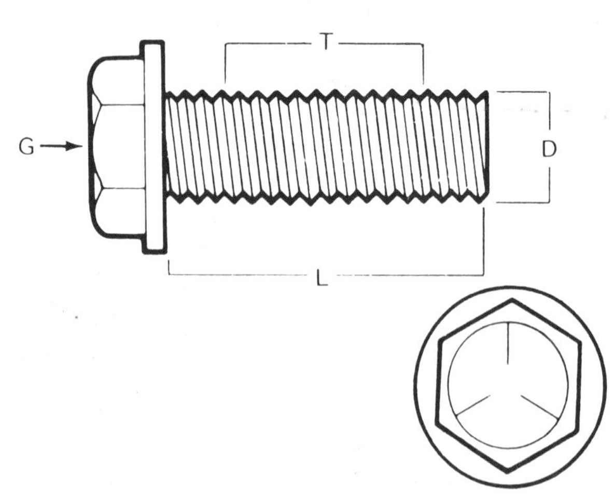

Standard (SAE and USS) bolt dimensions/grade marks

G Grade marks (bolt strength)
L Length (in inches)
T Thread pitch (number of threads per inch)
D Nominal diameter (in inches)

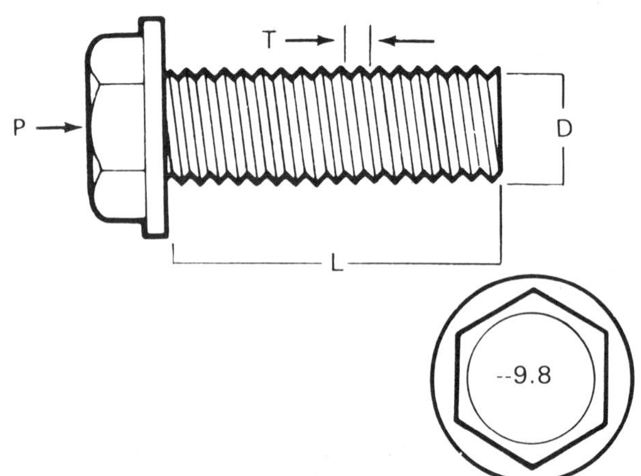

Metric bolt dimensions/grade marks

P Property class (bolt strength)
L Length (in millimeters)
T Thread pitch (distance between threads in millimeters)
D Diameter

for Grade 2 and Grade 3 fasteners. Higher grades can tolerate higher torque values.

Fasteners laid out in a pattern, such as cylinder head bolts, oil pan bolts, differential cover bolts, etc., must be loosened or tightened in sequence to avoid warping the component. This sequence will normally be shown in the appropriate Chapter. If a specific pattern is not given, the following procedures can be used to prevent warping.

Initially, the bolts or nuts should be assembled finger-tight only. Next, they should be tightened one full turn each, in a criss-cross or diagonal pattern. After each one has been tightened one full turn, return to the first one and tighten them all one-half turn, following the same pattern. Finally, tighten each of them one-quarter turn at a time until each fastener has been tightened to the proper torque. To loosen and remove the fasteners, the procedure would be reversed.

Component disassembly

Component disassembly should be done with care and purpose to help ensure that the parts go back together properly. Always keep track of the sequence in which parts are removed. Make note of special characteristics or marks on parts that can be installed more than one way, such as a grooved thrust washer on a shaft. It is a good idea to lay the disassembled parts out on a clean surface in the order that they were removed. It may also be helpful to make sketches or take instant photos of components before removal.

When removing fasteners from a component, keep track of their locations. Sometimes threading a bolt back in a part, or putting the washers and nut back on a stud, can prevent mix-ups later. If nuts and bolts cannot be returned to their original locations, they should be kept in a compartmented box or a series of small boxes. A cupcake or muffin tin is ideal for this purpose, since each cavity can hold the bolts and nuts from a particular area (i.e. oil pan bolts, valve cover bolts, engine mount bolts, etc.). A pan of this type is especially helpful when working on assemblies with very small parts, such as the carburetor, alternator, valve train or interior dash and trim pieces. The cavities can be marked with paint or tape to identify the contents.

Whenever wiring looms, harnesses or connectors are separated, it is a good idea to identify the two halves with numbered pieces of masking tape so they can be easily reconnected.

Gasket sealing surfaces

Throughout any vehicle, gaskets are used to seal the mating surfaces between two parts and keep lubricants, fluids, vacuum or pressure contained in an assembly.

Many times these gaskets are coated with a liquid or paste-type gasket sealing compound before assembly. Age, heat and pressure can sometimes cause the two parts to stick together so tightly that they are very difficult to separate. Often, the assembly can be loosened by striking it with a soft-face hammer near the mating surfaces. A regular hammer can be used if a block of wood is placed between the hammer and the part. Do not hammer on cast parts or parts that could be easily damaged. With any particularly stubborn part, always recheck to make sure that every fastener has been removed.

Avoid using a screwdriver or bar to pry apart an assembly, as they can easily mar the gasket sealing surfaces of the parts, which must remain smooth. If prying is absolutely necessary, use an old broom handle, but keep in mind that extra clean up will be necessary if the wood splinters.

After the parts are separated, the old gasket must be carefully scraped off and the gasket surfaces cleaned. Stubborn gasket material can be soaked with rust penetrant or treated with a special chemical to soften it so it can be easily scraped off. A scraper can be fashioned from a piece of copper tubing by flattening and sharpening one end. Copper is recommended because it is usually softer than the surfaces to be scraped, which reduces the chance of gouging the part. Some gaskets can be removed with a wire brush, but regardless of the method used, the mating surfaces must be left clean and smooth. If for some reason the gasket surface is gouged, then a gasket sealer thick enough to fill scratches will have to be used during reassembly of the components. For most applications, a non-drying (or semi-drying) gasket sealer should be used.

Hose removal tips

Warning: *If the vehicle is equipped with air conditioning, do not disconnect any of the A/C hoses without first having the system depressurized by a dealer service department or an air conditioning specialist.*

Hose removal precautions closely parallel gasket removal precautions. Avoid scratching or gouging the surface that the hose mates against or the connection may leak. This is especially true for radiator hoses. Because of various chemical reactions, the rubber in hoses can bond itself to the metal spigot that the hose fits over. To remove a hose, first loosen the hose clamps that secure it to the spigot. Then, with slip-joint pliers, grab the hose at the clamp and rotate it around the spigot. Work it back and forth until it is completely free, then pull it off. Silicone or other lubricants will ease removal if they can be applied between the hose and the outside of the spigot. Apply the same lubricant to the inside of the hose and the outside of the spigot to simplify installation.

As a last resort (and if the hose is to be replaced with a new one anyway), the rubber can be slit with a knife and the hose peeled from the spigot. If this must be done, be careful that the metal connection is not damaged.

If a hose clamp is broken or damaged, do not reuse it. Wire-type clamps usually weaken with age, so it is a good idea to replace them with screw-type clamps whenever a hose is removed.

Tools

A selection of good tools is a basic requirement for anyone who plans to maintain and repair his or her own vehicle. For the owner who has few tools, the initial investment might seem high, but when compared to the spiraling costs of professional auto maintenance and repair, it is a wise one.

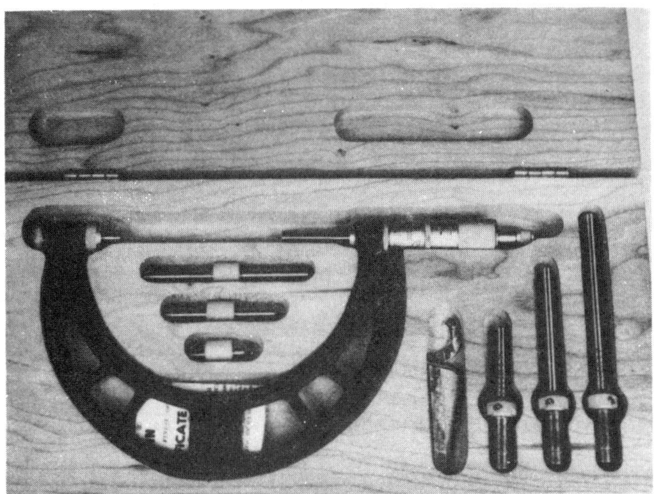

Micrometer set

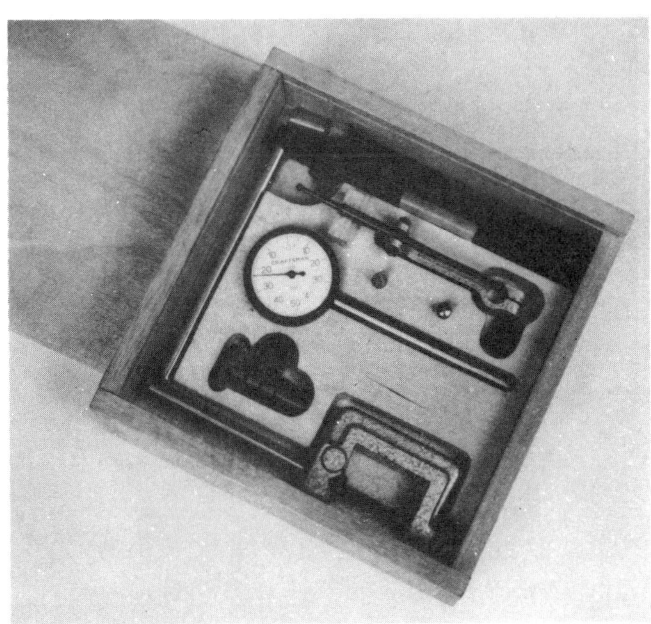

Dial indicator set

Dial caliper

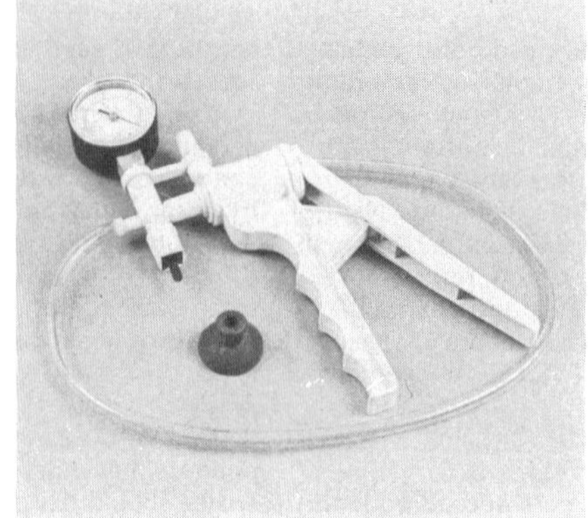

Hand-operated vacuum pump

Timing light

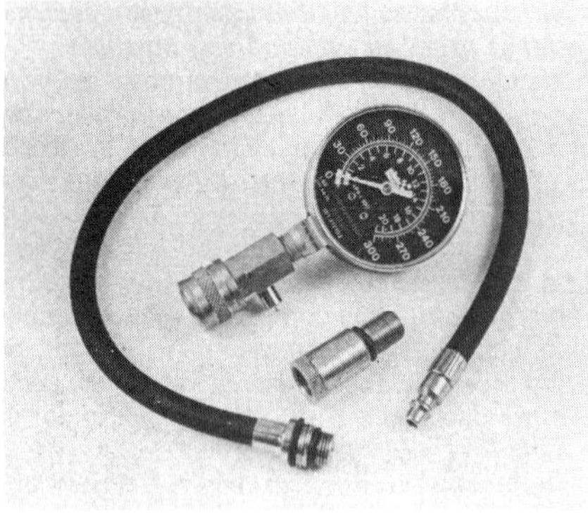

Compression gauge with spark plug hole adapter

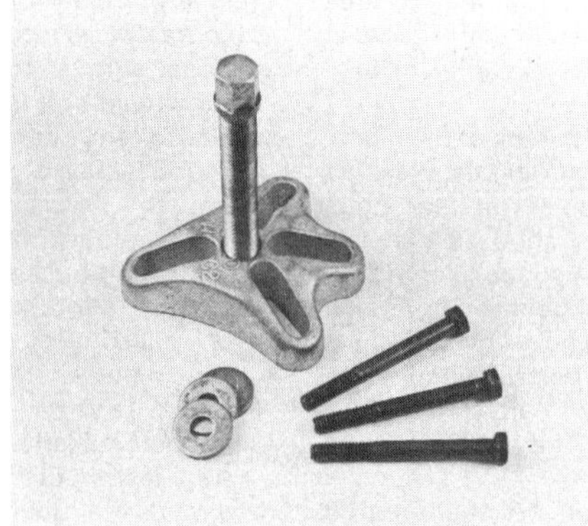

Damper/steering wheel puller

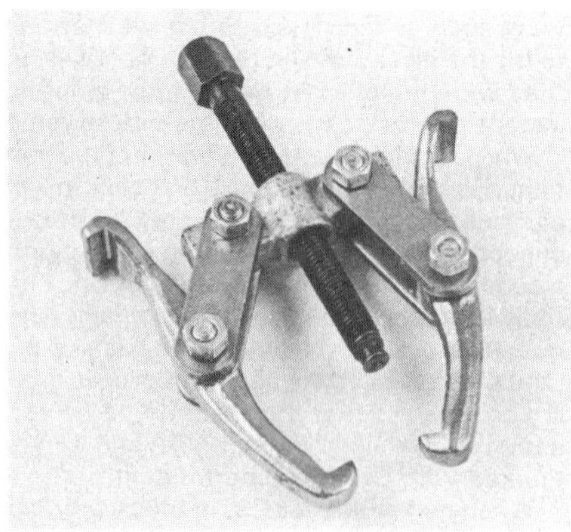

General purpose puller

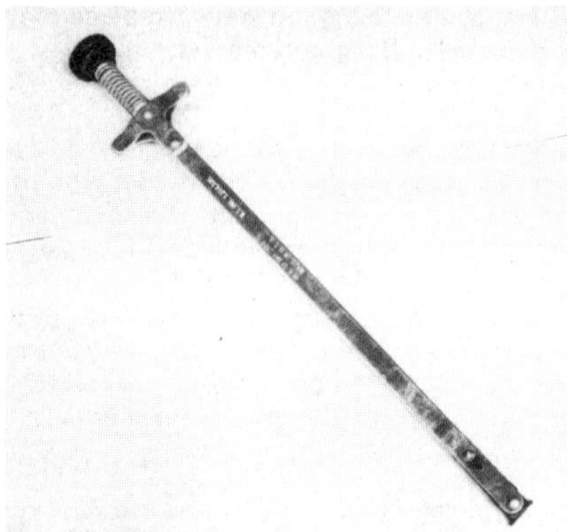

Hydraulic lifter removal tool

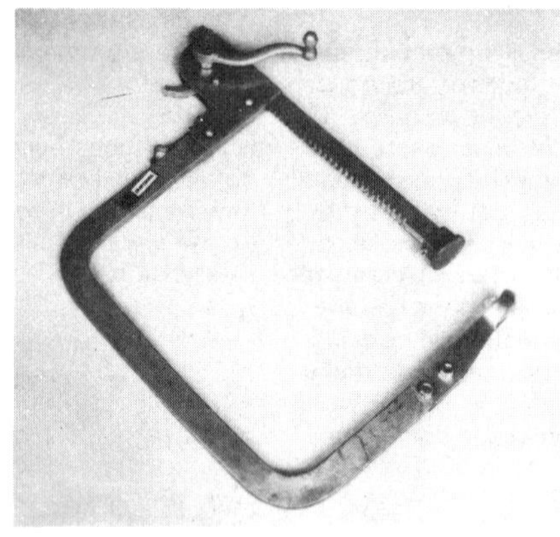

Valve spring compressor

Valve spring compressor

Ridge reamer

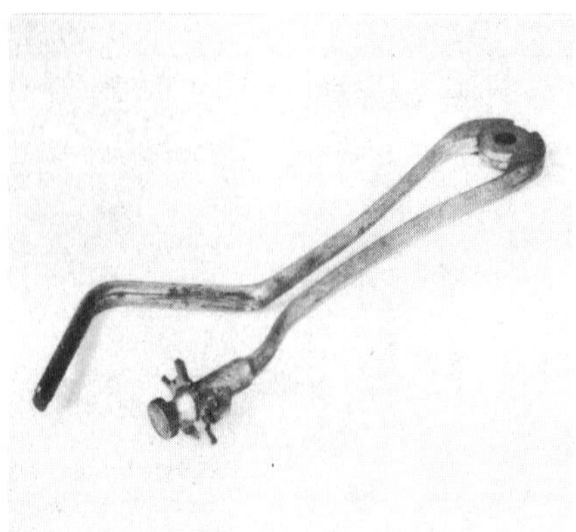

Piston ring groove cleaning tool

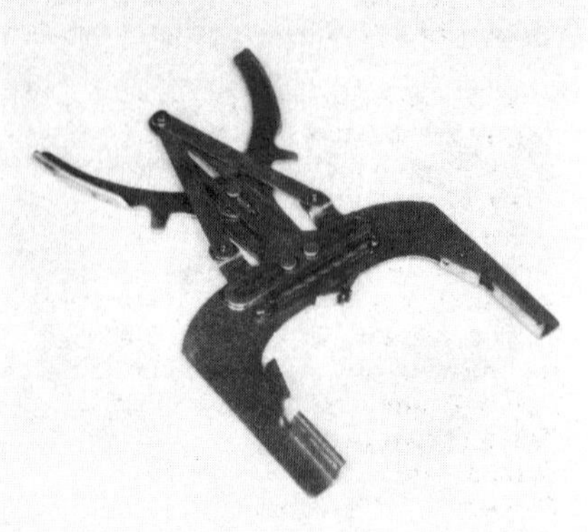

Ring removal/installation tool

Ring compressor

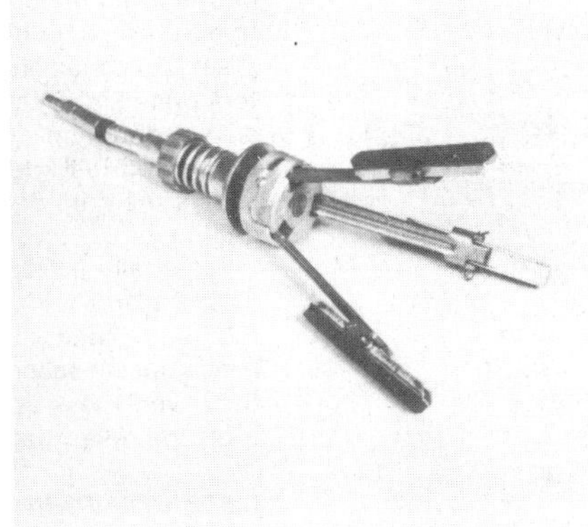
Cylinder hone

Brake hold-down spring tool

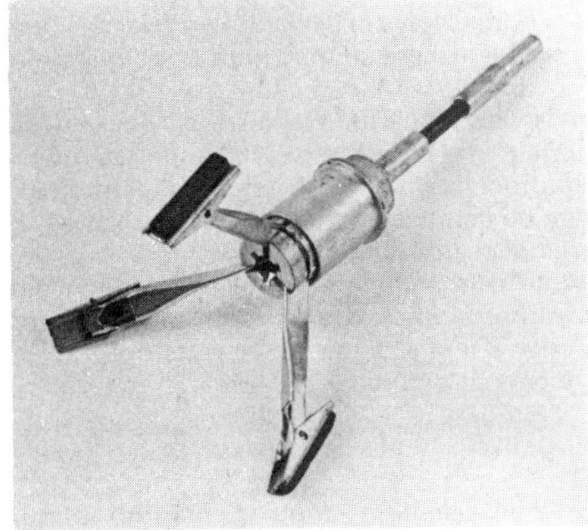
Brake cylinder hone

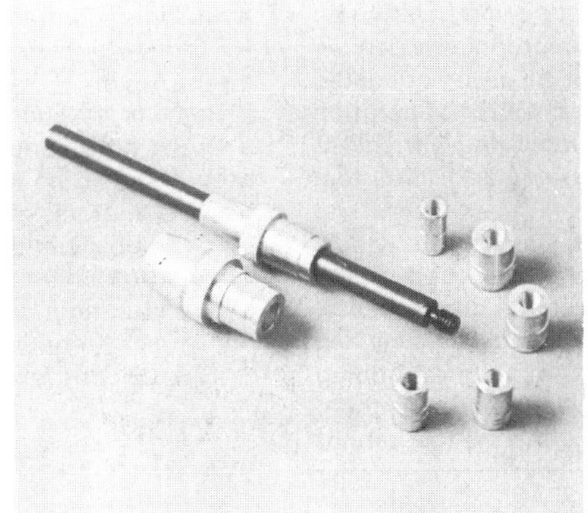
Clutch plate alignment tool

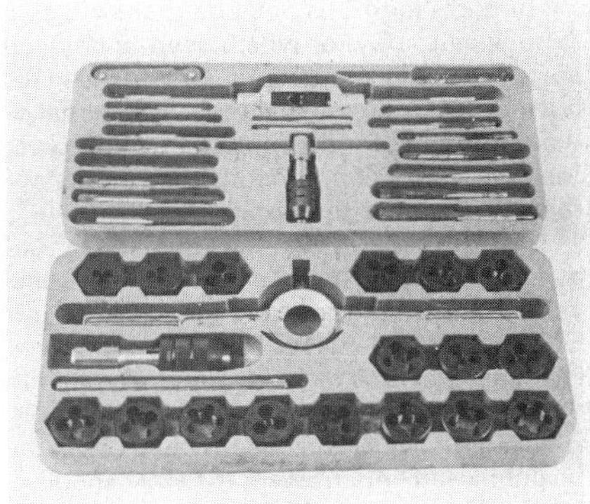
Tap and die set

To help the owner decide which tools are needed to perform the tasks detailed in this manual, the following tool lists are offered: *Maintenance and minor repair, Repair/overhaul* and *Special*.

The newcomer to practical mechanics should start off with the maintenance and minor repair tool kit, which is adequate for the simpler jobs performed on a vehicle. Then, as confidence and experience grow, the owner can tackle more difficult tasks, buying additional tools as they are needed. Eventually the basic kit will be expanded into the repair and overhaul tool set. Over a period of time, the experienced do-it-yourselfer will assemble a tool set complete enough for most repair and overhaul procedures and will add tools from the special category when it is felt that the expense is justified by the frequency of use.

Maintenance and minor repair tool kit

The tools in this list should be considered the minimum required for performance of routine maintenance, servicing and minor repair work. We recommend the purchase of combination wrenches (box-end and open-end combined in one wrench). While more expensive than open end wrenches, they offer the advantages of both types of wrench.

Combination wrench set (1/4-inch to 1 inch or 6 mm to 19 mm)
Adjustable wrench, 8 inch
Spark plug wrench with rubber insert
Spark plug gap adjusting tool
Feeler gauge set
Brake bleeder wrench
Standard screwdriver (5/16-inch x 6 inch)
Phillips screwdriver (No. 2 x 6 inch)
Combination pliers — 6 inch
Hacksaw and assortment of blades
Tire pressure gauge
Grease gun
Oil can
Fine emery cloth
Wire brush
Battery post and cable cleaning tool
Oil filter wrench
Funnel (medium size)
Safety goggles
Jackstands (2)
Drain pan

Note: *If basic tune-ups are going to be part of routine maintenance, it will be necessary to purchase a good quality stroboscopic timing light and combination tachometer/dwell meter. Although they are included in the list of special tools, it is mentioned here because they are absolutely necessary for tuning most vehicles properly.*

Repair and overhaul tool set

These tools are essential for anyone who plans to perform major repairs and are in addition to those in the maintenance and minor repair tool kit. Included is a comprehensive set of sockets which, though expensive, are invaluable because of their versatility, especially when various extensions and drives are available. We recommend the 1/2-inch drive over the 3/8-inch drive. Although the larger drive is bulky and more expensive, it has the capacity of accepting a very wide range of large sockets. Ideally, however, the mechanic should have a 3/8-inch drive set and a 1/2-inch drive set.

Socket set(s)
Reversible ratchet
Extension — 10 inch
Universal joint
Torque wrench (same size drive as sockets)
Ball peen hammer — 8 ounce
Soft-face hammer (plastic/rubber)
Standard screwdriver (1/4-inch x 6 inch)
Standard screwdriver (stubby — 5/16-inch)
Phillips screwdriver (No. 3 x 8 inch)
Phillips screwdriver (stubby — No. 2)

Pliers — vise grip
Pliers — lineman's
Pliers — needle nose
Pliers — snap-ring (internal and external)
Cold chisel — 1/2-inch
Scribe
Scraper (made from flattened copper tubing)
Centerpunch
Pin punches (1/16, 1/8, 3/16-inch)
Steel rule/straightedge — 12 inch
Allen wrench set (1/8 to 3/8-inch or 4 mm to 10 mm)
A selection of files
Wire brush (large)
Jackstands (second set)
Jack (scissor or hydraulic type)

Note: *Another tool which is often useful is an electric drill motor with a chuck capacity of 3/8-inch and a set of good quality drill bits.*

Special tools

The tools in this list include those which are not used regularly, are expensive to buy, or which need to be used in accordance with their manufacturer's instructions. Unless these tools will be used frequently, it is not very economical to purchase many of them. A consideration would be to split the cost and use between yourself and a friend or friends. In addition, most of these tools can be obtained from a tool rental shop on a temporary basis.

This list primarily contains only those tools and instruments widely available to the public, and not those special tools produced by the vehicle manufacturer for distribution to dealer service departments. Occasionally, references to the manufacturer's special tools are inluded in the text of this manual. Generally, an alternative method of doing the job without the special tool is offered. However, sometimes there is no alternative to their use. Where this is the case, and the tool cannot be purchased or borrowed, the work should be turned over to the dealer service department or an automotive repair shop.

Valve spring compressor
Piston ring groove cleaning tool
Piston ring compressor
Piston ring installation tool
Cylinder compression gauge
Cylinder ridge reamer
Cylinder surfacing hone
Cylinder bore gauge
Micrometers and/or dial calipers
Hydraulic lifter removal tool
Balljoint separator
Universal-type puller
Impact screwdriver
Dial indicator set
Stroboscopic timing light (inductive pick-up)
Hand operated vacuum/pressure pump
Tachometer/dwell meter
Universal electrical multimeter
Cable hoist
Brake spring removal and installation tools
Floor jack

Buying tools

For the do-it-yourselfer who is just starting to get involved in vehicle maintenance and repair, there are a number of options available when purchasing tools. If maintenance and minor repair is the extent of the work to be done, the purchase of individual tools is satisfactory. If, on the other hand, extensive work is planned, it would be a good idea to purchase a modest tool set from one of the large retail chain stores. A set can usually be bought at a substantial savings over the individual tool prices, and they often come with a tool box. As additional tools are needed, add-on sets, individual tools and a larger tool box can be purchased to expand the tool selection. Building a tool set gradually allows the cost of the tools to be spread over a longer period of time and gives the mechanic the freedom to choose only those tools that will actually be used.

Tool stores will often be the only source of some of the special tools that are needed, but regardless of where tools are bought, try to avoid cheap ones, especially when buying screwdrivers and sockets, because they won't last very long. The expense involved in replacing cheap tools will eventually be greater than the initial cost of quality tools.

Care and maintenance of tools

Good tools are expensive, so it makes sense to treat them with respect. Keep them clean and in usable condition and store them properly when not in use. Always wipe off any dirt, grease or metal chips before putting them away. Never leave tools lying around in the work area. Upon completion of a job, always check closely under the hood for tools that may have been left there so they won't get lost during a test drive.

Some tools, such as screwdrivers, pliers, wrenches and sockets, can be hung on a panel mounted on the garage or workshop wall, while others should be kept in a tool box or tray. Measuring instruments, gauges, meters, etc. must be carefully stored where they cannot be damaged by weather or impact from other tools.

When tools are used with care and stored properly, they will last a very long time. Even with the best of care, though, tools will wear out if used frequently. When a tool is damaged or worn out, replace it. Subsequent jobs will be safer and more enjoyable if you do.

Working facilities

Not to be overlooked when discussing tools is the workshop. If anything more than routine maintenance is to be carried out, some sort of suitable work area is essential.

It is understood, and appreciated, that many home mechanics do not have a good workshop or garage available, and end up removing an engine or doing major repairs outside. It is recommended, however, that the overhaul or repair be completed under the cover of a roof.

A clean, flat workbench or table of comfortable working height is an absolute necessity. The workbench should be equipped with a vise that has a jaw opening of at least four inches.

As mentioned previously, some clean, dry storage space is also required for tools, as well as the lubricants, fluids, cleaning solvents, etc. which will soon become necessary.

Sometimes waste oil and fluids, drained from the engine or cooling system during normal maintenance or repairs, present a disposal problem. To avoid pouring them on the ground or into a sewage system, pour the used fluids into large containers, seal them with caps and take them to an authorized disposal site or recycling center. Plastic jugs, such as old antifreeze containers, are ideal for this purpose.

Always keep a supply of old newspapers and clean rags available. Old towels are excellent for mopping up spills. Many mechanics use rolls of paper towels for most work because they are readily available and disposable. To help keep the area under the vehicle clean, a large cardboard box can be cut open and flattened to protect the garage or shop floor.

Whenever working over a painted surface, such as when leaning over a fender to service something under the hood, always cover it with an old blanket or bedspread to protect the finish. Vinyl covered pads, made especially for this purpose, are available at auto parts stores.

Booster battery (jump) starting

Certain precautions must be observed when using a booster battery to jump start a vehicle.

a) Before connecting the booster battery, make sure that the ignition switch is in the Off position.
b) Turn off the lights, heater and other electrical loads.
c) The eyes should be shielded. Safety goggles are a good idea.
d) Make sure the booster battery is the same voltage as the dead one in the vehicle.
e) The two vehicles must not touch each other.
f) Make sure the transaxle is in Neutral (manual transaxle) or Park (automatic transaxle).
g) If the booster battery is not a maintenance-free type, remove the vent caps and lay a cloth over the vent holes.

Connect the red jumper cable to the *positive* (+) terminals of each battery.

Connect one end of the black jumper cable to the *negative* (–) terminal of the booster battery. The other end of this cable should be connected to a good ground on the vehicle to be started, such as a bolt or bracket on the engine block. Use caution to insure that the cable will not come into contact with the fan, drivebelts or other moving parts of the engine.

Start the engine using the booster battery, then, with the engine running at idle speed, disconnect the jumper cables in the reverse order of connection.

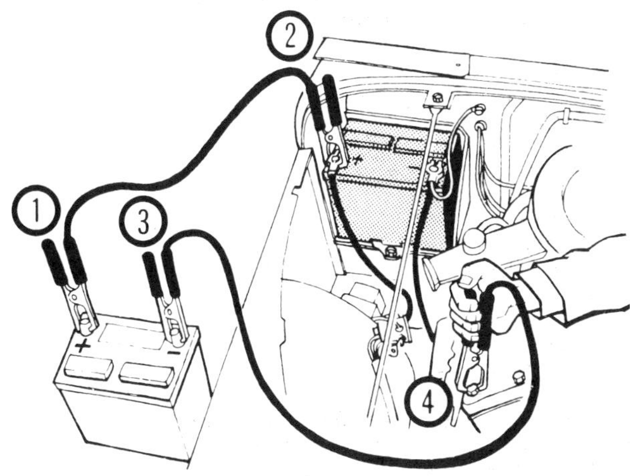

Make the booster battery cable connections in the numerical order shown (note that the negative cable of the booster battery is not attached to the negative terminal of the dead battery)

Jacking and towing

Jacking

The jack supplied with the vehicle should only be used for raising the vehicle when changing a tire or placing jackstands under the frame. **Warning:** *Never work under the vehicle or start the engine while this jack is being used as the only means of support.*

The vehicle should be on level ground with the wheels blocked and the transaxle in Park (automatic) or Reverse (manual). If the tire is to be changed, pry off the hub cap (if equipped) using the tapered end of the lug wrench. If the wheel is being replaced, loosen the wheel nuts one-half turn and leave them in place until the wheel is raised off the ground.

Place the jack under the side of the vehicle in the indicated position and raise it until the jack head hole fits over the rocker flange jack locator pin. Operate the jack with a slow, smooth motion until the wheel is raised off the ground. Refer to Chapter 10 for information related to removing and installing the tire.

Lower the vehicle, remove the jack and tighten the nuts (if loosened or removed) in a criss-cross pattern by turning the wrench clockwise. Replace the hub cap (if equipped) by placing it in position and using the heel of your hand or a rubber mallet to seat it.

Towing

Vehicles with an automatic transaxle can be towed with all four wheels on the ground, provided that speeds do not exceed 25 mph and the distance is not over 15 miles, otherwise transaxle damage can result. Vehicles with a manual transaxle can be towed at legal highway speeds for any distance. If the vehicle has a damaged transaxle, tow it only with the front wheels off the ground.

Towing equipment specifically designed for this purpose should be used and should be attached to the main structural members of the vehicle, not the bumper or brackets.

Safety is a major consideration when towing and all applicable state and local laws must be obeyed. A safety chain system must be used for all towing.

While towing, the parking brake should be released and the transmission must be in Neutral. The steering must be unlocked (ignition switch in the Off position). Remember that power steering and power brakes will not work with the engine off.

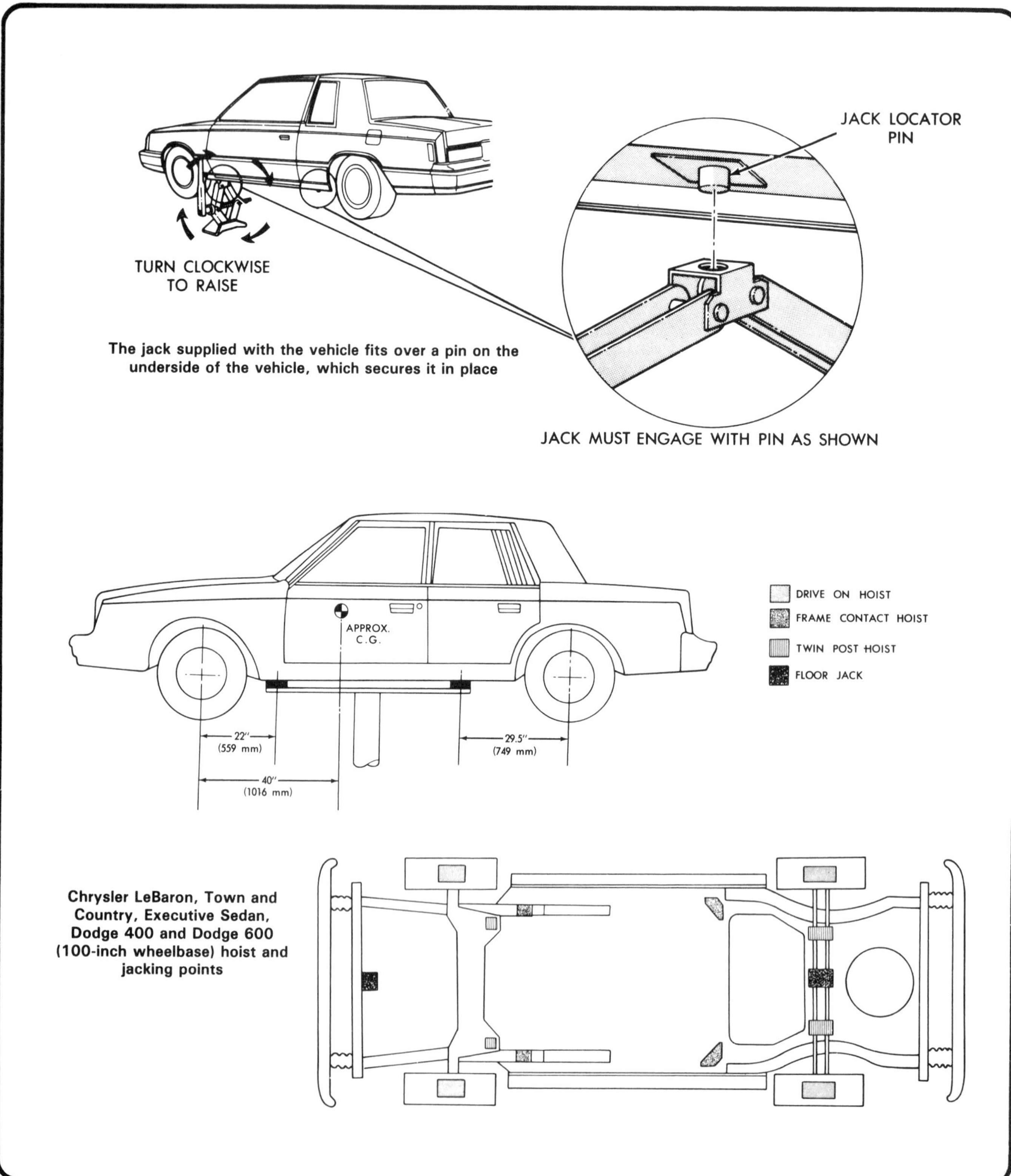

The jack supplied with the vehicle fits over a pin on the underside of the vehicle, which secures it in place

Chrysler LeBaron, Town and Country, Executive Sedan, Dodge 400 and Dodge 600 (100-inch wheelbase) hoist and jacking points

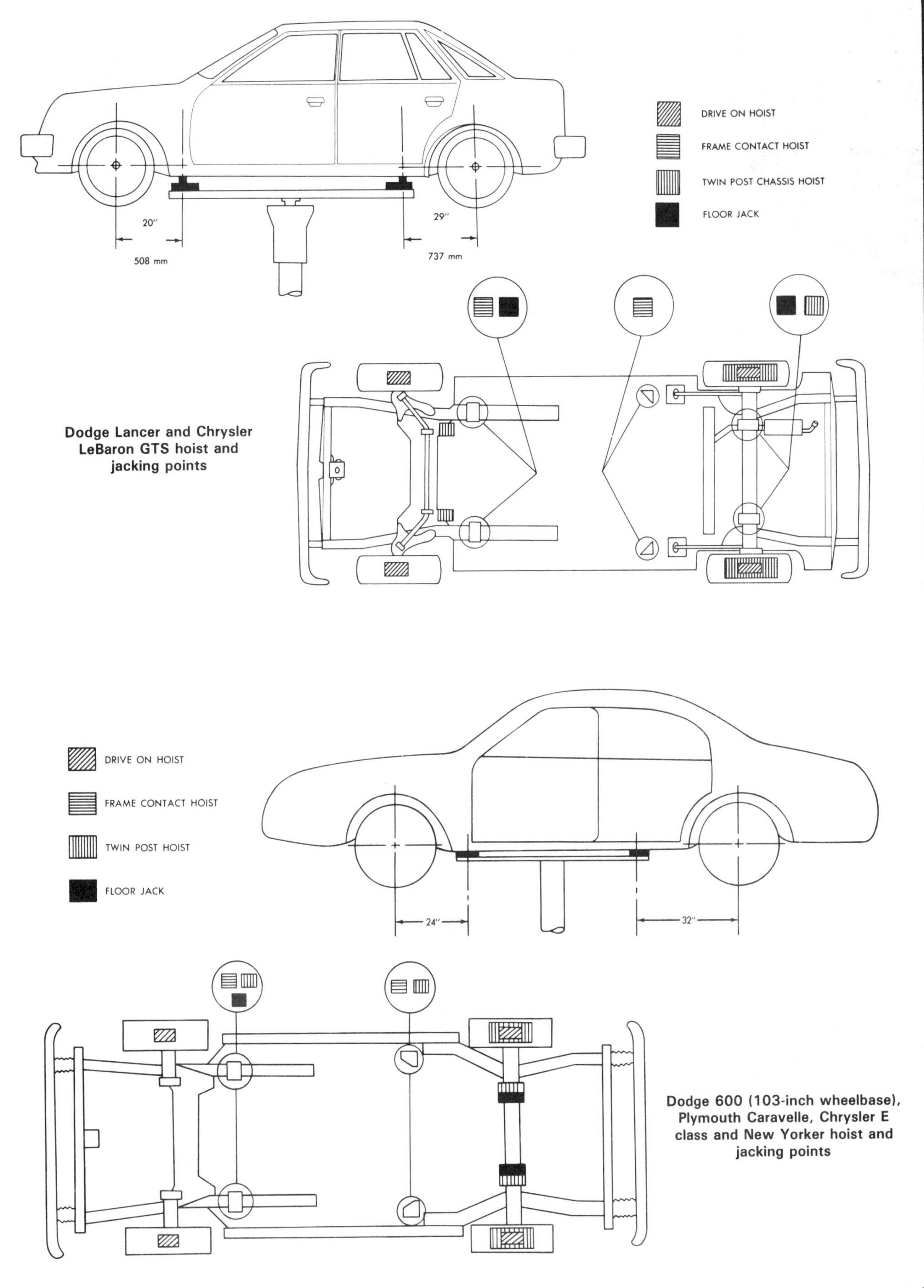

Dodge Lancer and Chrysler LeBaron GTS hoist and jacking points

Dodge 600 (103-inch wheelbase), Plymouth Caravelle, Chrysler E class and New Yorker hoist and jacking points

Safety first!

Regardless of how enthusiastic you may be about getting on with the job at hand, take the time to ensure that your safety is not jeopardized. A moment's lack of attention can result in an accident, as can failure to observe certain simple safety precautions. The possibility of an accident will always exist, and the following points should not be considered a comprehensive list of all dangers. Rather, they are intended to make you aware of the risks and to encourage a safety conscious approach to all work you carry out on your vehicle.

Essential DOs and DON'Ts

DON'T rely on a jack when working under the vehicle. Always use approved jackstands to support the weight of the vehicle and place them under the recommended lift or support points.
DON'T attempt to loosen extremely tight fasteners (i.e. wheel lug nuts) while the vehicle is on a jack — it may fall.
DON'T start the engine without first making sure that the transmission is in Neutral (or Park where applicable) and the parking brake is set.
DON'T remove the radiator cap from a hot cooling system — let it cool or cover it with a cloth and release the pressure gradually.
DON'T attempt to drain the engine oil until you are sure it has cooled to the point that it will not burn you.
DON'T touch any part of the engine or exhaust system until it has cooled sufficiently to avoid burns.
DON'T siphon toxic liquids such as gasoline, antifreeze and brake fluid by mouth, or allow them to remain on your skin.
DON'T inhale brake lining dust — it is potentially hazardous (see *Asbestos* below)
DON'T allow spilled oil or grease to remain on the floor — wipe it up before someone slips on it.
DON'T use loose fitting wrenches or other tools which may slip and cause injury.
DON'T push on wrenches when loosening or tightening nuts or bolts. Always try to pull the wrench toward you. If the situation calls for pushing the wrench away, push with an open hand to avoid scraped knuckles if the wrench should slip.
DON'T attempt to lift a heavy component alone — get someone to help you.
DON'T rush or take unsafe shortcuts to finish a job.
DON'T allow children or animals in or around the vehicle while you are working on it.
DO wear eye protection when using power tools such as a drill, sander, bench grinder, etc. and when working under a vehicle.
DO keep loose clothing and long hair well out of the way of moving parts.
DO make sure that any hoist used has a safe working load rating adequate for the job.
DO get someone to check on you periodically when working alone on a vehicle.
DO carry out work in a logical sequence and make sure that everything is correctly assembled and tightened.
DO keep chemicals and fluids tightly capped and out of the reach of children and pets.
DO remember that your vehicle's safety affects that of yourself and others. If in doubt on any point, get professional advice.

Asbestos

Certain friction, insulating, sealing, and other products — such as brake linings, brake bands, clutch linings, torque converters, gaskets, etc. — contain asbestos. *Extreme care must be taken to avoid inhalation of dust from such products since it is hazardous to health.* If in doubt, assume that they *do* contain asbestos.

Fire

Remember at all times that gasoline is highly flammable. Never smoke or have any kind of open flame around when working on a vehicle. But the risk does not end there. A spark caused by an electrical short circuit, by two metal surfaces contacting each other, or even by static electricity built up in your body under certain conditions, can ignite gasoline vapors, which in a confined space are highly explosive. Do not, under any circumstances, use gasoline for cleaning parts. Use an approved safety solvent.

Always disconnect the battery ground (–) cable *at the battery* before working on any part of the fuel system or electrical system. Never risk spilling fuel on a hot engine or exhaust component.

It is strongly recommended that a fire extinguisher suitable for use on fuel and electrical fires be kept handy in the garage or workshop at all times. Never try to extinguish a fuel or electrical fire with water.

Fumes

Certain fumes are highly toxic and can quickly cause unconsciousness and even death if inhaled to any extent. Gasoline vapor falls into this category, as do the vapors from some cleaning solvents. Any draining or pouring of such volatile fluids should be done in a well ventilated area.

When using cleaning fluids and solvents, read the instructions on the container carefully. Never use materials from unmarked containers.

Never run the engine in an enclosed space, such as a garage. Exhaust fumes contain carbon monoxide, which is extremely poisonous. If you need to run the engine, always do so in the open air, or at least have the rear of the vehicle outside the work area.

If you are fortunate enough to have the use of an inspection pit, never drain or pour gasoline and never run the engine while the vehicle is over the pit. The fumes, being heavier than air, will concentrate in the pit with possibly lethal results.

The battery

Never create a spark or allow a bare light bulb near the battery. The battery normally gives off a certain amount of hydrogen gas, which is highly explosive.

Always disconnect the battery ground (–) cable *at the battery* before working on the fuel or electrical systems.

If possible, loosen the filler caps or cover when charging the battery from an external source. Do not charge at an excessive rate or the battery may burst.

Take care when adding water and when carrying a battery. The electrolyte, even when diluted, is very corrosive and should not be allowed to contact clothing or skin.

Always wear eye protection when cleaning the battery to prevent the caustic deposits from entering your eyes.

Household current

When using an electric power tool, inspection light, etc., which operates on household current, always make sure that the tool is correctly connected to its plug and that, where necessary, it is properly grounded. Do not use such items in damp conditions and, again, do not create a spark or apply excessive heat in the vicinity of fuel or fuel vapor.

Secondary ignition system voltage

A severe electric shock can result from touching certain parts of the ignition system (such as the spark plug wires) when the engine is running or being cranked, particularly if components are damp or the insulation is defective. In the case of an electronic ignition system, the secondary system voltage is much higher and could prove fatal.

Automotive chemicals and lubricants

A number of automotive chemicals and lubricants are available for use during vehicle maintenance and repair. They include a wide variety of products ranging from cleaning solvents and degreasers to lubricants and protective sprays for rubber, plastic and vinyl.

Cleaners

Carburetor cleaner and choke cleaner is a strong solvent for gum, varnish and carbon. Most carburetor cleaners leave a dry-type lubricant film which will not harden or gum up. Because of this film it is not recommended for use on electrical components.

Brake system cleaner is used to remove grease and brake fluid from the brake system where clean surfaces are absolutely necessary. It leaves no residue and often eliminates brake squeal caused by contaminants.

Electrical cleaner removes oxidation, corrosion and carbon deposits from electrical contacts, restoring full current flow. It can also be used to clean spark plugs, carburetor jets, voltage regulators and other parts where an oil-free surface is desired.

Demoisturants remove water and moisture from electrical components such as alternators, voltage regulators, electrical connectors and fuse blocks. It is non-conductive, non-corrosive and non-flammable.

Degreasers are heavy-duty solvents used to remove grease from the outside of the engine and from chassis components. They can be sprayed or brushed on, and, depending on the type, are rinsed off either with water or solvent.

Lubricants

Motor oil is the lubricant formulated for use in engines. It normally contains a wide variety of additives to prevent corrosion and reduce foaming and wear. Motor oil comes in various weights (viscosity ratings) from 5 to 80. The recommended weight of the oil depends on the season, temperature and the demands on the engine. Light oil is used in cold climates and under light load conditions. Heavy oil is used in hot climates and where high loads are encountered. Multi-viscosity oils are designed to have characteristics of both light and heavy oils and are available in a number of weights from 5W-20 to 20W-50.

Gear oil is designed to be used in differentials, manual transaxles and other areas where high-temperature lubrication is required.

Chassis and wheel bearing grease is a heavy grease used where increased loads and friction are encountered, such as for wheel bearings, balljoints, tie rod ends and universal joints.

High temperature wheel bearing grease is designed to withstand the extreme temperatures encountered by wheel bearings in disc brake equipped vehicles. It usually contains molybdenun disulfide (moly), which is a dry-type lubricant.

White grease is a heavy grease for metal to metal applications where water is a problem. White grease stays soft under both low and high temperatures (usually from −100°F to +190°F), and will not wash off or dilute in the presence of water.

Assembly lube is a special extreme pressure lubricant, usually containing moly, used to lubricate high-load parts such as main and rod bearings and cam lobes for initial start-up of a new engine. The assembly lube lubricates the parts without being squeezed out or washed away until the engine oiling system begins to function.

Silicone lubricants are used to protect rubber, plastic, vinyl and nylon parts.

Graphite lubricants are used where oils cannot be used due to contamination problems, such as in locks. The dry graphite will lubricate metal parts while remaining uncontaminated by dirt, water, oil or acids. It is electrically conductive and will not foul electrical contacts in locks such as the ignition switch.

Moly penetrants loosen and lubricate frozen, rusted and corroded fasteners and prevent future rusting or freezing.

Heat-sink grease is a special electrically non-conductive grease that is used for mounting HEI ignition modules where it is essential that heat be transferred away from the module.

Sealants

RTV sealant is one of the most widely used gasket compounds. Made from silicone, RTV is air curing, it seals, bonds, waterproofs, fills surface irregularities, remains flexible, doesn't shrink, is relatively easy to remove, and is used as a supplementary sealer with almost all low and medium temperature gaskets.

Anaerobic sealant is much like RTV in that it can be used either to seal gaskets or to form gaskets by itself. It remains flexible, is solvent resistant and fills surface imperfections. The difference between an anaerobic sealant and an RTV-type sealant is in the curing. RTV cures when exposed to air, while an anaerobic sealant cures only in the absence of air. This means that an anaerobic sealant cures only after the assembly of parts, sealing them together.

Thread and pipe sealant is used for sealing hydraulic and pneumatic fittings and vacuum lines. It is usually made from a teflon compound, and comes in a spray, a paint-on liquid and as a wrap-around tape.

Chemicals

Anti-seize compound prevents seizing, galling, cold welding, rust and corrosion in fasteners. High temperature anti-seize, usually made with copper and graphite lubricants, is used for exhaust system and manifold bolts.

Anaerobic locking compounds are used to keep fasteners from vibrating or working loose, and cure only after installation, in the absence of air. Medium strength locking compound is used for small nuts, bolts and screws that you expect to be removing later. High strength locking compound is for large nuts, bolts and studs which you don't intend to be removing on a regular basis.

Oil additives range from viscosity index improvers to chemical treatments that claim to reduce internal engine friction. It should be noted that most oil manufacturers caution against using additives with their oils.

Gas additives perform several functions, depending on their chemical makeup. They usually contain solvents that help dissolve gum and varnish that build up on carburetor and intake parts. They also serve to break down carbon deposits that form on the inside surfaces of the combustion chambers. Some additives contain upper cylinder lubricants for valves and piston rings, and others chemicals to remove condensation from the gas tank.

Miscellaneous

Brake fluid is specially formulated hydraulic fluid that can withstand the heat and pressure encountered in brake systems. Care must be taken that this fluid does not come in contact with painted surfaces or plastics. An opened container should always be resealed to prevent contamination by water or dirt.

Weatherstrip adhesive is used to bond weatherstripping around doors, windows and trunk lids. It is sometimes used to attach trim pieces.

Undercoating is a petroleum-based tar-like substance that is designed to protect metal surfaces on the underside of the vehicle from corrosion. It also acts as a sound-deadening agent by insulating the bottom of the vehicle.

Waxes and polishes are used to help protect painted and plated surfaces from the weather. Different types of paint may require the use of different types of wax and polish. Some polishes utilize a chemical or abrasive cleaner to help remove the top layer of oxidized (dull) paint on older vehicles. In recent years many non-wax polishes that contain a wide variety of chemicals such as polymers and silicones have been introduced. These non-wax polishes are usually easier to apply and last longer than conventional waxes and polishes.

Conversion factors

Length (distance)					
Inches (in)	X 25.4	= Millimetres (mm)	X	0.0394	= Inches (in)
Feet (ft)	X 0.305	= Metres (m)	X	3.281	= Feet (ft)
Miles	X 1.609	= Kilometres (km)	X	0.621	= Miles
Volume (capacity)					
Cubic inches (cu in; in^3)	X 16.387	= Cubic centimetres (cc; cm^3)	X	0.061	= Cubic inches (cu in; in^3)
Imperial pints (Imp pt)	X 0.568	= Litres (l)	X	1.76	= Imperial pints (Imp pt)
Imperial quarts (Imp qt)	X 1.137	= Litres (l)	X	0.88	= Imperial quarts (Imp qt)
Imperial quarts (Imp qt)	X 1.201	= US quarts (US qt)	X	0.833	= Imperial quarts (Imp qt)
US quarts (US qt)	X 0.946	= Litres (l)	X	1.057	= US quarts (US qt)
Imperial gallons (Imp gal)	X 4.546	= Litres (l)	X	0.22	= Imperial gallons (Imp gal)
Imperial gallons (Imp gal)	X 1.201	= US gallons (US gal)	X	0.833	= Imperial gallons (Imp gal)
US gallons (US gal)	X 3.785	= Litres (l)	X	0.264	= US gallons (US gal)
Mass (weight)					
Ounces (oz)	X 28.35	= Grams (g)	X	0.035	= Ounces (oz)
Pounds (lb)	X 0.454	= Kilograms (kg)	X	2.205	= Pounds (lb)
Force					
Ounces-force (ozf; oz)	X 0.278	= Newtons (N)	X	3.6	= Ounces-force (ozf; oz)
Pounds-force (lbf; lb)	X 4.448	= Newtons (N)	X	0.225	= Pounds-force (lbf; lb)
Newtons (N)	X 0.1	= Kilograms-force (kgf; kg)	X	9.81	= Newtons (N)
Pressure					
Pounds-force per square inch (psi; lbf/in^2; lb/in^2)	X 0.070	= Kilograms-force per square centimetre (kgf/cm^2; kg/cm^2)	X	14.223	= Pounds-force per square inch (psi; lbf/in^2; lb/in^2)
Pounds-force per square inch (psi; lbf/in^2; lb/in^2)	X 0.068	= Atmospheres (atm)	X	14.696	= Pounds-force per square inch (psi; lbf/in^2; lb/in^2)
Pounds-force per square inch (psi; lbf/in^2; lb/in^2)	X 0.069	= Bars	X	14.5	= Pounds-force per square inch (psi; lbf/in^2; lb/in^2)
Pounds-force per square inch (psi; lbf/in^2; lb/in^2)	X 6.895	= Kilopascals (kPa)	X	0.145	= Pounds-force per square inch (psi; lbf/in^2; lb/in^2)
Kilopascals (kPa)	X 0.01	= Kilograms-force per square centimetre (kgf/cm^2; kg/cm^2)	X	98.1	= Kilopascals (kPa)
Torque (moment of force)					
Pounds-force inches (lbf in; lb in)	X 1.152	= Kilograms-force centimetre (kgf cm; kg cm)	X	0.868	= Pounds-force inches (lbf in; lb in)
Pounds-force inches (lbf in; lb in)	X 0.113	= Newton metres (Nm)	X	8.85	= Pounds-force inches (lbf in; lb in)
Pounds-force inches (lbf in; lb in)	X 0.083	= Pounds-force feet (lbf ft; lb ft)	X	12	= Pounds-force inches (lbf in; lb in)
Pounds-force feet (lbf ft; lb ft)	X 0.138	= Kilograms-force metres (kgf m; kg m)	X	7.233	= Pounds-force feet (lbf ft; lb ft)
Pounds-force feet (lbf ft; lb ft)	X 1.356	= Newton metres (Nm)	X	0.738	= Pounds-force feet (lbf ft; lb ft)
Newton metres (Nm)	X 0.102	= Kilograms-force metres (kgf m; kg m)	X	9.804	= Newton metres (Nm)
Power					
Horsepower (hp)	X 745.7	= Watts (W)	X	0.0013	= Horsepower (hp)
Velocity (speed)					
Miles per hour (miles/hr; mph)	X 1.609	= Kilometres per hour (km/hr; kph)	X	0.621	= Miles per hour (miles/hr; mph)
Fuel consumption*					
Miles per gallon, Imperial (mpg)	X 0.354	= Kilometres per litre (km/l)	X	2.825	= Miles per gallon, Imperial (mpg)
Miles per gallon, US (mpg)	X 0.425	= Kilometres per litre (km/l)	X	2.352	= Miles per gallon, US (mpg)

Temperature

Degrees Fahrenheit = (°C x 1.8) + 32

Degrees Celsius (Degrees Centigrade; °C) = (°F - 32) x 0.56

**It is common practice to convert from miles per gallon (mpg) to litres/100 kilometres (l/100km), where mpg (Imperial) x l/100 km = 282 and mpg (US) x l/100 km = 235*

Troubleshooting

Contents

This section provides an easy reference guide to the more common problems which may occur during the operation of your vehicle. These problems and possible causes are grouped under various components or systems; i.e. Engine, Cooling system, etc., and also refer to the Chapter and/or Section which deals with the problem.

Remember that successful troubleshooting is not a mysterious *black art* practiced only by professional mechanics. It's simply the result of a bit of knowledge combined with an intelligent, systematic approach to the problem. Always work by a process of elimination, starting with the simplest solution and working through to the most complex — and never overlook the obvious. Anyone can forget to fill the gas tank or leave the lights on overnight, so don't assume that you are above such oversights.

Finally, always get clear in your mind why a problem has occurred and take steps to ensure that it doesn't happen again. If the electrical system fails because of a poor connection, check all other connections in the system to make sure that they don't fail as well. If a particular fuse continues to blow, find out why — don't just go on replacing fuses. Remember, failure of a small component can often be indicative of potential failure or incorrect functioning of a more important component or system.

Engine

1 Engine will not rotate when attempting to start

1 Battery terminal connections loose or corroded. Check the cable terminals at the battery. Tighten the cable or remove corrosion as necessary.
2 Battery discharged or faulty. If the cable connections are clean and tight on the battery posts, turn the key to the On position and switch on the headlights and/or windshield wipers. If they fail to function, the battery is discharged.
3 Automatic transaxle not completely engaged in Park or clutch not completely depressed.
4 Broken, loose or disconnected wiring in the starting circuit. Inspect all wiring and connectors at the battery, starter solenoid and ignition switch.
5 Starter motor pinion jammed in flywheel ring gear. If manual transaxle, place transaxle in gear and rock the vehicle to manually turn the engine. Remove starter and inspect pinion and flywheel at earliest convenience.
6 Starter solenoid faulty (Chapter 5).
7 Starter motor faulty (Chapter 5).
8 Ignition switch faulty (Chapter 12).

2 Engine rotates but will not start

1 Fuel tank empty.
2 Battery discharged (engine rotates slowly). Check the operation of electrical components as described in previous Section.
3 Battery terminal connections loose or corroded. See previous Section.
4 Carburetor flooded and/or fuel level in carburetor incorrect. This will usually be accompanied by a strong fuel odor from under the hood. Wait a few minutes, depress the accelerator pedal all the way to the floor and attempt to start the engine.
5 Choke control inoperative (Chapter 1).
6 Fuel not reaching carburetor. With ignition switch in Off position, open hood, remove the top plate of air cleaner assembly and look into the top of the carburetor (manually move the choke plate back if necessary). Have an assistant depress the accelerator pedal and check that fuel spurts into the carburetor. If not, check the fuel filter (Chapter 1), fuel lines and fuel pump (Chapter 4).
7 Fuel injector or fuel pump faulty (fuel injected vehicles) (Chapter 4).
8 Excessive moisture on, or damage to, ignition components (Chapter 1).
9 Worn, faulty or incorrectly gapped spark plugs (Chapter 1).
10 Broken, loose or disconnected wiring in the starting circuit (see previous Section).
11 Distributor loose, causing ignition timing to change. Turn the distributor as necessary to start engine, then set ignition timing as soon as possible (Chapter 1).
12 Broken, loose or disconnected wires at the ignition coil or faulty coil (Chapter 5).

3 Starter motor operates without rotating engine

1 Starter pinion sticking. Remove the starter (Chapter 5) and inspect.
2 Starter pinion or flywheel teeth worn or broken. Remove the cover at the rear of the engine and inspect.

4 Engine hard to start when cold

1 Battery discharged or low. Check as described in Section 1.
2 Choke control inoperative or out of adjustment (Chapters 1 and 4).
3 Carburetor flooded (see Section 2).
4 Fuel supply not reaching the carburetor (see Section 2).
5 Carburetor/fuel injection system in need of overhaul (Chapter 4).
6 Distributor rotor carbon tracked and/or mechanical advance mechanism rusted (Chapter 5).

5 Engine hard to start when hot

1 Choke sticking in the closed position (Chapter 1).
2 Carburetor flooded (see Section 2).
3 Air filter clogged (Chapter 1).
4 Fuel not reaching the carburetor or fuel injection system (see Section 2).

6 Starter motor noisy or excessively rough in engagement

1 Pinion or flywheel gear teeth worn or broken. Remove the cover at the rear of the engine (if so equipped) and inspect.
2 Starter motor mounting bolts loose or missing.

7 Engine starts but stops immediately

1 Loose or faulty electrical connections at distributor, coil or alternator.
2 Insufficient fuel reaching the carburetor/fuel injector. Disconnect the fuel line at the carburetor/fuel injector and remove the filter (Chapter 1). Place a container under the disconnected fuel line. Note the flow of fuel from the line. If little or none at all, check for blockage in the lines and/or replace the fuel pump (Chapter 4).
3 Vacuum leak at the gasket surfaces of the intake manifold and/or carburetor/fuel injection unit (non-turbocharged models). Make sure that all mounting bolts/nuts are tightened securely and that all vacuum hoses connected to the carburetor/fuel injection unit and manifold are positioned properly and in good condition.

8 Engine lopes while idling or idles erratically

1 Vacuum leakage. Check mounting bolts/nuts at the carburetor/fuel injection unit and intake manifold for tightness. Make sure that all vacuum hoses are connected and in good condition. Use a stethoscope or a length of fuel hose held against your ear to listen for vacuum leaks while the engine is running. A hissing sound will be heard. A soapy water solution will also detect leaks. Check the carburetor/fuel injector and intake manifold gasket surfaces.
2 Leaking EGR valve or plugged PCV valve (see Chapters 1 and 6).
3 Air filter clogged (Chapter 1).
4 Fuel pump not delivering sufficient fuel to the carburetor/fuel injector (see Section 7).
5 Carburetor out of adjustment (Chapter 4).
6 Leaking head gasket. If this is suspected, take the vehicle to a repair shop or dealer where the engine can be pressure checked.
7 Timing chain and/or sprockets worn (Chapter 2).
8 Camshaft lobes worn (Chapter 2).

9 Engine misses at idle speed

1 Spark plugs worn or not gapped properly (Chapter 1).
2 Faulty spark plug wires (Chapter 1).
3 Choke not operating properly (Chapter 1).

10 Engine surges and/or misses at idle (1983 2.2L engine only)

A Chrysler Technical Service Bulletin concerning this problem has been issued. Take your vehicle to a dealer and inform him of the problem.

11 Engine misses throughout driving speed range

1 Fuel filter clogged and/or impurities in the fuel system (Chapter 1). Also check fuel output at the carburetor/fuel injector (see Section 7).
2 Faulty or incorrectly gapped spark plugs (Chapter 1).

3 Incorrect ignition timing (Chapter 1).
4 Check for cracked distributor cap, disconnected distributor wires and damaged distributor components (Chapter 1).
5 Leaking spark plug wires (Chapter 1).
6 Faulty emissions system components (Chapter 6).
7 Low or uneven cylinder compression pressures. Remove spark plugs and test compression with gauge (Chapter 2).
8 Weak or faulty ignition system (Chapter 5).
9 Vacuum leaks at carburetor/fuel injection unit, intake manifold or vacuum hoses (see Section 8).

12 Engine stalls

1 Idle speed incorrect (Chapter 1).
2 Fuel filter clogged and/or water and impurities in the fuel system (Chapter 1).
3 Choke improperly adjusted or sticking (Chapter 1).
4 Distributor components damp or damaged (Chapter 1).
5 Faulty emissions system components (Chapter 6).
6 Faulty or incorrectly gapped spark plugs. Also check spark plug wires (Chapter 1).
7 Vacuum leak at the carburetor/fuel injection unit, intake manifold or vacuum hoses. Check as described in Section 8.
8 Valve clearances incorrectly set (Chapter 2).

13 Engine lacks power

1 Incorrect ignition timing (Chapter 1).
2 Excessive play in distributor shaft. At the same time, check for worn rotor, faulty distributor cap, wires, etc. (Chapters 1 and 5).
3 Faulty or incorrectly gapped spark plugs (Chapter 1).
4 Carburetor/fuel injection unit not adjusted properly or excessively worn (Chapter 4).
5 Faulty coil (Chapter 5).
6 Brakes binding (Chapter 1).
7 Automatic transmission fluid level incorrect (Chapter 1).
8 Clutch slipping (Chapter 8).
9 Fuel filter clogged and/or impurities in the fuel system (Chapter 1).
10 Emissions control system not functioning properly (Chapter 6).
11 Use of substandard fuel. Fill tank with proper octane fuel.
12 Low or uneven cylinder compression pressures. Test with compression tester, which will detect leaking valves and/or blown head gasket (Chapter 2).

14 Engine backfires

1 Emissions system not functioning properly (Chapter 6).
2 Ignition timing incorrect (Chapter 1).
3 Faulty secondary ignition system (cracked spark plug insulator, faulty plug wires, distributor cap and/or rotor) (Chapters 1 and 5).
4 Carburetor/fuel injection unit in need of adjustment or worn excessively (Chapter 4).
5 Vacuum leak at carburetor/fuel injection unit(s), intake manifold or vacuum hoses. Check as described in Section 8.
6 Valve clearances incorrectly set, and/or valves sticking (Chapter 2).

15 Pinging or knocking engine sounds during acceleration or uphill

1 Incorrect grade of fuel. Fill tank with fuel of the proper octane rating.
2 Ignition timing incorrect (Chapter 1).
3 Carburetor/fuel injection unit in need of adjustment (Chapter 4).
4 Improper spark plugs. Check plug type against *Emission Control Information label* located in engine compartment. Also check plugs and wires for damage (Chapter 1).
5 Worn or damaged distributor components (Chapter 5).
6 Faulty emissions system (Chapter 6).
7 Vacuum leak. Check as described in Section 8.

16 Engine diesels (continues to run) after switching off

1 Idle speed too high (Chapter 1).
2 Electrical solenoid at side of carburetor not functioning properly (not all models, see Chapter 4).
3 Ignition timing incorrectly adjusted (Chapter 1).
4 Air cleaner heat valve not operating properly (Chapter 6).
5 Excessive engine operating temperature. Probable causes of this are malfunctioning thermostat, clogged radiator, faulty water pump (Chapter 3).

Engine electrical system

17 Battery will not hold a charge

1 Alternator drivebelt defective or not adjusted properly (Chapter 1).
2 Electrolyte level low or battery discharged (Chapter 1).
3 Battery terminals loose or corroded (Chapter 1).
4 Alternator not charging properly (Chapter 5).
5 Loose, broken or faulty wiring in the charging circuit (Chapter 5).
6 Short in vehicle wiring causing a continual drain on battery.
7 Battery defective internally.

18 Ignition light fails to go out

1 Fault in alternator or charging circuit (Chapter 5).
2 Alternator drivebelt defective or not properly adjusted (Chapter 1).

19 Ignition light fails to come on when key is turned on

1 Warning light bulb defective (Chapter 12).
2 Alternator faulty (Chapter 5).
3 Fault in the printed circuit, dash wiring or bulb holder (Chapter 12).

Fuel system

20 Excessive fuel consumption

1 Dirty or clogged air filter element (Chapter 1).
2 Incorrectly set ignition timing (Chapter 1).
3 Choke sticking or improperly adjusted (Chapter 1).
4 Emissions system not functioning properly (not all vehicles, see Chapter 6).
5 Carburetor idle speed and/or mixture not adjusted properly (Chapter 1).
6 Carburetor/fuel injection internal parts excessively worn or damaged (Chapter 4).
7 Low tire pressure or incorrect tire size (Chapter 1).

21 Fuel leakage and/or fuel odor

1 Leak in a fuel feed or vent line (Chapter 4).
2 Tank overfilled. Fill only to automatic shut-off.
3 Emissions system filter clogged (Chapter 1).
4 Vapor leaks from system lines (Chapter 4).
5 Carburetor/fuel injection internal parts excessively worn or out of adjustment (Chapter 4).

Cooling system

22 Overheating

1 Insufficient coolant in system (Chapter 1).
2 Water pump drivebelt defective or not adjusted properly (Chapter 1).
3 Radiator core blocked or radiator grille dirty and restricted (Chap-

ter 3).
4 Thermostat faulty (Chapter 3).
5 Electric cooling fan inoperative (Chapter 3).
6 Radiator cap not maintaining proper pressure. Have cap pressure tested by gas station or repair shop.
7 Ignition timing incorrect (Chapter 1).

23 Overcooling

1 Thermostat faulty (Chapter 3).
2 Inaccurate temperature gauge (Chapter 12).

24 Engine slow to warm up (1981 through 1983 2.2L engine only)

A Chrysler Technical Service Bulletin concerning this problem has been issued. Take your vehicle to a dealer and inform him of the problem.

25 External coolant leakage

1 Deteriorated or damaged hoses or loose clamps. Replace hoses and/or tighten clamps at hose connections (Chapter 1).
2 Water pump seals defective. If this is the case, coolant will drip from the weep hole in the water pump body (Chapter 1).
3 Leakage from radiator core or header tank. This will require the radiator to be professionally repaired (see Chapter 3 for removal procedures).
4 Engine drain plugs or water jacket core plugs leaking (see Chapter 2).

26 Internal coolant leakage

Note: *Internal coolant leaks can usually be detected by examining the oil. Check the dipstick and inside the cylinder head cover for water deposits and an oil consistency like that of a milkshake.*
1 Leaking cylinder head gasket. Have the cooling system pressure tested.
2 Cracked cylinder bore or cylinder head. Dismantle engine and inspect (Chapter 2).

27 Coolant loss

1 Too much coolant in system (Chapter 1).
2 Coolant boiling away due to overheating (see Section 22).
3 External or internal leakage (see Sections 25 and 26).
4 Faulty radiator cap. Have the cap pressure tested.

28 Poor coolant circulation

1 Inoperative water pump. A quick test is to pinch the top radiator hose closed with your hand while the engine is idling, then let it loose. You should feel a surge of coolant if the pump is working properly (Chapter 1).
2 Restriction in cooling system. Drain, flush and refill the system (Chapter 1). If necessary, remove the radiator (Chapter 3) and have it reverse flushed.
3 Water pump drivebelt defective or not adjusted properly (Chapter 1).
4 Thermostat sticking (Chapter 3).

Clutch

29 Fails to release (pedal pressed to the floor – shift lever does not move freely in and out of Reverse)

1 Improper linkage free play (Chapter 8).
2 Clutch fork off ball stud. Look under the vehicle, on the side of transmission.
3 Clutch plate warped or damaged (Chapter 8).

30 Clutch slips (engine speed increases with no increase in vehicle speed)

1 Linkage out of adjustment (Chapter 8).
2 Clutch plate oil soaked or lining worn. Remove clutch (Chapter 8) and inspect.
3 Clutch plate not seated. It may take 30 or 40 normal starts for a new one to seat.

31 Grabbing (chattering) as clutch is engaged

1 Oil on clutch plate lining. Remove and inspect (Chapter 8). Repair any leakage source.
2 Worn or loose engine or transaxle mounts. These units move slightly when clutch is released. Inspect mounts and bolts.
3 Worn splines on clutch plate hub. Remove clutch components (Chapter 8) and inspect.
4 Warped pressure plate or flywheel. Remove clutch components and inspect.

32 Squeal or rumble with clutch fully engaged (pedal released)

1 Improper adjustment; no free play (Chapter 1).
2 Release bearing binding on transaxle bearing retainer. Remove clutch components (Chapter 8) and check bearing. Remove any burrs or nicks, clean and relubricate before reinstallation.
3 Weak linkage return spring. Replace the spring.

33 Squeal or rumble with clutch fully disengaged (pedal depressed)

1 Worn, defective or broken release (throwout) bearing (Chapter 8).
2 Worn or broken pressure plate springs (or diaphragm fingers) (Chapter 8).

34 Clutch pedal stays on floor when depressed

1 Bind in linkage or release bearing. Inspect linkage or remove clutch components as necessary.
2 Linkage springs being over-extended. Check linkage for proper free play.

Manual transaxle

35 Noisy in Neutral with engine running

1 Input shaft bearing worn.
2 Damaged main drive gear bearing.
3 Worn countershaft bearings.
4 Worn or damaged countershaft end play shims.

36 Noisy in all gears

1 Any of the above causes, and/or:
2 Insufficient lubricant (see checking procedures in Chapter 1).

37 Noisy in one particular gear

1 Worn, damaged or chipped gear teeth for that particular gear.
2 Worn or damaged synchronizer for that particular gear.

38 Slips out of high gear

1 Transaxle loose on clutch housing (Chapter 7).
2 Shift linkage interfering with engine mounts or clutch lever (Chapter 7).
3 Shift rods or cables not working freely (Chapter 7).
4 Damaged mainshaft pilot bearing.
5 Dirt between transaxle case and engine or misalignment of transaxle (Chapter 7).
6 Worn or improperly adjusted linkage (Chapter 7).

39 Difficulty in engaging gears

1 Clutch not releasing completely (see clutch adjustment in Chapter 8).
2 Loose, damaged or out-of-adjustment shift linkage. Make a thorough inspection, replacing parts as necessary (Chapter 7).

40 Oil leakage

1 Excessive amount of lubricant in transaxle (see Chapter 1 for correct checking procedures). Drain lubricant as required.
2 Driveaxle oil seal or speedometer oil seal in need of replacement (Chapter 7).

Automatic transaxle

Note: *Due to the complexity of the automatic transaxle, it is difficult for the home mechanic to properly diagnose and service this component. For problems other than the following, the vehicle should be taken to a dealer or reputable mechanic.*

41 General shift mechanism problems

1 Chapter 7 deals with checking and adjusting the shift linkage on automatic transaxles. Common problems which may be attributed to poorly adjusted linkage are:

Engine starting in gears other than Park or Neutral
Indicator on shifter pointing to a gear other than the one actually being used
Vehicle moves when in Park

2 Refer to Chapter 7 to adjust the linkage.

42 Transaxle will not downshift with accelerator pedal pressed to the floor

Chapter 7 deals with adjusting the throttle cable to enable the transaxle to downshift properly.

43 Transaxle slips, shifts rough, is noisy or has no drive in forward or reverse gears

1 There are many probable causes for the above problems, but the home mechanic should be concerned with only one possibility — low fluid level.
2 Before taking the vehicle to a repair shop, check the level and condition of the fluid as described in Chapter 1. Add fluid as necessary or change the fluid and filter if needed. If the problem persists, have a professional diagnose the probable cause.

44 Fluid leakage

1 Automatic transaxle fluid is a deep red color. Fluid leaks should not be confused with engine oil, which can easily be blown by air flow to the transaxle.
2 To pinpoint a leak, first remove all built-up dirt and grime from around the transaxle. Degreasing agents and/or steam cleaning will achieve this. With the underside clean, drive the vehicle at low speeds so air flow will not blow the leak far from its source. Raise the vehicle and determine where the leak is coming from. Common areas of leakage are:

a) Pan: Tighten mounting bolts and/or replace pan gasket as necessary (see Chapters 1 and 7).
b) Transaxle oil lines: Tighten connectors where lines enter transaxle case and/or replace lines.
c) Vent: Transaxle overfilled and/or water in fluid (see checking procedures, Chapter 1).
d) Speedometer connector: Replace the O-ring where speedometer cable enters transaxle case (Chapter 7).

Driveaxles

45 Clicking noise in turns

Worn or damaged outboard joint. Check for cut or damaged boots. Repair as necessary (Chapter 8).

46 Knock or clunk when accelerating after coasting

Worn or damaged inboard joint. Check for cut or damaged boots. Repair as necessary (Chapter 8).

47 Shudder or vibration during acceleration

1 Excessive joint angle. Check and correct as necessary (Chapter 8).
2 Worn or damaged inboard or outboard joints. Repair or replace as necessary (Chapter 8).
3 Sticking inboard joint assembly. Correct or replace as necessary (Chapter 8).

Rear axle

48 Noise

1 Road noise. No corrective procedures available.
2 Tire noise. Inspect tires and check tire pressures (Chapter 1).
3 Rear wheel bearings loose, worn or damaged (Chapter 10).

Brakes

Note: *Before assuming that a brake problem exists, make sure that the tires are in good condition and inflated properly (see Chapter 1), that the front end alignment is correct and that the vehicle is not loaded with weight in an unequal manner.*

49 Vehicle pulls to one side during braking

1 Defective, damaged or oil contaminated disc brake pads on one side. Inspect as described in Chapter 1.
2 Excessive wear of brake pad material or disc on one side. Inspect and correct as necessary.
3 Loose or disconnected front suspension components. Inspect and tighten all bolts to the specified torque (Chapter 10).
4 Defective caliper assembly. Remove caliper and inspect for stuck piston or other damage (Chapter 9).

50 Noise (high-pitched squeal without the brakes applied)

Disc brake pads worn out. The noise comes from the rivets or pad backing plate rubbing against the disc. Replace pads with new ones immediately (Chapter 9).

51 Excessive brake pedal travel

1 Partial brake system failure. Inspect entire system (Chapter 9) and correct as required.
2 Insufficient fluid in master cylinder. Check (Chapter 1), add fluid and bleed system if necessary (Chapter 9).
3 Rear brakes not adjusting properly. Make a series of starts and stops while the vehicle is in Reverse. If this does not correct the situation, remove drums and inspect self-adjusters (Chapter 9).

52 Brake pedal feels spongy when depressed

1 Air in hydraulic lines. Bleed the brake system (Chapter 9).
2 Faulty flexible hoses. Inspect all system hoses and lines. Replace parts as necessary.
3 Master cylinder mounting bolts/nuts loose.
4 Master cylinder defective (Chapter 9).

53 Excessive effort required to stop vehicle

1 Power brake booster not operating properly (Chapter 9).
2 Excessively worn linings or pads. Inspect and replace if necessary (Chapter 9).
3 One or more caliper pistons or wheel cylinders seized or sticking. Inspect and rebuild as required (Chapter 9).
4 Brake linings or pads contaminated with oil or grease. Inspect and replace as required (Chapter 9).
5 New pads or shoes installed and not yet seated. It will take a while for the new material to seat against the disc or drum.

54 Pedal travels to the floor with little resistance

Little or no fluid in the master cylinder reservoir caused by leaking wheel cylinder(s), leaking caliper piston(s), loose, damaged or disconnected brake lines. Inspect entire system and correct as necessary.

55 Brake pedal pulsates during brake application

1 Wheel bearings not adjusted properly or in need of replacement (Chapter 10).
2 Caliper not sliding properly due to improper installation or obstructions. Remove and inspect (Chapter 9).
3 Disc defective. Remove the disc (Chapter 9) and check for excessive lateral runout and parallelism. Have the disc resurfaced or replace it with a new one.

Suspension and steering systems

56 Vehicle pulls to one side

1 Tire pressures uneven (Chapter 1).
2 Defective tire (Chapter 1).
3 Excessive wear in suspension or steering components (Chapter 10).
4 Front end in need of alignment.
5 Front brakes dragging. Inspect brakes as described in Chapter 9.

57 Shimmy, shake or vibration

1 Tire or wheel out-of-balance or out-of-round. Have professionally balanced.
2 Loose, worn or out-of-adjustment wheel bearings (Chapter 10).
3 Shock absorbers and/or suspension components worn or damaged (Chapter 10).

58 Excessive pitching and/or rolling around corners or during braking

1 Defective shock absorbers. Replace as a set (Chapter 10).
2 Broken or weak springs and/or suspension components. Inspect as described in Chapter 10.

59 Excessively stiff steering

1 Lack of fluid in power steering fluid reservoir (Chapter 1).
2 Incorrect tire pressures (Chapter 1).
3 Lack of lubrication at steering joints (Chapter 1).
4 Front end out of alignment.
5 See also section titled *Lack of power assistance.*

60 Excessive play in steering

1 Excessive wear in suspension or steering components (Chapter 10).
2 Steering gearbox out of adjustment (Chapter 10).

61 Lack of power assistance

1 Steering pump drivebelt faulty or not adjusted properly (Chapter 1).
2 Fluid level low (Chapter 1).
3 Hoses or lines restricted. Inspect and replace parts as necessary.
4 Air in power steering system. Bleed system (Chapter 10).

62 Excessive tire wear (not specific to one area)

1 Incorrect tire pressures (Chapter 1).
2 Tires out of balance. Have professionally balanced.
3 Wheels damaged. Inspect and replace as necessary.
4 Suspension or steering components excessively worn (Chapter 10).

63 Excessive tire wear on outside edge

1 Inflation pressures incorrect (Chapter 1).
2 Excessive speed in turns.
3 Front end alignment incorrect (excessive toe-in). Have professionally aligned.
4 Suspension arm bent or twisted (Chapter 10).

64 Excessive tire wear on inside edge

1 Inflation pressures incorrect (Chapter 1).
2 Front end alignment incorrect (toe-out). Have professionally aligned.
3 Loose or damaged steering components (Chapter 10).

65 Tire tread worn in one place

1 Tires out-of-balance.
2 Damaged or buckled wheel. Inspect and replace if necessary.
3 Defective tire (Chapter 1).

Chapter 1 Tune-up and routine maintenance

1

Contents

Specifications

Note: *Additional Specifications and torque figures can be found in individual Chapters.*

Recommended lubricants and fluids

Engine oil	Consult your owner's manual or local dealer for recommendations on the particular service grade and viscosity oil recommended for your area, special driving conditions and climate
Manual transaxle lubricant	
1982 through 1986	DEXRON II ATF (do not use gear oil!)
1987 on	SAE 5W-30 engine oil
Automatic transaxle fluid	DEXRON II ATF
Differential lubricant (1982 automatic transaxle equipped models only)	DEXRON II ATF (do not use gear oil!)
Transaxle shift linkage	NLGI No. 2 chassis grease
Clutch linkage	NLGI No. 2 chassis grease
Power steering reservoir	Mopar 4-253 power steering fluid or equivalent
Brake system and master cylinder	DOT 3 brake fluid
Carburetor choke shaft	Mopar combustion chamber conditioner No. 2933500 or 438001 or equivalent
Combustion chamber conditioner (Canadian models)	Autopar combustion chamber conditioner No. VU788 or equivalent
Engine coolant	50/50 mixture of ethylene glycol-based antifreeze and water
Parking brake mechanism	White lithium-based grease NLGI No. 2
Chassis lubrication	NLGI No. 2 EP grease
Steering shaft seal	NLGI No. 2 EP grease
Rear wheel bearing	NLGI No. 2 EP high temperature wheel bearing grease
Steering gear	API GL-4 SAE 90W oil
Hood and door hinges/liftgate hinges	Engine oil
Door hinge half and check spring	NLGI No. 2 multi-purpose grease
Key lock cylinders	Graphite spray
Hood latch assembly	Mopar Lubriplate or equivalent
Door latch striker	Mopar Door Ease No. 3744859 or equivalent

Quick reference capacities

	US	Metric
Engine oil (including filter)		
2.2L/2.5L non-turbocharged engine	4.0 qts	3.8 liters
2.2L turbocharged engine	5.0 qts	4.8 liters
2.6L engine	5.0 qts	4.8 liters
Fuel tank	14 gal	53.0 liters
Automatic transaxle		
From dry, including torque converter	8.9 qts	8.4 liters
Transaxle drain and refill	3.8 qts	3.6 liters
Manual transaxle		
4-speed	2.0 qts	1.8 liters
5-speed	2.3 qts	2.1 liters
Power steering system		
1982 through 1985	2.5 qts	2.4 liters
1986 on	1.6 qts	1.5 liters
Cooling system		
1982		
2.2L engine	7.0 qts	6.6 liters
2.6L engine	8.0 qts	7.5 liters
1983 on (all)	9.0 qts	8.5 liters

Ignition system

Spark plug type	See *Emission Control Information label* in engine compartment
Spark plug gap	See *Emission Control Information label* in engine compartment
Spark plug wire resistance	3000 ohms per foot minimum/7200 ohms per foot maximum
Ignition timing	See *Emission Control Information label* in engine compartment
Firing order	1-3-4-2

Drivebelt deflection

Alternator	
2.2L/2.5L engine	
New	1/8 in (3 mm)
Used	1/4 in (6 mm)
2.6L engine	
New	3/16 in (4 mm)
Used	1/4 in (6 mm)
Power steering pump	
2.2L/2.5L engine	
New	1/4 in (6 mm)
Used	7/16 in (11 mm)
2.6L engine	
New	1/4 in (6 mm)
Used	3/8 in (9 mm)
Water Pump	
2.2L/2.5L engine	
New	1/8 in (3 mm)
Used	1/4 in (6 mm)
2.6L engine	
New	5/16 in (8 mm)
Used	3/8 in (9 mm)
Air Pump	
2.2L/2.5L engine	
New	3/16 in (5 mm)
Used	1/4 in (6 mm)
Air conditioning compressor	
2.2L/2.5L engine	
New	5/16 in (8 mm)
Used	3/8 in (9 mm)
2.6L engine	
New	1/4 in (6 mm)
Used	5/16 in (8 mm)

Automatic transaxle band adjustment

Kickdown	
1982 and 1983	Back off 2-3/4 turns from 72 in-lb (8 Nm)
1984 on	Back off 2-1/2 turns from 72 in-lb (8 Nm)
Low-Reverse (rear)	Back off 3-1/2 turns from 41 in-lb (5 Nm)
Low-Reverse band end gap	0.080 in (2 mm)

Miscellaneous

2.6L engine valve clearance (hot engine)	
Intake and jet valves	0.006 in (0.15 mm)
Exhaust valves	0.010 in (0.25 mm)
Idle speed	See *Emission Control Information label* in engine compartment

Torque specifications	Ft-lbs *(unless otherwise indicated)*	Nm
Carburetor or fuel injection throttle body nuts	17	23
Manual transaxle fill plug	24	33
Oil pan drain plug		
2.2L/2.5L engine	20	27
2.6L engine	19	25
Spark plugs		
2.2L/2.5L engine	26	35
2.6L engine	25	34
Wheel lug nuts		
1982 and 1983	80	108
1984 on	95	129
Differential cover bolts	14	19
Oil pan bolts	14	19
Filter-to-valve body screws	40 in-lb	5
Kickdown band adjusting screw	72 in lb	8
Kickdown band locknut	35	47
Low-Reverse band adjusting screw	41 in-lb	5
Low-Reverse band locknut		
1982	20	27
1983 on	10	14

1 Introduction

This Chapter was designed to help the do-it-yourselfer perform routine maintenance procedures to attain maximum vehicle performance, economy, safety, reliability and longevity.

On the following pages you will find a maintenance schedule along with Sections which deal specifically with each item on the schedule. Included are visual checks, adjustments and item replacements. Refer to the accompanying underhood and underside illustrations to locate the various items mentioned in each procedure.

Servicing your vehicle using the time/mileage maintenance schedule and the sequenced Sections will result in a planned maintenance program. Keep in mind that it is a comprehensive plan; maintaining only a few items at the specified intervals will not produce the same results.

As you service your vehicle, you will discover that many of the procedures can — and should — be grouped together, due to the nature of the job at hand. For example, if the vehicle is raised for chassis lubrication, you should inspect the exhaust system, the steering and suspension systems and the fuel system while you're under the vehicle. When rotating the tires, it makes good sense to check the brakes and wheel bearings since the wheels are already removed. Finally, let's suppose you have to borrow or rent a torque wrench. Even if you only need to check the carburetor or throttle body mounting nuts, you might as well check the torque of as many critical fasteners as time allows.

The first step of this or any maintenance plan is to prepare yourself before the actual work begins. Read through the appropriate Sections for all work that is to be performed before you begin. Gather together all necessary parts and tools. If it appears you could have a problem during a particular job, don't hesitate to ask advice from your local parts man or dealer service department.

2 Routine maintenance schedule

The following recommendations are given with the assumption that the vehicle owner will be doing the maintenance or service work (as opposed to having a dealer service department do the work). The majority of the following intervals are factory recommendations; however, subject to the preference of the individual owner, in the interest of keeping his or her vehicle in peak condition at all times and with the vehicle's ultimate resale in mind, many of the operations may be performed more often. We encourage such owner initiative.

When the vehicle is new, it should be serviced initially by a factory authorized dealer service department to protect the factory warranty. In some cases the initial maintenance check is done at no cost to the owner.

Weekly or every 250 miles (400 km)

Check the engine oil level; add oil as necessary (Sec 4)
Check the wiper blade condition (Sec 7)
Check the engine coolant level; add water as necessary (Sec 4)
Check the tires and tire pressures (Sec 5)
Check the automatic transaxle fluid level (Sec 4)
Check the power steering fluid level (Sec 4)
Check the brake fluid level (Sec 4)
Check the battery condition (Sec 8)
Check the windshield washer fluid level (Sec 4)
Check the operation of all lights
Check the horn operation

Every 2000 miles (3200 km) or 2 months, whichever comes first

Change the engine oil and filter (all models) (Sec 9)
Check the suspension balljoint and steering linkage boots for damage and lubricant leakage (Sec 23)
Check the driveaxle CV joint boots for damage, wear and lubricant leakage (Sec 35)

Every 7500 miles (12,000 km) or 6 months, whichever comes first

Check the manual transaxle lubricant level (Sec 4)
Check the deflection of all drivebelts (Sec 14)
Check the differential lubricant level (1982 automatic transaxle models only) (Sec 4)
Check the fuel system hoses, lines and connections for leaks and damage (Sec 20)
Check the brake hoses and lines for leaks and damage (Sec 26)
Check the carburetor/fuel injection throttle body mounting nut torque (Sec 17)
Add combustion chamber conditioner to the engine (Canadian models only) (Sec 30)

Every 15,000 miles (24,000 km) or 12 months, whichever comes first

Check the cooling system hoses and connections for leaks and damage (Sec 21)
Check for free play in the steering linkage and balljoints (Sec 23)

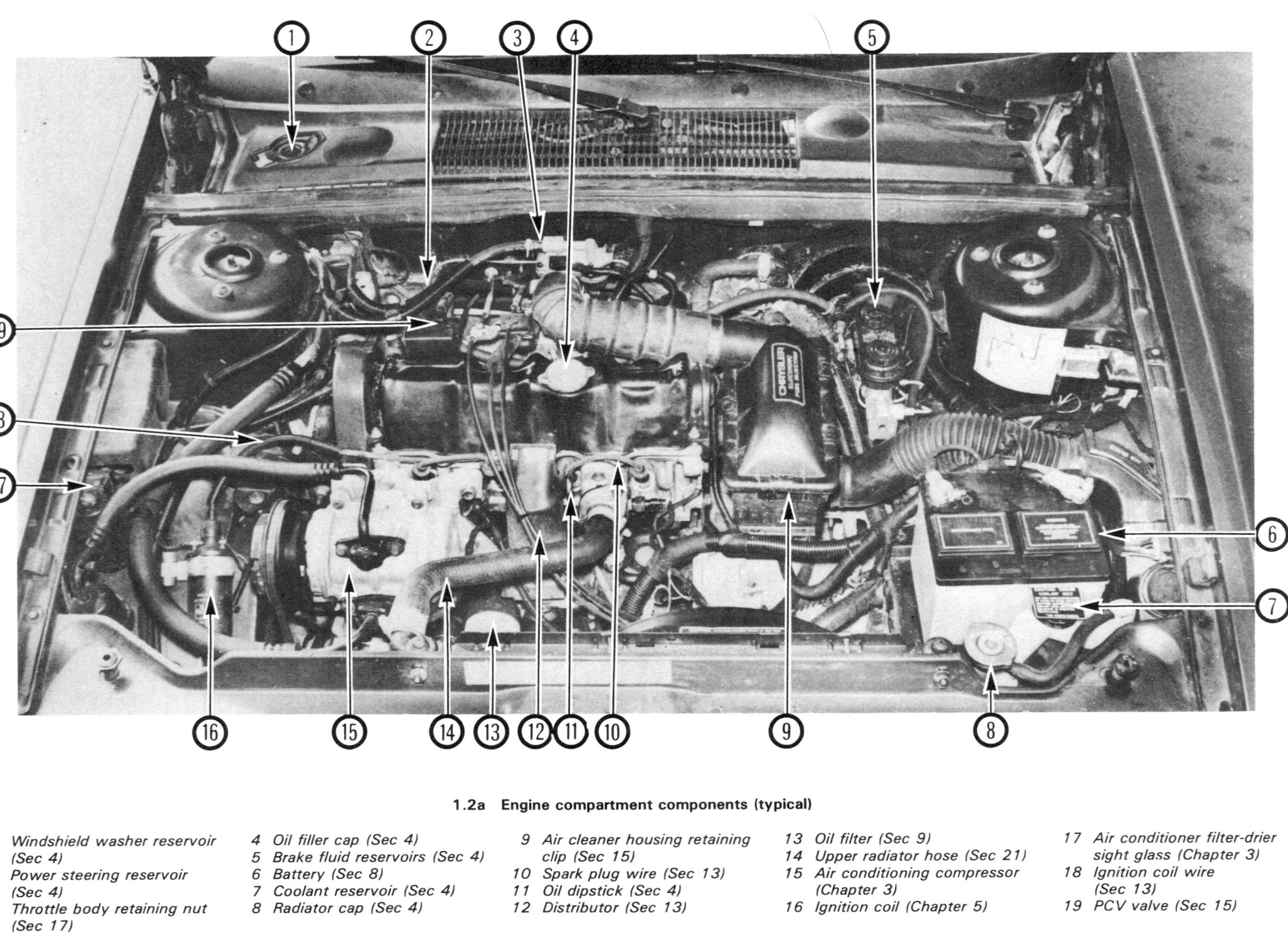

1.2a Engine compartment components (typical)

1 Windshield washer reservoir (Sec 4)
2 Power steering reservoir (Sec 4)
3 Throttle body retaining nut (Sec 17)
4 Oil filler cap (Sec 4)
5 Brake fluid reservoirs (Sec 4)
6 Battery (Sec 8)
7 Coolant reservoir (Sec 4)
8 Radiator cap (Sec 4)
9 Air cleaner housing retaining clip (Sec 15)
10 Spark plug wire (Sec 13)
11 Oil dipstick (Sec 4)
12 Distributor (Sec 13)
13 Oil filter (Sec 9)
14 Upper radiator hose (Sec 21)
15 Air conditioning compressor (Chapter 3)
16 Ignition coil (Chapter 5)
17 Air conditioner filter-drier sight glass (Chapter 3)
18 Ignition coil wire (Sec 13)
19 PCV valve (Sec 15)

1.2b Engine compartment underside components (turbocharged engine shown — others similar)

1 *Water pump*
2 *Alternator*
3 *Lower radiator hose (Sec 21)*
4 *Manual transaxle filler plug (Sec 4)*
5 *Brake hose (Sec 26)*
6 *Driveaxle CV joint boot (Sec 35)*
7 *Oil drain plug (Sec 9)*
8 *Intermediate shaft*
9 *Exhaust pipe-to-manifold flange bolt (Sec 22)*
10 *Brake caliper (Sec 26)*
11 *EVAP system canister (Chapter 6)*

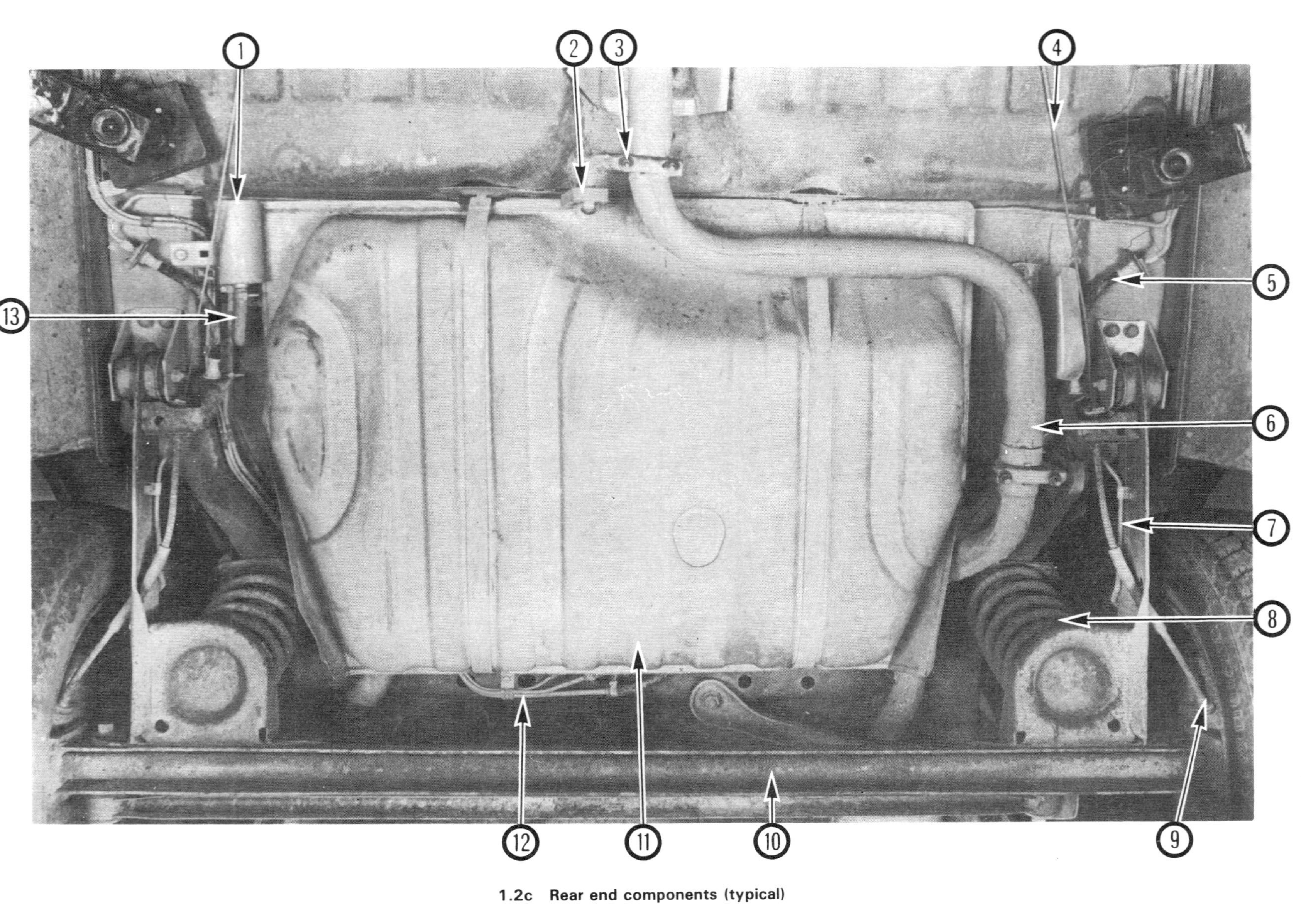

1.2c Rear end components (typical)

1 Fuel filter (Sec 10)
2 Exhaust pipe hanger (Sec 22)
3 Exhaust pipe U-bolt clamp nut (Sec 22)
4 Parking brake cable (Sec 26)
5 Brake hose (Sec 26)
6 Exhaust pipe (Sec 22)
7 Brake line (Sec 26)
8 Rear spring
9 Rear drum brake (Sec 26)
10 Rear axle
11 Fuel tank (Sec 20)
12 Fuel lines (Sec 16)
13 Fuel filter hose (Sec 10)

Check the fuel evaporative emission system hoses and connections (Section 16/Chapter 6)
Check the exhaust pipes and hangers (Sec 22)
Check the EGR system components for proper operation (Chapter 6)
Check the condition of all vacuum hoses and connections (Sec 16)
Check the condition of the wiring harness connections
Check and clean the battery (Sec 8)
Check the condition of the primary ignition wires and spark plug wires (Sec 13)
Check the distributor cap and rotor for cracks, wear and other damage (Sec 13)
Rotate the tires (Sec 6)
Check and adjust the valve clearances (2.6L engines only) (Sec 31)
Replace the spark plugs (vehicles *without* catalytic converter) (Sec 12)
Check/replace the wiper blade elements (Sec 7)

Every 22,500 miles (36,000 km) or 18 months, whichever comes first

Check the front disc brake pads (Sec 26)
Lubricate the front suspension and steering balljoints (Sec 11)
Check the air conditioning hoses, belts and sight glass (Section 14/Section 16/Chapter 3)
Replace the fuel filter (carburetor equipped models) (Sec 10)
Check the rear brake linings and drums for wear and damage (Sec 26)
Check and service the rear wheel bearings (Section 25/Chapter 10)

Every 30,000 miles (48,000 km) or 24 months, whichever comes first

Drain and replace the engine coolant (Sec 27)
Adjust the rear brake shoes (1982 models only) (Sec 26/Chapter 9)
Replace the air filter element (2.6L engines) (Sec 15)
Apply solvent to the carburetor choke shaft and sealing block (Sec 18)
Check the cylinder compression (Chapter 2C)
Check the choke for proper operation (Sec 18)
Change the automatic transaxle fluid (Section 33)
Adjust the automatic transaxle bands (Section 34)
Replace the air filter element (2.2L/2.5L engine) (Sec 15)
Check the EGR system (Canadian models only) (Chapter 6)
Check the parking brake operation (Section 26)
Check the steering shaft seal; lubricate as necessary (Sec 24)
Replace the spark plugs (vehicles *with* catalytic converter) (Sec 12)

Every 52,500 miles (84,000 km) or 60 months, whichever comes first

Inspect/replace the gas tank cap (Sec 20)
Replace the fuel filter (fuel injected models) (Sec 10)
Replace the spark plug wires, distributor cap and rotor (Sec 13)
Replace the oxygen sensor (Chapter 6)
Replace the PCV valve (Sec 15)

Severe operating conditions

Severe operating conditions are defined as:

Stop-and-go driving
Driving in dusty conditions
Extensive idling
Frequent short trips
Sustained high speed driving during hot weather (over 90°F/32°C)

Severe operating conditions maintenance intervals:

Change the automatic transaxle fluid and filter and adjust the bands every 15,000 miles (24,000 km)
Change the engine oil and filter every 2000 miles (3200 km) (turbo-charged engines — 1000 miles [1600 km])
Inspect the disc brake linings every 9000 miles (14,000 km)
Inspect the rear brake linings and drums every 9000 miles (14,000 km)
Lubricate and adjust the rear wheel bearings every 9000 miles (14,000 km)
Inspect the driveaxle CV joint boots and front suspension boots every 2000 miles (3200 km)
Lubricate the tie-rod ends every 15,000 miles (24,000 km)
Replace the air filter element every 15,000 miles (24,000 km)
Change the manual transaxle oil and clean the pan magnet every 15,000 miles (24,000 km)

3 Tune-up general information

The term *tune-up* is used in this manual to represent a combination of individual operations rather than one specific procedure.

If, from the time the vehicle is new, the routine maintenance schedule is followed closely and frequent checks are made of fluid levels and high wear items, as suggested throughout this manual, the engine will be kept in relatively good running condition and the need for additional work will be minimized.

More likely than not, however, there will be times when the engine is running poorly due to lack of regular maintenance. This is even more likely if a used vehicle, which has not received regular and frequent maintenance checks, is purchased. In such cases, an engine tune-up will be needed outside of the regular routine maintenance intervals.

The first step in any tune-up or engine diagnosis to help correct a poor running engine would be a cylinder compression check. A check of the engine compression will give valuable information regarding the overall performance of many internal components and should be used as a basis for tune-up and repair procedures. If, for instance, a compression check indicates serious internal engine wear, a conventional tune-up will not improve the running condition of the engine and would be a waste of time and money. Due to its importance, compression checking should be performed by someone who has the proper compression testing gauge and who is knowledgeable with its use. Further information on compression testing can be found in Chapter 2 of this manual.

The following series of operations are those most often needed to bring a generally poor running engine back into a proper state of tune:

Minor tune-up

Clean, inspect and test the battery
Check all engine related fluids
Check and adjust the drivebelts
Replace the spark plugs
Inspect the distributor cap and rotor
Inspect the spark plug and coil wires
Check and adjust the idle speed
Check and adjust the ignition timing
Check the PCV valve
Check the air filter
Check the cooling system
Check all underhood hoses

Major tune-up

All of the above plus . . .
Check the EGR system
Check the ignition system
Check the charging system
Check the fuel system
Replace the air filter
Replace the distributor cap and rotor
Replace the spark plug wires

4 Fluid level checks

Refer to illustrations 4.4, 4.5, 4.6, 4.8, 4.12, 4.15, 4.16, 4.24, 4.30, 4.31, 4.32, 4.36, 4.37, 4.42, 4.48a, 4.48b, 4.48c and 4.49

1 There are a number of components on a vehicle which rely on the use of fluids to perform their job. Through the normal operation of the vehicle, these fluids are used up and must be replenished before damage occurs. See *Recommended lubricants and fluids* for the specific fluid

4.4 The engine oil level dipstick is located on the front side of the engine

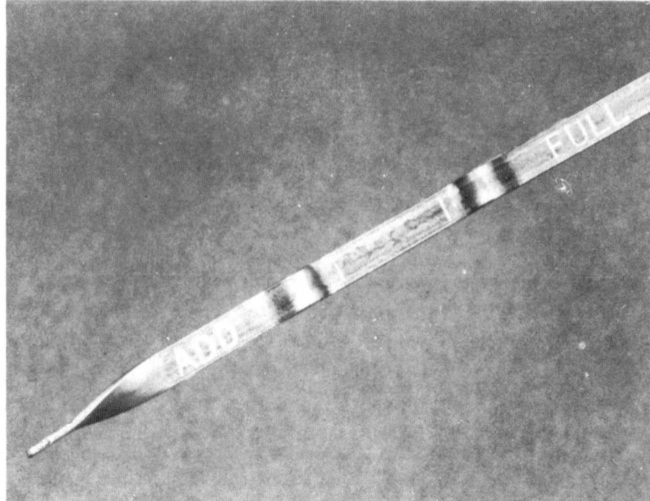

4.5 The oil level must be between the Add and Full marks (preferably in the Full range marked on the dipstick)

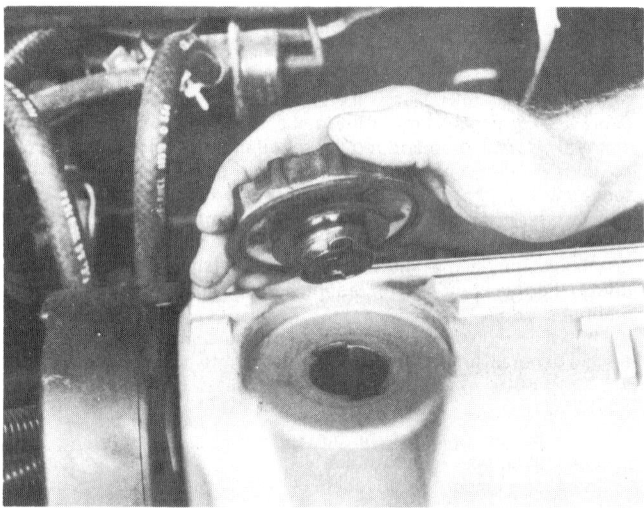

4.6 Oil is added to the engine through the filler cap on the cylinder head cover

4.8 The coolant level (which should be kept between the MIN and MAX marks) is checked at the reservoir — do not remove the radiator cap when the engine is hot!

to be used when adding is required. When checking fluid levels it is important that the vehicle is on a level surface.

Engine oil

2 The engine oil level is checked with a dipstick which is located at the front side of the engine block. The dipstick travels through a tube and into the oil pan at the bottom of the engine.
3 The oil level should be checked preferably before the vehicle has been driven, or about 15 minutes after the engine has been shut off. If the oil is checked immediately after driving the vehicle, some of the oil will remain in the upper engine components, giving an inaccurate reading on the dipstick.
4 Pull the dipstick from the tube **(see illustration)** and wipe all the oil from the end with a clean rag. Insert the clean dipstick all the way back into the tube, then pull it out again. Note the oil at the end of the dipstick. At its highest point, the level should be within the Full range mark.
5 It takes approximately one quart of oil to raise the level from the Add mark to the Full range mark on the dipstick **(see illustration)**. Do not allow the level to drop below the Add mark or engine damage may occur. On the other hand, do not overfill the engine by adding oil above the Full range mark; it may result in oil-fouled spark plugs, oil leaks and oil seal failures.
6 Oil is added to the engine after removing a twist-off cap located on the cylinder head cover. The cap will be marked "Engine oil" or something similar **(see illustration)**. A funnel will reduce spills as the oil is poured in.
7 Checking the oil level is an important part of the preventive maintenance program. If you notice the oil level dropping consistently, it is an indication of oil leakage or internal engine wear which should be corrected. If there are water droplets in the oil, or if it is milky looking, this also indicates component failure and the engine should be checked immediately. The condition of the oil should also be checked regularly. Each time you check the oil level, slide your thumb and index finger up the dipstick before wiping the oil off. If you see small dirt or metal particles clinging to the dipstick, the oil should be drained and fresh oil added (Section 9).

Engine coolant

8 All vehicles are equipped with a pressurized coolant recovery system which makes coolant level checks very easy. A coolant reservoir attached to the inner fender panel is connected by a hose to the radiator filler neck **(see illustration)**. As the engine heats up during operation, coolant is forced from the radiator, through the connecting tube and into the reservoir. As the engine cools, the coolant is automatically drawn back into the radiator to maintain the correct level.
9 The coolant level should be checked when the engine is idling and at normal operating temperature. Simply note the level of the fluid in

4.12 A funnel can be used to prevent spills when adding coolant to the reservoir

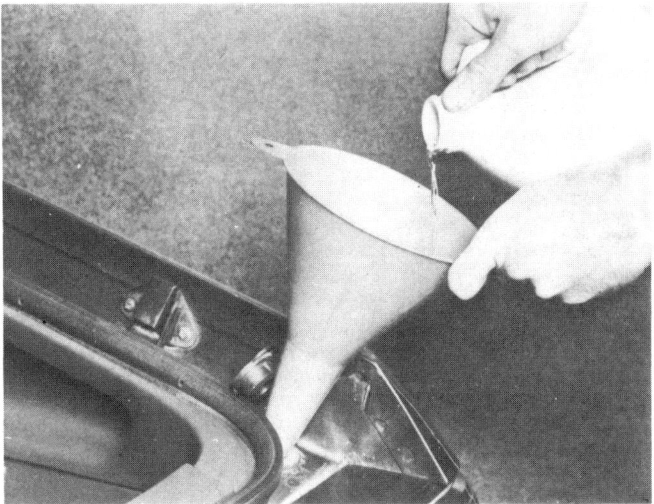

4.16 Use a funnel when adding fluid to the rear washer reservoir to avoid spilling

4.15 The windshield washer fluid reservoir (arrow) is located under the hood

the reservoir, which should be at or near the Max mark on the side of the reservoir.

10 The coolant level can also be checked by removing the radiator cap. **Warning:** *The cap should not, under any circumstances, be removed while the system is hot, as escaping steam could cause serious injury. Wait until the engine has cooled, then wrap a thick cloth around the cap and turn it to the first stop. If any steam escapes from the cap, allow the engine to cool further, then remove the cap and check the level in the radiator.*

11 If only a small amount of coolant is required to bring the system up to the proper level, regular water can be used. However, to maintain the proper antifreeze/water mixture in the system, both should be mixed together to replenish a low level. High-quality antifreeze/coolant should be mixed with water in the proportion specified on the antifreeze container. These vehicles have aluminium cylinder heads, so use of the proper coolant is critical to avoid corrosion. **Caution:** *Do not allow antifreeze to come into contact with your skin or painted surfaces of the vehicle. Flush contacted areas immediately with plenty of water.*

12 On systems with a reservoir, coolant should be added to the reservoir after removing the cap **(see illustration)**.

13 As the coolant level is checked, note the condition of the coolant as well. It should be relatively clear. If it is brown or rust colored, the system should be drained, flushed and refilled (Section 27).

14 If the cooling system requires repeated additions to maintain the proper level, have the radiator cap checked for proper sealing ability. Also check for leaks in the system (cracked hoses, loose hose connections, leaking gaskets, etc.).

Windshield and rear window washer fluid

15 The fluid for the windshield and (if equipped) rear window washer systems is located in plastic reservoirs. The level inside the reservoirs should be maintained about one inch below the filler cap. The reservoirs are accessible after opening the hood and rear hatch **(see illustration)**.

16 An approved windshield washer solvent should be added to the reservoir whenever replenishing is required **(see illustration)**. Do not use plain water alone in this system, especially in cold climates where the water could freeze.

Battery electrolyte

Warning: *Certain precautions must be followed when checking or servicing the battery. Hydrogen gas, which is highly flammable, is produced in the cells, so keep lighted tobacco, open flames, bare light bulbs and sparks away from the battery. The electrolyte inside the battery is dilute sulfuric acid, which can burn your skin and cause serious injury if splashed in the eyes (wear safety glasses). It will also ruin clothes and painted surfaces. Remove all metal jewelry which could contact the positive terminal and another grounded metal source, causing a short circuit.*

17 Vehicles equipped with maintenance-free batteries require no maintenance as the battery case is sealed and has no removable caps for adding water.

18 If a maintenance-type battery is installed, the caps on the top of the battery should be removed periodically to check for a low electrolyte level. This check will be more critical during the warm summer months.

19 Remove each of the caps and add distilled water to bring the level in each cell to the split ring in the filler opening.

20 At the same time the battery water level is checked, the overall condition of the battery and its related components should be noted. If corrosion is found on the cable ends or battery terminals, remove the cables and clean away all corrosion with a baking soda/water solution and a wire brush cleaning tool designed for this purpose. See Section 8 for complete battery check and maintenance procedures.

Brake fluid

21 The brake master cylinder is located on the left side of the engine compartment firewall and has two caps which must be removed to check the fluid level.

22 Before removing the caps, use a rag to clean all dirt, grease, etc. from the top of the reservoir. If any foreign matter enters the master cylinder with the caps removed, blockage in the brake system lines can occur. Also, make sure all painted surfaces around the master cylinder are covered, as brake fluid will ruin paint.

23 Unscrew the reservoir caps.

4.24 The brake fluid level in the master cylinder reservoirs must be maintained at the split rings

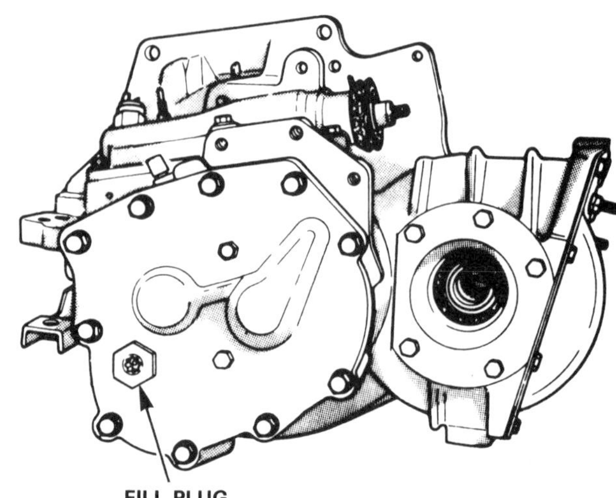

4.30 The manual transaxle lubricant level is checked by removing the fill plug

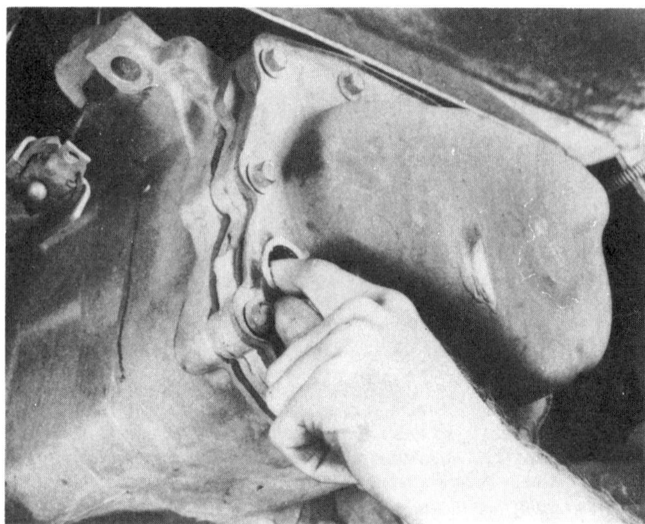

4.31 Use your finger as a dipstick to check the manual transaxle lubricant — it should be at the lower edge of the hole

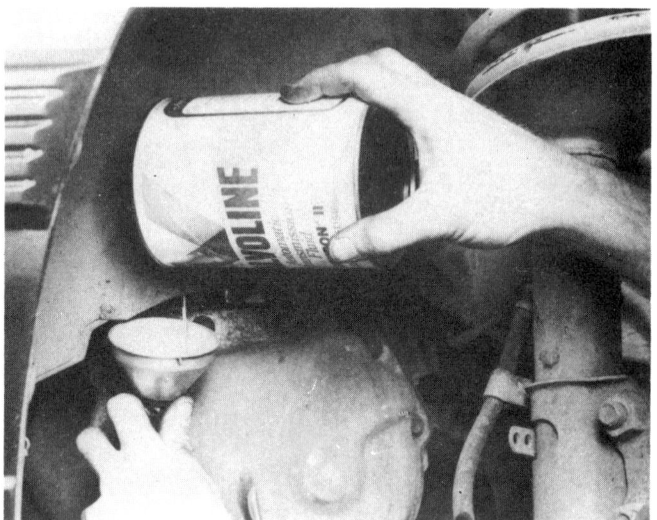

4.32 A funnel with a flexible spout or a syringe is necessary to replenish the manual transaxle lubricant

24 Note the fluid level **(see illustration)**. It should be at the bottom of the split rings.
25 If additional fluid is necessary to bring the level up to the specified point, carefully pour new, clean brake fluid into the master cylinder. Be careful not to spill the fluid on painted surfaces. Be sure the specified fluid is used; mixing different types of brake fluid can cause damage to the system. See *Recommended lubricants and fluids* or your owner's manual.
26 At this time the fluid and the master cylinder can be inspected for contamination. Normally the brake hydraulic system will not need periodic draining and refilling, but if rust deposits, dirt particles or water droplets are seen in the fluid, the system should be dismantled, drained and refilled with fresh fluid.
27 Reinstall the master cylinder caps.
28 The brake fluid in the master cylinder will drop slightly as the brake shoes or pads at each wheel wear down during normal operation. If the master cylinder requires repeated replenishing to keep it at the proper level, this is an indication of leakage in the brake system which should be corrected immediately. Check all brake lines and connections, along with the wheel cylinders and booster (see Chapter 9 for more information).
29 If, upon checking the fluid level, you discover one or both reservoirs empty or nearly empty, the brake system should be bled (Chapter 9).

Manual transaxle lubricant

30 Manual transaxles do not have a dipstick. The oil level is checked by removing a plug in the side of the transaxle case **(see illustration)**. Locate the plug and use a rag to clean the plug and the area around it. It may be necessary to remove the left inner fender well cover for access to the plug.
31 Check the level with the engine cold. Remove the plug. If oil immediately starts leaking out, thread the plug back into the transaxle — the oil level is alright. If there is no oil leakage, completely remove the plug and place a finger inside the hole **(see illustration)**. The oil level should be just at the bottom of the plug hole.
32 If the transaxle requires additional lubricant, use a funnel with a rubber filler tube or a syringe to pour or squeeze the recommended lubricant into the plug hole to restore the level **(see illustration)**. **Caution:** *Use only the specified transmission fluid; do not use gear oil (see Recommended lubricants and fluids).*
33 Thread the plug back into the transaxle and tighten it securely. Drive the vehicle and check for leaks around the plug.

Automatic transaxle fluid

34 The fluid inside the transaxle should be at normal operating temperature to get an accurate reading on the dipstick. This is done by driving the vehicle for several miles, making frequent starts and stops to allow

4.36 The automatic transaxle fluid level is checked by removing the dipstick — don't confuse it with the engine oil dipstick!

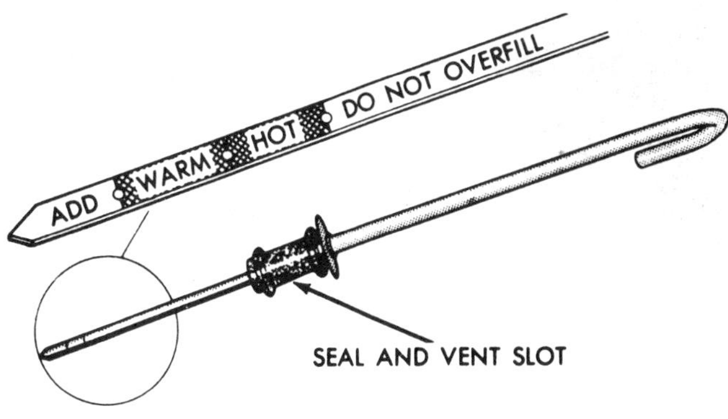

4.37 The automatic transaxle fluid level should be in the range indicated by the fluid temperature

1

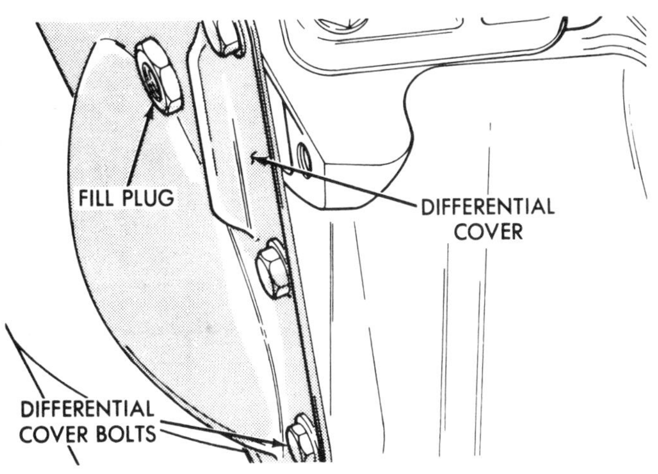

4.42 On 1982 models with an automatic transaxle, the differential lubricant is checked after removing the fill plug

4.48a The power steering fluid level should be checked with the engine off

the transaxle to shift through all gears.

35 Park the vehicle on a level surface, place the gear selector lever in Park and leave the engine running at an idle.

36 Remove the transaxle dipstick **(see illustration)** and wipe all the fluid from the end with a clean rag.

37 Push the dipstick back into the transaxle until the cap seats firmly on the dipstick tube. Remove the dipstick again and note the fluid on the end. The fluid level should be in the crosshatched area marked Hot (between the two upper holes in the dipstick) **(see illustration)**. If the fluid is not hot (temperature about 100°F), the level should be in the area marked Warm (between the two lower holes).

38 If the fluid level is at or below the Add mark on the dipstick, add enough fluid to raise the level to within the marks indicated for the appropriate temperature. Fluid should be added directly into the dipstick hole, using a funnel to prevent spills.

39 It is important that the transaxle not be overfilled. Under no circumstances should the fluid level be above the upper hole on the dipstick, as this could cause internal damage to the transaxle. The best way to prevent overfilling is to add fluid a little at a time, driving the vehicle and checking the level between additions.

40 Use only transaxle fluid specified by the manufacturer. This information can be found in the *Recommended lubricants and fluids* section of the Specifications.

41 The condition of the fluid should also be checked along with the level. If the fluid at the end of the dipstick is a dark reddish-brown color, or if it has a ''burnt'' smell, the transaxle fluid should be changed. If you are in doubt about the condition of the fluid, purchase some new fluid and compare the two for color and smell.

Differential lubricant (1982 automatic transaxles only)

42 On these models the differential lubricant must be checked separately from the transaxle. Raise the vehicle, support it securely and remove the differential fill plug **(see illustration)**.

43 The level must be within 3/8-inch of the bottom of the filler hole. If the level is low, add the specified lubricant with a syringe and install the plug.

Power steering fluid

44 Unlike manual steering, the power steering system relies on fluid which may, over a period of time, require replenishing.

45 The reservoir for the power steering pump is located on the rear side of the engine.

46 The power steering fluid level can be checked with the engine cold.

47 With the engine off, use a rag to clean the reservoir cap and the area around the cap. This will help prevent foreign material from falling into the reservoir when the cap is removed.

48 Turn and pull out the reservoir cap **(see illustration)**, which has a built-in dipstick attached to it. Remove the fluid at the bottom of the dipstick with a clean rag. Reinstall the cap/dipstick to get a fluid level

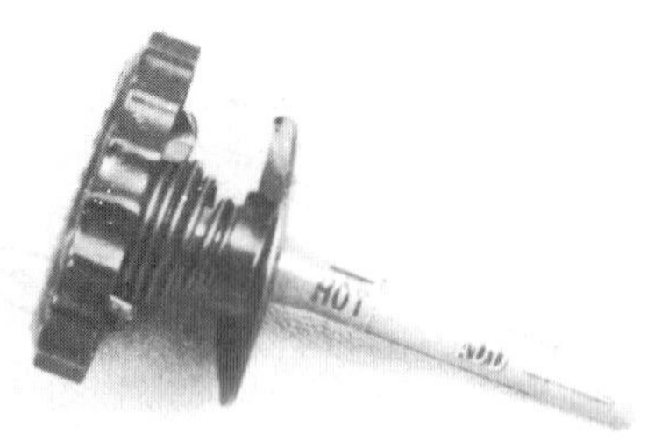

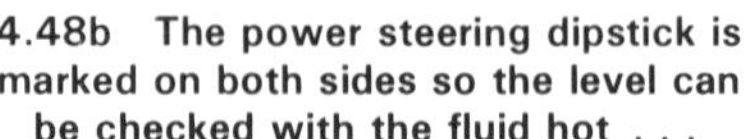
4.48b The power steering dipstick is marked on both sides so the level can be checked with the fluid hot . . .

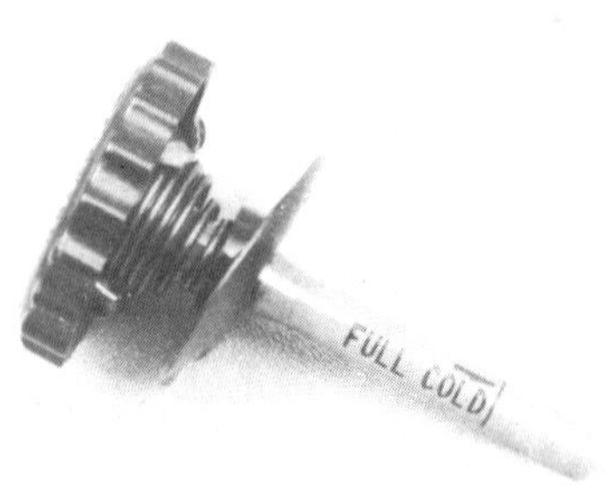

4.48c . . . or cold

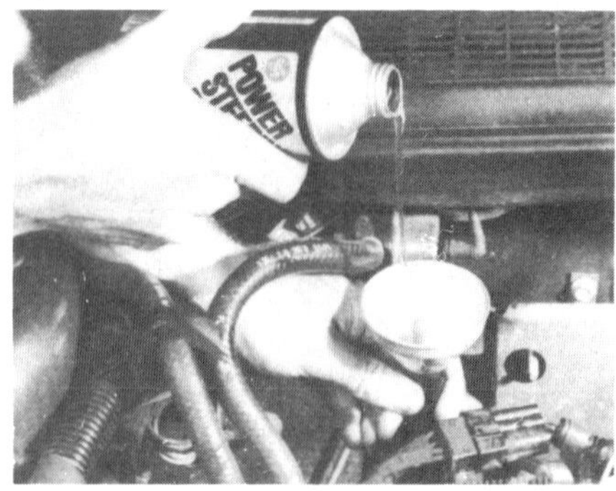

4.49 A funnel with a flexible spout or tube can be used to add fluid to the power steering reservoir

reading. Remove the dipstick and note the fluid level. It should be at the Full cold mark on the dipstick **(see illustrations)**.

49 If additional fluid is required, pour the specified type directly into the reservoir using a funnel to prevent spills **(see illustration)**.

50 If the reservoir requires frequent fluid additions, all power steering hoses, hose connections, the power steering pump and the steering box should be carefully checked for leaks.

5 Tire and tire pressure checks

Refer to illustration 5.3

1 Periodically inspecting the tires can prevent you from being stranded with a flat tire and can also give you clues as to possible problems with the steering and suspension systems before major damage occurs.

2 Proper tire inflation adds miles to the lifespan of the tires, allows the vehicle to achieve maximum miles per gallon figures and contributes to overall ride quality.

3 When inspecting a tire, first check for wear on the tread. Irregularities in the tread pattern (cupping, flat spots, more wear on one side than the other) are indications of front end alignment and/or balance problems. If any of these conditions are found, take the vehicle to a repair shop which can correct the problem **(see illustration)**.

4 Also check the tread area for cuts and punctures. Many times a nail or tack will embed itself in the tire tread and yet the tire will hold air pressure for a short time. In most cases, a repair shop or gas station can repair the punctured tire.

5 It is also important to check the sidewalls of the tire, both inside and outside. Check for deteriorated rubber, cuts and punctures. Also inspect the inboard side of the tire for signs of brake fluid, indicating a thorough brake inspection is needed immediately.

6 Incorrect tire pressure cannot be determined merely by looking at the tire. This is especially true for radial tires. A tire pressure gauge must be used. If you do not already have a reliable gauge, it is a good

Condition	Probable cause	Corrective action	Condition	Probable cause	Corrective action
Shoulder wear	• Underinflation (both sides wear) • Incorrect wheel camber (one side wear) • Hard cornering • Lack of rotation	• Measure and adjust pressure. • Repair or replace axle and suspension parts. • Reduce speed. • Rotate tires.	Feathered edge Toe wear	• Incorrect toe	• Adjust toe-in.
Center wear	• Overinflation • Lack of rotation	• Measure and adjust pressure. • Rotate tires.	Uneven wear	• Incorrect camber or caster • Malfunctioning suspension • Unbalanced wheel • Out-of-round brake drum • Lack of rotation	• Repair or replace axle and suspension parts. • Repair or replace suspension parts. • Balance or replace. • Turn or replace. • Rotate tires.

5.3 This chart will help you determine the condition of your tires, the probable cause(s) of abnormal wear and the corrective action necessary

idea to purchase one and keep it in the glove compartment. Built-in pressure gauges at gas stations are often unreliable. If you are in doubt as to the accuracy of your gauge, many repair shops have "master" pressure gauges which you can use for comparison purposes.

7 Always check tire inflation when the tires are cold. Cold, in this case, means the vehicle has not been driven more than one mile after sitting for three hours or more. It is normal for the pressure to increase four to eight pounds or more when the tires are hot.

8 Unscrew the valve cap protruding from the wheel or hubcap and firmly press the gauge onto the valve stem. Note the reading on the gauge and check it against the recommended tire pressure listed on the tire placard located on the jamb of the driver's door.

9 Check all tires and add air as necessary to bring all tires up to the recommended pressure levels. Don't forget the spare tire. Be sure to reinstall the valve caps, which keep dirt and moisture out of the valve stem mechanism.

6 Tire rotation

Refer to illustration 6.2

1 The tires should be rotated at the specified intervals and whenever uneven wear is noticed. Since the vehicle will be raised and the tires removed anyway, this is a good time to check the brakes (Section 26) and/or repack the wheel bearings. Read over the appropriate Sections if this is to be done at the same time.

2 The rotation pattern depends on whether or not the spare is included in the rotation **(see illustration)**.

3 See the information in *Jacking and towing* at the front of this manual for the proper procedures to follow when raising the vehicle and refer to Chapter 10 for changing a tire; however, if the brakes are to be checked, do not apply the parking brake as stated. Make sure the tires are blocked to prevent the vehicle from rolling.

4 Preferably, the entire vehicle should be raised at the same time. This can be done on a hoist or by jacking up each corner of the vehicle and lowering it onto jackstands. Always use four jackstands and make sure the vehicle is safely supported.

5 After the tire rotation, check and adjust the tire pressures as necessary and be sure to check wheel lug nut tightness.

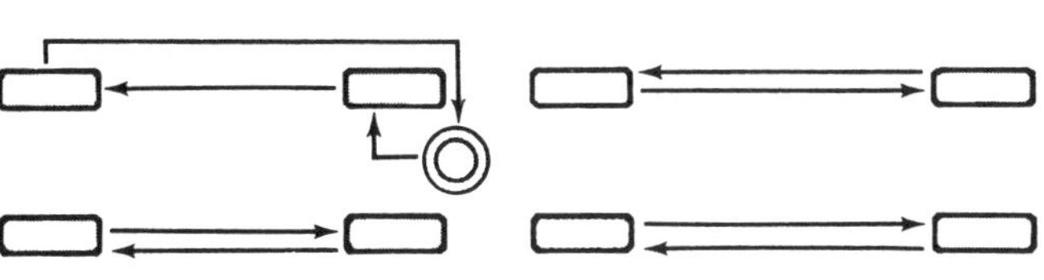

6.2 Tire rotation diagram

7 Wiper blade element replacement

Refer to illustrations 7.4, 7.5a, 7.5b, 7.5c, 7.7 and 7.8

1 The windshield and rear window wiper blade elements should be checked periodically for cracks and deterioration.

2 To gain access to the wiper blades, turn on the ignition switch and cycle the wipers to a position on the windshield or rear window where the work can be performed, then turn off the ignition.

3 Lift the wiper blade assembly away from the glass.

Type A

4 Use a screwdriver to lift the release tab and remove the wiper blade assembly from the arm **(see illustration)**.

5 Lift the lock tab on one of the end links, then squeeze the link to remove it from the center bridge. Slide the end link off the blade element and then slide the element from the claws of the other link **(see illustrations)**.

6 Installation is the reverse of removal.

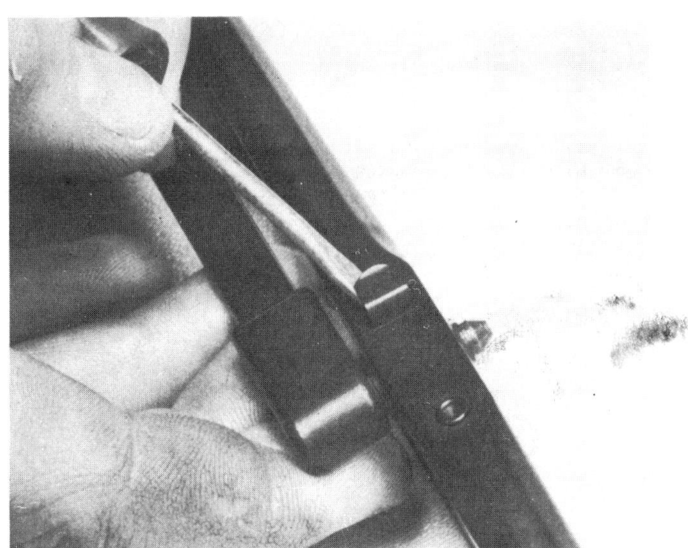

7.4 Lift the tabs with a small screwdriver and slide the wiper arm off the pin in the direction shown (type A wiper)

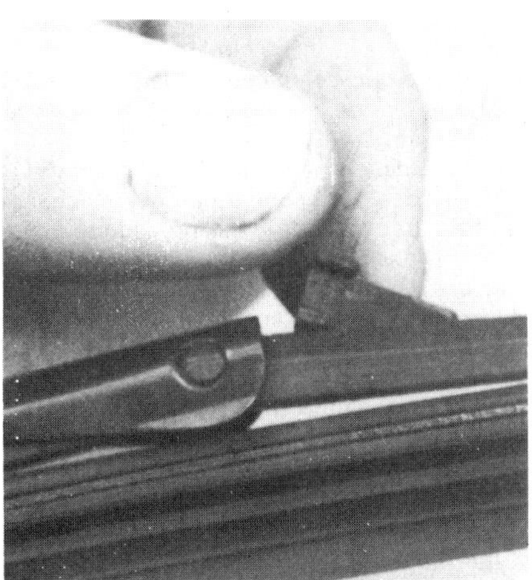

7.5a To remove the type A wiper element, lift the lock tabs at both ends and . . .

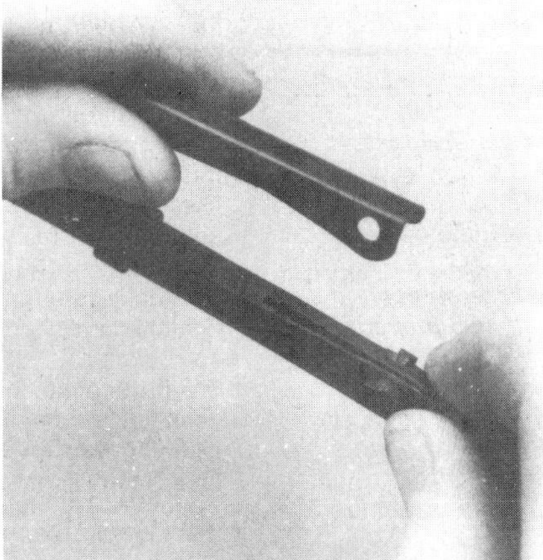

7.5b . . . squeeze the end links together, allowing . . .

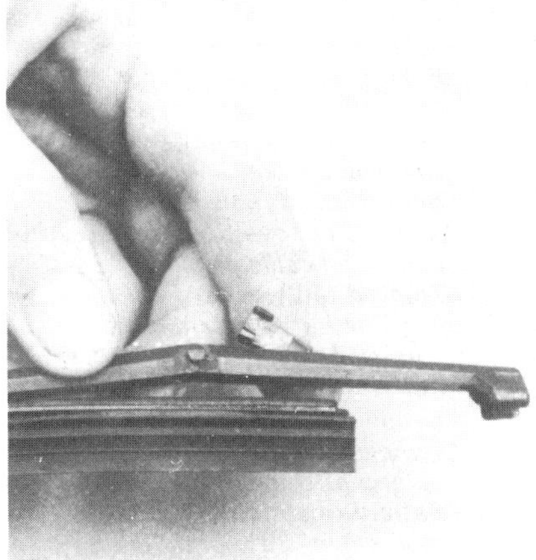

7.5c . . . the links to slide off

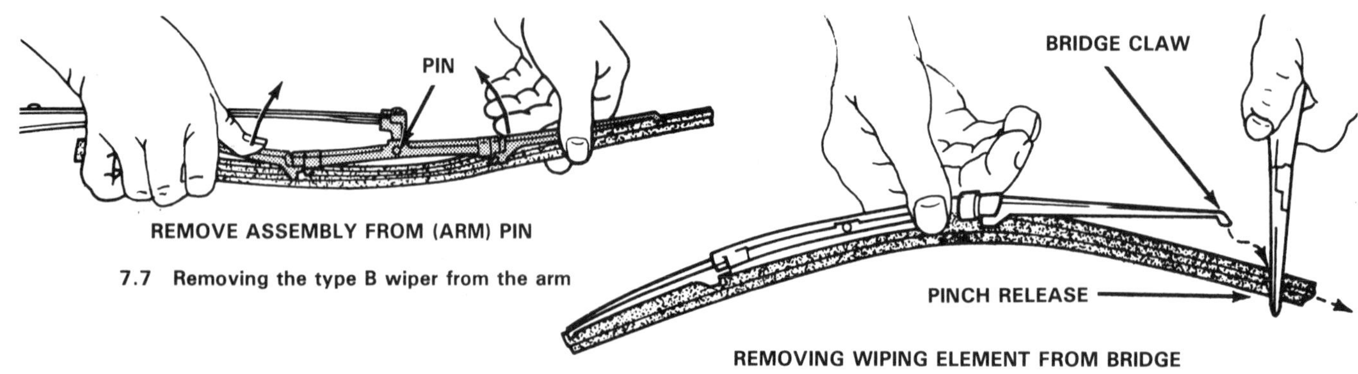

7.7 Removing the type B wiper from the arm

7.8 Use a pair of needle-nose pliers to slide the type B wiping element from the bridge

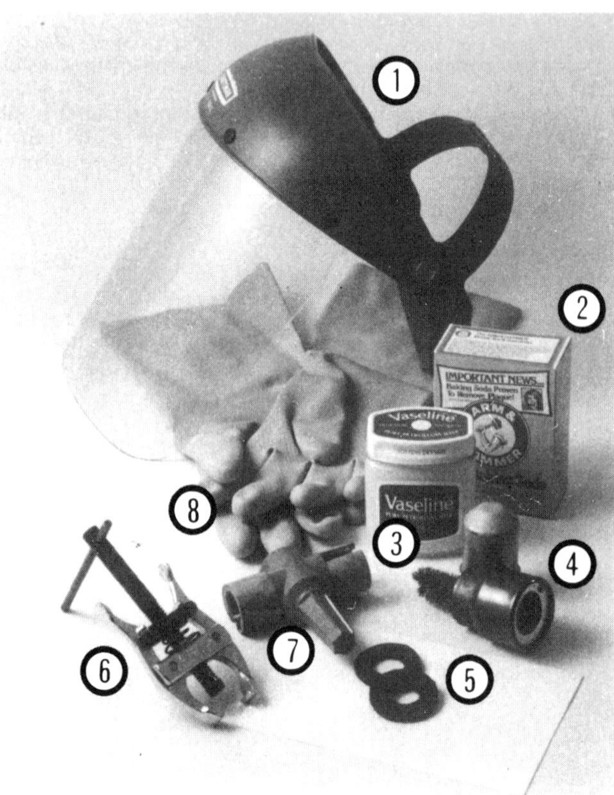

8.1 Tools and materials required for battery maintenance

1 **Face shield/safety goggles** — *When removing corrosion with a brush, the acidic particles can easily fly up into your eyes*
2 **Baking soda** — *A solution of baking soda and water can be used to neutralize corrosion*
3 **Petroleum jelly** — *A layer of this on the battery posts will help prevent corrosion*
4 **Battery post/cable cleaner** — *This wire brush cleaning tool will remove all traces of corrosion from the battery posts and cable clamps*
5 **Treated felt washers** — *Placing one of these on each post, directly under the cable clamps, will help prevent corrosion*
6 **Puller** — *Sometimes the cable clamps are very difficult to pull off the posts, even after the nut/bolt has been completely loosened. This tool pulls the clamp straight up and off the post without damage*
7 **Battery post/cable cleaner** — *Here is another cleaning tool which is a slightly different version of number 4 above, but it does the same thing*
8 **Rubber gloves** — *Another safety item to consider when servicing the battery; remember that's acid inside the battery!*

Type B

7 Apply reverse pressure to both wiper blade end bridges to disengage the blade assembly from the arm **(see illustration)**.
8 Use a pair of needle-nose pliers to pinch the lock on the end of the blade reinforcement and withdraw the element from the blade assembly **(see illustration)**.
9 Installation is the reverse of removal.

8 Battery check and maintenance

Refer to illustrations 8.1, 8.5a, 8.5b, 8.5c and 8.5d

Warning: *Certain precautions must be followed when checking or servicing the battery. Hydrogen gas, which is highly flammable, is produced in the cells, so keep lighted tobacco, open flames, bare light bulbs and sparks away from the battery. The electrolyte inside the battery is dilute sulfuric acid, which can burn your skin and cause serious injury if splashed in the eyes (wear safety glasses). It will also ruin clothes and painted surfaces. Remove all metal jewelry which could contact the positive terminal and another grounded metal source, causing a short circuit.*

1 Tools and materials required for battery maintenance include eye and hand protection, baking soda, petroleum jelly, a battery cable puller and a battery post/cable cleaning tool **(see illustration)**. In some cases where the cable clamp nuts are severely corroded and a wrench will not work to loosen them, a special battery terminal pliers may be needed.
2 These models are equipped with a maintenance-free battery, which doesn't require the addition of water. These batteries have built-in test indicators which display different colors depending on battery condition. If the indicator shows *green*, the battery is properly charged; if it is *red* or *black*, charging is required. A light *yellow* indicator means the battery must be replaced with a new one. **Warning:** *Do not charge, test or jump start a battery with a yellow indicator visible. If any doubt exists as to the battery state-of-charge, it should be tested by a dealer service department or service station.*
3 The top of the battery should be kept clean and free from dirt and moisture so that the battery does not become partially discharged. Clean the top and sides of the battery with a baking soda and water solution, but make sure that it does not enter the battery. After it is clean, check the case for cracks and other damage.
4 Make sure the cable clamps are tight to ensure good electrical connections and check the cables for cracked insulation, frayed wires and corrosion.
5 If the posts are corroded, remove the cables (negative first, then positive) and clean the clamps and battery posts with a battery terminal cleaning tool, then reinstall the cables (positive first, then negative) **(see illustrations)**. Apply petroleum jelly to the cable clamps and posts to keep corrosion to a minimum.
6 Make sure that the battery carrier is in good condition and that the hold-down clamp nut is tight. If the battery is removed, make sure that no parts remain in the bottom of the carrier when it is reinstalled. When reinstalling the clamp nut do not overtighten it.
7 Corrosion on the carrier and hold-down components can be re-

8.5a Battery terminal corrosion usually appears as light, fluffy powder

8.5b Removing the cable from a battery post with a wrench – sometimes a a special battery pliers is required for this procedure if corrosion has caused deterioration of the nut hex (always remove the ground cable first and hook it up last!)

8.5c Regardless of the type of tool used to clean the battery posts, a clean, shiny surface should be the result

8.5d When cleaning the cable clamps, all corrosion must be removed (the inside of the clamp is tapered to match the taper on the post, so don't remove too much material)

moved with a solution of baking soda and water. Rinse the treated areas with clean water, dry them thoroughly and apply zinc-based primer and paint.

9 Engine oil and filter change

Refer to illustrations 9.3, 9.9, 9.14 and 9.19

1 Frequent oil changes may be the best form of preventative maintenance available to the do-it-yourselfer. When engine oil ages it gets diluted and contaminated, which ultimately leads to premature engine wear.

2 Although some sources recommend oil filter changes every other oil change, we feel that the minimal cost of an oil filter and the relative ease with which it is installed dictate that a new filter be used whenever the oil is changed.

3 The tools necessary for a routine oil and filter change include a breaker bar and socket to fit the drain plug at the bottom of the oil pan, an oil filter wrench to remove the old filter, a container with at

least a five quart capacity to drain the old oil into and rubber gloves to protect your hands when draining the hot oil **(see illustration)**.

4 In addition, you should have plenty of clean rags and newspapers handy to mop up any spills. Access to the underside of the vehicle is greatly improved if it can be lifted on a hoist, driven onto ramps or supported by jackstands. **Warning:** *Do not work under a vehicle which is supported only by a jack.*

5 If this is your first oil change on the vehicle, it is a good idea to crawl underneath and familarize yourself with the locations of the oil drain plug and the oil filter. Since the engine and exhaust components will be warm during the actual work, it is a good idea to figure out any potential problems before the engine and exhaust system are hot.

6 Allow the engine to warm up to normal operating temperature. If oil or tools are needed, use the warm-up time to gather everything necessary for the job. The correct type of oil to buy for your application can be found in the *Recommended lubricants and fluids* section of the Specifications.

7 With the engine oil warm (warm oil will drain better and more built-up sludge will be removed with the oil), raise the vehicle and support it securely on jackstands. They should be placed under the portions of the body designated as hoisting and jacking points front and rear (see *Jacking and towing* at the front of this manual).

8 Move all necessary tools, rags and newspapers under the vehicle. Position the drain pan under the drain plug. Keep in mind that the oil will initially flow from the engine with some force, so locate the pan accordingly.

9 Being careful not to touch any of the hot exhaust components, use the breaker bar and socket to remove the drain plug near the bottom of the oil pan **(see illustration)**. Depending on how hot the oil is, you may want to wear gloves while unscrewing the plug the final few turns.

10 Allow the oil to drain into the pan. It may be necessary to move the pan further under the engine as the oil flow reduces to a trickle.

11 After all the oil has drained, clean the plug thoroughly with a rag. Small metal particles may cling to the plug and would immediately contaminate the new oil.

12 Clean the area around the oil pan opening and reinstall the plug. Tighten it securely.

13 Move the drain pan into position under the oil filter.

14 Now use the filter wrench to loosen the oil filter **(see illustration)**. Chain or metal band-type filter wrenches may distort the filter canister, but don't worry about it – the filter will be discarded anyway.

15 Sometimes the oil filter is on so tight it cannot be loosened, or it

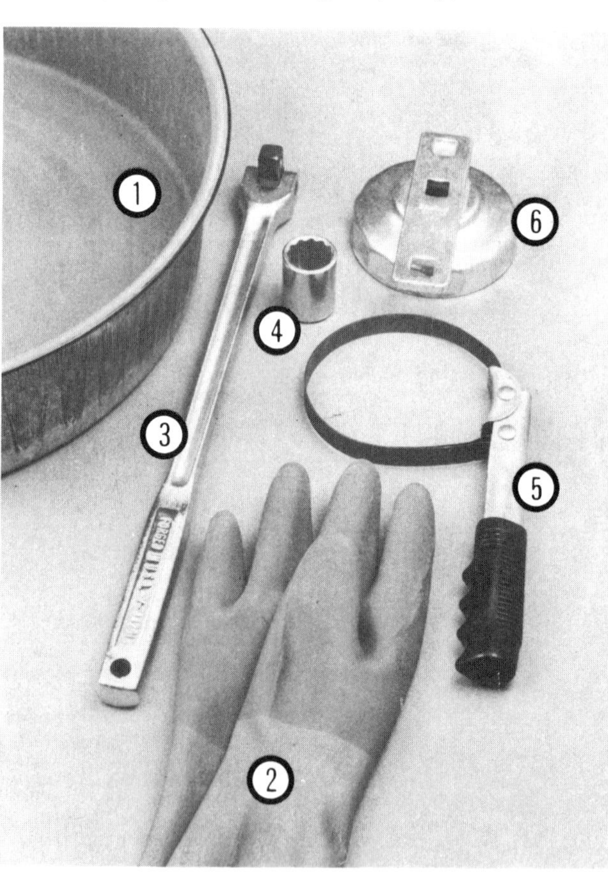

9.3 These tools are required when changing the engine oil and filter

1 **Drain pan** – *It should be fairly shallow in depth, but wide in order to prevent spills*
2 **Rubber gloves** – *When removing the drain plug and filter it is inevitable that you will get oil on your hands (the gloves will prevent burns)*
3 **Breaker bar** – *Sometimes the oil drain plug is pretty tight and a long breaker bar is needed to loosen it*
4 **Socket** – *To be used with the breaker bar or a ratchet (must be the correct size to fit the drain plug)*
5 **Filter wrench** – *This is a metal band-type wrench, which requires clearance around the filter to be effective*
6 **Filter wrench** – *This type fits on the bottom of the filter and can be turned with a ratchet or breaker bar (different size wrenches are available for different types of filters)*

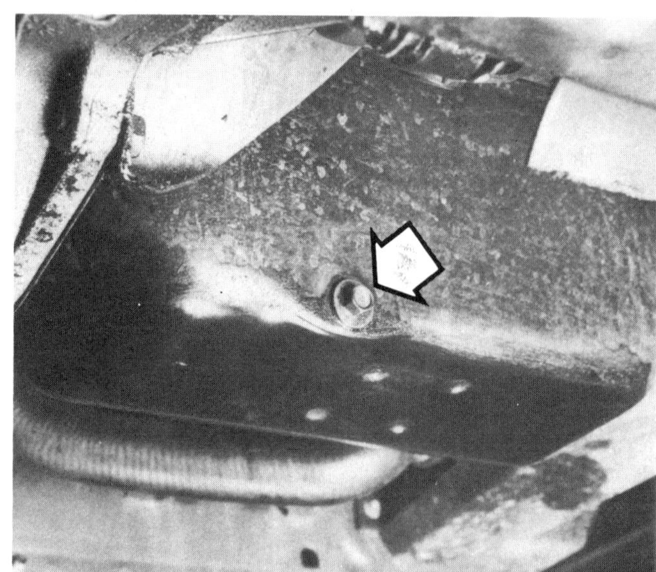

9.9 Use a six-point socket and breaker bar to remove the engine oil drain plug (it is usually very tight)

9.14 A strap-type wrench should be used to loosen the oil filter

is positioned in an area which is inaccessible with a conventional filter wrench. Other type of tools, which fit over the end of the filter and are turned with a ratchet/breaker bar, are available and may be better suited for removing the filter on your vehicle. If the filter is extremely tight, position the filter wrench near the threaded end of the filter, close to the engine.

16 Completely unscrew the old filter. Be careful, it is full of oil. Empty the old oil inside the filter into the drain pan.

17 Compare the old filter with the new one to make sure they are identical.

18 Use a clean rag to remove all oil, dirt and sludge from the area where the oil filter mounts on the engine. Check the old filter to make sure the rubber gasket is not stuck to the engine mounting surface. If the gasket is stuck to the engine (use a flashlight if necessary to check), remove it.

19 Open one of the containers of new oil and fill the new filter half full of oil. Also apply a light coat of oil to the rubber gasket on the new oil filter **(see illustration)**.

20 Attach the new filter to the engine following the tightening directions printed on the filter canister or packing box. Most filter manufacturers recommend against using a filter wrench due to the possibility of overtightening and damaging the canister.

9.19 Use your finger to apply a light coat of oil to the oil filter gasket

21 Remove all tools, and materials from under the vehicle, being careful not to spill the oil in the drain pan. Lower the vehicle off the jackstands.

22 Move to the engine compartment and locate the oil filler cap on the engine.

23 If an oil spout if used, push the spout into the top of the oil can and pour the fresh oil through the filler opening. A funnel placed in the opening may also be used.

24 Pour the specified amount of new oil into the engine. Wait a few minutes to allow the oil to drain to the pan, then check the level on the oil dipstick (see Section 4 if necessary). If the oil level is at or above the lower Add mark, start the engine and allow the new oil to circulate.

25 Run the engine for only about a minute, then shut it off. Immediately look under the vehicle and check for leaks at the oil pan drain plug and around the oil filter. If either one is leaking, tighten with a bit more force.

26 With the new oil circulated and the filter now completely full, recheck the level on the dipstick. If necessary, add enough oil to bring the level to the Full mark on the dipstick. 1

27 During the first few trips after an oil change, make it a point to check for leaks and keep a close watch on the oil level.

28 The old oil drained from the engine cannot be reused in its present state and should be disposed of. Oil reclamation centers, auto repair shops and gas stations will normally accept the oil (which can be refined and used again). After the oil has cooled, it should be drained into containers (plastic bottles with screw-on tops are preferred) for transport to a disposal site.

10 Fuel filter replacement

Refer to illustrations 10.1a, 10.1b, 10.11 and 10.12

Warning: *Gasoline is extremely flammable, so extra precautions must be taken when working on any part of the fuel system. Do not smoke or allow open flames or bare light bulbs near the vehicle. Also, do not work in a garage if a natural gas-type appliance with a pilot light is present.*

Carburetor equipped models

1 The fuel filter is a disposable paper element type and is located in the fuel line between the fuel pump and the carburetor **(see illustrations)**.

2 This job should be done with the engine cold (after sitting at least

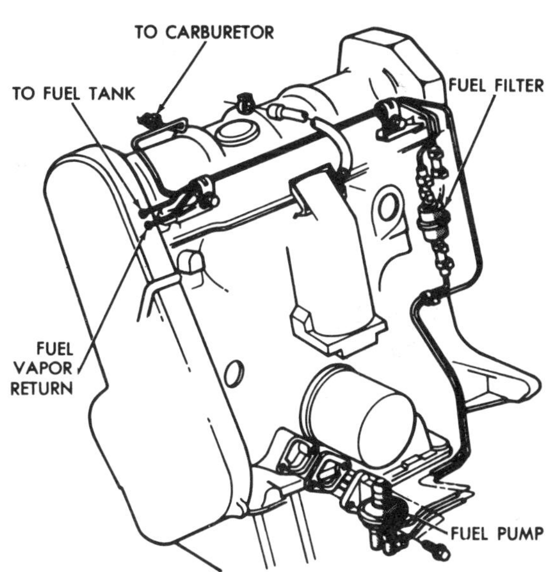

10.1a Fuel filter location — 2.2L engine

10.1b On 2.6L engines, the fuel filter is mounted near the carburetor

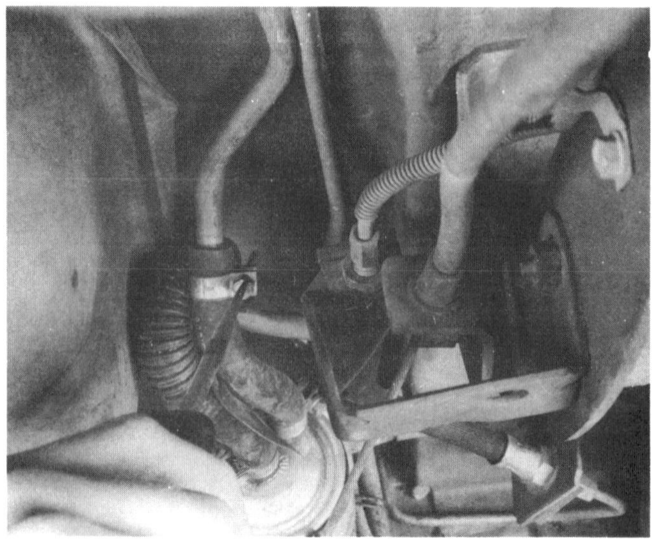

10.11 The new filter comes with this hose already mounted, so disconnect the old one at the fuel line (fuel injected models)

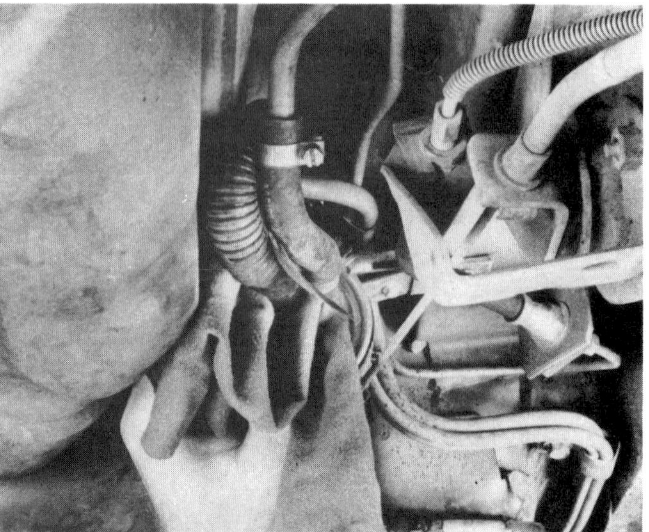

10.12 A cloth wrapped around the filter will keep the fuel from spurting out (fuel injected models)

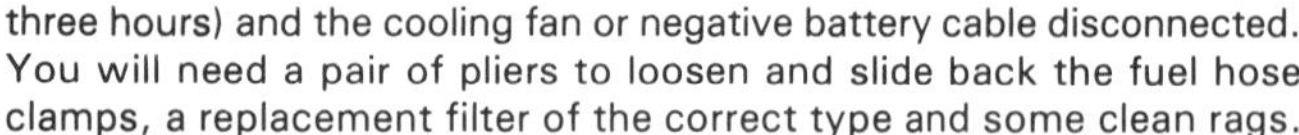

three hours) and the cooling fan or negative battery cable disconnected. You will need a pair of pliers to loosen and slide back the fuel hose clamps, a replacement filter of the correct type and some clean rags.
3 Place the rags under the fuel filter to catch any fuel that is spilled as the fuel hoses are disconnected.
4 Slide back the clamps, pull the hoses from the filter and remove the filter. On 2.6L engines it will also be necessary to disengage the mounting bracket.
5 Push the hoses onto the new filter and install the clamps.
6 Connect the battery and/or fan, start the engine, check for leaks and make sure the filter is securely mounted.
7 A second fuel filter is attached to the end of the fuel suction tube in the gas tank. It does not require routine replacement, but it may be serviced if it becomes clogged.

Fuel injected models

8 The fuel filter is a disposable canister type and is located in the fuel line under the rear of the vehicle, adjacent to the fuel tank.
9 Warning: Fuel injected models maintain pressure in the fuel system at all times so the system must be depressurized BEFORE any lines are disconnected to avoid the possibility of spraying fuel. Refer to Chapter 4 for the fuel pressure relief procedure.
10 Raise the rear of the vehicle and support it securely on jackstands.
11 Loosen the filter inlet and outlet hose clamps **(see illustration)**.
12 Wrap a cloth around the fuel filter to catch the residual fuel (which is under some pressure) and disconnect the hoses **(see illustration)**. It is a good idea to tie rags around your wrists to keep fuel from running down your arms.
13 Remove the bracket mounting bolt and detach the filter from the vehicle; hold your finger over the outlet to keep the residual fuel from running out.
14 Place the new filter in position, install the mounting bolt and tighten it securely.
15 Install new clamps and attach the hoses to the filter. Tighten the clamps securely.
16 Start the engine and check carefully for leaks at the hose connections.

11 Chassis lubrication

Refer to illustrations 11.1, 11.6a and 11.6b

1 A grease gun and a cartridge filled with the proper grease (see *Recommended lubricants and fluids*), graphite spray and an oil can filled with engine oil will be required to lubricate the chassis components **(see illustration)**. Occasionally, on later model vehicles, plugs will be installed rather than grease fittings. If so, grease fittings will have to be purchased and installed.
2 Look under the vehicle and see if grease fittings or plugs are installed. If there are plugs, remove them with a wrench and buy grease fittings which will thread into the component. A Chrysler dealer or auto parts store will be able to supply the correct fittings. Straight and angled

11.1 Materials required for chassis and body lubrication

1 ***Engine oil*** *— Light engine oil in a can like this can be used for door and hood hinges*
2 ***Graphite spray*** *— Used to lubricate lock cylinders*
3 ***Grease*** *— Grease, in a variety of types and weights, is available for use in a grease gun. Check the Specifications for your requirements*
4 ***Grease gun*** *— A common grease gun, shown here with a detachable hose and nozzle, is needed for chassis lubrication. After use, clean it thoroughly!*

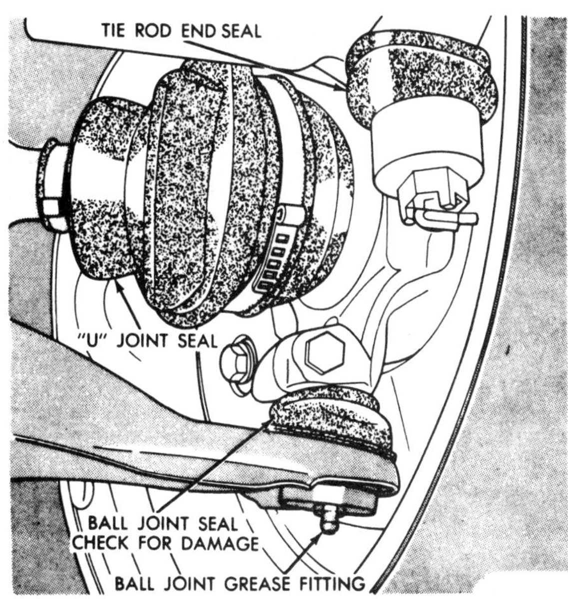

11.6a The suspension balljoints are usually equipped with grease fittings to ensure proper lubrication

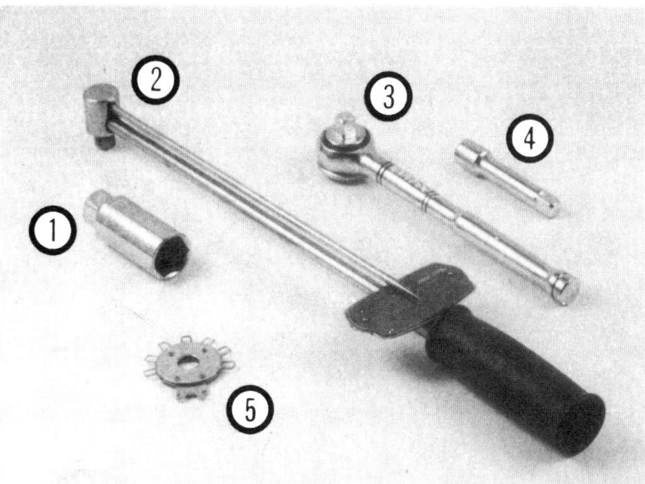

12.2 Tools required for changing spark plugs

1. ***Spark plug socket*** — *This will have special padding inside to protect the spark plug porcelain insulator*
2. ***Torque wrench*** — *Although not mandatory, use of this tool is the best way to ensure that the plugs are tightened properly*
3. ***Ratchet*** — *Standard hand tool to fit the plug socket*
4. ***Extension*** — *Depending on model and accessories, you may need special extensions and universal joints to reach one or more of the plugs*
5. ***Spark plug gap gauge*** — *This gauge for checking the gap comes in a variety of styles. Make sure the gap for your engine is included*

fittings are available.

3 For easier access under the vehicle, raise it with a jack and place jackstands under the portions of the body designated as hoisting and jacking points front and rear (see *Jacking and towing* at the front of this manual). Make sure it is securely supported by the stands.

4 Before beginning, force a little grease out of the nozzle to remove any dirt from the end of the gun. Wipe the nozzle clean with a rag.

5 With the grease gun and plenty of clean rags, crawl under the vehicle and begin lubricating the components.

6 Wipe the balljoint grease fitting clean and push the nozzle firmly

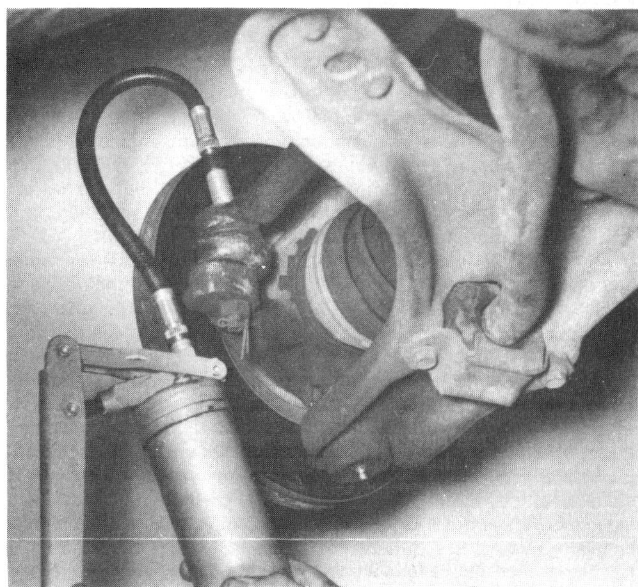

11.6b The steering system tie-rod end balljoint grease fittings are on the upper side and may be difficult to reach unless the grease gun is equipped with a flexible nozzle

over it **(see illustration)**. Operate the lever on the grease gun to force grease into the component. The balljoints should be lubricated until the rubber seal is firm to the touch. Do not pump too much grease into the fitting as it could rupture the seal **(see illustration)**. For all other suspension and steering components, continue pumping grease into the fitting until it oozes out of the joint between the two components. If grease escapes around the grease gun nozzle, the fitting is clogged or the nozzle is not completely seated on the fitting. Resecure the gun nozzle to the fitting and try again. If necessary, replace the fitting with a new one.

7 Wipe the excess grease from the components and the grease fitting. Repeat the procedure for the remaining fittings.

8 Lubricate the sliding contact and pivot points of the manual transaxle shift linkage with the specified grease. While you are under the vehicle, clean and lubricate the parking brake cable along with the cable guides and levers. This can be done by smearing some of the chassis grease onto the cable and related parts with your fingers. Lubricate the clutch adjuster and cable, as well as the cable positioner, with a thin film of multi-purpose grease.

9 Lower the vehicle to the ground.

10 Open the hood and smear a little chassis grease on the hood latch mechanism. Have an assistant pull the hood release lever from inside the vehicle as you lubricate the cable at the latch.

11 Lubricate all the hinges (door, hood, etc.) with the recommended lubricant to keep them in proper working order.

12 The key lock cylinders can be lubricated with spray-on graphite or silicone lubricant which is available at auto parts stores.

13 Lubricate the door weatherstripping with silicone spray. This will reduce chafing and retard wear.

12 Spark plug replacement

Refer to illustrations 12.2, 12.5a, 12.5b, 12.7 and 12.11

1 The spark plugs are located on the front side of the engine, facing the radiator grille on 2.2L/2.5L engines and on the back (firewall) side on 2.6L engines. **Caution:** *Before beginning work, disconnect the negative battery cable to prevent the electric cooling fan from coming on when working around the spark plugs.*

2 In most cases the tools necessary for spark plug replacement include a plug wrench or spark plug socket which fits onto a ratchet (this special socket will be padded inside to protect the porcelain insulators on the new plugs), various extensions and a feeler gauge to check and adjust the spark plug gap **(see illustration)**. A special plug wire removal tool is available for separating the wire boot from the spark plug, but

it is not absolutely necessary. Since these engines are equipped with an aluminum cylinder head, a torque wrench should be used for tightening the spark plugs.
3 The best approach when replacing the spark plugs is to purchase the new spark plugs beforehand, adjust them to the proper gap and then replace each plug one at a time. When buying the new spark plugs, be sure to obtain the correct plug for your specific engine. This information can be found on the *Emission Control Information label* located under the hood or in the factory owner's manual. If differences exist between the sources, purchase the spark plug type specified on the label as it was printed for your specific engine.
4 Allow the engine to cool completely before attempting to remove any of the plugs. During this cooling off time, each of the new spark plugs can be inspected for defects and the gaps can be checked.
5 The gap is checked by inserting the proper thickness gauge between the electrodes at the tip of the plug **(see illustration)**. The gap between the electrodes should be the same as that given in the Specifications or on the VECI label. The wire should touch each of the electrodes. If the gap is incorrect, use the adjuster on the thickness gauge body to bend the curved side electrode slightly until the proper gap is obtained **(see illustration)**. Also, at this time check for cracks in the spark plug body (if any are found, the plug should not be used). If the side electrode is not exactly over the center one, use the adjuster to align the two.
6 Cover the front of the vehicle to prevent damage to exterior paint.
7 With the engine cool, remove the spark plug wire from one spark plug. Pull only on the boot at the end of the wire; do not pull on the wire itself. Use a twisting motion to free the boot and wire from the plug. A plug wire removal tool (mentioned earlier) should be used if available **(see illustration)**.
8 If compressed air is available, use it to blow any dirt or foreign material away from the spark plug area. A common bicycle pump will also work. The idea here is to eliminate the possibility of material falling into the cylinder through the plug hole as the spark plug is removed.
9 Now place the spark plug socket over the plug and remove it from the engine by turning it in a counterclockwise direction.
10 Compare the spark plug with those shown in the accompanying color photos to get an indication of the overall running condition of the engine.
11 Thread one of the new plugs into the hole, tightening it as much as possible by hand. **Caution:** *Be extremely careful, as these engines have aluminum cylinder heads, which means that the spark plug hole threads can be stripped easily. It may be a good idea to slip a short length of rubber hose over the end of the plug to use as a tool to thread it into place. The hose will grip the plug well enough to turn it, but will start to slip on the plug if the plug begins to cross-thread in the hole — this will prevent damaged threads and the accompanying costs involved in repairing them* **(see illustration)**.
12 Attach the plug wire to the new spark plug, again using a twisting motion on the boot until it is seated on the spark plug.
13 Repeat the above procedure for the remaining spark plugs, replacing them one at a time to prevent mixing up the spark plug wires.

12.5a Spark plug manufacturers recommend using a wire-type gauge when checking the gap — if the wire does not slide between the electrodes with a slight drag, adjustment is required

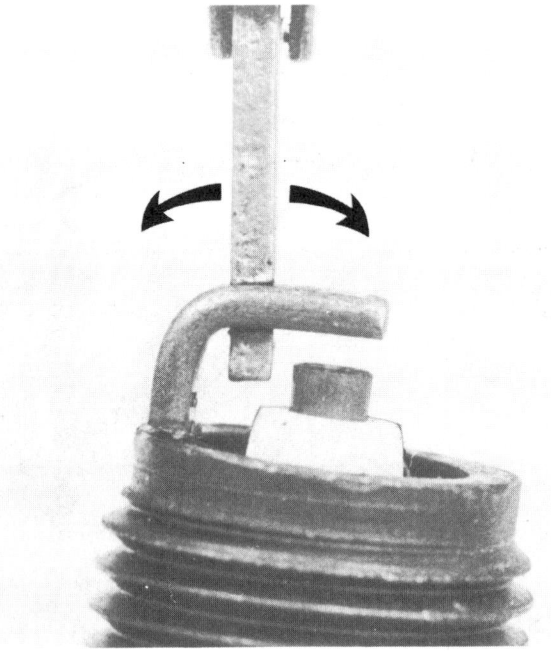

12.5b To change the gap, bend the *side* electrode only, as indicated by the arrows, and be very careful not to crack or chip the porcelain insulator surrounding the center electrode

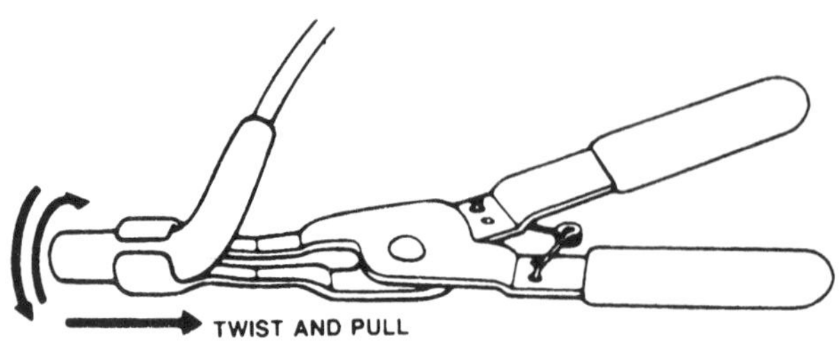

12.7 When removing the spark plug wires, pull only on the boot and use a twisting/pulling motion

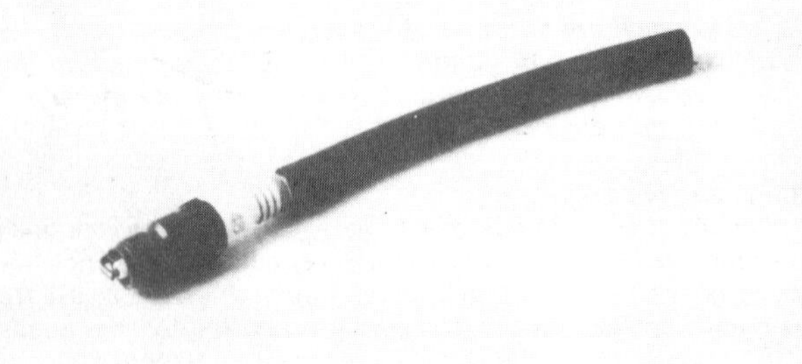

12.11 A length of 3/16-inch ID rubber hose will save time and prevent damaged threads when installing the spark plugs

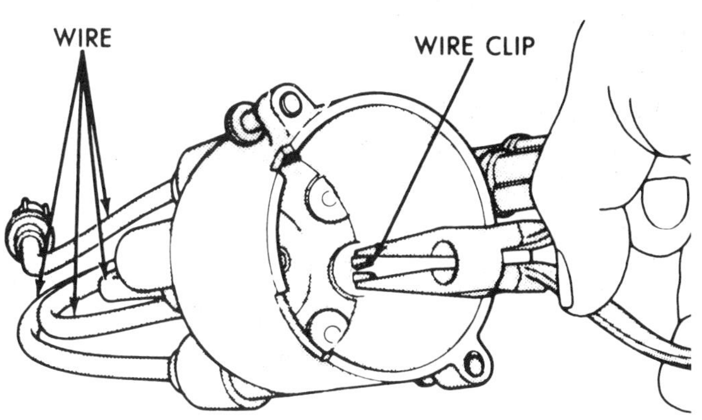

13.7 When replacing the spark plug wires on a 2.2L/2.5L engine, a pair of pliers must be used to compress the wire clips inside the distributor cap

13 Spark plug wire, distributor cap and rotor check and replacement

Refer to illustrations 13.7, 13.9 and 13.10

1 The spark plug wires should be checked at the recommended intervals or whenever new spark plugs are installed.

2 The wires should be inspected one at a time to prevent mixing up the order which is essential for proper engine operation.

3 Disconnect the plug wire from the spark plug. A removal tool can be used for this, or you can grab the rubber boot, twist slightly and then pull the wire free. *Do not pull on the wire itself, only on the rubber boot.*

4 Check inside the boot for corrosion, which will look like a white, crusty powder (don't mistake the white dielectric grease used on some plug wire boots for corrosion).

5 Now push the wire and boot back onto the end of the spark plug. It should be a tight fit on the plug end. If not, remove the wire and use a pair of pliers to carefully crimp the metal connector inside the wire boot until the fit is snug.

6 Now, using a cloth, clean each wire along its entire length. Remove all built-up dirt and grease. As this is done, inspect for burned areas, cracks and any other form of damage. Bend the wires in several places to ensure that the conductive material inside has not hardened. Repeat the procedure for the remaining wires (don't forget the distributor cap-to-coil wire).

7 Remove the distributor cap splash shield and check the wires at the cap, making sure they are not loose and that the wires and boots are not cracked or damaged. **Note:** *Do not attempt to pull the wires from the cap, as they are retained on the inside by wire clips. The manufacturer does not recommend removing the wires from the cap for inspection because this could damage the integrity of the boot seal. If the wires appear to be damaged, replace them with new ones. Remove the distributor cap, release the wire clips with a pair of pliers and remove the wires* **(see illustration)**. Insert the new wires into the cap while squeezing the boots to release any trapped air as you push them into place. Continue pushing until you feel the wire electrodes snap into position.

8 A visual check of the spark plug wires can also be made. In a darkened garage (make sure there is ventilation), start the engine and look at each plug wire. Be careful not to come into contact with any moving engine parts. If there is a break or fault in the wire, you will see arcing or a small spark at the damaged area.

9 Remove the distributor cap with the wires attached, and check the cap for cracks, carbon tracks and other damage. Examine the terminals inside the cap for corrosion (slight corrosion can be removed with a pocket knife) **(see illustration)**.

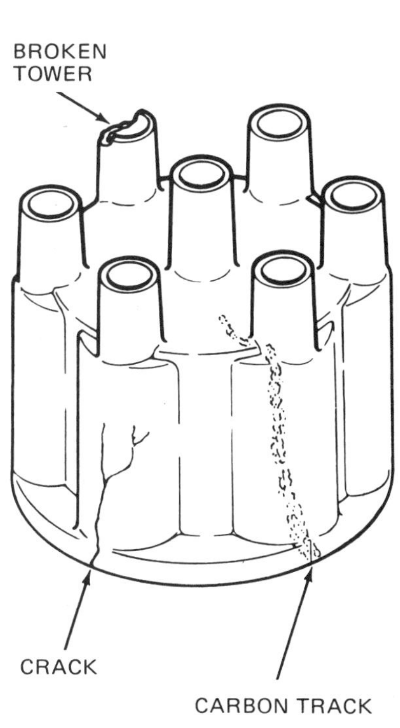

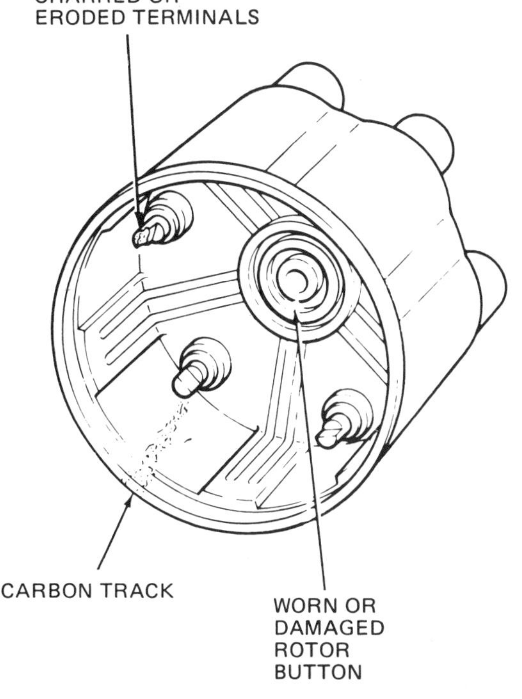

13.9 Shown here are some of the common defects to look for when inspecting the distributor cap (if in doubt about its condition, install a new one)

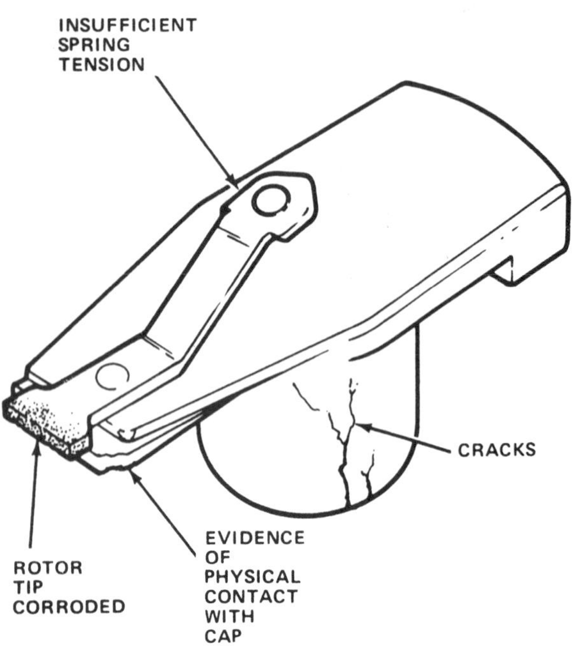

13.10 The ignition rotor should be checked for wear and corrosion as indicated here (if in doubt about its condition, buy a new one)

10 Check the rotor (now visible on the end of the distributor shaft) for cracks and a secure fit on the shaft. Make sure the terminals are not burned, corroded or pitted excessively. A small fine file can be used to restore the rotor terminals **(see illustration)**.

11 If new spark plug wires are needed, purchase a complete pre-cut set for your particular engine. The terminals and rubber boots should already be installed on the wires. Replace the wires one at a time to avoid mixing up the firing order and make sure the terminals are securely seated in the distributor cap and on the spark plugs.

14 Drivebelt check, adjustment and replacement

Refer to illustrations 14.3, 14.4, 14.5a, 14.5b, 14.5c and 14.5d

Caution: *The electric cooling fan on some models can activate at any time, even when the ignition switch is in the Off position. Disconnect the fan motor or negative battery cable when working in the vicinity of the fan.*

1 The drivebelts, or V-belts as they are sometimes called, at the front of the engine, play an important role in the overall operation of the vehicle and its components. Due to their function and material makeup, the belts are prone to failure after a period of time and should be inspected and adjusted periodically to prevent major damage.

2 The number of belts used on a particular engine depends on the accessories installed. Drivebelts are used to turn the alternator, AIR pump, power steering pump, water pump and air conditioning compressor. Depending on the pulley arrangement, a single belt may be used for more than one of these components.

3 With the engine off, open the hood and locate the various belts at the front of the engine. Using your fingers (and a flashlight if necessary), examine the belts. Check for cracks and separation of the plies. Look for contamination by grease or oil and glazed areas, which give the belt a shiny appearance. Both sides of each belt should be inspected, which means you will have to twist them to check the underside **(see illustration)**.

4 The tightness of each belt is checked by pushing on it at a distance halfway between the pulleys **(see illustration)**. Apply about 10 pounds of force with your thumb and see how much the belt moves down (deflects). Refer to the Specifications for the amount of deflection allowed in each belt.

5 If adjustment is necessary, it is done by moving the belt-driven accessory on the bracket **(see illustrations)**.

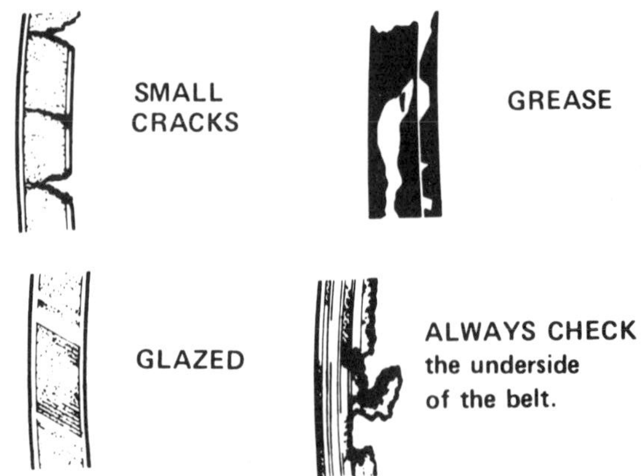

14.3 Here are some of the more common problems associated with drivebelts (check the belts very carefully to prevent an untimely breakdown)

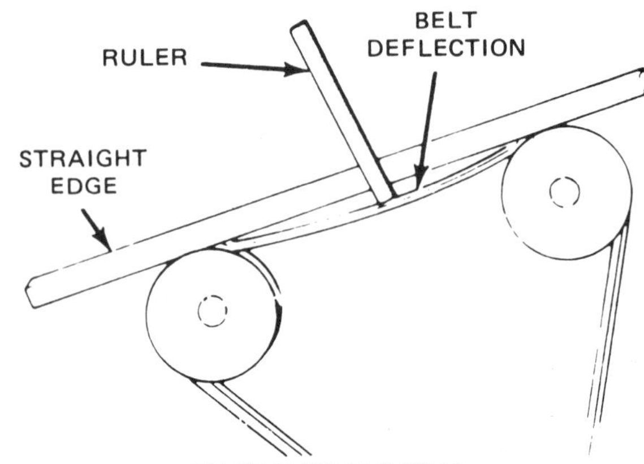

14.4 Measuring drivebelt deflection with a straightedge and ruler

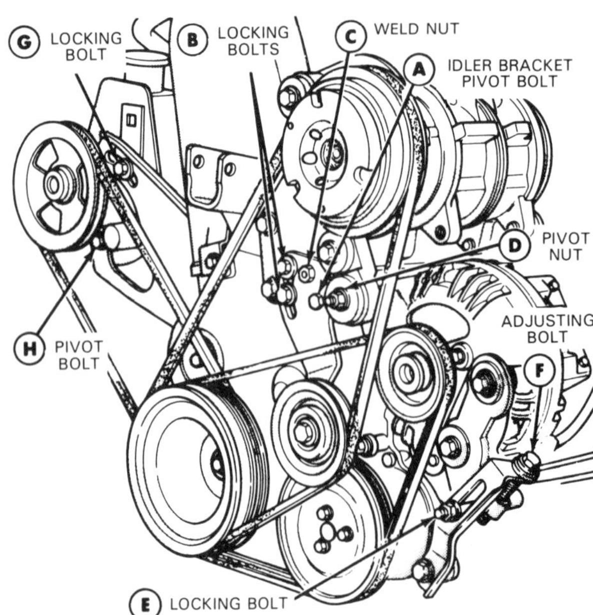

14.5a Typical engine drivebelt adjustment details showing the 2.2L/2.5L engine with a Chrysler alternator adjusting bracket

CARBON DEPOSITS

Symptoms: Dry sooty deposits indicate a rich mixture or weak ignition. Causes misfiring, hard starting and hesitation.

Recommendation: Check for a clogged air cleaner, high float level, sticky choke and worn ignition points. Use a spark plug with a longer core nose for greater anti-fouling protection.

OIL DEPOSITS

Symptoms: Oily coating caused by poor oil control. Oil is leaking past worn valve guides or piston rings into the combustion chamber. Causes hard starting, misfiring and hesition.

Recommendation: Correct the mechanical condition with necessary repairs and install new plugs.

TOO HOT

Symptoms: Blistered, white insulator, eroded electrode and absence of deposits. Results in shortened plug life.

Recommendation: Check for the correct plug heat range, over-advanced ignition timing, lean fuel mixture, intake manifold vacuum leaks and sticking valves. Check the coolant level and make sure the radiator is not clogged.

PREIGNITION

Symptoms: Melted electrodes. Insulators are white, but may be dirty due to misfiring or flying debris in the combustion chamber. Can lead to engine damage.

Recommendation: Check for the correct plug heat range, over-advanced ignition timing, lean fuel mixture, clogged cooling system and lack of lubrication.

HIGH SPEED GLAZING

Symptoms: Insulator has yellowish, glazed appearance. Indicates that combustion chamber temperatures have risen suddenly during hard acceleration. Normal deposits melt to form a conductive coating. Causes misfiring at high speeds.

Recommendation: Install new plugs. Consider using a colder plug if driving habits warrant.

GAP BRIDGING

Symptoms: Combustion deposits lodge between the electrodes. Heavy deposits accumulate and bridge the electrode gap. The plug ceases to fire, resulting in a dead cylinder.

Recommendation: Locate the faulty plug and remove the deposits from between the electrodes.

NORMAL

Symptoms: Brown to grayish-tan color and slight electrode wear. Correct heat range for engine and operating conditions.

Recommendation: When new spark plugs are installed, replace with plugs of the same heat range.

ASH DEPOSITS

Symptoms: Light brown deposits encrusted on the side or center electrodes or both. Derived from oil and/or fuel additives. Excessive amounts may mask the spark, causing misfiring and hesitation during acceleration.

Recommendation: If excessive deposits accumulate over a short time or low mileage, install new valve guide seals to prevent seepage of oil into the combustion chambers. Also try changing gasoline brands.

WORN

Symptoms: Rounded electrodes with a small amount of deposits on the firing end. Normal color. Causes hard starting in damp or cold weather and poor fuel economy.

Recommendation: Replace with new plugs of the same heat range.

DETONATION

Symptoms: Insulators may be cracked or chipped. Improper gap setting techniques can also result in a fractured insulator tip. Can lead to piston damage.

Recommendation: Make sure the fuel anti-knock values meet engine requirements. Use care when setting the gaps on new plugs. Avoid lugging the engine.

SPLASHED DEPOSITS

Symptoms: After long periods of misfiring, deposits can loosen when normal combustion temperature is restored by an overdue tune-up. At high speeds, deposits flake off the piston and are thrown against the hot insulator, causing misfiring.

Recommendation: Replace the plugs with new ones or clean and reinstall the originals.

MECHANICAL DAMAGE

Symptoms: May be caused by a foreign object in the combustion chamber or the piston striking an incorrect reach (too long) plug. Causes a dead cylinder and could result in piston damage.

Recommendation: Remove the foreign object from the engine and/or install the correct reach plug.

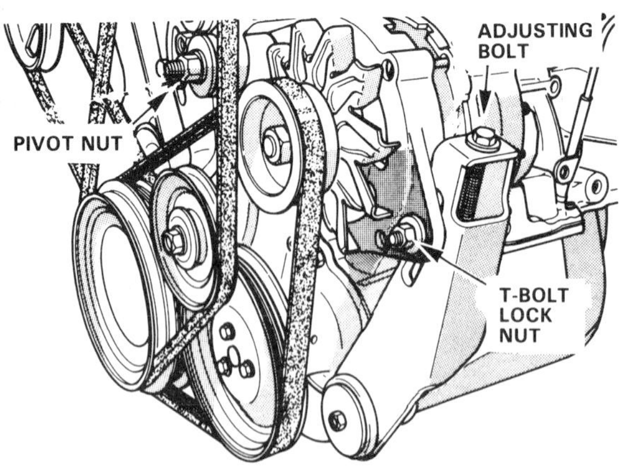

14.5b 2.2L/2.5L engines equipped with the Chrysler/Bosch alternator have a slightly different adjusting bracket, although the adjusting procedure is essentially the same

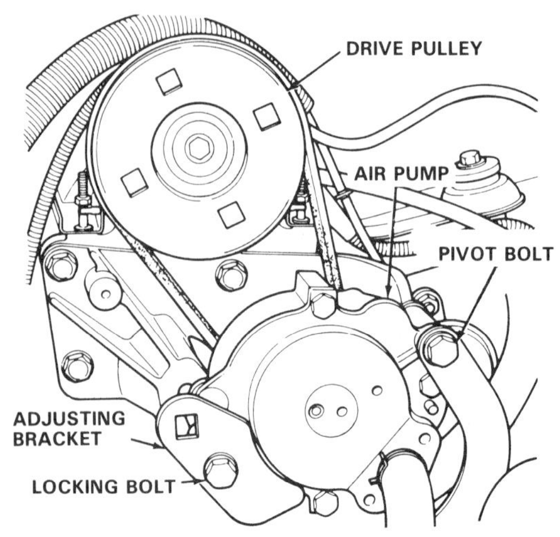

14.5c 2.2L engine air pump drivebelt adjustment details

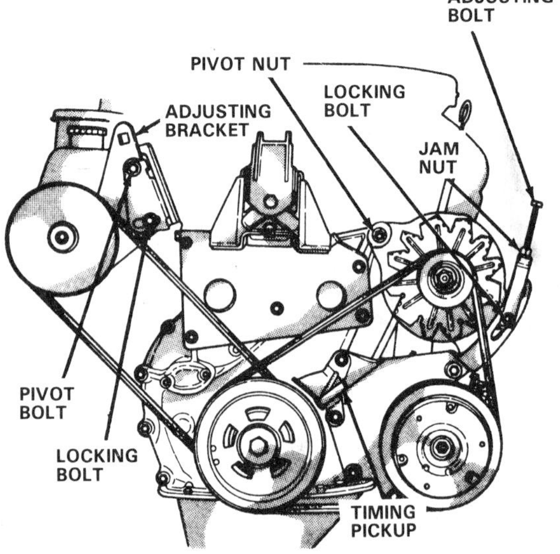

14.5d 2.6L engine drivebelt adjustment details

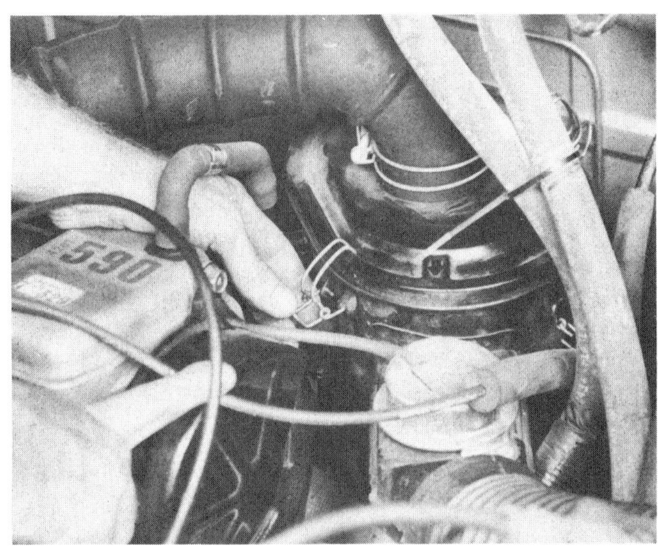

15.3a On 2.6L engines, release the clips, lift off the cover . . .

15.3b . . . and withdraw the air filter element

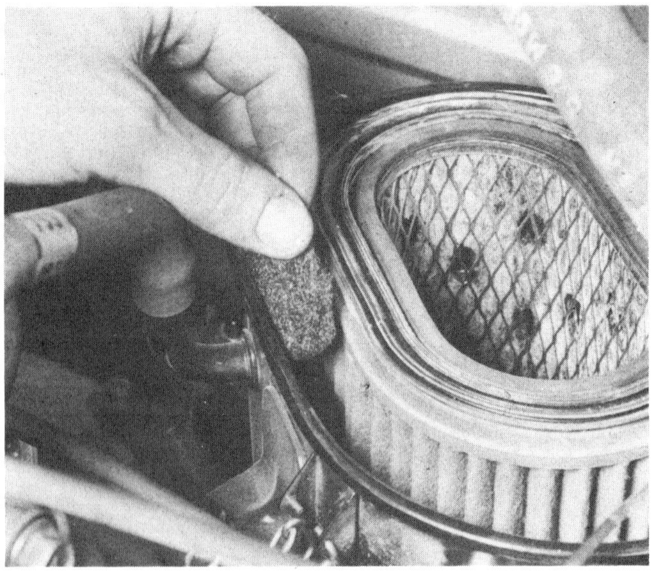

15.6 The PCV system filter must be replaced if it is dirty or clogged (2.6L engine)

6 For each component, there will be a locking bolt and a pivot bolt or nut. Both must be loosened slightly to enable you to move the component.

7 After the two bolts have been loosened, move the component away from the engine (to tighten the belt) or toward the engine (to loosen the belt). Many accessories are equipped with a square hole designed to accept a 3/8-inch or 1/2-inch square drive breaker bar. The bar can be used to lever the component and tension the drivebelt. Hold the accessory in position and check the belt tension. If it is correct, tighten the two bolts until snug, then recheck the tension. If it is alright, tighten the two bolts completely.

8 To adjust the alternator drivebelt, loosen the pivot nut and the locking screw or T-bolt locknut, then turn the adjusting bolt to tension the belt.

9 It may be necessary to use some sort of pry bar to move a component while the belt is adjusted. If this must be done, be very careful not to damage the component being moved, or the part being pried against.

10 Run the engine for about 15 minutes, then recheck the tension of the belts.

15 Air filter element, PCV valve and vent module maintenance

Refer to illustrations 15.3a, 15.3b, 15.6, 15.8, 15.9a, 15.9b, 15.9c, 15.10 and 15.18

1 At the specified intervals, the air filter element and PCV valve should be replaced with new ones and (if equipped) the crankcase vent module should be cleaned and inspected. In addition, they should be inspected periodically.

2 The air filter element is located inside a housing, adjacent to the engine.

Carburetor equipped models

3 To remove the filter element on 2.6L engines, release the clips, lift off the top plate and remove the element **(see illustrations)**. On 2.2L engines, remove the three wing nuts and three hold-down clips, lift off the air cleaner crossover cover and remove the filter element.

4 To check the filter, hold it up to sunlight or place a flashlight or droplight inside or behind the element. If you can see light coming through the paper element, the filter is alright.

5 Clean the inside of the housing with a rag.

6 Place the old filter (if in good condition) or the new filter (if the specified interval has elapsed) back into the air cleaner housing. Make sure it seats properly in the bottom of the housing. Replace the PCV system filter (2.6L engine only) if it is dirty **(see illustration)**. Apply a small amount of 30-weight oil to the new one before installation.

7 On the 2.6L engine, install the top plate and secure the hold-down clips.

8 On the 2.2L engine, the air cleaner crossover cover must be properly installed to prevent air leaks. Install the filter with the screen side up into the air cleaner housing bottom section. Place the steel top cover in place with the studs protruding and the hold-down clips aligned. Install and tighten the two plastic wing nuts securing the cover to the carburetor. Install the third wing nut which secures the air cleaner tab to the bracket and tighten it securely. Refasten the hold-down clips **(see illustration)**.

Fuel injected models

9 Loosen the clamps on the hose between the air cleaner housing and the throttle body. Release the air cleaner clips **(see illustration)**, pull the hose off the throttle body and lift the cover and hose off the bottom of the housing. On non-turbocharged models the cover can be rotated up without disconnecting the hose. Lift the air filter element out of the housing **(see illustrations)**.

1

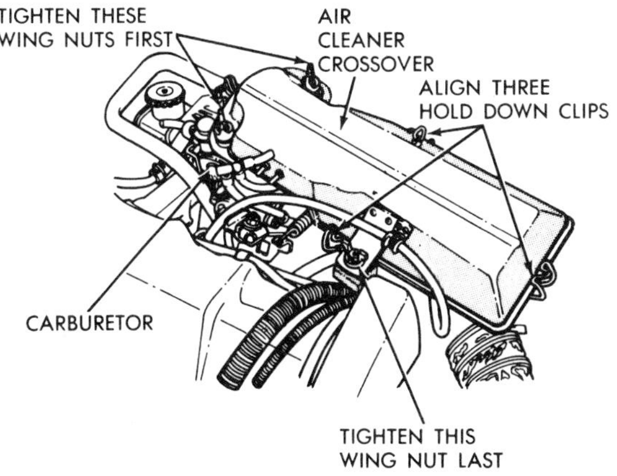

15.8 2.2L carburetor equipped engine air cleaner crossover installation details

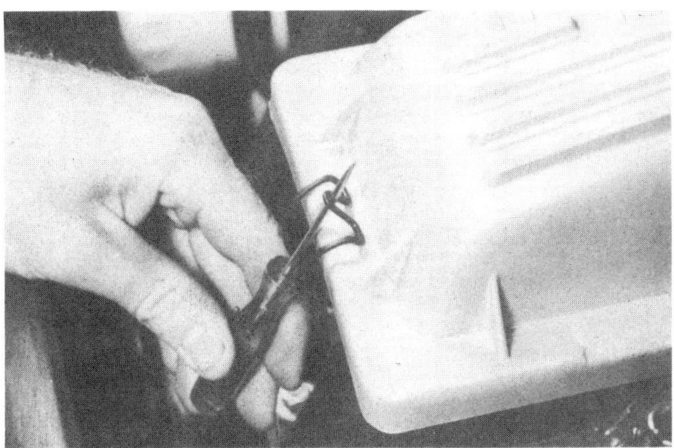

15.9a Use a small screwdriver to release the air cleaner housing cover clips

15.9b On turbocharged models, the filter element can be lifted out of the housing after completely removing the cover

15.9c On non-turbocharged models, the cover can be rotated away from the filter after loosening the hose clamp (arrow)

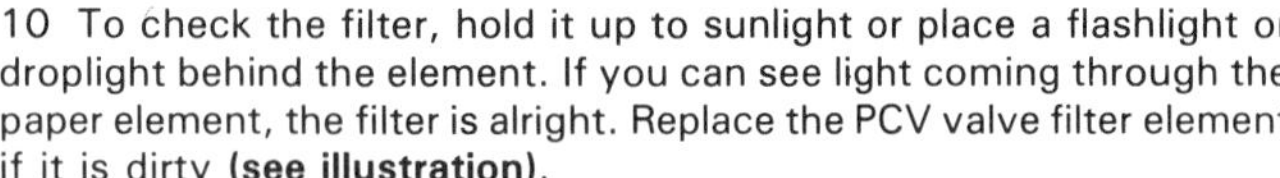

15.10 The PCV system filter must be replaced if it is dirty or clogged (fuel injected engine)

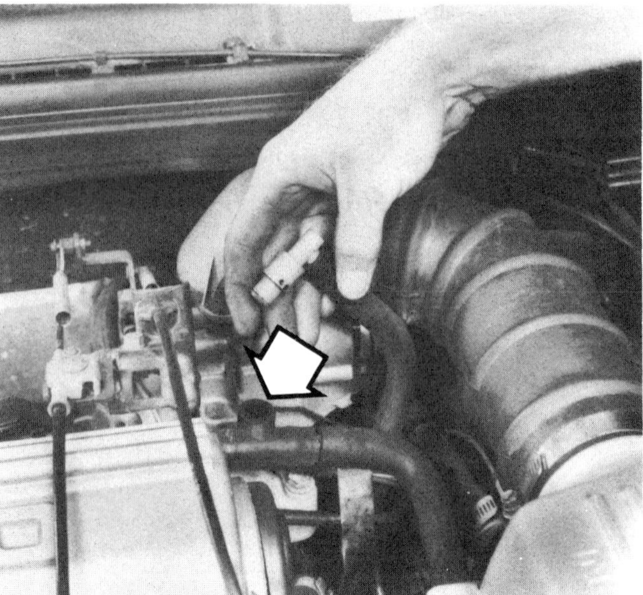

15.18 Make sure the grommet or hose (arrow) that seals around the PCV valve is in good condition to prevent air leaks that will affect engine performance

10 To check the filter, hold it up to sunlight or place a flashlight or droplight behind the element. If you can see light coming through the paper element, the filter is alright. Replace the PCV valve filter element if it is dirty **(see illustration)**.

11 Clean the inside of the housing with a rag.

12 Place the old filter (if in good condition) or the new filter (if the specified interval has elapsed) back into the air cleaner housing with the screen facing up. Make sure it seats properly in the bottom of the housing.

13 If the hose was removed from the throttle body, loosely install the clamp and then push the hose onto the throttle body.

14 Align the upper and lower halves of the air cleaner and connect the clips.

15 Tighten the clamp around the hose at the throttle body securely.

All models

16 The positive crankcase ventilation (PCV) valve should be replaced with a new one when the valve accumulates deposits which could cause it to stick. Refer to Chapter 6 for PCV valve checking procedures.

17 To replace the PCV valve, simply pull it from the hose or vent module and install a new one.

18 Inspect the hose prior to installation to ensure that it isn't plugged or damaged **(see illustration)**. Compare the new valve with the old one to make sure they are the same.

19 When replacing the PCV valve on 2.2L and 2.5L engines so equipped, inspect the vent module for cracks and damage and make sure the PCV system filter is clean. Remove the vent module and wash it thoroughly with kerosene or solvent. Prior to installation, invert the module and fill it with engine oil. Allow the oil to drain out through the vent at the top into a container. With the interior of the module now coated with oil, the module can be reinstalled.

16 Underhood hose check and replacement

Caution: *Replacement of air conditioning hoses must be left to a dealer service department or air conditioning shop that has the equipment to depressurize the system safely. Never remove air conditioning components or hoses until the system has been depressurized.*

General

1 High temperatures under the hood can cause the deterioration of the rubber and plastic hoses used for engine, accessory and emission systems operation. Periodic inspection should be made for cracks, loose clamps, material hardening and leaks.

2 Information specific to the cooling system hoses can be found in Section 9.

3 Some, but not all, hoses use clamps to secure the hoses to fittings. Where clamps are used, check to be sure they haven't lost their tension, allowing the hose to leak. Where clamps are not used, make sure the hose has not expanded and/or hardened where it slips over the fitting, allowing it to leak.

Vacuum hoses

4 It is quite common for vacuum hoses, especially those in the emissions system, to be color coded or identified by colored stripes molded into the hose. Various systems require hoses with different wall thicknesses, collapse resistance and temperature resistance. When replacing hoses, be sure to use the same hose material on the new hose.

5 Often the only effective way to check a hose is to remove it completely from the vehicle. Where more than one hose is removed, be sure to label the hoses and their attaching points to insure proper reattachment.

6 When checking vacuum hoses, be sure to include any plastic T-fittings in the check. Check the fittings for cracks and the hose where it fits over the fitting for enlargement, which could cause leakage.

7 A small piece of vacuum hose (1/4-inch inside diameter) can be used as a stethoscope to detect vacuum leaks. Hold one end of the hose to your ear and probe around vacuum hoses and fittings, listening for the "hissing" sound characteristic of a vacuum leak. **Warning:** *When probing with the vacuum hose stethoscope, be careful not to allow your body or the hose to come into contact with moving engine components such as the drivebelt, cooling fan, etc.*

Fuel hose

Warning: *There are certain precautions which must be taken when inspecting or servicing fuel system components. Work in a well ventilated area and do not allow open flames (cigarettes, appliance pilot lights, etc.) or bare light bulbs near the work area. Mop up any spills immediately and do not store fuel soaked rags where they could ignite. The fuel system is under pressure, so if any fuel lines are to be disconnected, the pressure in the system must be relieved (see Chapter 4 for more information).*

8 Check all rubber fuel lines for deterioration and chafing. Check especially for cracking in areas where the hose bends and just before clamping points, such as where a hose attaches to the fuel filter and fuel injection unit.

9 High quality fuel line, specifically designed for fuel injection

17.5 On turbocharged models, check the clamps (arrows) on the hoses between the throttle body and manifolds to make sure they are tight and in good condition

18.3 The choke plate is located in the carburetor throat and should be closed when the engine is cold

tems, should be used for fuel line replacement on vehicles equipped with EFI. Under no circumstances should unreinforced vacuum line, clear plastic tubing or water hose be used for fuel line replacement.
10 Spring-type clamps are commonly used on fuel lines. These clamps often lose their tension over a period of time, and can be "sprung" during the removal process. Therefore it is recommended that all spring-type clamps be replaced with screw clamps whenever a hose is replaced.

Metal lines

11 Sections of metal line are often used for fuel line between the fuel pump and fuel injection unit. Check carefully to be sure the line has not been bent and crimped and that cracks have not started in the line.
12 If a section of metal fuel line must be replaced, only seamless steel tubing should be used, since copper and aluminum tubing do not have the strength necessary to withstand normal engine operating vibration.
13 Check the metal brake lines where they enter the master cylinder and brake proportioning unit (if used) for cracks in the lines or loose fittings. Any sign of brake fluid leakage calls for an immediate thorough inspection of the brake system.

17 Carburetor/fuel injection throttle body mounting nut torque check

Refer to illustration 17.5

1 The carburetor or fuel injection throttle body is attached to the top of the intake manifold by nuts. These fasteners can sometimes work loose during normal engine operation and cause a vacuum leak.
2 To properly tighten the mounting nuts, a torque wrench is necessary. If you do not own one, they can usually be rented on a daily basis.
3 Remove the air cleaner assembly-to-carburetor or throttle body hose.
4 Locate the mounting nuts at the base of the carburetor or throttle body. Decide what special tools or adaptors will be be necessary, if any, to tighten the nuts with a socket and the torque wrench.
5 Tighten the nuts to the specified torque. Do not overtighten the nuts, as the threads may strip. On 2.2L engines, be careful not to bend the fast idle lever when tightening the nut next to it. Also, on turbocharged models, check the hoses and clamps between the throttle body and the turbocharger and the turbocharger and the intake manifold to make sure there are no leaks **(see illustration)**.
6 If you suspect a vacuum leak exists at the bottom of the carburetor or throttle body, obtain a short length of rubber hose. Start the engine and place one end of the hose next to your ear as you probe around the base of the carburetor or throttle body with the other end. You should hear a hissing sound if a leak exists.
7 If, after the nuts are properly tightened, a vacuum leak still exists, the carburetor or throttle body must be removed and a new gasket installed. See Chapter 4 for more information.
8 After tightening the nuts, reinstall the air cleaner hose.

18 Carburetor choke check

Refer to illustrations 18.3, 18.9a and 18.9b

1 The choke operates only when the engine is cold, so this check must be performed before the engine has been started for the day.
2 Open the hood and remove the top plate of the air cleaner assembly as described in Section 15. If any vacuum hoses must be disconnected, make sure you tag the hoses for reinstallation in their original positions.
3 Look at the top of the carburetor. You will notice a flat plate in each of the carburetor throats **(see illustration)**.
4 Have an assistant press the accelerator pedal to the floor. The plates should close completely. Start the engine while you watch the plates at the carburetor. **Warning:** *Do not position your face directly over the carburetor, as the engine could backfire, causing serious burns.* When the engine starts, the choke plates should open slightly.
5 Allow the engine to continue running at an idle speed. As the engine warms up to operating temperature, the plates should slowly open, allowing more air to enter through the top of the carburetor.
6 After a few minutes, the choke plates should be completely open to the vertical position.
7 You will notice that the engine speed corresponds with the plate opening. With the plates closed, the engine should run at a fast idle speed. As the plates open, the engine speed will decrease.
8 If the choke does not operate as described, refer to Chapter 4 for specific information on adjusting and servicing the choke components.

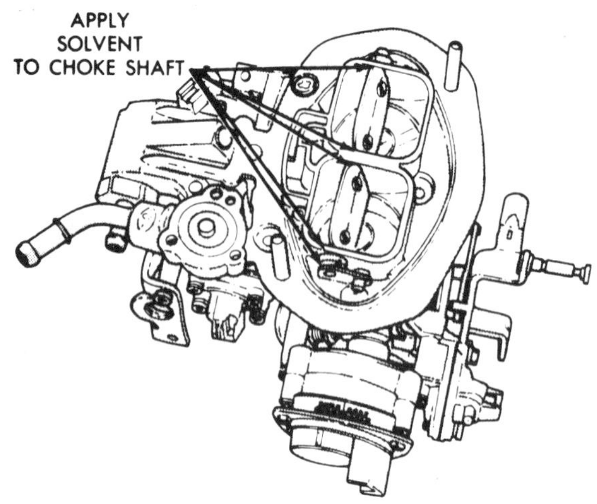

18.9a Solvent must be applied to the choke shaft in the areas indicated to prevent it from binding

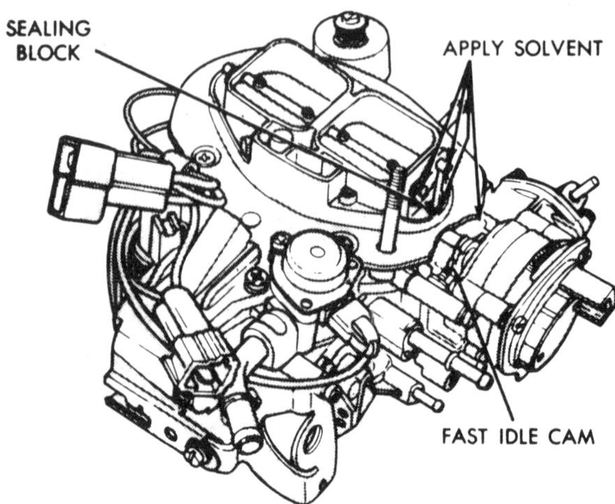

18.9b On 2.2L engines, apply solvent to the link between the choke shaft and thermostat and to the sealing block

9 At the recommended intervals, apply the specified solvent to the contact surfaces of the choke shaft to ensure free movement. Also, apply the solvent to the link connecting the choke shaft to the thermostat and the sealing block through which it passes **(see illustrations)**.

19 Heated inlet air system general check

Refer to illustration 19.3

1 All non-turbocharged models are equipped with a heated inlet air cleaner which draws air to the carburetor or fuel injection throttle body from different locations, depending on engine temperature.

2 This is a simple visual check; however, the outside air duct must be removed.

3 Locate the vacuum flapper door in the air cleaner assembly. It will be located inside the ''snorkel'' **(see illustration)**. Make sure that the flexible heat duct is securely attached and not damaged.

4 The check should be done when the engine and outside air are cold (less than 65°F). Start the engine and look through the snorkel at the flapper door (which should move to the Up or Heat on position). With the door up, air cannot enter through the end of the snorkel, but instead enters the air cleaner through the heat duct attached to the exhaust manifold.

5 As the engine warms up to operating temperature, the door should move to the Down or Heat off position to allow air through the snorkel end. Depending on outside air temperature, this may take 10 to 15 minutes. To speed up the check you can reconnect the outside air duct, drive the vehicle and then check to see if the door has moved down.

6 If the air cleaner is not operating properly, see Chapter 6 for more information.

19.3 The vacuum flapper door is located in the air cleaner housing snorkel (in this case it is in the Down or Heat off position)

20 Fuel system check

Refer to illustrations 20.4 and 20.6

Warning: *There are certain precautions to take when inspecting or servicing the fuel system components. Work in a well-ventilated area and do not allow open flames (cigarettes, appliance pilot lights, etc.) near the vehicle. Mop up spills immediately and do not store fuel-soaked rags where they could ignite.*

1 The fuel system on models which are equipped with Electronic Fuel Injection (EFI), is under pressure even when the engine is off. Consequently the EFI system must be depressurized (Chapter 4) whenever the fuel system is worked on. Even after depressurization, if any fuel lines are disconnected for servicing, be prepared to catch some fuel as it spurts out. Plug all disconnected fuel lines immediately to prevent the tank from emptying itself.

2 The fuel system is most easily checked with the vehicle raised on a hoist where the components on the underside are readily visible and accessible.

3 If the smell of gasoline is noticed while driving, or after the vehicle has been parked in the sun, the fuel system should be thoroughly inspected immediately.

4 Remove the gas tank cap and check for damage, corrosion and a proper sealing imprint on the gasket **(see illustration)**. Replace the cap with a new one if necessary.

5 Inspect the gas tank and filler neck for punctures, cracks and other damage. The connection between the filler neck and the tank is especially critical. Sometimes a rubber filler neck will leak due to loose clamps or deteriorated rubber; problems a home mechanic can usually rectify. **Warning:** *Do not, under any circumstances, try to repair a fuel tank yourself (except to replace rubber components) unless you have considerable experience. A welding torch or any open flame can easily cause the fuel vapors to explode if the proper precautions are not taken.*

6 Carefully check all rubber hoses and metal lines leading away from the fuel tank. Check for loose connections, deteriorated hoses, crimped lines and damage of any kind **(see illustration)**. Follow the lines up to the front of the vehicle, carefully inspecting them all the way. Repair or replace damaged sections as necessary (see Chapter 4).

21 Cooling system check

Refer to illustration 21.4

Warning: *The electric cooling fan on some models can activate at any*

20.4 Check the fuel cap gasket (arrow) to make sure there is an even sealing imprint all the way around

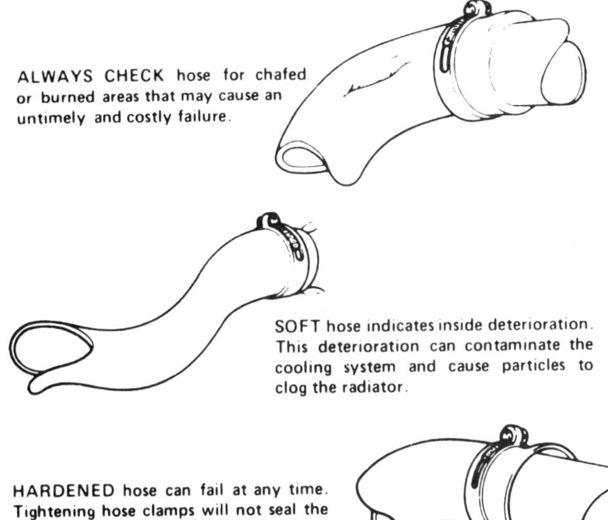

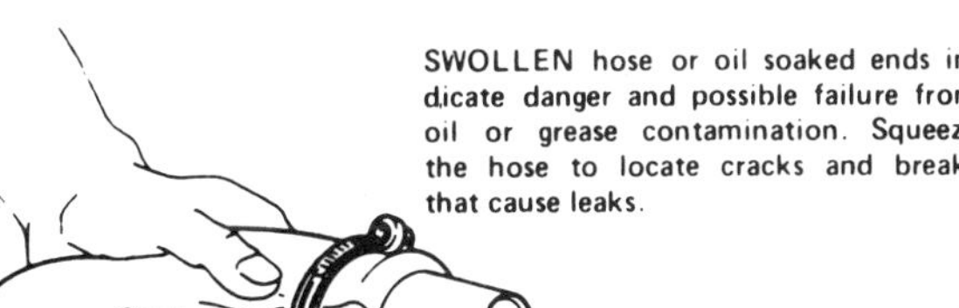

21.4 Hoses, like drivebelts, have a habit of failing at the worst possible time – to prevent the inconvenience of a blown radiator or heater hose, inspect them carefully as shown here

time, even when the Ignition switch is in the Off position. Disconnect the fan motor or the negative battery cable when working in the vicinity of the fan.

1 Many major engine failures can be attributed to a faulty cooling system. If the vehicle is equipped with an automatic transaxle, the cooling system is also used to cool the transaxle fluid.

2 The cooling system should be checked with the engine cold. Do this before the vehicle is driven for the day or after it has been shut off for three or four hours.

3 Remove the radiator cap and thoroughly clean the cap (inside and

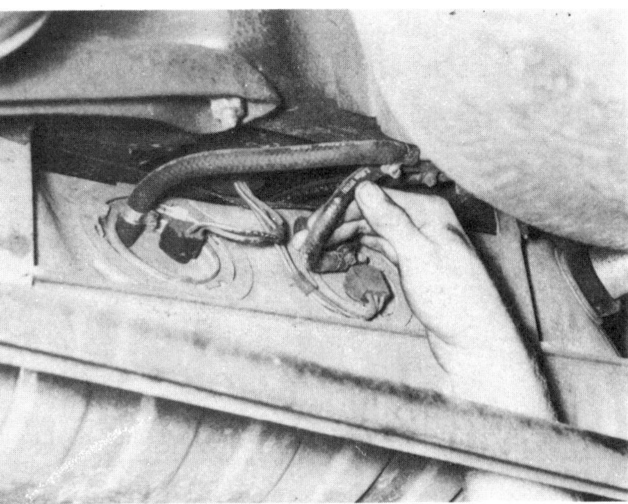

20.6 Move the fuel hoses back and forth to check for cracks

out) with water. Also clean the filler neck on the radiator. All traces of corrosion should be removed.

4 Carefully check the upper and lower radiator hoses along with the smaller diameter heater hoses. Inspect the entire length of each hose, replacing any that are cracked, swollen or deteriorated. Cracks may become more apparent when a hose is squeezed **(see illustration)**.

5 Also check that all hose connections are tight. A leak in the cooling system will usually show up as white or rust-colored deposits on the areas adjoining the leak.

6 Use compressed air or a soft brush to remove bugs, leaves, and other debris from the front of the radiator or air conditioning condenser. Be careful not to damage the delicate cooling fins, or cut yourself on them.

7 Finally, have the cap and system pressure tested. If you do not have a pressure tester, most gas stations and repair shops will do this for a minimal charge.

22 Exhaust system check

1 With the engine cold (at least three hours after the vehicle has been driven), check the complete exhaust system from its starting point at the engine to the end of the tailpipe. This should be done on a hoist where unrestricted access is available.

2 Check the pipes and connections for signs of leakage and/or corrosion indicating a potential failure. Make sure that all brackets and hangers are in good condition and tight.

3 At the same time, inspect the underside of the body for holes, corrosion and open seams which may allow exhaust gases to enter the passenger compartment. Seal all body openings with silicone or body putty.

4 Rattles and other noises can often be traced to the exhaust system, especially the mounts and hangers. Try to move the pipes, muffler and catalytic converter. If the components can come into contact with the body, secure the exhaust system with new mounts.

5 This is also an ideal time to check the running condition of the engine by inspecting the very end of the tailpipe. The exhaust deposits here are an indication of engine state-of-tune. If the pipe is black and sooty or coated with white deposits, the engine may be in need of a tune-up (including a thorough carburetor or fuel inection system inspection and adjustment).

23 Suspension and steering checks

Refer to illustrations 23.6a and 23.6b

1 Whenever the front of the vehicle is raised for service it is a good idea to visually check the suspension and steering components for wear and damage.

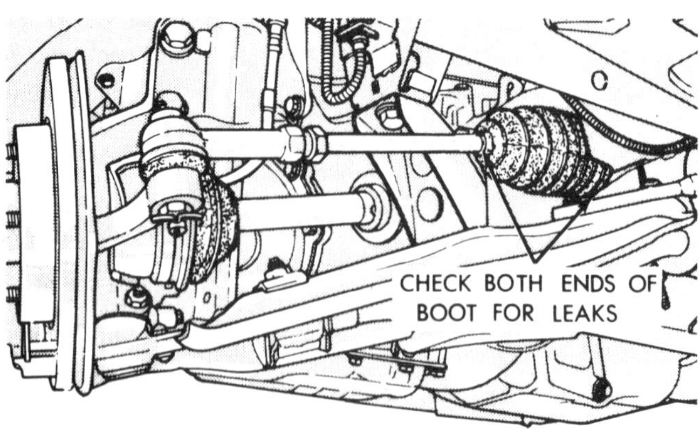

23.6a If the steering gear boots are leaking, they must be replaced with new ones

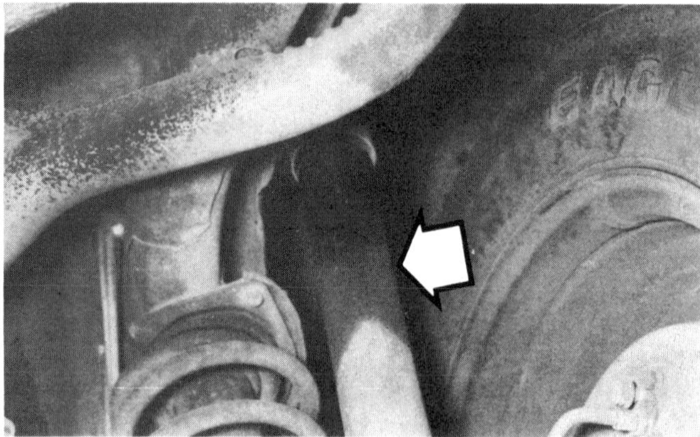

23.6b Fluid leakage (arrow) is a sure sign that a shock absorber has failed

2 Indications of wear and damage include excessive play in the steering wheel before the front wheels react, excessive sway around corners, body movement over rough roads or binding at some point as the steering wheel is turned.
3 Before the vehicle is raised for inspection, test the shock absorbers by pushing down to rock the vehicle at each corner. If it does not come back to a level position within one or two bounces, the shocks are worn and should be replaced. As this is done, check for squeaks and unusual noises from the suspension components. Information on shock absorbers and suspension components can be found in Chapter 10.
4 Now raise the front end of the vehicle and support it securely with jackstands placed under the jacking and hoisting points (see *Jacking and towing* at the front of this manual). Because of the work to be done, the vehicle must be stable and safely supported.
5 Check the front wheel hub nuts for correct tightness and make sure they are properly crimped in place.
6 Crawl under the vehicle and check for loose bolts, broken or disconnected parts and deteriorated rubber bushings on all suspension and steering components. Look for grease or fluid leaking from around the steering gear boots **(see illustration)**. Check the shock absorbers for signs of fluid leakage **(see illustration)**. Check the power steering hoses and connections for leaks. Check the steering joints for wear.
7 Have an assistant turn the steering wheel from side-to-side and check the steering components for free movement, chafing and binding. If the wheels do not respond to the movement of the steering wheel, try to determine where the slack is located.

24 Steering shaft seal lubrication

1 The steering shaft seal protects the steering shaft at the point where it passes through the firewall. Lubricate the inner circumference of the seal with the specified lubricant if the shaft makes noise or sticks to the seal when it is turned.
2 Raise the vehicle and support it securely.
3 Peel back the upper edge of the seal and apply a light coat of grease all the way around the inner circumference where it contacts the steering shaft.
4 Lower the vehicle.

25 Wheel bearing service

1 The front wheel bearings are adjusted and lubricated at the factory and normally only need to be checked for looseness, indicating bearing wear or an improperly tightened hub nut. Refer to Chapter 10 for checking and maintenance procedures for the front wheel bearings.
2 The rear wheel bearings should be checked at the specified intervals, or whenever the rear brake shoes are inspected. Adjustment, removal and installation and repacking procedures for the rear wheel bearings are also included in Chapter 10.

26.5 The brake pads can be checked after removing the wheels by looking through the inspection hole and the ends of each caliper (arrows)

26 Brake check

Refer to illustrations 26.5, 26.7, 26.14 and 26.16

1 The brakes should be inspected every time the wheels are removed or whenever a defect is suspected. Indications of a potential brake system problem include the vehicle pulling to one side when the brake pedal is depressed, noises coming from the brakes when they are applied, excessive brake pedal travel, pulsating pedal and leakage of fluid, usually seen on the inside of the tire or wheel.

Disc brakes

2 Disc brakes can be visually checked without removing any parts except the wheels.
3 Raise the vehicle and place it securely on jackstands. Remove the front wheels (see *Jacking and towing* at the front of this manual if necessary).
4 Now visible is the disc brake caliper which contains the pads. There is an outer brake pad and an inner pad. Both should be checked for wear.
5 Note the pad thickness by looking at each end of the caliper and through the inspection hole in the caliper body **(see illustration)**. If the combined thickness of the pad lining and metal shoe is 5/16-inch or less, the pads should be replaced.
6 Since it will be difficult, if not impossible, to measure the exact thickness of the pad, if you are in doubt as to the pad quality, remove them for further inspection or replacement. See Chapter 9 for disc brake pad replacement.

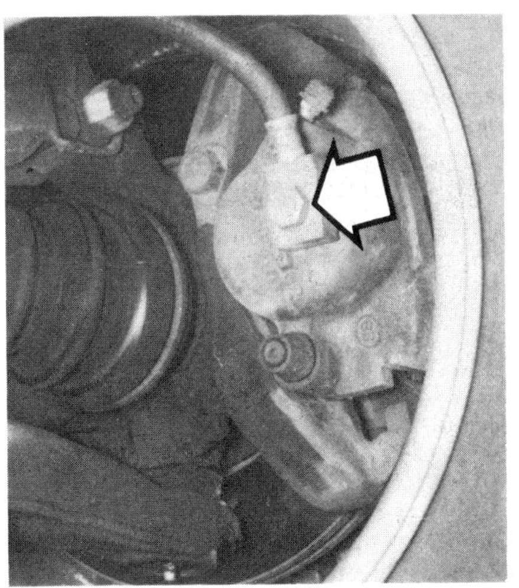

26.7 Check the front brake hoses and caliper connections for damage and leaks

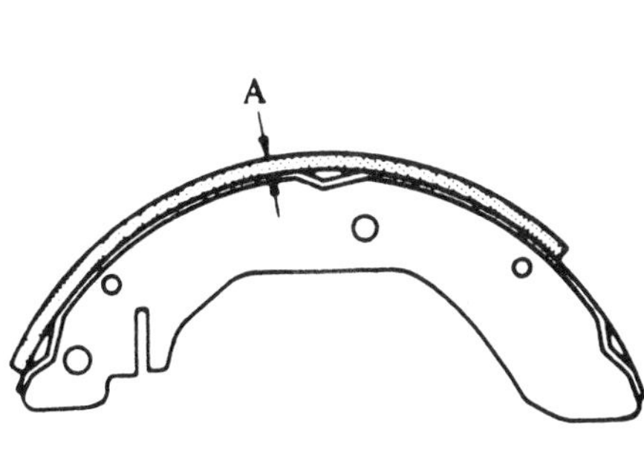

26.14 The rear brake shoe lining thickness (A) is measured from the outer surface of the lining to the metal shoe

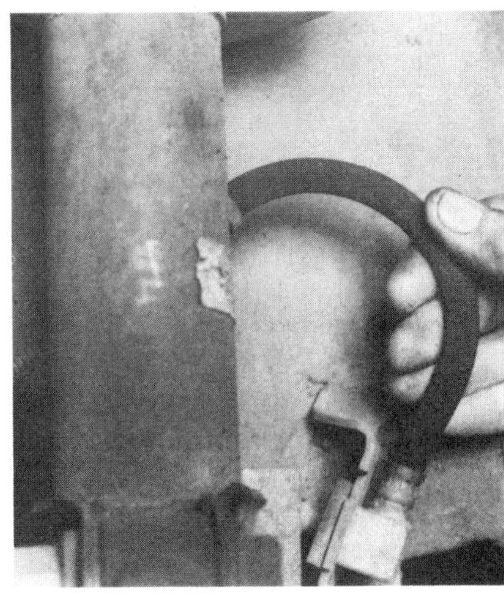

26.16 Check the rear brake hoses and connections for leaks and damage

7 Before installing the wheels, check for leakage around the brake hose connections leading to the caliper and for damaged brake hoses (cracks, leaks, chaffed areas, etc.) **(see illustration)**. Replace the hoses or fittings as necessary (see Chapter 9).
8 Also check the disc for score marks, wear and burned spots. If these conditions exist, the hub/disc assembly should be removed for servicing (Chapter 9).

Drum brakes (rear)

9 Raise the vehicle and support it securely on jackstands. Block the front tires to prevent the vehicle from rolling; however, do not apply the parking brake as it will lock the drums in place.
10 Remove the wheels, referring to *Jacking and towing* at the front of this manual if necessary.
11 Mark the hub so it can be reinstalled in the same position. Use a scribe, chalk, etc. on the drum, hub and backing plate.
12 Remove the brake drum as described in Chapter 10.
13 With the drum removed, carefully brush away any accumulations of dirt and dust. **Warning:** *Do not blow the dust out with compressed air. Make an effort not to inhale the dust as it contains asbestos, which is harmful to your health.*
14 Note the thickness of the lining material on both front and rear brake shoes. If the material has worn away to within 1/8-inch of the recessed rivets or metal backing, the shoes should be replaced **(see illustration)**. The shoes should also be replaced if they are cracked, glazed (shiny areas), or covered with brake fluid.
15 Make sure that all the brake assembly springs are connected and in good condition.
16 Check the brake components for signs of fluid leakage. With your finger, carefully pry back the rubber cups on the wheel cylinder located at the top of the brake shoes. Any leakage here is an indication that the wheel cylinders should be overhauled immediately (Chapter 9). Also check all hoses and connections for signs of leakage **(see illustration)**.
17 Wipe the inside of the drum with a clean rag and denatured alcohol. Again, be careful not to breathe the dangerous asbestos dust.
18 Check the inside of the drum for cracks, score marks, deep scratches and 'hard spots' which will appear as small discolored areas. If these imperfections cannot be removed with fine emery cloth, the drum must be taken to an automotive machine shop for resurfacing.
19 Repeat the procedure for the remaining wheel. If the inspection reveals that all parts are in good condition, reinstall the brake drums. Install the wheels and lower the vehicle to the ground.
20 On 1982 models, adjust the brake shoes (Chapter 9).

Parking brake

21 The easiest way to check the operation of the parking brake is to park the vehicle on a steep hill with the parking brake set and the transmission in Neutral. If the parking brake cannot prevent the vehicle from rolling, it is in need of adjustment (see Chapter 9).

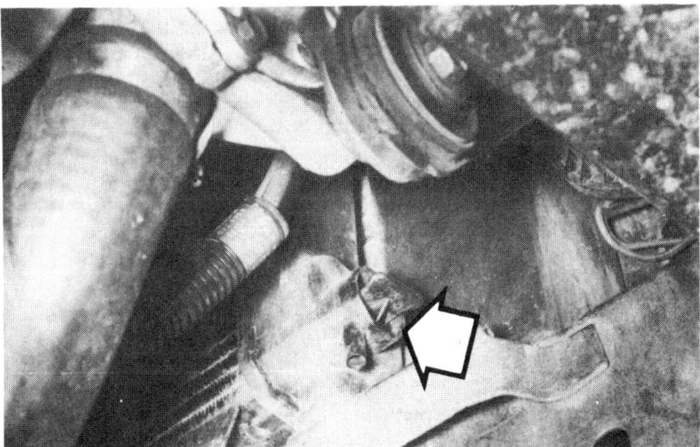

27.6 The radiator can be drained by opening the fitting (arrow) at the bottom

27 Cooling system servicing (draining, flushing and refilling)

Refer to illustration 27.6

Warning: *Since antifreeze is highly toxic, the radiator should always be drained into a container. Never allow the coolant to run onto the ground or driveway where a pet could drink it and be poisoned. The container should be capped and stored until it can be properly disposed of.*

1 The cooling system should be periodically drained, flushed and refilled to replenish the antifreeze mixture and prevent rust and corrosion, which can impair the performance of the cooling system and ultimately cause engine damage.
2 At the same time the cooling system is serviced, all hoses and the radiator cap should be inspected and replaced if faulty (see Section 21).
3 Antifreeze is a corrosive and poisonous solution, so be careful not to spill any of it on the vehicle's paint or your own skin. If this happens, rinse the affected area immediately with plenty of clean water. Also, consult your local authorities about the dumping of antifreeze before draining the cooling system. In many areas reclamation centers have been set up to collect automobile oil and coolant mixtures rather than allowing them to be added to the sewage and water facilities.
4 With the engine cold, remove the radiator cap and set the heater control to Heat (Max).
5 Move a large container under the radiator to catch the coolant mixture as it is drained.
6 Drain the radiator. Most models are equipped with a drain fitting at the bottom of the radiator **(see illustration)**. If the fitting has excessive

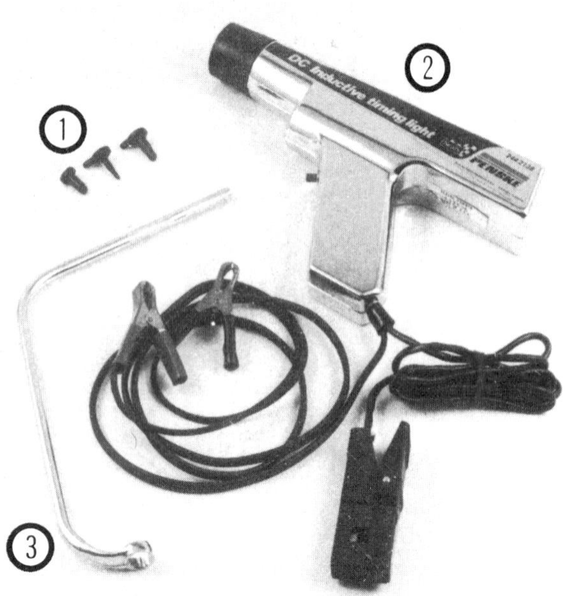

29.2 Tools needed to check and adjust the ignition timing

1 **Vacuum plugs** — *Vacuum hoses will, in most cases, have to be disconnected and plugged. Molded plugs in various shapes and sizes are available for this*
2 **Inductive pick-up timing light** — *Flashes a bright concentrated beam of light when the number one spark plug fires. Connect the leads according to the instructions supplied with the light*
3 **Distributor wrench** — *On some models, the hold-down bolt for the distributor is difficult to reach and turn with conventional wrenches or sockets. A special wrench like this must be used*

29.5a The timing light leads should be attached to the battery posts . . .

29.5b . . . and the number 1 spark plug wire (use an inductive pickup timing light only)

corrosion and cannot be turned easily, or the radiator is not equipped with one, detach the lower radiator hose to allow the coolant to drain. Wear safety goggles to prevent coolant from getting into your eyes. **Note:** *On 2.2L/2.5L engines, remove the vacuum switch or plug from the top of the thermostat housing on the engine.*
7 Disconnect the coolant reservoir hose, remove the reservoir and flush it with clean water.
8 Place a hose (a common garden hose is fine) in the radiator filler neck at the top of the radiator and flush the system until the water runs clear at all drain points.
9 In severe cases of contamination or clogging of the radiator, remove it (see Chapter 3) and reverse flush it. This involves simply inserting the hose in the bottom radiator outlet to allow the clean water to run against the normal flow, draining through the top. A radiator repair shop should be consulted if further cleaning or repair is necessary.
10 Where the coolant is regularly drained and the system refilled with the correct antifreeze mixture there should be no need to employ chemical cleaners or descalers.
11 Install the coolant reservoir, reconnect the hoses and close the drain fitting.
12 On 2.2L/2.5L engines, add coolant to the radiator until it reaches the bottom of the threaded hole in the thermostat housing. Reinstall the vacuum switch or plug in the hole and tighten it to 15 ft-lbs. Continue adding coolant to the radiator until it reaches the radiator cap seat.
13 On 2.6L engines, simply fill the radiator to the radiator cap seat.
14 On all models, add coolant to the reservoir until the level is between the Min and Max marks.
15 On 2.6L engines, install the cap and run the engine until the upper radiator hose feels hot. Turn the engine off and add coolant as necessary to completely fill the radiator.
16 On all other models run the engine until normal operating temperature is reached. With the engine idling, add coolant up to the correct level.
17 Always refill the system with a mixture of high quality antifreeze and water in the proportion called for on the antifreeze container or in your owner's manual. Chapter 3 also contains information on antifreeze mixtures.
18 Keep a close watch on the coolant level and the various cooling system hoses during the first few miles of driving. Tighten the hose clamps and/or add more coolant mixture as necessary.

28 Engine idle speed check and adjustment (carburetor equipped models only)

1 Engine idle speed is the speed at which the engine operates when no accelerator pedal pressure is applied. This speed is critical to the performance of the engine itself, as well as many other components.
2 A hand-held tachometer must be used when adjusting idle speed to get an accurate reading. The exact hook-up for these meters varies with the manufacturer, so follow the particular directions included.
3 The actual step-by-step idle speed adjusting procedure for each carburetor used on the vehicles covered by this manual is included in Chapter 4, along with specifications and illustrations. Each vehicle covered in this manual also has a *Vehicle Emission Control Information* label in the engine compartment. Printed instructions for setting idle speed on your particular engine can be found on the label (the instructions supersede any information included here or in Chapter 4).
4 Basically, on most models, the idle speed is set by turning an adjustment screw located at the side of the carburetor. The screw opens or closes the throttle plate, depending on how much it is turned and in which direction. The screw may be on the linkage itself or may be part of the idle stop solenoid. Refer to the emissions label or Chapter 4.

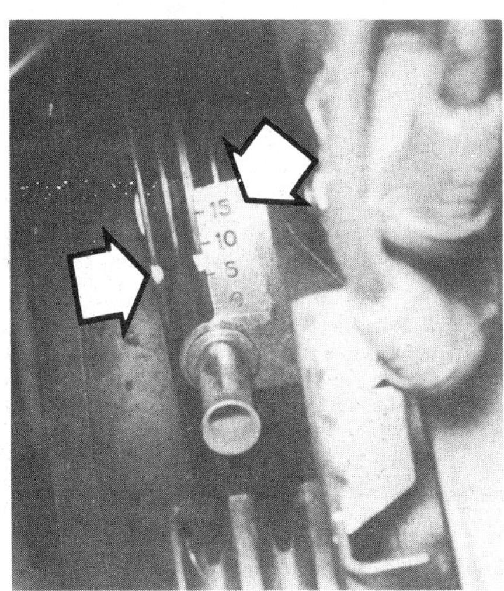

29.6a On the 2.6L engine, the timing marks are attached to the front of the engine and the crankshaft pulley has a groove in it for reference

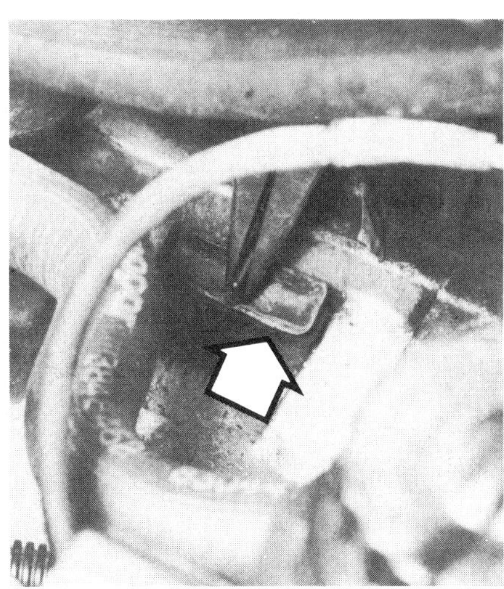

29.6b On 2.2L/2.5L engines, use a pair of needle-nose pliers to pull the timing window cover out (arrow)

29.8 Marking the notch (arrow) makes it easier to see during the timing adjustment procedure (2.2L engine shown)

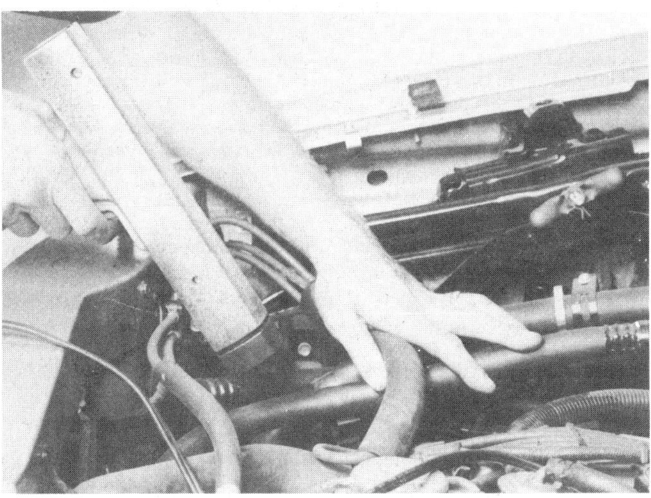

29.12 The timing marks should be aligned when the flashing light is pointed at them

5 Once you have found the idle speed screw, experiment with different length screwdrivers until the adjustments can be made easily, without coming into contact with hot or moving engine components.

6 Follow the instructions on the emissions label or in Chapter 4, which will probably include disconnecting certain vacuum or electrical connections. To plug a vacuum hose after disconnecting it, insert a golf tee or metal rod, or thoroughly wrap the open end with tape to prevent any vacuum loss through the hose.

7 Make sure the parking brake is set and the wheels blocked to prevent the vehicle from rolling. This is particularly important if the transaxle must be in Drive. An assistant inside the vehicle, pushing on the brake pedal, is the safest method.

8 For all applications, the engine must be completely warmed-up to operating temperature, which will automatically render the choke fast idle inoperative.

29 Ignition timing check and adjustment

Refer to illustrations 29.2, 29.5a, 29.5b, 29.6a, 29.6b, 29.8, 29.12 and 29.13

1 All vehicles are equipped with an *Emissions Control Information* label inside the engine compartment. The label contains important ignition timing specifications and the proper timing procedure for your specific vehicle. If the information on the emissions label is different from the information included in this Section, follow the procedure on the label.

2 At the specified intervals, or when the distributor has been removed, the ignition timing must be checked and adjusted if necessary. Tools required for this procedure include an inductive pick-up timing light, a tachometer, a distributor wrench and, in some cases, a means of plugging vacuum hoses **(see illustration)**.

3 Before you check the timing, make sure the idle speed is correct (carburetor equipped models only – Section 28) and the engine is at normal operating temperature.

4 On vehicles with a carburetor switch, connect a jumper wire between the switch and a good ground. Disconnect and plug the vacuum hose at the Spark Control Computer (2.2L engine) or at the distributor (2.6L engine). If the engine is already idling at or below the specified speed, proceed to the next Step. If the idle is too high, turn the idle speed adjusting screw until the specified curb idle is attained.

5 Connect a timing light in accordance with the manufacturer's instructions. Usually, the light must be connected to the battery and the number 1 spark plug in some fashion **(see illustrations)**. The number 1 spark plug wire or terminal should be marked at the distributor; trace it back to the spark plug and attach the timing light lead near the plug.

6 Locate the numbered timing tag on the front cover of the engine (2.6L engine) or at the timing window in the transaxle bellhousing (2.2L/2.5L engine) **(see illustrations)**.

7 Locate the notched groove across the crankshaft pulley or the flywheel. It may be necessary to have an assistant temporarily turn the ignition on and off in short bursts without starting the engine in order to bring the groove into a position where it can easily be cleaned and marked. **Warning:** *Stay clear of all moving engine components when the engine is turned over in this manner.*

8 Use white soap-stone, chalk or paint to mark the groove in the pulley or flywheel **(see illustration)**. Also, put a mark on the timing tag corresponding to the number of degrees specified on the *Emission Control Information* label in the engine compartment.

9 On fuel injected engines, connect a tachometer to the engine, setting the selector to the correct cylinder position.

10 Make sure that the wiring for the timing light is clear of all moving engine components, then start the engine.

11 On fuel injected engines, disconnect and then reconnect the water temperature sensor connector (located on the thermostat housing) by peeling back the boot with one hand while pulling the connector back with the other. The Power Loss/Power Limited light (Chapter 5) should light up and stay on and the engine speed should now be as specified on the *Emissions Control Information* label.

12 Aim the timing light at the marks **(see illustration)**, again being careful not to come into contact with moving parts. The marks you made should appear stationary. If the marks are in alignment, the timing is correct. If the marks are not aligned, turn off the engine.

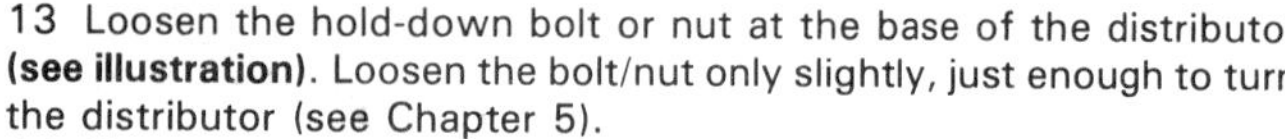

29.13 Loosen the bolt or nut and turn the distributor if the timing is not as specified (2.6L engine shown)

31.4a Using a feeler gauge and screwdriver to adjust the jet valve clearance

13 Loosen the hold-down bolt or nut at the base of the distributor **(see illustration)**. Loosen the bolt/nut only slightly, just enough to turn the distributor (see Chapter 5).
14 Now restart the engine and turn the distributor very slowly until the timing marks are aligned.
15 Shut off the engine and tighten the distributor bolt/nut, being careful not to move the distributor.
16 Start the engine and recheck the timing to make sure the marks are still in alignment.
17 On carburetor equipped models, remove the jumper wire from the carburetor switch (if equipped). Disconnect the timing light, unplug the vacuum hose and connect the hose to the distributor or computer port.
18 On carburetor equipped models, drive the vehicle and listen for "pinging" noises. They will be most noticeable when the engine is hot and under load (climbing a hill, accelerating from a stop). If you hear pinging, the ignition timing is advanced too much. Reconnect the timing light and turn the distributor to move the mark 1 or 2 degrees in the retard direction. Road test the vehicle again to check for proper operation.
19 On fuel injected models, turn the engine off, then disconnect and reconnect the positive battery cable quick disconnect. Start the vehicle and verify that the Power Loss/Power Limited light is off.
20 On fuel injected models, shut the engine off and turn the ignition on, off, on, off, on. The fault codes should clear with 88-51-55 (1984 and 1985 only) or 88-12-55 (1986 on) displayed.
21 On all models, to keep "pinging" at a minimum, yet still allow the engine to operate at the specified timing setting, use gasoline of the same octane at all times. Switching fuel brands and octane levels can decrease performance and economy and may possibly damage the engine.

30 Combustion chamber conditioner application (Canadian models only)

1 At the specified intervals combustion chamber conditioner (see *Recommended lubricants and fluids*) must be sprayed into the carburetor or fuel injection throttle body to help prevent the buildup of deposits in the combustion chamber and on the valves.
2 Remove the carburetor or throttle body air inlet hose.
3 With the engine idling at normal operating temperature, the transaxle in Park (automatic) or Neutral (manual) and the parking brake applied, spray a can of the specified conditioner into the carburetor or throttle body opening.
4 Reattach the hose to the air inlet.

31 Valve adjustment (2.6L engine only)

Refer to illustrations 31.4a and 31.4b

1 Remove the cylinder head cover (refer to Chapter 2 if necessary).
2 Adjust the valve clearances using the *hot engine* Specifications.
3 Put a wrench on the large bolt at the front of the crankshaft. Rotate the crankshaft in a clockwise direction while watching the number one cylinder rocker arms. Stop when the exhaust valve is closing and the intake valve has just begun to open (the intake valve is on the carburetor side of the engine, the exhaust valve is on the exhaust manifold side of the engine). Line up the notch in the pulley on the front of the crankshaft with the T or zero (0) on the timing mark tab on the timing chain case. At this point, the number 4 piston will be at top dead center (TDC) on the compression stroke and the number 4 cylinder valve clearances can be adjusted. **Note:** *The jet valve clearance is always adjusted before the intake and exhaust valve clearances.*
4 The intake valve and jet valve adjusting screws are located on a common rocker arm. Make sure the intake valve adjusting screw has been backed off at least two full turns, then loosen the locknut on the jet valve adjusting screw. Turn the jet valve adjusting screw counterclockwise and insert the appropriate size feeler gauge between the jet valve stem and the adjusting screw. Carefully tighten the adjusting screw until you can feel a slight drag on the feeler gauge as you withdraw it from between the stem and adjusting screw **(see illustration)**. Since the jet valve spring is relatively weak, use special care not to force the jet valve open. Be particularly careful if the adjusting screw is hard to turn. Hold the adjusting screw with a screwdriver (to keep it from turning) and tighten the locknut **(see illustration)**. Recheck the clearance to make sure it hasn't changed.
5 Next, adjust the intake valve clearance. Insert the appropriate size feeler gauge between the intake valve stem and the adjusting screw. Carefully tighten the adjusting screw until you can feel a slight drag on the feeler gauge as you withdraw it from between the stem and adjusting screw. Hold the screw with a screwdriver (to keep it from turning) and tighten the locknut, then recheck the clearance to make sure it hasn't changed.
6 Loosen the locknut on the exhaust valve adjusting screw. Turn the adjusting screw counterclockwise and insert the appropriate size feeler gauge between the valve stem and the adjusting screw. Carefully tighten the adjusting screw until you can feel a slight drag on the feeler gauge, as you withdraw it from between the stem and adjusting screw. Hold the adjusting screw with a screwdriver and tighten the locknut. Recheck the clearance to make sure it hasn't changed.
7 Repeat this procedure to adjust the valve clearances for cylinder numbers 1, 2 and 3. Use the following table for determining when the pistons are at TDC:

Exhaust valve closing — intake valve just opening:	Adjust valve clearances at:
No. 1 cylinder	No. 4 cylinder
No. 2 cylinder	No. 3 cylinder
No. 3 cylinder	No. 2 cylinder
No. 4 cylinder	No. 1 cylinder

Remember to align the notch in the crankshaft pulley with the T or zero on the timing mark tab before making the adjustments.
8 Install the cylinder head cover.

31.4b Hold the adjusting screw in position while tightening the locknut

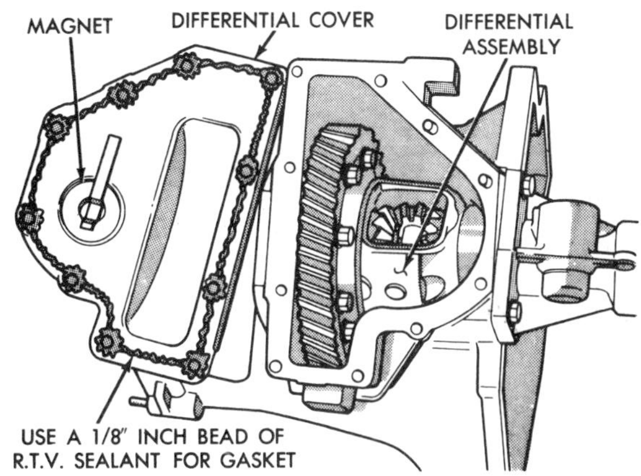

32.4 Apply RTV sealant to the mating surface of the differential cover prior to installation

33.3 Use a soft-face hammer to break the corner of the oil pan loose and drain the fluid

33.4 The filter screws may require a special Torx driver for removal

32 Manual transaxle oil change

Refer to illustration 32.4

1 Under normal operating conditions the lubricant added at the factory should last the life of the vehicle. If the vehicle is operated under severe conditions, the lubricant should be changed. Raise the front of the vehicle and support it securely on jackstands.

2 Remove the pan cover from the side of the differential and allow the fluid to drain into a container.

3 Attached to the inside of the pan cover is a small magnet, installed to trap metal particles before they can damage the trandsaxle bearings. Clean the magnet and the inside surface of the pan cover thoroughly.

4 Use RTV sealant to form a new gasket for the pan cover and install the cover on the differential **(see illustration)**. Tighten the bolts evenly and securely in a criss-cross pattern.

5 Fill the transaxle with the recommended lubricant until the level is at the bottom edge of the filler plug. Drive the vehicle and check the pan cover seal for leakage.

33 Automatic transaxle fluid and filter change

Refer to illustrations 33.3, 33.4, 33.6 and 33.8

1 The automatic transaxle fluid and filter should be changed, the magnet cleaned and the bands adjusted at the recommended intervals.

2 Raise the vehicle and support it securely.

3 Position container under the transaxle oil pan. Loosen the pan bolts. Completely remove the bolts along the rear of the pan. Tap the corner of the pan **(see illustration)** to break the seal and allow the fluid to drain into the container (the remaining bolts will prevent the pan from separating from the transaxle). Remove the remaining bolts and detach the pan.

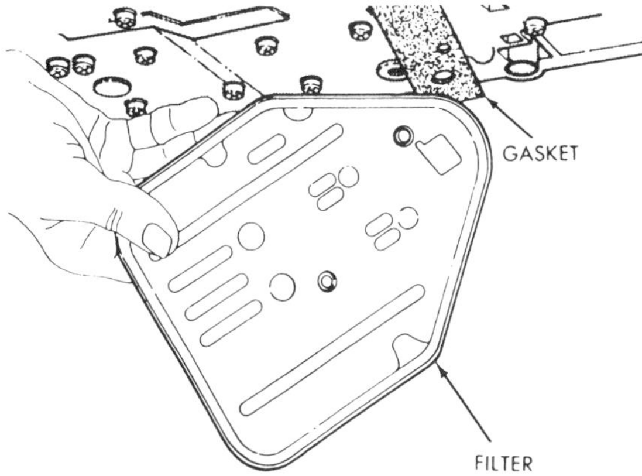

33.6 Be sure to install the new gasket before attaching the new filter to the transaxle

4 Remove the filter screws and detach the filter (a special Torx bit may be required for the screws) **(see illustration)**.

5 Refer to Section 34 and adjust the bands before proceeding with the fluid change.

6 Install the new gasket and filter and tighten the screws **(see illustration)**.

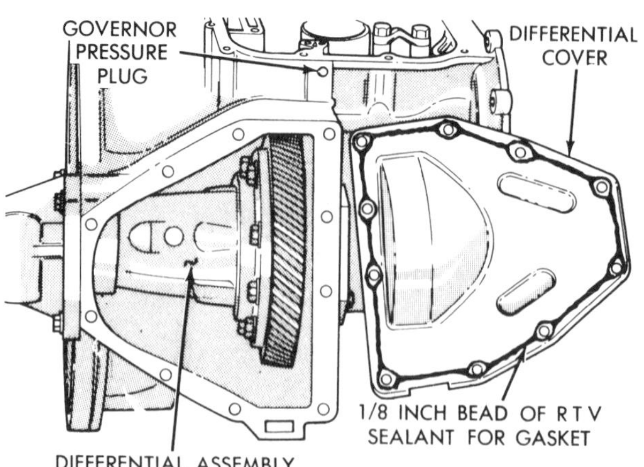

33.8 On models equipped with a magnet in the differential cover, apply RTV sealant to the cover as shown

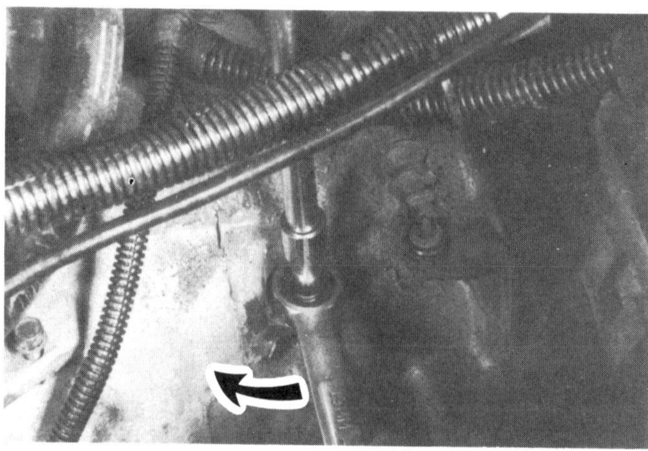

34.7 Tighten the kickdown band locknut with a box-end wrench while holding the screw so it doesn't turn

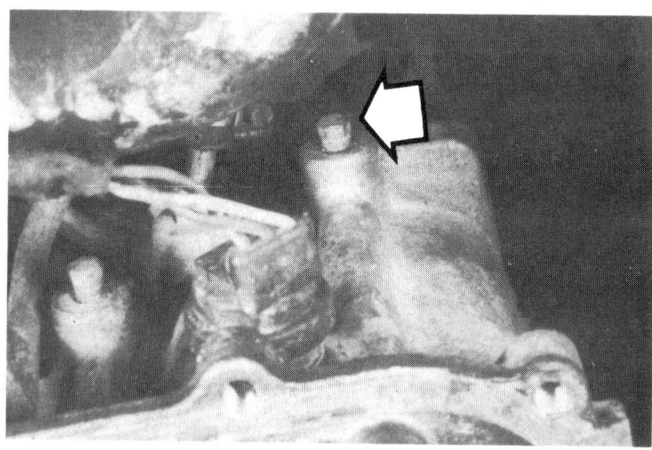

34.9 Low-Reverse pressure plug location (arrow)

7 Carefully remove all traces of old gasket sealant from the oil pan and the transaxle body (don't nick or gouge the sealing surfaces). Clean the magnet in the pan as well with a clean, lint-free cloth. On some models, the magnet is located in the differential cover. Remove the differential cover, take the magnet out of the recess and clean it.
8 Apply a 1/8-inch bead of RTV sealant to the oil pan gasket surface and position it on the transaxle. Install the bolts and tighten them to the specified torque following a criss-cross pattern. Work up to the final torque in three or four steps. On models so equipped, install the magnet in the differential cover, apply a 1/8-inch bead of RTV sealant to the mating surface and install it following the same procedure **(see illustration)**.
9 Lower the vehicle and add four quarts of the specified fluid to the transaxle. Start the engine and allow it to idle for at least one minute, then move the shift lever through each of the gear positions, ending in Park or Neutral. Check for fluid leakage around the oil pan and differential cover.
10 Add more fluid until the level is 1/8-inch below the Add mark on the dipstick.
11 Drive the vehicle until the fluid is hot, then recheck the level (see Section 4).
12 Make sure the dipstick is seated completely or dirt could get into the transaxle.

34 Automatic transaxle band adjustment

Refer to illustrations 34.7, 34.9, 34.10, 34.11a, 34.11b, 34.12 and 34.15

1 The transaxle bands should be adjusted when specified in the maintenance schedule or at the time of a fluid and filter change (Section 33).

Kickdown band

2 The kickdown band adjustment screw is located at the top left side of the transaxle case.
3 On some models the throttle cable may interfere with band adjustment. If so, mark its position and then remove the throttle cable adjustment bolt. Move the cable away from the band adjustment screw.
4 Loosen the locknut approximately five turns and make sure the adjusting screw turns freely.
5 Tighten the adjusting screw to the specified torque.
6 Back the adjusting screw off the specified number of turns.
7 Hold the screw in position and tighten the locknut securely **(see illustration)**.

Low-Reverse band

8 To gain access to the low-Reverse band, the oil pan must be removed (Section 33).
9 To determine if the band is worn excessively, remove the Low-Reverse pressure plug from the transaxle case and apply 30 psi of air pressure to the port **(see illustration)**.
10 Measure the gap between the band ends and compare it to the Specifications **(see illustration)**. If it is less than specified, the band should be replaced with a new one.
11 To proceed with adjustment, pry off the parking rod E-clip and remove the rod **(see illustrations)**.
12 Loosen the locknut approximately five turns. Use an in-lb torque wrench to tighten the adjusting screw to the specified torque **(see illustration)**.
13 Back the screw off the specified number of turns.
14 Hold the adjusting screw in position and tighten the locknut to the specified torque.
15 Push the shift pawl in the transaxle case to the rear and reinstall the parking rod **(see illustration)**.
16 Install the oil pan and refill the transaxle (Section 33).

35 Driveaxle CV joint boot check

Refer to illustration 35.3

1 If the driveaxle rubber boots are damaged or deteriorated, serious and costly damage can occur to the CV joints the rubber boots are designed to protect. The boots should be inspected very carefully at the recommended intervals.
2 Raise the front of the vehicle and support it securely on jackstands positioned under the hoisting and jacking points (see *Jacking and towing* at the front of this manual if necessary).
3 Crawl under the vehicle and check the four driveaxle boots (two on each driveaxle) very carefully for cracks, tears, holes, deteriorated rubber and loose or missing clamps **(see illustration)**. If the boots are dirty, wipe them clean before beginning the inspection.
4 If damage or deterioration is evident, replace the boots with new ones and check the CV joints for damage (Chapter 8).

34.10 Measuring the Low-Reverse band end clearance with a feeler gauge

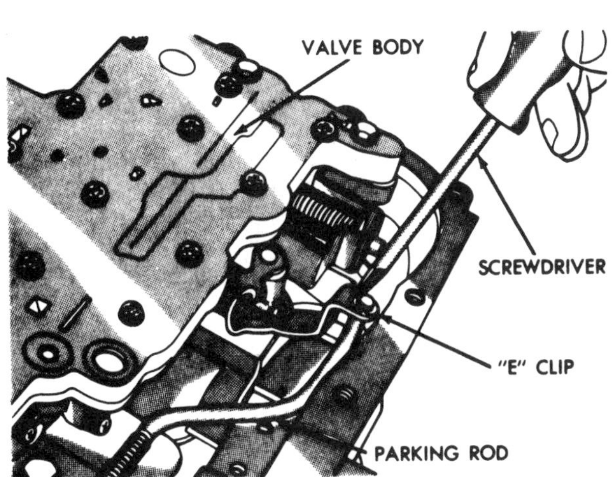

34.11a The parking rod E-clip can be removed with a screwdriver

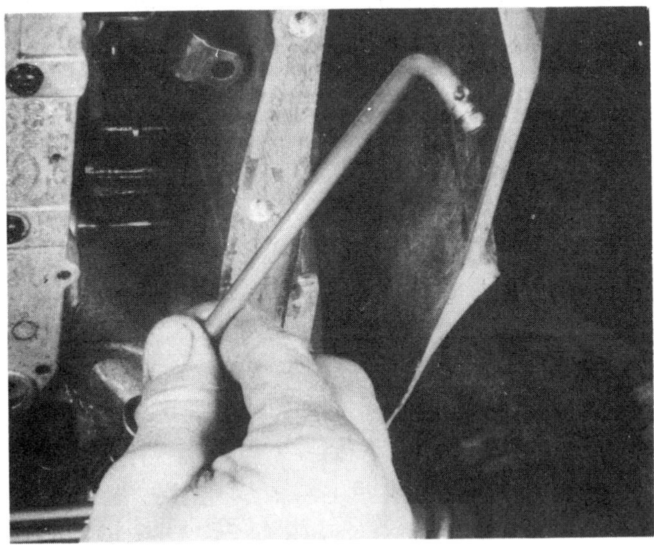

34.11b Removing the parking rod

34.12 Loosening the Low-Reverse band locknut

34.15 The shift pawl must be pushed back before the parking rod can be inserted

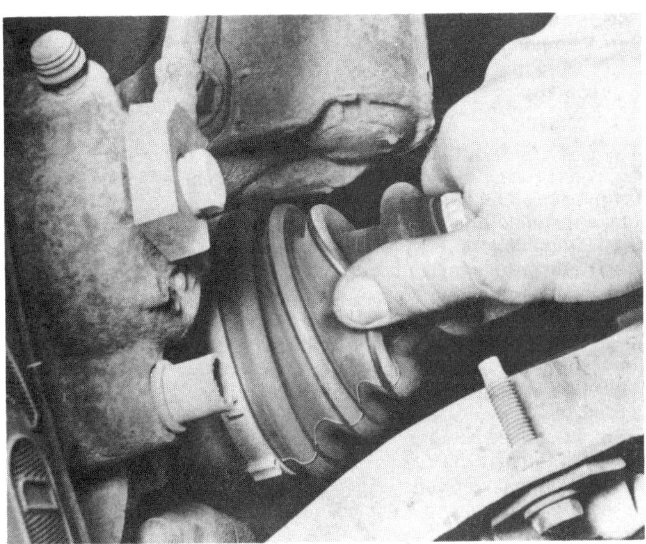

35.3 The driveaxle rubber boots should be flexed by hand to check for cracks, tears and holes

Chapter 2 Part A 2.6L engine

Contents

Specifications

Timing chain tensioner spring free length	2.587 in (65.7 mm)
Silent shaft	
front bearing journal diameter	0.906 in (23 mm)
front bearing oil clearance	0.0008 to 0.0024 in (0.02 to 0.06 mm)
rear bearing journal diameter	1.693 in (43 mm)
rear bearing oil clearance	0.0020 to 0.0035 in (0.05 to 0.09 mm)
Oil pump	
relief spring free length	1.850 in (47 mm)
gear-to-housing clearance	0.0043 to 0.0059 in (0.11 to 0.15 mm)
gear-to-pump body clearance	0.0008 to 0.0020 in (0.02 to 0.05 mm)
gear-to-pump cover bearing clearance	0.0016 to 0.0028 in (0.04 to 0.07 mm)
gear end play	
drive	0.0020 to 0.0043 in (0.05 to 0.11 mm)
driven	0.0016 to 0.0039 in (0.04 to 0.10 mm)
Camshaft end play	0.004 to 0.008 in (0.1 to 0.2 mm)

Torque specifications	**Ft-lbs**	**Nm**
Intake manifold nuts	12.5	17
Exhaust manifold nuts	12.5	17
Water pump drive pulley bolts	40	54
Water pump mounting bolts	17	23
Cylinder head-to-block bolts (HOT)	76	103
Cylinder head-to-block bolts (COLD)	69	94
Crankshaft sprocket/pulley bolt	87	118
Camshaft bearing cap bolts		
Step 1	7.5	10
Step 2	13.5	18
Flywheel to crankshaft bolt	65	88
Cylinder head cover bolts	4.5	6
Cylinder head-to-timing chain case bolts	13.5	18
Jet valves	14	19
Engine mount plate bolts	13.5	18
Engine-to-transaxle bolts	70	95

Front engine mount bolts		
Small bolts	40	54
Big bolts	45	61
Left engine mount bolts		
Small bolts	40	54
Big bolts	50	68
Right engine mount bolts		
Short bolts	21	28
Long bolts	75	102
Timing chain case cover bolts	13.5	18
Torque converter-to-driveplate bolts	40	54
Oil pan bolts	4.5	6
Camshaft sprocket/distributor drive gear bolt	40	54
Timing chain guide bolts	13.5	18
Silent Shaft chain guide bolts	13.5	18
Silent Shaft drive gear/oil pump sprocket bolt	25	34
Silent Shaft sprocket bolt	25	34
Engine mount through-bolts	40	54
Oil pump sprocket bolt	25	34
Oil pump mounting bolt	6	8

1 General information

The 2.6 liter engine is an inline vertical four, with a chain-driven overhead camshaft and a Silent Shaft counterbalancing system which cancels the engine's power pulses and produces relatively vibration-free operation. The crankshaft rides in five renewable insert-type main bearings, with the center bearing assigned the additional task of controlling crankshaft end play.

The pistons have two compression rings and one oil control ring. The semi-floating piston pins are press fitted into the small end of the connecting rod. The connecting rod big ends are also equipped with renewable insert-type plain bearings.

The engine is liquid-cooled, utilizing a centrifugal impeller-type pump, driven by a belt from the camshaft, to circulate coolant around the cylinders and combustion chambers and through the intake manifold.

Lubrication is handled by a gear-type oil pump mounted on the front of the engine under the timing chain cover. It is driven by the Silent Shaft chain. The oil is filtered continuously by a cartridge-type filter mounted on the radiator side of the engine.

2 Engine — removal

Refer to illustration 2.13

1 Disconnect the negative battery cable from the battery, then detach the positive cable and remove the battery.
2 Remove the hood (Chapter 11).
3 Drain the cooling system, remove the radiator hoses and disconnect the automatic transaxle cooler lines from the radiator. Drain the engine oil and remove the oil filter (Chapter 1).
4 Remove the radiator (Chapter 3), the air cleaner and hoses and the heater hoses.
5 If equipped, remove the air conditioning compressor *but do not disconnect any of the hoses as they are under high pressure*. Unbolt the power steering pump and move it out of the way (if equipped).
6 Detach all electrical connections at the engine, one at a time, marking them with pieces of tape or tags to simplify reinstallation.
7 Remove the alternator.
8 Disconnect and tag the fuel lines.
9 Disconnect the throttle cable from the carburetor.
10 Disconnect the exhaust pipe from the manifold.
11 Remove the starter (Chapter 5),
12 Remove the transaxle lower cover.
13 Mark the relationship of the driveplate to the torque converter (vehicles equipped with an automatic transmission) **(see illustration)**.
14 Remove the torque converter-to-driveplate bolts.
15 Retain the torque converter in place with a C-clamp so it will not fall during engine removal.
16 Support the transaxle with a jack.
17 Attach a lifting device to the engine and raise it enough to take up the slack in the chain and remove the weight from the engine mounts.
18 Remove the engine compartment right side inner splash shield.
19 Remove the engine-to-chassis ground strap.
20 Remove the right side engine mount-to-insulator through-bolt. If the insulator is removed, mark its position, as it must be reinstalled in the exact same position.
21 Remove the transaxle-to-engine block bolts.
22 Remove the front engine mount through-bolt.
23 Begin lifting the engine from the vehicle, making sure that there are no wires, hoses or other components still connected. Lift the engine clear of the vehicle and lower it to the floor or a workbench.

3 Flywheel/driveplate — removal and installation

1 Remove the bolts and separate the flywheel/driveplate from the crankshaft.
2 To install, hold the flywheel/driveplate in position and install the mounting bolts.

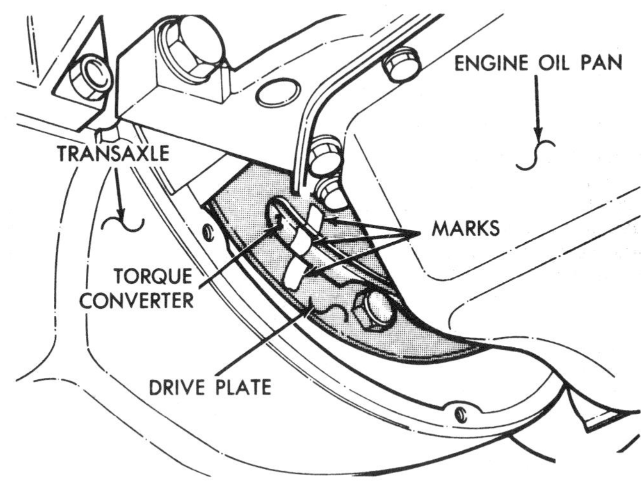

2.13 Mark the torque converter and driveplate to ensure that they are correctly mated when the engine is reinstalled

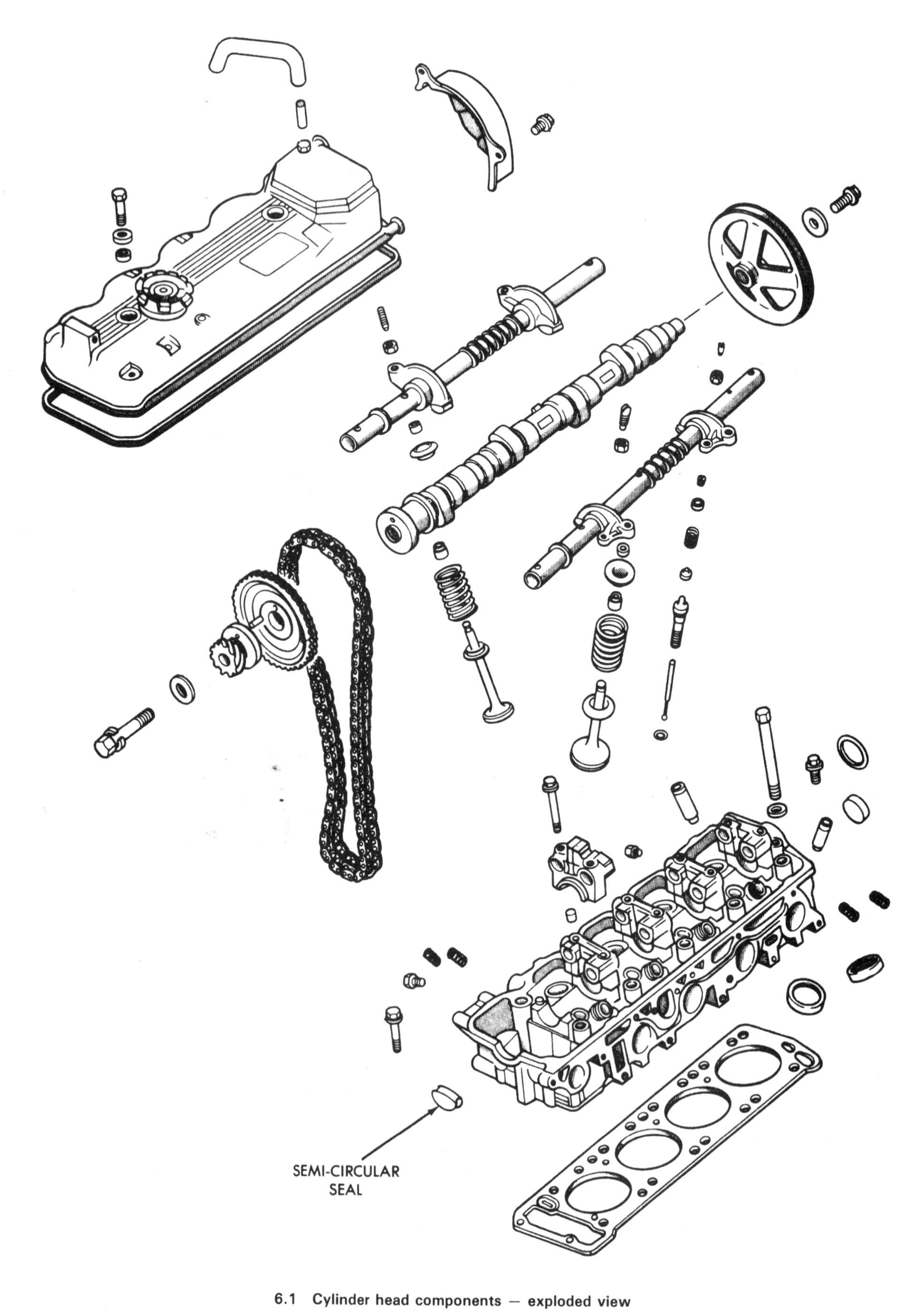

6.1 Cylinder head components — exploded view

3 While locking the crankshaft so it won't turn, tighten the bolts (following a criss-cross pattern) to the specified torque.

4 External engine components – removal

Note: *When removing the external components from the engine, pay close attention to details that may be helpful or important during installation. Look for the correct positioning of gaskets, seals, spacers, pins, washers, bolts and other small items.*

1 It is much easier to dismantle and repair the engine if it is mounted on a portable-type engine stand. These stands can often be rented, for a reasonable fee, from an equipment rental yard.

2 If a stand is not available, it is possible to dismantle the engine with it blocked up on a sturdy workbench or on the floor. Be extra careful not to tip or drop the engine when working without a stand.

3 Before the engine can be mounted on a stand, the flywheel/driveplate, the dust shield and the rear seal housing must be removed. Remove the flywheel/driveplate and dust shield (Section 3) then loosen and remove the seven bolts attaching the seal housing to the rear of the engine block and the oil pan. Carefully remove the housing (try not to let the oil separator inside the seal housing fall out of place). Note how the oil separator is installed, to prevent confusion during reassembly. You may have to tap the seal housing lightly with a soft-faced hammer to break it loose. Do not pry between the seal housing and engine block, as damage to the gasket sealing surfaces may result. At this point, the engine is ready to mount on the stand.

4 Remove the engine mounts and brackets. Store the right and left engine mount bracket components separately, to avoid confusion during reassembly. Be sure to inspect the metal parts for cracks and the rubber parts for deterioration and delamination from the metal. If any defects are found, replace the parts with new ones.

5 If your vehicle is equipped with air-conditioning, remove the upper and lower compressor brackets from the engine block.

6 Remove the bolts and detach the power steering pump bracket from the engine.

7 Remove the crankcase emissions control system components.

8 Remove the nine nuts and one bolt attaching the intake manifold to the cylinder head and lift the manifold and the carburetor, as an assembly, from the head. Note the position of the engine hoisting bracket attached to the rear intake manifold studs.

9 Remove the two nuts attaching the fuel pump to the cylinder head and slip off the fuel pump and the insulator.

10 Remove the distributor cap by depressing and turning the spring-loaded screws on the cap. Remove the distributor mounting nut and slip the distributor out of the engine by pulling straight out on it.

11 Remove the water pump (Chapter 3).

12 Unscrew and remove the oil pressure sending unit.

13 Remove the Pulse Air Feeder (PAF) system (Chapter 6).

14 Remove the four bolts attaching the spark plug wire brackets to the cylinder cover and lift the distributor cap and spark plug wires away from the engine as an assembly.

15 Take out the oil dipstick.

5 Oil pan – removal and installation

1 Remove the bolts securing the oil pan to the engine block.

2 Tap on the pan with a soft-faced hammer to break the gasket seal and lift the oil pan off the engine.

3 Using a gasket scraper, scrape off all traces of the old gasket from the engine block, the timing chain cover and the oil pan. Be especially careful not to nick or gouge the gasket sealing surface of the timing chain cover (it is made of aluminum and is quite soft).

4 Clean the oil pan with solvent and dry it thoroughly. Check the gasket sealing surfaces for distortion.

5 Before installing the oil pan, apply a thin coat of RTV-type gasket sealant to the engine block gasket sealing surfaces. Lay a new oil pan gasket in place and carefully apply a coat of gasket sealant to the exposed side of the gasket.

6 Gently lay the oil pan in place (do not disturb the gasket) and install the bolts. Start with the bolts closest to the center of the pan and tighten them to the specified torque using a criss-cross pattern. Do not overtighten them or leakage may occur.

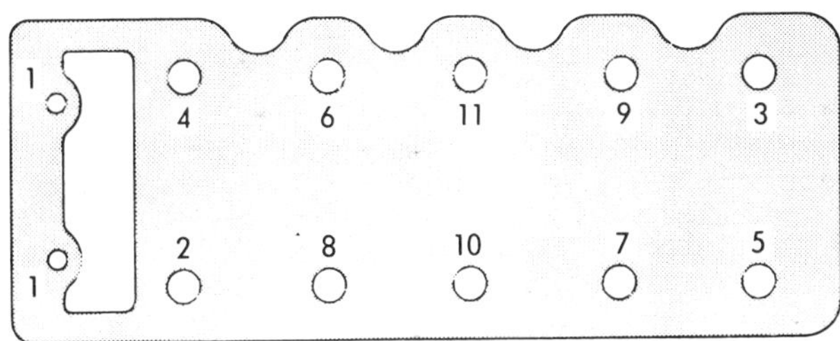

6.5 2.6L engine cylinder head bolt *loosening* sequence

6 Cylinder head – removal

Refer to illustrations 6.1 and 6.5

1 Remove the two bolts, washers and rubber seals attaching the cover to the cylinder head and lift off the cover. Remove the semi-circular seal from the front of the cylinder head. Remove the bolt and separate the water pump pulley and belt from the rear of the camshaft **(see illustration)**.

2 Rotate the crankshaft with a wrench on the large bolt at the front of the crankshaft until the number one piston is at top dead center on the compression stroke. To do this, watch the rocker arms for the number one cylinder valves while slowly rotating the crankshaft in a clockwise direction. When the intake valve closes, continue rotating the crankshaft until the mark on the pulley is aligned with the T or zero (0) on the timing tab.

3 Locate the timing mark on the camshaft sprocket and make sure the plated link of the cam chain is opposite the mark.

4 Remove the camshaft sprocket bolt from the front of the camshaft. To facilitate loosening the camshaft sprocket bolt, you can prevent the crankshaft from turning by holding the large bolt on the end of the crankshaft with a wrench. Remove the distributor drive gear from the front of the camshaft by tapping it with a soft-faced hammer. Pull the camshaft sprocket – with the chain in place – off the camshaft, and allow it to rest on the sprocket holder.

5 Loosen the ten camshaft bearing cap bolts, 1/2-turn each, in sequence, until all pressure from the valve springs has been released **(see illustration)**. Next remove the six inner bolts and lift the rocker arm shaft assembly away from the cylinder head with the four end bolts in place. No further disassembly of these components is necessary unless new parts are required. Carefully lift the camshaft out of the cylinder head and store it someplace where it will not be damaged.

6 Remove the two bolts attaching the cylinder head to the timing chain cover (at the very front of the cylinder head). Remove the ten bolts attaching the cylinder head to the engine block. Turn them 1/4-turn each, in the sequence shown, until they are all loose enough to remove by hand.

7 Remove the cylinder head by lifting it straight up and off the engine block. **Caution:** *Do not pry between the cylinder head and the engine block, as damage to the gasket sealing surfaces may result.* Instead, use a soft-faced hammer to tap the cylinder head and break the gasket seal.

8 Lift off the old head gasket.

7 Silent Shaft chain/sprockets – removal and inspection

Refer to illustration 7.5

1 Before attempting to remove the Silent Shaft chain and sprockets, you must remove the cylinder head and the oil pan (Sections 5 and 6).

2 Remove the large bolt at the front of the crankshaft and slide the pulley off.

3 Remove the bolts attaching the timing chain case to the engine block. Draw a simple diagram showing the location of each of the bolts so they can be returned to the same holes from which they were removed.

4 Tap the timing chain case with a soft-faced hammer to break the gasket seal, then remove the case from the engine block. **Caution:** *Prying between the case and the engine block can damage the gasket sealing surfaces.*

5 Remove the chain guides labeled A, B and C **(see illustration)**. Each guide is held in place by two bolts. Again, draw a simple diagram showing the location of each bolt so that it can be returned to the same hole from which it was removed.

6 Reinstall the large bolt in the end of the crankshaft. Hold it in place with a wrench to prevent the crankshaft from turning while loosening the bolt on the end of the rear (firewall side) Silent Shaft, the bolt attaching the rear Silent Shaft drive sprocket to the oil pump shaft and the bolt in the end of the front (radiator side) Silent Shaft. If the bolt in the end of the rear Silent Shaft is difficult to loosen, remove the oil pump and Silent Shaft as an assembly (see Section 10), then remove the bolt with the Silent Shaft securely clamped in a vise.

7 Slide the crankshaft sprocket, the Silent Shaft sprockets and the chain off the engine as an assembly. Leave the bolt in the end of the rear Silent Shaft in place. Do not lose the keys that index the sprockets to the shafts.

8 Check the sprocket teeth for wear and damage. Check the sprocket cushion rings and ring guides (Silent Shaft sprockets only) for wear and damage. Rotate the cushion rings and check for smooth operation. Inspect the chain for cracked side plates and pitted or worn rollers. Replace any defective or worn parts with new ones.

8 Timing chain/sprockets — removal, inspection and installation

Refer to illustrations 8.5, 8.6, 8.7, 8.8, 8.9a and 8.9b

1 The Silent Shaft chain and sprockets must be removed to gain access to the timing chain assembly (Section 7).

2 Depress the timing chain tensioner plunger on the oil pump and slide the camshaft sprocket, the crankshaft sprocket and the timing chain off the engine as an assembly. Do not lose the key that indexes the crankshaft sprocket in the proper place. Remove the timing chain tensioner plunger and spring from the oil pump.

3 Remove the camshaft sprocket holder and the right and left timing chain guides from the front of the engine block.

4 Inspect the sprocket teeth for wear and damage. Check the chain for cracked plates and pitted or worn rollers. Check the chain tensioner rubber shoe for wear and the tensioner spring for cracks and deterioration. Measure the tensioner spring free length and compare it to the Specifications. Check the chain guides for wear and damage. Replace any defective parts with new ones.

5 Install the sprocket holder **(see illustration)** and the right and left timing chain guides onto the engine block. Tighten the bolts securely. The upper bolt in the left timing chain guide should be installed finger-tight only. Then coat the entire length of the chain contact surfaces of the guides with clean, high-quality moly-based grease.

6 Turn the nose bolt on the crankshaft with a large wrench until the number one piston is at top dead center. The piston is at TDC when it's flush with the top of the engine block. Apply a layer of clean moly-based grease or engine assembly lube to the timing chain tensioner plunger and install the tensioner spring and plunger loosely into the oil pump body **(see illustration)**.

7 Position the timing chain sprocket on the end of the crankshaft with the wide shoulder facing out **(see illustration)**. Line up the keyway in the sprocket with the key on the crankshaft.

8 Install the camshaft sprocket onto the chain, lining up the plated link on the chain with the marked tooth on the sprocket **(see illustration)**.

9 Slip the chain over the crankshaft sprocket, lining up the plated link on the chain with the marked tooth on the sprocket **(see illustration)**. Slide the crankshaft sprocket all the way onto the crankshaft while depressing the chain tensioner so the chain fits into place in the guides. Rest the camshaft sprocket on the sprocket holder **(see illustration)** and make sure the plated links and mating marks are aligned properly. **Caution:** *Do not rotate the crankshaft for any reason until the cylinder head and camshaft have been properly installed.*

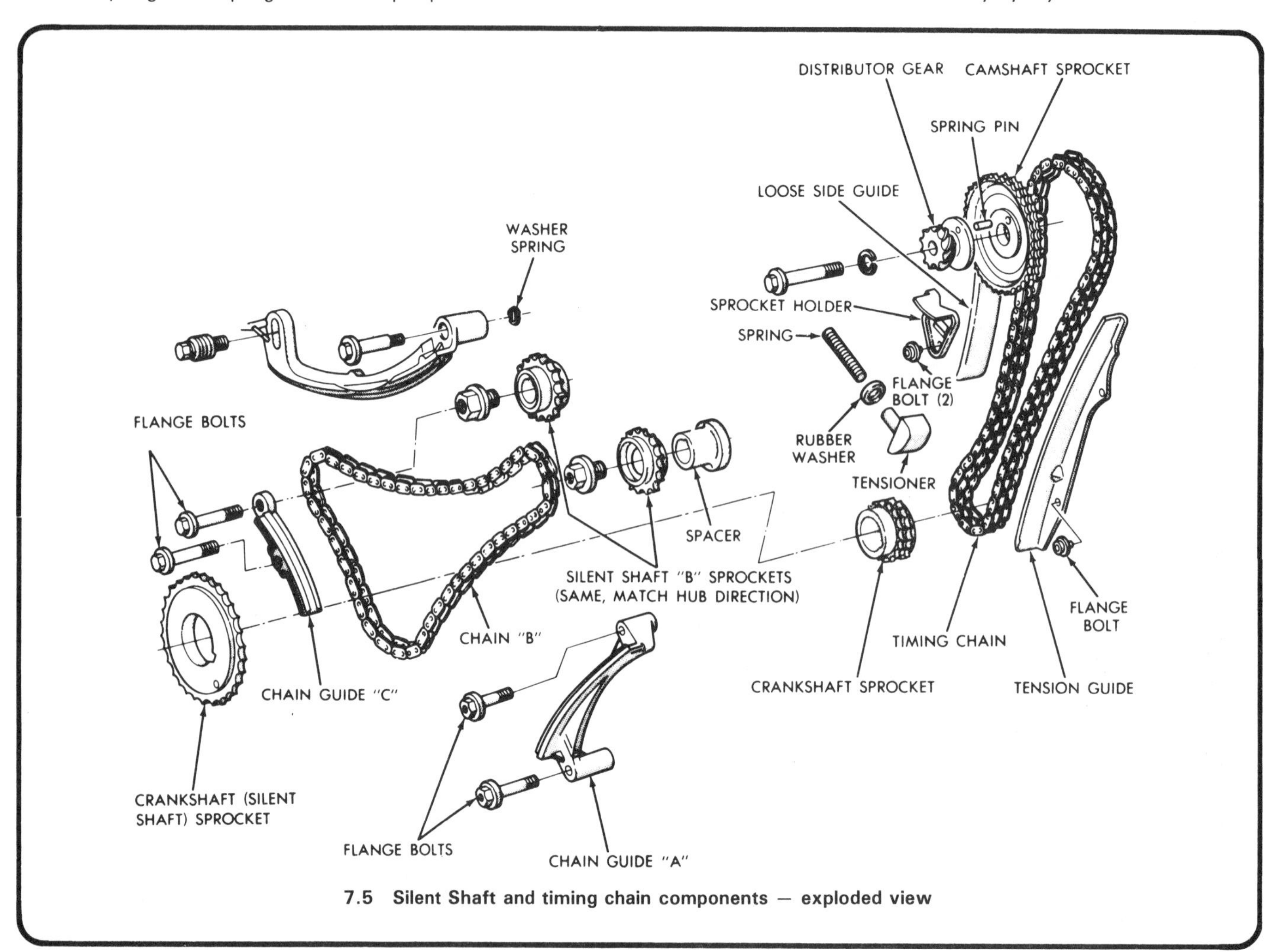

7.5 Silent Shaft and timing chain components — exploded view

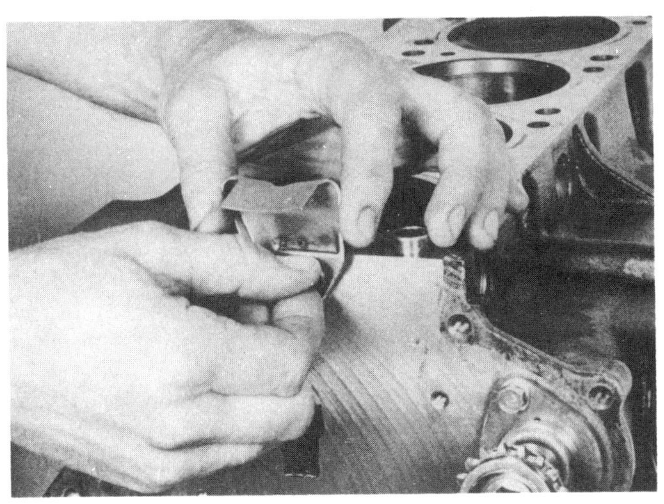
8.5 Installing the camshaft sprocket holder on the engine block

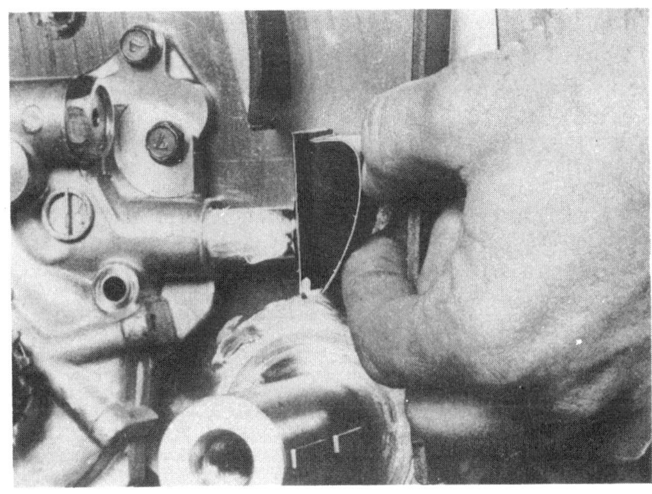
8.6 Lubricate the timing chain tensioner plunger and install it in the oil pump bore

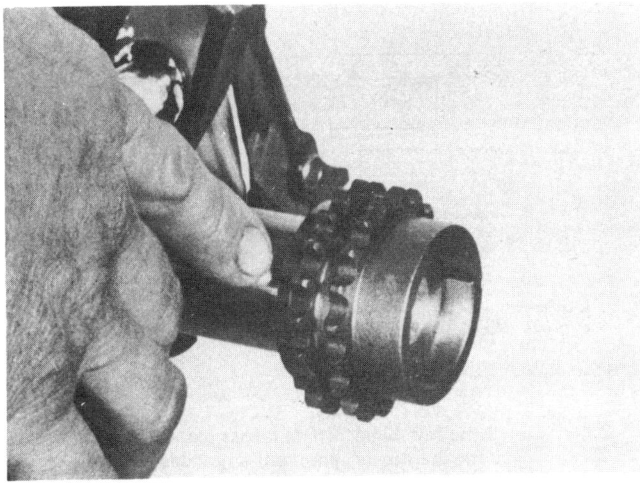
8.7 Install the timing chain sprocket on the end of the crankshaft with the wide shoulder facing out

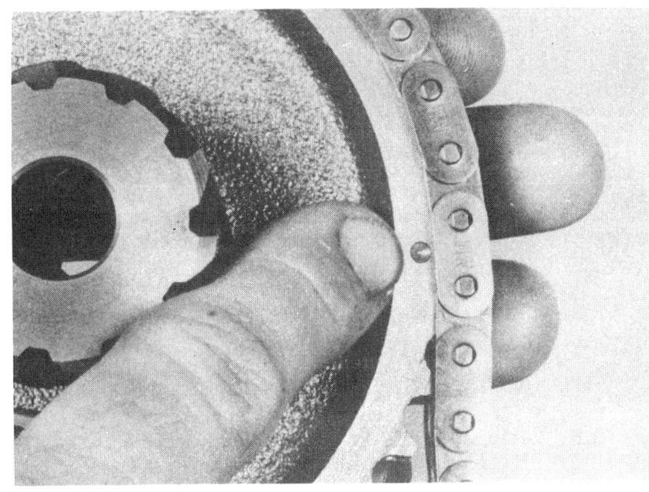
8.8 Mesh the camshaft sprocket and the timing chain with the mark on the sprocket directly opposite the plated link on the chain

8.9a Installing the timing chain on the crankshaft sprocket (note that the sprocket mark and the plated link are opposite each other)

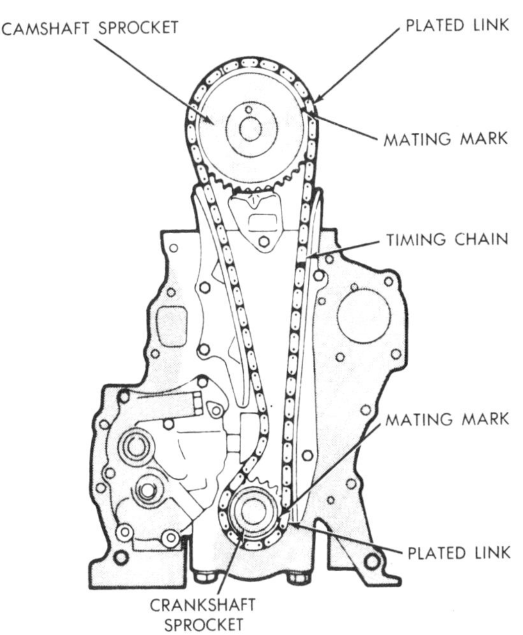

8.9b Correct timing chain and sprocket relationship

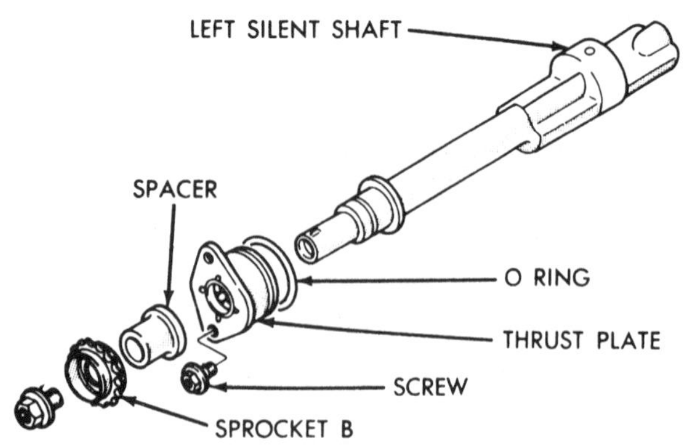

9.5 Left Silent Shaft components — exploded view

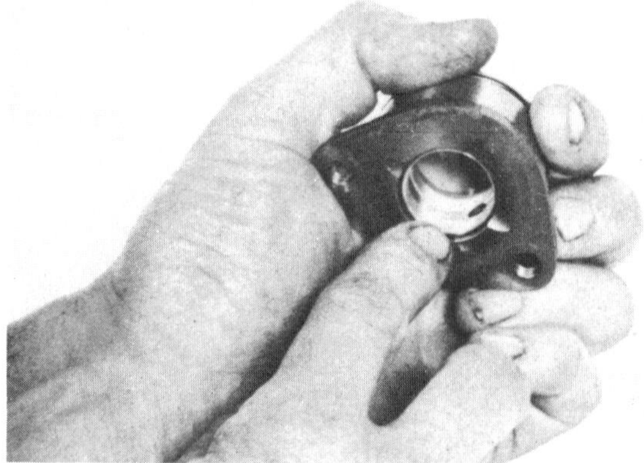

9.7 Checking the bearing in the thrust plate for wear and damage

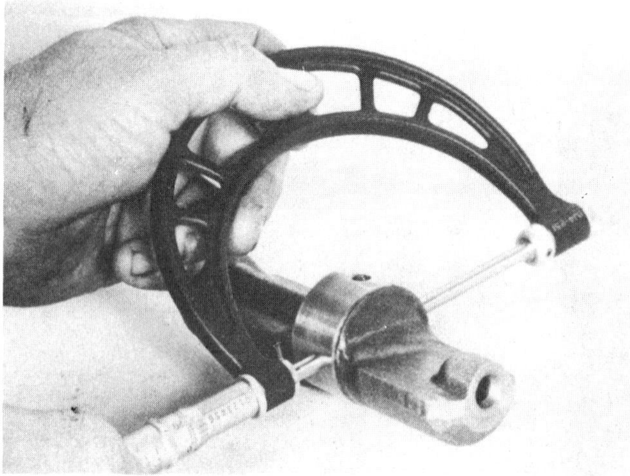

9.8 Measuring the Silent Shaft bearing journal outside diameter with a micrometer

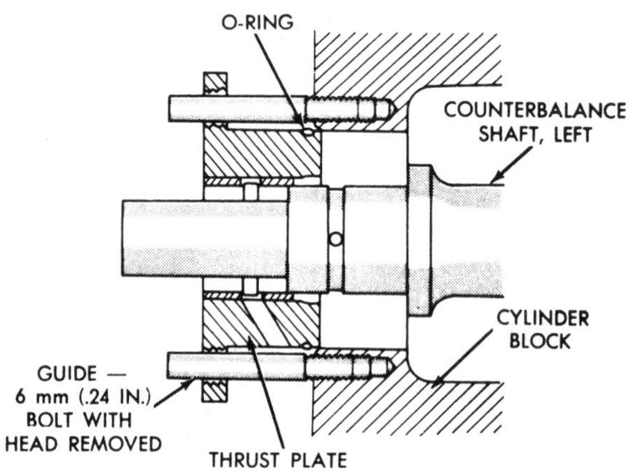

9.11 Install the left Silent Shaft thrust plate using bolts (with the heads removed) as guides

9 Silent Shafts — removal, inspection and installation

Refer to illustrations 9.5, 9.7, 9.8 and 9.11

1 The Silent Shaft chain and sprockets, the timing chain and sprockets and the oil pump should be removed before the Silent Shafts.

2 Remove the front Silent Shaft chamber cover plate from the engine block. It is held in place with two bolts. You may have to tap the cover with a soft-faced hammer to break the gasket seal.

3 Remove the two bolts attaching the front Silent Shaft thrust plate to the engine block, then carefully pull out the thrust plate and the Silent Shaft as an assembly. Support the rear of the shaft (by reaching through the access hole) to prevent damage to the rear bearing as the shaft is withdrawn from the engine. If the thrust plate proves to be difficult to pull out, screw an appropriate size bolt into each of the threaded holes in the thrust plate flange until they bottom on the engine block. Continue turning them with a wrench, one turn at a time, alternating between the two, until the thrust plate is backed out of the engine block. Remove the bolts from the thrust plate flange.

4 The rear Silent Shaft is removed with the oil pump (see Section 10).

5 To disassemble the front Silent Shaft, slip off the spacer and the thrust plate/bearing assembly. Do not lose the key in the end of the shaft. Remove the O-ring from the thrust plate **(see illustration)**.

6 Clean the components with solvent and dry them thoroughly. Make sure that the oil holes in the shafts and thrust plate are clean and clear.

7 Check both Silent Shafts and the thrust plate for cracks and other damage. Check the bearings in the engine block and the thrust plate **(see illustration)** for scratches, scoring and excessive wear. Check the bearing journals on the Silent Shafts for excessive wear and scoring.

8 Measure the outside diameter of each bearing journal **(see illustration)** and the inside diameter of each bearing. Subtract the journal diameter from the bearing diameter to obtain the bearing oil clearance. Compare the measured clearance to the Specifications. If it is excessive, have an automotive machine shop or dealer service department replace the bearings with new ones. If new bearings do not restore the oil clearance, or if the bearing journals on the shafts are damaged or worn, replace the shafts too. If the bearing in the front Silent Shaft thrust plate is bad, replace the bearing and thrust plate as an assembly.

9 Apply a thin layer of clean moly-based grease (or engine assembly lube) to the bearing journals on the front Silent Shaft, then carefully insert it into the engine block. Support the rear of the shaft so the rear bearing is not scratched or gouged as the shaft is inserted into its chamber.

10 Install a new O-ring onto the outside of the thrust plate and lubricate it with clean multi-purpose grease. Also, apply a layer of grease to the thrust plate Silent Shaft bearing.

11 Cut the heads off two 6 x 50 mm bolts and install the bolts in the thrust plate mounting bolt holes. Using the bolts as a guide, carefully slide the thrust plate into position in the engine block **(see illustration)**. The guides are necessary to keep the bolt holes in the thrust plate aligned with the holes in the engine block. If the thrust plate is turned to align the holes, the O-ring could be twisted or damaged.

12 Remove the guide bolts, install the mounting bolts and tighten them securely.

13 Slip the spacer onto the end of the Silent Shaft (make sure that the key is in place).

14 Turn the shaft by hand and check for smooth operation.

15 Using a new rubber gasket and RTV-type gasket sealant, as well as new O-rings on the bolts, install the front Silent Shaft chamber cover plate and tighten the bolts securely.

16 The rear Silent Shaft is installed with the oil pump.

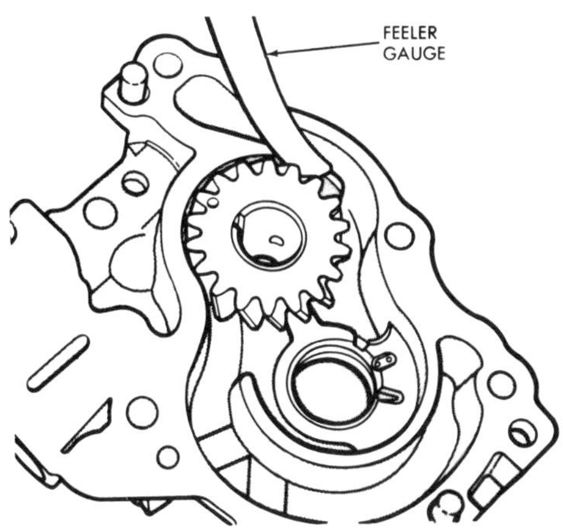

10.10a Checking the driven gear-to-housing clearance with a feeler gauge

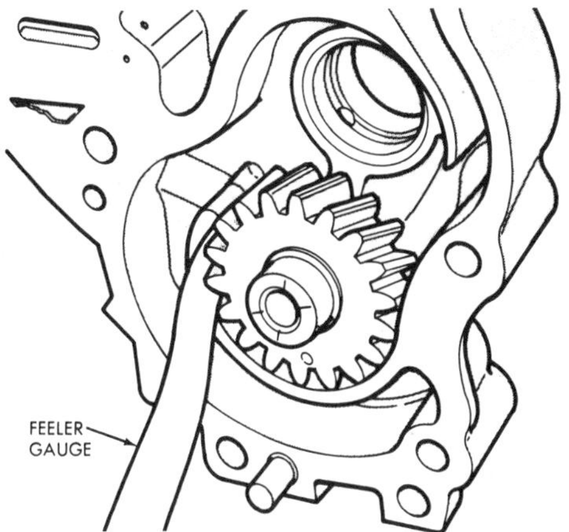

10.10b Checking the drive gear-to-housing clearance with a feeler gauge

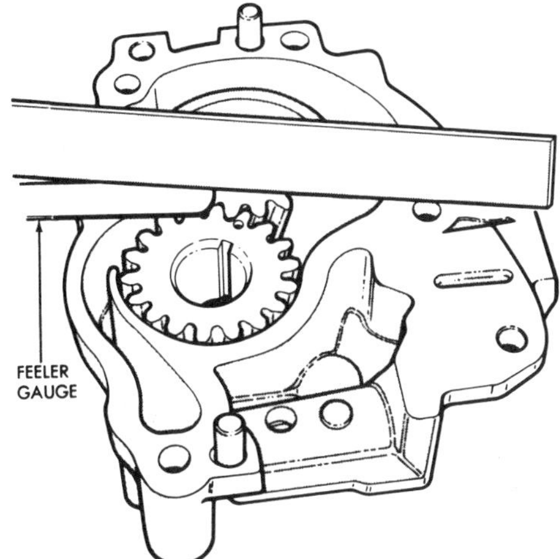

10.10c Checking gear end play with a feeler gauge and straightedge

11.3 Be sure to align the marks on the oil pump gears before installing the cover

10 Oil pump – removal, disassembly and inspection

Refer to illustrations 10.10a, 10.10b and 10.10c

1 The oil pump and rear Silent Shaft are removed from the engine as an assembly.

2 Remove the bolt attaching the oil pump to the engine block. Some of the Silent Shaft chain guide mounting bolts also serve as oil pump mounting bolts; they have already been removed. Leave the Phillips head screw in the front side of the pump in place.

3 Carefully pull straight ahead on the oil pump and remove it, along with the right Silent Shaft, from the engine block. You may have to tap gently on the oil pump body with a soft-faced hammer to break the gasket seal. **Caution:** *Prying between the oil pump and engine block could result in damage to the engine body.*

4 Remove the bolt from the nose of the rear Silent Shaft and pull the shaft out of the oil pump from the rear (do not lose the key in the nose of the shaft). Refer to Section 9 for Silent Shaft inspection procedures.

5 Remove the plug from the upper side of the pump body and withdraw the relief spring and plunger. You may have to mount the pump body in a vise equipped with soft jaws to loosen the plug. If so, do not apply excessive pressure to the pump body.

6 Remove the Philips head screw from the left side of the pump. Separate the oil pump cover from the body and lift out the two pump gears. Do not lose the key in the lower gear shaft. **Caution:** *Prying between the cover and body may result in damage to the pump body.*

7 Clean the parts with solvent and dry them thoroughly. Use compressed air to blow out all of the oil holes and passages.

8 Check the entire pump body and cover for cracks and excessive wear. Look closely for a ridge where the gears contact the body and cover.

9 Insert the relief plunger into the pump body and check to see if it slides smoothly. Look for cracks in the relief spring and measure its free length. Inspect the timing chain tensioner plunger sleeve for noticeable wear and the rubber pad for cracks and excessive wear. Measure the tensioner spring free length and compare it to the Specifications.

10 Measure the inside diameter of the bearing surfaces and the outside diameter of each gear shaft. Subtract the two to obtain the gear-to-bearing clearance. Measure the gear-to-housing clearance with a feeler gauge and the gear end play with a feeler gauge and straightedge **(see illustrations)**. Compare the measured clearances to the Specifications.

11 If the oil pump clearances are excessive, or if excessive wear is evident, replace the oil pump as a unit.

11 Oil pump – reassembly and installation

Refer to illustration 11.3

1 The oil pump and rear Silent Shaft are installed as a unit.

2 Coat the oil pump relief plunger with clean moly-based grease and insert the plunger and spring into the oil pump body. Install the cap and tighten it securely.

3 Apply a layer of moly-based grease to the gear teeth, the sides of the gears and the bearing surfaces in the pump body and cover. Lay the gears in place in the body with the mating marks aligned **(see illustration)**. If the mating marks are not properly aligned, the rear Silent Shaft will be out of phase and engine vibration will result.

12.5 Installing the Silent Shaft chain guides

4 Lay the cover in place using the dowel pins to align it properly. Install the Phillips head screw in the left side of the pump, but do not tighten it completely at this time. Make sure the gears rotate smoothly without binding.
5 Lay a new gasket in place on the cover. It's not necessary to use sealant. The dowel pins will align the gasket properly and hold it in place.
6 Make sure the key is in place in the nose of the shaft, then slip the rear Silent Shaft through the oil pump driven gear as you line up the key in the shaft with the keyway in the gear. Once the shaft and gear are properly mated, clamp the counterweight end of the shaft in a vise equipped with soft jaws, install the bolt in the front end of the shaft and tighten it to the specified torque.
7 Apply a thin layer of clean moly-based grease (or engine assembly lube) to the rear bearing journal of the rear Silent Shaft.
8 Hold the pump upright and fill it with a minimum of 10cc of engine oil. Insert the Silent Shaft into the engine block and through the rear bearing. Be careful not to scratch or gouge the bearing as the shaft is installed.
9 Make sure the pump is seated against the engine block, then install the mounting bolts and tighten them evenly and securely. Do not forget to tighten the Phillips head screw. The remaining pump mounting bolts will be installed with the chain guides.
10 Temporarily slip the Silent Shaft drive sprocket onto the lower pump gear shaft and use it to rotate the pump gears/Silent Shaft. Check for any obvious binding.

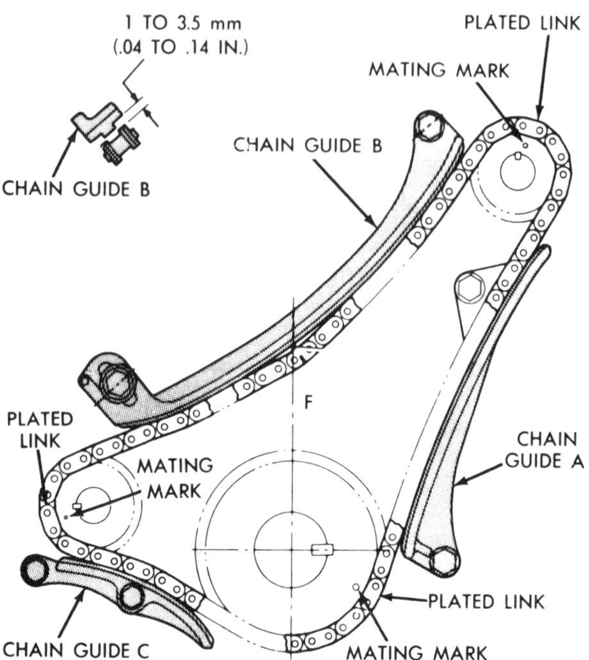

12.6a Silent Shaft and chain installation and adjustment details

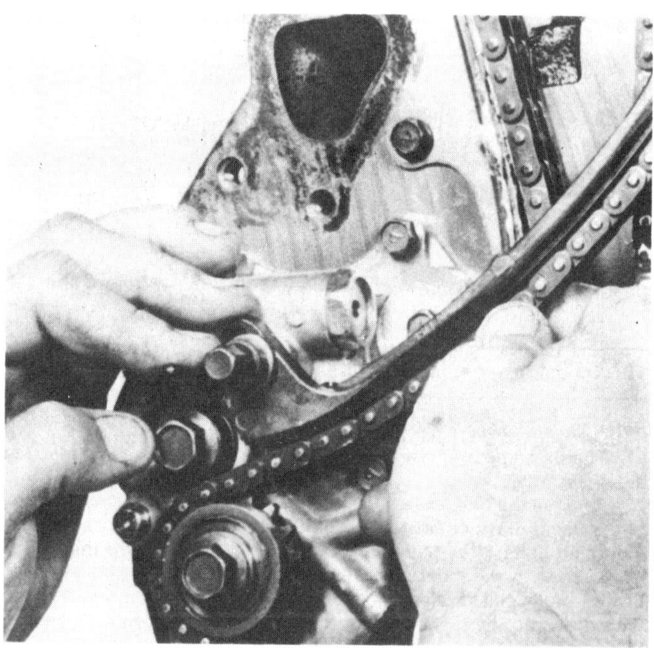

12.6b Adjusting the Silent Shaft chain slack

12 Silent Shaft chain/sprockets – installation

Refer to illustrations 12.5, 12.6a, 12.6b, 12.8, 12.10, 12.11 and 12.12

1 Before installing the Silent Shaft chain and sprockets, the timing chain must be properly installed and the number one piston must be at TDC on the compression stroke. Both Silent Shafts and the oil pump should also be in place.
2 Slide the crankshaft sprocket part way onto the front of the crankshaft by lining up the keyway in the sprocket with the key on the shaft.
3 Install the Silent Shaft chain onto the crankshaft sprocket and the front Silent Shaft sprocket. The dished or recessed side of the front Silent Shaft sprocket must face out. Line up the plated links on the chain with the mating marks stamped into the sprockets.
4 With the dished or recessed side facing in, slide the rear Silent Shaft sprocket part way onto the lower oil pump gear shaft. Line up the plated link on the chain with the mating mark on the sprocket. Push the Silent Shaft sprockets all the way onto their respective shafts, lining up the keyways in the sprockets with the keys on the shafts. Simultaneously, push the crankshaft sprocket back until it bottoms on the crankshaft timing chain sprocket. Recheck the position of the mating marks on the chain and sprockets, then install the Silent Shaft sprocket bolts and tighten them to the specified torque.
5 Install the chain guides labeled A, B and C **(see illustration)** and tighten the mounting bolts for chain guides A and C securely (leave the mounting bolts for chain guide B finger-tight). Note the difference between the upper and lower chain guide B mounting bolts. Make sure they are installed in the proper location.
6 Adjust the chain slack as follows: rotate the rear Silent Shaft clockwise and the front Silent Shaft counterclockwise so the chain slack is collected at point P **(see illustration)**. Pull the chain with your finger tips in the direction of arrow F, then move the lower end of the chain

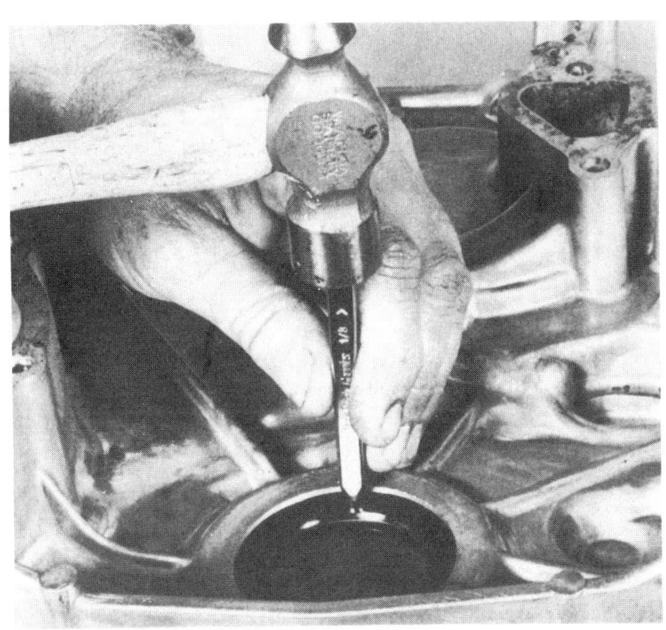
12.8 Drive the old oil seal out of the timing chain cover with a hammer and punch

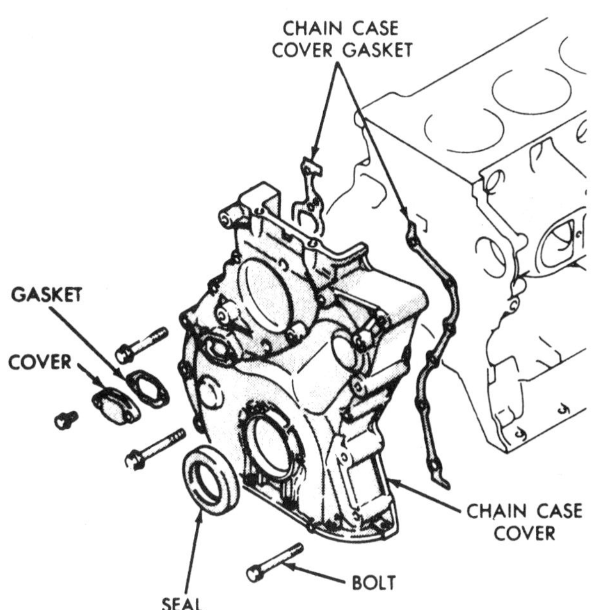

12.10 Timing chain cover components — exploded view

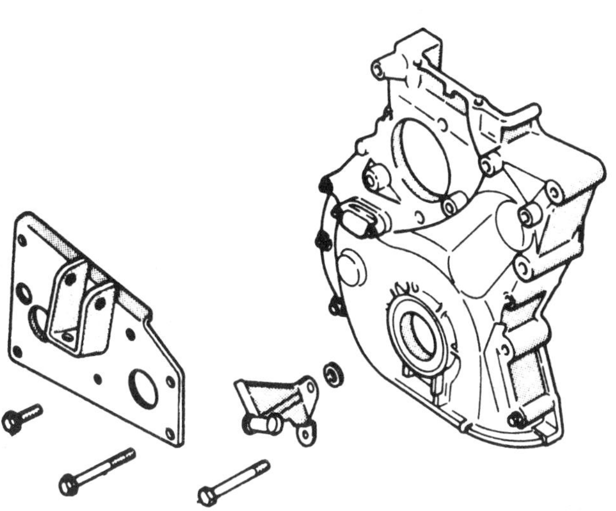
12.11 Install this mounting plate to the face of the timing chain case

12.12 Apply a thin layer of grease to the seal contact surface of the crankshaft pulley prior to installation

guide B up or down, as required, until the clearance between the chain and the guide (chain slack) is as specified **(see illustration)**. Tighten the chain guide B mounting bolts securely, then recheck the slack to make sure it has not changed. If the chain is not tensioned properly, engine noise will result.

7 Apply a coat of clean moly-based grease to the chain and chain guides.

8 Using a hammer and punch, drive the oil seal out of the timing chain case **(see illustration)**.

9 Lay a new seal in place — make sure the lip faces inward — and tap around its circumference with a block of wood and a hammer until it is properly seated.

10 Using a new gasket and RTV-type gasket sealant, fit the timing chain case onto the engine **(see illustration)**. Install the bolts in a criss-cross pattern and tighten them as specified. If the gasket protrudes beyond the top or bottom of the case and engine block, trim off the excess with a razor blade.

11 Install the engine mounting plate onto the face of the timing chain case **(see illustration)**. Tighten to the specified torque.

12 Apply a thin layer of clean moly-based grease to the seal contact surface of the crankshaft pulley **(see illustration)**, then slide it onto the crankshaft. Install the bolt and tighten it finger-tight only. **Note:** *The bolt should be tightened to the specified torque only after the cylinder head and camshaft have been installed.*

13 Cylinder head — installation

Refer to illustrations 13.2, 13.4, 13.7, 13.11 and 13.16

1 Before installing the cylinder head, the timing chain and sprockets, the Silent Shaft chain and sprockets and the timing chain case must be in place on the engine.

2 Make sure the gasket sealing surfaces of the engine block and cylinder head are clean and oil-free, then lay the new head gasket in place on the block with the manufacturer's stamped mark facing up

13.2 DO NOT use sealant on the new head gasket

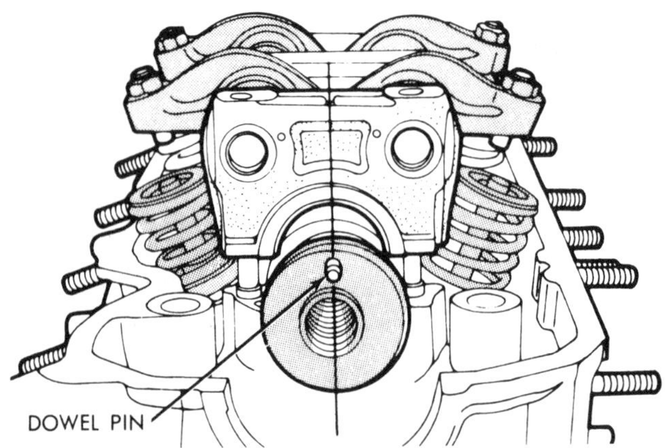

13.7 Position the camshaft with the dowel pin at the top before installing the rocker arm assembly

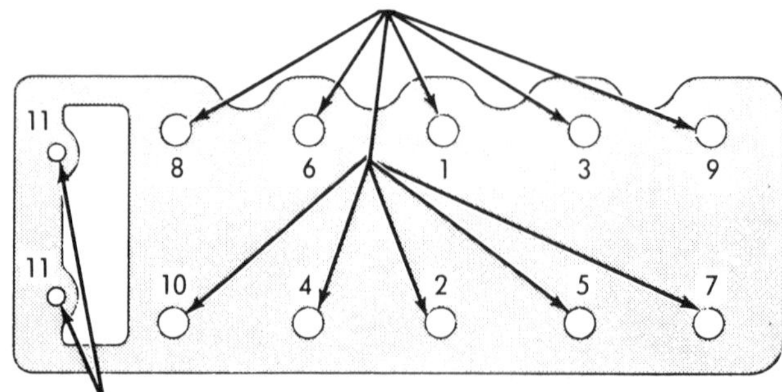

13.4 2.6L engine cylinder head bolt *tightening* sequence

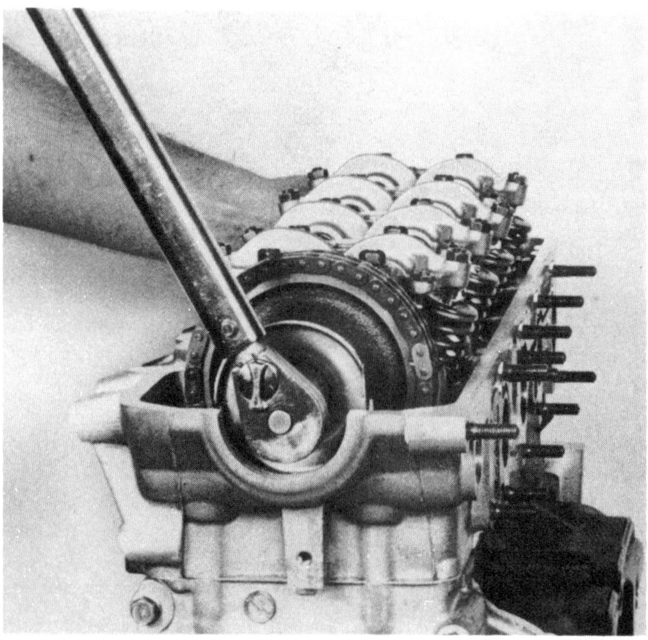

13.11 Tightening the camshaft sprocket bolt with a torque wrench (hold the crankshaft bolt with a wrench to keep the camshaft from turning)

(see illustration). Do not use any sealant. Use the dowel pins in the top of the block to properly locate the gasket.

3 Carefully set the cylinder head in place on the block. Use the dowel pins to properly align it.

4 Install the ten head bolts and tighten them in sequence **(see illustration)**, to 1/3 of the specified torque. Repeat the procedure, using the same sequence, tightening them to 2/3 of the specified torque. Repeat the procedure one last time, tightening them to the final specified torque.

5 Install the two small head bolts (with washers) in the very front of the head and tighten them to the specified torque. Install a new seal in the rear of the head (make sure it is seated in the opening). Apply grease to the seal lips.

6 Wipe the camshaft bearing surfaces in the cylinder head clean and apply a coat of clean moly-based grease (or engine assembly lube) to each of them.

7 Make sure the camshaft bearing journals are clean, then carefully lay the camshaft in place in the head. Do not lubricate the cam lobes at this time. Rotate the camshaft until the dowel pin on the front is positioned at 12 o'clock **(see illustration)**.

8 Loosen the jam nuts on the valve clearance adjusting bolts and back the adjusting bolts out a minimum of two full turns.

9 Wipe the camshaft bearing cap bearing surfaces clean and apply a coat of clean moly-based grease (or engine assembly lube) to each of them. Also, apply a very small amount of grease to the end of each valve stem. Lay the rocker arm shaft assembly in place with the number one bearing cap toward the timing chain. Install the camshaft bearing cap bolts and tighten them to the initial specified torque in the following order: center, number two, number four, front, rear. Repeat the procedure, tightening them to the final specified torque.

10 Next, lift up on the camshaft sprocket (with the chain attached) and slip it into place on the end of the camshaft. The dowel pin on the cam should slip into the hole in the sprocket.

11 Install the distributor drive gear (again, line up the dowel pin and hole) and the bolt. Tighten the bolt to the specified torque **(see illustration)**. To keep the camshaft and crankshaft from turning, install two of the flywheel mounting bolts in the rear flange of the crankshaft (180° apart), then wedge a large screwdriver between the bolts. Also, tighten the large bolt in the nose of the crankshaft to the specified torque at this time.

12 Camshaft end play can be checked with a dial indicator set or a feeler gauge.

13 If a feeler gauge is used, gently pry the camshaft all the way toward the front of the engine. Slip a feeler gauge between the flange at the front of the camshaft and the number one (front) cam bearing cap. Compare the measured end play to the Specifications.

14 If a dial indicator is used, mount it at the front of the engine with the indicator stem touching the head of the bolt that attaches the sprocket to the camshaft. Carefully pry the camshaft all the way toward the front of the engine, then zero the dial indicator. Gently pry the camshaft as far as possible in the opposite direction and observe the needle movement on the dial indicator, which will indicate the amount of end play. Compare it to the Specifications.

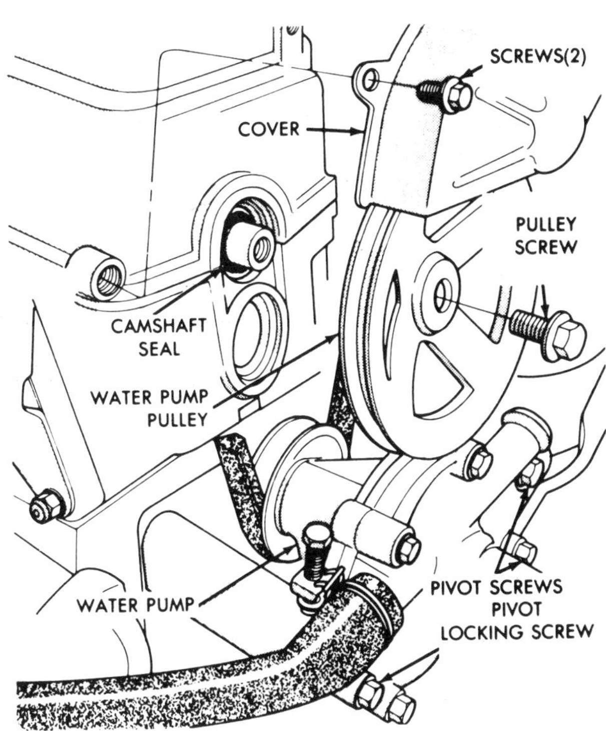

13.16 Installing the water pump pulley, bolt and pulley cover

15 Adjust the valve clearances as described in Chapter 1.
16 Slip the water pump pulley and belt onto the rear of the camshaft, then install the bolt and tighten it to the specified torque **(see illustration)**.
17 Temporarily install the cylinder head cover to keep dirt and other foreign objects out of the valve gear.

14 External engine components – installation

Refer to illustrations 14.4, 14.5 and 14.13

1 Once the engine has been assembled to the point where all internal parts, the timing chain cover, the oil pan and the cylinder head are in place, the exterior components can be installed. If the engine is mounted on a stand, it must be removed from the stand so the rear oil seal housing can be installed.
2 Lubricate the seal contact surface of the flange at the rear of the crankshaft with moly-based grease.
3 After noting which side is facing out, use a hammer and punch to drive the oil seal out of the housing. Lay a new seal in place (with the correct side out) and seat it in the housing with a hammer and a block of wood. Tap the seal along its circumference to seat it squarely in the housing.
4 Place the oil separator into the housing with the oil hole facing downward, toward the bottom of the case, and the tabs pointing out **(see illustration)**. One or two strategically placed dabs of heavy grease will help keep the separator positioned properly.
5 Apply a thin, even coat of RTV-type gasket sealant to both sides of the new gasket and to the exposed portion of the oil pan gasket, then install the oil seal housing. Make sure the oil separator does not fall out of place. Tap the seal housing very gently with a soft-faced hammer **(see illustration)** to seat it properly. Install and tighten the mounting bolts.
6 Install the flywheel/driveplate (Section 3) and slip the oil dipstick into the tube.
7 After coating the threads with a thread sealant, or sealing tape, screw the oil pressure sending unit into the block and tighten it securely.
8 Install the engine mount brackets. Tighten the bolts/nuts to the specified torque.
9 Attach the air conditioner compressor brackets (if applicable) to the block and tighten the bolts securely.
10 Install the water pump.
11 Install the air conditioner idler pulley and the power steering pump bracket (if applicable).
12 Next, install the fuel pump. Use a new gasket and coat both sides with RTV-type gasket sealant. Tighten the mounting nuts securely.
13 Coat both sides of the areas immediately around the coolant passages in the intake manifold gasket with RTV-type gasket sealant **(see illustration)**, then install the intake manifold/carburetor assembly on the engine. Do not allow any gasket sealer to get in the jet air passages in the manifold and head.
14 Slip the engine hoisting bracket into place on the rear studs then install the nuts (and the one bolt) and tighten them to the specified

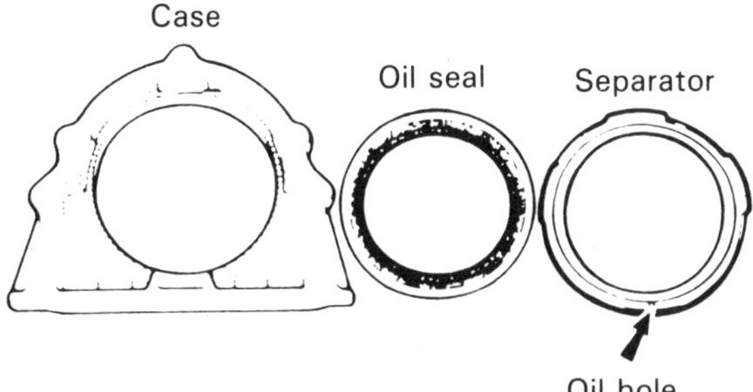

14.4 When installing the rear oil seal housing, make sure the separator oil hole is at the bottom

14.5 Tap the rear oil seal housing with a soft-faced hammer to seat it on the engine block and oil pan before installing the bolts

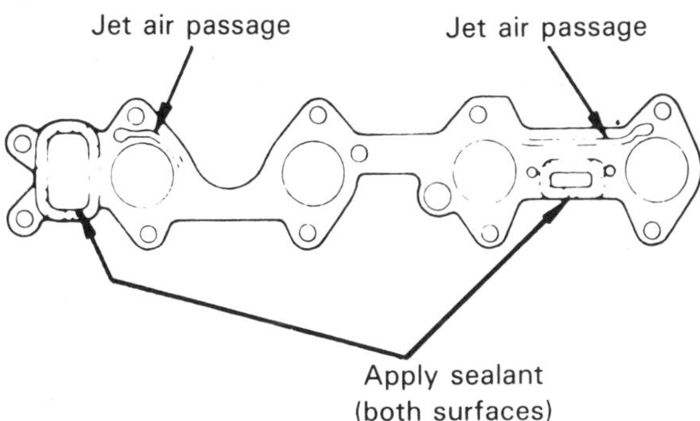

14.13 Before installing the intake manifold, coat the areas around the gasket coolant passages with RTV-type sealant

2A

torque. When tightening, start at the center of the manifold and work out toward the ends. Tighten each fastener in sequence, a little at a time, until they are all at the specified torque.

15 Slip the rubber coolant hose onto the intake manifold spigot and tighten the hose clamps securely.

16 Using a new gasket, install the exhaust manifold and tighten the nuts to the specified torque. Be sure to install the engine hoist bracket at the front. When tightening, start at the center of the manifold and work out toward the ends. Tighten each nut in sequence, a little at a time, until they are all at the specified torque.

17 Attach the heat cowl to the exhaust manifold.

18 Install the Pulse Air Feeder (PAF) system (Chapter 6).

19 Make sure the number one piston is at top dead center on the compression stroke, then install the distributor. Line up the mating marks on the distributor housing (a line) and the driven gear (a punch mark). Slide the distributor into place in the cylider head while lining up the mark on the distributor hold-down flange with the center of the stud. Make sure the distributor is completely seated, then install the mounting nut and tighten it securely.

20 Remove the cylinder head cover. Coat the gasket sealing surfaces of the head with RTV-type gasket sealant.

21 Coat the edges of a new semi-circular seal with RTV-type sealant, then install it in the recess at the front of the head. Make sure the rear seal (water pump pulley) is seated in the head, then position a new gasket in the cover and install the cylinder head cover on the engine.

22 Attach new seals to the bolts, then install the bolts and tighten them evenly and securely.

15 Engine – installation

Refer to illustrations 15.4a, 15.4b, 15.4c, 15.7, 15.11, 15.12, 15.14, 15.15, 15.16 and 15.18

1 Attach the lifting hook to the chain and raise the engine until it clears the front of the vehicle. **Caution:** *Do not let the engine swing freely.*

2 Lower the engine carefully into place. Work slowly and direct the engine into place on the mounts.

3 If the engine mounts have been removed, make sure they are installed in the exact original positions, otherwise the driveaxle alignment could be affected.

4 Install *all* of the engine mount through-bolts and nuts and then tighten them to the specified torque **(see illustrations)**.

5 Install the engine-to-transaxle bolts and tighten them to the specified torque.

6 Remove the lifting chain.

7 Connect the ground strap and install the right inner splash shield **(see illustration)**.

8 Install the starter.

9 Connect the exhaust system and tighten the nuts.

10 Remove the C-clamp retaining the torque converter, align the driveplate with the marks made during removal, install the bolts and tighten them to the specified torque.

11 Install the alternator **(see illustration)**.

12 Connect the fuel and heater hoses **(see illustration)**.

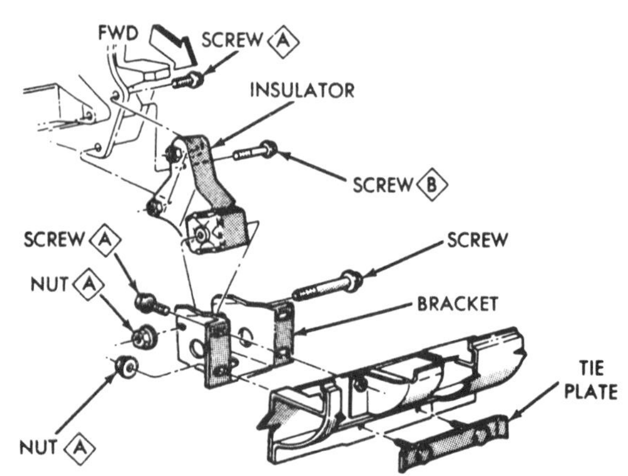

15.4a Exploded view of the front engine mount hardware

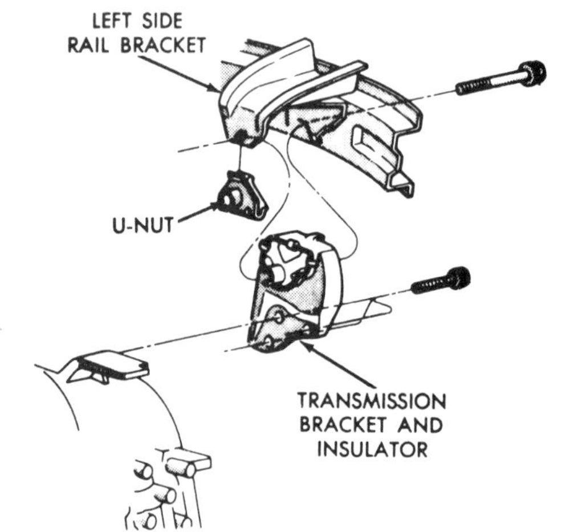

15.4b Exploded view of the left engine mount hardware

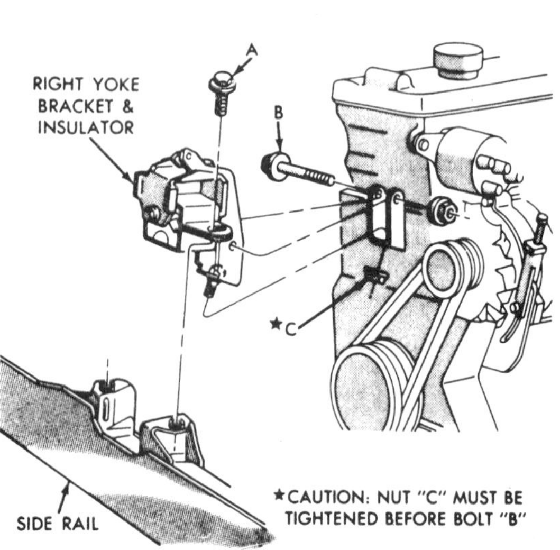

15.4c Right engine mount hardware

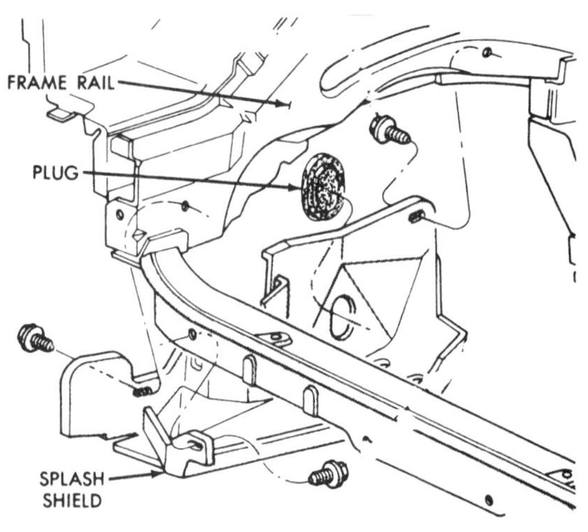

15.7 Right inner splash shield hardware

13 Connect the throttle cable to the carburetor **(see illustration 15.12)**.
14 Connect all of the electrical wires to the engine and components **(see illustration)**.
15 Install the power steering pump (if equipped) and fill it with the specified fluid **(see illustration)**.
16 Install the air conditioning compressor (if equipped) and adjust all the drivebelts **(see illustration)**.
17 Install the air cleaner assembly and hoses.
18 Install the radiator and shroud, connect the hoses and fill the cooling system with the specified coolant **(see illustration)**.
19 Install the hood and the battery. Hook up the positive cable first, then the negative cable.
20 Double-check all nuts and bolts for tightness and make sure all hoses, electrical wiring and other components are properly installed.
21 Install a new oil filter (Chapter 1) and add new oil to the specified level.

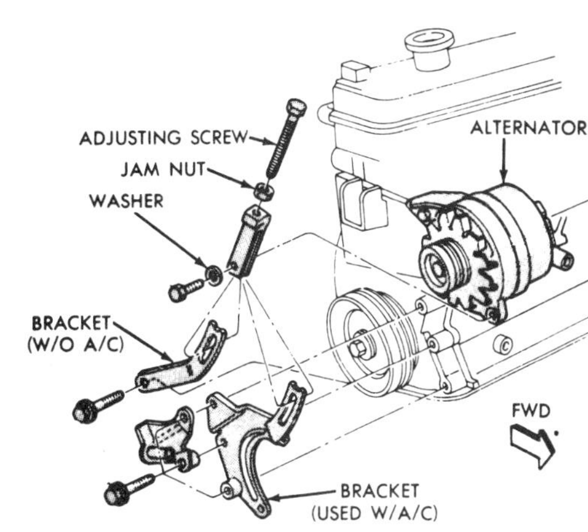

15.11 Exploded view of alternator mounting brackets

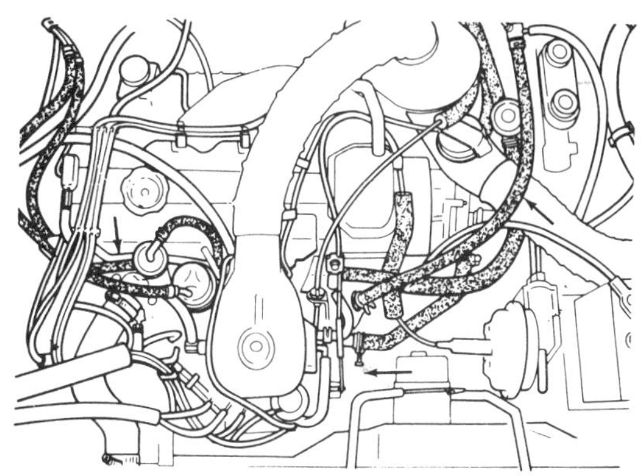

15.12 Fuel line, heater hose and throttle cable routing

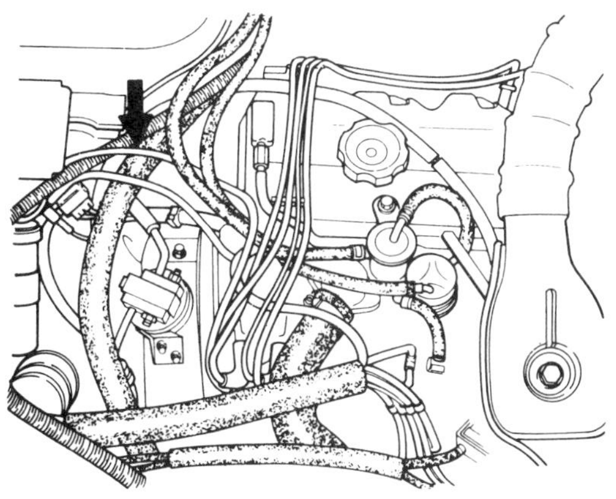

15.14 Electrical connections routing

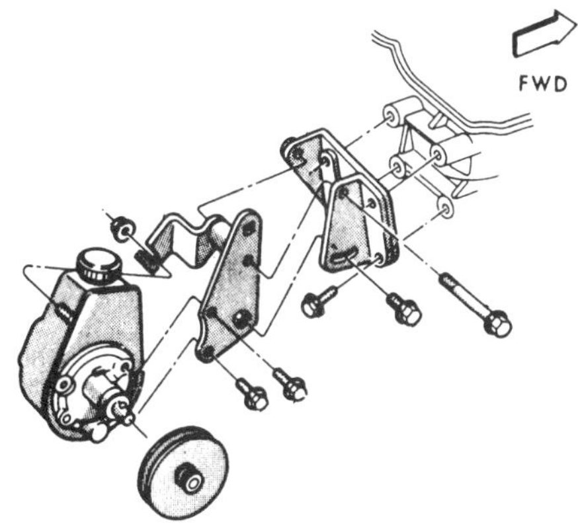

15.15 Exploded view of power steering pump mounting brackets

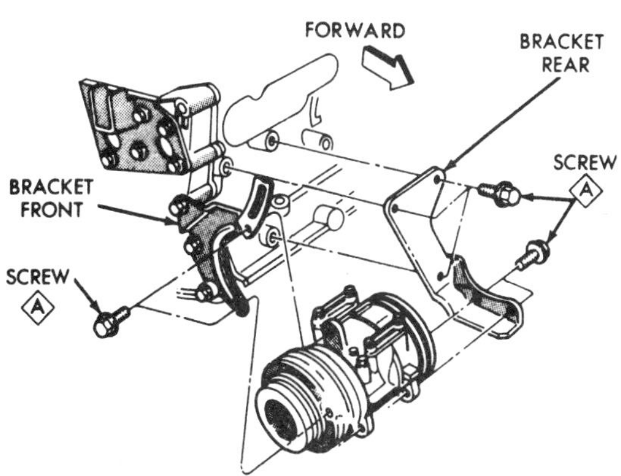

15.16 Exploded view of air conditioner compressor mounting brackets

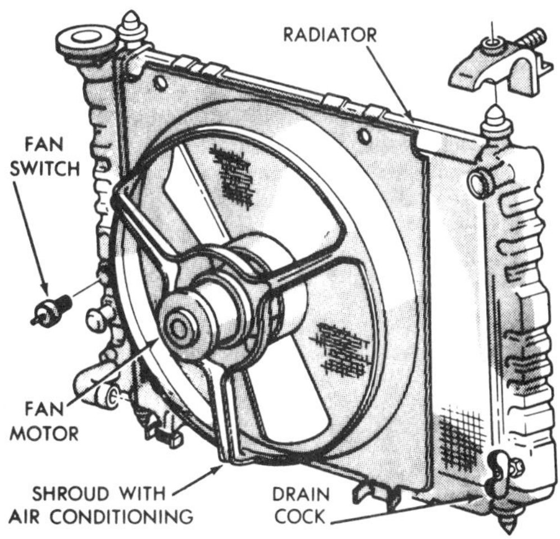

15.18 Typical radiator and shroud assembly

Chapter 2 Part B 2.2L and 2.5L engines

Contents

Specifications

Camshaft

End play	
standard	0.005 to 0.013 in (0.13 to 0.33 mm)
service limit	0.020 in (0.50 mm)

Oil Pump

Outer rotor-to-housing bore clearance	
standard	0.010 in (0.25 mm)
service limit	0.014 in (0.35 mm)
Outer rotor thickness	
1982 through 1985	
standard	0.826 to 0.827 in (20.98 to 21.00 mm)
service limit	0.825 in (20.96 mm)
1986 on	
standard	0.944 to 0.946 in (23.97 to 24.00 mm)
service limit	0.944 in (23.97 mm)
Inner rotor-to-outer rotor tip clearance	
1982 through 1985 limit	0.010 in (0.25 mm)
1986 on	
standard	0.008 in (0.20 mm)
service limit	0.010 in (0.25 mm)
Rotor-to-housing clearance	
standard	0.001 to 0.003 in (0.03 to 0.08 mm)
service limit	0.004 in (0.10 mm)
Pump cover warpage	
standard	0.010 in (0.25 mm)
service limit	0.015 in (0.38 mm)
Relief spring free length	1.95 in (49.5 mm)
Relief spring load	15 to 25 lbs @ 1.34 in (67 to 89 N @ 34 mm)
Relief valve opening pressure	80 psi

Torque specifications	**Ft-lbs**	**Nm**
Balance shaft carrier		
front chain cover bolt	9	12
chain tensioner adjustment bolt	9	12
chain tensioner pivot bolt	9	12
chain snubber stud	9	12
chain snubber nut	9	12
gear cover bolt	9	12
gear cover double-ended stud	9	12
gear and sprocket-to-balance shaft bolt	21	28
sprocket-to-crankshaft Torx drive bolt	11.1	15
rear cover bolt	9	12
carrier-to-cylinder block bolt	40	54

Cylinder head bolts (1982 through 1985)		
step 1	30	41
step 2	45	61
step 3	45	61
step 4	1/4-additional turn after reaching torque specified in step 3	
Cylinder head bolts (1986 on)		
step 1	45	61
step 2	65	88
step 3	65	88
step 4	1/4-additional turn after reaching torque specified in step 3	
Camshaft cover bolts	9	12
Camshaft sprocket bolt	65	88
Camshaft bearing cap nut	14	19
Crankshaft sprocket bolt	50	68
Main bearing cap bolt	30*	41*
Connecting rod bearing cap nut	40*	54*
Front crankshaft oil seal housing bolt	9	12
Rear crankshaft oil seal housing bolt	9	12
Intermediate shaft oil seal retainer bolt	9	12
Intermediate shaft sprocket bolt	65	88
Upper timimg belt cover bolt	3.5	4
Lower timing belt cover bolt	3.5	4
Exhaust manifold nut	17	23
Intake manifold bolt	17	23
Turbocharger-to-exhaust manifold nut	40	54
Turbocharger heat shield screw	9	12
Turbocharger fuel injection fuel rail screw	21	28
Turbocharger coolant tube nut	30	41
Turbocharger oil line tube nut	11	15
Thermostat housing bolt	21	28
Water pump housing bolt		
upper	21	28
lower	40	54
Oil pan bolt		
6 mm	9	12
8 mm	17	23
Oil pump mounting bolt	17	23
Oil pump cover bolt	9	12
Oil pump brace mounting bolt	9	12
Right engine bracket through-bolt	75	102
Right engine bracket insulator nut	75	102
Right engine bracket bolt	21	28
Transaxle-to-engine bolts	70	95
Turbocharger damper nut	16	22
Turbocharger damper mount bolt and nut	21	28
Left engine mount insulator bolt	40	54
Left engine mount through bolt	50	68
Anti-roll strut through-bolt	40	54
Anti-roll strut mount nut	21	28
Clutch pressure plate-to-flywheel bolts	21	28
Flywheel or driveplate-to-crankshaft bolts		
1982 through 1985	65	88
1986 on	70	95
Torque converter-to-driveplate bolts		
1982 through 1985	40	54
1986 on	55	74

* *Plus an additional 1/4-turn*

2B

1 General information

The 2.2 and 2.5 liter engines used in these models are virtually identical in design except that the 2.5 liter engine features a longer stroke (for increased displacement) and a chain driven, counterrotating balance shaft device mounted below the crankshaft (to reduce vibration). The majority of the 2.5 liter engine operations are the same as for the 2.2 liter engine except those affected by the balance shaft assembly.

The 2.2L/2.5L engine is an inline four with a belt-driven overhead camshaft. The belt also turns an intermediate shaft, mounted low in the block, which drives the oil pump and distributor.

The aluminum cylinder head has removable valve guides and valve seat inserts. The intake and exhaust ports are located on the rear (firewall) side with the spark plugs on the front (radiator) side of the cylinder head.

The crankshaft rides in five replaceable insert-type bearings. No vibration damper is used and a sintered iron timing belt sprocket is mounted on the front of the crankshaft.

The balance shaft and carrier assembly is bolted to the crankcase below the crankshaft and contains two counter-rotating shafts. The shafts are geared together and are turned at twice crankshaft speed by a crankshaft-driven roller chain.

The pistons have two compression rings and one oil control ring. The piston pins are semi-floating and press fit into the small end of the connecting rod. The big ends of the connecting rods are equipped with insert-type bearings.

The engine is liquid cooled. Coolant is circulated around the cylinders and combustion chambers and through the intake manifold by a centrifugal impeller-type pump which is driven by a belt from the crankshaft.

Lubrication is handled by an eccentric rotor-type oil pump mounted in the oil pan and driven by the intermediate shaft.

2 Engine – removal

Refer to illustrations 2.3, 2.6, 2.8, 2.12 and 2.17

Warning: *Before beginning any service procedure under the hood, always disconnect the negative cable at the battery. Place the cable out of the way so it cannot accidentally come in contact with the negative terminal of the battery, as this would once again allow power into the electrical system of the vehicle.*

1 Remove the hood as described in Chapter 11.
2 Drain the cooling system (Chapter 1).
3 Remove the radiator hoses, followed by the radiator and fan assembly **(see illustration)**.
4 Remove the air cleaner assembly and hoses.
5 Detach the throttle cable from the linkage and bracket.
6 **Warning:** *Be sure to relieve the fuel system pressure as described in Chapter 4 before disconnecting any fuel lines or hoses.* Disconnect and plug the fuel and heater hoses at the engine **(see illustration)**. Remove the oil filter.
7 Unbolt the air conditioning compressor and set it aside, but do not disconnect the hoses. **Caution:** *On vehicles equipped with an air conditioner, the system must be evacuated by a dealer service department or air conditioning repair shop before any refrigerant lines are disconnected. Do not attempt to do this yourself as injury could result.*
8 Disconnect all electrical wires from the engine, fuel injection and alternator, then remove the alternator. Be sure to tag all wires to ensure correct reinstallation **(see illustration)**.
9 Remove the power steering pump with the hoses attached and set it aside.
10 Disconnect the heater hoses at the firewall fittings.
11 Disconnect the exhaust pipe at the manifold and remove the lower transaxle case cover.
12 On vehicles with a manual transaxle, disconnect the clutch cable **(see illustration)**.
13 On vehicles with an automatic transaxle, mark the driveplate and torque converter so they can be mated correctly during installation, then remove the bolts. Attach a large C-clamp to the front edge of the torque converter housing to prevent the torque converter from falling out.
14 Support the transaxle with a jack or blocks, then remove the starter

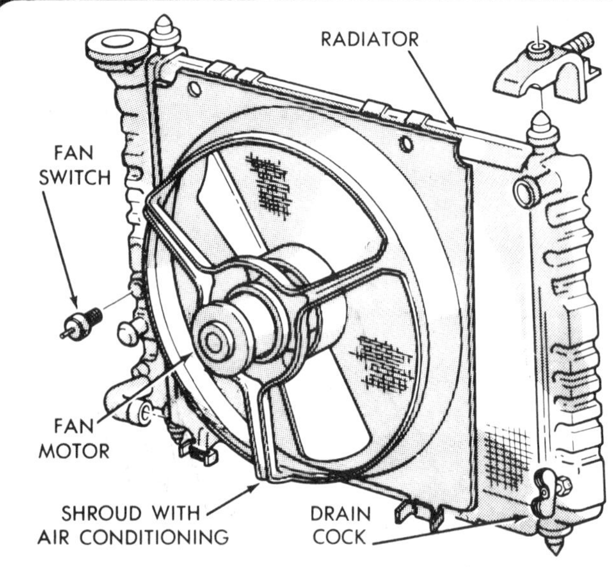

2.3 After detaching all cooling hoses, remove the radiator and fan assembly

2.6 Be sure to plug the fuel and vapor lines (arrows) as you remove them

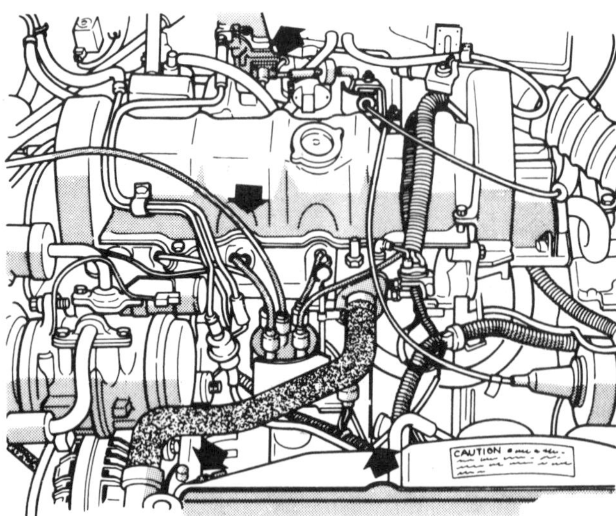

2.8 Alternator, carburetor and engine electrical connections (arrows) must be tagged for correct reassembly

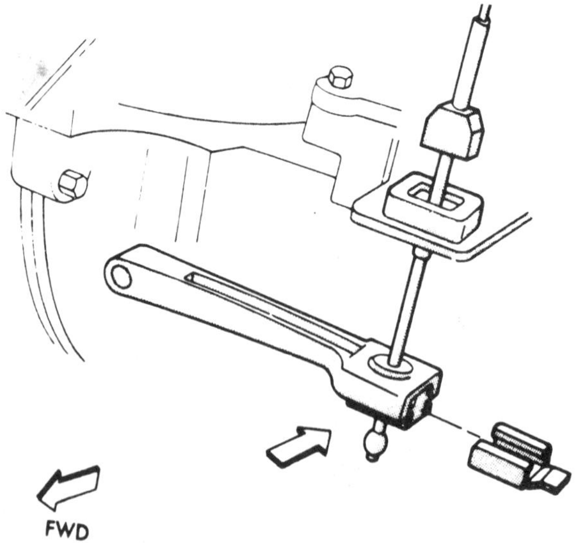

2.12 Remove the retainer to detach the clutch cable from the release arm

motor (Chapter 5) and the right inner splash shield.
15 Attach a chain to the engine lifting hooks and support the engine with a hoist.
16 Remove the engine ground strap between the cylinder head and the firewall.
17 Remove the through-bolt and nut and the insulator nut from the engine mount yoke at the timing belt end of the engine **(see illustration)**. **Caution:** *Do not remove the insulator bolts from the body unless the insulator is marked to ensure installation in the exact same position.*
18 Remove the transaxle-to-engine bolts and the front engine mount through-bolt and nut.
19 If you have a manual transaxle model, remove the anti-roll strut or damper (see illustration 2.17).
20 Unbolt and remove the left side engine and transaxle mount (see illustration 2.17).
21 Lift the engine slowly and carefully up and out of the engine compartment.

3 Automatic transaxle driveplate — removal and installation

1 Remove the bolts and separate the driveplate from the crankshaft.
2 To install, hold the driveplate in position and thread the mounting bolts into place.
3 While locking the crankshaft so it won't turn, tighten the bolts (following a criss-cross pattern) to the specified torque.

4 Clutch and flywheel — removal and installation

1 Remove the clutch cover and clutch disc assembly (Chapter 8).
2 Remove the bolts and separate the flywheel from the crankshaft.
3 Hold the flywheel in position and install the bolts in the end of the crankshaft.
4 While holding the flywheel so that it doesn't turn, tighten the bolts (using a criss-cross pattern) to the specified torque.
5 Install the clutch disc and clutch cover assembly (Chapter 8).

5 Manifolds/external engine components — removal

Refer to illustrations 5.15 and 5.16

Note: *When removing the external components from the engine, pay close attention to details that may be helpful or important during installation. Note the locations of gaskets, seals, spacers, pins, washers, bolts and other small parts.*

1 It is much easier to dismantle and repair the engine if it is mounted on an engine stand. These stands can often be rented, for a reasonable fee, from an equipment rental yard.
2 If a stand isn't available you can dismantle the engine while it is blocked up on a sturdy workbench or on the floor. Be extra careful not to tip or drop the engine when working without a stand.
3 Remove the oxygen sensor from the exhaust manifold (Chapter 6).
4 Unscrew the oil pressure sending unit. Remove the dipstick, grasp the tube and pull it out of the engine block.
5 Disconnect the water hose from the water box and unscrew the adapter and coolant sensor.
6 Remove the thermostat and cover.
7 Remove the temperature vacuum switches (TVS) (if equipped) from the thermostat housing. Mark them for installation in the same locations.
8 Remove the two screws at the base and lift off the distributor cap shield.
9 Disconnect the spark plug wires and coil wire from the retainer on the valve cover.

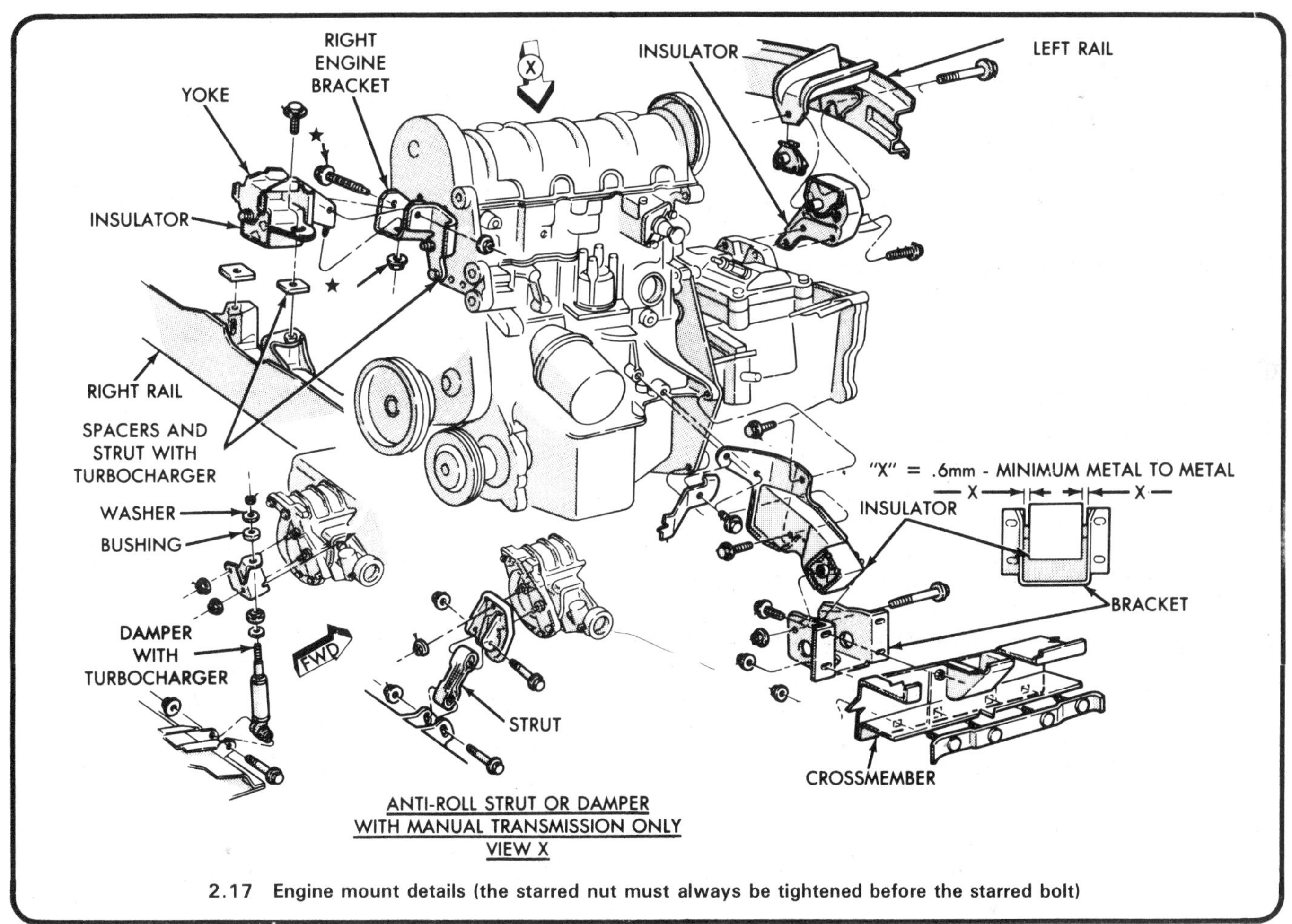

2.17 Engine mount details (the starred nut must always be tightened before the starred bolt)

10 Remove the distributor cap and distributor (Chapter 5).
11 Unscrew the coolant temperature sending unit from the cylinder head.
12 Disconnect the fuel lines from the carburetor or fuel injection assembly. On carburetor equipped models, remove the fuel pump.
13 Remove the spark plugs. On turbocharged models, remove the turbocharger-to-engine block bracket. Remove the oil drain back tube and disconnect the coolant tube (refer to Chapter 4B if necessary).
14 Remove the water pump (Chapter 3).
15 Remove the crankshaft pulley **(see illustration)**.
16 Remove the upper and lower timing belt covers **(see illustration)**.
17 Remove the right engine bracket.
18 Remove the ground strap from the intake manifold.
19 Remove the PCV valve, vent module (if equipped) and hose.
20 Remove the carburetor or fuel injection throttle body (Chapter 4).
21 Remove the air cleaner heat tube from the exhaust manifold (if equipped).
22 Disconnect the EGR tube from the intake manifold (if equipped).
23 Unbolt and remove the EGR valve assembly (Chapter 6).
24 On turbocharged models, remove the turbocharger assembly. Remove the fuel rail and injectors (Chapter 4).
25 Loosen the intake manifold bolts (work from the middle out and loosen them a little at a time).
26 Remove the intake manifold.
27 Remove the exhaust manifold, loosening the bolts in the same manner as for the intake manifold.
28 Remove the two engine mount brackets (if equipped) at the bottom edge of the block.
29 Remove the air injection pump (if equipped).

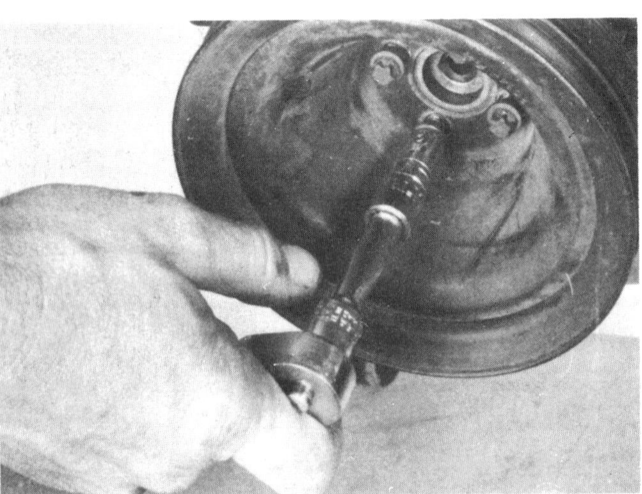

5.15 A Torx head socket is required to remove the small crankshaft pulley bolts after the large center bolt has been removed

6 Timing belt and sprockets — removal, inspection and installation

Refer to illustrations 6.1, 6.2, 6.3, 6.4, 6.5, 6.11, 6.12, 6.14, 6.17 and 6.19

1 Locate the number one piston at top dead center on the compression stroke by removing the spark plug, placing your finger over the hole and turning the crankshaft until pressure is felt. The marks on the crankshaft and intermediate shaft sprocket will be aligned **(see illustration)** and the arrows on the camshaft sprocket will line up with the bearing cap parting line (see illustration 6.14).

2 Use one wrench to hold the offset tensioner pulley bolt while using another wrench or socket to loosen the center bolt, releasing the tension from the timing belt. Remove the belt **(see illustration)**. Remove the tensioner pulley assembly.

3 Remove the intermediate shaft sprocket bolt while holding the sprocket with the special tool (no. C-4687) or a homemade substitute **(see illustration)**. Pull the sprocket off the shaft.

4 Remove the bolt and use a puller to remove the crankshaft sprocket **(see illustration)**.

5 Hold the camshaft sprocket as described in Step 3 and remove the bolt **(see illustration)**, then detach the sprocket from the cam.

6 Inspect the timing belt for wear, signs of stretching and damaged teeth. Check for signs of contamination by oil, gasoline, coolant and other liquids, which could cause the belt to break down and stretch. **Note:** *Unless the vehicle has very low mileage, it is a good idea to replace the timing belt with a new one any time it is removed.*

7 Inspect the tensioner pulley for damage, distortion and nicked or bent flanges. Replace the tensioner with a new one if necessary.

8 Inspect the camshaft, crankshaft and intermediate shaft sprockets for wear, damage, cracks, corrosion and rounding of the teeth. Replace them with new ones if necessary as damaged or worn sprockets could cause the belt to slip and alter camshaft timing (which could cause internal engine damage).

9 Inspect the crankshaft and intermediate shaft seals for signs of oil leakage and replace them with new ones if necessary (Sections 10 and 12).

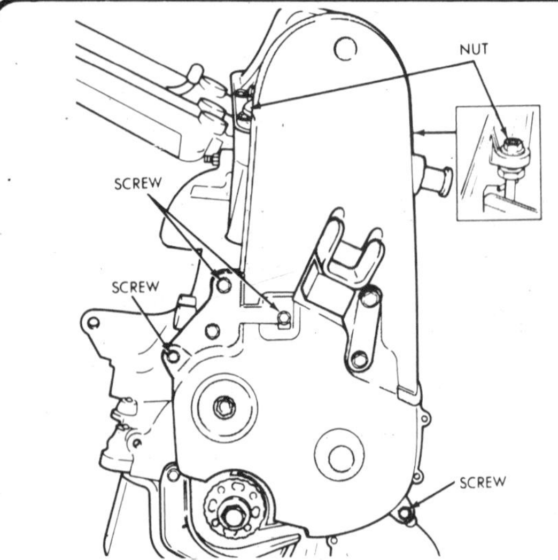

5.16 The timing belt cover is detached in two sections after removing the bolts

6.1 Correct alignment of the crankshaft and intermediate shaft sprocket marks (arrows) with the number 1 piston at TDC on the compression stroke

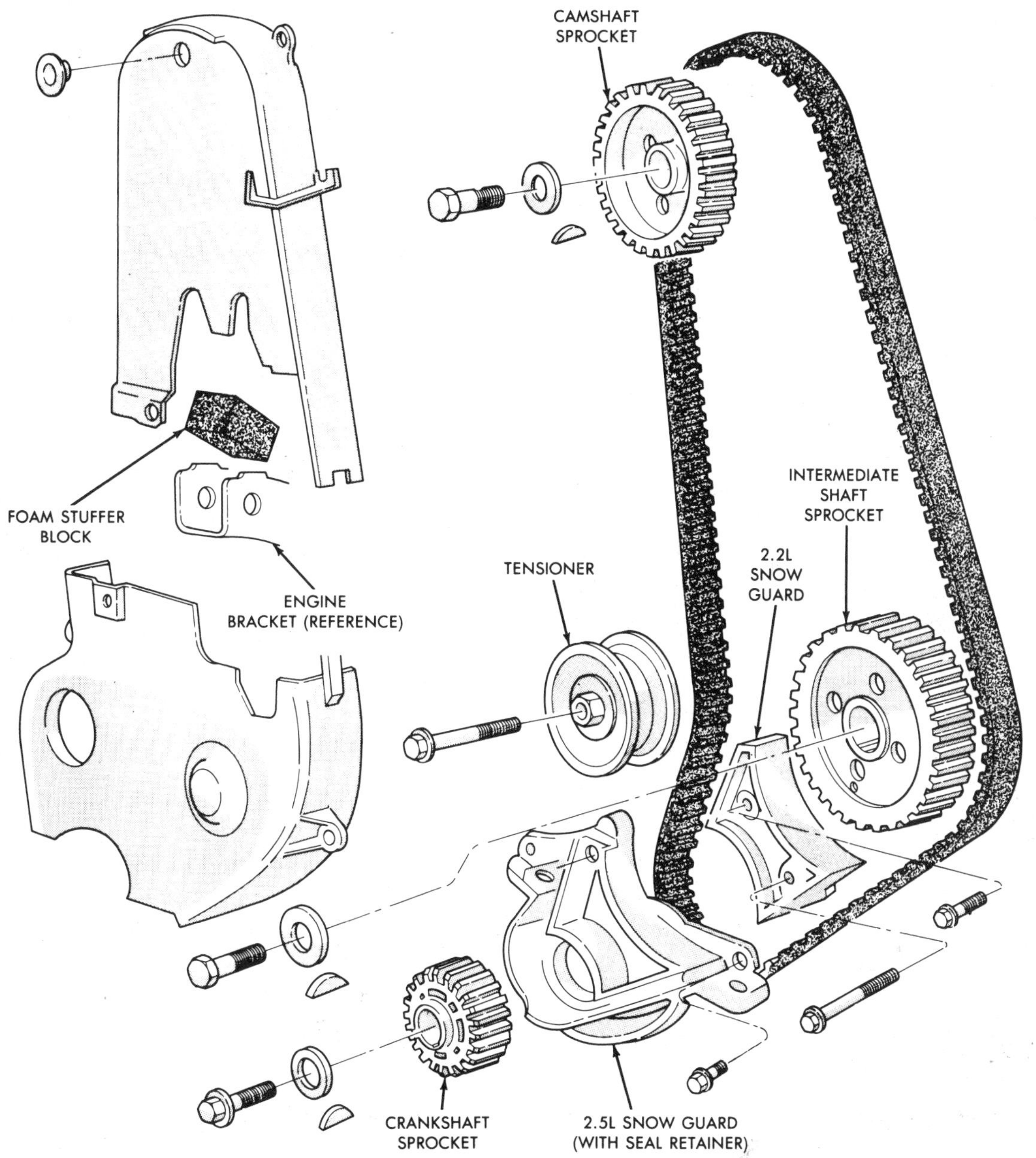

CAMSHAFT SPROCKET
FOAM STUFFER BLOCK
ENGINE BRACKET (REFERENCE)
TENSIONER
INTERMEDIATE SHAFT SPROCKET
2.2L SNOW GUARD
CRANKSHAFT SPROCKET
2.5L SNOW GUARD (WITH SEAL RETAINER)

6.2 Timing belt and sprocket components — exploded view

6.3 Hold the intermediate shaft sprocket with a tool to keep it from turning as the bolt is loosened

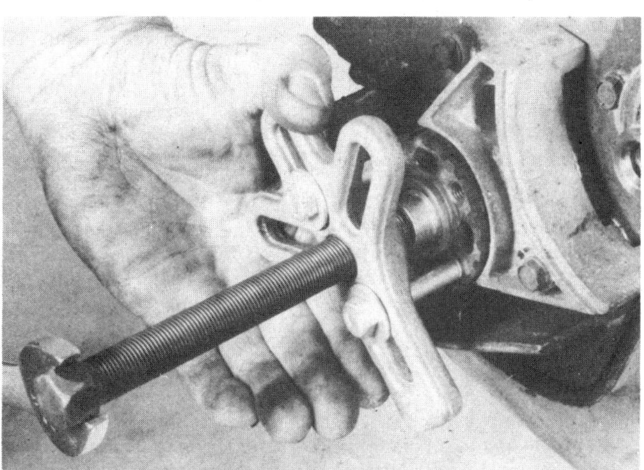

6.4 A puller must be used to remove the crankshaft sprocket

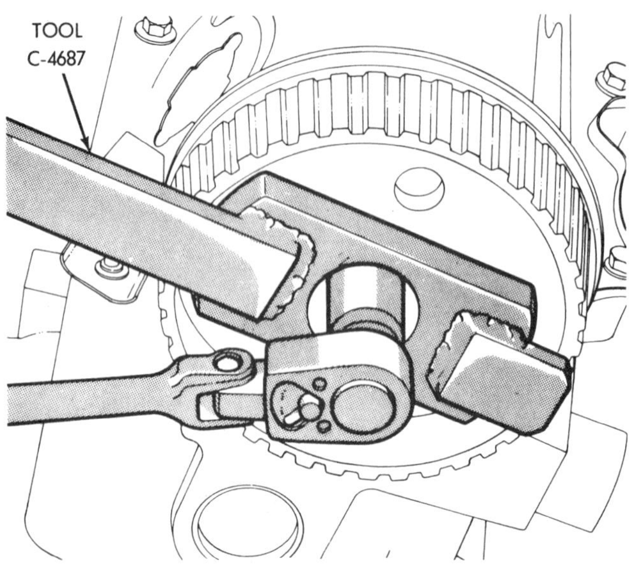

6.5 Removing the camshaft sprocket bolt using a special tool to keep the sprocket from turning

6.11 Use a straightedge to make sure the marks line up with the centers of the sprocket bolt holes

6.12 Install and tighten the crankshaft sprocket bolt

6.14 The small hole must be at the top and the arrows on the camshaft sprocket hub must be aligned with the bearing cap parting line when installing the timing belt

10 When installing the timing belt, the keys on all shafts must be at the 12 o'clock position (facing up).

11 Install the crankshaft and intermediate shaft sprockets, then turn the shafts until the marks are aligned **(see illustration)**.

12 Install the crankshaft sprocket bolt, lock the crankshaft to keep it from rotating and tighten the bolt to the specified torque **(see illustration)**.

13 Install the intermediate shaft sprocket bolt and tighten it to the specified torque. Double-check to make sure the marks are aligned as shown in illustration 6.11.

14 Install the camshaft sprocket and bolt. Tighten the bolt to the specified torque. The arrows on the sprocket hub must align with the camshaft bearing cap parting line **(see illustration)**.

15 Install the timing belt without turning any of the sprockets.

16 Install the tensioner pulley with the bolt finger tight.

17 With the help of an assistant, apply tension to the timing belt and temporarily tighten the tensioner bolt. Measure the deflection of the belt between the camshaft and tensioner pulley. Adjust the tensioner until belt deflection is approximately 5/16-inch **(see illustration)**.

18 Turn the crankshaft two complete revolutions. This will align the belt on the pulleys. Recheck the belt deflection and tighten the tensioner pulley.

19 Recheck the camshaft timing with the timing belt cover installed and the number one piston at TDC on the compression stroke. The small hole in the camshaft sprocket must be centered in the timing belt cover hole **(see illustration)**.

7 Oil pan – removal and installation

Refer to illustration 7.5

1 Remove the bolts securing the oil pan to the engine block.

2 Tap on the pan with a soft-face hammer to break the gasket seal and lift the oil pan off the engine.

3 Using a gasket scraper, scrape off all traces of the old gasket from the engine block and oil pan. Remove the end seals from the oil seal retainers.

4 Clean the oil pan with solvent and dry it thoroughly. Check the gasket sealing surfaces for distortion.

5 Before installing the oil pan, install new end seals in the oil seal retainers. Apply a 3/16-inch bead of RTV sealant completely around

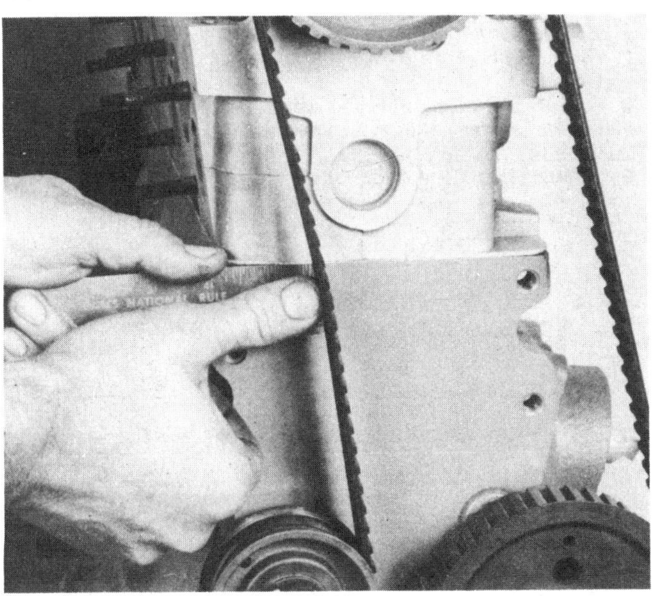
6.17 Use a ruler to measure timing belt deflection

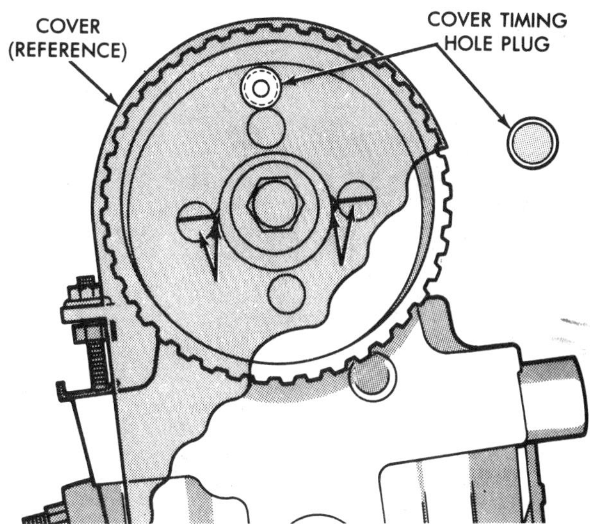

6.19 To check the cam timing with the cover in place, see if the small hole in the camshaft sprocket is aligned with the hole in the cover – this is done with the number 1 piston at TDC on the compression stroke

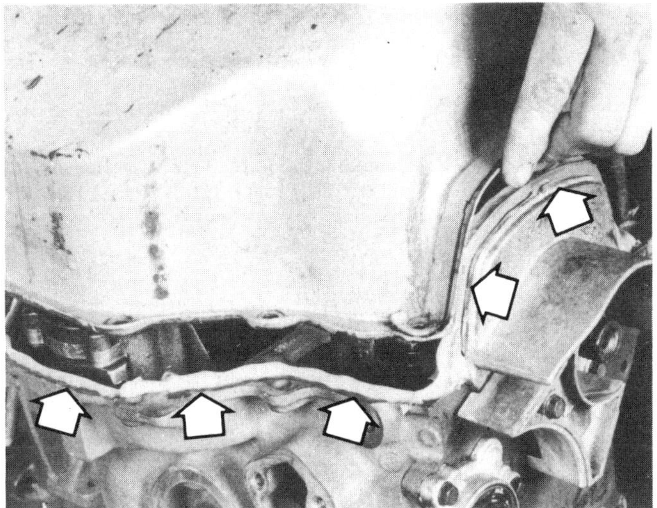
7.5 Apply a continuous bead (arrows) of RTV-type sealant to the block and end seals before installing the oil pan

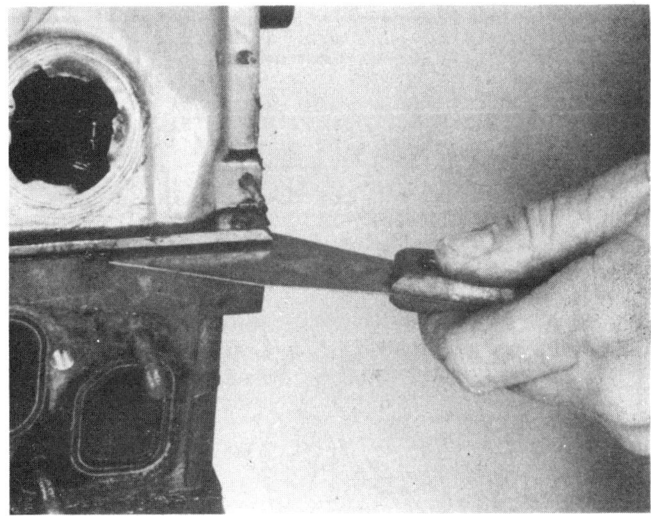
8.3 Carefully slip a putty knife under the valve cover to break the seal (don't nick or otherwise damage the head)

the oil pan gasket surface of the engine block, including the end seals **(see illustration)**.

6 Gently lay the oil pan in place.

7 Install the bolts and tighten them to the specified torque, starting with the bolts closest to the center of the pan and working out in a criss-cross pattern. *Do not overtighten them or leakage may occur.*

8 Cylinder head and camshaft – removal

Refer to illustrations 8.3, 8.5, 8.6 and 8.9

1 Remove the timing belt (Section 6).

2 Remove the camshaft sprocket (Section 6).

3 Remove the bolts and work carefully around the cover with a scraper or putty knife **(see illustration)** to release it from the sealant. Lift the cover off.

4 **Note:** *Removal of the cylinder head does not require removal of the camshaft, so you may skip the following steps pertaining to camshaft removal if you're just removing the head.* Loosen the camshaft bearing cap nuts, working from the ends toward the center, in 1/4-turn increments, until they can be removed by hand.

5 Lift off the cam bearing caps. It may be necessary to tap the camshaft lightly with a soft-faced hammer to loosen them **(see illustration)**.

8.5 Tap the rear of the camshaft *lightly* with a soft-face hammer to dislodge the bearing caps

8.6 Lift straight up on the camshaft to avoid damage to the thrust bearing surfaces

6 Remove the camshaft **(see illustration)**. **Caution:** *If the camshaft is cocked as it is removed the thrust bearings could be damaged.*

7 Reinstall the caps temporarily to protect the studs and bearing surfaces.

8 Lift off the rocker arms and either mark them or place them in a marked container so they will be reinstalled in their original locations. Remove the lash adjusters.

9 Starting from the outside, loosen the head bolts, 1/8-turn at a time each in the sequence shown **(see illustration)**. Remove the bolts and washers.

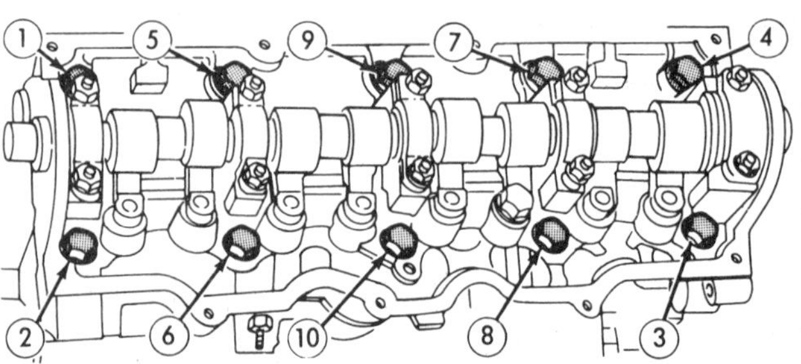

8.9 To avoid warping the head, *loosen* the head bolts a little at a time in the sequence shown until they can be removed

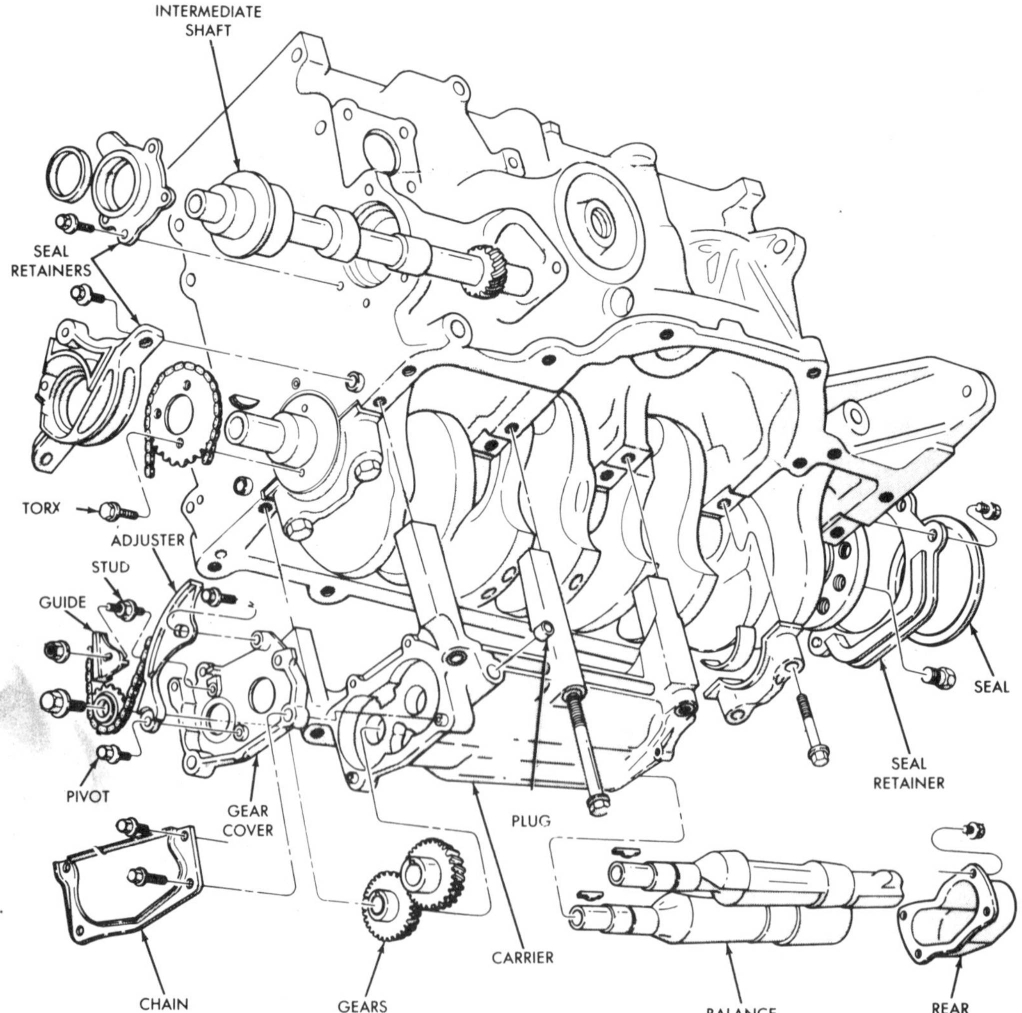

INTERMEDIATE SHAFT
SEAL RETAINERS
TORX
ADJUSTER
STUD
GUIDE
PIVOT
GEAR COVER
PLUG
SEAL
SEAL RETAINER
CHAIN COVER
GEARS
CARRIER
BALANCE SHAFTS
REAR COVER

9.1 2.5L engine balance shaft assembly component layout

10 Use a soft-face hammer, if necessary, to tap the cylinder head and break the gasket seal. Do not pry between the cylinder head and the engine block. Remove the cylinder head.
11 Remove the gasket.

9 Balance shaft assembly — removal and installation

Refer to illustrations 9.1, 9.2, 9.3, 9.4, 9.5, 9.14, 9.17 and 9.23

1 Remove the oil pan, oil pickup, timing belt cover, timing belt, crankshaft sprocket and front oil seal retainer **(see illustration)**.

Balance shafts — removal and installation

2 Remove the balance shaft assembly chain cover, guide and tensioner **(see illustration)**. Remove the bolt from the end of the left shaft.
3 Remove the bolts retaining the balance shaft sprockets and remove the chain and sprockets as an assembly **(see illustration)**. The bolts in the crankshaft sprocket may require a special tool for removal.
4 Remove the balance shaft drive gear cover double ended retaining stud and remove the cover and gears **(see illustration)**.
5 Unbolt and remove the rear cover and slide the balance shafts out of the carrier **(see illustration)**.
6 Remove the six bolts and separate the carrier from the crankcase.
7 Installation is the reverse of removal.

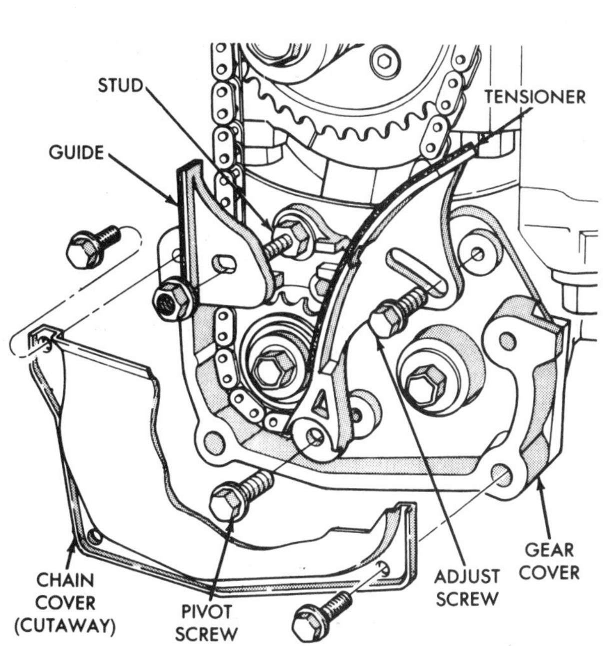

9.2 Balance shaft chain cover, guide and tensioner details

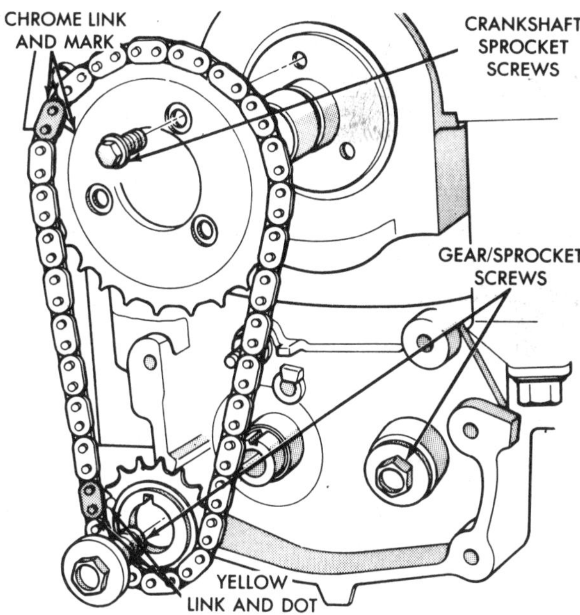

9.3 Balance shaft assembly drive chain and sprocket layout

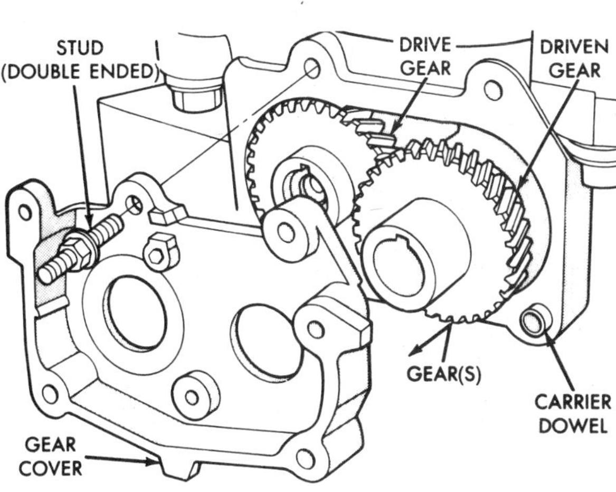

9.4 Balance shaft assembly drive gear and cover removal or installation details

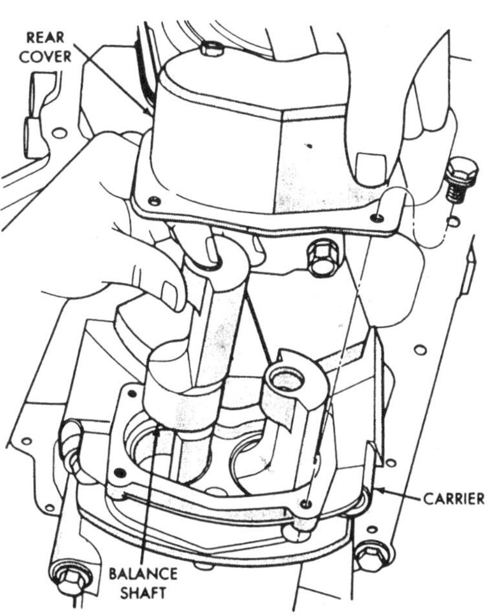

9.5 Removal/installation of the balance shafts

2B

Carrier assembly — removal and installation

8 The carrier can be removed as an assembly with the gear cover, gears, balance shafts and rear cover intact.

9 Remove the chain cover, followed by the bolt from the balance shaft driven gear.

10 Loosen the tensioner pivot and adjusting bolts and push the driven balance shaft in and through the driven chain sprocket so the sprocket is hanging in the lower chain loop.

11 Remove the bolts and detach the carrier assembly from the crankcase.

12 Installation is the reverse of removal. Note that the crankshaft-to-balancer shaft timing must be established as described below.

Balance shaft timing

13 With the balance shafts installed in the carrier, place the carrier in position on the crankcase and install the bolts. Tighten the bolts to the specified torque.

14 Rotate the balance shafts until both keyways face up (in line with the centerline of the engine block) and install the gears. The short hub drive gear goes on the sprocket driven shaft and the long hub gear goes on the gear driven shaft. After installation the alignment dots must be directly opposite each other **(see illustration)**.

15 Install the gear cover and tighten the double-ended stud to the specified torque.

16 Install the crankshaft sprocket and tighten the bolts to the specified torque.

17 Rotate the crankshaft until the number one piston is at Top Dead Center (TDC). The timing marks on the chain sprocket should now be aligned with the parting line on the left side of the number one main bearing cap **(see illustration)**. Place the timing chain over the crankshaft sprocket so that the nickel plated (bright) link is over the timing mark on the crankshaft sprocket as shown in the illustration.

18 Place the balance shaft sprocket in position in the timing chain, making sure the yellow timing mark on the sprocket mates with the yellow painted link on the chain. The mark on the sprocket should also line up with the notch in the cover (see illustration 9.17).

19 Make sure the balance shaft keyways are pointing straight up, then slide the sprocket onto the nose of the balance shaft. It may be necessary to push the balance shaft in slightly to obtain sufficient clearance. At this point the timing mark on the sprocket and the notch

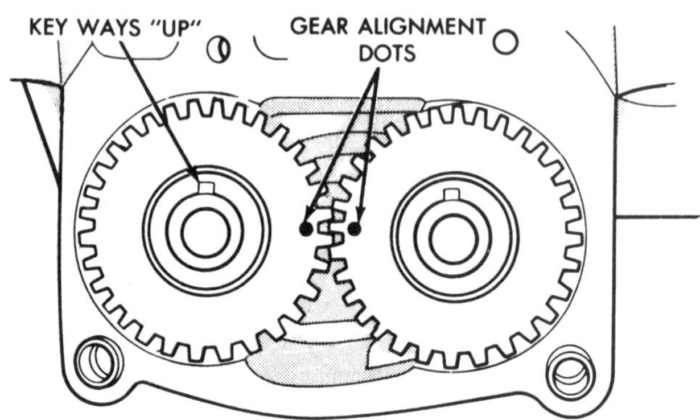

9.14 The balance shaft gear keyways must point directly up and the gear dots must be aligned for correct gear timing

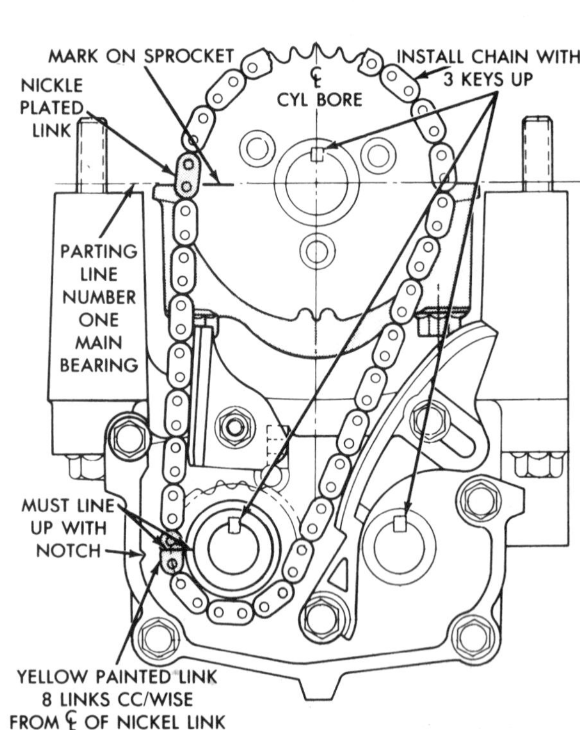

9.17 Balance shaft assembly shaft, gear and chain alignment details

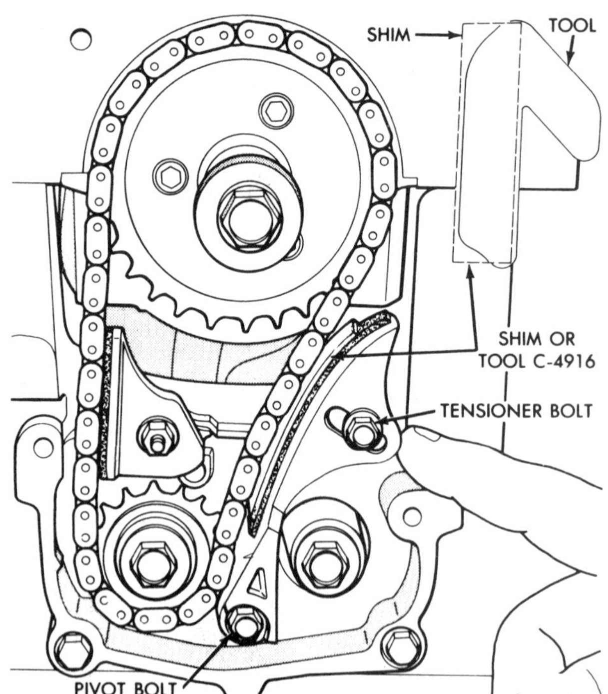

9.23 Balance shaft chain tension adjustment details

on the side of the gear cover must be aligned if the balance shafts are timed correctly.

20 Install the balance shaft bolts. Place a wood block between the crankshaft counterweight and the crankcase, to keep the crankshaft and gear from rotating, and tighten the bolts to the specified torque.

Balance shaft chain tensioning

21 Install the chain tensioner assembly with the bolts finger tight.

22 Place a piece of shim stock measuring 0.039-inch (1mm) thick and 2.75-inch (70 mm) long or factory tool number C-4916 between the tensioner and the chain.

23 Push the tensioner and shim (or tool) up against the chain. Maintain pressure by pressing the tensioner directly behind the adjustment slot so that all slack is taken up as shown **(see illustration)**.

24 With the tension maintained, tighten first the top and then the bottom tensioner bolts to the specified torque. Remove the shim.

25 Place the guide in position on the double-ended stud, making sure the tab on the guide fits into the slot on the gear cover. Install the nut and washer and tighten the nut to the specified torque.

26 Install the balance shaft assembly covers and tighten the bolts to the specified torque.

10 Intermediate shaft and seal – removal, inspection and installation

Refer to illustrations 10.4, 10.5, 10.7 and 10.8

1 Remove the timing belt (Section 6).

2 Remove the sprocket (Section 6).

3 Inspect the sprocket as described in Section 6.

4 Unbolt and remove the shaft retainer **(see illustration)**.

5 Grasp the shaft and carefully withdraw it from the engine **(see illustration)**.

6 Clean the shaft thoroughly with solvent and inspect the gear, bearing surfaces and lobes for wear and damage.

7 Use a punch to drive the old oil seal out of the retainer. Apply a thin coat of RTV sealant to the inner surface of the retainer and tap the new seal into place with a soft-face hammer **(see illustration)**.

8 Lightly lubricate the gear, lobes and bearing surfaces with engine assembly lubricant and carefully insert the shaft into place. After installation, make sure the shaft is securely in place in the oil pump. The oil pump slot must be parallel to the crankshaft centerline and the intermediate shaft keyway must be in the 12 o'clock position **(see illustration)**.

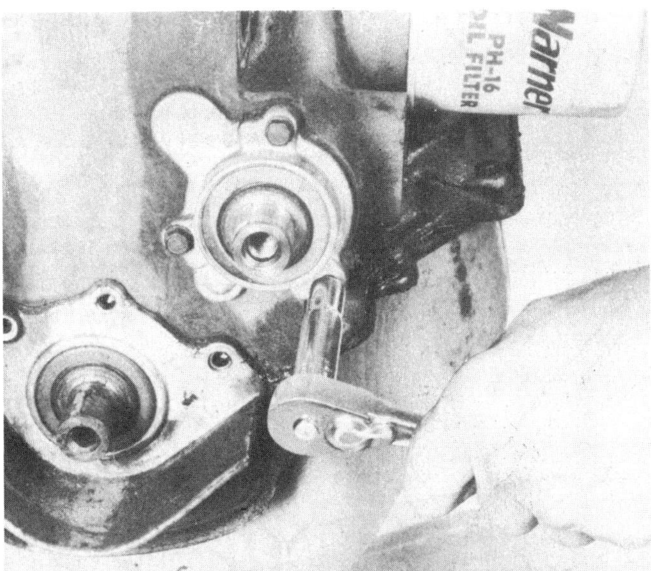

10.4 The retainer must be removed to withdraw the intermediate shaft

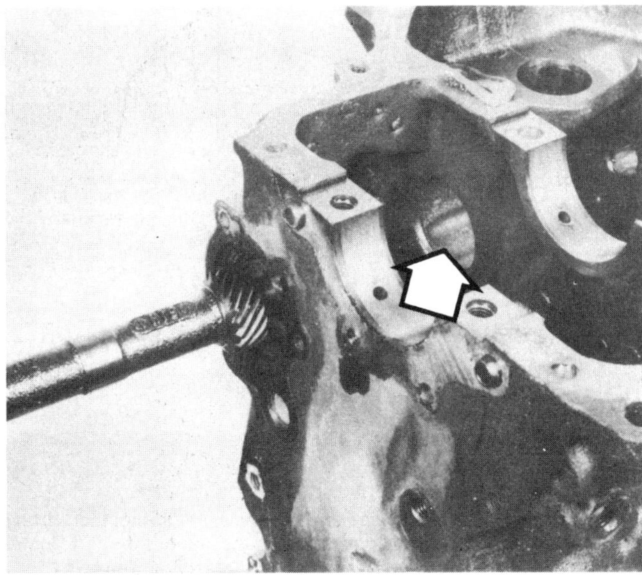

10.5 Be careful not to nick or gouge the bearings as the intermediate shaft is removed

10.7 With the retainer on a flat surface, carefully tap the new seal into place with a soft-face hammer

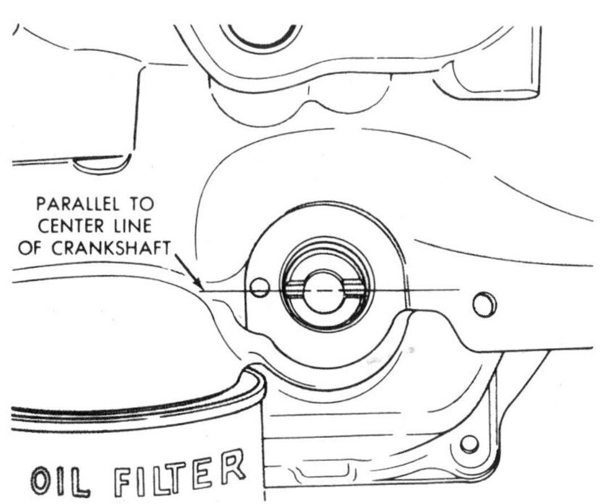

10.8 When viewed through the distributor hole, the oil pump shaft slot must be parallel to the crankshaft centerline

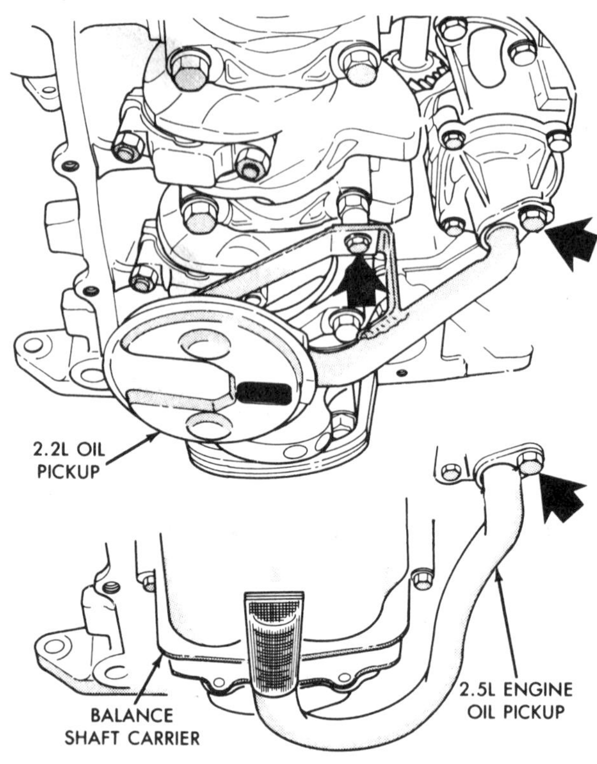

11.1 The 2.2L (top) and 2.5L oil pickup bolts (arrows)

9 Apply a 1 mm wide bead of *anaerobic* sealant to the contact surface of the retainer and place it in position over the end of the shaft. Install the retaining bolts and tighten them to the specified torque.
10 Install the sprocket as described in Section 6.
11 Install the timing belt (Section 6).

11 Oil pump – removal, disassembly and inspection

Refer to illustrations 11.1, 11.4, 11.5, 11.6, 11.7, 11.8 and 11.9

1 Unbolt and remove the oil pickup **(see illustration)**.
2 Unbolt and remove the oil pump.
3 Remove the retaining bolts and lift off the oil pump cover.
4 Check the end play of the rotors, using a feeler gauge and a straightedge **(see illustration)**. Compare the measurement to the Specifications.
5 Remove the outer rotor and measure its thickness **(see illustration)**. **Caution:** *Install the rotor with the large chamfered edge facing the pump body.*
6 Check the clearance between the rotors with a feeler gauge **(see illustration)** and compare the results to the Specifications.
7 Measure the outer rotor-to-body clearance **(see illustration)** and compare it to the Specifications.
8 Check the oil pump cover for warpage with a feeler gauge and a straightedge to make sure it is as specified **(see illustration)**.
9 Measure the oil pressure relief valve spring to ensure that it is the specified length **(see illustration)**.
10 If any components are worn beyond the specified limit, the oil pump will have to be replaced with a new one.

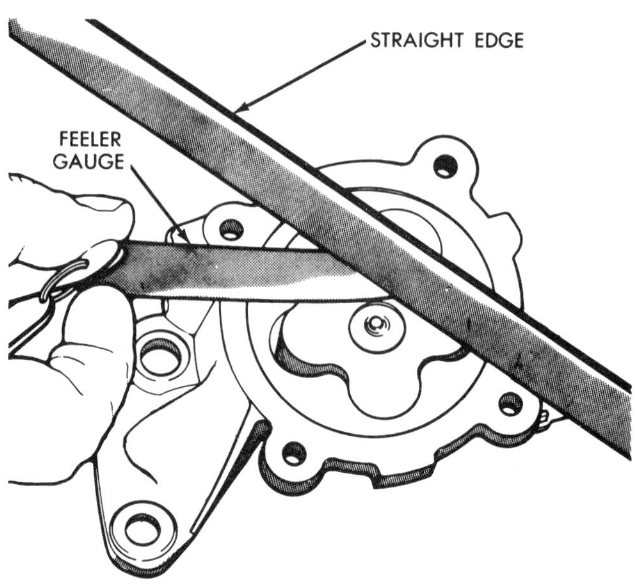

11.4 Checking oil pump rotor end play with a straightedge and feeler gauge

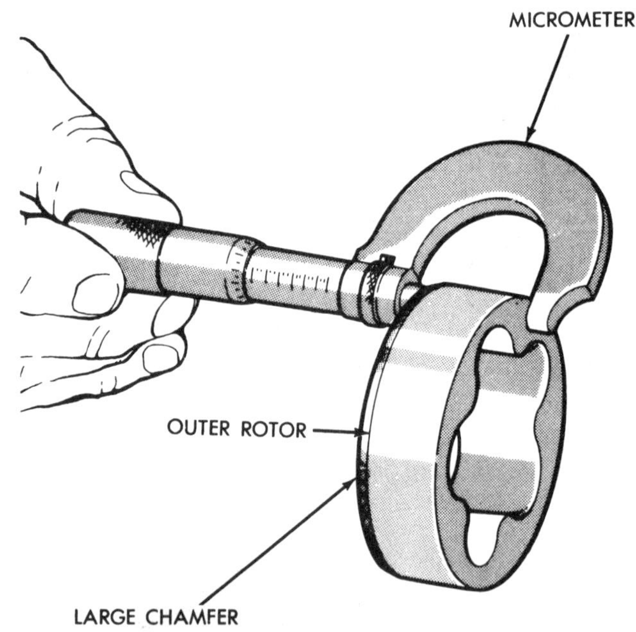

11.5 Measuring the oil pump rotor thickness with a micrometer

12 Front oil seal and housing – removal and installation

Refer to illustrations 12.1 and 12.3

1 With the timing belt and sprockets, the oil pan and the intermediate shaft sprocket removed for access, unbolt and remove the oil seal housing **(see illustration)**.
2 Use a punch and hammer to drive the old oil seal from the housing.

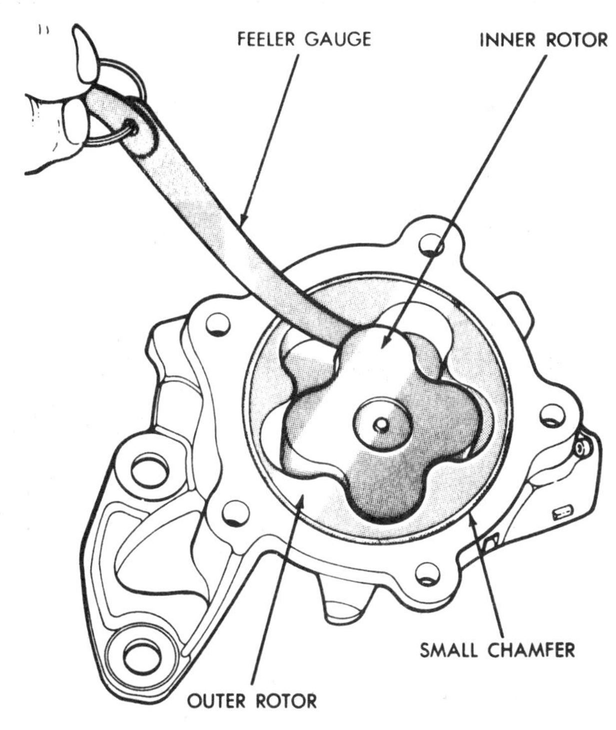

11.6 Checking the oil pump rotor clearance

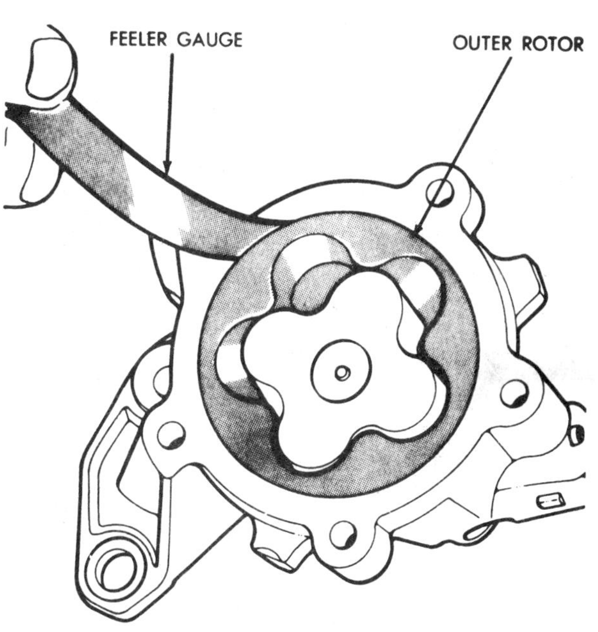

11.7 Checking the outer rotor-to-pump body clearance

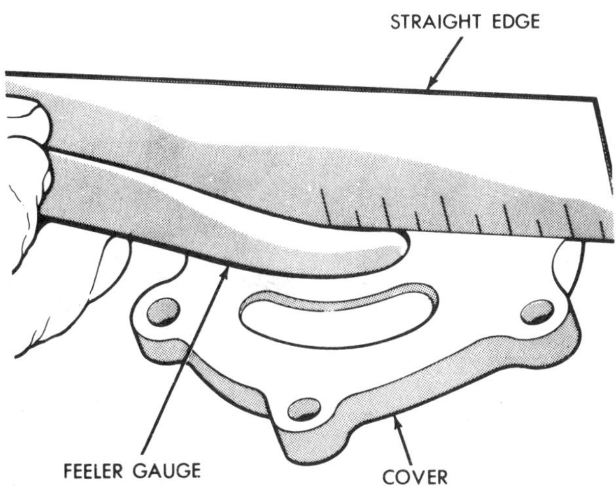

11.8 Checking the oil pump cover for warpage with a straightedge and feeler gauge

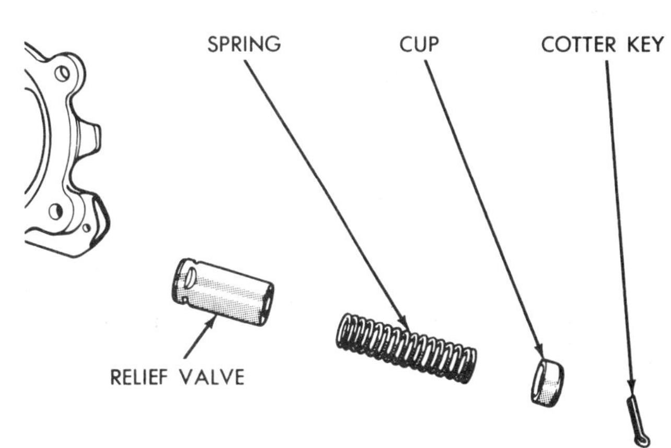

11.9 Oil pressure relief valve components — exploded view

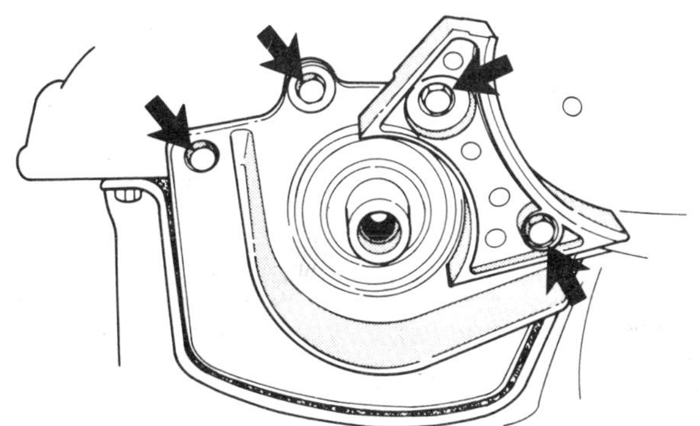

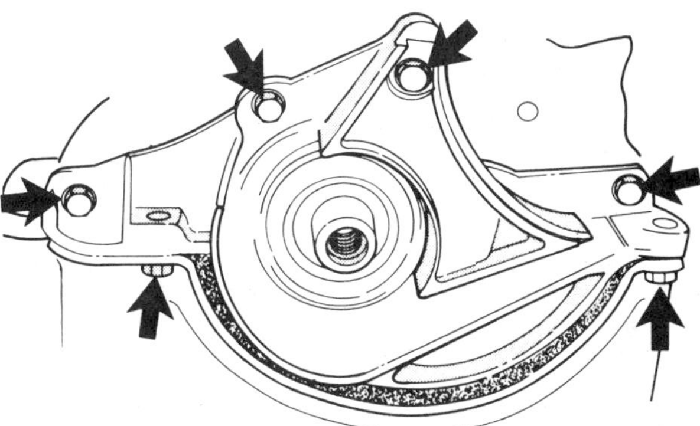

12.1 2.2L (left) and 2.5L front oil seal housing retaining bolts (arrows)

3 Apply a thin coat of RTV sealant to the inner surface of the housing, place the new seal in place and carefully tap it into position with a soft-face hammer **(see illustration)**.

4 Lubricate the inner circumference of the seal with white lithium-base grease and apply a 1 mm bead of *anaerobic* gasket sealant to the engine block mating surfaces of the seal housing. Position the housing on the engine. Install the retaining bolts and tighten them to the specified torque.

13 Rear oil seal and housing – removal and installation

Refer to illustrations 13.1 and 13.4

1 Remove the four bolts and detach the housing and seal from the rear of the engine block **(see illustration)**.

2 Drive the old seal from the housing.

3 Clean the seal surface thoroughly with solvent and inspect it for nicks and other damage.

4 Apply a thin coat of RTV sealant to the inner circumference of the housing, lay the new seal in place and tap it squarely into position with a soft-face hammer **(see illustration)**.

5 Lubricate the seal inner surface with white lithium-base grease.

6 Apply a 1mm bead of anaerobic gasket sealant to the engine block mating surfaces of the seal housing.

7 Place the assembly in position, install the bolts and tighten them to the specified torque.

14 Oil pump – reassembly and installation

Refer to illustrations 14.4 and 14.6

1 Install the rotor (large chamfered edge toward the pump body) and oil pressure relief valve and spring assembly.

2 Install the pump cover and tighten the bolts to the specified torque.

3 Apply a thin coat of RTV sealant to the contact surface of the pump and lower it fully into position. Rotate it back and forth slightly to make sure there is positive contact between the pump and the cylinder block. While holding the pump securely in place, coat the threads of the retaining bolts with sealant and install and tighten them to the specified torque. The slot in the oil pump shaft must be parallel to the crankshaft centerline when viewed through the distributor opening (see illustration 10.8).

4 Install a new O-ring in the oil pump pickup opening **(see illustration)**.

5 Carefully work the pickup into the pump, install the retaining bolts and tighten them to the specified torque.

6 On 2.2 liter engines, install the brace bolt and tighten it securely **(see illustration)**.

15 Cylinder head and camshaft – installation

Refer to illustrations 15.5, 15.7, 15.8, 15.12, 15.14, 15.15 and 15.18

1 Before installing the cylinder head, check to make sure the number one (front) piston is at top dead center, the timing belt sprockets are properly aligned (Section 6) and the oil pump shaft slot (viewed through the distributor installation hole) is parallel to the crankshaft centerline.

2 Place the head gasket in position on the engine block and press it into place over the alignment dowels.

3 Place the cylinder head in position.

4 Apply a thin coat of sealant to the threads of the head bolts and

12.3 Tap the new front crankshaft oil seal into place with a soft-face hammer

13.1 Pull the rear crankshaft oil seal housing away from the crankshaft and detach it from the engine

13.4 Tap the new rear oil seal squarely into place with a soft-face hammer

install the bolts finger tight. **Caution:** *Head bolts used in 1986 and later models are 11 mm in diameter and have an 11 on the bolt head. The 10 mm bolts used in previous years will thread into the 11 mm holes, but will strip the threads when they are tightened.*

5 Tighten the head bolts to the specified torque, following the sequence shown **(see illustration)**. **Caution:** *Bolt torque after the final 1/4-turn (Step 4) must be over 90 ft-lbs on 1986 and later models. If it isn't, replace the bolt(s).*

6 Lubricate the valve lash adjusters with engine oil and insert them into the bores.

7 Lightly lubricate the contact points of the valve stems and lash adjusters with assembly lube **(see illustration)**.

8 Install the rocker arms **(see illustration)**.

9 Lubricate the contact surfaces on the top side of the rocker arms with assembly lube.

10 Lubricate the camshaft bearing surfaces in the head with assembly lube. Wipe the camshaft carefully with a clean, dry, lint-free cloth.

11 Lubricate the camshaft lobes with assembly lubricant and lower it into position with the sprocket keyway facing up.

14.4 Lubricate the new O-ring and install it in the oil pump before attaching the pickup assembly

14.6 Don't forget to tighten the pickup brace bolt on 2.2L engines

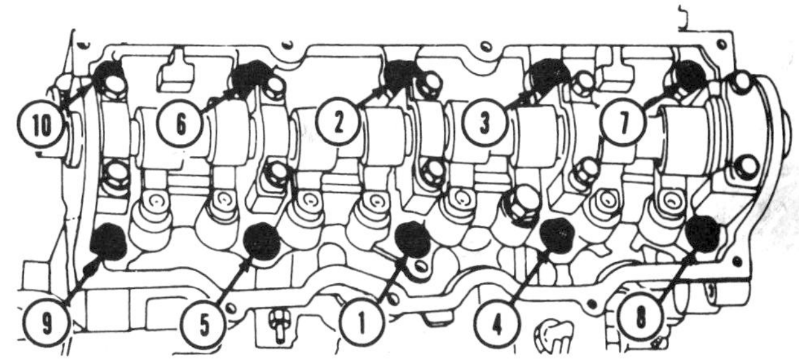

15.5 Cylinder head bolt *tightening* sequence

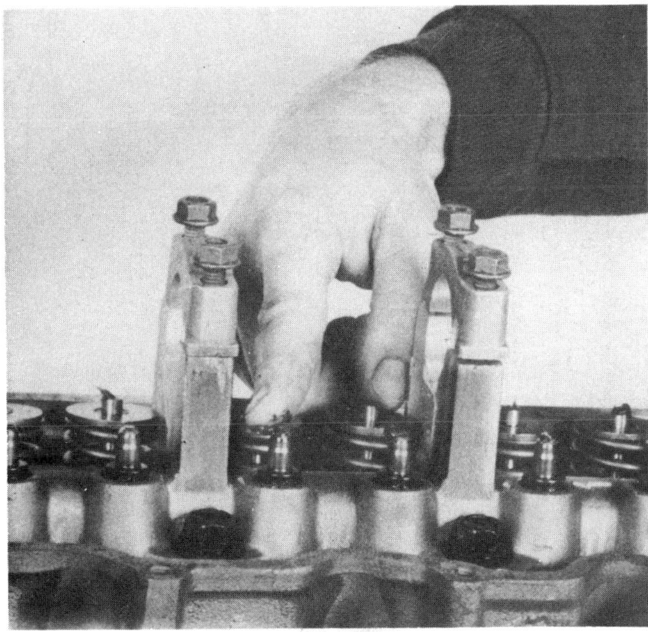

15.7 Apply assembly lubricant to the lash adjusters and the ends of the valve stems

15.8 Seat the rocker arms on the valves and adjusters, then apply assembly lubricant to the cam lobe contact surfaces

2B

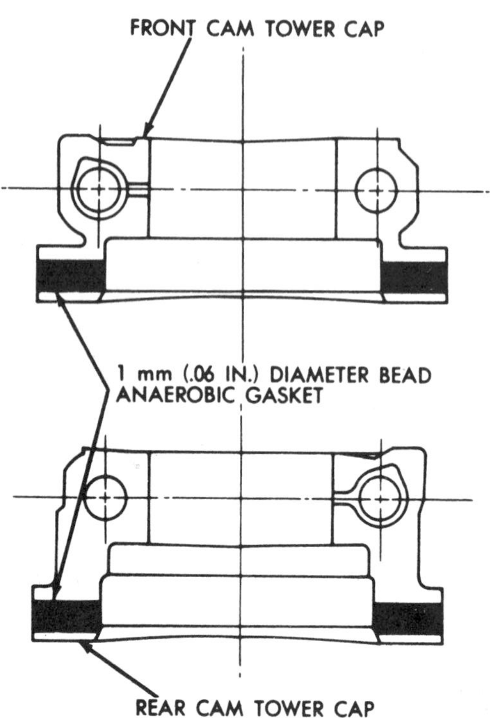

15.12 Apply anaerobic-type gasket sealant to the dark areas of the front and rear camshaft bearing caps (do not get it in the oil passages)

15.14 Use a small screwdriver to remove excess sealant from the bearing cap seal surfaces

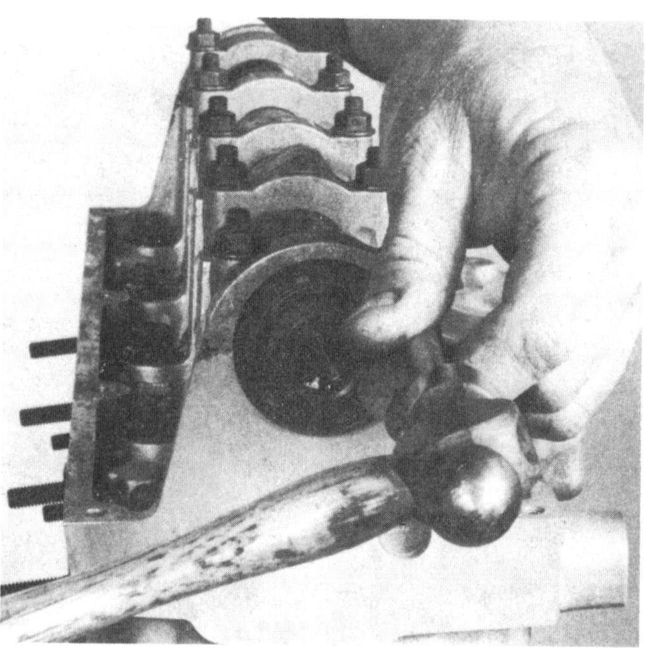

15.15 Tap the new camshaft seal into place with the broad end of a punch and a hammer

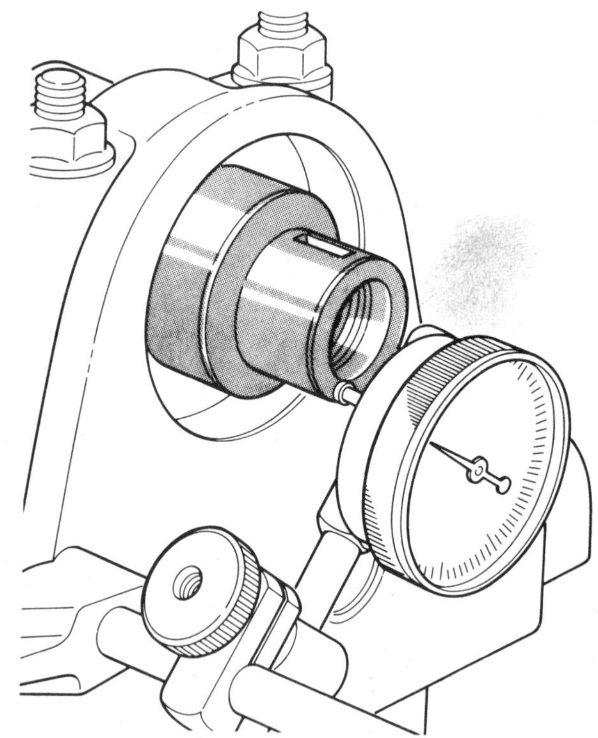

15.18 Measuring camshaft end play with a dial indicator

12 Apply a thin coat of assembly lubricant to the camshaft bearing caps and install them on their respective pedestals (the arrows must point toward the timing belt). Apply *anaerobic-type* sealant to the contact surfaces of the two end bearing caps **(see illustration)**.
13 Install the bearing cap nuts and tighten them with your fingers until they are snug. Tighten the nuts evenly, in 1/4-turn increments, to the specified torque.
14 Remove any excess sealant from the two end bearing caps **(see illustration)**.
15 Press the camshaft seals into the end bearing caps and seat them in place with a hammer and the large end of a drift punch **(see illustration)**.
16 The camshaft end play can be checked with a dial indicator set or a feeler gauge.
17 If a feeler gauge is used, gently pry the camshaft all the way toward the front of the engine. Slip a feeler gauge between the flange at the front of the camshaft and the front bearing cap. Compare the measured end play to the Specifications.
18 If a dial indicator is used, mount it at the front of the engine with the indicator stem touching the end of the camshaft. Carefully pry the

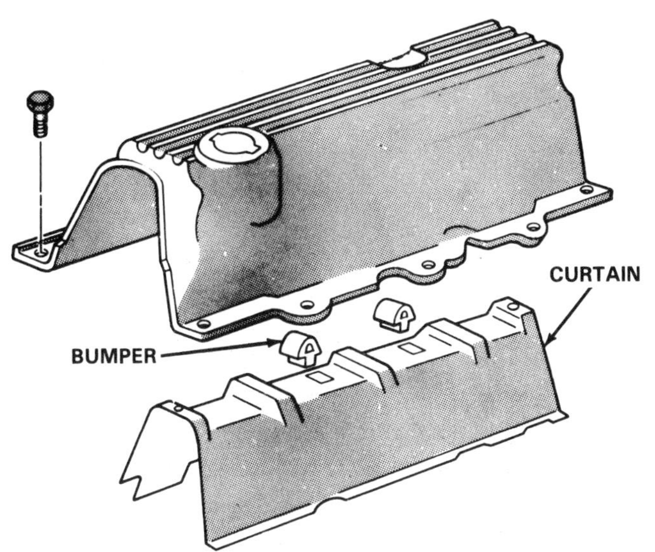

16.5 EFI equipped engine valve cover installation details

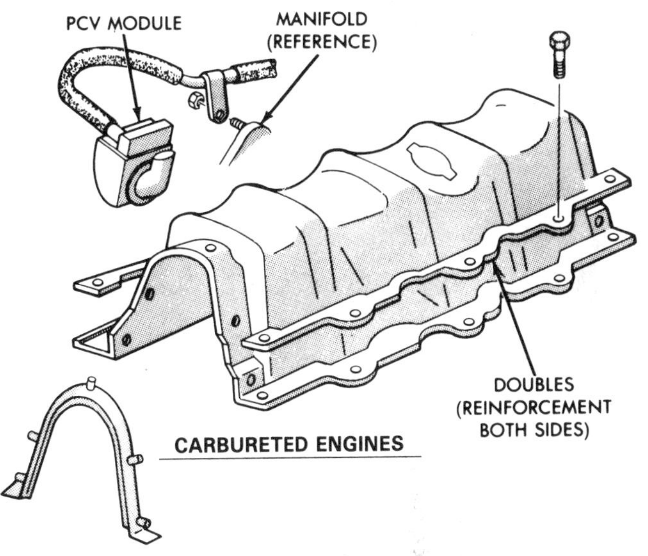

16.7 Carburetor equipped engine valve cover installation details

2B

camshaft all the way toward the front of the engine, then zero the indicator. Gently pry the camshaft as far as possible in the opposite direction and observe the needle movement on the dial indicator, which will indicate the amount of end play. Compare the reading to the Specifications **(see illustration)**.

16 Manifolds/external engine components — installation

Refer to illustrations 16.5 and 16.7

1 Install the camshaft drivebelt sprocket, making sure it is properly aligned (Section 6). Install the retaining bolt finger tight.
2 Install the air injection pump pulley and bolt (if equipped). Lock the pulley to keep it from turning and tighten the bolt to the specified torque.
3 On air pump equipped models, lock the air pump pulley to keep it from turning or use the special tool (Chrysler no. C-4687 or equivalent) to hold the camshaft timing belt sprocket, install the bolt and tighten it to the specified torque.
4 Install and adjust the timing belt (Section 6).
5 On TBI equipped models, attach the rubber bumpers in the valve cover curtain and place the curtain in position on the cylinder head with the clearance cutouts facing the manifold **(see illustration)**.
6 Apply a 1/8-inch bead of RTV sealant around the sealing surface of the cover.
7 Place the valve cover in position and press down to seat it. On carburated models, place the reinforcements in position **(see illustration)**. Install the retaining bolts and tighten them to the specified torque.
8 On non-turbocharged engines, apply a thin coat of gasket sealant to the new intake/exhaust manifold gaskets and place them in position. On turbocharged engines, position a new Grafoil-type gasket in place. *Do not use sealant on this type of gasket.*
9 Place the exhaust manifold in position, lubricate the mounting stud threads with lithium-base grease and install the nuts. Tighten them to the specified torque, working from the center out toward the ends.
10 Install the intake manifold and bolts. Tighten the bolts to the specified torque working from the center out toward the ends.
11 Install the turbocharger assembly (if equipped), the fuel rail and injectors (Chapter 4).
12 Install the EGR valve (Chapter 6).
13 Install the oxygen sensor (Chapter 6).
14 Apply RTV sealant to both sides of the carburetor spacer. Place the spacer in position, install the nuts and tighten them securely.
15 Install the carburetor or the fuel injection throttle body.
16 Install the PCV valve and hose assembly.
17 Attach the engine mount to the front of the engine.
18 Install the lower timing belt cover, followed by the upper cover.
19 Connect the fuel lines to the carburetor or fuel injection unit.
20 On turbocharged models, install the turbocharger-to-engine block bracket. Install the oil drain back tube and connect the turbocharger coolant tube.
21 Install the water pump (Chapter 3).
22 Lubricate the O-ring on the distributor shaft with lithium-base grease and install the distributor (Chapter 5).
23 Install the thermostat, gasket and cover (Chapter 3).
24 Install the heater water outlet.
25 Install the coolant temperature switch(es) in the water outlet housing.
26 Install the oil pressure switch.
27 Install the coolant temperature sensor in the cylinder head.

17 Engine — installation

1 Attach the hoist to the engine, carefully lower the engine into the engine compartment and line up the transaxle and engine bolt holes.
2 Align the engine mounts and install all bolts/nuts finger tight. *Do not tighten any of the bolts/nuts until all of them have been installed.*
3 Install the transaxle-to-engine bolts and tighten them securely. Remove the hoist and the transaxle supports.
4 Attach the engine ground strap and install the right engine splash shield.
5 Install the starter and connect the exhaust pipe to the manifold.
6 On vehicles with a manual transaxle, install the lower transmission case cover and hook up the clutch cable.
7 On vehicles with an automatic transaxle, remove the C-clamp from the housing and align the driveplate and torque converter. Install the bolts and tighten them to the specified torque, then install the lower transmission case cover.
8 Install the power steering pump and drivebelt.
9 Install the alternator and drivebelt.
10 Hook up the fuel and vapor lines, the throttle cable and the heater hoses.
11 Reattach the wires to the engine, carburetor or fuel injection unit and alternator.
12 Install a new oil filter and fill the crankcase with the specified oil (Chapter 1).
13 Install the air conditioning compressor and drivebelt.
14 Install the radiator and fan assembly and hook up the radiator hoses, then refill the cooling system (Chapter 1).
15 Install the air cleaner assembly and the hoses.
16 Install the battery and connect the cables (positive first, then negative).
17 Install the hood (Chapter 11).

Chapter 2 Part C
General engine overhaul procedures

Contents

Specifications

2.6L engine

General

Displacement	2.6 liters (156 cu in)
Bore and stroke	3.59 x 3.86 in (91.19 x 98.04 mm)
Firing order	1-3-4-2
Compression ratio	8.7:1
Compression pressure	149 psi at 250 rpm
Oil pressure (engine warm)	45 to 90 psi at 3000 rpm (6 psi at idle)

Engine block

Cylinder bore diameter	3.59 in (91.2 mm)
Taper and out-of-round limit	0.0008 in (0.020 mm)

Silent Shaft

Front bearing journal diameter	0.906 in (23.01 mm)
Front bearing oil clearance	0.0008 to 0.0024 in (0.020 to 0.061 mm)
Rear bearing journal diameter	1.693 in (43.00 mm)
Rear bearing oil clearance	0.0020 to 0.0035 in (0.051 to 0.089 mm)

Pistons and rings

Piston diameter	3.5866 in (91.100 mm)
Piston ring-to-groove clearance	
Standard	
Top ring	0.0024 to 0.0039 in (0.061 to 0.099 mm)
Second ring	0.008 to 0.0024 in (0.02 to 0.061 mm)
Oil ring	Side rails must rotate freely after assembly
Service limit	
Top ring	0.006 in (0.15 mm)
Second ring	0.0039 in (0.099 mm)
Piston ring end gap	
Standard	
Top ring	0.010 to 0.018 in (0.25 to 0.46 mm)
Second ring	0.010 to 0.018 in (0.25 to 0.46 mm)
Oil ring	0.008 to 0.035 in (0.20 to 0.89 mm)
Service limit	
Top ring	0.039 in (0.99 mm)
Second ring	0.039 in (0.99 mm)
Oil ring	0.059 in (1.50 mm)

Crankshaft and flywheel	
Main journal diameter	2.3622 in (60.000 mm)
Taper and out-of-round limit	0.0004 in (0.010 mm)
Main bearing oil clearance	0.0008 to 0.003 in (0.020 to 0.0711 mm)
Connecting rod journal diameter	2.0866 in (53.000 mm)
Connecting rod bearing oil clearance	0.0008 to 0.0028 in (0.020 to 0.071 mm)
Connecting rod side clearance	0.004 to 0.010 in (0.10 to 0.25 mm)
Crankshaft end play	0.002 to 0.007 in (0.05 to 0.18 mm)
Flywheel clutch face runout limit	0.020 in (0.51 mm)
Camshaft	
Bearing oil clearance	0.002 to 0.004 in (0.05 to 0.10 mm)
Lobe height (intake and exhaust)	
Standard	1.6614 in (42.200 mm)
Service limit	1.6414 in (41.692 mm)
End play	0.004 to 0.008 in (0.10 to 0.20 mm)
Cylinder head and valve train	
Head warpage limit	0.004 in (0.10 mm)
Valve seat angle	45°
Valve seat margin width	
Intake	0.028 to 0.047 in (0.71 to 1.19 mm)
Exhaust	0.039 to 0.079 in (0.99 to 2.01 mm)
Valve stem-to-guide clearance	
Intake	
Standard	0.0012 to 0.0024 in (0.031 to 0.061 mm)
Service limit	0.004 in (0.10 mm)
Exhaust	
Standard	0.0020 to 0.0035 in (0.051 to 0.089 mm)
Service limit	0.006 in (0.15 mm)
Valve spring free length	
Standard	1.869 in (47.47 mm)
Service limit	1.479 in (46.57 mm)
Valve spring pressure (lbs at specified length)	61 lbs at 1.59 in (273 N at 40.4 mm)
Out-of-square service limit	3° max
Valve spring installed height	
Standard	1.590 in (40.39 mm)
Service limit	1.629 in (41.38 mm)
Jet Valve	
Stem diameter	0.1693 in (4.300 mm)
Seat angle	45°
Spring free length	1.165 in (29.59 mm)
Spring pressure	5.5 lbs at 0.846 in (24.5 Nm at 21.49 mm)
Valve clearance (HOT engine)	
Intake	0.006 in (0.15 mm)
Exhaust	0.010 in (0.25 mm)
Jet valve	0.006 on (0.15 mm)
Timing belt tensioner	
Spring free length	2.587 in (65.71 mm)
Spring load	4.4 lbs at 1.453 in (19.6 N at 36.91 mm)
Oil Pump	
Relief valve opening pressure	49.8 to 64.0 psi (343.4 to 441.3 kPa)
Gear-to-housing clearance	0.0043 to 0.0059 in (0.109 to 0.150 mm)
Gear-to-pump body bearing clearance	0.0008 to 0.0020 in (0.020 to 0.051 mm)
Gear-to-pump cover bearing clearance	0.0016 to 0.0028 in (0.041 to 0.071 mm)
Gear end play	
Drive	0.0020 to 0.0043 in (0.051 to 0.109 mm)
Driven	0.0016 to 0.0039 in (0.041 to 0.099 mm)
Relief spring free length	1.850 in (46.99 mm)
Relief spring load	9.5 lbs at 1.575 in (42.3 N at 40.01 mm)
Oil pressure switch minimum actuating pressure	4 psi (28 kPa) or less

Torque specifications	Ft-lbs	Nm
Main bearing cap bolts	58	79
Connecting rod bearing cap nuts	34	46

2.2L/2.5L engine

General

Displacement	
2.2L	135 cu in (2.2 liters)
2.5L	153 cu in (2.5 liters)
Bore and stroke	
2.2L	3.44 x 3.62 in (87.4 x 92.0 mm)
2.5L	3.44 x 4.09 in (87.4 x 104 mm)

2C

2.2L/2.5L engine (continued)

Compression pressure	130 to 150 psi (896 to 1034 kPa)
Maximum variation between cylinders	20 psi (138 kpa)
Oil pressure	
1982 through 1984 (at 2000 rpm)	40 psi (276 kPa)
1985 (at 3000 rpm)	25 to 90 psi (172 to 620 kPa)
1986 (at 3000 rpm)	25 to 80 psi (172 to 552 kPa)

Engine block

Cylinder bore diameter	3.44 in (87.4 mm)
Taper limit	
1982 through 1984	0.010 in (0.25 mm)
1985 on	0.005 in (0.127 mm)
Out-of-round limit	
1982 through 1984	0.005 in (0.127 mm)
1985 on	0.002 in (0.05 mm)

Pistons and rings

Piston diameter	
Non-turbocharged engine	3.443 to 3.445 in (87.45 to 87.50 mm)
Turbocharged engine	3.416 to 3.444 in (87.465 to 87.4815 mm)
Piston ring-to-groove clearance	
Standard	
Top ring	0.0015 to 0.0031 in (0.038 to 0.079 mm)
2nd ring	0.0015 to 0.0037 in (0.038 to 0.094 mm)
Oil ring	0.008 in (0.20 mm)
Service limit	
Top ring	0.004 in (0.10 mm)
2nd ring	0.004 in (0.10 mm)
Piston ring end gap (non-turbocharged engine)	
Top ring	
Standard	0.011 to 0.021 in (0.28 to 0.53 mm)
Service limit	0.039 in (1.0 mm)
2nd ring	
Standard	0.011 to 0.021 in (0.28 to 0.53 mm)
Service limit	0.039 in (1.0 mm)
Oil ring	
Standard	0.015 to 0.055 in (0.38 to 1.40 mm)
Service limit	0.074 in (1.88 mm)
Piston ring end gap (turbocharged engine)	
Top ring	
Standard	0.010 to 0.020 in (0.25 to 0.51 mm)
Service limit	0.038 in (0.98 mm)
2nd ring	
Standard	0.009 to 0.019 in (0.23 to 0.48 mm)
Service limit	0.037 in (0.95 mm)
Oil ring	
Standard	0.015 to 0.55 in (0.38 to 1.40 mm)
Service limit	0.074 in (1.88 mm)

Crankshaft and flywheel

Main journal diameter	
Non-turbocharged engine	2.362 to 2.363 in (59.987 to 60.020 mm)
Turbocharged engine	2.3622 to 2.3627 in (60.000 to 60.013 mm)
Taper limit	0.0004 in (0.010 mm)
Out-of-round limit	0.012 in (0.03 mm)
Main bearing oil clearance (non-turbocharged engine)	
Standard	0.0003 to 0.0031 in (0.007 to 0.080 mm)
Service limit	0.004 in (0.10 mm)
Main bearing oil clearance (turbocharged engine)	0.0004 to 0.0023 in (0.011 to 0.058 mm)
Connecting rod journal diameter	1.968 to 1.969 in (49.979 to 50.005 mm)
Connecting rod bearing oil clearance (non-turbocharged engine)	
Standard	0.0008 to 0.0034 in (0.019 to 0.087 mm)
Service limit	0.004 in (0.10 mm)
Connecting rod bearing oil clearance (turbocharged engine)	0.0008 to 0.0031 in (0.019 to 0.079 mm)
Connecting rod side clearance	0.005 to 0.013 in (0.13 to 0.32 mm)
Crankshaft end play	
Standard	0.002 to 0.007 in (0.05 to 0.18 mm)
Service limit	0.014 in (0.35 mm)

Camshaft

End play	
Standard	0.005 to 0.013 in (0.13 to 0.33 mm)
Service limit	0.020 in (0.51 mm)
Bearing journal diameter	1.375 to 1.376 in (34.93 to 34.95 mm)

Camshaft lobe wear limit	
1982 through 1984	0.005 in (0.13 mm)
1985 on	0.010 in (0.25 mm)

Cylinder head and valve train

Head warpage limit	0.004 in (0.10 mm)
Valve seat angle	45°
Valve seat width	
Intake	0.069 to 0.088 in (1.75 to 2.24 mm)
Exhaust	0.059 to 0.078 in (1.50 to 1.98 mm)
Valve face angle	45°
Valve margin width (minimum)	
Intake	1/32 in (0.79 mm)
Exhaust	3/64 in (1.19 mm)
Valve stem diameter	
Intake	0.3124 in (7.935 mm)
Exhaust	0.3103 in (7.882 mm)
Valve head diameter	
Intake	1.60 in (40.6 mm)
Exhaust	1.39 in (35.3 mm)
Valve stem-to-guide clearance	
Intake	0.0009 to 0.0026 in (0.023 to 0.066 mm)
Exhaust	0.0030 to 0.0047 in (0.076 to 0.119 mm)
Valve spring free length	
1982 through 1984	2.28 in (57.9 mm)
1985 on	
Non-turbocharged engine	2.39 in (60.7 mm)
Turbocharged engine	2.28 in (57.9 mm)
Valve spring installed height	
Intake	1.62 to 1.68 in (41.2 to 42.7 mm)
Exhaust	1.62 to 1.68 in (41.2 to 42.7 mm)
Valve lash adjustment	Hydraulic
Collapsed tappet gap	0.024 to 0.060 in (0.61 to 1.52 mm)
Spring seat-to-valve tip dimension*	1.960 to 2.009 in (49.76 to 51.04 mm)

* *Must be checked if valve faces or seats are reground*

Intermediate shaft

Journal diameter	
Large	1.6812 to 1.6822 in (42.67 to 42.70 mm)
Small	0.775 to 0.776 in (19.67 to 19.70 mm)
Bearing inside diameter	
Large	1.6836 to 1.6844 in (42.73 to 42.75 mm)
Small	0.777 to 0.778 in (19.72 to 19.75 mm)
Oil clearance	0.08 mm maximum

Torque specifications	**Ft-lbs**	**Nm**
Main bearing cap bolt	30*	41*
Connecting rod bearing cap nut	40*	54*

* *Plus 1/4-turn*

2C

1 General information

Included in this part of Chapter 2 are the general overhaul procedures for the cylinder head and internal engine components. This information ranges from advice about preparing for an overhaul and the purchase of replacement parts to detailed, step-by-step procedures covering removal and installation of internal engine components and the inspection of parts.

In the following Sections, it is assumed that the engine has been removed from the vehicle. For information concerning removal and installation of the engine and its external components, see Part A or B of this Chapter and Section 2 of this Part.

The specifications included here in Part B are only those necessary for the inspection and overhaul procedures which follow. Refer to Part A or B for additional specifications.

2 Repair operations possible with the engine in the vehicle

Many major repair operations can be accomplished without removing the engine from the vehicle.

It is a very good idea to clean the engine compartment and the exterior of the engine with some type of pressure washer before any work is begun. A clean engine will make the job easier and will prevent the possibility of getting dirt into internal areas of the engine.

Remove the hood (Chapter 11) and cover the fenders to provide as much working room as possible and to prevent damage to the painted surfaces.

If oil or coolant leaks develop, indicating a need for gasket or seal replacement, the repairs can generally be made with the engine in the vehicle. The oil pan gasket, the cylinder head gasket, intake and exhaust manifold gaskets, timing cover gaskets and the front crankshaft oil seal are accessible with the engine in place.

Exterior engine components, such as the water pump, the starter motor, the alternator, the distributor, the fuel pump and the carburetor, as well as the fuel injection components and the intake and exhaust manifolds, are quite easily removed for repair with the engine in place.

Since the cylinder head can be removed without pulling the engine, valve component servicing can also be accomplished with the engine in the vehicle.

Replacement of, repairs to or inspection of the timing sprockets and chain or belt, the Silent Shaft and chain assembly, the oil pump and front cover seals are all possible with the engine in place.

In extreme cases caused by a lack of necessary equipment, repair or replacement of piston rings, pistons, connecting rods and rod bearings and reconditioning of the cylinder bores is possible with the engine in the vehicle. However, this practice is not recommended because of the cleaning and preparation work that must be done to the components involved.

Detailed removal, inspection, repair and installation procedures for the above mentioned components can be found in the appropriate Part of Chapter 2 or the other Chapters in this manual.

3 Engine overhaul – general information

It is not always easy to determine when, or if, an engine should be completely overhauled, as a number of factors must be considered.

High mileage is not necessarily an indication that an overhaul is needed, while low mileage does not preclude the need for an overhaul. Frequency of servicing is probably the most important consideration. An engine which has had regular and frequent oil and filter changes, as well as other required maintenance, will most likely give many thousands of miles of reliable service. Conversely, a neglected engine may require an overhaul very early in its life.

Excessive oil consumption is an indication that piston rings and/or valve guides are in need of attention. Make sure that oil leaks are not responsible before deciding that the rings and guides are bad. Have a cylinder compression or leakdown test performed by an experienced tune-up mechanic to determine the extent of the work required.

If the engine is making obvious knocking or rumbling noises, the connecting rod and/or main bearings are probably at fault. Check the oil pressure with a gauge installed in place of the oil pressure sending unit and compare it to the Specifications. If it is extremely low, the bearings and/or oil pump are probably worn out.

Loss of power, rough running, excessive valve train noise and high fuel consumption rates may also point to the need for an overhaul, especially if they are all present at the same time. If a complete tune-up does not remedy the situation, major mechanical work is the only solution.

An engine overhaul involves restoring the internal parts to the specifications of a new engine. During an overhaul, the piston rings are replaced and the cylinder walls are reconditioned (rebored and/or honed). If a rebore is done, new pistons are required. The main and connecting rod bearings are replaced with new ones and, if necessary, the crankshaft may be reground to restore the journals. Generally, the valves are serviced as well, since they are usually in less-than-perfect condition at this point. While the engine is being overhauled, other components, such as the carburetor, distributor, starter and alternator, can be rebuilt as well. The end result should be a like new engine that will give many trouble free miles.

Before beginning the engine overhaul, read through the entire procedure to familiarize yourself with the scope and requirements of the job. Overhauling an engine is not difficult, but it is time consuming. Plan on the vehicle being tied up for a minimum of two weeks, especially if parts must be taken to an automotive machine shop for repair or reconditioning. Check on availability of parts and make sure that any necessary special tools and equipment are obtained in advance. Most work can be done with typical hand tools, although a number of precision measuring tools are required for inspecting parts to determine if they must be replaced. Often an automotive machine shop will handle the inspection of parts and offer advice concerning reconditioning and replacement. **Note:** *Always wait until the engine has been completely disassembled and all components, especially the engine block, have been inspected before deciding what service and repair operations must be performed by an automotive machine shop.* Since the condition of the block will be the major factor to consider when determining whether to overhaul the original engine or buy a rebuilt one, never purchase parts or have machine work done on other components until the block has been thoroughly inspected. As a general rule, time is the primary cost of an overhaul, so it does not pay to install worn or substandard parts.

As a final note, to ensure maximum life and minimum trouble from a rebuilt engine, everything must be assembled with care in a spotlessly clean environment.

4 Engine rebuilding alternatives

The do-it-yourselfer is faced with a number of options when performing an engine overhaul. The decision to replace the engine block, piston/connecting rod assemblies and crankshaft depends on a number of factors, especially the condition of the block. Other considerations are cost, access to machine shop facilities, parts availability, time required to complete the project and experience.

Some of the rebuilding alternatives include:

Individual parts – If the inspection procedures reveal that the engine block and most engine components are in reusable condition, purchasing individual parts may be the most economical alternative. The block, crankshaft and piston/connecting rod assemblies should all be inspected carefully. Even if the block shows little wear, the cylinder bores should receive a finish hone.

Crankshaft kit – This rebuild package consists of a reground crankshaft and a matched set of pistons and connecting rods. The pistons will already be installed on the connecting rods. Piston rings and the necessary bearings will be included in the kit. These kits are commonly available for standard cylinder bores, as well as for engine blocks which have been bored to a regular oversize.

Short block – A short block consists of an engine block with a crankshaft and piston/connecting rod assemblies already installed. All new bearings are incorporated and all clearances will be correct. The existing camshaft, valve train components, cylinder head and external parts can be bolted to the short block with little or no machine shop work necessary.

Long block – A long block consists of a short block plus an oil pump, oil pan, cylinder head, cylinder head cover, camshaft and valve train components, timing sprockets and belt/chain and timing cover. All components are installed with new bearings, seals and gaskets incorporated throughout. The installation of manifolds and external parts is all that is necessary.

Give careful thought to which alternative is best for you and discuss the situation with local automotive machine shops, auto parts dealers or parts store countermen before ordering or purchasing replacement parts.

5 Engine removal – methods and precautions

If it has been decided that an engine must be removed for overhaul or major repair work, certain preliminary steps should be taken.

Locating a suitable work area is extremely important. A shop is, of course, the most desirable place to work. Adequate work space, along with storage space for the vehicle, is very important. If a shop or garage is not available, use a flat, level, clean work surface made of concrete or asphalt.

Cleaning the engine compartment and engine prior to removal will help keep tools clean and organized.

An engine hoist or A-frame will also be necessary. Make sure that the equipment is rated in excess of the combined weight of the engine and its accessories. Safety is of primary importance, considering the potential hazards involved in lifting the engine out of the vehicle.

If the engine is being removed by a novice, a helper should be available. Advice and aid from someone more experienced would also be helpful. There are many instances in which one person cannot simultaneously perform all of the operations necessary to lift the engine out of the vehicle.

Plan the operation ahead of time. Obtain all of the tools and equipment you will need--or know where to get them--prior to beginning the job. Some of the equipment necessary for safe and easy engine removal and installation are an engine hoist, a heavy duty floor jack, complete sets of wrenches and sockets as described in the front of this manual, wooden blocks and plenty of rags and cleaning solvent for mopping up the inevitable spills. If you plan to rent a hoist, arrange for it in advance and perform all of the operations possible without it beforehand. This will save you money and time.

Plan for the vehicle to be out of use for a considerable period of time. A machine shop is a must for that work which you cannot accomplish without special skills and equipment. Machine shops often have busy schedules, so it's a good idea to coordinate your plans for overhaul work with your local shop. Careful planning will result in less down time for your vehicle.

Always use extreme caution when removing and installing the engine. Serious injury can result from careless actions. Plan ahead. If you take your time and think out each step before you proceed, even a job of this magnitude can be accomplished successfully.

6 Engine overhaul — disassembly sequence

1 It is much easier to disassemble and work on the engine if it is mounted on a portable engine stand, which can usually be rented for a reasonable fee from an equipment rental yard. Before the engine is mounted on a stand, the flywheel/driveplate should be removed from the engine (refer to Part A or B).

2 If you can't find a stand suitable for your engine, you can block it up on a sturdy workbench or on the floor. If you elect to work on the engine in this manner, be extra careful not to tip or drop it.

3 If you are performing a complete engine rebuild yourself, the following external components will have to come off. Even if you are going to obtain a rebuilt engine, the same components must still be removed from the old engine so they can be installed on the rebuilt. In general, this includes:

Alternator and brackets
Emissions control components
Distributor, spark plug wires and spark plugs
Thermostat and housing
Water pump
Carburetor/EFI components
Turbocharger (if equipped)
Intake/exhaust manifolds
Oil filter
Fuel pump
Engine mounts
Flywheel/driveplate

Note: *When removing the external components from the engine, pay close attention to details that may be helpful or important during installation. Note the installed position of gaskets, seals, spacers, pins, washers, bolts and other small items.*

4 If you are obtaining a short block, which consists of the engine block, crankshaft, pistons and connecting rods all assembled, then the cylinder head, oil pan and oil pump will also have to be removed from the old engine. See Section 4 for additional information regarding the alternatives.

5 If you are planning a complete overhaul, the engine must be disassembled in the following order:

External engine components
Oil pan
Cylinder head cover
Timing cover
Silent Shaft chain and sprockets (2.6L engine only)
Balance shaft and carrier assembly (2.5L engine only)
Timing belt/chain and sprockets
Intermediate shaft and sprocket (2.2L/2.5L engine only)
Cylinder head and camshaft
Oil pump (2.2L/2.5L engine only)
Piston/connecting rod assemblies
Front oil seal housing (2.2L/2.5L engine only)
Rear oil seal housing
Crankshaft
Left Silent Shaft (2.6L engine only)
Oil pump/right Silent Shaft (2.6L engine only)

6 Before beginning the disassembly and overhaul procedures, make sure the following items are available:

Common hand tools
Small cardboard boxes or plastic bags for storing parts
Gasket scraper
Ridge reamer
Vibration damper puller
Micrometers
Telescoping gauges
Dial indicator set
Valve spring compressor
Cylinder surfacing hone
Piston ring groove cleaning tool
Electric drill motor
Tap and die set
Wire brushes
Cleaning solvent

7 Cylinder head — disassembly

Refer to illustrations 7.2a, 7.2b and 7.3

Note: *Cylinder head service involves removal and disassembly of the intake and exhaust valves and their related components. Because some specialized tools are necessary for disassembly and inspection and because replacement parts are not always readily available, it may be more practical and economical for the home mechanic to purchase a replacement head rather than taking the time to disassemble, inspect and recondition the original head. New and rebuilt cylinder heads for most engines are usually available at dealerships and auto parts stores.*

2C

1 The jet valves should be removed from the cylinder head of the 2.6L engine before removal of the intake and exhaust valves. Use a six-point socket and a breaker bar to unscrew them. **Caution:** *Do not tilt the socket — excessive force exerted on the valve spring retainers can easily bend the jet valve stems.* Label each jet valve to ensure installation in its original position. The jet valves can be disassembled by carefully compressing the spring and removing the keepers, the retainer and the spring. Slide the valve out of the body and pull off the seal with a pair of pliers. Discard the old seals. Use new ones during reassembly. Do not allow the parts for one jet valve assembly to become accidentally interchanged with those of another.

2 Before removing the valves, arrange to label and store them, along with their related components, so they can be stored separately and reinstalled in the same valve guides from which they are removed. Measure the valve spring installed height of each valve and compare it to the Specifications **(see illustration)**. If it is greater than specified,

7.2a Measuring the valve spring installed height with a dial caliper

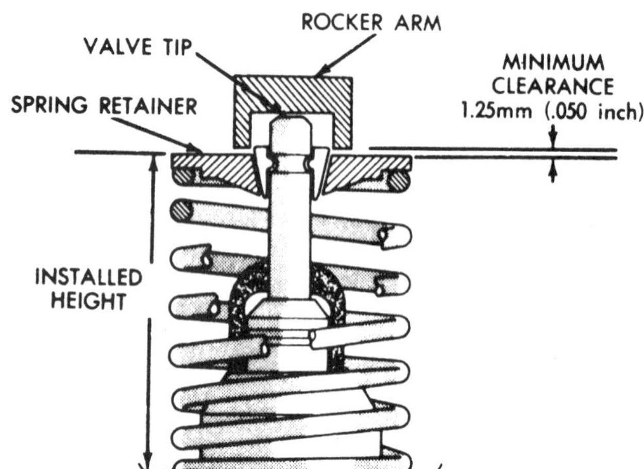

7.2b On 2.2L/2.5L engines, the valve spring installed height is measured from the upper edge of the retainer (note the minimum clearance required between the rocker arm and retainer – if the valves are serviced, the clearance may not be correct)

7.3 Use a valve spring compressor to compress the valve springs, then remove the keepers from the valve stem (a magnet or needle-nose pliers may be needed) (2.6L engine shown)

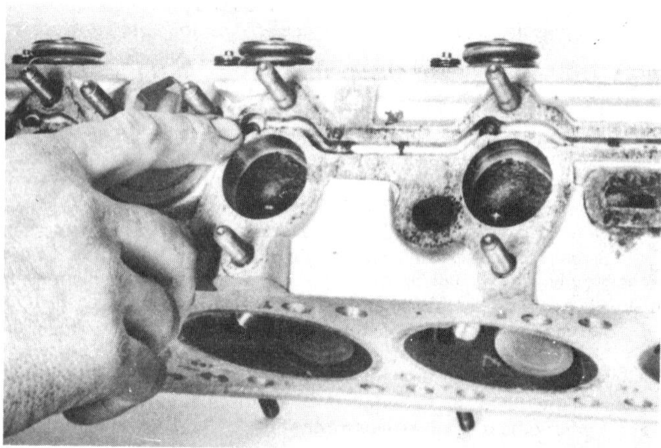

8.4 The Jet air passages, EGR ports and oil holes must be clean and clear (2.6L engine shown)

the valve seats and faces need attention. **Note:** *On 2.2L/2.5L engines, the valve spring installed height is measured from the bottom of the spring to the upper edge of the retainer* ***(see illustration)***.

3 Compress the valve springs on the first valve with a spring compressor and remove the keepers **(see illustration)**. Carefully release the valve spring compressor and remove the retainer, the springs, the valve stem seal, the spring seat and the valve from the head. If the valve binds in the guide and won't come out, push it back into the head and deburr the area around the keeper groove with a fine file or whetstone.

4 Repeat this procedure for each of the remaining valves. Remember to keep all the parts for each valve together so they can be reinstalled in the same locations.

5 Once the valves have been removed and safely stored, the head should be thoroughly cleaned and inspected. If a complete engine overhaul is being done, finish the engine disassembly procedures before beginning the cylinder head cleaning and inspection process.

8 Cylinder head – cleaning and inspection

Refer to illustrations 8.4, 8.11, 8.12, 8.14, 8.16, 8.18, 8.19a, 8.19b, 8.20, 8.21, 8.22, 8.24a, 8.24b, 8.25a and 8.25b

1 Thorough cleaning of the cylinder head and related valve train components, followed by a detailed inspection, will enable you to decide how much valve service work must be done during the engine overhaul.

Cleaning

2 Scrape away all traces of old gasket material and sealing compound from the head gasket, intake manifold and exhaust manifold sealing surfaces. **Caution:** *Do not gouge the cylinder head.* Special gasket removal solvents which dissolve the gasket, making removal much easier, are available at auto parts stores.

3 Remove any built up scale around the coolant passages.

4 Run a stiff wire brush through the oil holes, the EGR gas ports and the jet air passages to remove any deposits that may have formed in them **(see illustration)**.

5 Run an appropriate size tap into each of the threaded holes to remove any corrosion and thread sealant that may be present. If compressed air is available, use it to clear the holes of debris produced by this operation. **Warning:** *Always wear safety goggles when using compressed air to blow away debris.*

6 Clean the exhaust and intake manifold stud threads with an appropriate size die. Clean the rocker arm pivot bolt or stud threads with a wire brush.

7 Clean the cylinder head with solvent and dry it thoroughly. Compressed air will speed the drying process and ensure that all holes and recessed areas are clean. **Note:** *Decarbonizing chemicals may prove helpful for cleaning cylinder heads and valve train components. They are very caustic and should be used with caution. Be sure to follow the instructions on the container.*

8 Without dismantling the rocker arm assembly, clean the rocker arms and shafts with solvent and dry them thoroughly. Compressed air will speed the drying process and can be used to clean out the oil passages.

9 Clean all the valve springs, keepers and retainers with solvent and dry them thoroughly. Clean these assemblies one at a time to avoid mixing up the parts.

10 Scrape off any heavy deposits that may have formed on the valves, then use a motorized wire brush to remove the remaining deposits from the valve heads and stems. Again, do not mix up the valves. If you are servicing the 2.6L cylinder head, you will also want to clean the jet valve components with solvent. Do one jet valve assembly at a time so that the parts are not accidentally interchanged. Carefully remove any deposits from the stems and valve heads with a fine wire brush. **Caution:** *Do not bend the valve stems of the jet valves while cleaning them.*

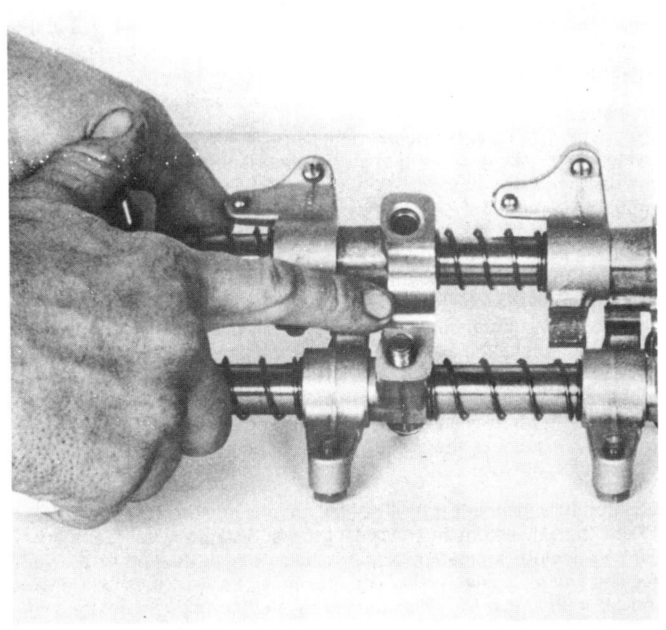

8.11 Inspect the camshaft bearing caps for signs of wear and damage such as galling and pitting

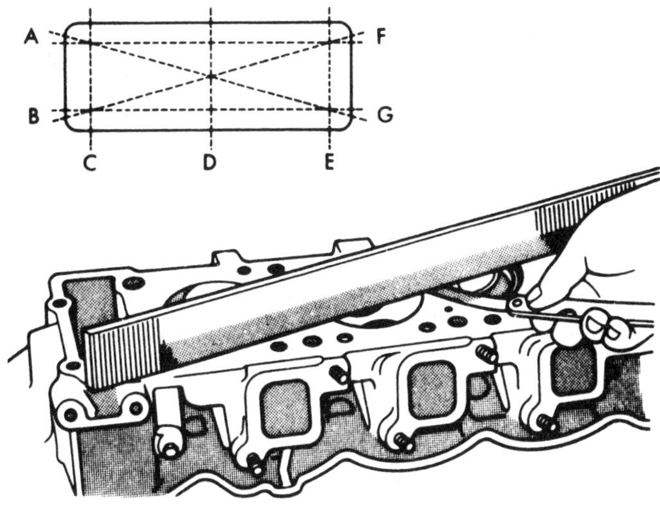

8.12 The cylinder head can be checked for warpage with a straightedge and feeler gauges

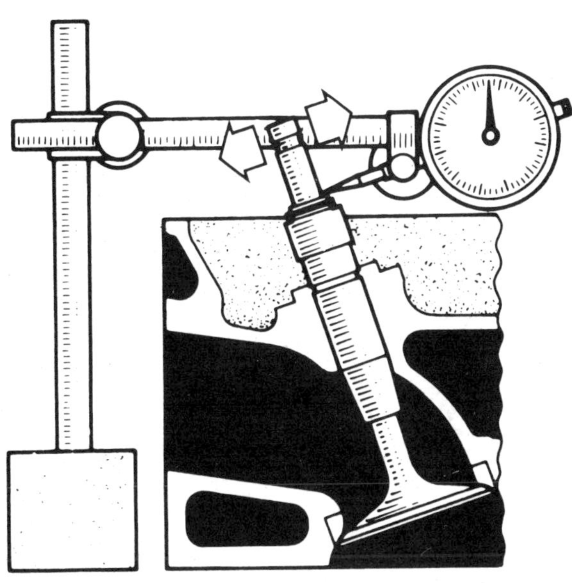

8.14 A dial indicator can be used to check for excessive valve stem-to-guide clearance

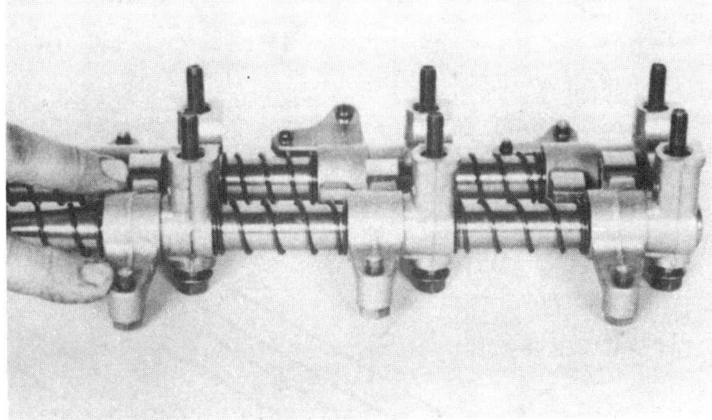

8.16 Look for wear and damage on the rocker arm and adjusting screw surfaces that contact the cam lobe and valve

Inspection

Cylinder head

11 Inspect the head very carefully for cracks, evidence of coolant leakage and other damage. If cracks are discovered, a new cylinder head must be obtained. Check the camshaft bearing surfaces in the head and the bearing caps **(see illustration)**. If there is evidence of excessive cam bearing galling or scoring, the head must be replaced. Failure to do so can lead to camshaft seizure.

12 Using a straightedge and feeler gauge, check the head gasket mating surface for warpage **(see illustration)**. If the warpage exceeds the specified amount, the head should be resurfaced at an automotive machine shop.

13 Examine the valve seats in each of the combustion chambers. If they are pitted, cracked or burned, take the head to an automotive machine shop for a valve job. This procedure is beyond the scope of the home mechanic.

14 Check the valve stem-to-valve guide clearance. Use a dial indicator to measure the lateral movement of each valve stem with the valve in the guide and raised off the seat slightly **(see illustration)**. If there is still some doubt regarding the condition of the valve guides after this check, the exact clearance and condition of the guides can be checked by an automotive machine shop.

Rocker arm assembly (2.2L/2.5L engine)

15 The rocker arms on the 2.2L/2.5L engine ride below the camshaft and contact the valve stem at one end and the hydraulic lash adjuster at the other end. Check each rocker arm for wear, galling and pitting of the contact surfaces. Inspect the lash adjuster contact surfaces for pitting and wear as well.

Rocker arm assembly (2.6L engine)

16 The rocker arms on the 2.6L engine are mounted on shafts that rest in the camshaft bearing caps. The rocker arms contact the valve on one end and the camshaft on the other end. Check the rocker arm faces that contact the camshaft lobes and the ends of the adjusting screws that contact the valve stems. Look for pitting, excessive wear and roughness **(see illustration)**.

17 Check the adjusting screw threads for damage. Make sure they can be threaded in and out of the rocker arms.

18 Slide each rocker arm along the shaft, against the locating spring pressure, and check the shaft for excessive wear and evidence of scoring in the areas that normally contact the rocker arms **(see illustration)**.

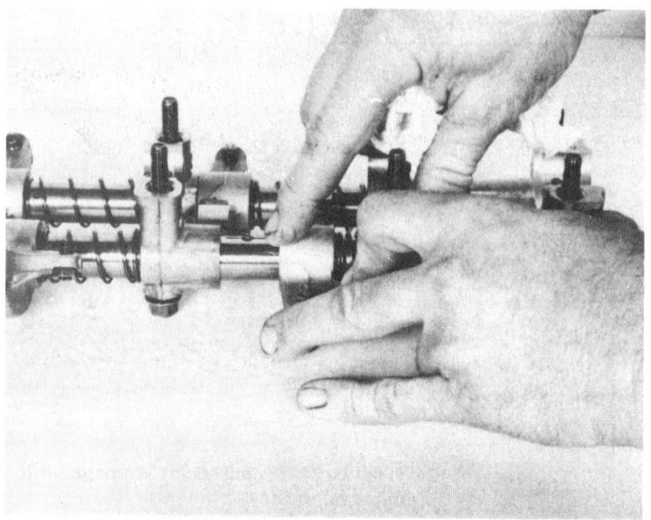

8.18 Check the rocker arm shafts for wear and damage

19 Any damaged or excessively worn parts must be replaced with new ones. Refer to the accompanying exploded view of the rocker arm assembly components for the correct sequence of disassembly and reassembly **(see illustrations)**.

Camshaft

20 Inspect the camshaft bearing journals for excessive wear and evidence of galling, scoring or seizure **(see illustration)**. If the journals are damaged, the bearing surfaces in the head and bearing caps are probably damaged as well. Both the camshaft and cylinder head will have to be replaced.

21 Check the cam lobes for grooves, flaking, pitting and scoring. Measure the cam lobe height and compare it to the Specifications **(see illustration)**. If the lobe height is less than the minimum specified, and/or the lobes are damaged, get a new camshaft.

22 To determine the extent of cam lobe wear on the 2.2L/2.5L engine, measure the height of each lobe at the edge, in the unworn area, and in the center, where the rocker arm contacts the lobe **(see illustration)**. Subtract the center measurement from the edge measurement to obtain the wear, Compare the results to the Specifications.

Valves

23 Carefully inspect each valve face for cracks, pits and burned spots. Check the valve stem and neck for cracks. Rotate the valve and check for any obvious indication that it is bent. Check the end of the stem for pits and excessive wear. The presence of any of these conditions indicates the need for valve service by an automotive machine shop.

24 Measure the width of the valve margin on each valve **(see illustrations)** and compare it to Specifications. Any valve with a margin narrower than specified will have to be replaced with a new one.

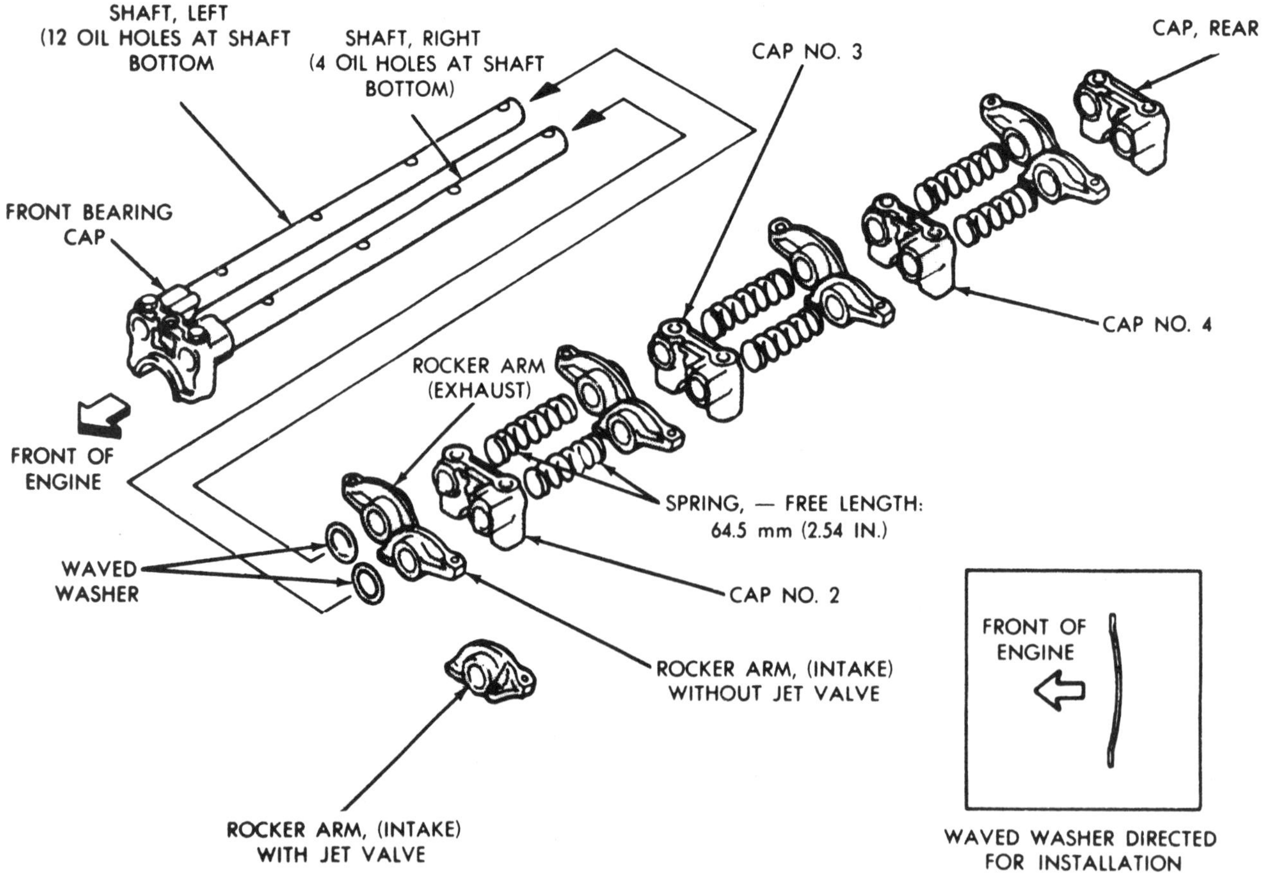

SHAFT, LEFT (12 OIL HOLES AT SHAFT BOTTOM
SHAFT, RIGHT (4 OIL HOLES AT SHAFT BOTTOM)
CAP NO. 3
CAP, REAR
FRONT BEARING CAP
CAP NO. 4
ROCKER ARM (EXHAUST)
FRONT OF ENGINE
SPRING, — FREE LENGTH: 64.5 mm (2.54 IN.)
WAVED WASHER
CAP NO. 2
FRONT OF ENGINE
ROCKER ARM, (INTAKE) WITHOUT JET VALVE
ROCKER ARM, (INTAKE) WITH JET VALVE
WAVED WASHER DIRECTED FOR INSTALLATION

8.19a 2.6L engine rocker arm shaft components — exploded view

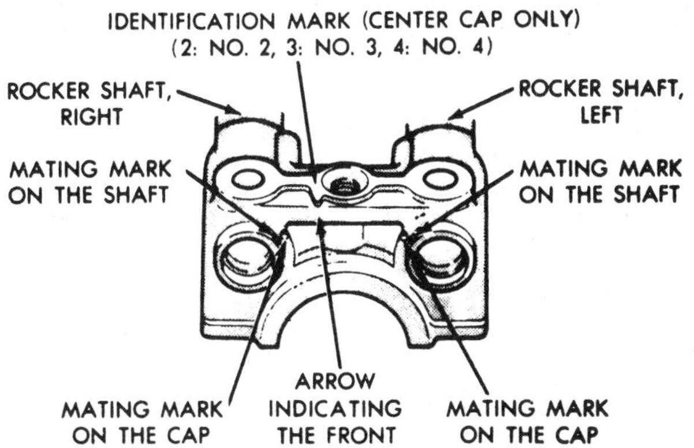

8.19b 2.6L engine camshaft bearing cap marks

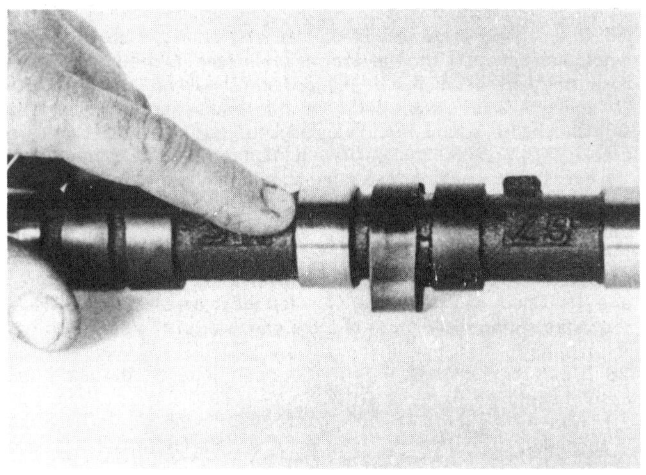

8.20 If the camshaft bearing journals are worn, scored or pitted, a new camshaft is required

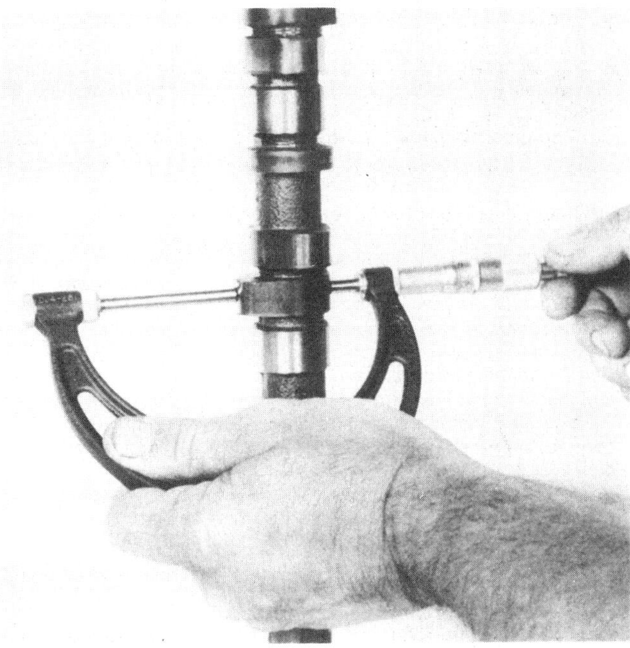

8.21 Measuring camshaft lobe height (2.6L engine)

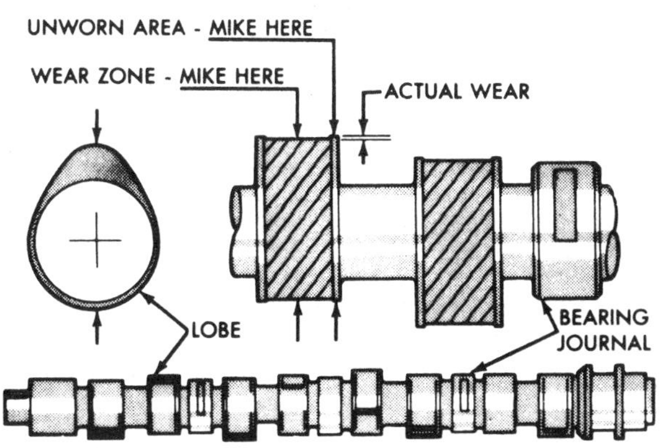

8.22 2.2L/2.5L engine cam lobe wear can be determined by measuring each lobe at the edge and in the center and subtracting the two measurements

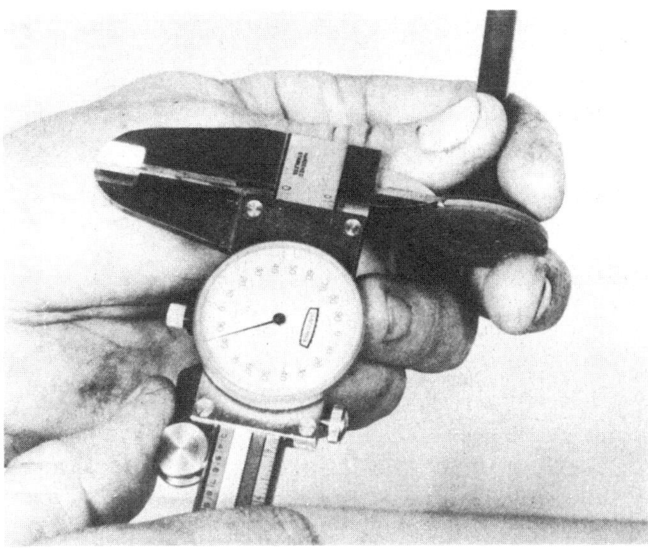

8.24a Measuring valve margin width with a dial caliper

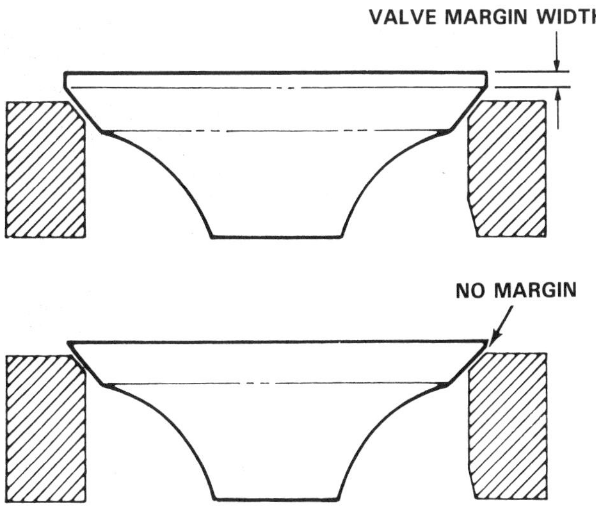

8.24b The margin width on each valve must be as specified (if no margin exists, the valve cannot be reused)

Valve components

25 Check each valve spring for wear and pitting. Measure the free length and compare it to the Specifications **(see illustration)**. If a spring is shorter than specified, it has sagged and should not be reused. Stand the spring on a flat surface and check it for squareness **(see illustration)**.

26 Check the spring retainers and keepers for obvious wear and cracks. Any questionable parts should be replaced with new ones. In the event that a retainer or keeper should fail during operation of the engine, extensive damage will occur.

Jet valve assemblies (2.6L engine)

27 Make sure the valves slide freely in their respective bodies, with no detectable side play. Check each valve head and seat for cracks and pits. Check each spring for wear (on the ends) and cracks. Measure the valve spring free length and the diameter of the stem. Compare the results to the Specifications.

28 If defects are found in any of the components, the entire valve assembly should be replaced with a new one.

29 If the inspection process indicates that the valve components are in generally poor condition and worn beyond the limits specified, which is often the case in an engine being overhauled, reassemble the valves in the cylinder head and refer to Section 9 for valve servicing recommendations.

30 If the inspection turns up no excessively worn parts, and if the valve faces and seats are in good condition, the valve train components can be reinstalled in the cylinder head without major servicing. Refer to the appropriate Section for cylinder head reassembly procedures.

9 Valves – servicing

1 Because of the complex nature of the job and the special tools and equipment needed, servicing of the valves, the valve seats and the valve guides, commonly known as a 'valve job,' is best left to a professional.

2 The home mechanic can remove and disassemble the head, do the initial cleaning and inspection, then reassemble and deliver the head to a dealer service department or an automotive machine shop for the actual valve servicing.

3 The dealer service department or automotive machine shop will remove the valves and springs, recondition or replace the valves and valve seats, recondition the valve guides, check and replace the valve springs, spring retainers and keepers (as necessary), replace the valve seals with new ones, reassemble the valve components and make sure the installed spring height is correct. The cylinder head gasket surface will also be resurfaced if it is warped.

4 After the valve job has been performed by a professional, the head will be in "like new" condition. When the head is returned, be sure to clean it again – with compressed air, if available – to remove any metal particles and abrasive grit that may still be present from the valve service or head resurfacing operations. If you have compressed air, use it blow out all the oil holes and passages too.

10 Cylinder head – reassembly

Refer to illustration 10.3

1 Regardless of whether or not the head was sent to an automotive machine shop for valve servicing, make sure it is clean before beginning reassembly.

2 If the head was sent out for valve servicing, the valves and related components will already be in place. Begin the reassembly procedure with Step 6.

3 Lay all of the spring seats in position, then install new seals on each of the valve guides. Use a soft faced hammer and a deep socket to gently tap each seal into place until it is properly seated on the guide **(see illustration)**. Do not twist or cock the seals during installation or they will not seal properly against the valve stems.

4 Install the valves, taking care not to damage the new valve stem oil seals, the valve springs and the retainers. Coat the valve stems with engine assembly lube or moly-based grease before slipping them into the guides and install the springs with the painted side next to the retainer.

5 Compress the spring with a valve compressor tool and install the keepers. Do not allow the retainer to touch the seal. Release the compressor, making sure the keepers are seated properly in the valve stem groove(s). If necessary, grease can be used to hold the keepers in place until the compressor is released.

6 Double check the installed valve spring height (if it was correct before disassembly, it should still be within the specified limits). **Note:** *On 2.2L/2.5L engines, the spring height is measured from the bottom of the spring to the upper edge of the spring retainer.*

7 Install new seals on each of the jet valve bodies (2.6L engine only). Gently tap them into place with a hammer and deep socket. Lubricate and install the valves and make sure the stems slide smoothly in the valve bodies. Install the springs, the retainers and the keepers. When compressing the springs, be careful not to damage the valve stems or the new seals.

8 Install a new O-ring on each jet valve body and apply a thin coat of clean engine oil or grease to each O-ring, the jet valve threads and the seating surfaces.

9 Carefully thread the jet valve assemblies into the cylinder head and tighten them to the specified torque. **Caution:** *Do not tilt the socket – the valve stems bend very easily.*

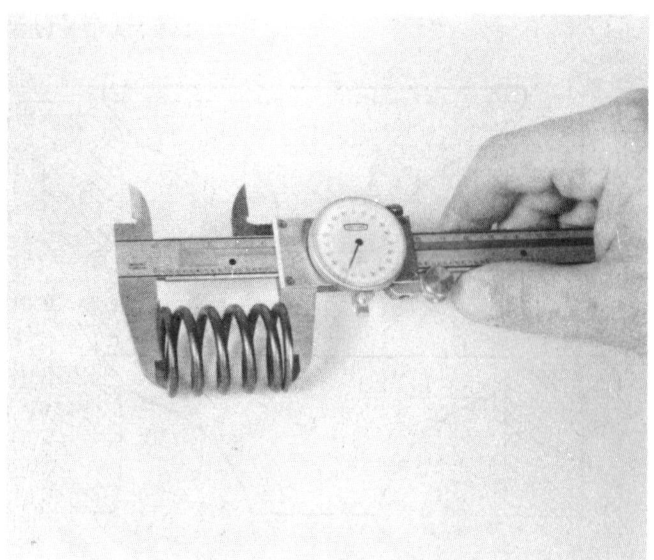

8.25a Measure the free length of each valve spring with a dial or vernier caliper

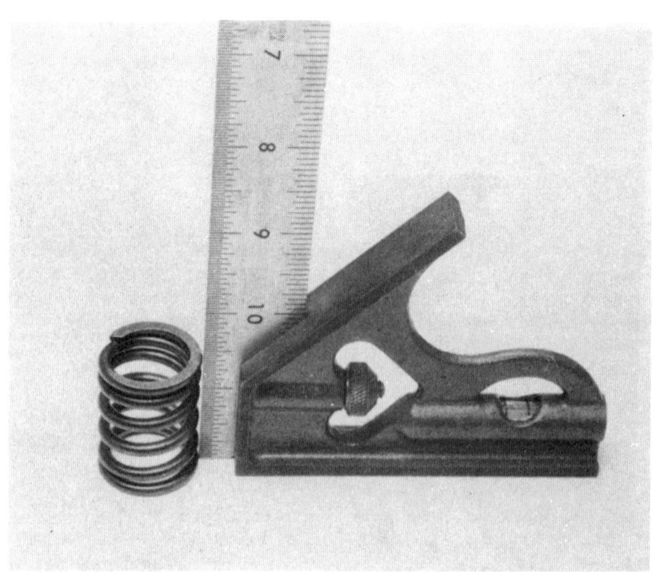

8.25b Check each valve spring for squareness

11 Piston/connecting rod assembly – removal

Refer to illustrations 11.1, 11.5 and 11.7

1 Using a ridge reamer, completely remove the ridge at the top of each cylinder **(see illustration)**. Follow the manufacturer's instructions provided with the ridge reaming tool. **Caution:** *Failure to remove the ridge before attempting to remove the piston/connecting rod assemblies will result in piston breakage.*

2 With the engine in the upside-down position, remove the oil pickup tube and screen assembly from the bottom of the engine block. It is held in place with two bolts.

3 Before the connecting rod caps are removed, check the rod end play. Mount a dial indicator with its stem in line with the crankshaft and touching the side of the number one connecting rod cap.

4 Push the connecting rod backward, as far as possible, and zero the dial indicator. Next, push the connecting rod all the way to the front and check the reading on the dial indicator. The distance that it moves is the end play. If the end play exceeds the service limit, a new connecting rod will be required. Repeat the procedure for the remaining connecting rods.

5 An alternative method is to slip feeler gauges between the connecting rod and the crankshaft throw until the play is removed **(see illustration)**. The end play is equal to the thickness of the feeler gauge(s).

6 Check the connecting rods and connecting rod caps for identification marks. If they are not plainly marked, use a small punch or scribe to label them correctly so that they will be reinstalled to the same cylinder from which they were removed.

7 Loosen each of the connecting rod cap nuts 1/2-turn. Remove the number one connecting rod cap and bearing insert. Do not drop the bearing insert out of the cap. Slip a short length of plastic or rubber hose over each connecting rod cap bolt to protect the crankshaft journal and cylinder wall when the piston is removed **(see illustration)** and push the connecting rod/piston assembly out through the top of the engine.

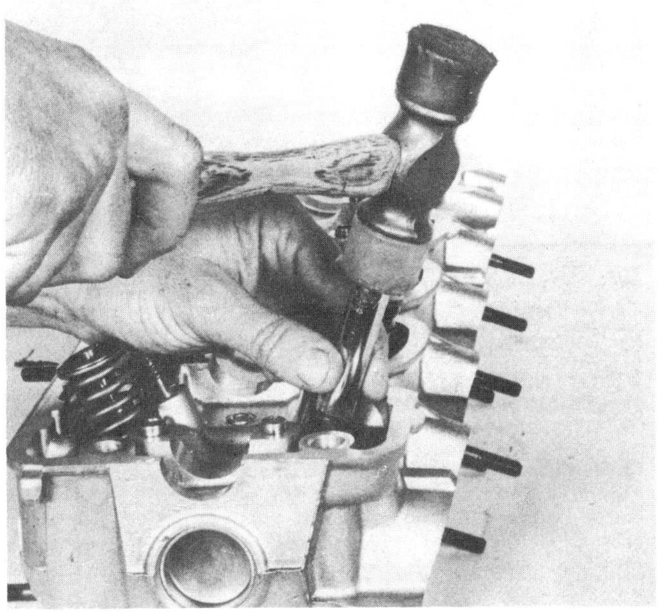

10.3 Install the new valve guide seals with a hammer and deep socket

11.1 A special tool is required to remove the ridge from the top of each cylinder

2C

11.5 Checking connecting rod end play with a feeler gauge

11.7 To prevent damage to the crankshaft journals and cylinder walls, slip sections of hose over the rod bolts before removing the pistons

12.1 Checking crankshaft end play with a dial indicator

12.3 Checking crankshaft end play with a feeler gauge

Use a wooden tool to push on the upper bearing insert in the connecting rod. If resistance is felt, double-check to make sure that the ridge has been completely removed from the cylinder.

8 Repeat this procedure for each of the remaining cylinders. After removal, reattach the connecting rod caps and bearing inserts to their respective connecting rods and install the cap nuts finger-tight. Leaving the old bearing inserts in place until reassembly will help prevent the connecting rod bearing surfaces from being accidentally nicked or gouged.

12 Crankshaft – removal

Refer to illustrations 12.1, 12.3 and 12.4

Note: *The front crankshaft oil seal housing (2.2L/2.5L engine), the rear crankshaft oil seal housing and the oil pickup tube and screen assembly must be removed before the crankshaft is removed.*

1 Before the crankshaft is removed, check the end play. Mount a dial indicator with the stem in line with the crankshaft and just touching one of the crank throws **(see illustration)**.

2 Push the crankshaft all the way to the rear and zero the diai indicator. Next, pry the crankshaft to the front as far as possible and check the reading on the dial indicator. The distance that it moves is the end play. If it is greater than specified, check the crankshaft thrust surfaces for wear. If no wear is apparent, new main bearings should correct the end play.

3 If a dial indicator is not available, feeler gauges can be used. Gently pry or push the crankshaft all the way to the front of the engine. Slip feeler gauges between the crankshaft and the front face of the thrust main bearing to determine the clearance **(see illustration)**.

4 Loosen each of the main bearing cap bolts 1/4-turn at a time, until they can be removed by hand. Check the main bearing caps to see if they are marked correctly with respect to their locations. They are usually numbered consecutively from the front of the engine to the rear and may have arrows which point to the front of the engine. If they are not marked, label them with number stamping dies or a center punch **(see illustration)**.

5 Gently tap the caps with a soft-faced hammer, then separate them from the engine block. If necessary, use the main bearing cap bolts as levers to remove the caps. Sometimes the bearing inserts come out with the caps. If they do, don't drop them.

6 Carefully lift the crankshaft out of the engine. It is a good idea to have an assistant available, since the crankshaft is quite heavy. With the bearing inserts in place in the engine block and in the main bearing caps, return the caps to their respective locations on the engine block and tighten the bolts finger tight.

12.4 Mark the main bearing caps with a center punch before removing them

13 Engine block – cleaning

Refer to illustrations 13.1a, 13.1b and 13.10

1 Remove the soft plugs from the engine block. To do this, knock the plugs into the block, using a hammer and punch, then grasp them with a large pair of pliers and pull them back through the holes **(see illustrations)**.

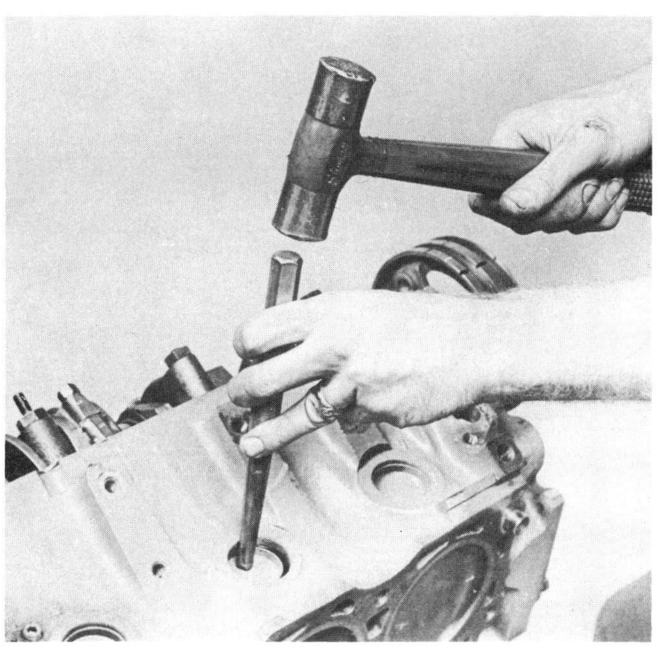

13.1a Drive each soft plug into the block with a large punch and hammer, . . .

13.1b . . . then grip it with a pair of pliers and lever it out of the hole

13.10 A large socket, mounted on an extension, can be used to drive the new soft plugs into the block

2 Using a gasket scraper, remove all traces of gasket material from the engine block. Be very careful not to nick or gouge the gasket sealing surfaces.

3 Remove the main bearing caps and separate the bearing inserts from the caps and the engine block. Tag the bearings to indicate the cap or block from which they were removed and the cylinder to which they must be returned. Set them aside.

4 Using an allen wrench of the correct size, remove any threaded oil gallery plugs from the block.

5 If the engine is extremely dirty it should be taken to an automotive machine shop to be steam cleaned or hot tanked.

6 After the block is returned, clean all oil holes and oil galleries one more time. Brushes for cleaning oil holes and galleries are available at most auto parts stores. Flush the passages with warm water until the water runs clear, dry the block thoroughly and wipe all machined surfaces with a light, rust preventive oil. If you have access to compressed air, use it to speed the drying process and to blow out all the oil holes and galleries.

7 If the block is not extremely dirty or sludged up, you can do an adequate cleaning job with warm soapy water and a stiff brush. Take plenty of time and do a thorough job. Regardless of the method used, thoroughly clean all oil holes and galleries, dry the block completely and coat all machined surfaces with light oil.

8 The threaded holes in the block must be clean to ensure accurate torque readings during reassembly. Run the proper size tap into each of the holes to remove any rust, corrosion, thread sealant or sludge and to restore any damaged threads. If possible, use compressed air to clear the holes of debris produced by this operation. Thoroughly clean the threads on the head bolts and the main bearing cap bolts as well.

9 Reinstall the main bearing caps and tighten the bolts finger-tight.

10 After coating the sealing surfaces of the new soft plugs with a good quality gasket sealer, install them in the engine block **(see illustration)**. Make sure they are driven in straight and seated properly or leakage could result. Special tools are available for this job, but equally good results can be obtained with a hammer and large socket. The outside diameter of the socket should just slip into the soft plug.

11 If the engine is not going to be reassembled right away, cover it with a large plastic trash bag to keep it clean.

14 Engine block – inspection

Refer to illustrations 14.4a, 14.4b, 14.4c, 14.7a and 14.7b

1 Thoroughly clean the engine block as described in Section 13 and double-check to make sure that the ridge at the top of each cylinder has been completely removed.

2 Visually check the block for cracks, rust and corrosion. Look for stripped threads in the threaded holes. It is also a good idea to have the block checked for hidden cracks by an automotive machine shop that has the special equipment to do this type of work. If defects are found, have the block repaired. If this isn't possible, replace it.

3 Check the cylinder bores for scuffing and scoring.

4 Measure each cylinder's diameter at the top (just under the ridge),

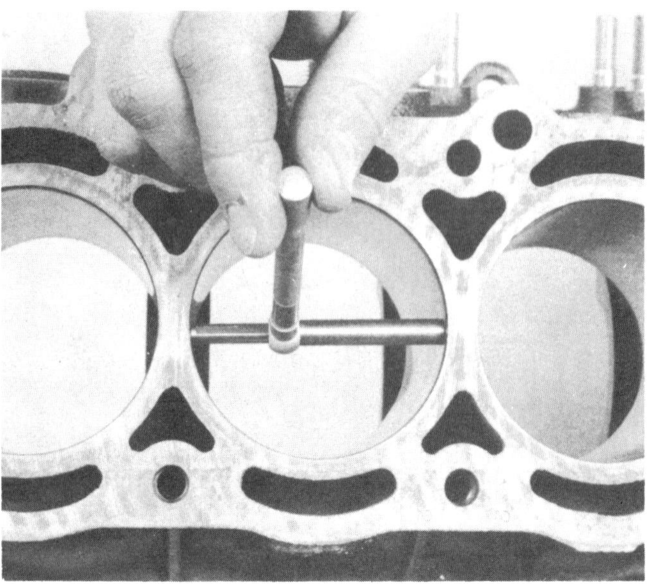
14.4a Use a telescoping gauge to determine the cylinder bore size, . . .

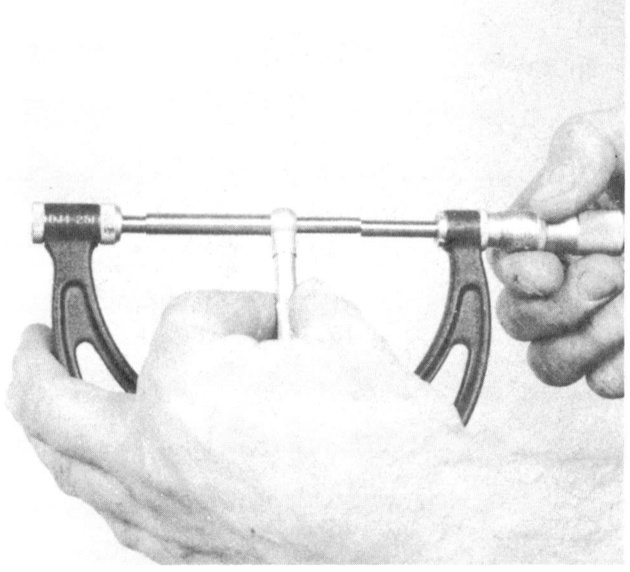
14.4b . . . then measure the gauge with a micrometer to obtain the diameter in inches

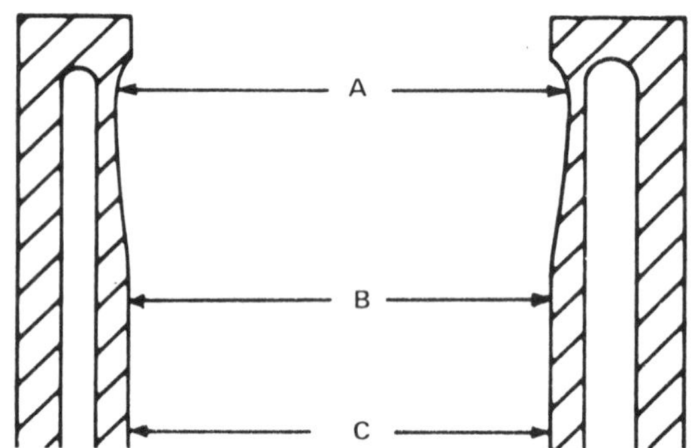

14.4c Measure the diameter of each cylinder just under the wear ridge (A), at the center (B) and at the bottom (C)

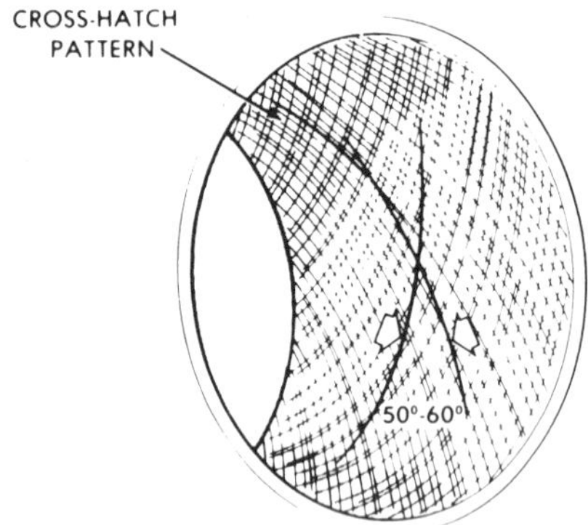

14.7b The cylinder hone should leave a cross-hatch pattern with the lines intersecting at approximately a 60° angle

14.7a A surfacing hone should be used to prepare the cylinders for the new rings

center and bottom of the cylinder bore, parallel to the crankshaft axis **(see illustrations)**. Next, measure each cylinder's diameter at the same three locations across the crankshaft axis. Compare the results to the Specifications. If the cylinder walls are badly scuffed or scored, or if they are out of round or tapered beyond the specified limits, have the engine block rebored and honed at an automotive machine shop. If the block is rebored, you will have to obtain correctly oversized pistons and rings.

5 If the cylinders are in reasonably good condition and not worn to the outside of the limits, and if the piston-to-cylinder clearances can be maintained properly, then they do not have to be rebored. But they still must be honed.

6 Before honing the cylinders, install the main bearing caps and tighten the bolts to the specified torque.

7 To perform the honing operation you will need the proper size flexible hone and fine stones, plenty of light oil or honing oil, some rags and an electric drill motor. Mount the hone in the drill motor, compress the stones and slip the hone into the first cylinder **(see illustration)**. Lubricate the cylinder thoroughly, turn on the drill and move the hone up and down in the cylinder at a pace which will produce a fine crosshatch pattern on the cylinder walls with the crosshatch lines intersecting at approximately a 60° angle **(see illustration)**. Be sure to use plenty of lubricant. Do not withdraw the hone from the cylinder while it is running. Instead, shut off the drill and continue moving the hone up and down in the cylinder until it comes to a complete stop, then compress the stones and withdraw the hone. Wipe the oil out of the cylinder and repeat the procedure on the remaining cylinders. If you

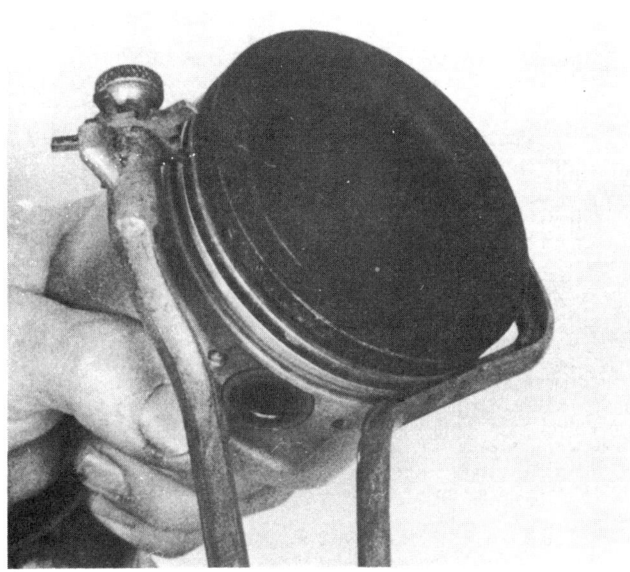
15.4a If available, a ring groove cleaning tool can be used to remove carbon from the ring grooves

15.4b Or use a piece of broken piston ring (use caution not to remove any of the piston material)

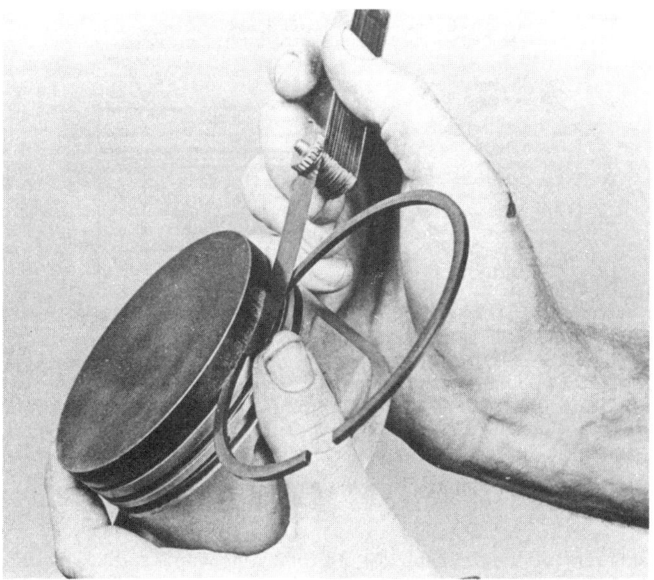
15.10 Checking the piston ring side clearance with a feeler gauge

do not have the tools or do not desire to perform the honing operation, most automotive machine shops will do it for a reasonable fee.

8 After the honing job is complete, chamfer the top edges of the cylinder bores with a small file so the rings will not catch when the pistons are installed.

9 The entire engine block must be thoroughly washed again with warm, soapy water to remove all traces of the abrasive grit produced during the honing operation. Be sure to run a brush through all oil holes and galleries and flush them with running water. After rinsing, dry the block and apply a coat of light rust preventative oil to all machined surfaces. Wrap the block in a plastic trash bag to keep it clean and set it aside until reassembly.

15 Piston/connecting rod assembly — inspection

Refer to illustrations 15.4a, 15.4b, 15.10, 15.11a, 15.11b, 15.11c and 15.11d

1 Before the inspection process can be carried out, the piston/connecting rod assemblies must be cleaned and the original piston rings removed from the pistons. **Note:** *Always use new piston rings when the engine is reassembled.*

2 Using a piston ring installation tool, carefully remove the rings from the pistons. Do not nick or gouge the pistons in the process.

3 Scrape all traces of carbon from the top (or crown) of the piston. A hand-held wire brush or a piece of fine emery cloth can be used once the majority of the deposits have been scraped away. **Caution:** *Do not, under any circumstances, use a wire brush mounted in a drill motor to remove deposits from the pistons. The piston material is soft and will be eroded away by the wire brush.*

4 Use a piston ring groove cleaning tool to remove any carbon deposits from the ring grooves **(see illustration)**. If a tool is not available, a broken piece of the old ring will do the job **(see illustration)**. Be very careful to remove only the carbon deposits. Do not remove any metal and do not nick or scratch the sides of the ring grooves.

5 Once the deposits have been removed, clean the piston/rod assemblies with solvent and dry them thoroughly. Make sure that the oil return holes in the back sides of the lower ring grooves are clear.

6 Normal piston wear is indicated by even vertical lines on the piston thrust surfaces and slight looseness of the top ring in its groove. If the pistons are not damaged or worn excessively and if the engine block is not rebored, new pistons will not be necessary. However, new piston rings should always be used when an engine is rebuilt.

7 Carefully inspect each piston for cracks around the skirt, at the pin bosses and at the ring lands.

8 Look for scoring and scuffing on the thrust faces of the skirt, holes in the piston crown and burned areas at the edge of the crown. If the skirt is scored or scuffed, the engine may have been suffering from overheating and/or abnormal combustion which caused excessively high operating temperatures. The cooling and lubrication systems should be checked thoroughly. A hole in the piston crown is an indication that abnormal combustion (preignition) was occurring. Burned areas at the edge of the piston crown are usually evidence of spark knock (detonation). If any of the above problems exist, the causes must be corrected or the damage will occur again.

9 Corrosion of the piston, evidenced by pitting, indicates that coolant is leaking into the combustion chamber and/or the crankcase. Again, the cause must be corrected or the problem will persist in the rebuilt engine.

10 Measure the piston ring side clearance by laying a new piston ring in each ring groove and slipping a feeler gauge between the ring and the edge of the ring groove **(see illustration)**. Check the clearance at three or four locations around each groove. Be sure to use the correct ring for each groove; they are different. If the side clearance is greater than specified, new pistons will have to be used.

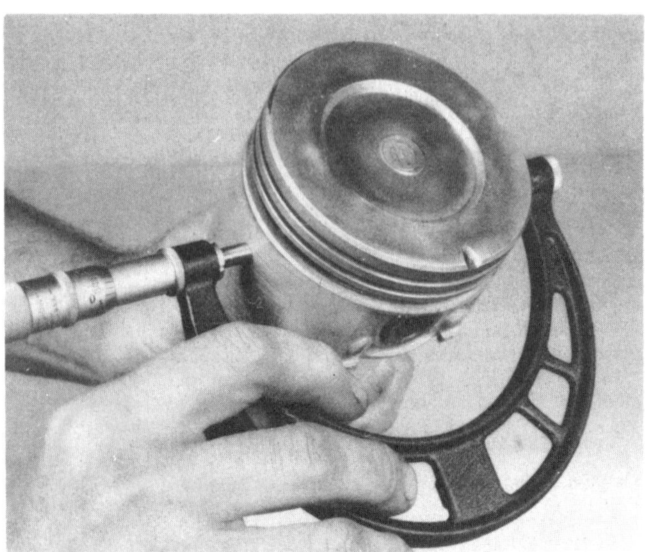

15.11a Measure the piston diameter at the point indicated in the text

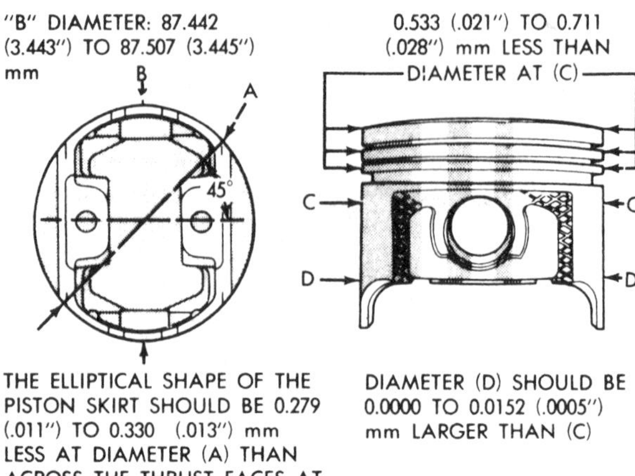

15.11b 1982 and 1983 2.2L engine piston measurement details

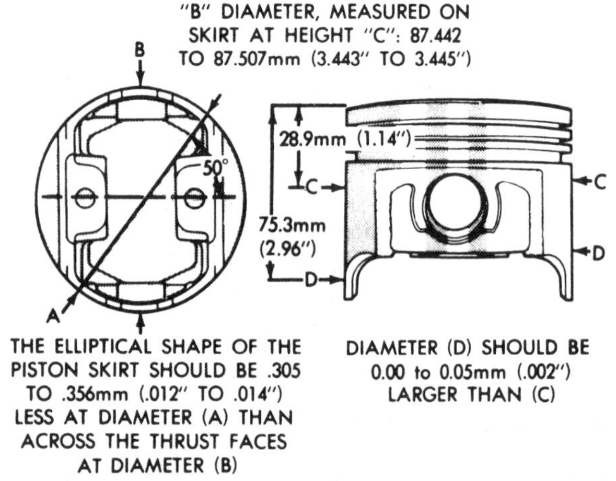

15.11c 1984 and later 2.2L/2.5L engine piston measurement details (non-turbocharged)

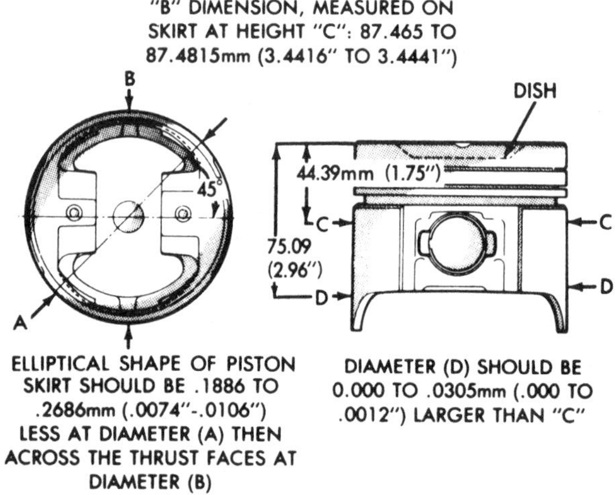

15.11d Turbocharged engine piston measurement details

11 Check the piston-to-bore clearance by measuring the bore (see Section 14) and the piston diameter **(see illustration)**. Make sure that the pistons and bores are correctly matched. Measure the piston across the skirt, on the thrust faces (at an angle to the piston pin). On *2.6L engines*, take the measurement about 0.080-inch (2 mm) up from the bottom of the skirt. On *2.2L/2.5L engines*, the diameter must be measured 1.140-inches (28.9 mm) down from the edge of the crown (non-turbocharged engine). On turbocharged engines, take the measurement 1.750-inches (44.39 mm) down from the edge **(see illustrations)**. Subtract the piston diameter from the bore diameter to obtain the clearance. If it is greater than specified, the block will have to be rebored and new pistons and rings installed. Check the piston-to-rod clearance by twisting the piston and rod in opposite directions. Any noticeable play indicates that there is excessive wear, which must be corrected. The piston/connecting rod assemblies should be taken to an automotive machine shop to have the pistons and connecting rods rebored and new pins installed.

12 If the pistons must be removed from the connecting rods – for instance, when new pistons must be installed – or if the piston pins have too much play in them, they should be taken to an automotive machine shop. Have them checked for bend and twist too. Automotive machine shops have special equipment for this purpose. Unless new pistons or connecting rods must be installed, do not disassemble the pistons from the connecting rods.

13 Check the connecting rods for cracks and other damage. Temporarily remove the rod caps, lift out the old bearing inserts, wipe the rod and cap bearing surfaces clean and inspect them for nicks, gouges and scratches. After checking the rods, replace the old bearings, slip the caps into place and tighten the nuts finger-tight.

16 Crankshaft – inspection

Refer to illustration 16.2

1 Clean the crankshaft with solvent and dry it thoroughly. Be sure to clean the oil holes with a stiff brush and flush them with solvent. Check the main and connecting rod bearing journals for uneven wear, scoring, pitting and cracks. Check the remainder of the crankshaft for cracks and damage.

2 Measure the diameter of the main and connecting rod journals with a micrometer **(see illustration)** and compare the results to the Specifications. By measuring the diameter at a number of points around the journal's circumference, you will be able to determine whether or not the journal is out-of-round. Take the measurement at each end of the journal, near the crank counterweights, to determine whether the journal is tapered.

3 If the crankshaft journals are damaged, tapered, out-of-round or worn beyond the limits given in the Specifications, have the crankshaft reground by an automotive machine shop. Be sure to use the correct

16.2 Measure the diameter of each crankshaft journal at several points to detect taper and out-of-round conditions

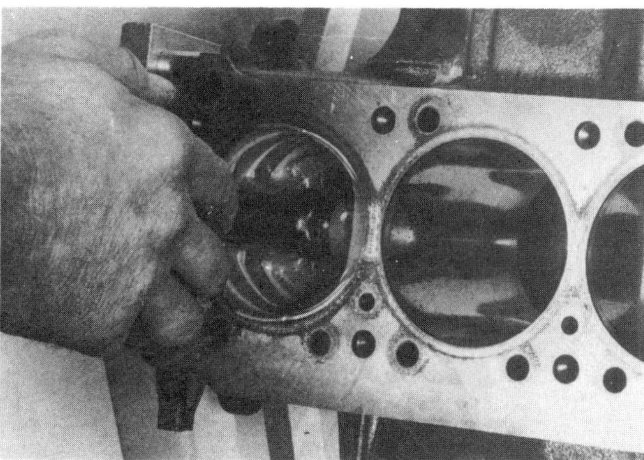

18.3a Use the piston to square up the ring in the cylinder prior to checking the ring end gap

size bearing inserts if the crankshaft is reconditioned.

4 Refer to Section 17 and examine the main and rod bearing inserts.

17 Main and connecting rod bearings — inspection

Caution: *On turbocharged engines, whenever main, connecting rod or cam bearings are replaced, the turbocharger must be flushed with clean engine oil.*

1 The main and connecting rod bearings should always be replaced with new ones when the engine is overhauled. But don't discard the old bearings. They can reveal valuable information about the condition of the engine.

2 Bearing failure occurs because of lack of lubrication, the presence of dirt or other foreign particles, overloading the engine and corrosion. Regardless of the cause of bearing failure, it must be corrected before the engine is reassembled to prevent it from happening again.

3 When examining the bearings, remove them from the engine block, the main bearing caps, the connecting rods and the rod caps and lay them out on a clean surface in the same order and location which they occupied in the engine. This is the only way you can match a bearing problem to its corresponding crankshaft journal.

4 Dirt and other foreign particles get into the engine in a number of ways. Sometimes it isn't removed from the engine during assembly. Or it enters through filters or breathers. Either way, it gets into the oil and then into the bearings. Metal chips from machining operations and normal engine wear invade the oil too. Abrasives are sometimes left in engine components after reconditioning, especially when parts are not thoroughly cleaned using the proper cleaning methods. No matter where it comes from, this stuff usually finds its way into bearing clearances, where it embeds itself into soft bearing material. This kind of problem is easy to identify. Larger particles, however, will not embed in the bearing. They will score or gouge the bearing and shaft. So even though the cause itself may not be visible, the effect will be just as easy to see as smaller embedded particles. The best, and really the only, prevention for either of these causes of bearing failure is to clean all parts thoroughly and keep everything spotlessly clean during engine assembly. Frequent and regular engine oil and filter changes are also recommended.

5 Lack of lubrication (or lubrication breakdown) has a number of interrelated causes. Excessive engine operation heat thins the oil. Overloading between journals and bearing surfaces sometimes squeezes the thin film of oil from the bearing face. Oil leakage or throw off from excessive bearing clearances, worn oil pump or high engine speeds all contribute to lubrication breakdown. Blocked oil passages, which usually are the result of misaligned oil holes in a bearing shell, will also oil starve a bearing and destroy it. When lack of lubrication is the cause of bearing failure, the bearing material is wiped or extruded from the steel backing of the bearing. Temperatures may increase to the point where the steel backing turns blue from overheating.

6 Driving habits can have a definite effect on bearing life. Full throttle, low speed operation, lugging the engine, puts very high loads on bearings, which tends to squeeze out the oil film. These loads cause the bearings to flex, which produces fine cracks in the bearing face (fatigue failure). Eventually the bearing material will loosen in pieces and tear away from the steel backing. Short trip driving leads to corrosion of bearings because insufficient engine heat is produced to drive off the condensed water and corrosive gases. These products collect in the engine oil, forming acid and sludge. As the oil is carried to the engine bearings, the acid attacks and corrodes the bearing material.

18.3b Measure the ring end gap with a feeler gauge

7 Incorrect bearing installation during engine assembly will lead to bearing failure as well. Tight fitting bearings leave insufficient bearing oil clearance and will result in oil starvation. Dirt or foreign particles trapped behind a bearing insert result in high spots on the bearing which lead to failure.

18 Piston rings — installation

Refer to illustrations 18.3a, 18.3b, 18.9a, 18.9b, 18.10, 18.11 and 18.12

1 Before installing the new piston rings, the ring end gaps must be checked. It is assumed that the piston ring side clearance has been measured and verified to be correct (Section 15).

2 Lay out the piston/connecting rod assemblies and the new ring sets so the ring sets will be matched with the same piston and cylinder during the end gap measurement and engine assembly.

3 Insert the top (number one) ring into the first cylinder and square it up with the cylinder walls by pushing it in with the top of the piston **(see illustration)**. The ring should be near the bottom of the cylinder at the lower limit of ring travel. To measure the end gap, slip a feeler gauge between the ends of the ring **(see illustration)**. Compare the measurement to the Specifications.

18.9a Installing the spacer/expander in the oil control ring groove

18.9b *Do not* use a piston ring tool when installing the oil ring side rails

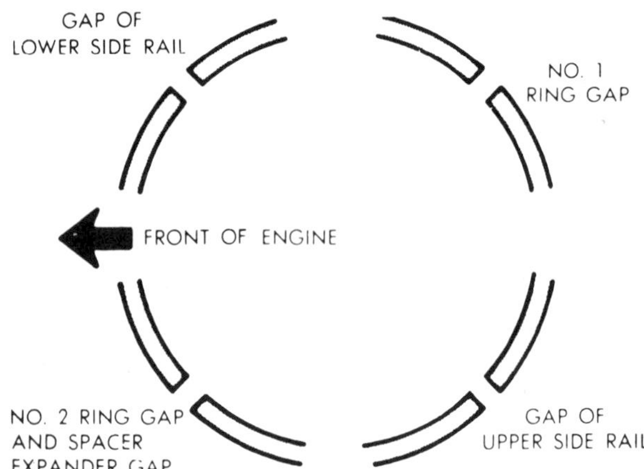

18.10 Position the ring end gaps as shown here before installing the pistons in the block

18.11 The compression rings must be installed with the marks facing the top of the engine

4 If the gap is larger or smaller than specified, double-check to make sure that you have the correct rings before proceeding.

5 If the gap is too small, it must be enlarged or the ring ends may come in contact with each other during engine operation, which can cause serious damage to the engine. The end gap can be increased by filing the ring ends very carefully with a fine file. Mount the file in a vise equipped with soft jaws, slip the ring over the file with the ends contacting the file face and slowly move the ring to remove material from the ends. When performing this operation, file only from the outside in.

6 Excess end gap is not critical unless it is greater than 0.040-inch (1 mm). Again, double-check to make sure you have the correct rings for your engine.

7 Repeat the procedure for each ring that will be installed in the first cylinder and for each ring in the remaining cylinders. Remember to keep rings, pistons and cylinders matched up.

8 Once the ring end gaps have been checked and corrected, the rings can be installed on the pistons.

9 The oil control ring (lowest one on the piston) is installed first. It is composed of three separate components. Slip the spacer/expander into the groove **(see illustration)**, then install the lower side rail with the size mark and manufacturer's stamp facing up. Do not use a piston ring installation tool on the oil ring side rails, as they may be damaged. Instead, place one end of the side rail into the groove between the spacer/expander and the ring land, hold it firmly in place and slide a finger around the piston while pushing the rail into the groove **(see illustration)**. Next, install the upper side rail in the same manner.

10 After the three oil ring components have been installed, check to make sure that both the upper and lower side rails can be turned smoothly in the ring groove. Position the end gaps correctly **(see illustration)**.

11 The number two (middle) ring is installed next. It is stamped with a mark which should face toward the top of the piston **(see illustration)**. **Note:** *Always follow the instructions printed on the ring package or box. Different manufacturers may specify slight variations in method of installation. Do not mix up the top and middle rings--they have different cross-sections.*

12 Use a piston ring installation tool and make sure that the identification mark is facing the top of the piston, then slip the ring into the middle groove on the piston **(see illustration)**. Do not expand the ring any more than is necessary to slide it over the piston.

13 Install the number one (top) ring in the same manner. Make sure the identifying mark is facing up. Be careful not to confuse the number one and number two rings. Refer to the illustration for ring gap positioning.

14 Repeat this procedure for the remaining pistons and rings.

19 Crankshaft — installation and main bearing oil clearance check

Refer to illustrations 19.11 and 19.14

1 Crankshaft installation is generally one of the first steps in engine reassembly. It is assumed at this point that the engine block and

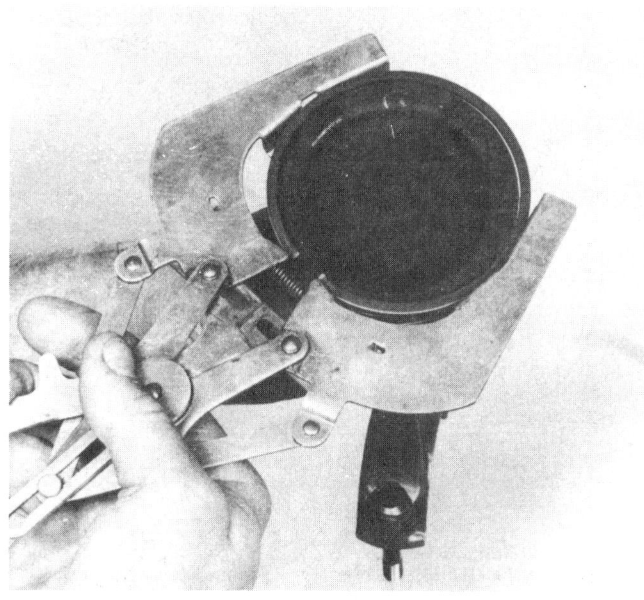

18.12 Install the compression rings with a ring expander

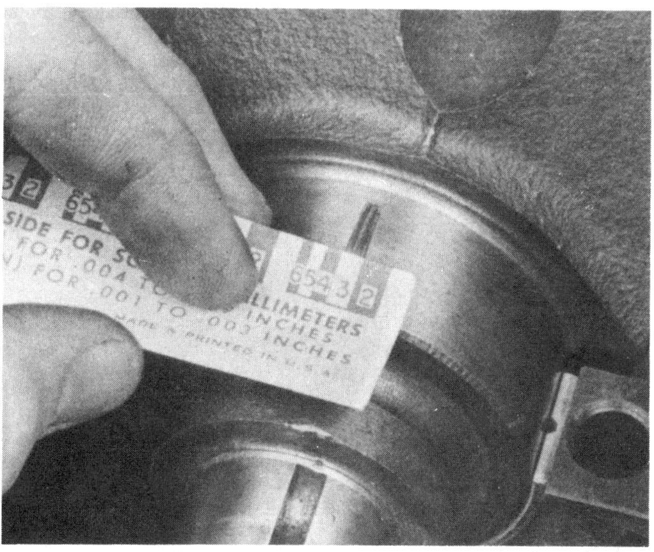

19.14 The crushed Plastigage is compared to the scale printed on the container to obtain the main bearing oil clearance (be sure to use the correct scale – standard and metric scales are included)

crankshaft have been cleaned, inspected and repaired or reconditioned.
2 Position the engine with the bottom facing up.
3 Remove the main bearing cap bolts and lift out the caps. Lay them out in the proper order to ensure that they are installed correctly.
4 If they are still in place, remove the old bearing inserts from the block and the main bearing caps. Wipe the main bearing surfaces of the block and caps with a clean, lint-free cloth. They must be kept spotlessly clean.
5 Clean the back sides of the new main bearing inserts and lay one bearing half in each main bearing saddle in the block. Lay the other bearing half from each bearing set in the corresponding main bearing cap. Make sure the tab on the bearing insert fits into the recess in the block or cap. Also, the oil holes in the block must line up with the oil holes in the bearing insert. Do not hammer the bearing into place and do not nick or gouge the bearing faces. No lubrication should be used at this time.
6 The flanged thrust bearing must be installed in the number three (center) cap and saddle.
7 Clean the faces of the bearings in the block and the crankshaft

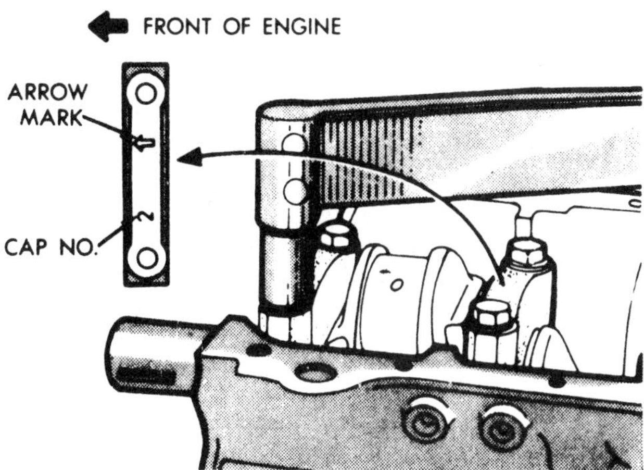

19.11 On 2.6L engines, the main bearing caps are marked with an arrow which must point toward the front of the engine

main bearing journals with a clean, lint-free cloth. Check or clean the oil holes in the crankshaft, as any dirt here can go only one way – straight through the new bearings.

8 Once you are certain that the crankshaft is clean, carefully lay it in position (an assistant would be very helpful here) in the main bearings.
9 Before the crankshaft can be permanently installed, the main bearing oil clearance must be checked.
10 Trim several pieces of the appropriate size of Plastigage so they are slightly shorter than the width of the main bearings, and place one piece on each crankshaft main bearing journal, parallel with the journal axis.
11 Clean the faces of the bearings in the caps and install the caps in their respective positions (do not mix them up) with the arrows pointing toward the front of the engine **(see illustration)**. Do not disturb the Plastigage.
12 Starting with the center main and working out toward the ends, tighten the main bearing cap bolts, in three steps, to the specified torque. **Note:** *Do not rotate the crankshaft at any time during this operation.*
13 Remove the bolts and carefully lift off the main bearing caps. Keep them in order. Do not disturb the Plastigage or rotate the crankshaft. If any of the main bearing caps are difficult to remove, tap them gently from side-to-side with a soft-faced hammer to loosen them.
14 Compare the width of the crushed Plastigage on each journal to the scale printed on the Plastigage wrapper to obtain the main bearing oil clearance **(see illustration)**. Check the Specifications to make sure your measurement is correct.
15 If the clearance is not correct, double-check to make sure you have the right size bearing inserts. Also, make sure that no dirt or oil was between the bearing inserts and the main bearing caps or the block when the clearance was measured.
16 Carefully scrape all traces of the Plastigage material off the main bearing journals and/or the bearing faces. Do not nick or scratch the bearing faces.
17 Carefully lift the crankshaft out of the engine. Clean the bearing faces in the block, then apply a thin, uniform layer of clean, high quality moly-based grease or engine assembly lube to each of the bearing surfaces. Be sure to coat the thrust faces as well as the journal face of the thrust bearing.
18 Make sure the crankshaft journals are clean, then lay the crankshaft back in place in the block. Clean the faces of the bearings in the caps, then apply a thin, uniform layer of clean, moly-based grease or engine assembly lube to each of the bearing faces. Install the caps in their respective positions with the arrows pointing toward the front of the engine. Install the bolts and tighten them to the specified torque, starting with the center main and working out toward the ends. Work up to the final torque in three steps.
19 On manual transaxle models, install a new pilot bearing in the end of the crankshaft. Lubricate the crankshaft cavity and the outer circum-

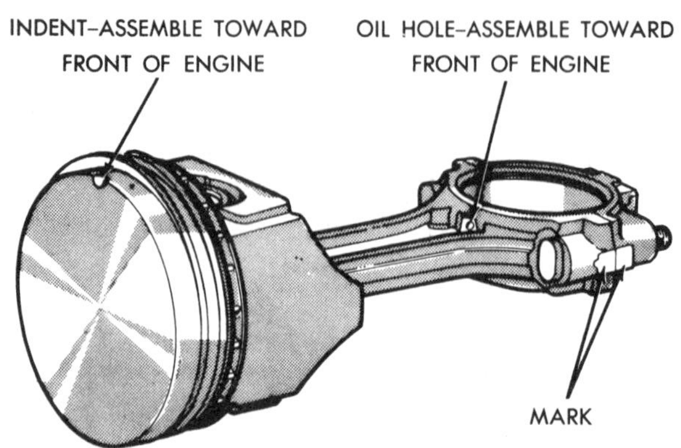

20.8a On 1982 through 1985 2.2L/2.5L engines, the indent on the piston and the oil hole in the rod must face the front of the engine

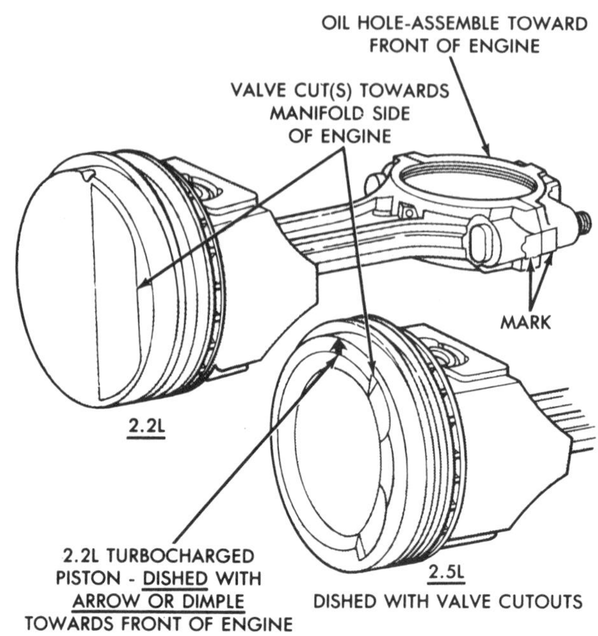

20.8b 1986 and later model 2.2L/2.5L piston installation details

ference of the bearing with clean engine oil and place the bearing in position. Tap it fully and evenly into the cavity using a section of pipe and a hammer. Lubricate the inside of the bearing with grease.

20 Rotate the crankshaft a number of times by hand to check for any obvious binding.

21 The final step is to check crankshaft end play with a feeler gauge or a dial indicator (Section 12).

20 Piston/connecting rod assembly — installation and rod bearing oil clearance check

Refer to illustrations 20.8a, 20.8b, 20.8c, 20.9, 20.11 and 20.13

Note: *Since the rod bolt nuts on 2.2L/2.5L engines are tightened using a new method, they should be examined carefully before installing the pistons/rods. If the rod bolt threads are "necked down" they should be replaced with new ones. To check them, hold a scale or straightedge against the threads or run a 3/8 x 24 nut down each bolt the full length of the threads. If all the threads do not contact the straightedge or if the nut does not run down smoothly, the bolt should be rejected.*

1 Before installing the piston/connecting rod assemblies, the cylinder walls must be perfectly clean, the top edge of each cylinder must be chamfered, and the crankshaft must be in place.

2 Remove the connecting rod cap from the end of the number one connecting rod. Remove the old bearing inserts and wipe the bearing surfaces of the connecting rod and cap with a clean, lint free cloth. Everything must be spotlessly clean.

3 Clean the back side of the new upper bearing half, then lay it in place in the connecting rod. Make sure that the tab on the bearing fits into the recess in the rod. Do not hammer the bearing insert into place and be very careful not to nick or gouge the bearing face. Do not lubricate the bearing at this time.

4 Clean the back side of the other bearing insert and install it in the rod cap. Again, make sure the tab on the bearing fits into the recess in the cap, and do not apply any lubricant. It is critically important that the mating surfaces of the bearing and connecting rod are perfectly clean and oil free when they are assembled.

5 Position the piston ring gaps as shown in the accompanying illustration, then slip a section of plastic or rubber hose over the connecting rod cap bolts.

6 Lubricate the piston and rings with clean engine oil and attach a piston ring compressor to the piston. Leave the skirt protruding about 1/4-inch to guide the piston into the cylinder. The rings must be compressed as far as possible.

7 Rotate the crankshaft until the number one connecting rod journal is as far from the number one cylinder as possible (bottom dead center), and apply a coat of engine oil to the cylinder walls.

8 On *2.2L/2.5L engines*, the indent on the piston and oil hole in the connecting rod big end must face the front of the engine. On 1986 and later models, the valve relief on the piston crown must be on the manifold side of the engine **(see illustrations)**. Turbocharged engines may have pistons marked with an arrow which must point toward the front of the engine. On *2.6L engines*, the arrow on the piston crown must point toward the front of the engine. Gently place the piston/connecting rod assembly into the number one cylinder bore **(see illustration)** and rest the bottom edge of the ring compressor on the engine block. Tap the top edge of the ring compressor to make sure it contacts the block around its entire circumference.

9 Carefully tap on the top of the piston with the end of a wooden hammer handle **(see illustration)** while guiding the end of the connecting rod into place on the crankshaft journal. The piston rings may try to pop out of the ring compressor just before entering the cylinder bore, so keep some downward pressure on the ring compressor. Work slowly, and if any resistance is felt as the piston enters the cylinder, stop immediately. Find out what is hanging up and fix it before proceeding. **Caution:** *Do not, for any reason, force the piston into the cylinder. If you force it, you will break a ring and/or the piston.*

10 Once the piston/connecting rod assembly is installed, the connecting rod bearing oil clearance must be checked before the rod cap is permanently bolted in place.

11 Cut a piece of the appropriate size Plastigage slightly shorter than the width of the connecting rod bearing and lay it in place on the number one connecting rod journal, parallel with the journal axis **(see illustration)**. It should not cross the oil hole in the journal.

12 Clean the connecting rod cap bearing face, remove the protective hoses from the connecting rod bolts and install the rod cap. Make sure the mating mark on the cap is on the same side as the mark on the connecting rod. Install the nuts and tighten them to the specified torque, working up to it in three steps. On 2.2L/2.5L engines, apply a small amount of engine oil to the rod bolt threads before installing the nuts. **Note:** *Do not rotate the crankshaft at any time during this operation.*

13 Remove the rod cap, being very careful not to disturb the Plastigage. Compare the width of the crushed Plastigage to the scale printed on the Plastigage container to obtain the oil clearance **(see illustration)**. Compare it to the Specifications to make sure the clearance is correct. If the clearance is not correct, double-check to make sure that you have the correct size bearing inserts. Also, recheck the crankshaft connecting rod journal diameter and make sure that no dirt or oil was between the bearing inserts and the connecting rod or cap when the clearance was measured.

14 Carefully scrape all traces of the Plastigage material off the rod journal and/or bearing face. Be very careful not to scratch the bearing — use your fingernail or a piece of hardwood. Make sure the bearing faces are perfectly clean, then apply a uniform layer of clean, high quality moly-based grease or engine assembly lube to both of them. You

20.8c Leave the piston protruding about 1/4-inch out of the bottom of the ring compressor to align it in the bore

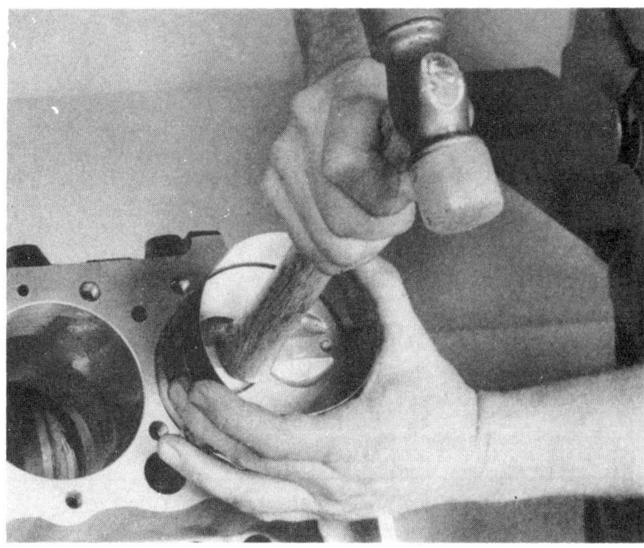

20.9 If resistance is encountered when tapping the piston into the block, *stop immediately* and make sure the rings are fully compressed

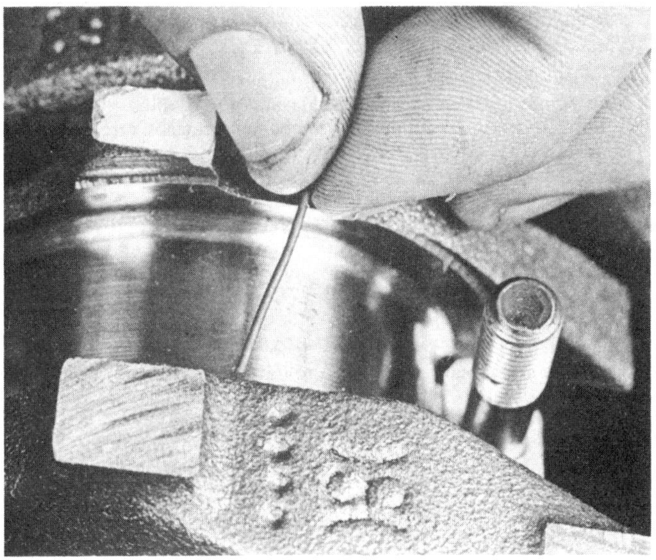

20.11 Carefully lay the Plastigage on the crankshaft rod journal

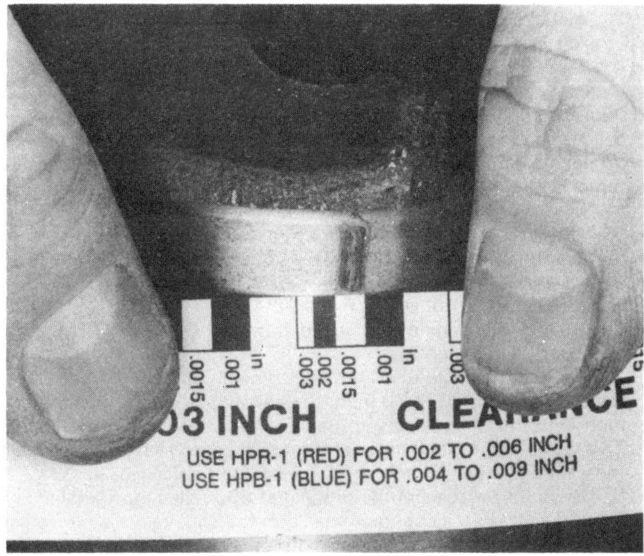

20.13 The crushed Plastigage is compared to the scale printed on the container to obtain the rod bearing oil clearance (be sure to use the correct scale — standard and metric scales are included)

will have to push the piston into the cylinder to expose the face of the bearing insert in the connecting rod. Be sure to slip the protective hoses over the rod bolts first.

15 Slide the connecting rod back into place on the journal, remove the protective hoses from the rod cap bolts, install the rod cap and tighten the nuts to the specified torque. Again, work up to the torque in three steps.

16 Repeat the entire procedure for the remaining piston/connecting rod assemblies. Keep the back sides of the bearing inserts and the inside of the connecting rod and cap perfectly clean when assembling them. Make sure you have the piston matched to the correct cylinder. Use plenty of oil to lubricate the piston before installing the ring compressor. Also, when installing the rod caps for the final time, be sure to lubricate the bearing faces adequately.

17 After all the piston/connecting rod assemblies have been properly installed, rotate the crankshaft a number of times by hand to check for any obvious binding.

18 As a final step, the connecting rod end play must be checked (Section 11). Compare the measured end play to the Specifications to make sure it is correct.

21 Engine overhaul — reassembly sequence

1 Before beginning engine reassembly, make sure you have all the necessary new parts, gaskets and seals as well as the following items on hand:

Common hand tools
A 1/2-inch drive torque wrench
Piston ring installation tool
Piston ring compressor
Short lengths of rubber or plastic hose to fit over connecting rod bolts
Plastigage
Feeler gauges
A fine-tooth file
New engine oil
Engine assembly lube or moly-based grease
RTV-type gasket sealant
Anaerobic-type gasket sealant
Thread locking compound

2 In order to save time and avoid problems, engine reassembly must be done in the following order.

Crankshaft and main bearings
Piston rings
Piston/connecting rod assemblies
Balance shaft and carrier assembly (2.5L engine only)
Oil pump and oil strainer (2.2L/2.5L engine only)
Front oil seal housing (2.2L/2.5L engine only)
Rear oil seal housing
Oil pan
Flywheel/driveplate
Cylinder head
Camshaft/rocker arm assembly
Timing belt or chain, sprockets and tensioner
Silent Shaft chain and sprockets (2.6L engine only)
Timing cover
Cylinder head cover
Oil pan
External components

22 Initial start-up and break-in after overhaul

1 Once the engine has been properly installed in the vehicle, double-check the engine oil and coolant levels.
2 With the spark plugs out of the engine and the coil high tension lead grounded to the engine block, crank the engine until oil pressure registers on the gauge (if so equipped) or until the oil light goes off.
3 Install the spark plugs, hook up the plug wires and the coil high tension lead.
4 Make sure the carburetor choke plate is closed, then start the engine. It may take a few moments for the gasoline to reach the carburetor, but the engine should start without a great deal of effort.
5 As soon as the engine starts it should be set at a fast idle to ensure proper oil circulation and allowed to warm up to normal operating temperature. While the engine is warming up, make a thorough check for oil and coolant leaks.
6 After the engine reaches normal operating temperature, shut it off, remove the cylinder head cover, retorque the head bolts and recheck the valve clearances. Install the cylinder head cover and recheck the engine oil and coolant levels. Restart the engine and check the ignition timing and the engine idle speed (refer to Chapter 1). Make any necessary adjustments.
7 Drive the vehicle to an area with minimum traffic, accelerate at full throttle from 30 to 50 mph, then allow the vehicle to slow to 30 mph with the throttle closed. Repeat the procedure 10 or 12 times. This will load the piston rings and cause them to seat properly against the cylinder walls. Check again for oil and coolant leaks.
8 Drive the vehicle gently for the first 500 miles (no sustained high speeds) and keep a constant check on the oil level. It is not unusual for an engine to use oil during the break-in period.
9 At approximately 500 to 600 miles, change the oil and filter, retorque the cylinder head bolts and recheck the valve clearances (if applicable).
10 For the next few hundred miles, drive the vehicle normally. Do not pamper it or abuse it.
11 After 2000 miles, change the oil and filter again and consider the engine fully broken in.

23 Cylinder compression check

1 A compression check will tell you a lot about the mechanical condition of your engine. For instance, it can tell you if compression is low because of leakage caused by worn piston rings, defective valves and seats or a blown head gasket.
2 Warm the engine to normal operating temperature, shut it off and allow it to sit for ten minutes to allow the catalytic converter temperature to drop.
3 Begin by cleaning the area around the spark plugs before you remove them. This will prevent dirt from falling into the cylinders while you are checking compression.
4 Remove the high-tension lead from the distributor and ground it on the engine block. Block the throttle and choke valves wide open. Or depress the accelerator pedal all the way to the floor.
5 With the compression gauge in the number one cylinder's spark plug hole, crank the engine over at least four compression strokes and observe the gauge (compression should build up quickly in a healthy engine). Low compression on the first stroke, followed by gradually increasing pressure on successive strokes, indicates worn piston rings. A low compression reading on the first stroke, which does not build up during successive strokes, indicates leaking valves or a defective head gasket. Record the highest gauge reading that you obtained.
6 Repeat this procedure for the remaining cylinders and compare the results to the Specifications. Compression readings 10% above or below the specified amount can be considered normal.
7 Pour a couple of teaspoons of engine oil (a squirt can works great) into each cylinder, through the spark plug hole, and repeat the test.
8 If the compression increases after oil is added, the piston rings are definitely worn. If the compression does not increase significantly, the leakage is occurring at the valves or head gasket.
9 If two adjacent cylinders have equally low compression, there is a strong possibility that the head gasket between them is blown. The appearance of coolant in the combustion chamber or the crankcase will verify this condition.
10 If the compression is higher than normal, the combustion chambers are probably coated with carbon deposits. If that is the case, the cylinder head should be removed and decarbonized.
11 If compression is way down, or varies greatly between cylinders, it's a good idea to have a ''leak-down'' test performed by a reputable automotive repair shop. This test will pinpoint exactly where the leakage is occurring and how severe it it.

24 Top Dead Center (TDC) for number 1 piston – locating

1 Top Dead Center (TDC) is the highest point in the cylinder that each piston reaches as it travels up-and-down when the crankshaft turns. Each piston reaches TDC on the compression stroke and again on the exhaust stroke, but TDC generally refers to piston position on the compression stroke. The timing marks are referenced to the number 1 piston at TDC on the compression stroke.
2 Positioning the piston(s) at TDC is an essential part of many procedures such as valve adjustment, timing chain/belt and sprocket replacement and distributor removal.
3 In order to bring any piston to TDC, the crankshaft must be turned using one of the methods outlined below. When looking at the front of the engine, normal crankshaft rotation is *clockwise.*

a) The preferred method is to turn the crankshaft with a large socket and breaker bar attached to the vibration damper bolt that is threaded into the front of the crankshaft.
b) A remote starter switch, which may save some time, can also be used. Attach the switch leads to the ignition switch and battery terminals on the starter motor. Once the piston is close to TDC, use a socket and breaker bar as described in the previous paragraph.
c) If an assistant is available to turn the ignition switch to the Start position in short bursts, you can get the piston close to TDC without a remote starter switch. Use a socket and breaker bar as described in Paragraph a to complete the procedure.

4 Locate the number 1 cylinder spark plug wire and trace it back to the distributor cap. The number 1 cylinder is located at the timing belt or chain end of the engine (opposite the transaxle.)
5 Using a felt tip pen, make a mark on the engine directly in line with the number 1 spark plug wire terminal on the distributor cap.
6 Remove the distributor cap as described in Chapter 1.
7 Turn the crankshaft (see Paragraph 3 above) until the line on the vibration damper or flywheel is aligned with the zero mark on the timing scale.
8 The rotor should now be pointing directly at the mark on the engine (made in Step 5). If it isn't, the piston is at TDC on the exhaust stroke.
9 To get the piston to TDC on the compression stroke, turn the crankshaft one complete turn (360°) clockwise. The rotor should now be pointing at the mark. When the rotor is pointing at the number 1 spark plug wire terminal in the distributor cap (which is indicated by the mark on the engine) and the timing marks are aligned, the number 1 piston is at TDC on the compression stroke.
10 After the number 1 piston has been positioned at TDC on the compression stroke, TDC for any of the remaining cylinders can be located by turning the crankshaft 180° at a time and following the firing order (refer to the Specifications).

Chapter 3
Cooling, heating and air conditioning systems

Contents

Specifications

General

Radiator pressure cap rating	14 to 18 psi

Thermostat rating

2.2L/2.5L engine	195 °F (91 °C)
2.6L engine	
California models	180 °F (83 °C)
All others	190 °F (88 °C)

Torque specifications	**Ft-lbs**	**Nm**
Turbocharger coolant tube connections	30	41
Thermostat housing bolts		
2.2L/2.5L engine		
1982 through 1985	15	20
1986 on	20	28
2.6L engine (all)	15	20
Water pump cover-to-housing bolts (2.2L/2.5L engine)	10	12
Water pump-to-housing bolts (2.6L engine)	7	9
Water pump mounting bolts		
2.2L/2.5L engine		
Upper three bolts	20	28
Lower bolt		
1982 through 1985	50	68
1986 on	40	72
2.6L engine (all)	17	23
Water pump pulley bolts	10	13

1 General information

Warning: *When working in the vicinity of the fan, always make sure the ignition is turned off and the negative battery cable is disconnected.*

The cooling system on all models consists of a radiator, an electrically-driven fan mounted in the radiator shroud, a thermostat, a water pump and a coolant reservoir.

Coolant is circulated through the radiator tubes and is cooled by air passing through the cooling fins. The coolant is circulated by a pump mounted on the engine and driven by a belt.

A thermostat allows the engine to warm up by remaining closed until the coolant in the engine is at operating temperature. The thermostat then opens, allowing full circulation of the coolant throughout the cooling system.

The electric fan is actuated by a thermal switch or on-board computer (fuel injected models) or when the air conditioning system is on. This aids cooling by drawing air through the radiator.

The radiator cap contains a vent valve which allows coolant to escape through a tube to the reservoir. When the engine cools, vacuum in the

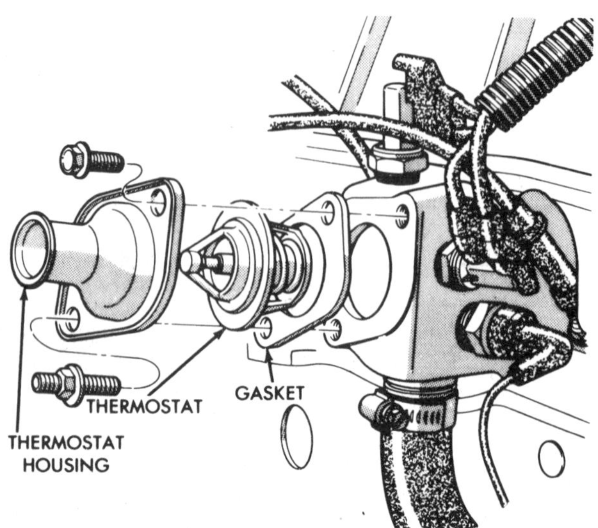

3.5a 2.2L/2.5L engine thermostat and related components — exploded view

radiator draws the coolant back from the reservoir so the coolant level remains constant.

On turbocharged models, coolant is circulated from the cylinder head through the turbocharger housing (to cool the center bearing) and back to the cylinder head water box.

The heating system operates by directing air through the heater core mounted in the dash and then to the interior of the vehicle by a system of ducts. Temperature is controlled by mixing heated air with fresh air, using a system of flapper doors in the ducts, and a heater motor.

Some models are equipped with an air conditioner/heater system consisting of an evaporator core and ducts in the dash and a compressor in the engine compartment.

2 Antifreeze — general information

Warning: *Do not allow antifreeze to contact your skin or the painted surfaces of the vehicle. Flush contacted areas immediately with water. Antifreeze can be fatal to children and pets (they like its sweet taste). Wipe up garage floor and drip pan coolant spills immediately. Keep antifreeze containers covered and repair leaks in vehicle cooling systems as quickly as possible.*

The cooling system should be filled with a water/ethylene glycol-based antifreeze solution, which will give protection down to at least −20°F at all times (even lower in cold climates). It also provides protection against corrosion and increases the coolant boiling point.

The cooling system should be drained, flushed and refilled at least every other year. The use of antifreeze solutions for periods longer than two years is likely to cause damage and encourage the formation of rust and scale in the system.

Before adding antifreeze to the system, check all hose connections (antifreeze tends to search out and leak through very minute openings).

The exact mixture of antifreeze-to-water which you should use depends upon the relative weather conditions. The mixture should contain at least 50 percent antifreeze, but should never contain more than 70 percent antifreeze.

3 Thermostat — removal and installation

Refer to illustrations 3.5a, 3.5b, 3.6, 3.7 and 3.10

Warning: *The engine must be completely cool before beginning this procedure.*

1 A faulty thermostat is indicated by failure of the engine to reach operating temperature or requiring longer than normal time to do so.

2 Disconnect the negative cable at the battery. Place the cable out of the way so it cannot accidentally come in contact with the negative terminal of the battery, as this would once again allow power into the electrical system of the vehicle.

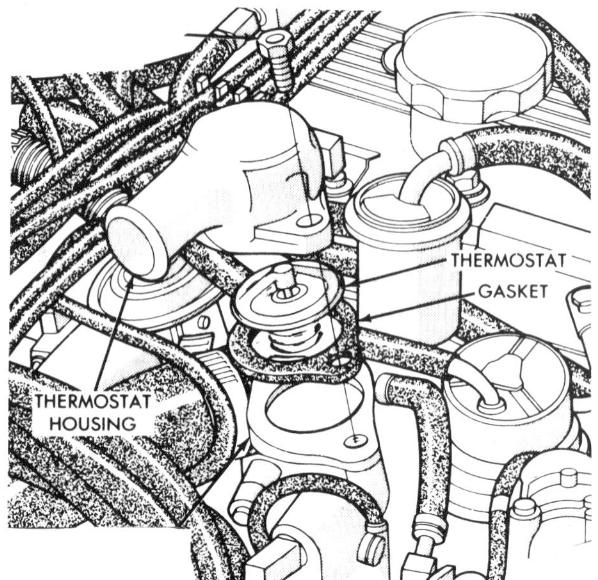

3.5b 2.6L engine thermostat and related components — exploded view

3.6 Grasp the thermostat housing and rock it back and forth to break the gasket seal (2.2L/2.5L engine shown)

3 Drain the coolant (see Chapter 1).

4 Detach the upper radiator hose from the thermostat housing.

5 Remove the thermostat housing mounting bolts. On 2.6L engines, the fuel filter and hoses may have to be removed as well **(see illustrations)**.

6 Grasp the thermostat housing securely, break it loose from the gasket by rocking it back and forth and remove it **(see illustration)**.

7 Use a screwdriver to dislodge it, then lift the thermostat out of the engine **(see illustration)**.

8 Clean all traces of gasket from the housing and engine mating surfaces with a scraper, taking care not to gouge or nick them.

9 Coat both sides of the new gasket with a thin layer of RTV sealant, then position the gasket on the engine.

10 Install the new thermostat in the engine **(see illustration)**. **Note:** *Make sure the spring side faces into the engine and center the thermostat in the gasket.*

11 Install the housing and bolts. Tighten the bolts to the specified torque.

3.7 Dislodge the thermostat by inserting a screwdriver behind it (2.2L/2.5L engine shown)

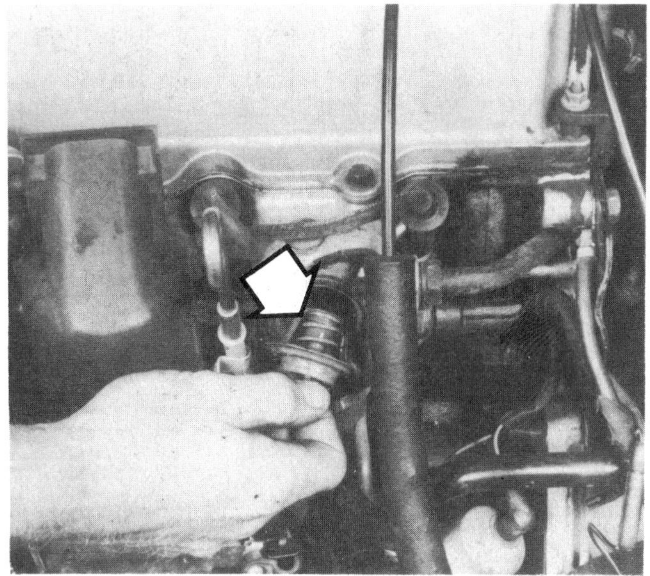

3.10 Make sure the spring on the thermostat (arrow) is installed facing into the engine (2.2L/2.5L engine shown)

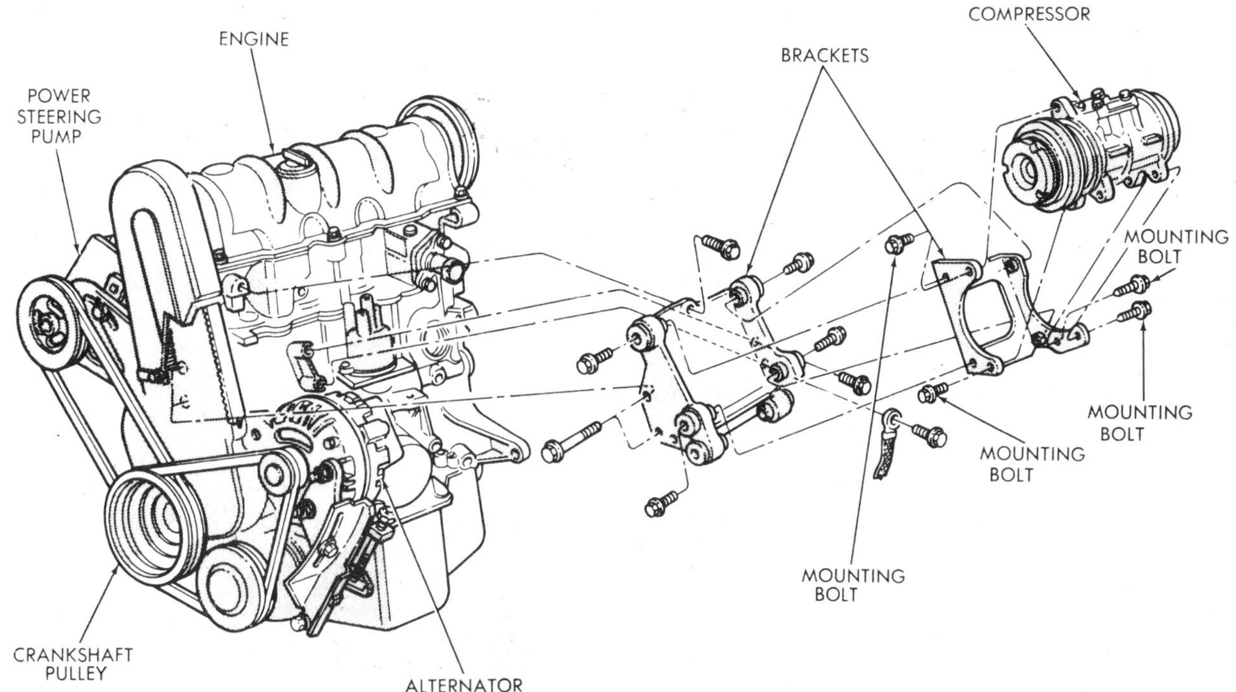

4.7 Air conditioner compressor mounting details (2.2L/2.5L engine)

12 Install the hose, refill the radiator with the specified coolant and connect the negative battery cable.
13 Start the engine and check for coolant leaks around the thermostat housing.

4 Water pump (2.2L/2.5L engine) – removal and installation

Refer to illustrations 4.7, 4.8, 4.9, 4.10, 4.12, 4.13a and 4.13b

Warning: *The engine must be completely cool before beginning this procedure.*

1 Disconnect the negative cable at the battery. Place the cable out of the way so it cannot accidentally come in contact with the negative terminal of the battery, as this would once again allow power into the electrical system of the vehicle.
2 Drain the coolant (see Chapter 1) and remove the upper radiator hose.
3 On air conditioner equipped models, loosen the compressor idler pulley bolt and release the drivebelt tension. Unplug the air conditioner electrical connector, unbolt the compresser and secure it out of the way. **Warning:** *Do not disconnect or kink the hoses, as serious injury could result.*
4 Detach the wires from the alternator.
5 Loosen the alternator drivebelt adjuster and slip off the drivebelt.
6 Remove the alternator through-bolt and detach the alternator.
7 Unbolt and remove the air conditioner compressor bracket (if equipped) **(see illustration)**.

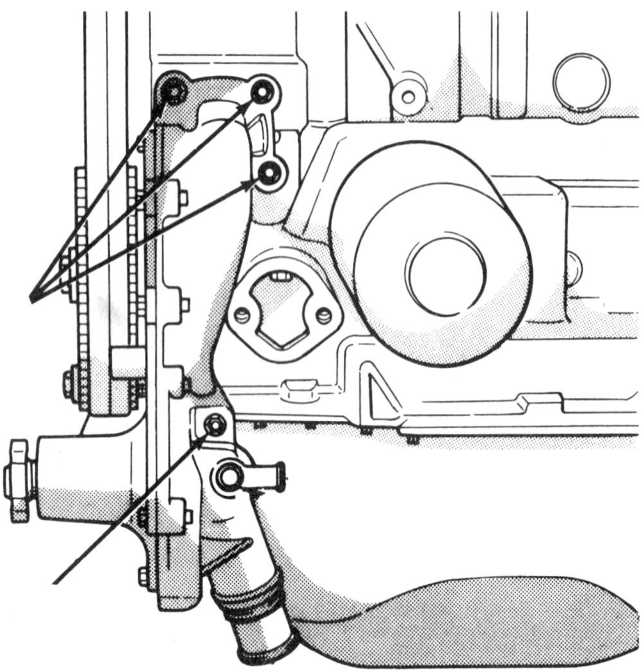

4.8 Water pump mounting bolt locations (2.2L/2.5L engine)

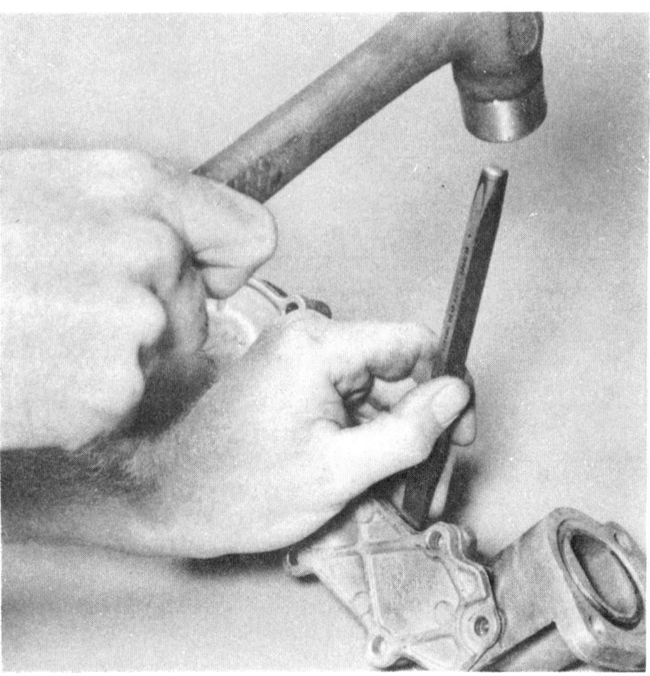

4.9 Separate the water pump and housing using a hammer and chisel (2.2L/2.5L engine)

4.10 Scrape the old sealant material off the engine and housing (2.2L/2.5L engine)

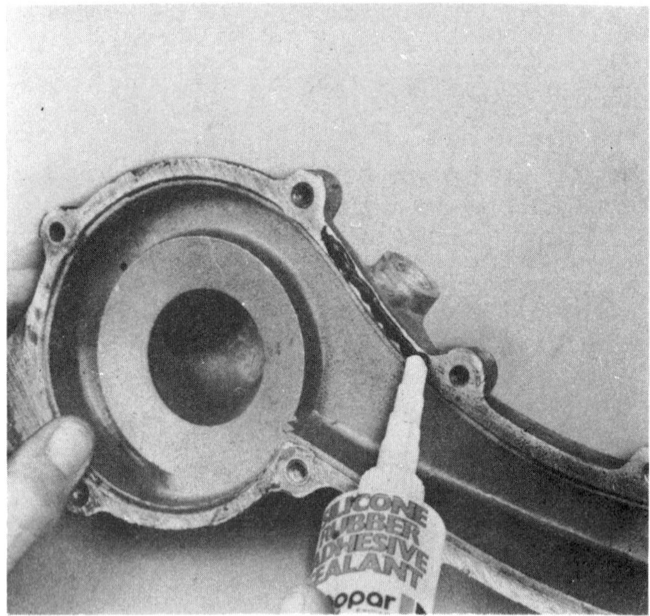

4.12a Carefully apply RTV sealant to the mating surface of the water pump . . .

8 Disconnect the lower radiator hose, remove the water pump and housing assembly mounting nuts and bolts **(see illustration)** and detach the assembly from the engine.

9 Remove the bolts (noting their locations for reinstallation in the same positions) and separate the water pump from the housing. It may be necessary to use a hammer and chisel to carefully break the seal **(see illustration)**.

10 Clean the mating surfaces of the water pump and housing to remove the old sealant material **(see illustration)**. Remove the O-ring from the housing.

11 If a new water pump is being installed, transfer the pulley to the new pump.

12 Apply a bead of RTV sealant to the housing mating surface and attach the pump **(see illustrations)**. Install the bolts and tighten them to the specified torque.

13 Clean the groove in the housing and press the new O-ring into place **(see illustration)**.

14 Make sure the O-ring is still in place, then attach the pump and housing assembly to the engine. Tighten the bolts to the specified torque. Install the radiator and heater hoses.

15 Install the air conditioner bracket and alternator and adjust the drivebelt.

16 Connect the wires to the alternator.

17 Install the air conditioner compressor (if removed) and adjust the drivebelt.

18 Refill the cooling system with the specified coolant (see Chapter 1).

19 Connect the negative battery cable.

20 Start the engine and check for coolant leaks at the water pump.

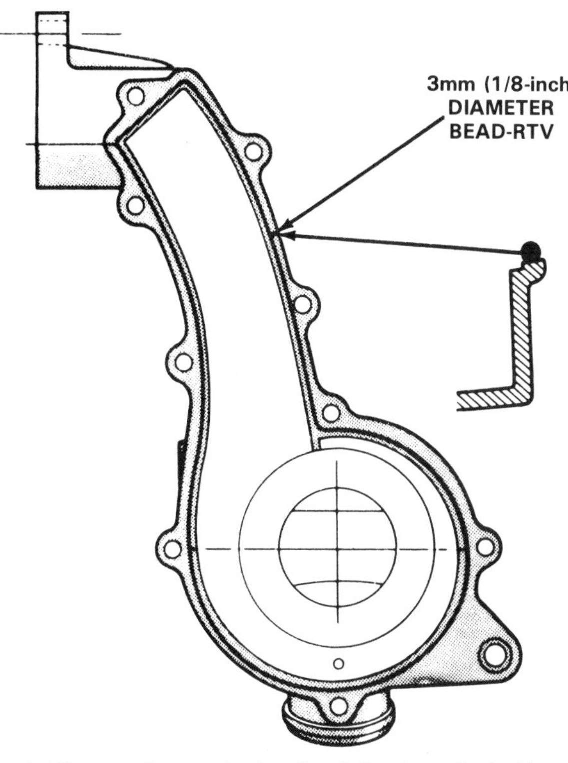

4.12b ... in an unbroken bead that is to the inside of the bolt holes (note the specified bead width)

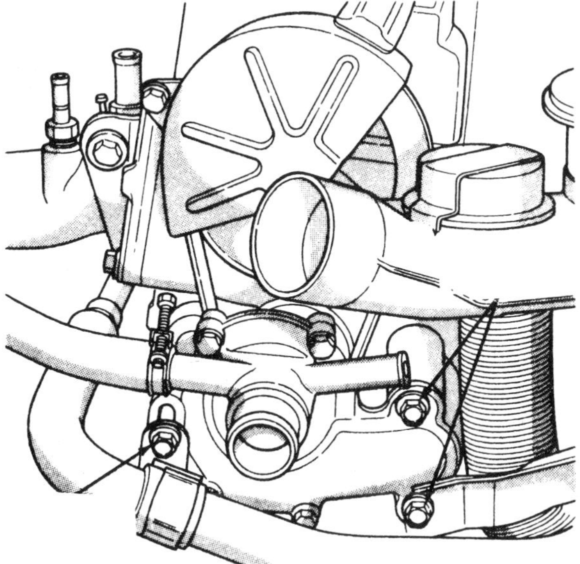

5.5 Water pump mounting bolt locations (2.6L engine)

5 Water pump (2.6L engine) – removal and installation

Refer to illustrations 5.5 and 5.8

Warning: *The engine must be completely cool before beginning this procedure.*

1 Disconnect the negative cable at the battery. Place the cable out of the way so it cannot accidentally come in contact with the negative terminal of the battery, as this would once again allow power into the electrical system of the vehicle.
2 Drain the cooling system (see Chapter 1).
3 Disconnect the radiator, by-pass and heater hoses from the water pump.
4 Remove the drivebelt pulley shield.
5 Remove the water pump bolts **(see illustration)**, detach the drivebelt

4.13 Press the O-ring evenly into the water pump housing groove (2.2L/2.5L engine)

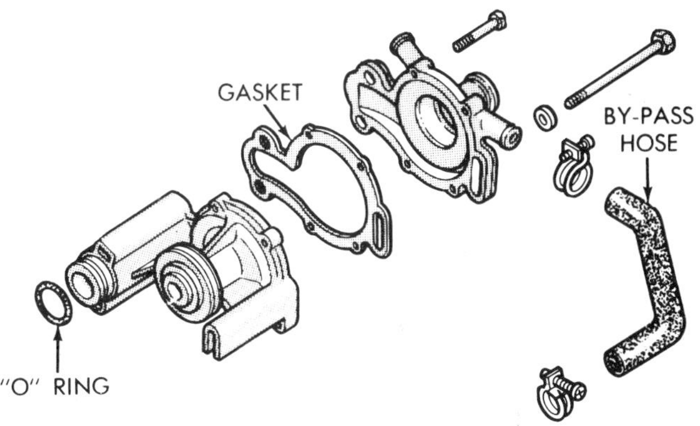

5.8 2.6L engine water pump – exploded view

and separate the water pump and housing assembly from the engine.
6 Remove the bolts and separate the water pump from the housing.
7 Discard the gasket and clean the mating surfaces to remove any remaining gasket material.
8 Remove the O-ring from the housing and carefully clean out the groove **(see illustration)**.
9 Coat both sides of the new gasket with a thin layer of RTV sealant and attach the gasket to the water pump body. Attach the pump body to the housing and tighten the bolts to the specified torque.
10 Press the new O-ring into the groove.
11 Install the water pump assembly on the engine with the bolts finger tight.
12 Install the drivebelt, adjust it to the proper tension (Chapter 1) and tighten the water pump bolts to the specified torque.
13 Install the drivebelt pulley shield.
14 Attach the radiator, by-pass and heater hoses to the water pump.
15 Refill the cooling system with coolant (Chapter 1).
16 Connect the negative battery cable.
17 Start the engine and check for coolant leaks at the water pump.

6 Radiator – removal and installation

Refer to illustrations 6.3, 6.6a, 6.6b and 6.10

Warning: *The engine must be completely cool before beginning this procedure.*

1 Disconnect the negative cable at the battery. Place the cable out

3

6.3 Use a screwdriver to pry the overflow hose off the radiator fitting

6.6a Radiator mounting nuts (arrows)

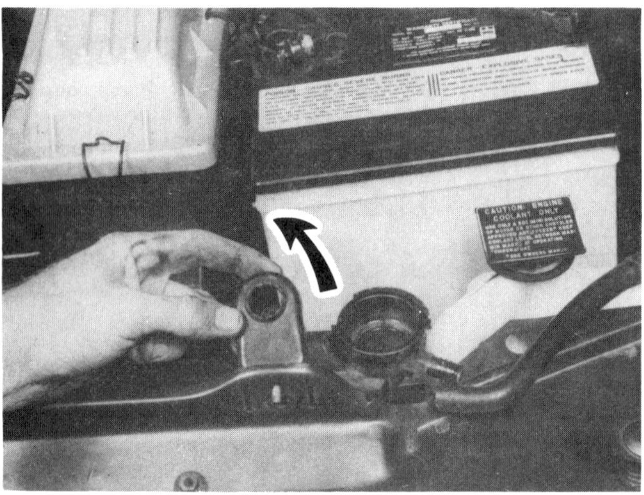

6.6b Rotate the retaining brackets up and out of the mounts

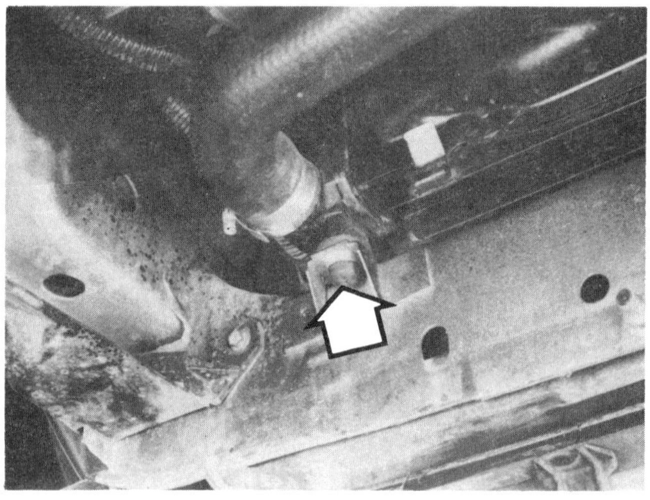

6.10 Make sure the radiator tabs seat securely in the rubber grommet (arrow)

of the way so it cannot accidentally come in contact with the negative terminal of the battery, as this would once again allow power into the electrical system of the vehicle.

2 Drain the cooling system (Chapter 1).

3 Remove the radiator hoses and the coolant reservoir hose **(see illustration)**.

4 Unplug the radiator fan switch connector.

5 Remove the fan motor and shroud assembly (Section 9).

6 Remove the two upper mounting nuts and the radiator retaining brackets **(see illustrations)**.

7 Grasp the radiator securely and work it from side to side while pulling up to disengage the mounting tabs from the rubber grommets at the bottom. Once it is disengaged, the radiator can be lifted straight up, out of the engine compartment.

8 Inspect the radiator for leaks, bent fins, damaged tubes, cracks around the tanks and signs of corrosion.

9 Lubricate all of the hose fittings lightly with white lithium grease to ease hose installation.

10 Lower the radiator into place and push down to seat the tabs in the rubber grommets **(see illustration)**.

11 Install the bolts and tighten them securely.

12 Install the radiator, heater and reservoir hoses. Be sure not to over-tighten the hose clamps. Also, make sure that the radiator hoses are securely mounted in the clips.

13 Install the fan motor and shroud assembly.

14 Refill the cooling system with the specified coolant.

15 Connect the negative battery cable.

16 Start the engine and check for coolant leaks at the hose fittings.

7 Radiator — inspection

1 The radiator should be kept free of obstructions such as leaves, paper, insects, mud and other debris which could affect the flow of air through it.

2 Periodically inspect the radiator for bent cooling fins or tubes, signs of coolant leakage and cracks around the upper and lower tanks.

3 Check the filler neck sealing surface for dents which could affect the radiator cap sealing effectiveness.

8 Drivebelts — inspection, replacement and adjustment

1 The drivebelts should be inspected periodically for wear, cuts and contamination by oil, gasoline or coolant as well as for signs of glazing, indicating improper adjustment.

2 To replace a drivebelt, loosen the bolts and push the pivoting component away from the belt until it can be removed. Do not pry on the pulley surface as this could cause nicks or gouges which will damage the new belt.

3 Install the new belt and adjust it as described in Chapter 1.

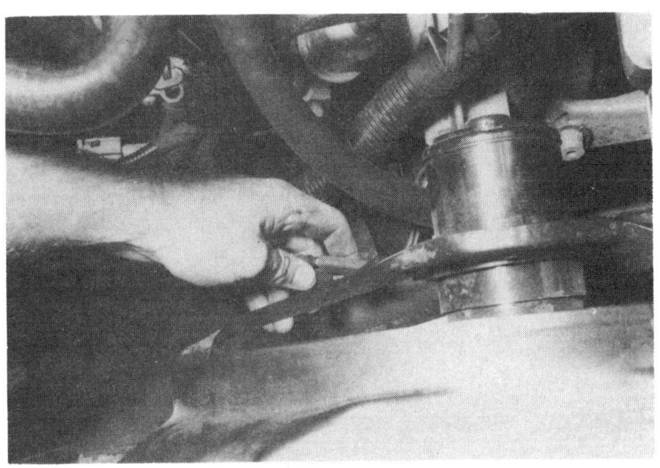

9.2 Unplug the fan motor at the connector nearest the motor

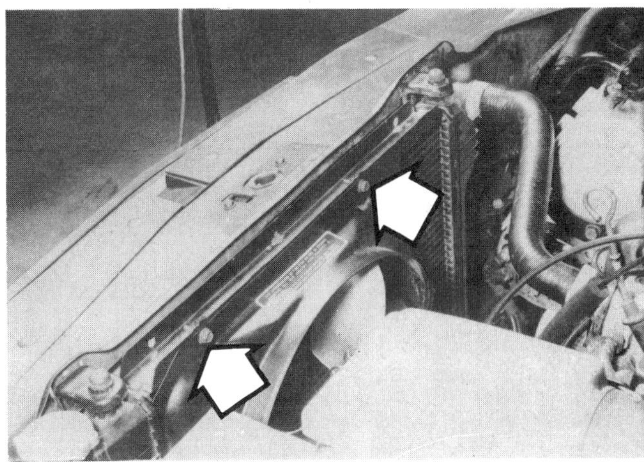

9.3 Fan shroud retaining bolts (arrows)

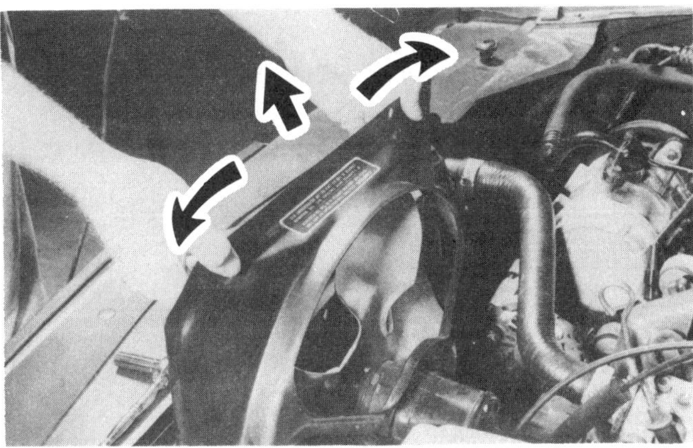

9.4 Rock the fan shroud from side to side while pulling up to disengage the clips

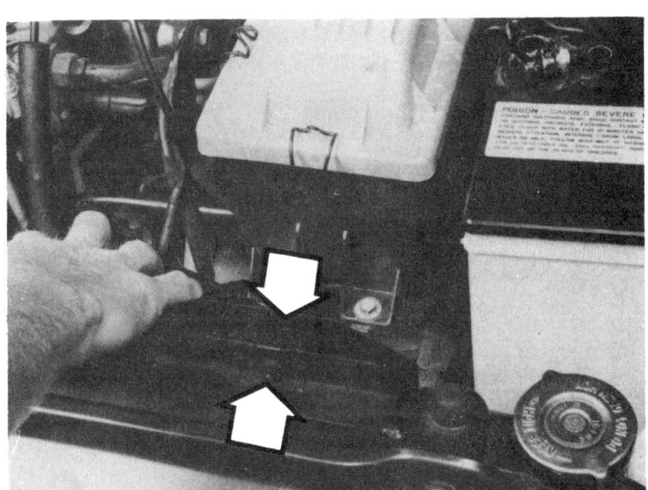

9.5 Lower the motor and shroud assembly into the clips until the bolt holes (arrows) line up

9 Fan motor and shroud assembly – removal and installation

Refer to illustrations 9.2, 9.3, 9.4 and 9.5

1 Disconnect the negative cable at the battery. Place the cable out of the way so it cannot accidentally come in contact with the negative terminal of the battery, as this would once again allow power into the electrical system of the vehicle.

2 Unplug the fan motor wiring connector **(see illustration)**.

3 Remove the two fan shroud retaining bolts **(see illustration)**.

4 Pull the assembly up, working it from side to side to disengage the shroud from the clips at the bottom of the radiator and lift it from the engine compartment **(see illustration)**.

5 To install it, lower the motor and shroud assembly into position, line up the bolt holes and push down to seat it in the clips **(see illustration)**.

6 Install the bolts and tighten them securely.

7 Plug in the fan motor wiring connector and reattach the negative battery cable.

10 Fan motor and shroud assembly – disassembly, inspection and reassembly

Refer to illustrations 10.2 and 10.3

1 Remove the assembly from the vehicle (Section 9) and place it on a workbench. Be very careful not to bend the fan blades.

2 Remove the clip and slide the fan off the motor shaft **(see illustration)**.

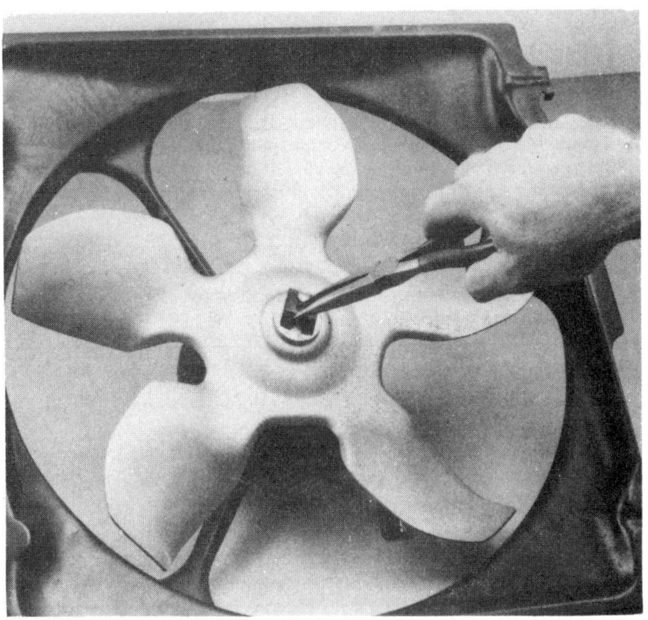

10.2 The fan retaining clip can be removed with a pair of needle-nose pliers

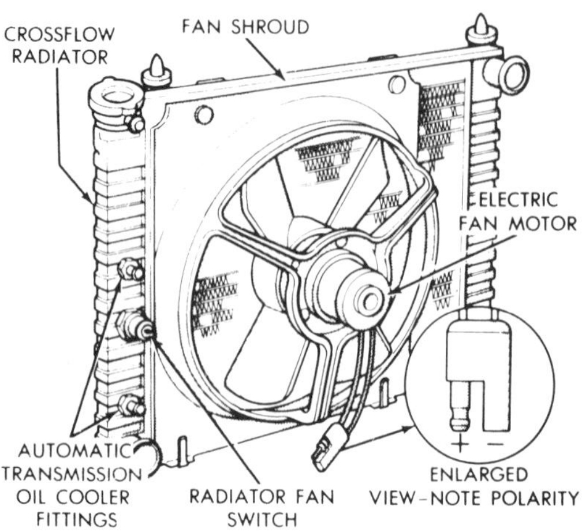

10.3 Cooling fan connector terminal polarity

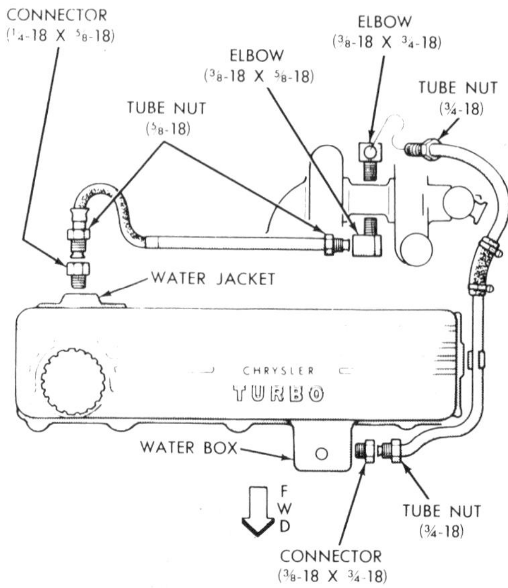

11.2 Turbocharger coolant hose and tube details

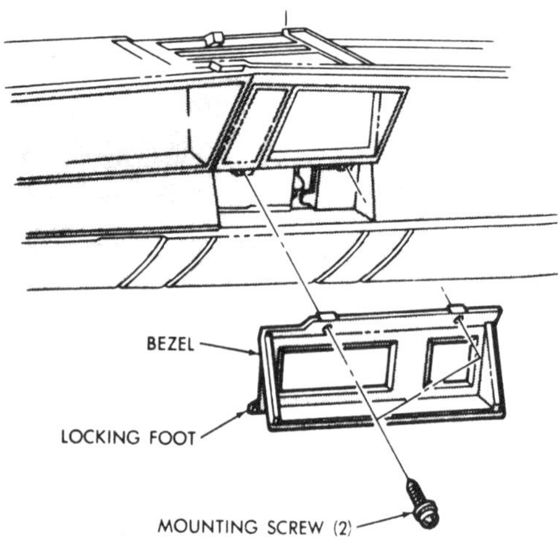

12.2 Standard model heater/air conditioner control bezel details

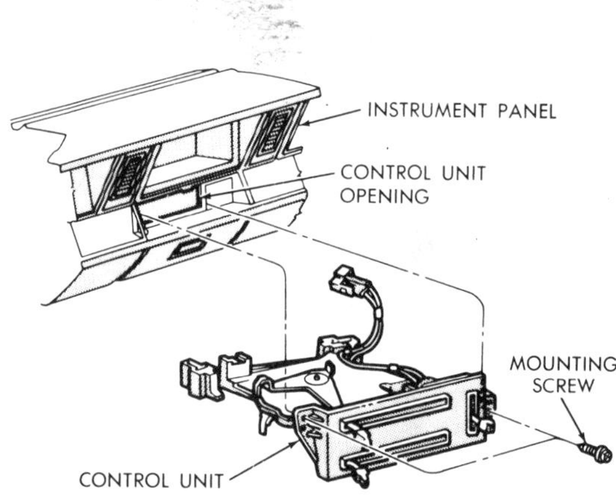

12.3 Standard model instrument panel heater/air conditioner control unit details

3 Inspect the motor for a bent shaft, damage and worn wiring insulation. Check the motor by inserting two 14 gauge wires into the connector and attaching them to the battery posts **(see illustration)**. Replace the motor with a new one if it does not run and the wiring and connector are in good condition. Inspect the fan for warping, cracks and damage. Replace it with a new one of the same design if necessary.
4 Slide the fan onto the shaft and retain it with the clip.
5 Install the assembly.

11 Turbocharger coolant hose and tube assembly – check and replacement

Refer to illustration 11.2

1 Check the hoses, tubes and connections for cracks, damage and leaks. Replace any damaged components.
2 When installing new components, apply thread sealant the full length of all screw-in connections which thread into coolant passages and tighten the fittings to the specified torque **(see illustration)**.

12 Heater and air conditioner control – removal and installation

Refer to illustrations 12.2, 12.3, 12.8a, 12.8b and 12.8c

1 Disconnect the negative cable at the battery. Place the cable out of the way so it cannot accidentally come in contact with the negative terminal of the battery, as this would once again allow power into the electrical system of the vehicle.

Standard models

2 Remove the two screws, disengage the locking feet at the bottom and rotate the bezel up and out of the instrument panel **(see illustration)**.
3 Remove the two mounting screws and slide the control out of the instrument panel, then disconnect the cables, vacuum hoses and wiring connectors **(see illustration)**.
4 To install it, place the assembly in position and connect the cables, vacuum hoses and wires.
5 Install the screws and bezel and connect the battery cable.

Console equipped models

6 Remove the two screws at the base of the heater control bezel, grasp the base of the bezel and pull out sharply to disengage the clips.
7 Remove the screws that hold the control base to the instrument panel.
8 Withdraw the assembly from the dash and disengage the control cable **(see illustrations)**. Unplug the electrical connectors. Some connectors are retained by clips which can be released using a small screwdriver **(see illustration)**.
9 Remove the control assembly from the vehicle.
10 To install it, place the assembly in position and connect the vacuum

12.8a Squeeze the control cable flag tab to release it from the receiver, lift it up . . .

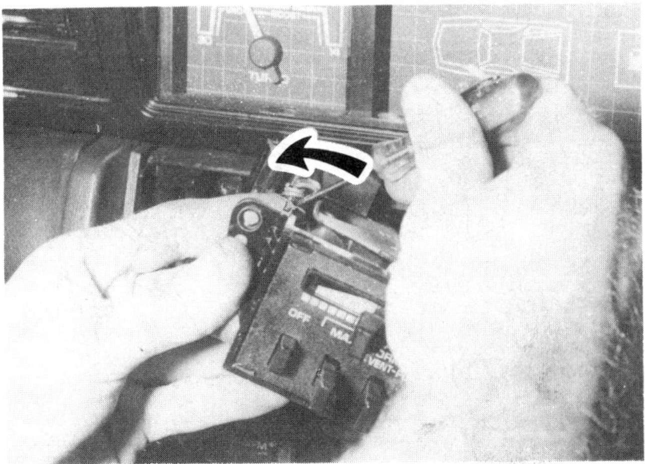

12.8b . . . and pry the clip off the end of the cable with a screwdriver

and electrical connectors. Hook up the control cable.

11 Install the control base screws and bezel and connect the negative battery cable.

13 Heater and air conditioner evaporator assembly — removal and installation

Refer to illustrations 13.3, 13.8, 13.9, 13.11 and 13.15

Caution: *On vehicles equipped with an air conditioner, the system must be evacuated by a dealer service department or air conditioning repair shop before any refrigerant lines are disconnected. Do not attempt to do this yourself as serious injury could result.*

1 Refer to Chapter 1 and drain the cooling system.

2 Disconnect the battery cables (negative first, then positive). Place the cables out of the way so they cannot accidentally come in contact with the terminals of the battery, as this would once again allow power into the electrical system of the vehicle.

3 Disconnect the heater hoses at the core fittings on the firewall. Plug the core fittings to prevent coolant from spilling out when the assembly is removed **(see illustration)**.

12.8c Use a small screwdriver to lift the locking tab and release the connector

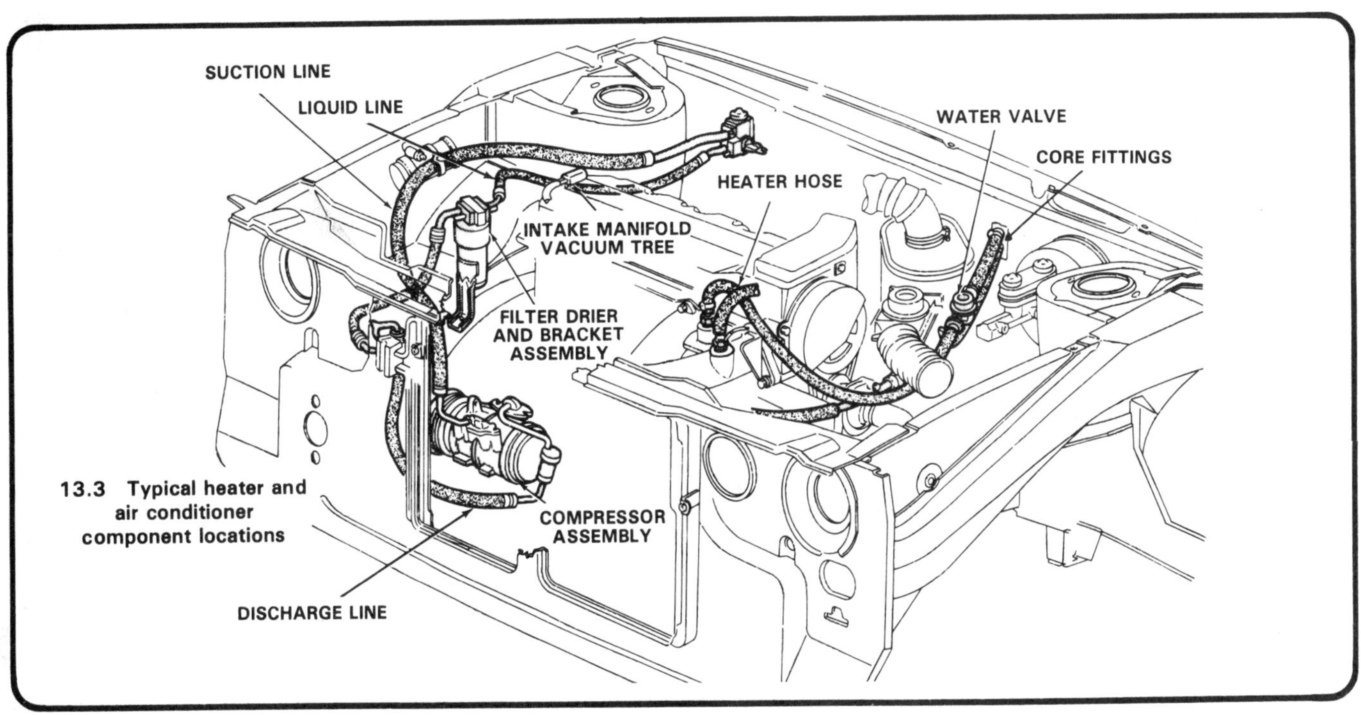

13.3 Typical heater and air conditioner component locations

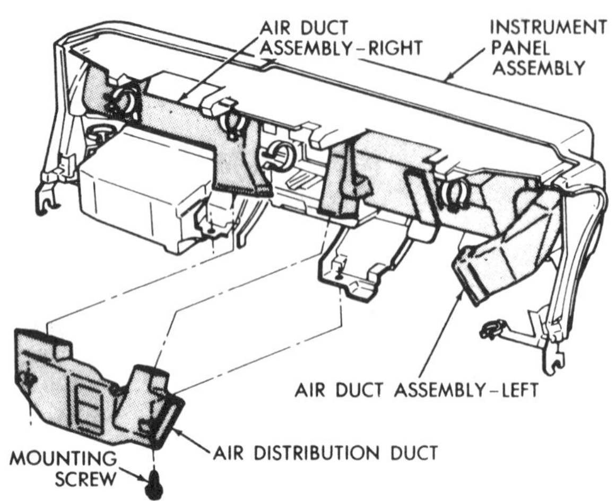

13.8 Center air distribution duct installation details (later models)

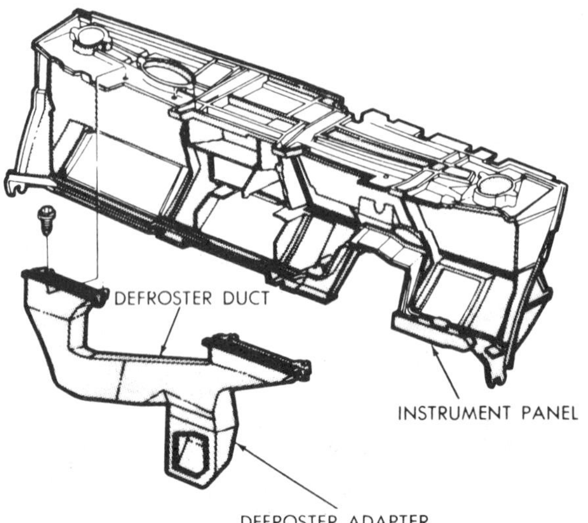

13.9 Defroster duct mounting details

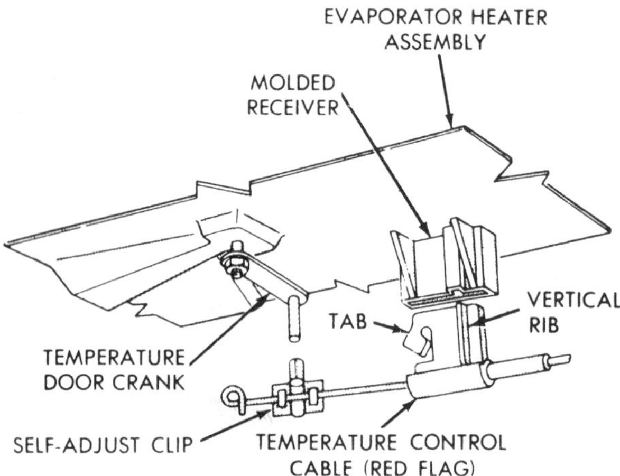

13.11 Heater/air conditioner control cable mount details

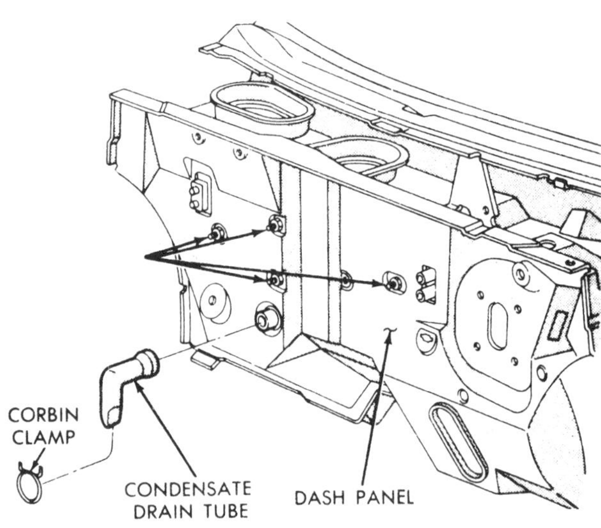

13.15 The heater/air conditioner evaporator retaining nuts (arrows) are accessible from the engine compartment

4 Disconnect the vacuum lines at the intake manifold and heater water valve.
5 Remove the cowl side trim panel and the glove box.
6 Remove the heater/air conditioner control (Section 12).
7 On models so equipped, remove the console and forward console mounting bracket.
8 Remove the center air distribution duct **(see illustration)**.
9 Pull the defroster adapter out from under the instrument panel **(see illustration)**.
10 Remove the clamp, pull off the condensate drain tube, then remove the evaporator/heater assembly-to-dash retaining nuts.
11 Unplug the wiring harnesses, then remove the control cable by depressing the tab on the flag and pulling the flag out of the receiver **(see illustration)**.
12 Disconnect the wiring harness from the assembly.
13 Remove the right side cowl-to-plenum brace and pull the carpet back from under the evaporator unit.
14 Remove the evaporator/hanger strap and swing it out of the way.
15 Remove the heat shield (if equipped) and remove the nuts in the engine compartment retaining the air conditioning unit to the dash panel **(see illustration)**.
16 On convertible models, remove the floor air distribution duct from the housing. Remove the upper instrument pad and the instrument panel mounting screws along the windshield. With the help of an assistant, lift up on the dash assembly while pulling the evaporator assembly back and rotating it out from under the dash.
17 On all other models, pull the unit to the rear and remove it from the vehicle.
18 Installation is the reverse of removal. **Note:** *Care must be taken not to hang the vacuum lines up on the accelerator or trap them between the evaporator/heater assembly and the dash. If they are, they will be kinked and the evaporator/heater assembly will have to be removed again. Proper routing of the lines may require two people. Be sure to hook the black vacuum line to the brake booster and the gray one to the water valve.*

14 Heater core, evaporator core and blower motor – removal and installation

Refer to illustrations 14.2, 14.4 and 14.10

1 Position the heater assembly on a workbench (as it would be viewed by a front seat passenger).
2 Remove the mode door actuator arm nut and squeeze the arm off the shaft with a pair of pliers **(see illustration)**.
3 Remove the screws and detach the cover. The mode door will come out with the cover (it can be removed if repair is necessary).
4 Remove the screw from the heater core tube retaining bracket and lift the core out of the housing. The evaporator core can be lifted out of the housing as well after the expansion seal and bracket screw have been removed **(see illustration)**.

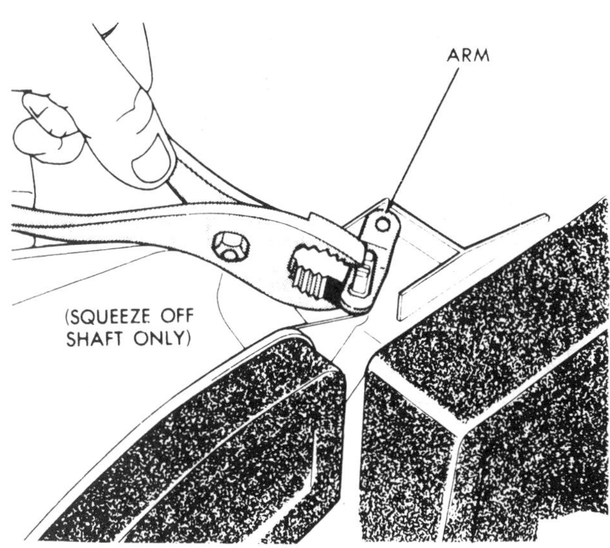

14.2 Remove the actuator arm by squeezing it off the shaft with a pair of pliers

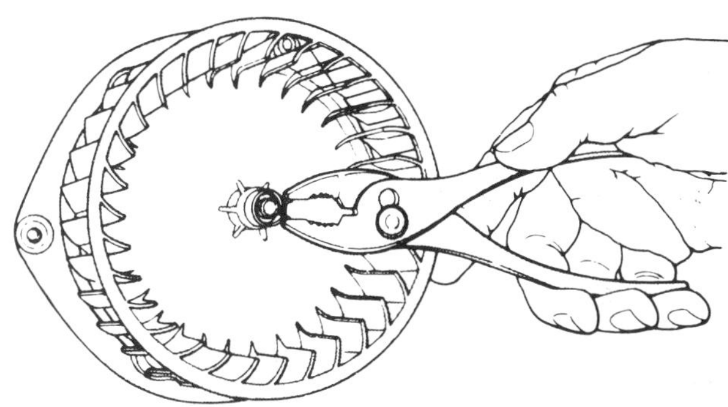

14.10 To remove the blower fan, use a pair of pliers to release the clamp, then slide the clamp and blower off the motor shaft

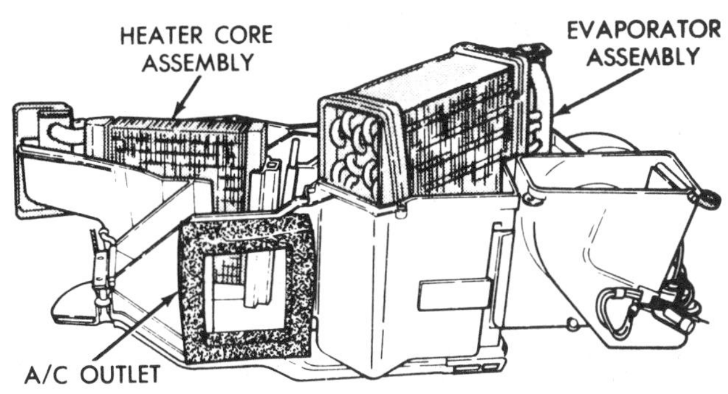

14.4 Heater core/evaporator locations

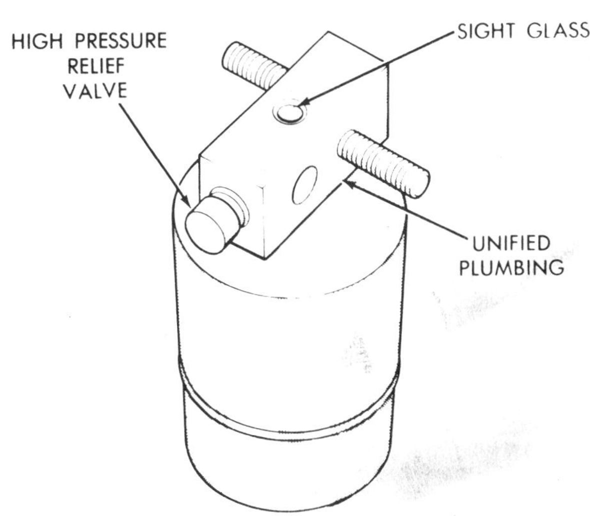

15.4 Air conditioner filter-drier sight glass location

5 Disconnect the actuator linkage from the recirculation door and the vacuum lines from the actuator. Remove the nuts and detach the actuator.
6 Remove the screws and detach the recirculation cover from the housing.
7 The recirculation door can now be removed from the housing as well.
8 Remove the evaporator/heater housing vent tube.
9 Remove the screws and lift out the blower motor and fan assembly.
10 To detach the fan, remove the retaining clamp and slide it off the motor shaft **(see illustration)**.
11 The motor is held in place with three screws.
12 Installation is the reverse of removal.

15 Air conditioning system – description and check

Refer to illustrations 13.3 and 15.4

Caution: *The air conditioning system is pressurized at the factory and requires special equipment for service and repair. Any work should be left to your dealer or an air conditioning shop. Do not, under any circumstances, disconnect the air conditioning hoses while the system is under pressure.*

1 The air conditioning system consists of a condenser mounted in front of the radiator, an evaporator mounted under the dash, a belt-driven compressor incorporating a clutch, a filter-drier which contains a high pressure relief valve and associated hoses.
2 The temperature in the passenger compartment is lowered by transferring the heat in the air to the refrigerant in the evaporator and then passing the refrigerant through the filter-drier to the condenser.
3 Maintenance is confined to keeping the system properly charged with refrigerant, the compressor drivebelt adjusted properly and making sure the condenser is free of leaves and other debris.
4 The sight glass located on the top of the filter-drier can give some indication of the refrigerant level **(see illustration)**.
5 With the control on A/C, the fan switch on High and the temperature lever on Cool, run the system for several minutes. The temperature in the vehicle should be approximately 70°F (21°C).
6 The system has a full refrigerant charge if the sight glass is clear, the air conditioner compressor clutch is engaged, the inlet line to the compressor is cool and the discharge line is warm.
7 If the glass is clear, the clutch is engaged but there is no difference in temperature between the inlet and discharge lines, the refrigerant charge is very low.
8 Continuous foam or bubbles in the sight glass is another symptom of low refrigerant. Occasional foam or bubbles under certain conditions, such as very high or low temperatures in the vehicle interior, is acceptable.

3

Chapter 4 Part A Fuel and exhaust systems

Contents

Specifications

Carburetor adjustments

Curb idle speed	See *Emissions Control Information label* in engine compartment
Fast idle speed	See *Emissions Control Information label* in engine compartment
2.2L engine choke vacuum kick adjustment	
Carburetor number	
1982	
R9582-A	0.060 in (1.5 mm)
R9583-A	
R9584-A	
R9585-A	
R9582-A	0.080 in (2 mm)
R9822-A	
R9823-A	
R9513A	0.120 in (3.05 mm)
R9514A	
R9499A	0.130 in (3.30 mm)
R9511A	
R9512A	
R9824A	0.065 in (1.65 mm)
R9503A	0.085 in (2.15 mm)
R9504A	
R9750A	
R9751A	

R9505A	0.100 in (2.55 mm)
R9506A	
R9752A	
R9753A	
1983	
R400203A	0.055 in (1.35 mm)
R40022A	
R40023A	0.070 in (1.80 mm)
R40024A	
R40025A	
R40026A	
R40141A	
R40003A	
R40007A	
R40008A	
R40012A	
R40004A	0.080 in (2 mm)
R40005A	
R40006A	
R40010A	
R40014A	
R40080A	0.45 in (1.20 mm)
R40081A	
1984	
R40060A	0.055 in (1.35 mm)
R400851A	0.040 in (1.05 mm)
R40170A	0.060 in (1.5 mm)
R40171A	
R400671A	0.070 in (1.80 mm)
R40068A	
R400581A	
R400641A	0.080 in (2 mm)
R400651A	
R400811A	
R400821A	
R40071A	
R40122A	
2.2L engine float drop	1-7/8 in (47.6 mm)
2.2L engine dry float level	0.480 in (12.2 mm)
2.6L engine dry float level	0.780 ± 0.039 in (20 ± 1 mm)

Torque specifications	**Ft-lbs** *(unless otherwise noted)*	**Nm**
Carburetor mounting nuts		
2.2L engine	17	23
2.6L engine	12.5	17
2.6L engine exhaust manifold-to-catalytic converter bolts	24	32
Single-point EFI system		
Automatic Idle Speed (AIS) motor Torx screws	20 in-lbs	2
Throttle body-to-manifold bolts/nuts		
Through 1987	17	23
1988 on	15	20
Pressure regulator screws	4	5
Throttle position sensor screws	20 in-lbs	2
Fuel injector Torx screws	4	5
Fuel line fittings	15	20
Multi-point EFI system		
Fuel rail bolts	19	25
Throttle body-to-intake manifold bolts	54	40
Throttle position sensor screws	17 in-lbs	2
Fuel line fittings	15	20

1 General information

These models may be equipped with either a carburetor or an Electronic Fuel Injection (EFI) system. The fuel system consists of a rear mounted fuel tank, a mechanical (mounted on the engine — carbureted models) or electric (located in the fuel tank — EFI models) fuel pump which supplies fuel to the carburetor or fuel injection system, and associated hoses, lines and filters. The exhaust system is made up of pipes, heat shields, a muffler and catalytic converters. The use of catalytic converters requires that only unleaded fuel be used in the vehicle.

2 Air conditioning idle speed (2.2L carburetor equipped engine) — check

1 Air conditioned models are equipped with a system which increases idle speed when the air conditioning compressor engages, putting a greater load on the engine. Prior to checking the air conditioning idle speed, check the curb idle and timing (Chapter 1) to make sure they are correct. The checks should be made with the engine at normal operating temperature.
2 When the air conditioner is engaged, the idle speed is increased

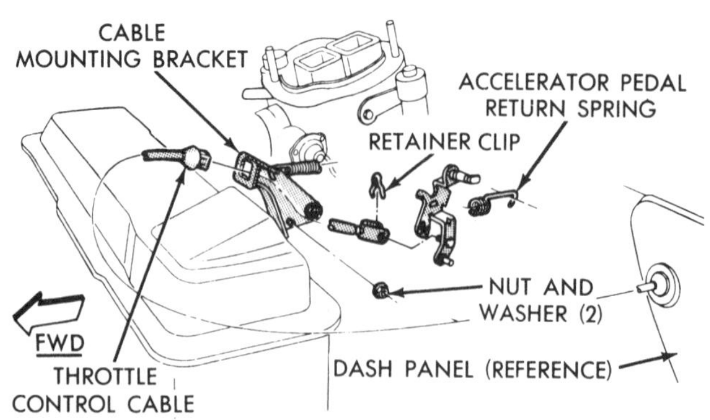

3.2a 2.2L carburetor equipped engine throttle cable installation details

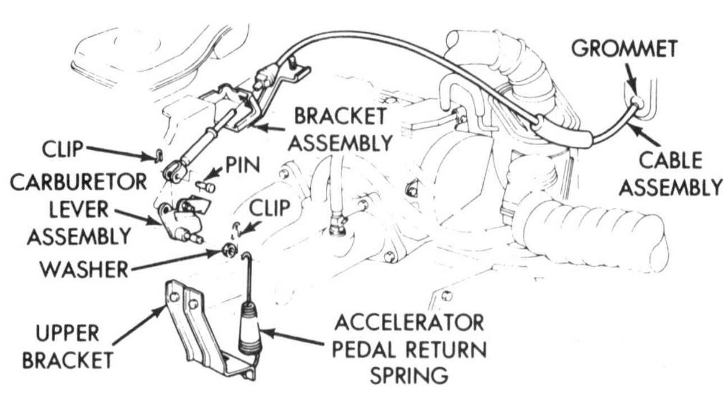

3.2b 2.6L engine throttle cable installation details

3.7a Pull the throttle cable retainer clip off with a pair of needle-nose pliers

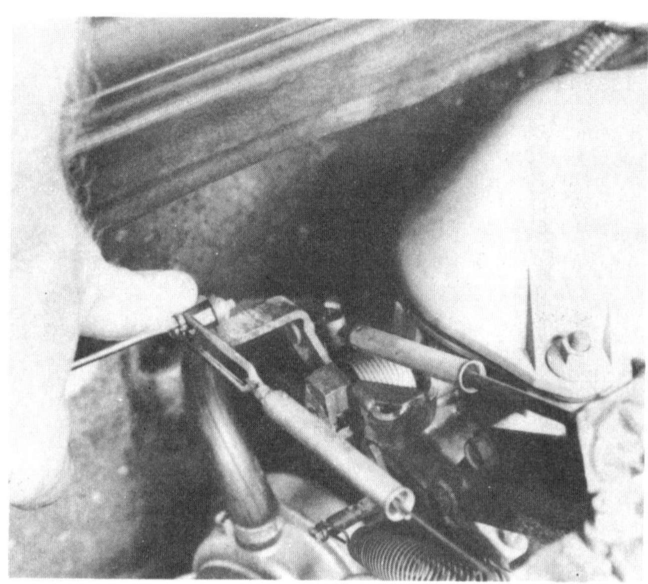

3.7b Use a small screwdriver to pry off the cruise control cable clip

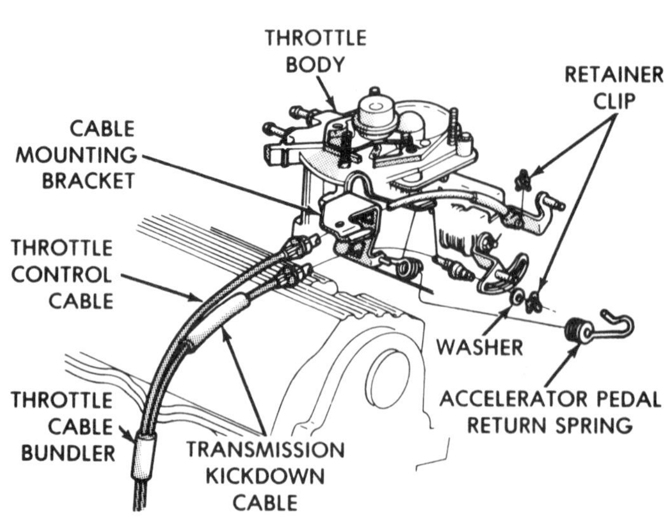

3.7c Single-point EFI throttle cable installation details

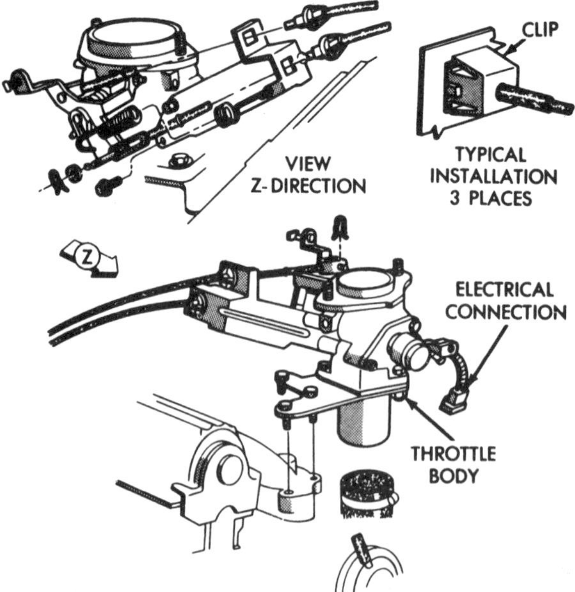

3.7d Multi-point EFI throttle cable installation details

by a vacuum or solenoid type kicker.
3 Kicker operation can be checked by running the engine (at normal operating temperature), moving the temperature control to the coldest setting and then turning the air conditioning on. The kicker plunger should move in and out as the compressor clutch engages and disengages. Remove the air cleaner for better visual access to the kicker, if necessary (also, see illustration 11.8).
4 If the idle speed doesn't change as the air conditioner cycles on and off, check the system hoses and diaphragm for leaks and make sure the vacuum solenoid (which directs vacuum to the kicker) is operating. If no defective parts are found, replace the kicker with a new one and repeat the check.

3 Throttle cable – removal and installation

Refer to illustrations 3.2a, 3.2b, 3.7a, 3.7b, 3.7c and 3.7d

Carburetor equipped models

1 Working inside the vehicle, remove the retaining plug and detach the cable end from the accelerator pedal shaft (see illustration 4.1). Remove the retainer clip from the cable assembly housing at the grommet.
2 Working in the engine compartment, remove the retainer clip and separate the cable from the pin or stud, then detach the cable from the mounting bracket **(see illustrations)**. Compress the cable-to-bracket fitting with a pair of pliers that has wide jaws.
3 Pull the cable assembly into the engine compartment and remove it from the vehicle. Make sure the grommet remains in place in the dash panel.
4 Installation is the reverse of removal.

Fuel injection equipped models

5 Working inside the vehicle, disconnect the throttle cable from the pedal shaft (Section 4). Working inside the vehicle, remove the retainer clip from the cable assembly housing at the grommet **(see illustration 4.1)**.
6 Working in the engine compartment, pull the cable housing end fitting out of the dash panel grommet, making sure the grommet remains in place.
7 Remove the retainer clips and disconnect the throttle cable and cruise control cable (if equipped) from the throttle body **(see illustrations)**. Use a pair of pliers to compress the end fitting tabs so the cable can then be separated from the mounting bracket.
8 To install the cable, insert the housing into the cable mounting bracket on the engine and attach the cable clevis to the throttle body with the retainer clip. Insert the cable through the dash panel grommet and connect it to the throttle pedal.

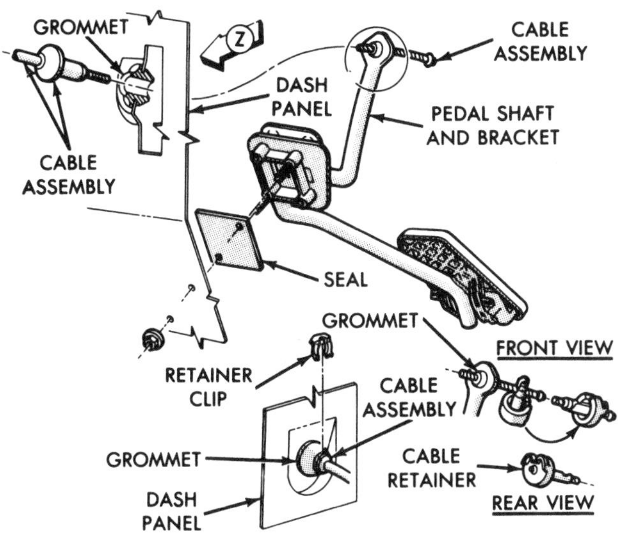

4.1 Throttle pedal installation details

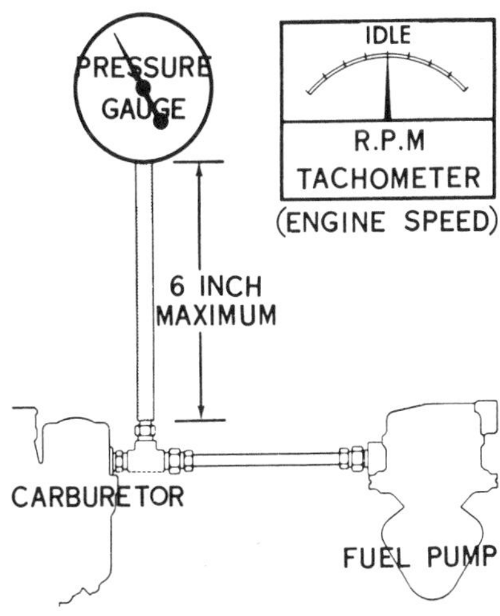

5.1 Attach the T-fitting as close to the carburetor as possible and use a 6-inch maximum length of hose when hooking up the pressure gauge to check the fuel pump pressure

4 Throttle pedal – removal and installation

Refer to illustration 4.1

1 Remove the cable retainer and disengage the throttle cable from the pedal shaft and bracket **(see illustration)**.
2 Working in the engine compartment, remove the pedal assembly retaining nuts.
3 Working inside the vehicle, detach the pedal assembly from the dash panel and remove it.
4 Installation is the reverse of removal.

4A

5 Fuel pump (2.2L carburetor equipped engine) – check

Refer to illustration 5.1

Warning: *Gasoline is extremely flammable, so extra precautions must be taken when working on any part of the fuel system. Do not smoke or allow open flames or bare light bulbs near the work area. Also, do not work in a garage if a natural gas-type appliance with a pilot light is present.*

1 Disconnect the fuel line from the carburetor and install a T-fitting **(see illustration)**. Connect a fuel system pressure gauge to the T-fitting with a section of fuel hose that is no longer than six inches.
2 Disconnect the gauge from the end of the fuel hose and direct the end of the hose into a metal container. Operate the starter for a few seconds, until fuel spurts out of the hose, to vent the pump (this eliminates any air in the fuel chamber, which could affect the pressure reading). Reattach the gauge to the fuel hose.
3 Start the engine and allow it to idle. The pressure on the gauge should be 4.5 to 6 psi, remain constant and return to zero slowly when the engine is shut off.
4 An instant pressure drop indicates a faulty outlet valve. If this occurs, or if the pressure is too high or low, replace the fuel pump with a new one. **Note:** *If the pressure is too high, check the air vent to see if it is plugged before replacing the pump.*

6 Fuel pump (2.2L carburetor equipped engine) – removal and installation

Refer to illustration 6.1

Warning: *Gasoline is extremely flammable, so extra precautions must be taken when working on any part of the fuel system. Do not smoke or allow open flames or bare light bulbs near the work area. Also, do not work in a garage if a natural gas-type appliance with a pilot light is present.*

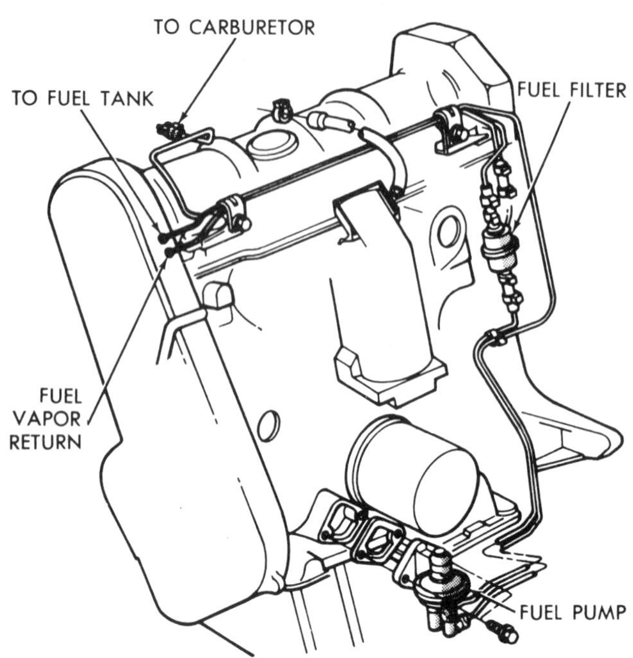

6.1 2.2L carburetor equipped engine fuel pump location and fuel line routing

1 The fuel pump is bolted to the engine block adjacent to the oil filter **(see illustration)**.
2 Place clean rags or newspaper under the fuel pump to catch any gasoline which is spilled during removal.
3 Carefully loosen and unscrew the fuel line fittings and detach the lines from the pump. A flare-nut wrench should be used to prevent damage to the line fittings.
4 Unbolt and remove the fuel pump.
5 Before installation, coat both sides of the spacer block with RTV sealant, position the fuel pump and spacer in place and install the bolts.
6 Attach the lines to the pump and tighten the fittings securely (use a flare-nut wrench, if one is available, to prevent damage to the fittings).
7 Run the engine and check for leaks.

7 Fuel pump (2.6L engine) — removal and installation

Refer to illustrations 7.1 and 7.12

Warning: *Gasoline is extremely flammable, so extra precautions must be taken when working on any part of the fuel system. Do not smoke or allow open flames or bare light bulbs near the work area. Also, do not work in a garage if a natural gas-type appliance with a pilot light is present.*

1 The fuel pump is mounted on the cylinder head, adjacent to the carburetor **(see illustration)**. It is held in place with two nuts.
2 Pull the coil high-tension lead out of the distributor and ground it on the engine block. Remove the spark plugs and wires (refer to Chapter 1 if necessary).
3 Place your thumb over the number one cylinder spark plug hole and rotate the crankshaft in a clockwise direction (with a wrench on the large bolt attaching the pulley to the front of the crankshaft) until you can feel the compression pressure rising in the number one cylinder.
4 Continue rotating the crankshaft until the notch on the crankshaft pulley lines up with the T or zero on the timing mark tab on the timing chain case. At this point, the lift of the fuel pump drive cam is reduced to a minimum, which will make the pump easier to remove.
5 Install the spark plugs and hook up the wires. Don't forget the coil high-tension lead.
6 Remove the air intake housing and carburetor-to-cylinder head cover bracket, then remove the fuel filter mounting bolt. Loosen the hose clamps and remove the fuel hoses from the pump fittings. Plug

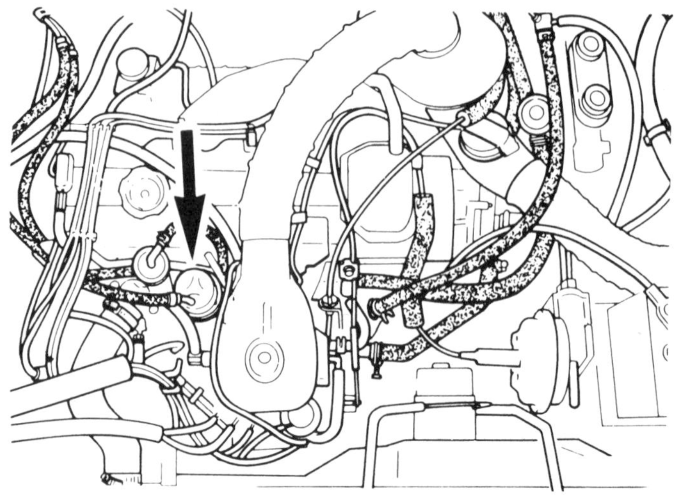

7.1 2.6L engine fuel pump location (arrow)

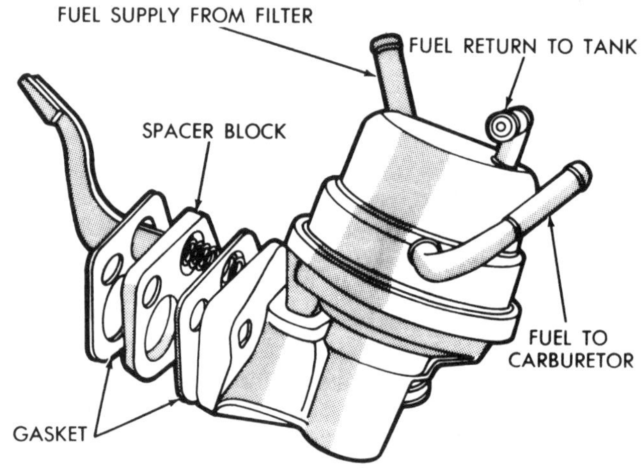

7.12 2.6L engine fuel pump mounting details

the ends of the hoses.
7 Remove the fuel pump mounting nuts and pull the pump off the engine. You may have to tap the pump body with a soft-face hammer to break the gasket seal.
8 If the pump is difficult to remove, take off the cylinder head cover (see Chapter 2) and guide the pump rocker arm out of the head from the inside.
9 Remove the spacer block and scrape off all traces of the old gaskets and sealer.
10 Before installing the new pump, make sure that the rocker arm moves up and down without binding or sticking.
11 Coat both sides of the new gaskets with RTV gasket sealant before installation.
12 Slip the first gasket, the spacer block and the second gasket (in that order) onto the fuel pump mounting studs **(see illustration)**.
13 Install the fuel pump. It may be necessary to guide the rocker arm into place from inside the head. Work slowly; there is not much clearance between the rocker arm and the valve gear.
14 Once the fuel pump is properly seated, install the mounting nuts and tighten them evenly. Do not overtighten them or the spacer block may crack.
15 Install the cylinder head cover if it was removed.
16 Install the hoses (after inspecting them for cracks) and new hose clamps.
17 Install the filter mounting bolt, the bracket and the air intake housing.

18 Start the engine and check for fuel leaks at the hose fittings. Check for oil leaks where the fuel pump mounts on the cylinder head.

8 Carburetor overhaul

A thorough road test and check of carburetor adjustments should be done before any major carburetor service. Specifications for some adjustments are listed on the vehicle *Emission Control Information label* found in the engine compartment.

Some performance complaints directed at the carburetor are actually a result of loose, misadjusted or malfunctioning engine or electrical components. Others develop when vacuum hoses leak, are disconnected or are incorrectly routed, The proper approach to analyzing carburetor problems should include a routine check of the following areas:

a) Inspect all vacuum hoses and actuators for leaks and proper installation (see Chapter 6).
b) Tighten the intake manifold nuts and carburetor mounting nuts evenly and securely.
c) Perform a cylinder compression test.
d) Clean or replace the spark plugs as necessary.
e) Check the resistance of the spark plug wires.
f) Inspect the ignition primary wires and check the vacuum advance operation. Replace any defective parts.
g) Check the ignition timing as described in Chapter 1.
h) Inspect the heat control valve in the air cleaner for proper operation (refer to Chapter 1).
i) Remove the carburetor air filter element and blow out any dirt with compressed air. If the filter is extremely dirty, replace it with a new one.
j) Inspect the crankcase ventilation system (see Chapter 1).

Carburetor problems usually show up as flooding, hard starting, stalling, severe backfiring and poor acceleration. A carburetor that is leaking fuel and/or covered with wet-looking deposits definitely needs attention.

Diagnosing carburetor problems may require that the engine be started and run with the air cleaner removed. While running the engine without the air cleaner it is possible that it could backfire. A backfiring situation is likely to occur if the carburetor is malfunctioning, but removal of the air cleaner alone can lean the fuel/air mixture enough to produce an engine backfire. **Warning:** *Do not position your face directly over the carburetor opening.*

Once it is determined that the carburetor is in need of work or an overhaul, several alternatives should be considered. If you are going to attempt to overhaul the carburetor yourself, first obtain a good quality carburetor rebuild kit, which will include all necessary gaskets, internal parts, complete instructions and a parts list. You will also need carburetor cleaning solvent and some means of blowing out the internal passages of the carburetor with air.

Due to the many configurations and variations of carburetors offered on the range of vehicles covered in this book, it is not possible to include a step-by-step overhaul of each type. You will receive a detailed set of instructions with any quality carburetor overhaul kit; they will apply in a more specific manner to the carburetor on your vehicle.

Another alternative is to obtain a new or rebuilt carburetor. These are readily available from dealers and auto parts stores for all engines covered in this manual. The important fact when purchasing one of these units is to make sure the exchange carburetor is identical to the original. Usually a tag is attached to the top of the carburetor. The tag will aid in determining the exact type of carburetor you have. When obtaining a rebuilt carburetor or a rebuild kit, take time to ascertain that the kit or carburetor matches your application exactly. Seemingly insignificant differences can make a considerable difference in the overall performance of your engine.

If you choose to overhaul your own carburetor, allow enough time to disassemble the carburetor carefully, soak the necessary parts in the cleaning solvent (usually for at least one half day or according to the instructions listed on the carburetor cleaner) and reassemble it, which will usually take much longer than disassembly. When you are disassembling the carburetor, match each part with the illustration in the carburetor kit and lay the parts out in order on a clean work surface. Overhauls by amateurs sometimes result in an engine which runs poorly, or not at all. To avoid this happening to you, use care and patience when disassembling the carburetor so you can reassemble it correctly.

9 Carburetor (2.2L engine) – removal and installation

Warning: *Gasoline is extremely flammable, so extra precautions must be taken when working on any part of the fuel system. Do not smoke or allow open flames or bare light bulbs near the work area. Also, do not work in a garage if a natural gas-type appliance with a pilot light is present.*

Removal

1 Disconnect the negative cable at the battery. Place the cable out of the way so it cannot accidentally come in contact with the negative terminal of the battery, as this would once again allow power into the electrical system of the vehicle.
2 Remove the air cleaner assembly.
3 Remove the fuel tank filler cap as the tank could be under some pressure.
4 Place a metal container under the fuel inlet fitting and disconnect the fitting.
5 Disconnect the wiring harness from the carburetor.
6 Disconnect the throttle linkage.
7 Tag and remove all hoses from the carburetor.
8 Remove the mounting nuts and carefully detach the carburetor from the manifold, taking care to hold it level. Do not remove the isolator mounting screws unless the isolator must be replaced with a new one.

Installation

9 Inspect the mating surfaces of the carburetor and the isolator for nicks, burrs and debris that could cause air leaks.
10 Place the carburetor in position and install the mounting nuts, taking care not to damage the fast idle lever.
11 Tighten the nuts to the specified torque, following a criss-cross pattern.
12 Check all of the vacuum hoses and connections for damage, replacing them with new parts if necessary, and install them.
13 Connect the throttle linkage and the fuel line.
14 Check the operation of the throttle linkage and the choke plate.
15 Connect the wiring harness and install the air cleaner.
16 Connect the negative battery cable.
17 Start the engine and check for fuel leaks.
18 Check the engine idle speed.

10 Carburetor (2.6L engine) – removal and installation

Warning: *Gasoline is extremely flammable, so extra precautions must be taken when working on any part of the fuel system. Do not smoke or allow open flames or bare light bulbs near the work area. Also, do not work in a garage if a natural gas-type appliance with a pilot light is present.*

Removal

1 Disconnect the negative cable at the battery. Place the cable out of the way so it cannot accidentally come in contact with the negative terminal of the battery, as this would once again allow power into the electrical system of the vehicle.
2 Remove the intake housing from the carburetor air horn.
3 Release any pressure which may exist in the fuel tank by removing the filler cap.
4 Drain the radiator (see Chapter 1).
5 Remove the carburetor protector, tag the locations of the vacuum and coolant hoses and detach them from the carburetor.
6 Unplug the carburetor wiring harness connectors.
7 Place a metal container under the carburetor fuel inlet to catch any residual fuel and disconnect the fuel hose from the inlet fitting.
8 Disconnect the throttle linkage.
9 Remove the mounting bolt and nuts and carefully detach the carburetor from the manifold. Keep the carburetor level to avoid spilling fuel.

Installation

10 Check the mating surfaces of the carburetor and intake manifold for nicks, burrs and old gasket material which could cause air leaks.
11 Using a new gasket, place the carburetor in position and install the mounting nuts and bolt. Tighten them to the specified torque,

following a criss-cross pattern.
12 Connect the throttle linkage and the fuel hose.
13 Connect the coolant and vacuum hoses and install the carburetor protector.
14 Refill the radiator with the specified coolant.
15 Check the operation of the throttle linkage and choke plate.
16 Install the air intake housing and the fuel tank cap.
17 Connect the negative battery cable.
18 Start the engine and check for fuel leaks.
19 Check the engine idle speed.

11 Carburetor (2.2L engine) — idle speed adjustment

Refer to illustration 11.8

Note: *Refer to Section 2 for the air conditioning idle speed check procedure.*

1 Start the engine and run it until normal operating temperature is reached.
2 Check the ignition timing and adjust as necessary (Chapter 1), then shut off the engine.
3 On 1983 and 1984 models, disconnect and plug the vacuum connector at the CVSCC (see Chapter 6 if necessary). On all 6520 feedback carburetor equipped models, disconnect the oxygen feedback system test connector located on the left fender shield.
4 Unplug the fan wire connector and install a jumper wire so the fan will run continuously.
5 Remove the PCV valve from the vent module so the valve will draw air from the engine compartment.
6 Leave the air cleaner in place and connect a tachometer. Ground the carburetor switch with a jumper wire.
7 Start the engine.
8 Check the idle speed reading on the tachometer and compare it to the *Emissions Control Information label* under the hood. Turn the idle speed screw **(see illustration)** as necessary to achieve the specified idle speed.
9 Shut off the engine and remove the tachometer.
10 Remove the carburetor switch jumper wire, plug in the fan connector, install the PCV valve and reconnect any vacuum hoses and wires which were disconnected.

12 Carburetor (2.2L engine) — fast idle adjustment

Refer to illustration 12.3

1 Perform Steps 1 through 6 in Section 11.
2 On 1982 feedback carburetors, disconnect the red and tan wires at the carburetor.
3 Start the engine, open the throttle slightly and set the fast idle screw on the slowest step of the fast idle cam **(see illustration)**.

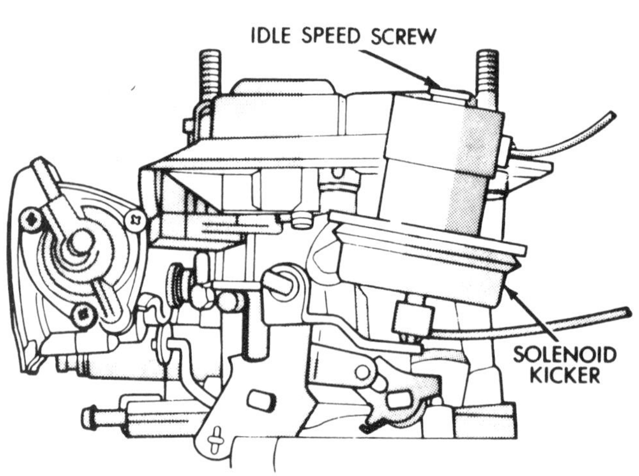

11.8 Idle speed adjusting screw location — 2.2L engine

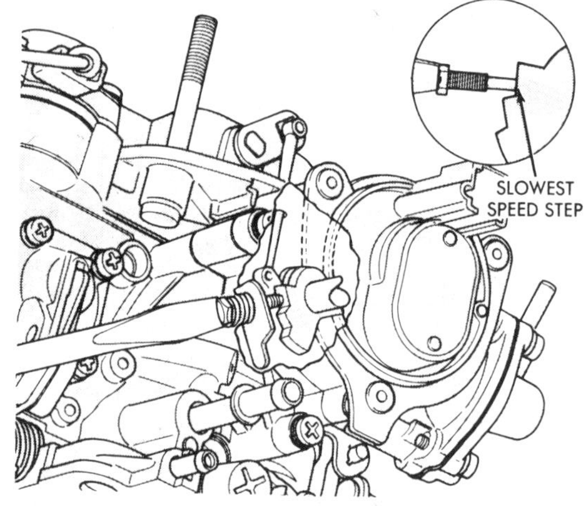

12.3 Fast idle speed adjustment details — 2.2L engine

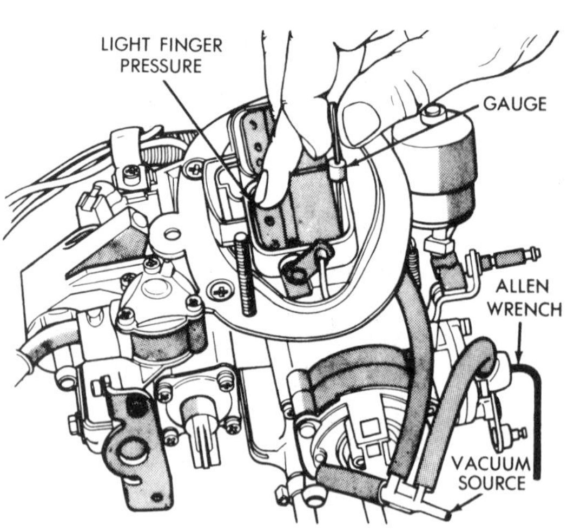

13.5a 1982 model 2.2L engine choke vacuum kick adjustment details

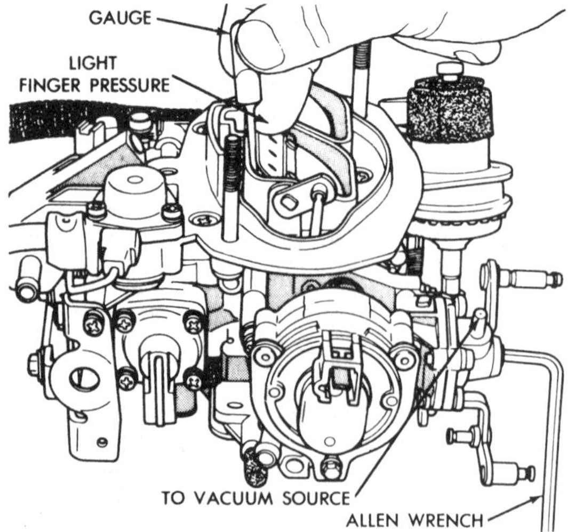

13.5b 1983 and 1984 model 2.2L engine choke vacuum kick adjustment details

4 With the choke valve completely open, adjust the fast idle speed to the specification on the *Emissions Control Information label* by turning the adjustment screw.
5 Return the engine to idle, then reposition the fast idle screw on the slowest step of the fast idle cam to verify the fast idle speed. Adjust as necessary.
6 Turn off the engine, remove the tachometer and reconnect all components removed for the adjustment procedure.

13 Carburetor (2.2L engine) – choke vacuum kick adjustment

Refer to illustrations 13.5a and 13.5b

1 Remove the air cleaner.
2 Open the throttle, close the choke and then close the throttle so the fast idle system is trapped at the closed choke position.

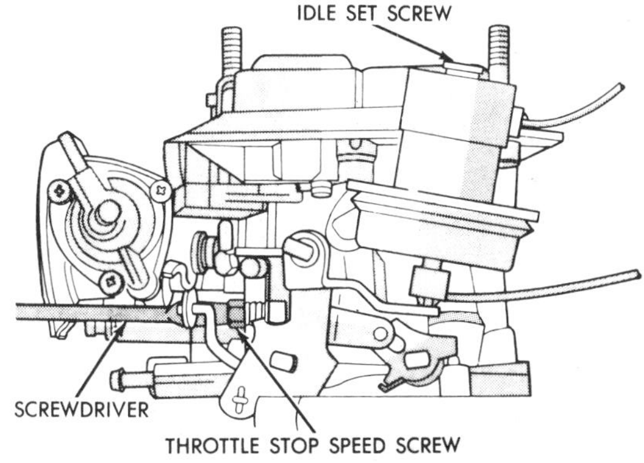

14.4 Anti-diesel adjustment details – 2.2L engine

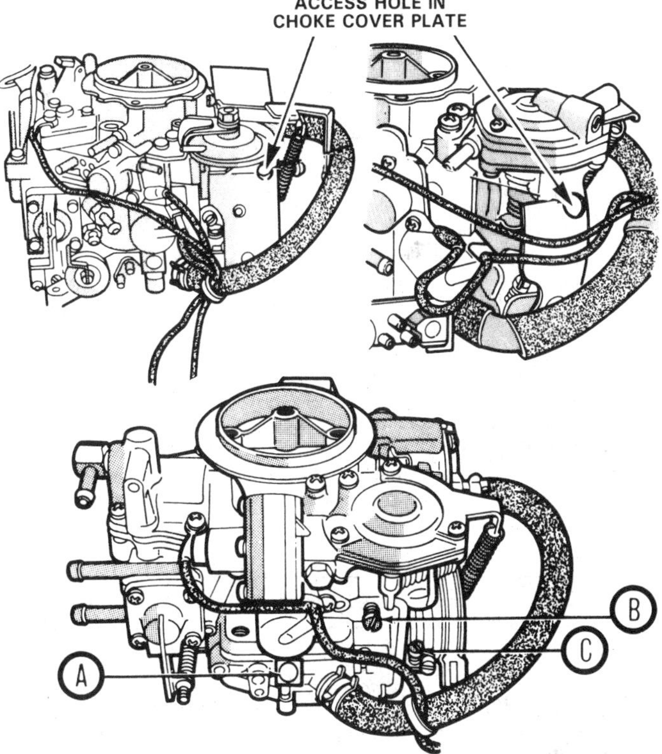

15.5a 1982 model non-feedback carburetor adjustment screw location – 2.6L engine

A Mixture adjustment screw (behind concealment plug)
B Idle speed adjusting screw (accessible through the hole in the choke cover plate)
C Idle up adjusting screw

3 Disconnect the carburetor vacuum hose, connect a vacuum pump and apply 15-inches of vacuum.
4 Push the choke closed so the plates are at their smallest opening (use very light pressure and do not distort the linkage). The choke system internal spring will now be compressed.
5 Insert the appropriate size drill bit or gauge between the plate and the air horn wall at the primary throttle end of the carburetor. Check the clearance against the Specifications and adjust as necessary by turning an Allen wrench inserted into the diaphragm **(see illustrations)**.
6 After adjustment, replace the vacuum hose and the air cleaner assembly.

14 Carburetor (2.2L engine) – anti-diesel adjustment

Refer to illustration 14.4

1 Warm up the engine to operating temperature, check the ignition timing (Chapter 1), then shut it off. Connect a tachometer.
2 On 1983 and 1984 models, remove the red wire from the 6-way connector on the carburetor side of the connector.
3 With the transaxle in Neutral, the parking brake set securely and the wheels blocked to prevent any movement, ground the carburetor idle stop switch with a jumper wire and make sure the headlights are off. Start the engine.
4 Adjust the throttle stop speed screw **(see illustration)** to achieve an idle speed of 700 rpm.
5 Shut off the engine, remove the tachometer, remove the jumper wire and connect the carburetor idle stop switch wire.

15 Carburetor (2.6L engine) – idle speed adjustment

Refer to illustrations 15.5a, 15.5b and 15.6

1 With the transaxle in Neutral, the parking brake set and the wheels blocked to prevent any movement, unplug the cooling fan wire, turn off the lights and all accessories. Connect a tachometer to the engine, start the engine and allow it to warm up to normal operating temperature so the choke is fully open. Check the ignition timing (Chapter 1).
2 On 1984 feedback models, turn the engine off, disconnect the negative battery cable for three seconds and then reconnect it. Carefully unplug the engine wiring harness from the oxygen sensor bullet-type connector located nearest to the sensor. **Caution:** *Be careful working in this area as the exhaust manifold is very hot and could cause burns.*
3 Start the engine. On 1982 and 1983 models, allow the engine to idle for one minute. On 1984 and 1985 models, open the throttle and run the engine at 2500 rpm for 10 seconds, then return the engine to idle and wait two minutes.
4 After waiting one minute (1982 and 1983 models) or two minutes (1984 and 1985 models) with the curb idle stabilized, check the rpm indicated on the tachometer and make sure it is the same as specified on the *Emissions Control Information label.*
5 If it isn't, turn the idle speed screw to bring the rpm to the proper curb idle setting **(see illustrations)**. On feedback carburetors, it will be necessary to unplug the idle switch connector for access to the idle adjusting screw.

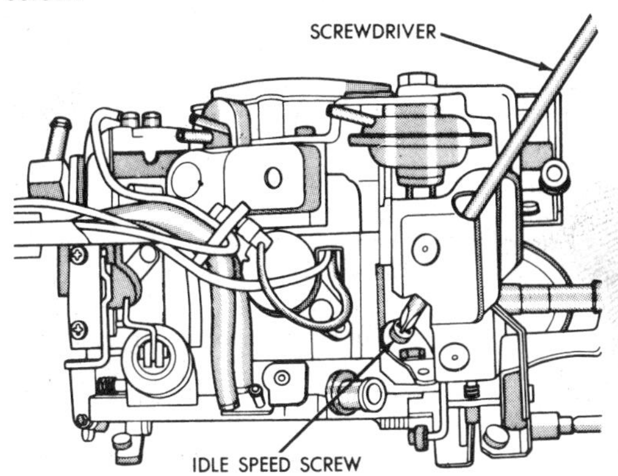

15.5b Idle speed adjusting screw location – later model 2.6L engine

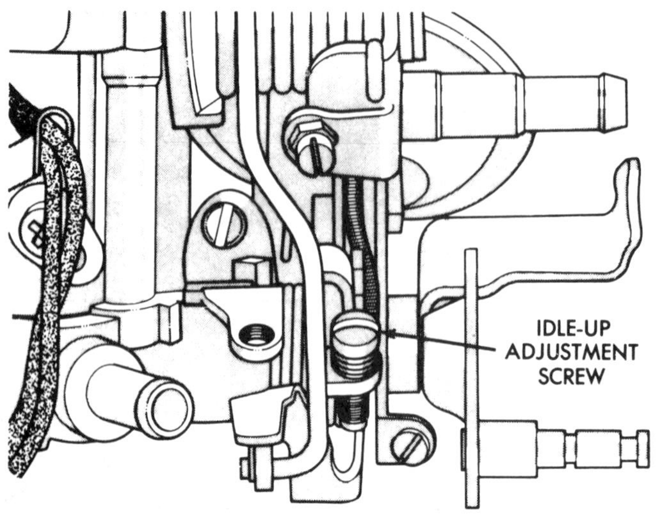

15.6 Air conditioner idle-up adjustment screw location — later model 2.6L engine

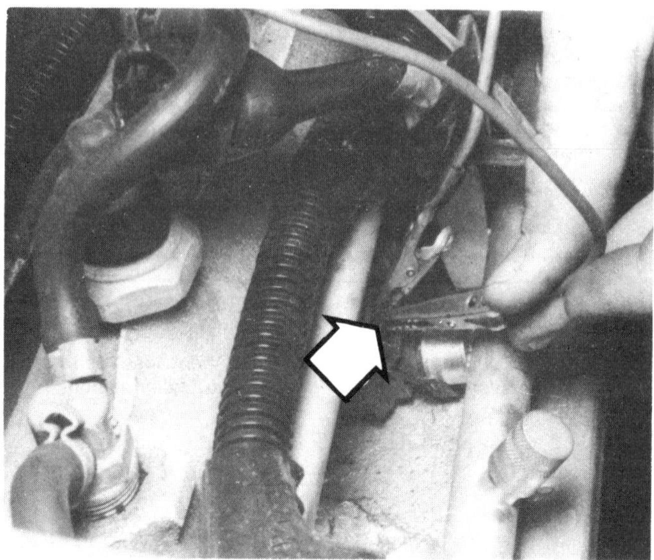

16.5 Bleed the fuel pressure in short bursts by touching the fuel injector terminal (arrow) with the jumper wire clip (multi-point EFI shown)

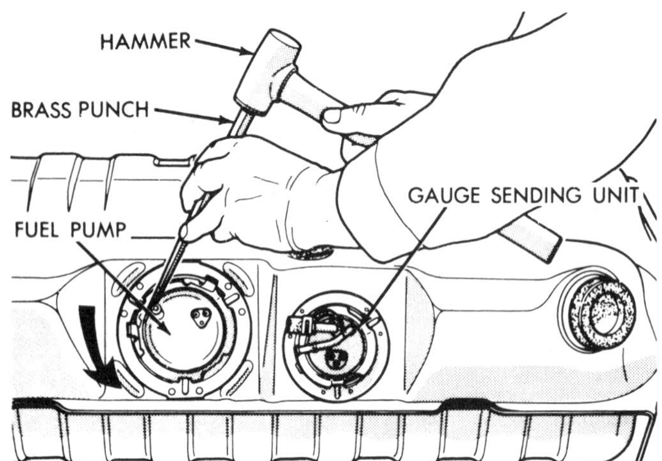

17.2 Use a hammer and a *brass* drift punch to unscrew the fuel pump locking ring

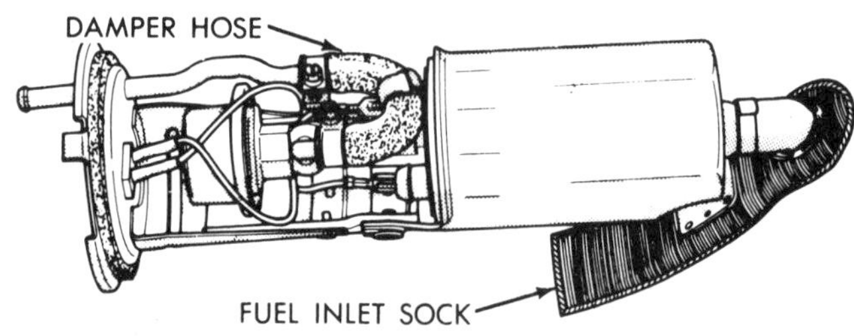

17.4 Inspect the fuel pump damper hose and the fuel inlet filter sock for damage

6 On air conditioned models, turn on the air conditioner and, with the compressor running, adjust the idle speed to the specified rpm by turning the idle-up adjustment screw **(see illustration)**.
7 Shut off the engine, reconnect the cooling fan and oxygen sensor and remove the tachometer.

16 Electronic Fuel Injection (EFI) system – pressure release

Refer to illustration 16.5

Warning: *Gasoline is extremely flammable, so extra precautions must be taken when working on any part of the fuel system. Do not smoke or allow open flames or bare light bulbs near the work area. Also, do not work in a garage if a natural gas-type appliance with a pilot light is present.*

1 The fuel system on fuel injected models is pressurized, even when the engine is off. Consequently, any time the fuel system is worked on (such as when the fuel filter is replaced) the system must be depressurized to avoid the dangerous release of fuel when a component is disconnected.
2 Loosen the fuel tank cap to release any pressure in the tank.
3 Unplug the harness connector at the throttle body (single-point) or one of the fuel injectors (multi-point).
4 Ground one of the injector terminals and connect a jumper wire between the other terminal and the positive (+) post of the battery. Be very careful not to create a direct short by touching the jumper wires together.
5 Connect the jumper wire to the terminal for no longer than five seconds to depressurize the fuel system **(see illustration)**. **Caution:** *Do not ground the injector terminal for more than five seconds. To avoid damage to the fuel injector, it is recommended that the pressure be bled in several spurts of one to two seconds to make sure the expensive injector system is not damaged. The fuel pressure can be heard escaping into the throttle body or combustion chamber; when the sound is no longer heard, the system is depressurized.*

17 Fuel pump (EFI equipped engine) – removal and installation

Refer to illustrations 17.2 and 17.4

Warning: *Gasoline is extremely flammable, so extra precautions must be taken when working on any part of the fuel system. Do not smoke or allow open flames or bare light bulbs near the work area. Also, do not work in a garage if a natural gas-type appliance with a pilot light is present.*

1 Remove the fuel tank (Section 31).
2 Use a hammer and a **brass** punch to remove the fuel pump locking ring by tapping it in a *counterclockwise* direction until it can be unscrewed **(see illustration)**.
3 Lift the fuel pump and O-ring from the fuel tank.

4 Clean the sealing area of the fuel tank and install a new O-ring on the fuel pump. Prior to installation, inspect the sock-like filter on the fuel pump suction tube for damage and contamination. Replace it with a new one if necessary **(see illustration)**.
5 Place the fuel pump in position in the tank, install the locking ring and use the hammer and **brass** punch to lock the pump in place.
6 Install the fuel tank.

18 Electronic Fuel Injection (EFI) system — description and check

Two types of Electronic Fuel Injection (EFI) systems are used on these models: single-point and multi-point. Single-point EFI is used on non-turbocharged models and multi-point on turbocharged models.

Both types are similar in operation and are controlled by the logic module and power module or the single module engine controller (SMEC) (1988 models only) (see Chapter 5) in combination with a variety of sensors and switches. On both the single and multi-point systems the conventional carburetor is replaced by a throttle body which is capable of very precise fuel metering for every driving condition. On single-point EFI the fuel is mixed with air and sprayed into the intake manifold, which directs it to the intake ports and cylinders. On multi-port EFI the fuel is sprayed directly into the ports by fuel injectors with the intake manifold supplying only the air.

The EFI system consists of a throttle body mounted on the intake manifold (single-point) or adjacent to the fuel rail (multi-point) which houses the fuel injector (single-point system only), pressure regulator, Throttle Position Sensor (TPS), Automatic Idle Speed (IAS) motor and throttle body temperature sensor, all of which interact with the power module and the logic module or the SMEC.

Due to the complexity of the EFI system, the home mechanic can do very little in the way of diagnosis because of the special techniques and equipment required. However, checking of the EFI system components and electrical and vacuum connections to make sure they are secure and not obviously damaged is one thing the home mechanic can do which can often detect a potential or current problem. Since the logic and power modules are completely dependent on the information provided by the many sensors and vacuum connections, a simple visual check and tightening of loose connections can save diagnostic time and possibly an unneccessary trip to the dealer service department.

Damaged or faulty EFI components can be replaced using the procedures in the following Sections. Further information on the logic and power modules and the EFI system can be found in Chapter 5.

19 Electronic Fuel Injection (EFI) system fuel lines and fittings — replacement

Warning: *Gasoline is extremely flammable, so extra precautions must be taken when working on any part of the fuel system. Do not smoke or allow open flames or bare light bulbs near the work area. Also, do not work in a garage if a natural gas-type appliance with a pilot light is present.*

Note: *Since the EFI system is under considerable pressure, always replace any clamp which is loosened or removed with a new one.*

1 Remove the air cleaner assembly.
2 Release the fuel system pressure (Section 16).
3 Disconnect the negative cable at the battery. Place the cable out of the way so it cannot accidentally come in contact with the negative terminal of the battery, as this would once again allow power into the electrical system of the vehicle.
4 Loosen the hose clamps, wrap a cloth around each end of the hose to catch the residual fuel and twist and pull to remove the hose.
5 Remove the fuel fittings. Note the inlet diameter and remove the copper washers.
6 When installing fuel fittings, make sure the inlet diameters match and always use **new** copper washers. Tighten the fittings to the specified torque.
7 When replacing hoses, always use hoses marked EFI/EFM and new original equipment-type clamps only. **Warning:** *Do not use fuel hose that is designed for carburetor equipped systems.*
8 Connect the negative battery cable, start the engine and check for leaks.
9 Install the air cleaner assembly.

20 Single-point EFI throttle body — removal and installation

Refer to illustrations 20.4a, 20.4b and 20.4c

Warning: *Gasoline is extremely flammable, so extra precautions must be taken when working on any part of the fuel system. Do not smoke or allow open flames or bare light bulbs near the work area. Also, do not work in a garage if a natural gas-type appliance with a pilot light is present.*

Removal

1 Remove the air cleaner assembly.
2 Release the fuel system pressure (Section 16).
3 Disconnect the negative cable at the battery. Place the cable out of the way so it cannot accidentally come in contact with the negative terminal of the battery, as this would once again allow power into the electrical system of the vehicle.
4 Disconnect the vacuum hoses and electrical connectors **(see illustrations)**.
5 Disconnect the throttle linkage and (if equipped) the cruise control and transaxle kickdown cables.
6 Remove the throttle return spring.
7 Place rags or newspapers under the fuel hoses to catch the residual fuel. Loosen the clamps, wrap a cloth around each fuel hose and remove each hose. Remove the copper washers from the hoses, noting their locations.
8 Remove the mounting bolts or nuts and detach the throttle body from the manifold.

Installation

9 Inspect the mating surfaces of the throttle body and the manifold for nicks, burrs and debris that could cause air leaks.
10 Using a new gasket, place the throttle body in position and install the mounting bolts or nuts.
11 Tighten the bolts or nuts to the specified torque, following a criss-cross pattern.
12 Check all of the vacuum hoses and electrical connectors for damage, replacing them with new parts if necessary, then install them.
13 Connect the throttle linkage and (if equipped) cruise control and kickdown cables.
14 Connect the throttle return spring.
15 Using **new** clamps and copper washers, install the fuel hoses.
16 Check the operation of the throttle linkage.
17 Install the air cleaner assembly.
18 Connect the negative battery cable.
19 Start the engine and check for fuel leaks.

21 Single-point EFI fuel pressure regulator — removal and installation

Warning: *Gasoline is extremely flammable, so extra precautions must be taken when working on any part of the fuel system. Do not smoke or allow open flames or bare light bulbs near the work area. Also, do not work in a garage if a natural gas-type appliance with a pilot light is present.*

Removal

1 Remove the air cleaner assembly.
2 Release the fuel system pressure (Section 16).
3 Disconnect the negative cable at the battery. Place the cable out of the way so it cannot accidentally come in contact with the negative terminal of the battery, as this would once again allow power into the electrical system of the vehicle.
4 On 1984 and 1985 models, remove the fuel inlet chamber (refer to illustrations 20.4a and 20.4b.
5 On 1984 and 1985 models, remove the vacuum tube from the regulator and throttle body.
6 Wrap a cloth around the fuel inlet chamber to catch any residual fuel, which is under pressure.
7 Withdraw the pressure regulator from the throttle body.
8 Carefully remove the O-ring from the pressure regulator, followed by the gasket.

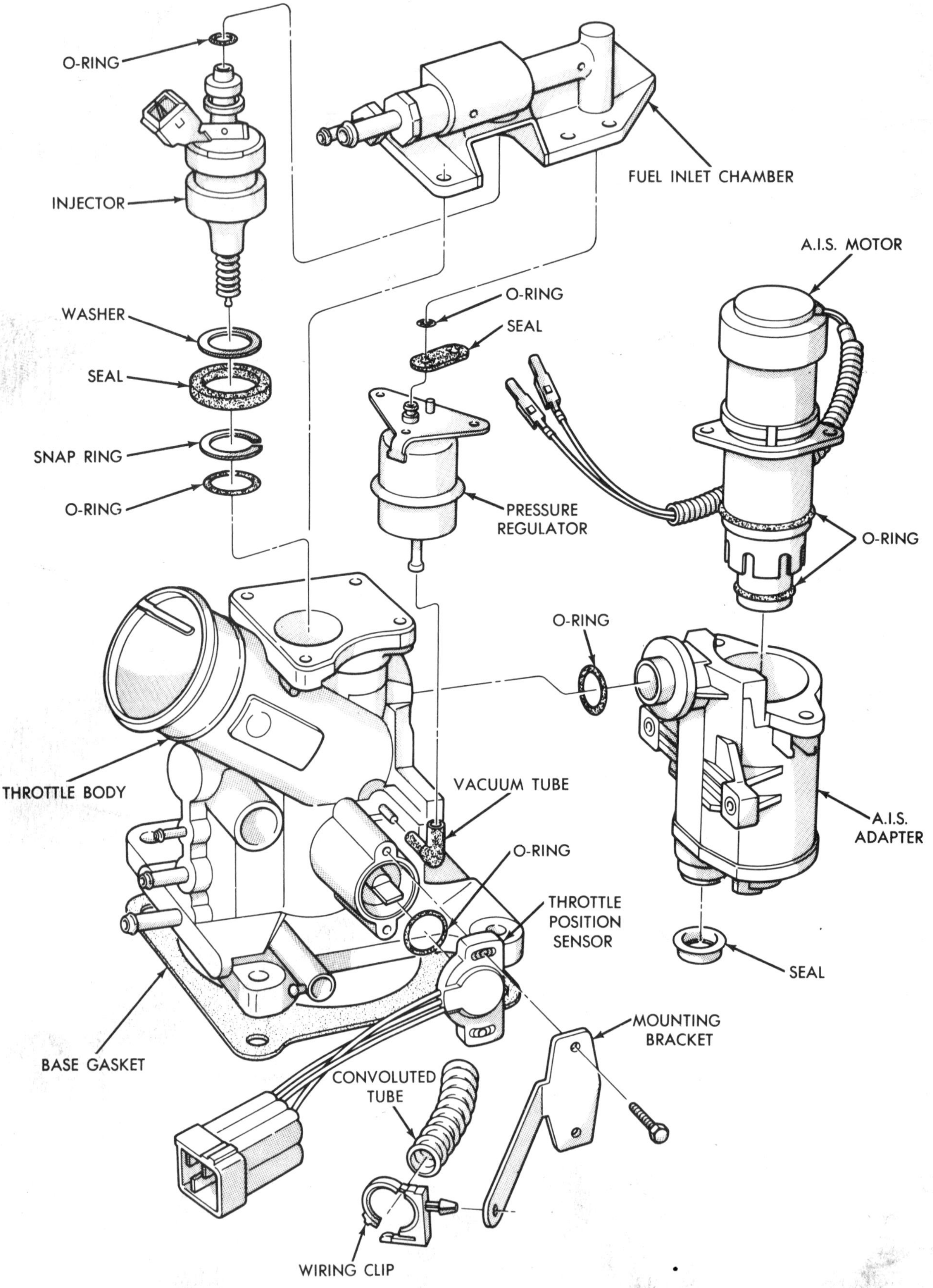

O-RING
INJECTOR
FUEL INLET CHAMBER
A.I.S. MOTOR
O-RING
SEAL
WASHER
SEAL
SNAP RING
O-RING
PRESSURE REGULATOR
O-RING
O-RING
THROTTLE BODY
VACUUM TUBE
A.I.S. ADAPTER
O-RING
THROTTLE POSITION SENSOR
SEAL
MOUNTING BRACKET
BASE GASKET
CONVOLUTED TUBE
WIRING CLIP

20.4a 1984 and 1985 model single-point EFI throttle body — exploded view

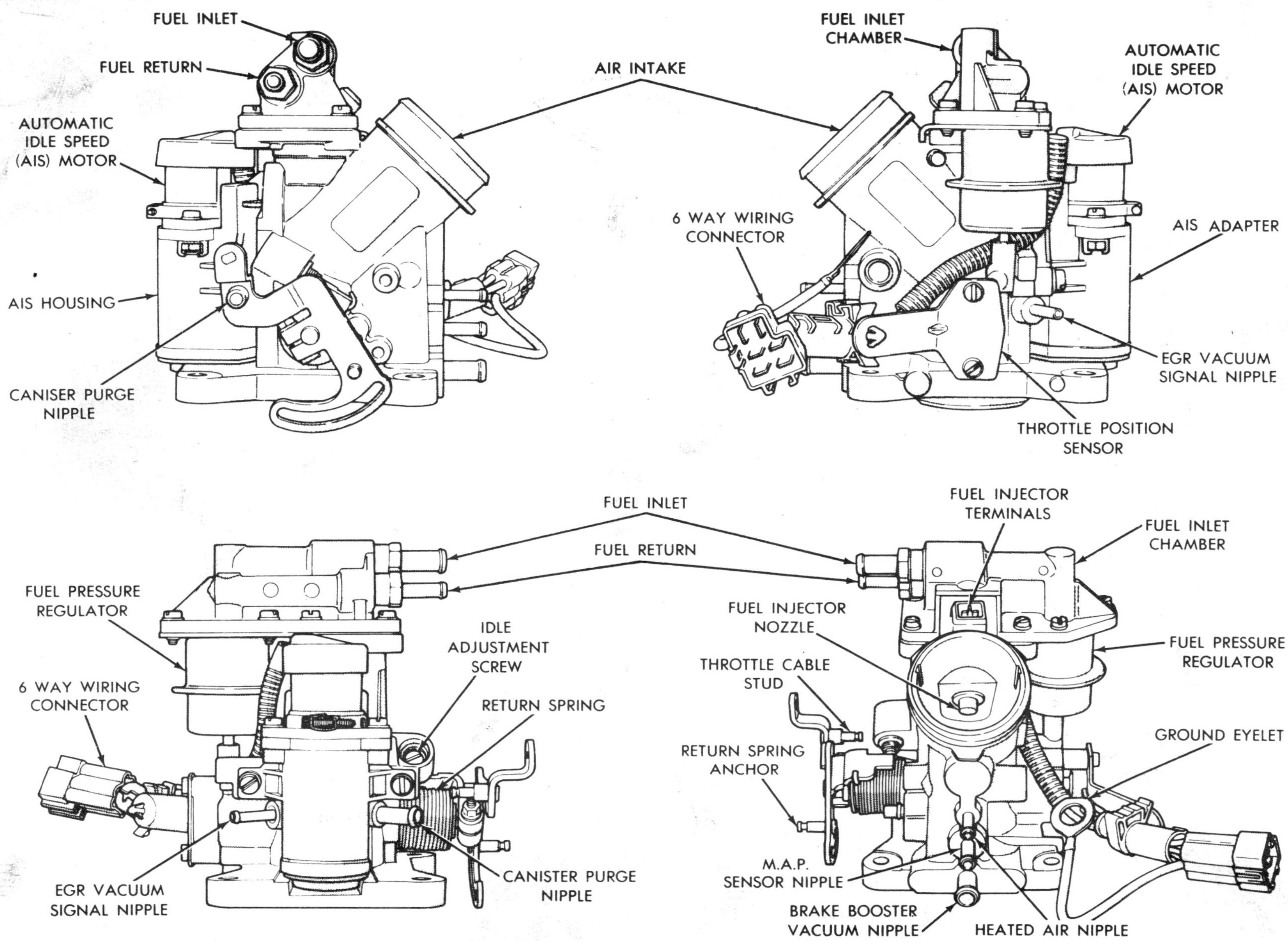

20.4b 1984 and 1985 model single-point EFI throttle body external details

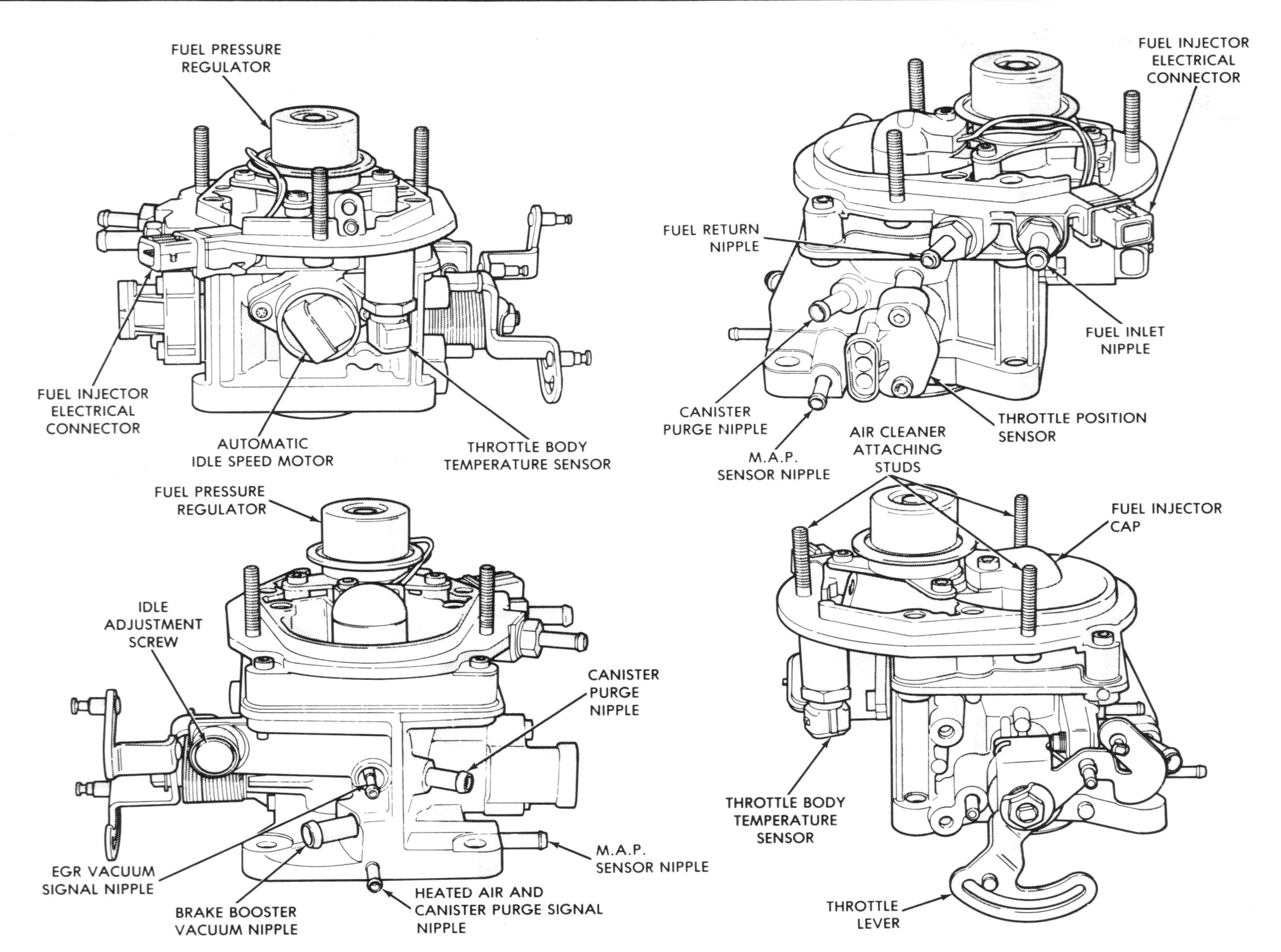

20.4c 1986 and later model single-point EFI throttle body external details

Installation

9 Place a new gasket in position on the pressure regulator and carefully install a new O-ring.
10 On 1986 models, place the pressure regulator in position on the throttle body, press it into position and install the three retaining screws. Tighten the screws to the specified torque.
11 On 1984 and 1985 models, install the vacuum tube.
12 On 1984 and 1985 models, install the fuel inlet chamber.
13 Connect the negative battery cable.
14 Install the air cleaner assembly.
15 Start the engine and check for fuel leaks.

22 Single-point EFI fuel injector — removal and installation

Warning: *Gasoline is extremely flammable, so extra precautions must be taken when working on any part of the fuel system. Do not smoke or allow open flames or bare light bulbs near the work area. Also, do not work in a garage if a natural gas-type appliance with a pilot light is present.*

Removal

All models

1 Remove the air cleaner assembly.
2 Release the fuel system pressure (Section 16).
3 Disconnect the negative cable at the battery. Place the cable out of the way so it cannot accidentally come in contact with the negative terminal of the battery, as this would once again allow power into the electrical system of the vehicle.

1984 and 1985 models

4 Remove the four screws retaining the fuel inlet chamber to the throttle body.
5 Remove the fuel pressure regulator-to-throttle body vacuum tube.
6 Wrap a cloth around the fuel inlet chamber to catch the residual fuel and lift the inlet chamber and injector off the throttle body.
7 Withdraw the injector from the inlet chamber (see illustration 20.4a).
8 Peel the upper and lower O-rings from the fuel injector.
9 Remove the snap-ring retaining the seal and washer on the injector, followed by the seal and washer.

1986 and later models

10 Remove the bolt retaining the injector cap and lift the cap off the injector using two screwdrivers inserted in the slots provided for this purpose (see illustration 20.4c).
11 Pry the injector from the pod using a screwdriver inserted in the holes in the side of the electrical connector. After removal, make sure the lower injector O-ring is removed from the pod.

Installation

1984 and 1985 models

12 Install a new O-ring, washer and seal on the injector, retaining them with the snap-ring.
13 Insert the injector into the fuel inlet chamber.
14 Place the injector/fuel inlet chamber in position on the throttle body and install the pressure regulator-to-throttle body vacuum tube.
15 Place the assembly in the throttle body and install the retaining screws. Tighten the screws to the specified torque.

1986 and later models

16 Install new O-rings on the injector and injector cap (a new injector should already have the upper O-ring installed).
17 Place the injector in the pod and position the injector so the cap (which is keyed to the injector) can be installed without interference.
18 Rotate the cap and injector so they line up with the attachment hole, push down to ensure a good seal and install the retaining screws. Tighten the screws to the specified torque.

All models

19 Connect the negative battery cable, start the engine and check for leaks.
20 Turn off the engine and install the air cleaner assembly.

23 Single-point EFI Throttle Position Sensor (TPS) — removal and installation

Warning: *Gasoline is extremely flammable, so extra precautions must be taken when working on any part of the fuel system. Do not smoke or allow open flames or bare light bulbs near the work area. Also, do not work in a garage if a natural gas-type appliance with a pilot light is present.*

Removal

All models

1 Disconnect the negative cable at the battery. Place the cable out of the way so it cannot accidentally come in contact with the negative terminal of the battery, as this would once again allow power into the electrical system of the vehicle.
2 Remove the air cleaner assembly.

1984 and 1985 models

3 Unplug the 6-way wiring connector (see illustrations 20.4a and 20.4b).
4 Remove the two TPS-to-throttle body retaining screws, undo the wiring clip from the convoluted tube and remove the mounting bracket (see illustration 20.4b).
5 Detach the TPS from the throttle shaft and remove the O-ring.
6 Pull the three TPS wires from the convoluted tube.
7 Look inside the 6-way connector and use a small screwdriver to lift the locking tab for each of the TPS wire blade terminals. Disconnect each TPS blade (noting their positions to simplify reinstallation).

1986 and later models

8 Disconnect the throttle cables and unplug the electrical connector.
9 Remove the two TPS-to-throttle body screws.
10 Pull the TPS off the throttle shaft.
11 Remove the O-ring.

Installation

1984 and 1985 models

12 Making sure they go into the proper locations, insert the wire blade terminals into the throttle body connector.
13 Insert the TPS wires into the convoluted tube.
14 Place the TPS and new O-ring in position with the mounting bracket on the throttle body and install the retaining screws. Tighten the screws to the specified torque.
15 Attach the wiring clips to the convoluted tube and connect the 6-way connector.

1986 and later models

16 Install the TPS with a new O-ring on the throttle body and install the retaining screws. Tighten the screws to the specified torque.
17 Plug in the electrical connector and connect the throttle cable.

All models

18 Install the air cleaner.
19 Connect the negative battery cable.

24 Single-point EFI Automatic Idle Speed (AIS) motor — removal and installation

Warning: *Gasoline is extremely flammable, so extra precautions must be taken when working on any part of the fuel system. Do not smoke or allow open flames or bare light bulbs near the work area. Also, do not work in a garage if a natural gas-type appliance with a pilot light is present.*

Removal

All models

1 Disconnect the negative cable at the battery. Place the cable out of the way so it cannot accidentally come in contact with the negative terminal of the battery, as this would once again allow power into the electrical system of the vehicle.
2 Remove the air cleaner assembly.

1984 and 1985 models

3 Remove the two screws retaining the AIS adapter to the throttle body (see illustration 20.4a).
4 Remove the wiring clips and the two AIS wires from the throttle body connector. Use a small screwdriver to lift each locking tab (noting the position of each wire to simplify reinstallation) and disconnect each blade terminal.
5 Carefully withdraw the assembly from the rear of the throttle body. Note that the O-ring at the top and the seal at the bottom may fall off the adapter so it is important to keep track of them.
6 Remove the O-ring and seal.

7 To separate the motor from the adapter, remove the two retaining screws (but not the clamp), lift the motor out and remove the O-ring.

1986 and later models

8 Unplug the 4-pin connector on the AIS.
9 Remove the throttle body temperature sensor (Section 25).
10 Remove the two retaining screws.
11 Withdraw the AIS from the throttle body, making sure that the O-ring does not fall into the throttle body opening.

Installation

1984 and 1985 models

12 If the AIS motor has been removed from the adapter, install new O-rings and carefully work the motor into the adaptor and install the retaining screws. Tighten the screws to the specified torque.
13 To install the AIS motor/adaptor assembly, first install a new O-ring and seal on the adaptor.
14 Place the assembly carefully in position on the back of the throttle body, making sure the O-ring and seal are in place and install the retaining screws. Tighten the screws to the specified torque.

1986 and later models

15 Prior to installation, make sure the pintle is in the retracted position. If the retracted pintle measurement is more than 1.26-inches (32 mm), the AIS must be taken to a dealer or properly equipped shop to be retracted.
16 Install a new O-ring and insert the AIS into the housing, making sure the O-ring is not dislodged.
17 Install the two retaining screws. Tighten the screws to the specified torque.
18 Plug the 4-pin connector into the AIS.
19 Install the throttle body temperature sensor (Section 25).

All models

20 Install the air cleaner assembly and connect the negative battery cable.

25 Single-point EFI throttle body temperature sensor (1986 and later models only) — removal and installation

Warning: *Gasoline is extremely flammable, so extra precautions must be taken when working on any part of the fuel system. Do not smoke or allow open flames or bare light bulbs near the work area. Also, do not work in a garage if a natural gas-type appliance with a pilot light is present.*

Removal

1 Disconnect the negative cable at the battery. Place the cable out of the way so it cannot accidentally come in contact with the negative terminal of the battery, as this would once again allow power into the electrical system of the vehicle.
2 Remove the air cleaner assembly.
3 Disconnect the throttle cable from the throttle body, remove the two cable bracket screws and lay the bracket aside.
4 Unplug the wiring connector by pulling down on it.
5 Remove the sensor by unscrewing it (see illustration 20.4c).

Installation

6 Apply a thin coat of heat transfer compound to the tip of the new sensor.
7 Screw the sensor into the throttle body and tighten it securely.
8 Plug in the wiring connector.
9 Connect the throttle linkage.
10 Install the air cleaner and connect the negative battery cable.

26 Multi-point (EFI) throttle body — removal and installation

Refer to illustrations 26.2, 26.4, 26.5, 26.8 and 26.11

Warning: *Gasoline is extremely flammable, so extra precautions must be taken when working on any part of the fuel system. Do not smoke or allow open flames or bare light bulbs near the work area. Also, do not work in a garage if a natural gas-type appliance with a pilot light is present.*

Removal

1 Disconnect the negative cable at the battery. Place the cable out of the way so it cannot accidentally come in contact with the negative terminal of the battery, as this would once again allow power into the electrical system of the vehicle.
2 Remove the air cleaner hose and the throttle body adapter **(see illustration)**.
3 Remove the return spring, disconnect the throttle cable and remove (if equipped) the cruise control and automatic transaxle kickdown cables.
4 Unbolt and remove the throttle cable bracket **(see illustration)**.
5 Unplug the electrical connector **(see illustration)**.
6 Disconnect the vacuum hoses from the throttle body.
7 Loosen the turbocharger-to-throttle body hose clamp.
8 Remove the retaining bolts and nuts and detach the throttle body from the intake manifold **(see illustration)**.

Installation

9 Place the throttle body in position and install the mounting bolts/nuts. Tighten them securely in a criss-cross pattern to the specified torque.
10 Tighten the turbocharger hose clamp.
11 Connect the vacuum hoses **(see illustration)**.
12 Plug in the electrical connector.
13 Install the throttle bracket and connect the throttle cable, return spring and (if equipped) the cruise control and automatic transaxle kickdown cables.
14 Install the air cleaner hose and adapter.
15 Connect the negative battery cable.

27 Multi-point EFI Throttle Position Sensor (TPS) — removal and installation

Refer to illustration 27.3

Removal

1 Disconnect the negative cable at the battery. Place the cable out of the way so it cannot accidentally come in contact with the negative terminal of the battery, as this would once again allow power into the electrical system of the vehicle.
2 Unplug the 6-way electrical connector.
3 Remove the TPS-to-throttle body retaining screws **(see illustration)**.
4 Unclip the convoluted plastic wiring tube and remove the mounting bracket.
5 Withdraw the TPS from the throttle shaft and remove the O-ring.
6 Look inside the 6-way connector and locate the TPS wire blade terminals. After noting their locations to ensure installation in the same positions, use a small screwdriver to lift each locking tab and disconnect the TPS.

Installation

7 Insert the TPS blade terminals into the 6-way connector.
8 Push the TPS wires into the convoluted plastic wiring tube.
9 Install the TPS and a new O-ring, along with the mounting bracket, on the throttle body. Tighten the screws securely.
10 Install the clips on the convoluted plastic wiring tube.
11 Plug in the 6-way connector and connect the negative battery cable.

28 Multi-point EFI Automatic Idle Speed (AIS) motor — removal and installation

Removal

1 Disconnect the negative cable at the battery. Place the cable out of the way so it cannot accidentally come in contact with the negative terminal of the battery, as this would once again allow power into the electrical system of the vehicle.
2 Unplug the 6-way electrical connector.
3 Remove the wiring clips and then detach the two AIS wires from the 6-way connector. Using a small screwdriver, lift each locking tab and remove each blade terminal.
4 Remove the two AIS motor-to-throttle body retaining screws. Do not remove the clamp (see illustration 27.3).

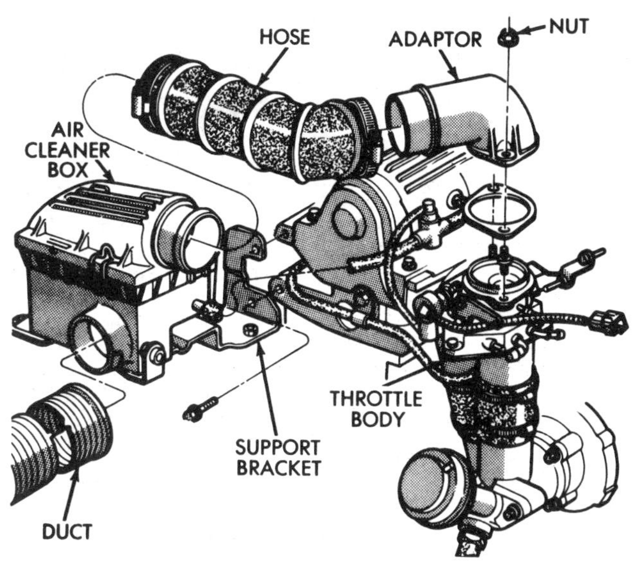

26.2 Multi-port EFI throttle body air cleaner hose and adapter locations

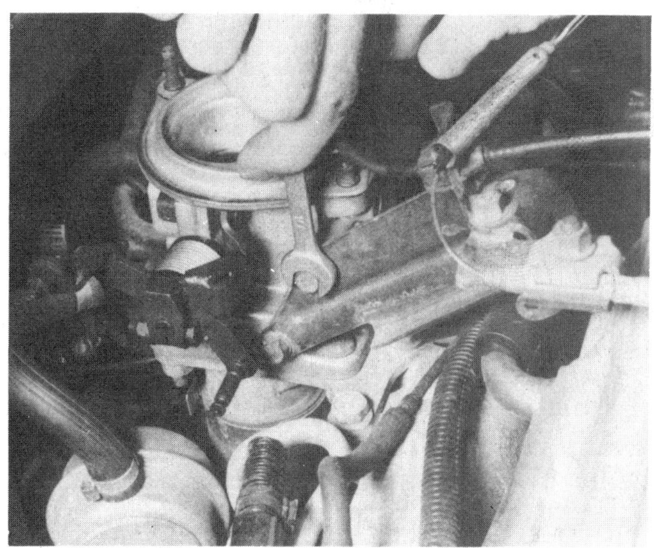

26.4 Remove the two throttle cable bracket bolts, . . .

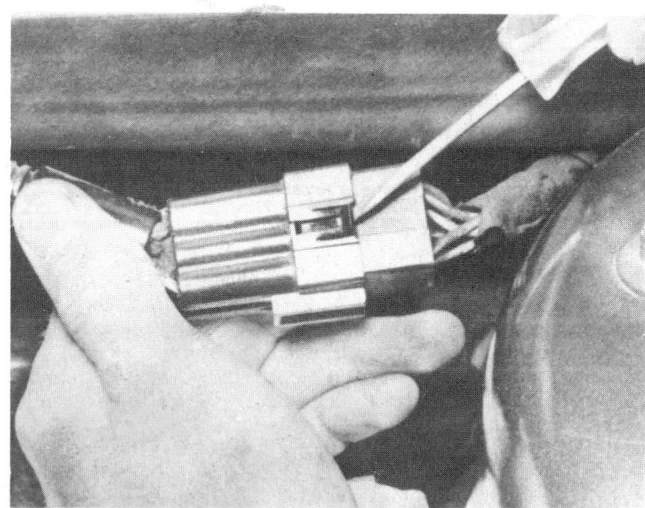

26.5 . . . then bend the clip up with a small screwdriver before separating the electrical connector sections

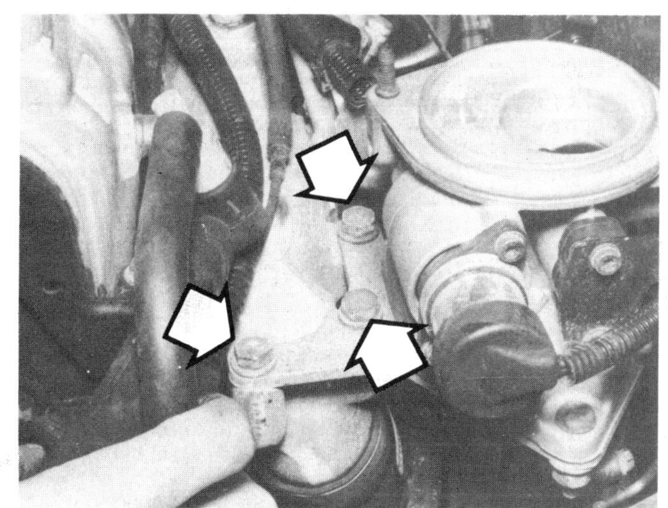

26.8 Multi-point throttle body retaining bolt locations (arrows)

4A

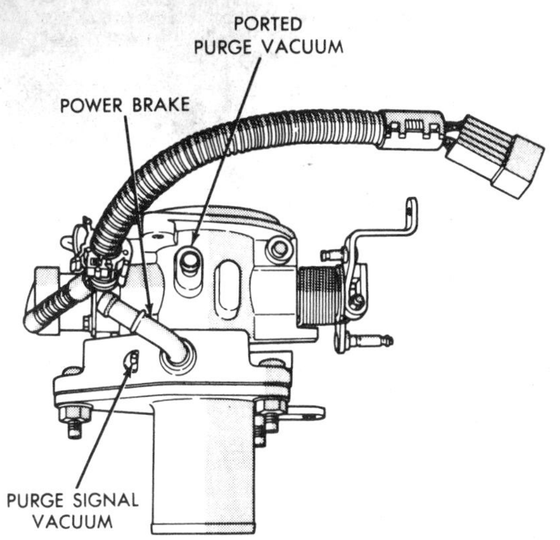

26.11 Multi-point EFI throttle body vacuum connections

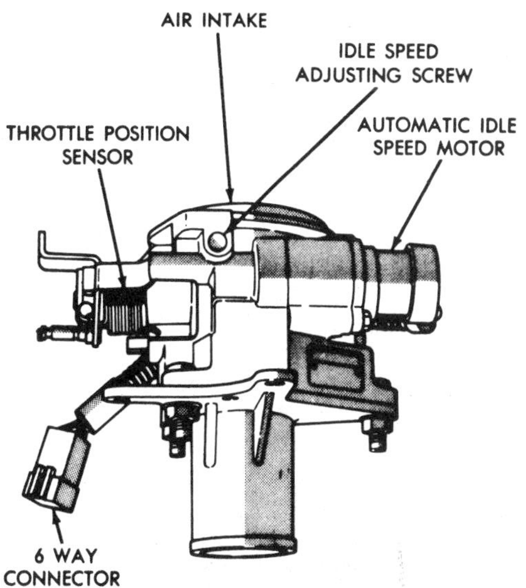

27.3 Multi-point EFI throttle body component layout

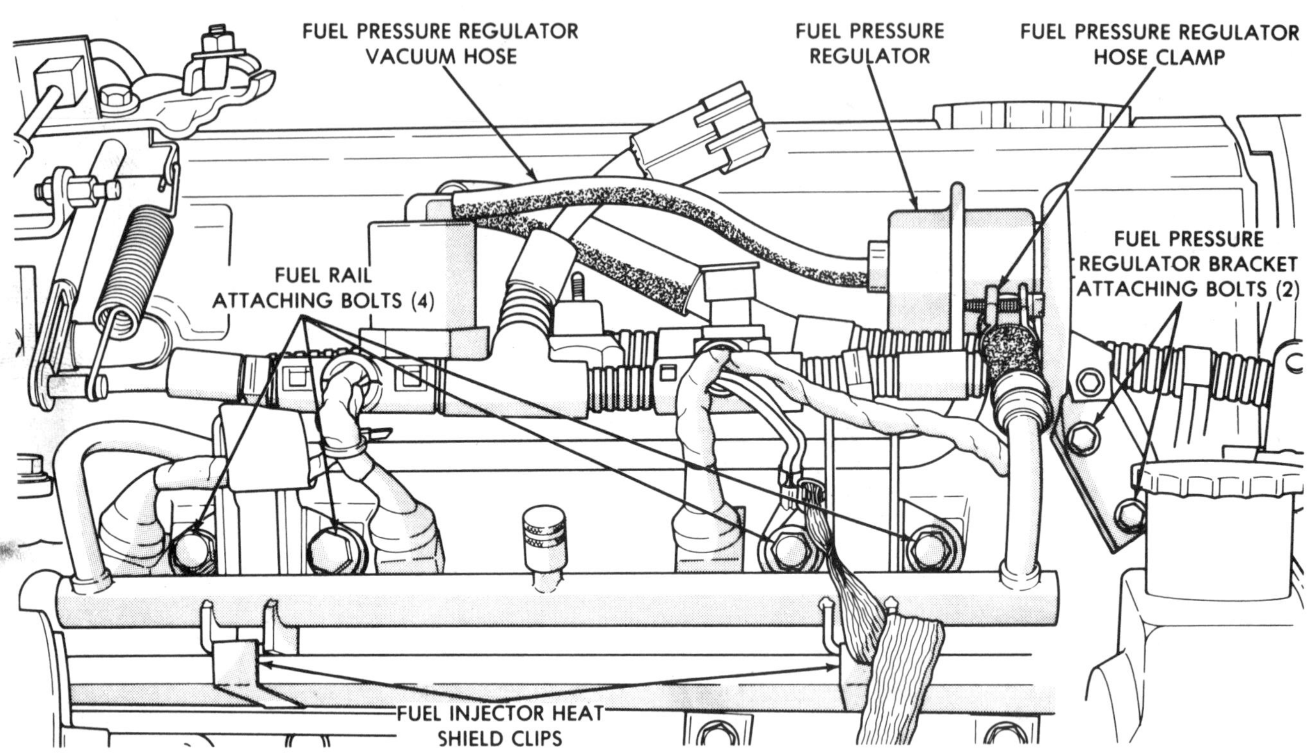

29.4 1986 and later multi-point EFI fuel pressure regulator component layout

5 Detach the AIS motor from the throttle body, making sure that both O-rings remain on the motor.

Installation

6 Carefully position the AIS motor (using new O-rings — a new motor should already be equipped with O-rings) in place in the throttle body.
7 Install the mounting screws and tighten them securely.
8 Route the AIS wiring to the connector and plug in the AIS blade terminals in the correct positions.
9 Connect the wiring clips and plug in the 6-way connector.
10 Connect the negative battery cable.

29 Multi-point EFI fuel injector rail assembly — removal and installation

Refer to illustrations 29.4, 29.7, 29.9 and 29.10

Warning: *Gasoline is extremely flammable, so extra precautions must be taken when working on any part of the fuel system. Do not smoke or allow open flames or bare light bulbs near the work area. Also, do not work in a garage if a natural gas-type appliance with a pilot light is present.*

Removal

1 Release the fuel system pressure (Section 16).
2 Disconnect the negative cable at the battery. Place the cable out of the way so it cannot accidentally come in contact with the negative terminal of the battery, as this would once again allow power into the electrical system of the vehicle.
3 Loosen the supply hose clamp at the fuel rail inlet and pull the hose off the fitting.
4 On 1986 models, disconnect the fuel pressure regulator vacuum hose, remove the two bracket bolts, loosen the regulator hose clamp at the end of the rail and then remove the hose and regulator **(see illustration)**.
5 Remove the fuel rail-to-camshaft cover bracket bolt.
6 Unplug the fuel injector wiring connector.

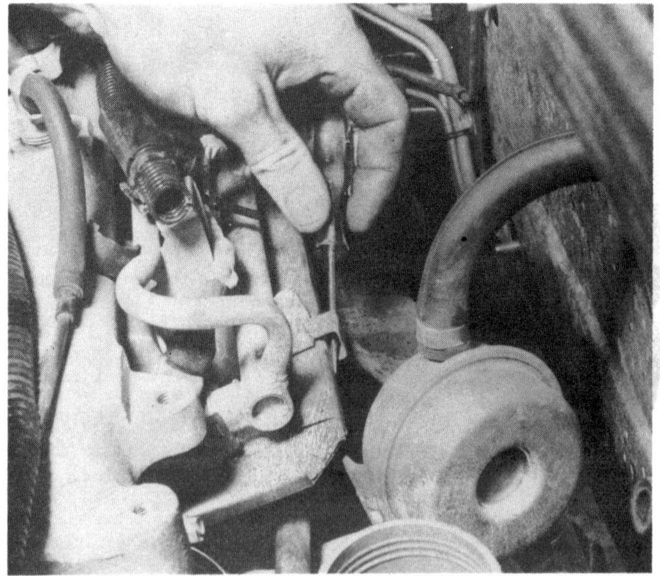

29.7 A small screwdriver can be used to pry off the fuel rail clips

7 Remove the fuel injector heat shield clips with a small screwdriver **(see illustration)**.
8 Remove the four fuel rail attaching bolts.
9 Grasp the fuel rail and injector assembly securely and pull the injectors straight out of the ports. Taking care not to damage the rubber injector O-rings, remove the rail assembly from the vehicle **(see illustration)**. The fuel injectors must not be removed until the fuel rail is detached from the vehicle.
10 Support the fuel rail and disconnect the remaining fuel hoses **(see illustration)**.

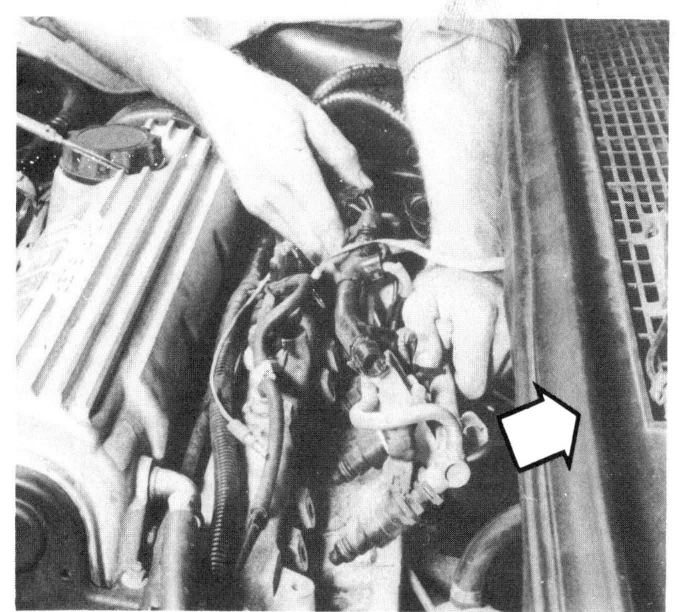

29.9 Grasp the fuel rail securely and pull the injectors straight out of the intake manifold

29.10 With the fuel rail supported out of the way, loosen the fuel hose clamps

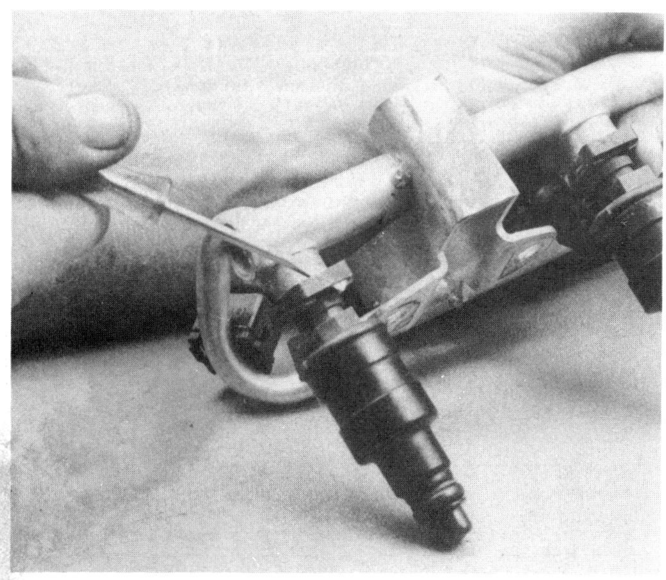

30.3a Insert a small screwdriver under the clip and pry it off

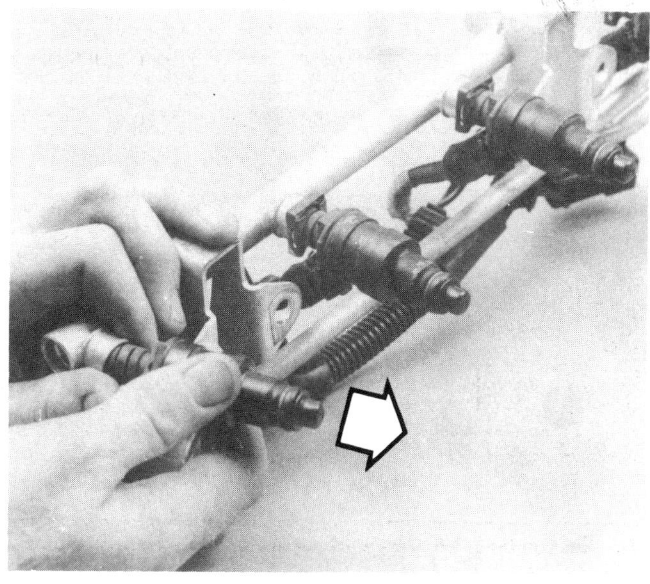

30.3b Pull the injector straight out of the fuel rail receiver cup

Installation

11 Prior to installation, make sure the injectors are securely seated in the receiver cup with the lock ring in place.
12 Inspect the injector holes to make sure they are clean.
13 Lubricate the injector O-rings with clean engine oil.
14 Insert the injector assemblies carefully into the holes and install the bolts and ground straps. Tighten the bolts evenly in a criss-cross pattern so the injectors are drawn into place and seated evenly. Once the injectors are seated, tighten the fuel rail bolts to the specified torque.
15 Connect the injector wiring harness to the injectors and fasten it into the wiring clips.
16 Install the heat shield clips and connect the wiring harness.
17 Install the fuel rail-to-camshaft cover bracket bolt.
18 On 1986 models, connect the fuel pressure regulator vacuum hose.
19 Install the fuel supply hose and clamp on the rail and tighten the clamp securely.
20 Check to make sure that the ground straps, hoses and wiring harnesses and connectors are securely installed in their original locations.
21 Connect the negative battery cable.

30 Multi-point EFI fuel injectors – removal and installation

Refer to illustrations 30.3a, 30.3b, 30.4a, 30.4b, 30.4c, 30.4d and 30.6

Removal

1 Remove the fuel rail assembly (Section 29).
2 Place the fuel rail assembly on a clean work surface so the fuel injectors are accessible.
3 Remove the injector clip from the fuel rail and injector by prying it off with a small screwdriver, then pull the injector straight out of the receiver cup **(see illustrations)**.

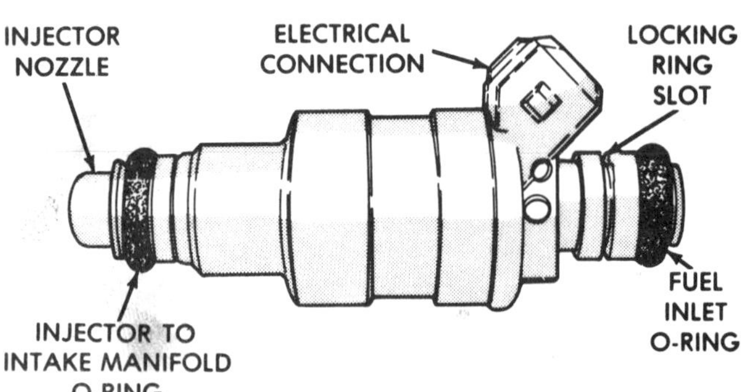

30.4a Two different size O-rings are installed on the injectors

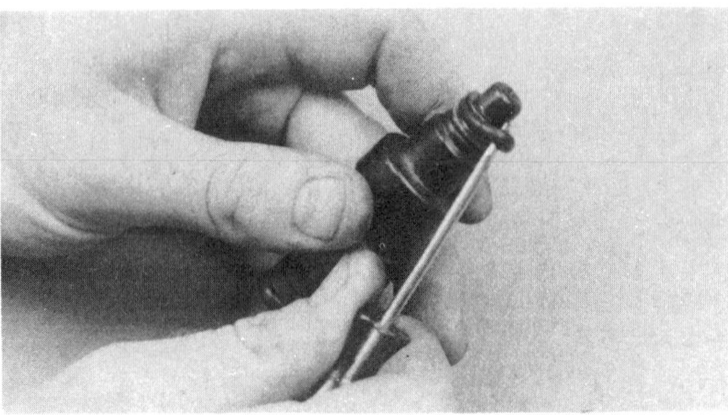

30.4b Insert a small screwdriver under the O-ring and pry it off — be careful not to damage the injector tip

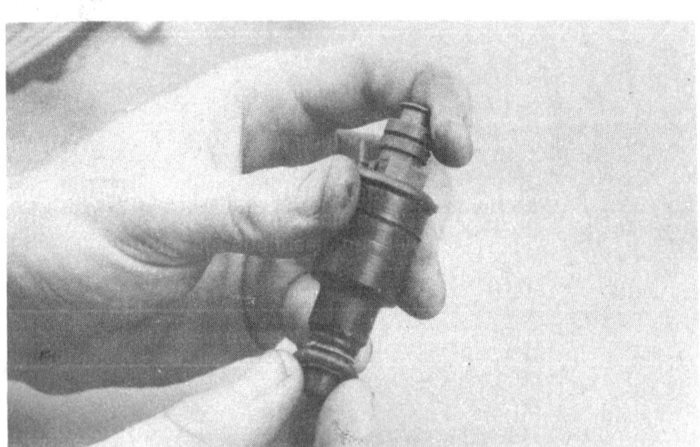

30.4c Push the new O-ring over the tip of the injector and into the groove

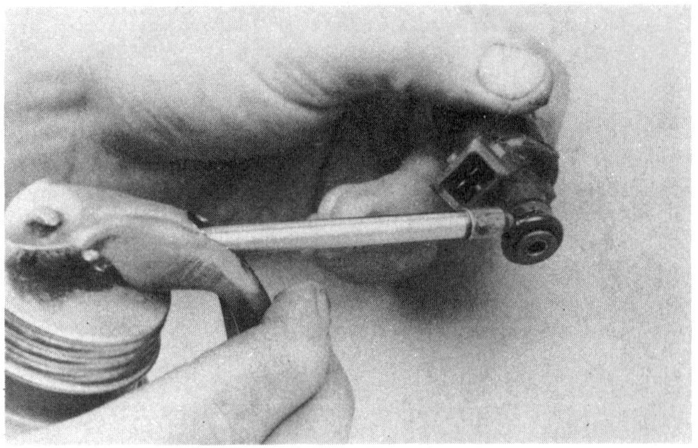

30.4d A drop of clean engine oil will allow the injector to seat more easily

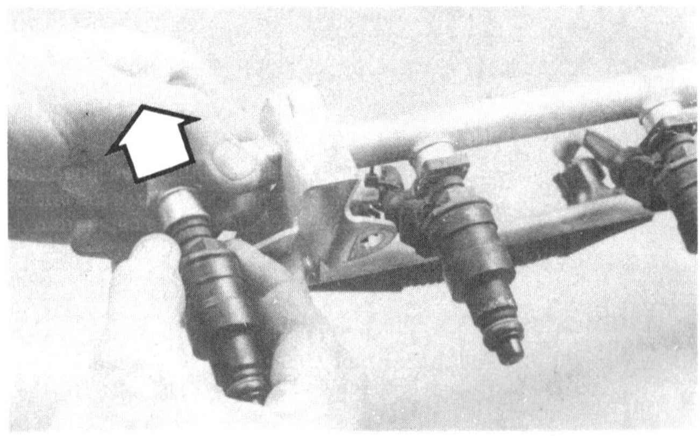

30.6 Insert the injector carefully so that it goes straight into the receiver cup

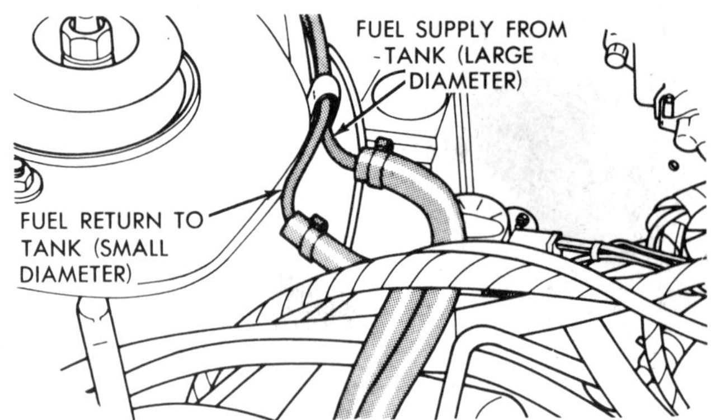

31.5 The fuel system can be drained or siphoned at the supply hose (large diameter)

4 Inspect the injector O-rings for damage. Replace them with new ones if necessary **(see illustration)**. To replace the O-rings, use a small screwdriver to remove the old one, then roll the new one into the groove. Apply a drop of engine oil to the O-ring **(see illustrations)**. Protect the injector tip so that it is not damaged if the injector is to be reused.

Installation

5 Prior to installation, lubricate the O-ring with a drop of clean engine oil if you have not already done so.

6 Install the top end of the injector carefully into the fuel rail receiver cup, taking care not to damage the O-ring **(see illustration)**.

7 Slide the open end of the injector clip into the top slot of the injector, onto the receiver cup ridge and into the side slots of the clip (see illustrations 30.3a and 30.3b).

8 Install the fuel rail (Section 29).

31 Fuel tank — removal and installation

Refer to illustrations 31.5, 31.6 and 31.13

Warning: *Gasoline is extremely flammable, so extra precautions must be taken when working on any part of the fuel system. Do not smoke or allow open flames or bare light bulbs near the work area. Also, do not work in a garage if a natural gas-type appliance with a pilot light is present.*

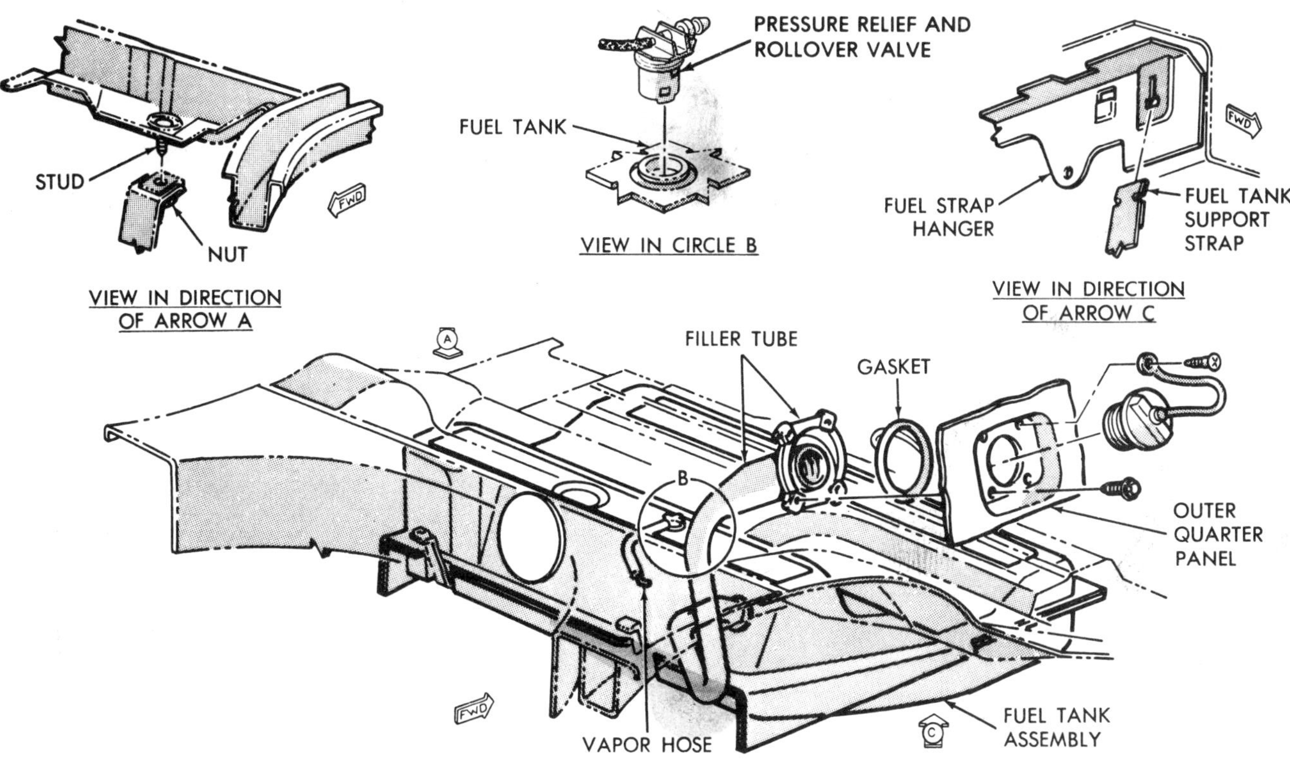

31.6 Fuel filler tube and tank details

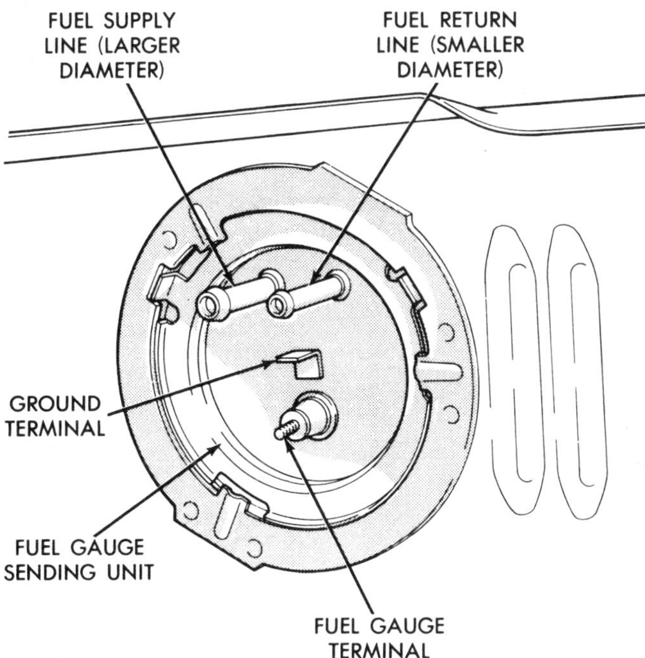

31.13 Fuel tank connection details

Removal

1 On fuel injection models, release the fuel system pressure (Section 16).

2 Disconnect the negative cable at the battery. Place the cable out of the way so it cannot accidentally come in contact with the negative terminal of the battery, as this would once again allow power into the electrical system of the vehicle.

3 Raise the rear of the vehicle and support it securely on jackstands.

4 Remove the gas cap.

5 Disconnect the fuel feed line (the large diameter supply line leading to the carburetor or fuel injection unit) located in the engine compartment **(see illustration)**, connect a hose and drain or siphon the tank into a metal container. **Warning:** *Do not use your mouth to start the siphoning action.*

6 Remove the screws retaining the filler tube to the body **(see illustration)**. It may be necessary to remove the right rear wheel to provide access to the filler tube.

7 Disconnect all wires and hoses from the tank (label them first to avoid problems during installation).

8 Support the tank with a floor jack (use a section of plywood as a platform). Remove the mounting strap retaining nuts, lower the tank slightly and remove the filler tube.

9 Lower the tank further and support it while disconnecting the rollover/vapor separator valve hose.

10 Remove the tank and insulator pad.

Installation

11 To install the tank, raise it into position with a jack, connect the rollover/vapor separator valve hose and place the insulator pad on the top. Connect the filler tube. **Caution:** *Be sure the vapor vent hose is not pinched between the tank and floor pan.*

12 Raise the tank with the jack, connect the retaining strap and install the retaining nuts. Tighten them securely.

13 Connect the fuel lines and wiring **(see illustration)** and install the filler tube retaining screws.

14 Fill the fuel tank, install the cap, connect the negative battery cable and check for leaks.

32 Exhaust system – removal and installation

Refer to illustrations 32.4a, 32.4b, 32.4c and 32.4d

1 The exhaust system should be inspected periodically for leaks, cracks and damaged or worn components (Chapter 1).

2 Allow the exhaust system to cool for at least three hours prior to inspecting or beginning work on it.

3 Raise the vehicle and support it securely on jackstands.
4 Exhaust system components can be removed by removing the heat shields, unbolting and/or disengaging them from the hangers and removing them from the vehicle **(see illustrations)**. Pipes on either side of the muffler must be removed by cutting with a hacksaw. Install the new muffler using new U-bolts. If parts are rusted together, apply a penetrating oil (available at auto supply stores) and allow it to soak in prior to attempting removal.
5 After replacing any part of the exhaust system, check carefully for leaks before driving the vehicle.

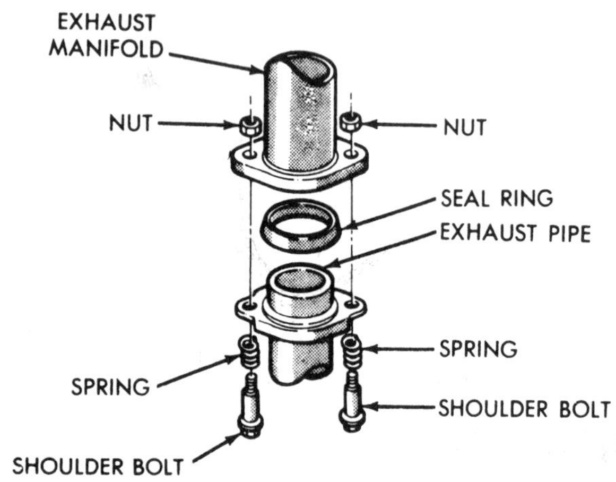

32.4a Exhaust manifold-to-pipe connection details

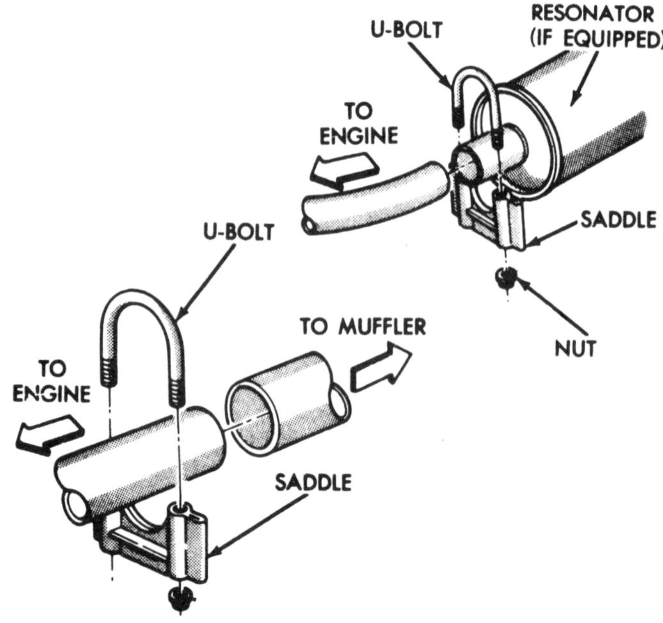

32.4b Typical exhaust system front slip joint connection details

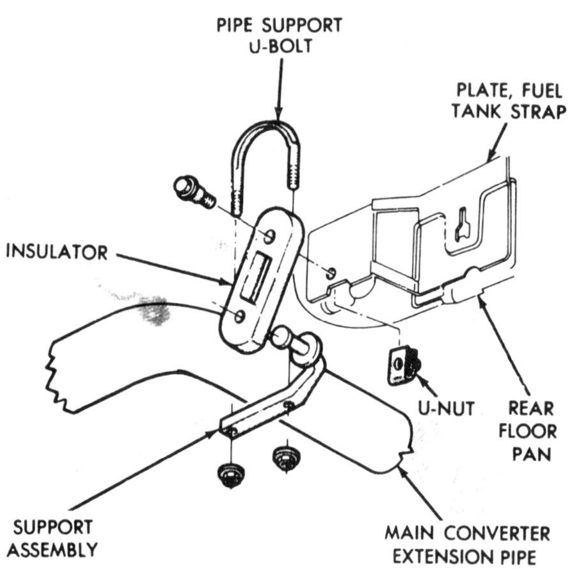

32.4c Typical catalytic converter mount details

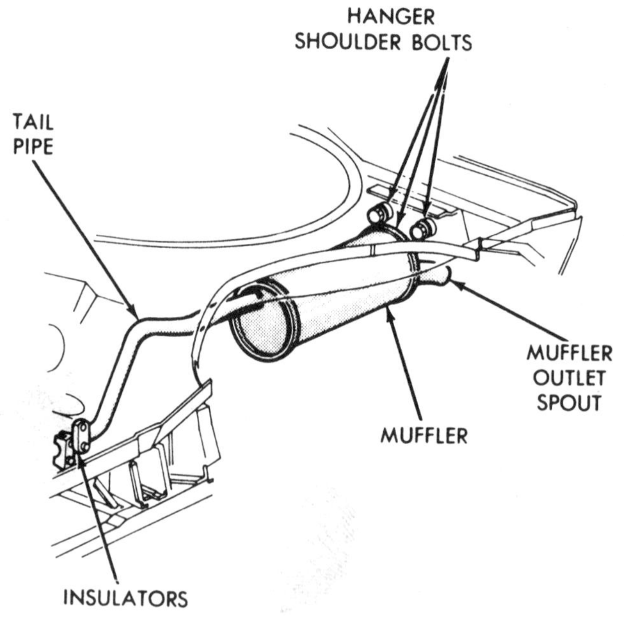

32.4d Typical tailpipe and muffler details

Chapter 4 Part B Turbocharger

Contents

Specifications

Torque specifications	Ft-lbs	Nm
Air cleaner box support bracket bolt	40	54
Coolant tube fitting	30	41
Exhaust pipe-to-manifold bolt/nut	20	28
Oil line tube fitting	11	14
Throttle body-to-intake manifold bolts	40	54
Turbocharger-to-exhaust manifold nuts	40	54
Turbocharger fuel rail bolts	20	28
Turbocharger support bracket		
to engine block bolt	40	54
to turbocharger bolt	20	28

1 General information

The turbocharger increases power by using an exhaust gas-driven turbine to pressurize the fuel/air mixture before it enters the combustion chambers. The amount of boost (intake manifold pressure) is controlled by the wastegate (exhaust bypass valve). The wastegate is operated by a spring-loaded actuator assembly which controls the maximum boost level by allowing some of the exhaust gas to bypass the turbine. The wastegate is controlled by the logic module.

2 Turbocharger — check

1 While it is a comparatively simple device, the turbocharger is also a precision component which can be severely damaged by an interrupted oil or coolant supply or loose or damaged ducts.
2 Due to the special techniques and equipment required, checking and diagnosis of suspected problems should be left to a dealer service department. The home mechanic can, however, check the connections and linkages for security, damage and other obvious problems.
3 Because each turbocharger has its own distinctive sound, a change in the noise level can be a sign of potential problems.
4 A high-pitched or whistling sound is a symptom of an inlet air or exhaust gas leak.
5 If an unusual sound comes from the vicinity of the turbine, the turbocharger can be removed and the turbine wheel inspected. **Caution:** *All checks must be made with the engine off and cool to the touch and the turbocharger stopped or personal injury could result. Operating the engine without all the turbocharger ducts and filters installed is also dangerous and can result in damage to the turbine wheel blades.*
6 Reach inside the housing and turn the turbine wheel to make sure it spins freely. If it doesn't, it is possible that the cooling oil has sludged or coked from overheating. Push in on the turbine wheel and check for binding. The turbine should rotate freely with no binding or rubbing on the housing.
7 Check the exhaust manifold for cracks and loose connections.
8 Because the turbine wheel rotates at speeds up to 140,000 rpm,

severe damage can result from the interruption of coolant or contamination of the oil supply to the turbine bearings. Check for leaks in the coolant and oil inlet lines and obstructions in the oil drain back line, as this can cause severe oil loss through the turbocharger seals. Burned oil on the turbine housing is a sign of this. **Caution:** *Whenever a major engine bearing such as a main, connecting rod or camshaft bearing is replaced, the turbocharger should be flushed with clean oil.*

3 Turbocharger – removal and installation

Refer to illustrations 3.4, 3.5, 3.6 and 3.13

Removal

1 Disconnect the negative cable at the battery. Place the cable out of the way so it cannot accidentally come in contact with the negative terminal of the battery, as this would once again allow power into the electrical system of the vehicle.

3.4 Exhaust pipe bolt and oxygen sensor wire connector locations (arrows)

2 Drain the cooling system (Chapter 1).
3 Raise the front of the vehicle and support it securely on jackstands.
4 Working under the engine compartment, disconnect the exhaust pipe and unplug the oxygen sensor connector **(see illustration)**.
5 Remove the turbocharger housing-to-engine block bracket support at the block **(see illustration)**.
6 Loosen the oil drain back hose clamps and push the hose down on the block fitting with a screwdriver **(see illustration)**.
7 Disconnect the turbocharger coolant tube fitting at the block outlet (located below the power steering pump bracket) and detach the tube support bracket from the block.
8 Lower the vehicle.
9 Working in the engine compartment, remove the air cleaner assembly, along with the throttle body adapter, the hose and the air cleaner box and support.
10 Disconnect the throttle linkage, wire connectors and vacuum hoses from the throttle body. Label the wires and hoses if there is any possibility of confusion during installation.
11 Loosen the turbocharger-to-throttle body hose clamps. Because the clamps are difficult to reach, a small wrench or socket will make the job easier.
12 Remove the three retaining bolts and detach the throttle body.
13 Loosen, but do not remove, the turbocharger discharge hose clamps **(see illustration)**.
14 Position the fuel rail, injectors, wiring harness and fuel lines out of the way by removing the hose retainer bracket screw, the four bracket screws from the intake manifold and the two bracket retaining clips.
15 Disconnect the oil line at the turbocharger bearing housing.
16 Remove the three screws and detach the heat shield.
17 Disconnect the coolant return tube and hose assembly from the turbocharger and water box and remove the tube support bracket.
18 Remove the four turbocharger-to-exhaust manifold retaining nuts. To make this job easier, it is a good idea to apply penetrating oil to the exposed threads and allow it to soak in for a few minutes.
19 To remove the turbocharger, lift the assembly off the exhaust manifold studs, then push it down toward the passenger side and lift it up and out of the engine compartment.

Installation

20 Carefully clean the mating surfaces of the turbocharger and manifold.
21 Place the turbocharger in positon on the manifold studs, making sure the discharge tube is in place between the manifold and turbo-

3.6 Disconnect the turbocharger oil drain back hose at the block fitting (arrow) and push it down in the direction shown with a screwdriver

3.13 The two turbocharger discharge hose clamps (arrows) should be loosened, but not removed

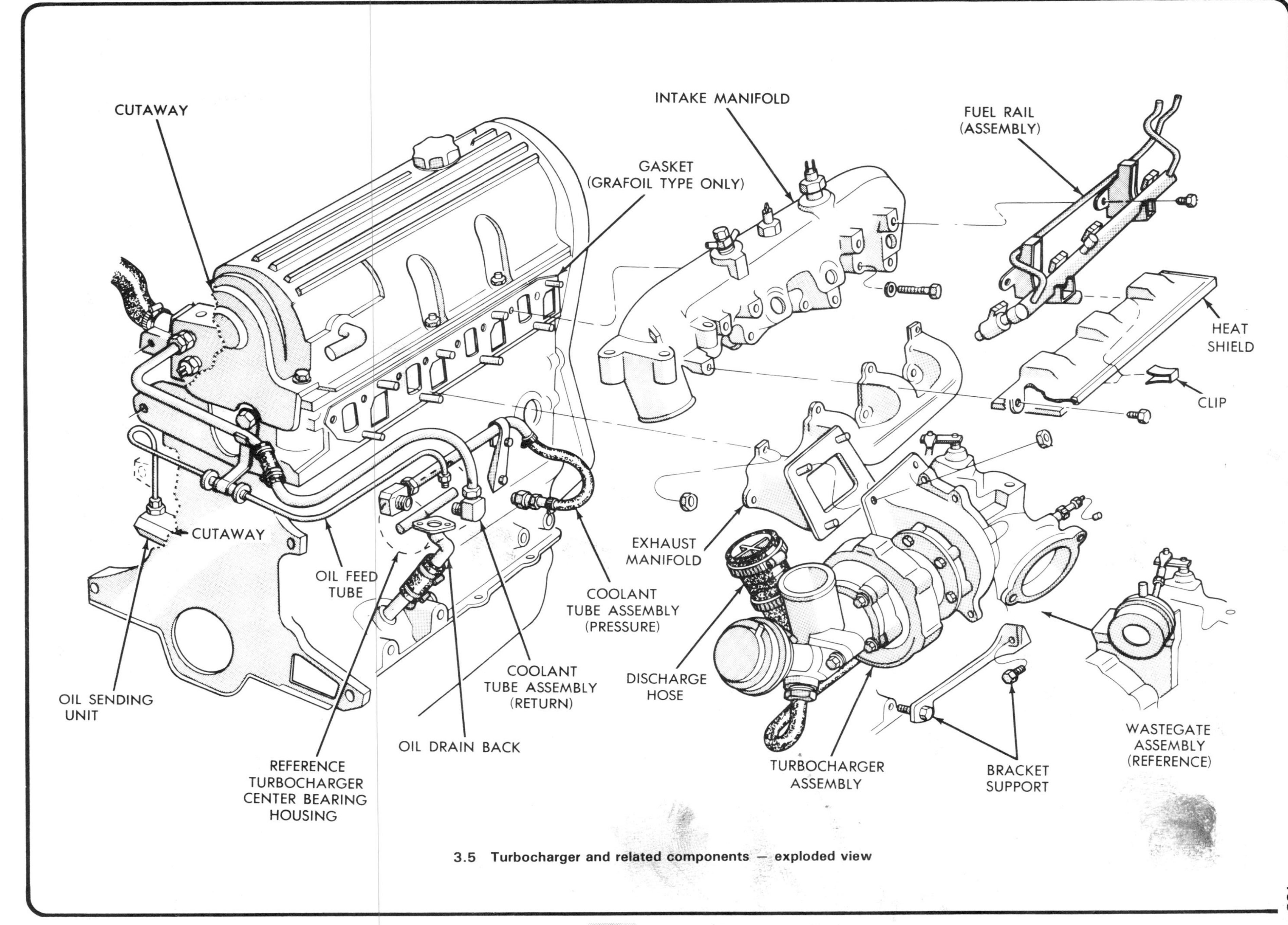

3.5 Turbocharger and related components — exploded view

charger.
22 Apply anti-seize compound to the studs and install the nuts. Tighten the nuts to the specified torque.
23 Connect the oil line and tighten the fitting securely.
24 Attach the bracket to the turbocharger and tighten the bolt to the specified torque.
25 Install the heat shield.
26 Connect the coolant tube and tighten the fitting.
27 Install the bracket-to-engine bolt and tighten it to the specified torque.
28 Install the fuel rail (refer to Part A of this Chapter).
29 Tighten the turbocharger discharge hose clamp securely.
30 Place the throttle body in position and install the bolts. Tighten the bolts to the specified torque.
31 Connect the throttle body hose and tighten the clamp screw securely.
32 Connect the throttle linkage, wire connectors and vacuum hoses to the throttle body.
33 Install the throttle body adapter, the hose and air cleaner box, the support and the air cleaner assembly.
34 Raise the front of the vehicle and support it securely on jackstands.
35 From under the vehicle, connect the coolant tube and tighten the fitting securely.
36 Connect the oil drain back hose.
37 Install the turbocharger housing-to-engine block support bracket with the bolts finger tight. Tighten the block bolt first, followed by the turbocharger bolt, to the specified torque.
38 Connect the exhaust pipe and install the exhaust pipe articulated joint shoulder bolts. Tighten the bolts to the specified torque.
39 Connect the oxygen sensor wire.
40 Lower the front of the vehicle.
41 Fill the cooling system and connect the negative battery cable.

Chapter 5 Engine electrical systems

Contents

Specifications

Ignition system

Firing order	1-3-4-2
Cylinder number one location	Timing belt or chain end of engine
Distributor	
Direction of rotation	Clockwise
Shaft side play (maximum)	
2.2L/2.5L engine	0.004 in (0.1 mm)
2.6L engine	0.002 in (0.05 mm)
Ignition coil resistance @ 70° to 80°F (21° to 27°C)	
1982 through 1985	
Primary resistance	
2.2L engine (Echlin or Essex)	1.41 to 1.62 ohms
2.2L engine (Prestolite)	1.60 to 1.79 ohms
2.6L engine	0.7 to 0.85 ohms
Secondary resistance	
2.2L engine (Echlin or Essex)	9 to 12.2 K ohms
2.2L engine (Prestolite)	9.4 to 11.7 K ohms
2.6L engine	9 to 11 K ohms
1986 on	
Primary resistance	
2.2L/2.5L engine (Essex)	1.34 to 1.55 ohms
2.2L/2.5L engine (Prestolite)	1.34 to 1.55 ohms
Secondary resistance	
2.2L/2.5L engine (Essex)	9 to 12.2 K ohms
2.2L/2.5L engine (Prestolite)	9.4 to 11.7 K ohms

Charging system

Regulated voltage (battery specific gravity above 1.200)

Temperature*	Voltage range
-20°F	14.9 to 15.9
80°F	13.9 to 14.6
140°F	13.3 to 13.9
Above 140°F	Less than 13.9

* *Ambient temperature 1/4-inch from regulator*

Brush length service limit	
2.2L/2.5L engine	0.197 in (5 mm)
2.6L engine	0.315 in (8 mm)
2.6L engine alternator-to-timing chain case mount clearance	0.008 in (0.2 mm)

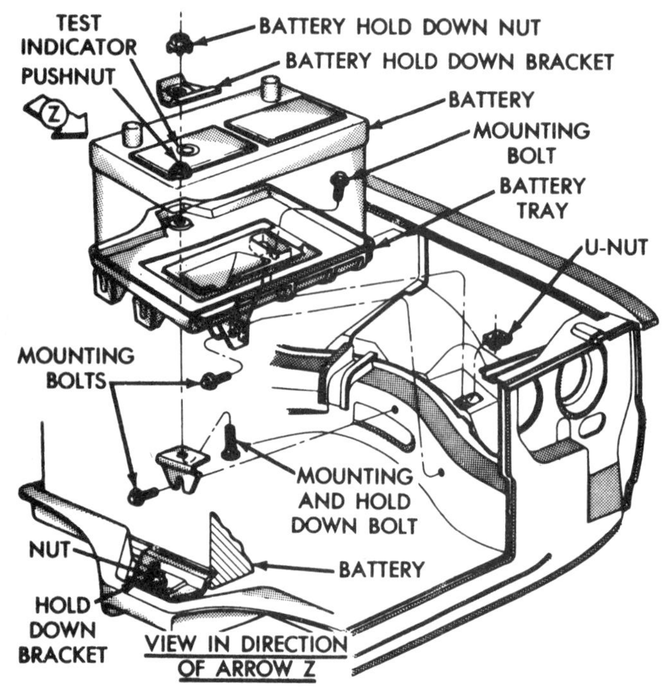

2.1a Battery mount — exploded view

2.1b The hold-down nut (arrow) is located at the base of the battery

1 General information

Caution: *Whenever the electrical system is being worked on, the negative battery cable should be disconnected from the battery.*

The engine electrical system includes the battery, charging system, starter, Electronic Fuel Injection (EFI) system (if equipped) and ignition system. The EFI system consists of the power module, logic module, (or single module engine controller — SMEC — 1988 models only) oxygen sensor, the fuel injectors and associated sensors. The electrical system is 12-volt with a negative ground.

The charging system consists of the alternator, voltage regulator and battery. On some fuel injected models the EFI system handles the voltage regulator functions.

The starter is operated by the battery's electrical power through the starter relay.

The ignition system includes the distributor, Spark Control Computer (SCC) on 2.2L carburetor equipped models, power and logic modules or SMEC (1988 only) (EFI models), IC igniter (electronic control unit) on 2.6L engines, the ignition coil, spark plugs and associated wires.

Information on the routine maintenance of the ignition, starting and charging systems and the battery can be found in Chapter 1.

2 Battery — removal and installation

Refer to illustrations 2.1a and 2.1b

Caution: *Certain precautions must be followed when checking or servicing the battery. Hydrogen gas, which is very flammable, is produced in the cells, so keep lighted tobacco, open flames and sparks away from the battery. The electrolyte inside is actually dilute sulfuric acid, which can burn skin and cause serious injury if splashed in the eyes. It will also ruin clothes and painted surfaces.*

1 The battery is located at the left front corner of the engine compartment and is held in place by a hold-down clamp at its base **(see illustrations)**.

2 Always disconnect the negative (–) battery cable first, followed by the positive (+) cable.

3 After the cables are disconnected, remove the nut and hold-down clamp.

4 Lift out the battery. **Note:** *When lifting the battery from the engine compartment, be careful not to twist the case as acid could spurt out of the vent openings.*

5 Installation is the reverse of removal. Be careful not to overtighten the retaining nut as the clamp could damage the battery case.

3 Alternator — general information

The alternator is operated by a drivebelt turned by the crankshaft pulley. The rotor turns inside the stator to produce an alternating current, which is then converted to direct current by diodes. The current is adjusted to battery requirements by an electronic voltage regulator or, on fuel injected models, the EFI system.

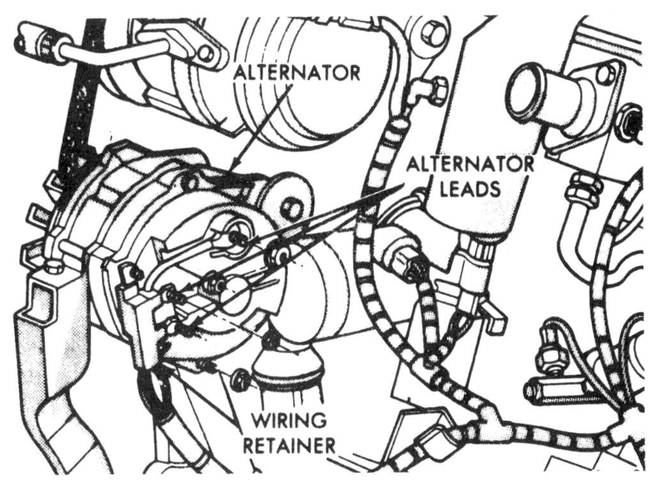

7.2a Typical 2.2L/2.5L non-turbocharged engine alternator wiring connections

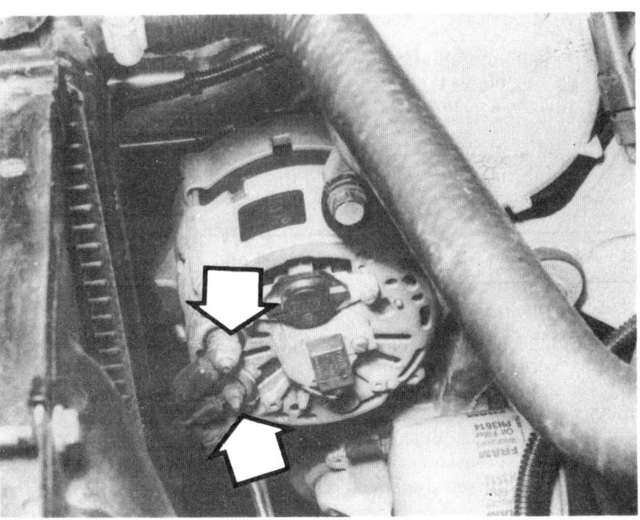

7.2b Typical 2.2L turbocharged engine alternator wiring connections (arrows)

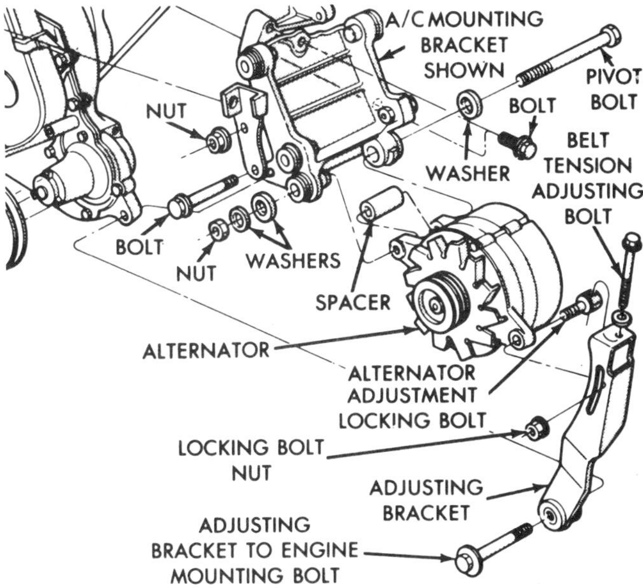

7.3 2.2L/2.5L engine alternator mount components — exploded view

4 Alternator — maintenance

1 The alternator requires very little maintenance because the only components subject to wear are the brushes and bearings. The bearings are sealed for life. The brushes should be inspected for wear after about 75,000 miles (120,000 km) and the length compared to the Specifications.

2 Regular maintenance consists of cleaning to remove grease and dirt, checking the electrical connections for tightness and adjusting the drivebelt for proper tension (see Chapter 1).

5 Alternator — special precautions

Whenever the electrical system is being worked on or a booster battery is used to start the engine, certain precautions must be observed to avoid damaging the alternator:

a) Make sure that the battery cables are never reversed or damage to the alternator diodes will result. The negative (–) cable must always be grounded.
b) The output (B) cable must never be grounded; it should always be connected to the positive battery terminal.
c) Never use a high voltage tester on the alternator.
d) Do not operate the engine with the voltage regulator plug disconnected.
e) When the alternator is to be removed or its wiring disconnected, always disconnect the negative battery cable first.
f) The engine must never be operated with the battery-to-alternator cable disconnected.
g) Disconnect the battery cables before charging the battery from an external source.
h) If a booster battery or charger is used, be sure to observe correct polarity.

6 Alternator — troubleshooting and repair

5

1 The most obvious sign of a problem is the alternator warning light on the instrument panel coming on, particularly at low speeds. This indicates that the alternator is not charging. Other symptoms are a low battery state-of-charge, evidenced by dim headlights and the starter motor turning the engine over slowly.

2 The first check should always be of the drivebelt tension (Chapter 1), followed by making sure that all electrical connections are secure and free of dirt and corrosion.

3 If the drivebelt tension, electrical connections and battery are good, an internal fault in the alternator or voltage regulator is indicated.

4 Due to the special skills and equipment required to check the alternator, diagnosis and repair should be left to a dealer service department or properly equipped shop. If the vehicle has a lot of miles on it, a good alternative is to replace the alternator with a rebuilt unit.

7 Alternator (2.2L/2.5L engine) — removal and installation

Refer to illustrations 7.2a, 7.2b and 7.3

1 With the ignition switch in the Off position, disconnect the negative cable at the battery. Place the cable out of the way so it cannot accidentally come in contact with the negative terminal of the battery, as this would once again allow power into the electrical system of the vehicle.

2 Disconnect the alternator wires **(see illustrations)**. Mark each wire and terminal to ensure correct reinstallation.

3 Loosen the pivot bolt/nut, the locking bolt nut and the belt tension adjusting bolt, then remove the drivebelt **(see illustration)**.

4 Remove the belt tension adjusting bolt and the adjustment locking bolt/nut.

5 Remove the pivot bolt and nut and separate the alternator from the engine.
6 To install the alternator, place it in position and install the pivot bolt and nut finger-tight.
7 Install the adjustment locking bolt/nut and the belt tension adjusting bolt.
8 Install and adjust the drivebelt (Chapter 1).
9 Tighten the pivot bolt/nut and the adjustment locking bolt nut.

8 Alternator (2.6L engine) – removal end installation

Refer to illustrations 8.2, 8.3 and 8.6

1 With the ignition switch in the Off position, disconnect the negative battery cable from the battery.
2 Disconnect the wires from the alternator (mark the wires and terminals to ensure correct reinstallation) **(see illustration)**.
3 Loosen the locknut and adjusting bolt, as well as the adjusting clevis bolt and the alternator-to-engine block support (pivot) bolt nut **(see illustration)**. Loosen the adjusting strap bolt, then remove the drivebelt(s).
4 Withdraw the support bolt and remove the adjusting clevis bolt, then detach the alternator.
5 To install the alternator, place it in position and insert the support bolt from the front of the bracket.
6 Install the drivebelt(s) and push the alternator forward. Measure the clearance between the alternator yoke leg and the timing chain case **(see illustration)** and compare it to the Specifications. If the gap is too large, install spacers as required.
7 Install the adjusting clevis bolt.
8 Adjust the drivebelt tension (Chapter 1), then tighten the support bolt nut and the adjusting clevis bolt. The adjusting bolt locknut must be tightened as well as the support bolt.
9 Connect the wires to the alternator terminals.
10 Connect the negative battery cable.

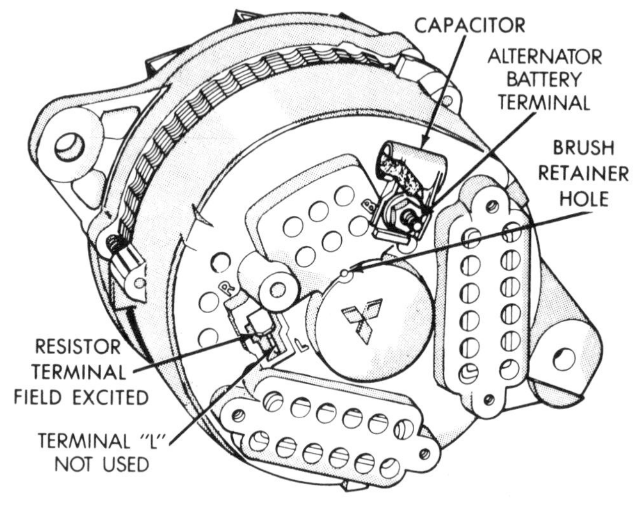

8.2 Alternator wiring connections – 2.6L engine

9 Alternator brushes (2.2L/2.5L engine) – removal, inspection and installation

Refer to illustrations 9.2, 9.3, 9.5, 9.6, 9.11, 9.16, 9.17a, 9.17b and 9.18

1 Disconnect the negative cable at the battery. Place the cable out of the way so it cannot accidentally come in contact with the negative terminal of the battery, as this would once again allow power into the electrical system of the vehicle. Label the wires and detach them from the alternator terminals.

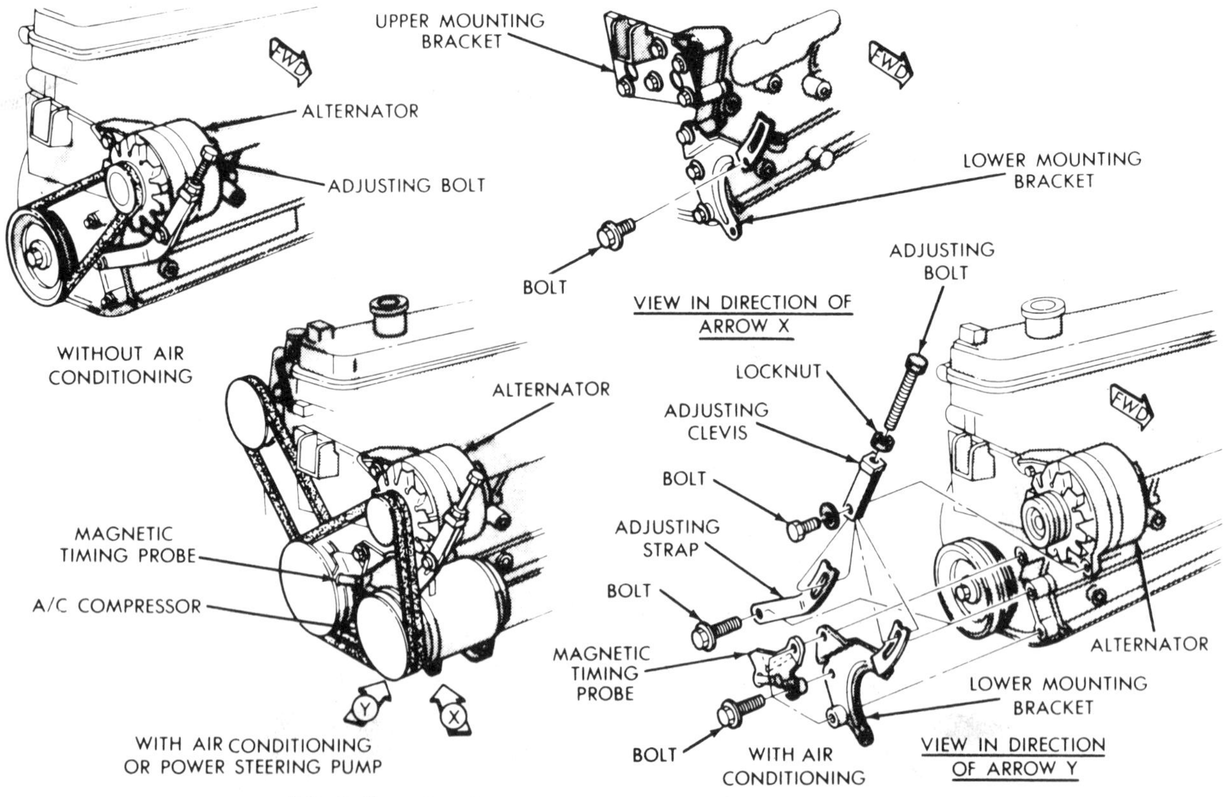

8.3 2.6L engine alternator mount components – exploded view

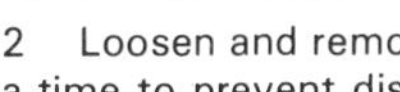

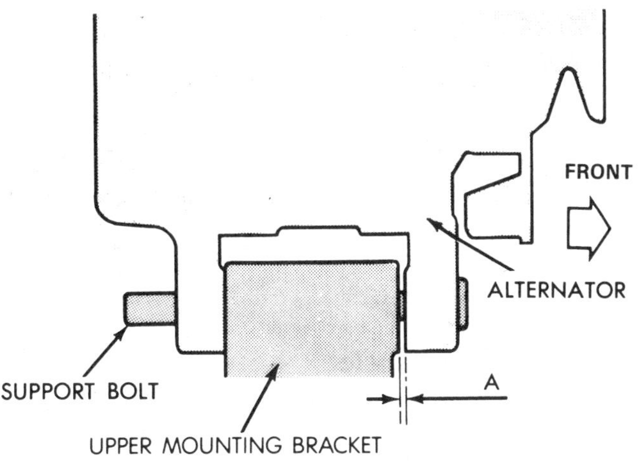

8.6 When installing the 2.6L engine alternator, the clearance A must be as specified or spacers must be added to close the gap

Bosch alternator

2 Loosen and remove the brush holder mounting screws a little at a time to prevent distortion of the holder **(see illustration)**.

3 Rotate the brush holder and separate it from the rear of the alternator **(see illustration)**.

4 If the brushes are worn beyond the specified limit, or if they do not move smoothly in the brush holder, replace the brush holder assembly with a new one.

5 Before installing the brush holder assembly, check for continuity between each brush and the appropriate field terminal **(see illustration)**.

6 Insert the holder into position, making sure the brushes seat correctly **(see illustration)**

7 Hold the brush holder securely in place and install the screws. Tighten them evenly, a little at a time, so the holder is not distorted. Once the screws are snug, tighten them securely.

8 Connect the negative battery cable.

Chrysler 60 and 78 amp alternators

9 Remove the alternator.

10 The brushes are mounted in plastic holders which locate them in the proper position.

11 Remove the brush mounting screws and insulating washers and

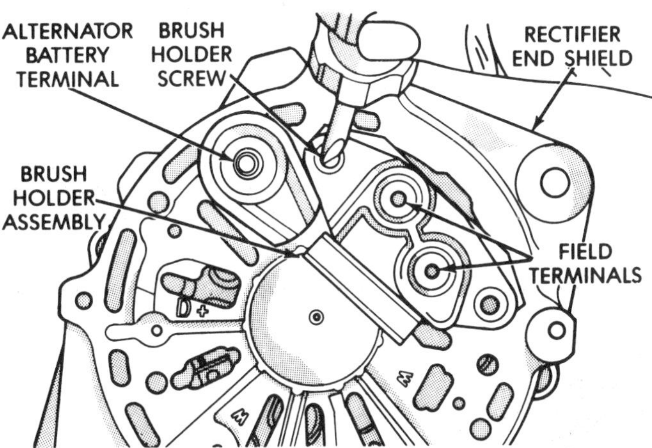

9.2 On Bosch alternators, remove the screws evenly so the holder won't be damaged . . .

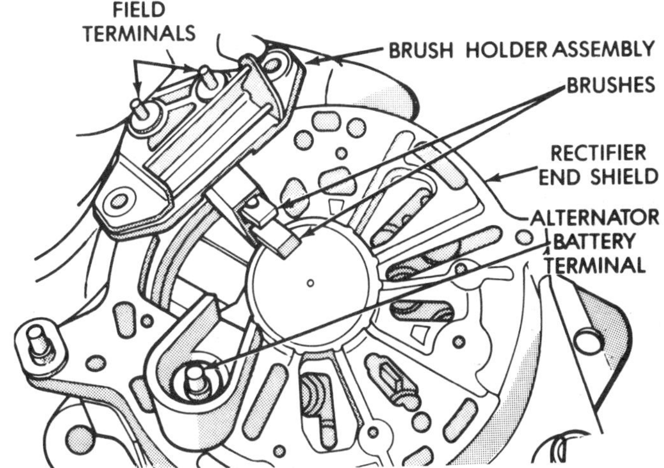

9.3 . . . and rotate the brush holder out of the alternator housing

5

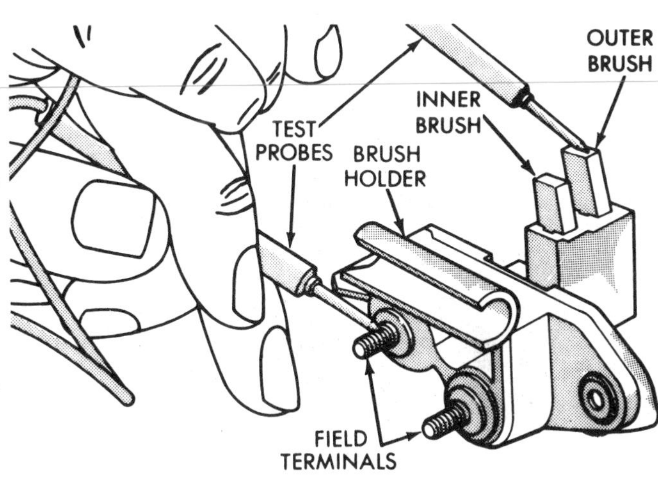

9.5 Be sure continuity exists between each brush and the appropriate field terminal before installing the brush holder assembly (Bosch alternator shown)

9.6 Push the brush holder into place making sure the brushes (which are spring loaded) seat securely (Bosch alternator shown)

separate the brush assemblies from the rectifier end shield **(see illustration)**.
12 Measure the length of each brush and compare it to the Specifications. If the brushes are worn beyond the specified limit or are oil soaked or damaged, replace them with new ones.
13 Make sure the brushes move smoothly in the holders with no binding.

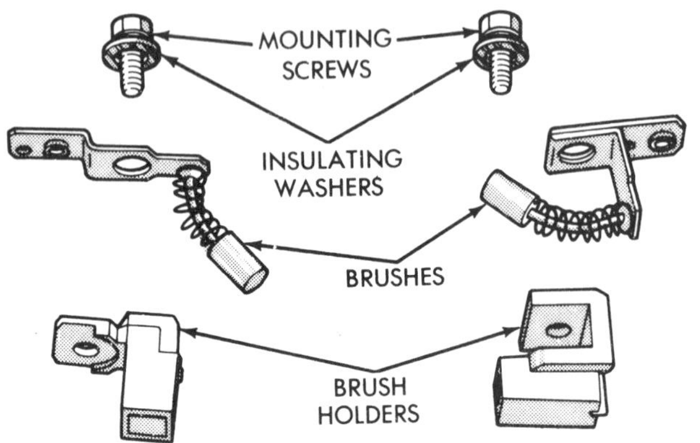

9.11 On 60/78 amp alternators, the insulating washers must be in place when the brushes are installed

14 Insert the brush assemblies into the rectifier end shield and install the screws and washers. Tighten the screws securely. Make sure the brushes are not grounded.
15 Install the alternator.

Chrysler 40 and 90 amp alternators

16 Remove the nut and detach the dust cover from the rear of the alternator **(see illustration)**.
17 Remove the brush holder mounting screws and separate the brush holder from the end shield **(see illustrations)**.
18 Before installing the new brush holder assembly, check for continuity between each brush and the appropriate field terminal **(see illustration)**.
19 Installation is the reverse of removal. Be careful when slipping the brushes over the slip rings and do not overtighten the brush holder screws.

10 Alternator brushes (2.6L engine) — removal, inspection and installation

Refer to illustrations 10.3, 10.4, 10.5 and 10.6

1 Remove the alternator from the vehicle.
2 Mount the alternator in a vise, using blocks of wood to protect it.
3 Remove the through bolts retaining the drive end shield to the stator and rectifier end shield assembly **(see illustration)**.
4 Use two screwdrivers to separate the two sections of the alter-

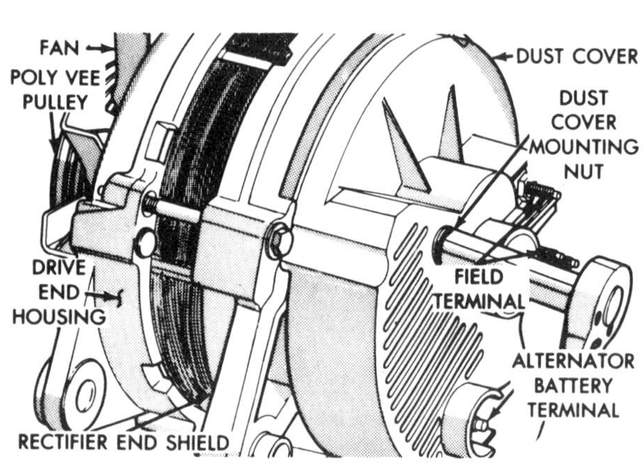

9.16 Remove the nut and detach the dust cover . . .

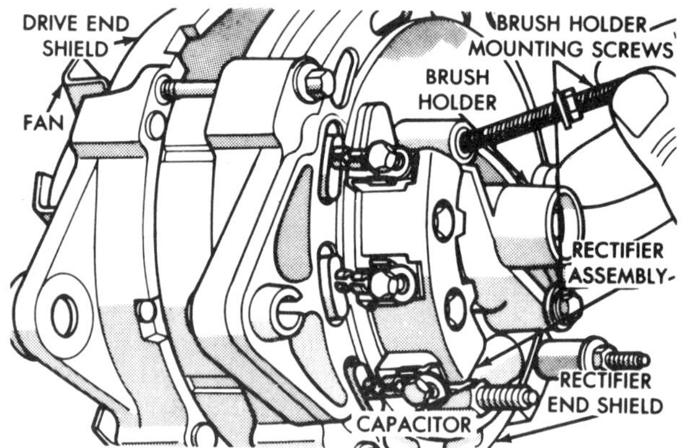

9.17a . . . then remove the brush holder mounting screws . . .

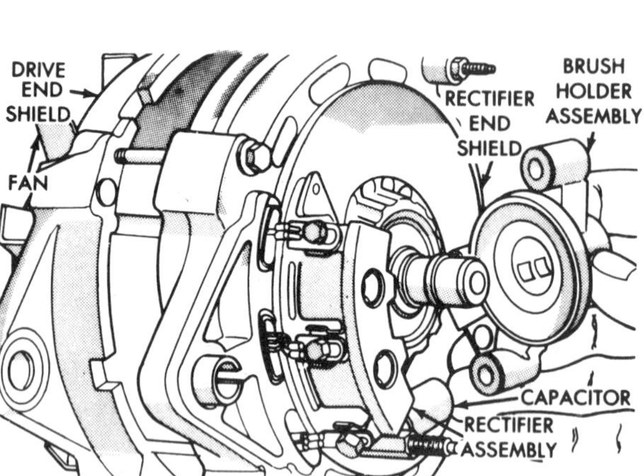

9.17b . . . and detach the brush holder to service the brushes on 40/90 amp alternators

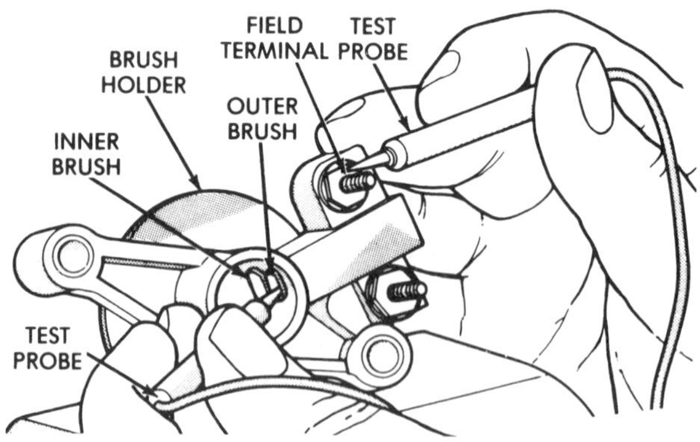

9.18 Be sure continuity exists between each brush and the appropriate field terminal before installing the brush holder assembly on 40/90 amp alternators

nator assembly and remove the rectifier end assembly **(see illustration)**.

5 Remove the brushes and springs from the rectifier and shield assembly. Measure the length of the brushes **(see illustration)**. If they are shorter than specified, replace them with new ones.

6 Push the brushes into the brush holder and insert a piece of wire to hold them in place **(see illustration)**.

7 Carefully slide the drive end shield and the rotor assembly into the rectifier end assembly. Line up the bolt holes and install the three through bolts. Tighten them evenly and securely.

8 Remove the wire retaining the brushes.

9 Install the alternator.

11 Voltage regulator – general information

The voltage regulator controls the charging system voltage by limiting the alternator output voltage. The regulator is a sealed unit and is not adjustable.

If the ammeter fails to register a charge rate or the red warning light on the dash comes on and the alternator, battery, drivebelt tension and electrical connections seem to be fine, have the regulator checked by a dealer service department or a repair shop.

The voltage regulator on 2.2L carburetor equipped vehicles is located on the left-hand inner fender panel (under a cover on some models) in the engine compartment. To replace the regulator, unplug the wiring connector, remove the retaining screws and detach it. Installation is the reverse of removal.

Some Bosch alternators incorporate an integral voltage regulator which is part of the brush assembly.

The voltage regulator on 2.6L engines is integral with the alternator. In the event of regulator failure, the alternator will have to be replaced with a new or rebuilt unit.

On fuel injected models the voltage regulator is incorporated into the logic and power module/EFI system and consequently all diagnosis and repair must be left to a dealer service department or repair shop.

12 Starting system – general information

The starting system is made up of the motor, battery, starter switch, starter relay and associated wiring.

When the ignition switch is turned to the Start position, the relay is energized through the control circuit. The relay then connects the battery to the starter motor.

13 Starter motor – in-vehicle check

1 If the starter motor fails to operate, check the condition of the battery by turning on the headlights. If they glow brightly for several seconds and then gradually dim, the battery is in an uncharged condition.

2 If the headlights continue to glow brightly and it is obvious that the battery is in good condition, then check the tightness of the battery cables and the starter wiring. Check the tightness of the connections at the rear of the solenoid.

3 If the battery is fully charged and the wiring is in order, and the starter still fails to operate, then it will have to be removed from the engine for examination. Before this is done, however, make sure that the pinion gear has not jammed in mesh with the ring gear due either to a broken solenoid spring or dirty pinion gear splines. To release the

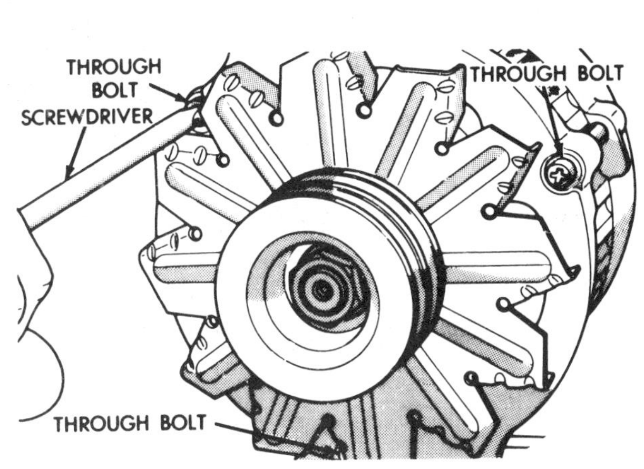

10.3 To gain access to the 2.6L engine alternator brushes, remove the through-bolts, . . .

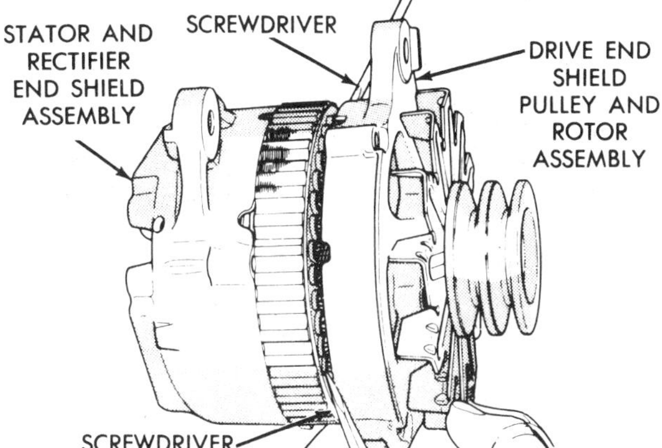

10.4 . . . carefully separate the alternator components and detach the brush holder

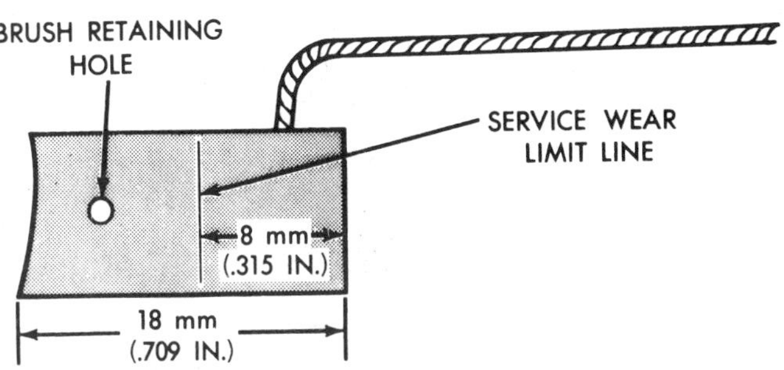

10.5 If the service wear limit line on the brushes is visible, replace the brush holder assembly with a new one

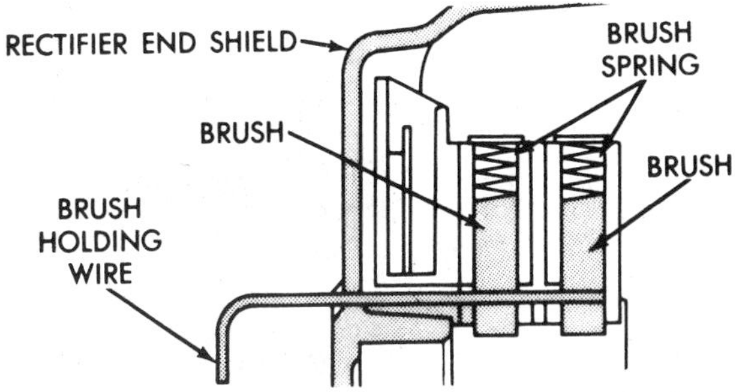

10.6 Insert a wire (a paper clip works great for this) through the end shield and the brush holes to keep them retracted as the alternator components are rejoined

5

pinion, engage a low gear (manual transaxle) and with the ignition switched off, rock the vehicle backwards and forwards. This should release the pinion from mesh with the ring gear; if the pinion still remains jammed, the starter motor must be removed.

14 Starter motor (2.2L/2.5L engine) – removal and installation

Refer to illustrations 14.5a, 14.5b, 14.6 and 14.7

Removal

1 Disconnect the negative cable at the battery. Place the cable out of the way so it cannot accidentally come in contact with the negative terminal of the battery, as this would once again allow power into the electrical system of the vehicle.
2 Raise the front of the vehicle and support it securely on jackstands.
3 Remove the right side driveaxle (non-turbocharged models) or intermediate shaft (turbocharged models).
4 On turbocharged models it will be necessary to unbolt the turbocharger brace at the lower starter motor-to-block mount and swivel it out of the way.
5 Remove the heat shield (if equipped) **(see illustrations)**.
6 Remove the nuts and detach the battery cable and solenoid wire from the starter **(see illustration)**.
7 Remove the mounting bolts/nuts and separate the starter from the bellhousing **(see illustration)**.

Installation

8 To install the starter, place it in position on the studs, install the mounting bolts/nuts and tighten them securely.
9 Connect the starter cable and solenoid wire.
10 Install the heat shield (if equipped).
11 Lower the front of the vehicle.
12 Connect the negative battery cable.

15 Starter motor (2.6L engine) – removal and installation

Refer to illustration 15.2

1 Disconnect the negative battery cable from the battery.
2 Remove the starter cable and solenoid wire from the motor terminals **(see illustration)**.
3 Remove the mounting bolts and detach the starter motor.
4 To install the starter, hold it in place, install the mounting bolts and tighten them securely.
5 Connect the starter cable and solenoid wire.
6 Connect the negative battery cable.

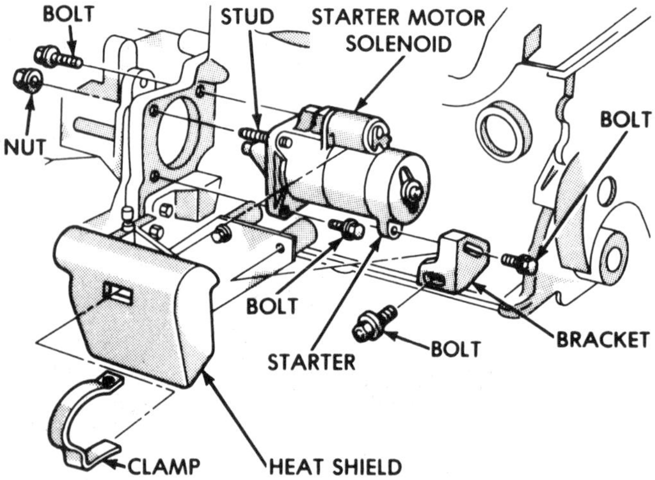

14.5a Typical starter motor installation details

14.5b Remove the heat shield clamp by squeezing and pulling it off

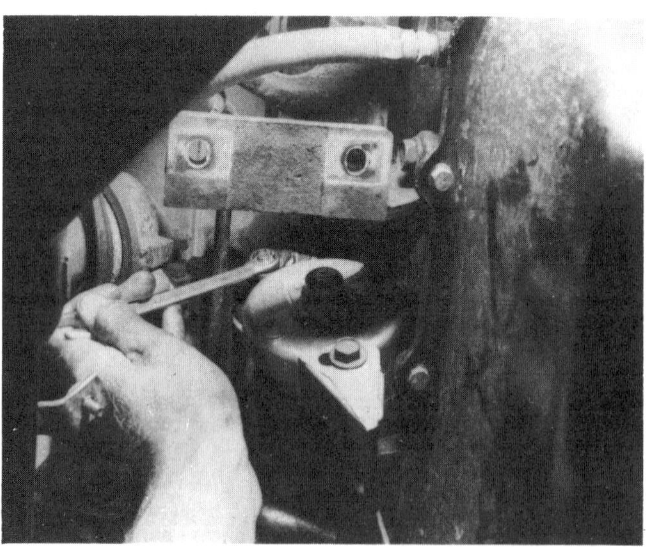

14.6 Removing the battery cable and solenoid wire terminal nuts from the starter motor

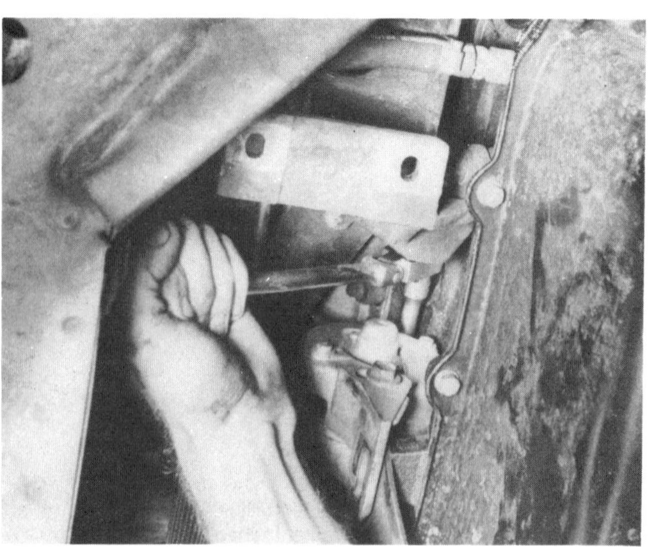

14.7 A socket and long extension are necessary for removing the starter motor-to-bellhousing bolts

16 Ignition system – general information

The ignition system is designed to ignite the fuel/air charge entering each cylinder at just the right moment. It does this by producing a high-voltage electrical spark between the electrodes of each spark plug.

On vehicles equipped with 2.2L carbureted engines, the ignition system consists of a switch, the ignition coil, the distributor and a Spark Control Computer (SCC). The spark timing is constantly adjusted by the computer and distributor in response to input from the various sensors located on the engine.

On fuel injection equipped vehicles the ignition system and the Electronic Fuel Injection (EFI) system interact through the logic and power modules to provide the proper fuel flow and ignition curve for all conditions (see Section 27). The ignition system consists of a switch, the ignition coil, the distributor and the logic and power modules. The spark timing is constantly adjusted by the logic and power modules and distributor in response to input from the various sensors located on the engine.

On 2.6L engines the ignition system is made up of the switch, coil, distributor and an electronic control unit (igniter). Ignition advance is varied according to driving conditions by centrifugal and vacuum advance mechanisms which are integral with the distributor.

17 Spark Control Computer (SCC) (2.2L carburetor equipped engine) – removal and installation

Refer to illustration 17.2

1 Disconnect the negative battery cable, followed by the positive cable, then remove the battery.

2 Disconnect the vacuum hose from the transducer and unplug the electrical connectors **(see illustration)**. Disengage the assembly from the outside air duct.

3 Remove the three mounting screws and detach the SCC assembly from the vehicle.

4 To install the computer, place it in position, engage it with the air duct and install the screws. Connect the vacuum hose and plug in the electrical connectors. Do not remove the grease from the connector or cavity. There should be at least 1/8-inch of grease in the cavity to prevent the intrusion of moisture. If there is not, apply multi-purpose grease to the cavity.

5 Install the battery.

18 Spark Control Computer (SCC) (2.2L carburetor equipped engine) – check

Refer to illustrations 18.2a, 18.2b, 18.4, 18.8, 18.11, 18.13, 18.14, 18.16, 18.17, 18.18, 18.19, 18.21 and 18.22

1 Prior to testing the spark control computer (SCC), check the coil and battery to make sure they are in good operating condition. Inspect the electrical harness and wires for shorts, cracked and worn insulation and all connectors for security. Check the vacuum hose for kinks, damage and secure connection.

2 Connect the special test tool **(see illustration)** to the negative terminal of the coil and ground the other end. Pull the coil wire from the distributor and place it 1/4-inch from a good ground **(see illustration)**. With the ignition switch on, momentarily touch the remaining test lead to the negative coil terminal. A spark should jump from the coil wire

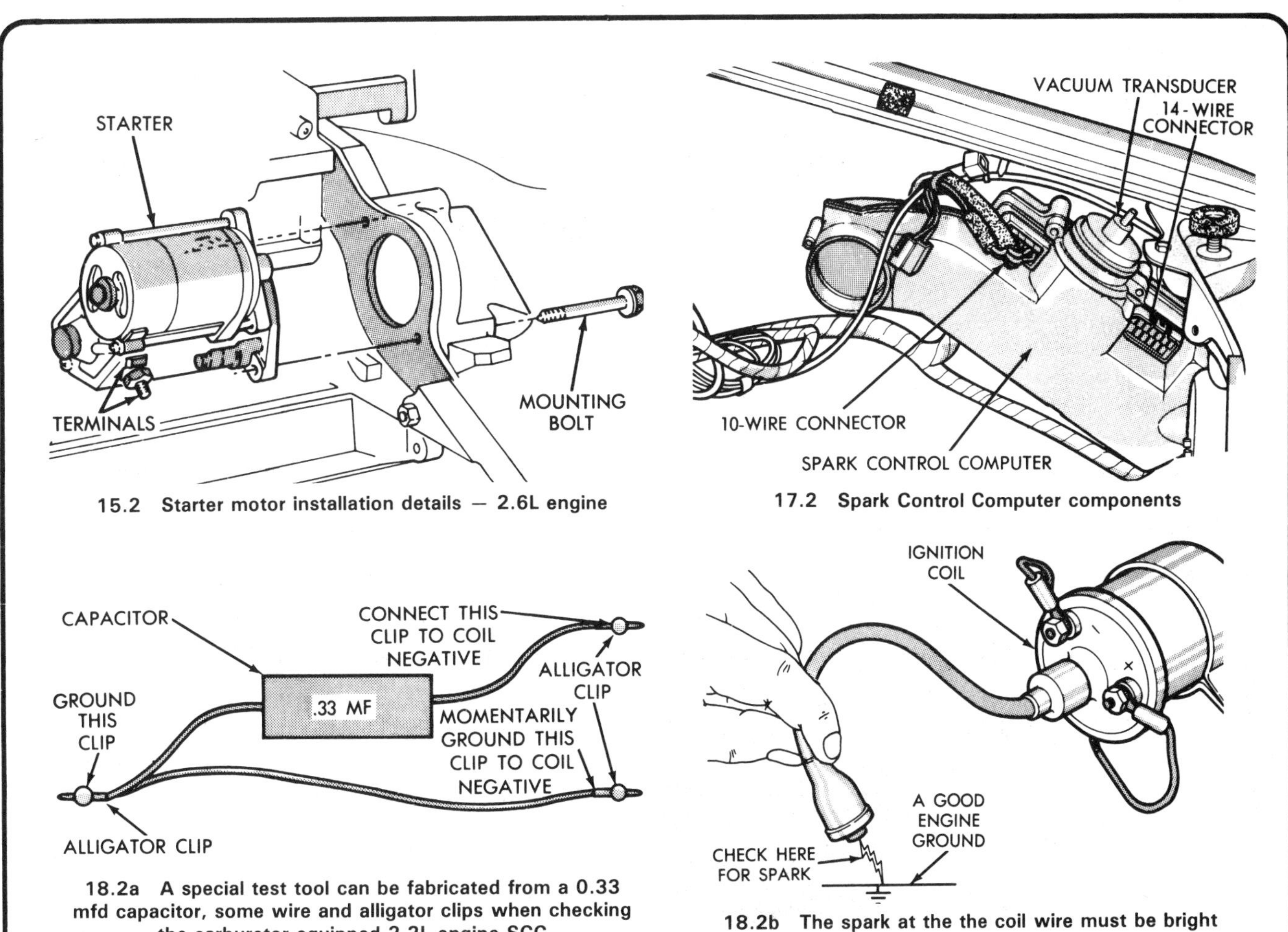

15.2 Starter motor installation details – 2.6L engine

17.2 Spark Control Computer components

18.2a A special test tool can be fabricated from a 0.33 mfd capacitor, some wire and alligator clips when checking the carburetor equipped 2.2L engine SCC

18.2b The spark at the the coil wire must be bright blue and well defined

5

to ground.

3 If there is a spark, proceed to Step 8.

4 If there is no spark, turn off the ignition switch, disconnect the ten wire harness connector at the SCC **(see illustration)** and repeat the test. If a spark is now produced, the computer output is shorted and the spark control computer must be replaced with a new one.

5 If there was still no spark, check the voltage at the coil positive terminal to make sure it is within one volt of battery voltage.

6 If there was no voltage reading, check the wiring between the battery and the positive terminal of the coil.

7 If there was a proper voltage reading, check the voltage at the coil negative terminal. This reading should also be within one volt of the battery voltage. If there is no voltage or there is voltage but no spark was produced when performing the test in Step 2, replace the coil with

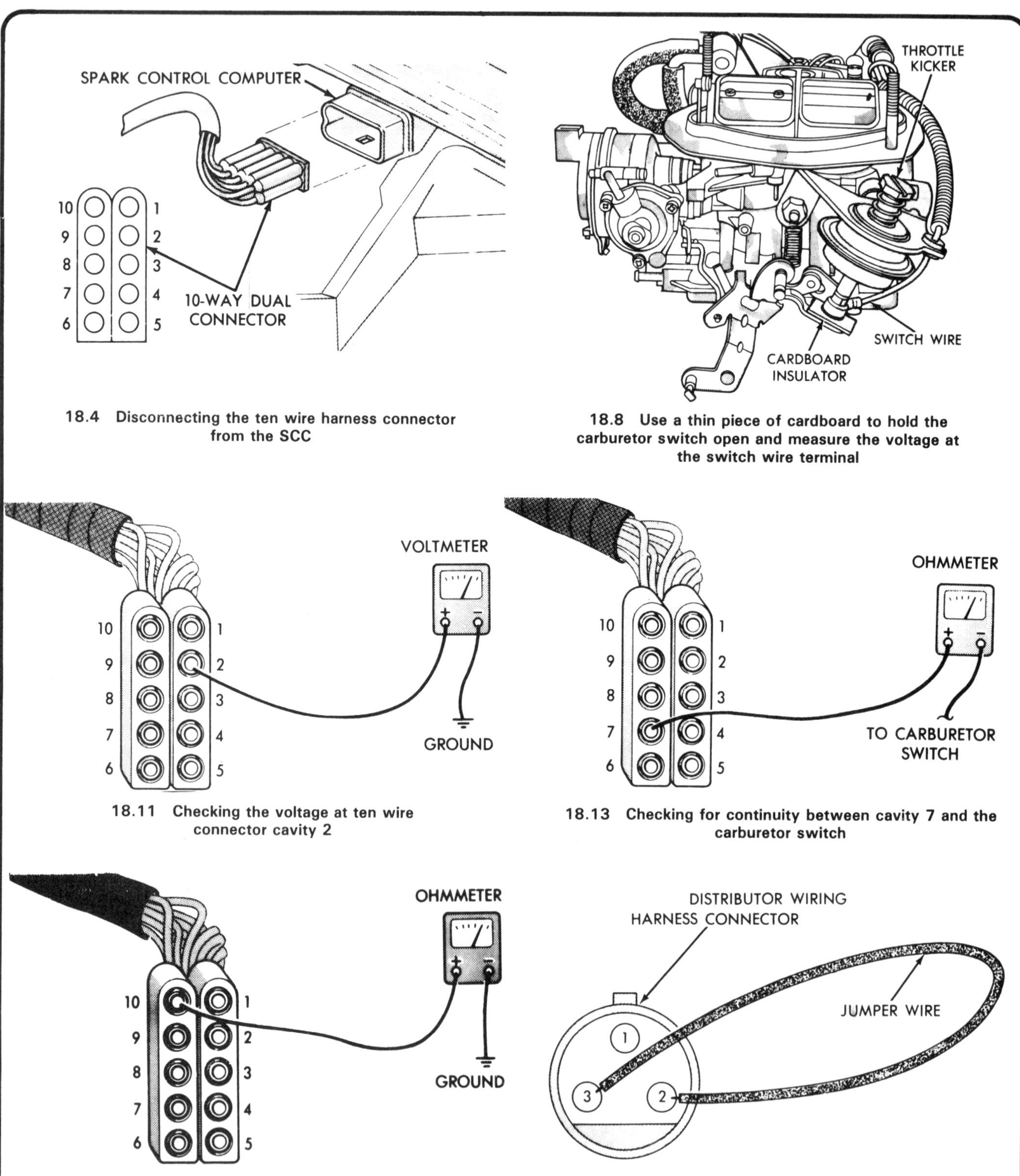

18.4 Disconnecting the ten wire harness connector from the SCC

18.8 Use a thin piece of cardboard to hold the carburetor switch open and measure the voltage at the switch wire terminal

18.11 Checking the voltage at ten wire connector cavity 2

18.13 Checking for continuity between cavity 7 and the carburetor switch

18.14 Checking for continuity between cavity 10 and a good ground

18.16 The jumper wire must be connected between cavities 2 and 3 in the distributor wiring harness connector

a new one.

8 If there is a voltage reading but the engine will not start, use a thin piece of cardboard to hold the carburetor switch open **(see illustration)** and measure the voltage at the switch. The reading should be at least five volts.

9 If the voltage reading is correct, go on to Step 16.

10 If there is no voltage, turn off the ignition switch and unplug the SCC ten wire connector.

11 Turn the switch on and check the voltage at cavity 2 of the connector **(see illustration)**. It should be within one volt of battery voltage.

12 If there is no voltage reading, check for continuity between cavity 2 and the battery. Repair the circuit and repeat the test in Step 11.

13 If there is voltage present, turn off the ignition switch and check for continuity between cavity 7 and the carburetor switch **(see illustration)**. If no continuity is present, check for an open wire between cavity 7 and the carburetor switch and repair the circuit.

14 If there is continuity present, check for continuity between cavity 10 and a good ground **(see illustration)**. If there is continuity, it will be necessary to replace the computer with a new one as power is going into it but not out. Repeat the test in Step 8.

15 If continuity is not present, check for an open wire.

16 If the wiring is alright and the engine will not start, plug the ten wire connector into the computer and unplug the distributor wire harness connector. Connect a jumper wire between cavities 2 and 3 of the connector **(see illustration)**. Hold the coil wire near a good ground, turn the ignition switch on and break the circuit at cavity 2 or 3 several times. A bright blue spark should occur at the coil wire.

17 If sparks are produced but the engine still does not start, replace the distributor pick-up assembly (also called a Hall Effect switch), making sure the shutter blades are grounded **(see illustration)**. With the ignition switched off, check for a good ground on the distributor shaft with an ohmmeter. It may be necessary to seat the rotor securely on the shaft to obtain a good ground. Connect one lead of the ohmmeter to the shutter blade and the other to a good ground and make sure there is continuity. If there is none, push the rotor down on the shaft until continuity is indicated. Replacement rotors should always have ESA stamped on the top.

18 Repeat the test in Step 16 and if there is no spark present, measure the voltage at cavity 1 of the distributor connector **(see illustration)**. It should be within one volt of battery voltage.

19 If the voltage is correct, turn off the ignition, unplug the ten wire connector from the computer and check for continuity between cavity 2 of the distributor harness and cavity 9 of the computer connector. Follow this by checking between cavity 3 of the distributor harness and cavity 5 of the computer connector **(see illustration)**. If there is no continuity, find and repair the fault in the harness. If there is continuity, replace the computer with a new one as power is going into it but not coming out.

20 Repeat the test in Step 16.

21 If no voltage is present when making the check in Step 18, turn off the ignition, unplug the computer ten wire connector and check for continuity between cavity 1 of the distributor harness connector and cavity 3 of the computer connector **(see illustration)**. If there is no continuity, repair the wire and repeat the test in Step 16.

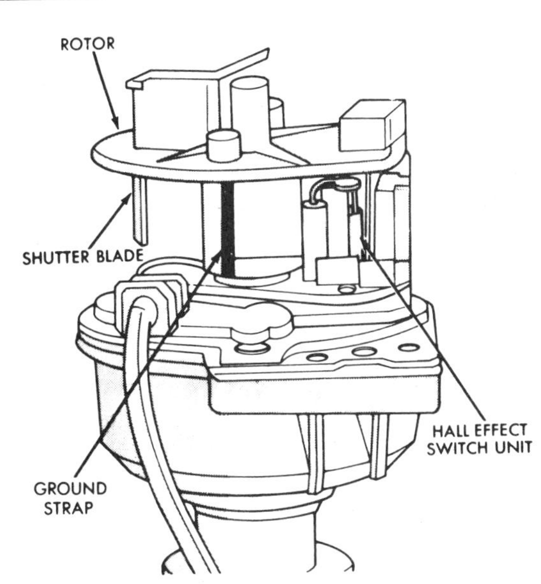

18.17 Rotor shutter blade and ground strap locations

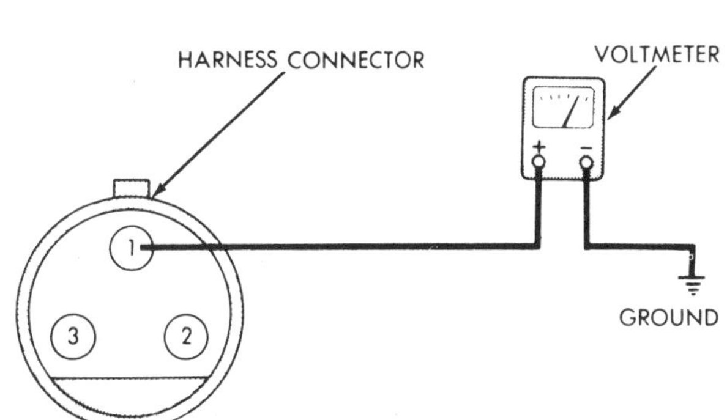

18.18 Checking for voltage between the distributor harness connector cavity 1 and a good ground

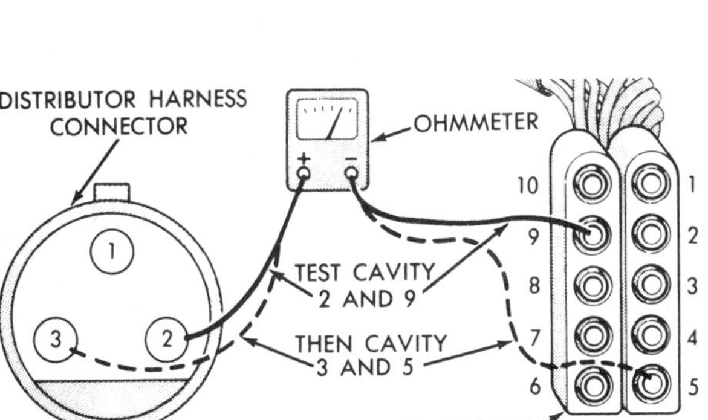

18.19 Checking for continuity between the distributor and SCC connector cavities

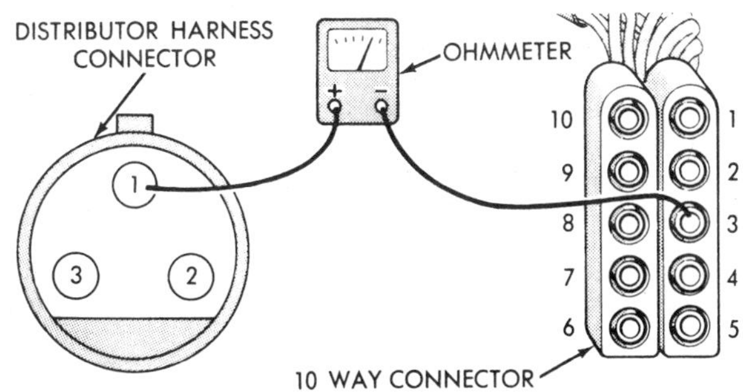

18.21 Checking for continuity between the distributor harness connector cavity 1 and the SCC connector cavity 3

5

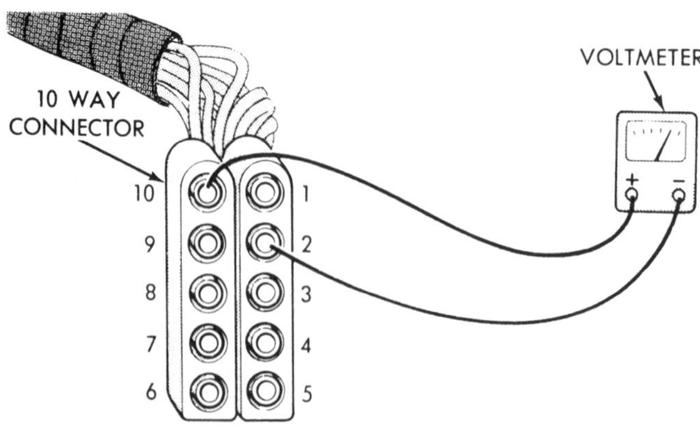

18.22 Checking for voltage between SCC connector cavities 10 and 2

22 If there is continuity, turn on the ignition switch and check for voltage between cavities 2 and 10 of the computer connector **(see illustration)**. If there is voltage, the computer is faulty and must be replaced with a new one. Repeat the test in Step 16.
23 If there is no voltage, check and repair the ground wire, as the computer is not grounded. Repeat the Step 16 test.

19 Ignition system (2.6L engine) – check

1 Remove the high voltage coil wire from the distributor cap and hold the end about 1/4-inch from a good engine ground with an insulated plug wire tool. Operate the starter and look for a series of bright blue sparks at the coil wire.
2 If sparks occur, and they are bright blue and well defined, continue to operate the starter while slowly moving the coil wire away from the ground. As this is done, look for arcing and sparking at the coil tower. If it occurs, replace the coil with a new one. If arcing does not occur at the coil tower, the ignition system is producing the necessary high secondary voltage. However, make sure the voltage is getting to the spark plugs by checking the rotor, distributor cap, spark plug wires and spark plugs as described in Chapter 1. If the results are positive, the ignition system is not the reason the engine will not start.
3 If no sparks occurred, or if they were weak or intermittent, measure the voltage at the ignition coil negative terminal with the ignition switch on. It should be the same as battery voltage. If it is three volts or less, the igniter is defective. If no voltage was present, check the coil and wires for an open circuit.
4 Refer to Step 2 in Section 18 and perform the check described there.
5 If no spark was produced, check for voltage at the positive coil terminal with the ignition switch on. Battery voltage should be indicated. If it is, the coil is defective. If no voltage is present, check the associated wires and connections.

20 Centrifugal advance (2.6L engine) – check

1 Refer to Chapter 1, *Ignition timing check and adjustment*, and hook up a timing light as described there.
2 With the engine running at idle speed and the timing light properly connected, remove the vacuum hose from the vacuum advance control unit on the distributor.
3 Watch the timing marks on the front of the engine and slowly increase engine speed. The timing mark on the crankshaft pulley should appear to move smoothly in a direction away from the stationary mark on the timing tab (when the engine is running at 3000 rpm, 10° of advance should be indicated). Then, when the engine is slowed down, the mark should return to its original position.
4 If the above conditions are not met, the advance mechanism inside the distributor should be checked for broken governor springs and sticking weights.

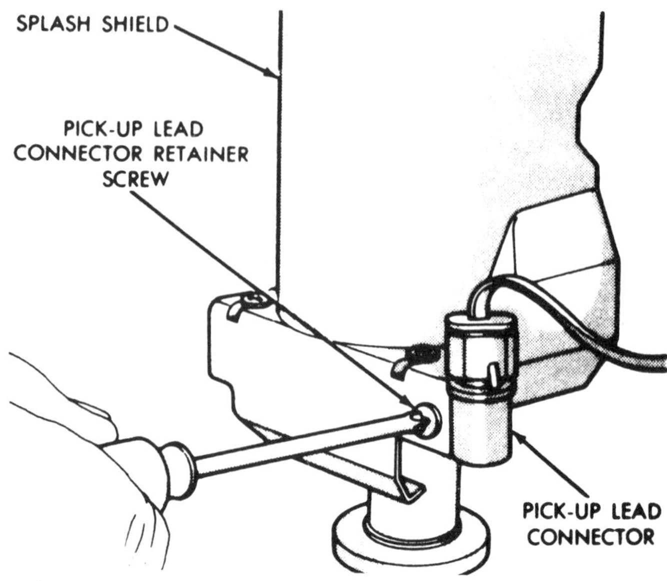

22.3 After unplugging the distributor wire harness connector, remove the screw and detach the connector from the distributor (1982 through 1985 models)

21 Vacuum advance (2.6L engine) – check

1 Refer to Chapter 1, *Ignition timing check and adjustment*, and hook up a timing light as described there.
2 Start the engine and set the speed at approximately 2500 rpm.
3 Watch the timing marks at the front of the engine and remove the vacuum hose from the vacuum advance control unit on the distributor. When the hose is removed, the timing mark on the crankshaft pulley should appear to move closer to the stationary mark on the timing tab. When the hose is reconnected, the mark should move away again.
4 If reconnecting the vacuum hose produces an abrupt increase in advance, or none at all, the vacuum advance control unit is probably defective.

22 Distributor (2.2L/2.5L engine) – removal and installation

Refer to illustrations 22.3, 22.7a and 22.7b

Removal

1 Disconnect the negative cable at the battery. Place the cable out of the way so it cannot accidentally come in contact with the negative terminal of the battery, as this would once again allow power into the electrical system of the vehicle.
2 Unplug the distributor pick-up coil lead wire at the harness connector.
3 On 1982 through 1985 models, remove the retaining screw and separate the pick-up lead connector from the retainer **(see illustration)**.
4 Remove the distributor splash shield.
5 Loosen the two screws and detach the distributor cap.
6 Refer to Chapter 2, Part C, and position the number one piston at TDC on the compression stroke.
7 Remove the hold-down screw or bolt and carefully lift the distributor out of the engine **(see illustrations)**. **Note:** *Do not turn the crankshaft with the distributor out of the engine.*

Installation

8 To install the distributor, lower it into position, making sure the gasket or O-ring is seated properly. Engage the distributor drive with the auxiliary shaft so that the rotor is aligned with the mark on the engine block made during removal.
9 If the crankshaft was turned while the distributor was out of the engine, it will be necessary to establish the proper relationship between the distributor and the number one piston position. Remove the number

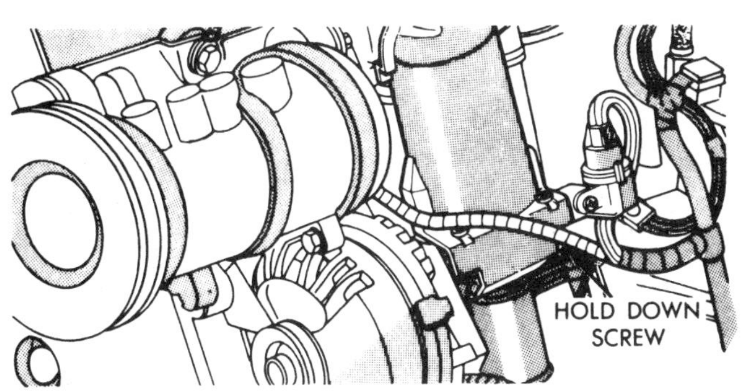

22.7a Distributor hold-down screw or bolt location (1982 through 1985 models)

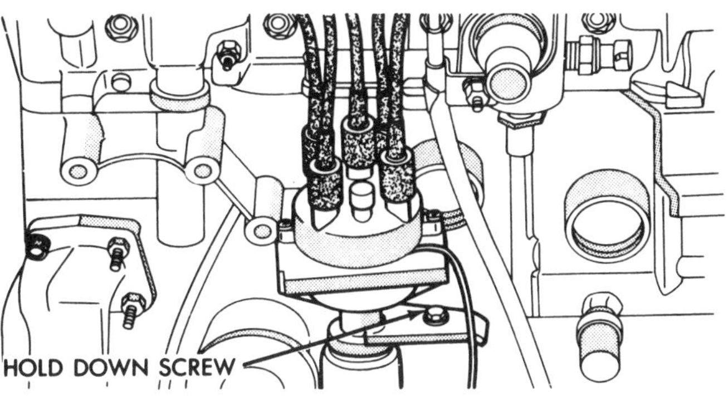

22.7b 1986 and later model distributor hold-down screw or bolt location

23.3 The rotor can be simply pulled off the distributor shaft (1982 through 1985 models)

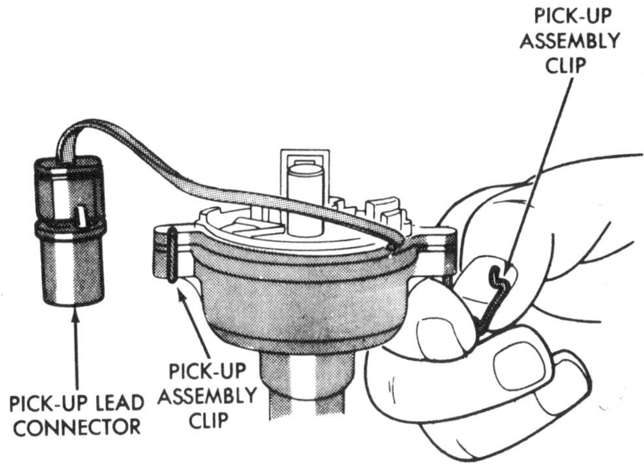

23.4a On some models the retaining clips must be removed before the pick-up assembly can be removed

one cylinder spark plug, place your finger over the plug hole and rotate the crankshaft until pressure is felt, indicating that the piston is at top dead center on the compression stroke. The pointer on the bellhousing should be aligned with the 0 (TDC) mark on the flywheel. If it is not, continue to turn the crankshaft until the mark and the 0 are lined up.
10 Install the distributor cap.
11 Install the hold-down bolt.
12 Install the splash shield.
13 Install the pick-up coil lead and plug the wire into the harness. Connect the negative battery cable.
14 Check the timing (Chapter 1) and tighten the distributor hold-down bolt securely.

23 Hall Effect pick-up assembly (2.2L/2.5L engine) – removal and installation

Refer to illustrations 23.3, 23.4a, 23.4b, 23.6a, and 23.6b

1 Disconnect the negative cable at the battery. Place the cable out of the way so it cannot accidentally come in contact with the negative terminal of the battery, as this would once again allow power into the electrical system of the vehicle.
2 Remove the distributor splash shield and cap.

1982 through 1985 models

3 Remove the rotor **(see illustration)**.
4 Remove the clips (if equipped) and lift the pick-up assembly off the distributor shaft **(see illustrations)**.
5 To install the pick-up assembly, place it carefully into position, making sure the electrical lead retainer is in the locating hole. Install the

23.4b Lift the Hall Effect pick-up assembly off the distributor shaft

5

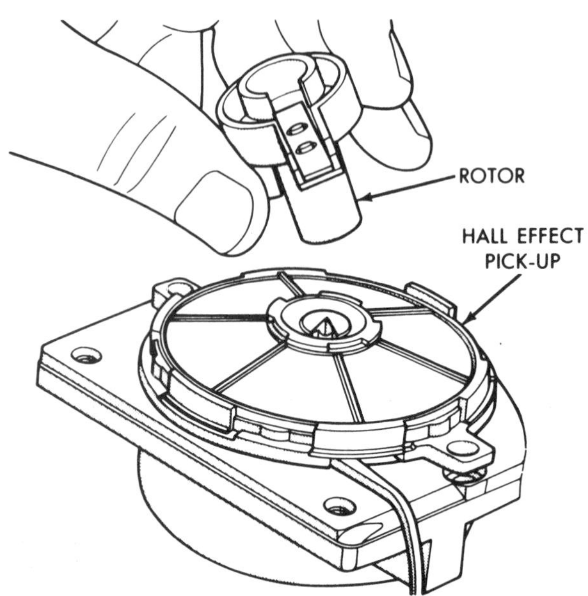

23.6a Remove the 1986 model distributor rotor by lifting it off the Hall Effect pick-up

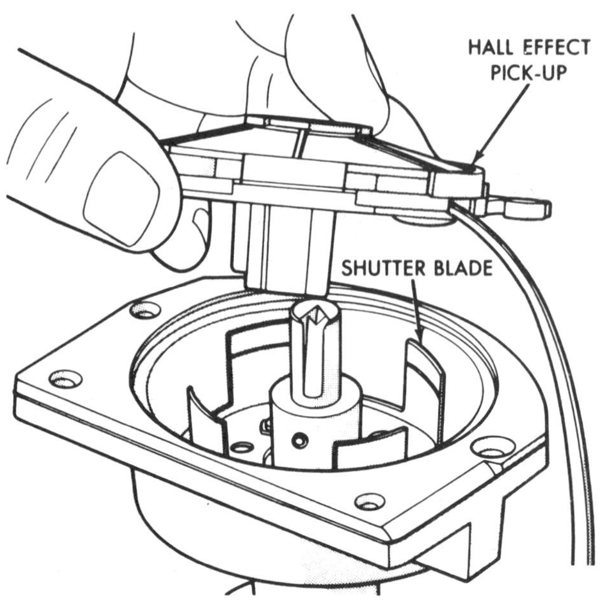

23.6b Lift the Hall Effect pick-up straight up, off the distributor shaft (1986 models)

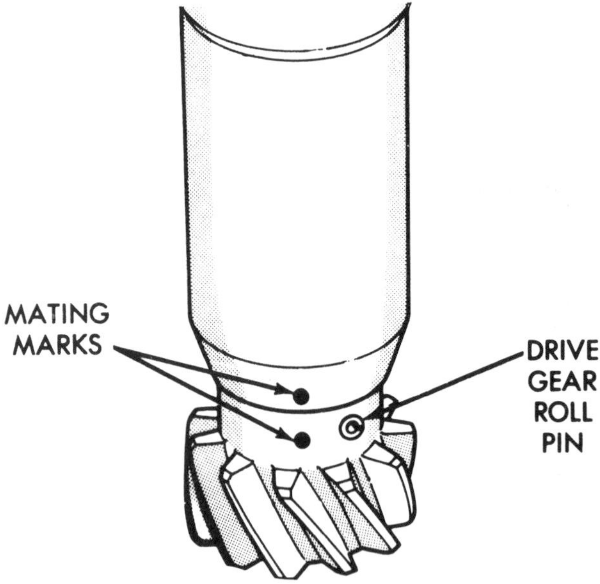

24.7a Align the marks on the distributor housing and the gear before installing the distributor (2.6L engine)

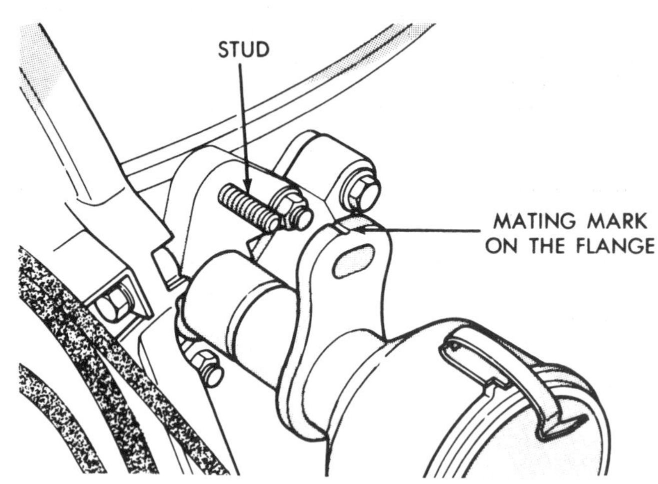

24.7b Line up the mark on the distributor flange with the center of the stud as the distributor is installed (2.6L engine)

retaining clips (if equipped) and the rotor, with the ESA marking on top. After installation check for continuity between the distributor rotor and shaft with an ohmmeter.

1986 and later models

6 Lift the rotor off the shaft, followed by the pick-up assembly **(see illustrations)**.

7 To install the pickup assembly, place it carefully into position, making sure the electrical lead retainer is in the locating hole. Install the rotor, with the ESA marking on top.

All models

8 Install the distributor cap and splash shield and connect the negative battery cable.

24 Distributor (2.6L engine) – removal and installation

Refer to illustrations 24.7a and 24.7b

1 Disconnect the negative battery cable from the battery. Unplug the distributor wiring harness and remove the distributor cap by depressing and turning the spring-loaded screws.

2 Disconnect the vacuum hose from the vacuum advance control unit on the distributor.

3 Pull the spark plug wires off the spark plugs. Pull only on the rubber boot or damage to the spark plug wire could result.

4 Refer to Chapter 2, Part C, and position the number one piston at TDC on the compression stroke.

5 Remove the distributor mounting nut and pull straight out on the distributor.

6 Do not allow the engine to be cranked until the distributor has been reinstalled.

7 To install the distributor, line up the mating marks on the distributor housing and the distributor-driven gear (punch marks) **(see illustration)**. Slide the distributor into place in the cylinder head while lining up the mark on the distributor hold-down flange with the center of the stud **(see illustration)**. Make sure the distributor is completely seated, then install the nut and tighten it finger-tight.
8 Replace the spark plugs and install the plug wires.
9 Install the distributor cap, plug in the wiring harness and connect the vacuum hose to the vacuum control unit.
10 Connect the negative battery cable to the battery and check the ignition timing as described in Chapter 1. Don't forget to tighten the distributor nut securely when finished.

25 Ignition coil – check

1 Mark the wires and terminals with pieces of numbered tape, then remove the primary wires and the high-tension lead from the coil.
2 Remove the coil from the mount, clean the outer case and check it for cracks and other damage.
3 Clean the primary coil terminals and check the coil tower terminal for corrosion. Clean it with a wire brush if any corrosion is found.
4 Check the primary coil resistance by attaching the leads of an ohmmeter to the positive and negative terminals. Compare the measured resistance to the Specifications.
5 Check the secondary coil resistance by hooking one of the ohmmeter leads to one of the primary terminals and the other ohmmeter lead to the large center terminal. Compare the measured resistance to the Specifications.
6 If the measured resistances are not as specified, the coil is probably defective and should be replaced with a new one.
7 It is essential for proper ignition system operation that all coil terminals and wire leads be kept clean and dry.
8 Install the coil in the vehicle and hook up the wires.

26 Power Loss or Power Limited light (EFI models) – general information

On EFI-equipped models, the Power Loss/Power Limited light, located in the instrument panel, ordinarily flashes on briefly and then goes out when the engine is started. The light comes on and stays on when there is a fault in the EFI system and can also be used to diagnose problems in the EFI system (Section 27).

27 Logic module and power module/SMEC (EFI models) – description and check

1 The logic module, located in the passenger compartment behind the right kick panel, is a digital computer containing a microprocessor. The power module is located in the left front corner of the engine compartment and works in conjunction with the logic module, handling the heavier electric currents, including the ground for the ignition coil and power for the fuel injection. It directs the voltage to the logic module and the Hall Effect pick-up assembly in the distributor (which then directs voltage to the spark plugs) and the automatic shutdown relay which energizes the fuel tank mounted electric fuel pump. The logic module receives the input signals from all of the sensors and switches which monitor the engine and then determines the fuel injector operation as well as the spark advance, ignition coil dwell, idle speed, canister purge solenoid, cooling fan operation and alternator charge rate. The electric fuel pump which delivers fuel to the injectors and maintains pressure in the system, is located in the fuel tank (Chapter 4).
2 Four components which provide basic information so the logic module can operate the EFI system are the Manifold Absolute Pressure (MAP) sensor, Throttle Position Sensor (TPS), oxygen sensor and the coolant temperature sensor. The MAP sensor is located on or adjacent to the logic module, is connected to the throttle body by a vacuum line and monitors the manifold vacuum. The TPS is located in the throttle body and monitors the actual position of the throttle lever which is connected to the throttle pedal. The oxygen sensor (located in the exhaust manifold) provides information on the exhaust gas makeup and the temperature sensor (threaded into the water box) monitors engine operating temperature.
3 Because the EFI system is controlled by the logic module and power module or SMEC in combination with a variety of sensors and switches, the home mechanic can do very little in the way of diagnosis without factory Diagnostic Read Out Tool number C-4805 or its equivalent. Consequently, diagnosis should be confined to inspection and checking of all electrical and vacuum connections to make sure they are secure and not obviously damaged.
4 The logic module is self-testing and a problem in the system will be indicated by the Power Loss/Limited light on the dash. The Power Loss/Limited light will come on when there is electrical system voltage fluctuation or a fault in the MAP, throttle position or coolant temperature sensor circuits. If the fault is severe enough to affect driveability, the logic module will go into a "limp-in" mode so the vehicle can still be driven.
5 The logic module stores trouble codes which can be checked using the Power Loss/Limited light. Within a five second period, turn the ignition key On-Off-On-Off-On. The Power Loss/Limited light will then flash fault codes indicating the area of the fault. The codes are two digit numbers and the start of test (88) for example, will be indicated by eight flashes, a pause and eight more flashes. If there is more than one code, the light will flash them in order, ending with the end of message code (55). Because the fault codes indicate the general location of a fault, simply checking and tightening a vacuum hose or electrical connector can often correct a problem. Any further checking of fault codes should be left to a dealer service department or properly equipped shop.

Fault codes

88 Start of test
11 Engine not cranked since battery disconnected
12 Memory standby power lost
13* MAP sensor pneumatic circuit
14* MAP sensor electrical circuit
15 Vehicle speed/distance sensor circuit
16* Loss of battery voltage
17 Engine running too cold
21 Oxygen sensor circuit
22* Coolant sensor circuit
23 Throttle body temperature circuit
24* Throttle position circuit
25 Automatic Idle Speed (AIS) motor driver circuit
26 Peak injector circuit has not been reached
27 Logic module fuel circuit internal problem
31 Purge solenoid circuit
33 Air conditioning cutout relay circuit
35 Cooling fan relay circuit
37 Shift indicator light circuit
41 Charging system excess or lack of field current
42 Automatic shutdown relay driver circuit
43 Spark interface circuit
44 Battery temperature out of range
46* Battery voltage too high
47 Battery voltage too low
51 Oxygen sensor stuck at lean position
52 Oxygen sensor stuck at rich position
53 Logic module internal problem
55 End of message
* *Activates Power Loss/Limited light*

28 Logic module (EFI models) – removal and installation

Refer to illustrations 28.2 and 28.3

Removal

1 Disconnect the negative cable at the battery. Place the cable out of the way so it cannot accidentally come in contact with the negative terminal of the battery, as this would once again allow power into the electrical system of the vehicle.

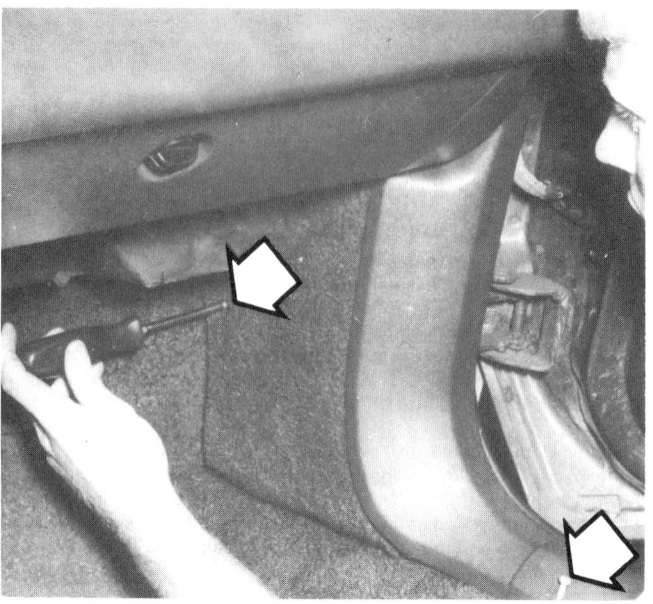
28.2 The cowl trim panel covering the logic module is held in place by two screws (arrows)

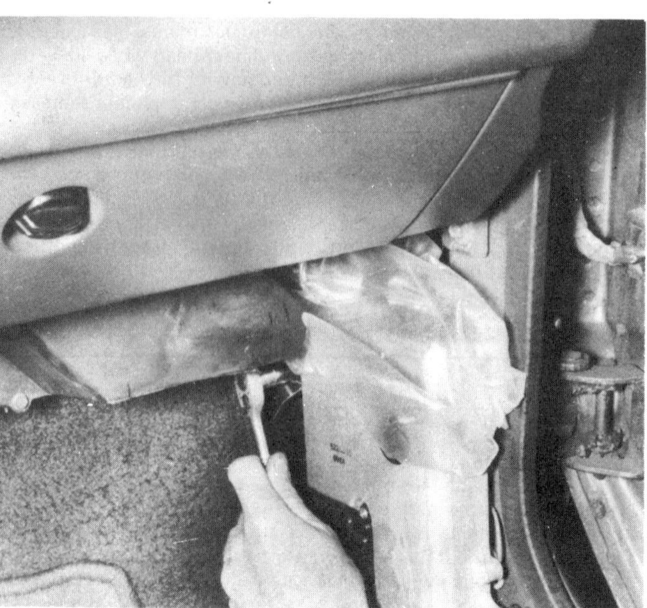
28.3 Use a ratchet and deep socket to remove the logic module mounting bolts

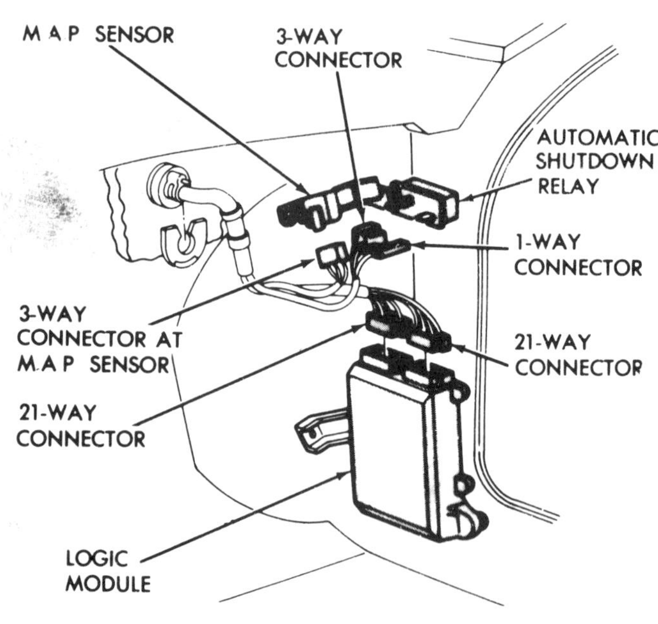

29.3 The MAP sensor and Automatic Shutdown Relay are located adjacent to the logic module on 1984 models

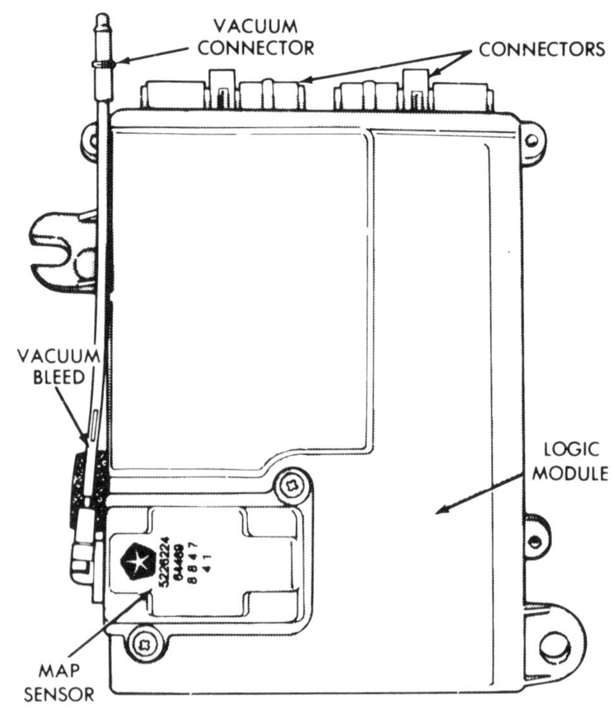

29.6 On 1985 and 1986 models the MAP sensor is located on the logic module

2 Remove the passenger's side cowl trim panel **(see illustration)**.
3 Remove the nuts, lift the logic module off the studs, unplug the connectors and remove the module from the vehicle **(see illustration)**.

Installation

4 Place the logic module in position, plug in the connectors and install the mounting nuts. Tighten the nuts securely.
5 Install the trim panel and connect the negative battery cable.

29 Manifold Absolute Pressure (MAP) sensor (EFI models) – removal and installation

Refer to illustrations 29.3 and 29.6

1 Disconnect the negative cable at the battery. Place the cable out of the way so it cannot accidentally come in contact with the negative terminal of the battery, as this would once again allow power into the electrical system of the vehicle.

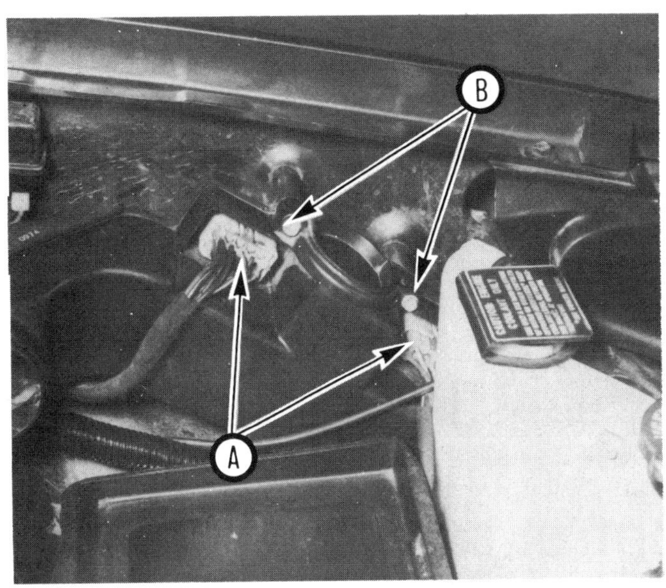

31.4 The power module can be removed after unplugging the electrical connectors (A) and removing the retaining bolts (B)

1984 models

2 Remove the glove box for access to the MAP sensor.
3 Unplug the vacuum hose and wiring connector, remove the retaining bolts and withdraw the sensor from under the instrument panel **(see illustration)**.
4 To install the sensor, place it in position and install the retaining bolts. Tighten the bolts securely and install the glove box.

1985 and later models

5 Remove the logic module (Section 28).
6 Remove the two screws and detach the MAP sensor from the logic module **(see illustration)**.
7 To install the sensor, place it in position on the logic module and install the screws. Tighten them securely.

30 Automatic shutdown relay (EFI models) – removal and installation

1 Disconnect the negative cable at the battery. Place the cable out of the way so it cannot accidentally come in contact with the negative terminal of the battery, as this would once again allow power into the electrical system of the vehicle.

1984 models

2 Remove the glove box.
3 Unplug the wiring harness connector, remove the retaining bolt and lower the relay from under the dash (see illustration 29.3).
4 Installation is the reverse of removal.

1988 models

5 The relay on these models is mounted behind the single module engine controller (SMEC – the same as the power module), next to the A/C clutch cutout relay in the engine compartment.
6 Remove the bolt and detach the relay and bracket, then unplug the wire harness.
7 Installation is the reverse of removal.

31 Power module/SMEC (EFI models) – removal and installation

Refer to illustration 31.4

Removal

1 Disconnect the battery cables (negative first, followed by the positive cable).
2 Disconnect the air cleaner duct from the module.
3 Remove the battery (Section 2).
4 Remove the retaining screws, unplug the connectors and remove the power module/SMEC from the engine compartment **(see illustration)**.

Installation

5 Place the module in position, install the retaining screws and plug in the connectors.
6 Connect the air cleaner duct.
7 Install the battery and connect the battery cables.

Chapter 6 Emissions control systems

Contents

Specifications

General (2.2/2.5L engines only)

Charcoal canister delay valve vacuum	10 in of vacuum
EGR valve test vacuum	10 in of vacuum
EGR valve travel	1/8 in (3 mm)

Torque specifications *(2.2L/2.5L engines only)*	**Ft-lbs**	**Nm**
Air injection check valve tube-to-manifold	25 to 35	34 to 47
Air injection pump pulley bolts	6	8
Air injection relief valve-to-pump bolts	8	11
Air pump bracket-to-transaxle bolts	40	54
Air pump mounting bolts	29	40
Catalytic converter clamp nut	22	30
Oxygen sensor-to-catalytic converter	20	27

1 General information

Refer to illustrations 1.6a and 1.6b

Since these vehicles are equipped with 2.2L/2.5L engines with either a carburetor or EFI and carbureted 2.6L engines, many emission control devices are used. Some of these devices or systems are exclusive to a particular engine, while others are applicable to all vehicles. All systems will be described in this Chapter so that all vehicles will be covered.

All engines are equipped with a Fuel Evaporative Emissions Control (EVAP) system, an Exhaust Gas Recirculation (EGR) system, a Positive Crankcase Ventilation (PCV) system, a heated inlet air system (except turbocharged models) and a catalytic converter. Carbureted models are equipped with automatic chokes. Some models are also equipped with an air aspirator system.

Vehicles with a 2.2L carburetor equipped engine use an air injection system and some models have an electronic feedback carburetor. The electronic feedback carburetor works in conjunction with an oxygen

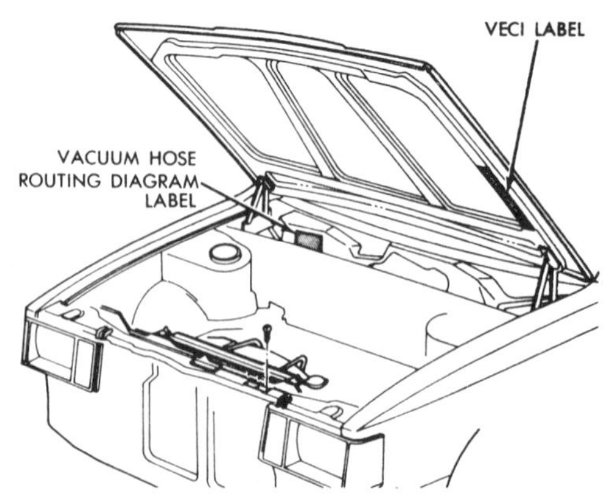

1.6a Vacuum hose routing label and Vehicle Emission Control Information (VECI) label locations

4288955
CATALYST

CHRYSLER CORPORATION | VEHICLE EMISSION CONTROL INFORMATION

THIS VEHICLE CONFORMS TO U.S. EPA REGULATIONS APPLICABLE TO 1986 MODEL YEAR NEW MOTOR VEHICLES AT ALL ALTITUDES.

2.5 LITER GCR2.5V5HCFX GCRVB	SPARK PLUGS .035 IN. GAP RN12YC

*BASIC IGNITION TIMING AND FUEL INJECTION MIXTURE HAVE BEEN PRESET AT THE FACTORY. SEE THE SERVICE MANUAL FOR PROPER PROCEDURES AND OTHER ADDITIONAL INFORMATION.

*ADJUSTMENTS MADE BY OTHER THAN APPROVED SERVICE MANUAL PROCEDURES MAY VIOLATE FEDERAL AND STATE LAWS.

IDLE SETTINGS *	MAN.	AUTO
TIMING BTC	12 *	12 *
IDLE RPM	900	700

1.6b Typical Vehicle Emission Control Information label

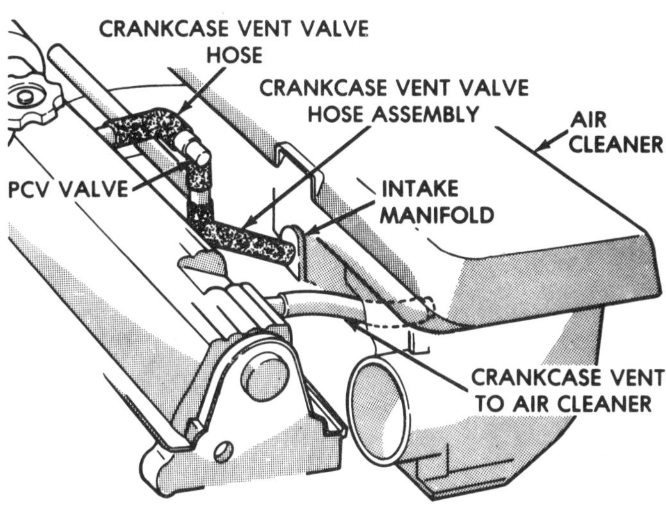

2.2 Typical PCV system component locations

sensor located in the exhaust system and a spark control computer. The three work together to constantly monitor exhaust gas oxygen content and vary the spark timing and fuel mixture so that emissions are always within prescribed limits.

The 2.6L engine features a Pulse Air Feeder (PAF) air injection system which injects air into the exhaust system between the front and rear catalytic converters to reduce emissions. Also, a Jet valve system is used to inject a very lean fuel mixture into the combustion chamber and improve efficiency and thus emissions.

The operation of the Electronic Fuel Injection (EFI) system used on fuel injected models places the control of virtually every component having to do with the engine and to some degree the electrical system under the logic module and the power module or SMEC microprocessors (Chapter 5). This system works in conjunction with an oxygen sensor located in the exhaust system to constantly monitor exhaust gas oxygen content and vary the spark timing and fuel mixture so that emissions are always within limits.

Vehicle Emission Control Information (VECI) and vacuum hose routing labels with information on your particular vehicle are located under the hood **(see illustrations)**.

Before assuming that an emission control system is malfunctioning, check the fuel and ignition systems carefully. In some cases, special tools and equipment, as well as specialized training, are required to accurately diagnose the causes of a rough running or difficult to start engine. If checking and servicing become too difficult, or if a procedure is beyond the scope of the home mechanic, consult your Chrysler dealer service department or a reputable repair shop. This does not necessarily mean, however, that the emission control systems are all particularly difficult to maintain and repair. You can quickly and easily perform many checks and do most (if not all) of the regular maintenance at home with common tune-up and hand tools. **Note:** *The most frequent cause of emission system problems is simply a loose or broken vacuum hose or wiring connection. Therefore, always check hose and wiring connections first.*

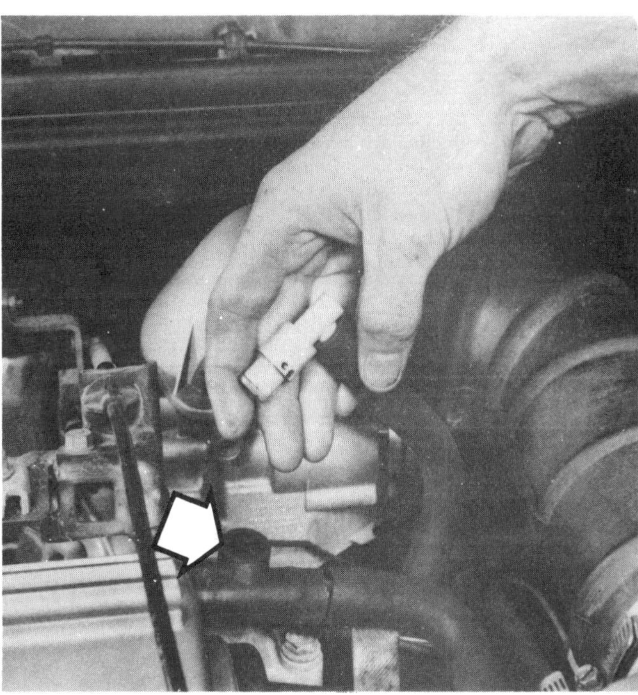

2.3 Checking the PCV valve (make sure the hose or grommet [arrow] which seals around the PCV valve is in good condition to prevent air leaks which would affect engine performance)

6

2 Positive Crankcase Ventilation (PCV) system

Refer to illustrations 2.2 and 2.3

General description

1 This system is designed to reduce hydrocarbon emissions (HC) by routing blow-by gases (fuel/air mixture that escapes from the combustion chamber past the piston rings into the crankcase) from the crankcase to the intake manifold and combustion chambers, where they are burned during engine operation.

2 The system is very simple and consists of rubber hoses and a small, replaceable metering valve (PCV valve) **(see illustration)**.

Checking and component replacement

3 With the engine running at idle, pull the PCV valve out of the mount or hose and place your finger over the valve inlet **(see illustration)**. A strong vacuum will be felt and a hissing noise will be heard if the valve

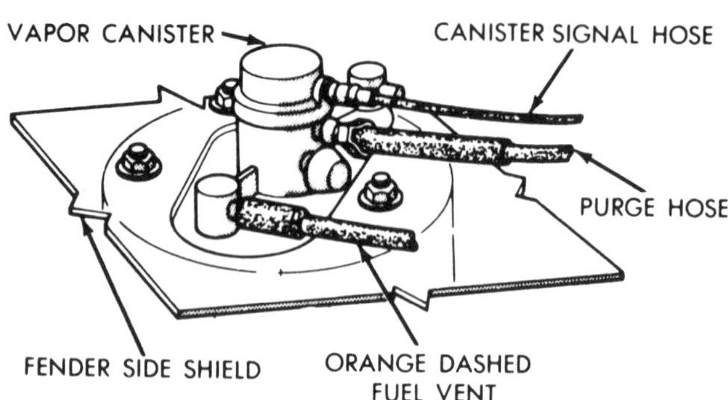

3.7 Check the EVAP canister hoses to make sure they are undamaged and properly installed

is operating properly. Replace the valve with a new one if it is not functioning as described. Do not attempt to clean the old valve.
4 To replace the PCV valve, simply pull it from the hose or vent module and install a new one.
5 Inspect the hose prior to installation to ensure that it isn't plugged or damaged. Compare the new valve with the old one to make sure they are the same. Chapter 1 contains additional PCV valve information.

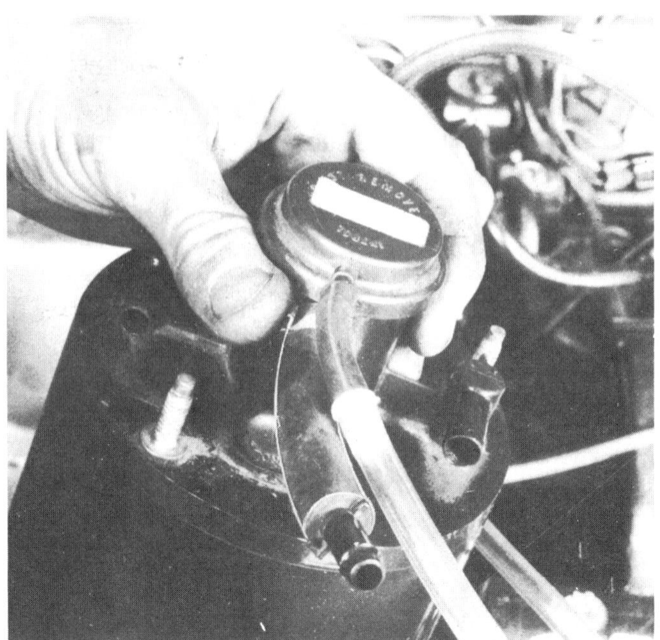

3.9 Apply vacuum with a hand pump to check the canister delay valve

3 Fuel Evaporative Emission Control (EVAP) system

Refer to illustrations 3.7, 3.9, 3.13 and 3.14

General description

1 This system is designed to trap and store fuel that evaporates from the fuel system that would normally enter the atmosphere in the form of hydrocarbon (HC) emissions.
2 The system is very simple and consists of a charcoal-filled canister, a damping canister, a purge solenoid (some models), a combination rollover/separator valve and connecting lines and hoses. Later models may also have a valve in the fuel tank vent line which retains vapor until it can be drawn into the canister when the engine is running.
3 When the engine is off and pressure begins to build up in the fuel tank (caused by fuel evaporation), the charcoal in the canister absorbs the fuel vapor. When the engine is started (cold), the charcoal continues to absorb and store fuel vapor. As the engine warms up, the stored fuel vapors are routed to the intake manifold or air cleaner and ombustion chambers where they are burned during normal engine operation.
4 The canister is purged using air from the air injection pump delay or purge valve (carbureted models) or engine vacuum by the purge solenoid which is controlled by the logic module (EFI models). On EFI models, when the engine coolant temperature is below 70°F (21°C) the logic module energizes the solenoid by grounding it so that vacuum will not flow through it to the vacuum canister. Once the coolant temperature rises above 70°F the solenoid is de-energized and vacuum then acts on the canister.
5 On 2.6L engines a damping canister serves as a purge control device. The fuel vapors released from the main canister pass through the damping canister and are momentarily held before passing to the intake manifold. When the engine is shut off, a bowl vent valve opens so that the carburetor is vented directly to the main canister.
6 The relief valve, which is mounted in the fuel tank filler cap, is calibrated to open when the fuel tank vacuum or pressure reaches a certain level. This vents the fuel tank and relieves the high vacuum or pressure.

Checking

Canister, lines, hoses, fuel filler cap and relief valve

7 Check the canister, hoses and lines for cracks and other damage **(see illustration)**.
8 To check the filler cap, look for a damaged or deformed gasket as described in Chapter 1.

Canister delay valve (carburetor equipped models)

9 A symptom of a failed delay valve is difficulty in starting the engine when it is hot. Disconnect the top vacuum hose **(see illustration)** and connect a vacuum pump to it. If the valve cannot hold the specified vacuum, replace the canister with a new one.

Component replacement

Canister

10 The canister is located in the right front corner of the engine compartment, behind the headlight.
11 To replace the canister, disconnect the vacuum hoses, remove the mounting nuts and lower the canister, removing it from beneath the vehicle.
12 Installation is the reverse of removal.

Canister purge/EGR solenoid (EFI models)

13 The canister purge solenoid is located under a cover in the engine compartment on the right inner fender panel. On models equipped with an EGR solenoid, this solenoid is mounted together with the canister purge solenoid **(see illustration)**.
14 To gain access to the solenoid(s), remove the cover. On early models this is accomplished by grasping it securely and pulling it off **(see illustration)**. On later models the cover is retained by a nut.
15 Disconnect the vacuum hose(s), unplug the electrical connector(s), remove the retaining bolt and detach the solenoid(s) and bracket assembly from the fender panel.
16 Installation is the reverse of removal.

4 Catalytic converter

General description

1 The catalytic converter is designed to reduce hydrocarbon (HC) and carbon monoxide (CO) pollutants in the exhaust gases. The converter oxidizes these components and converts them to water and carbon dioxide.
2 If large amounts of unburned gasoline enter the catalyst, it may overheat and cause a fire. Always observe the following precautions:

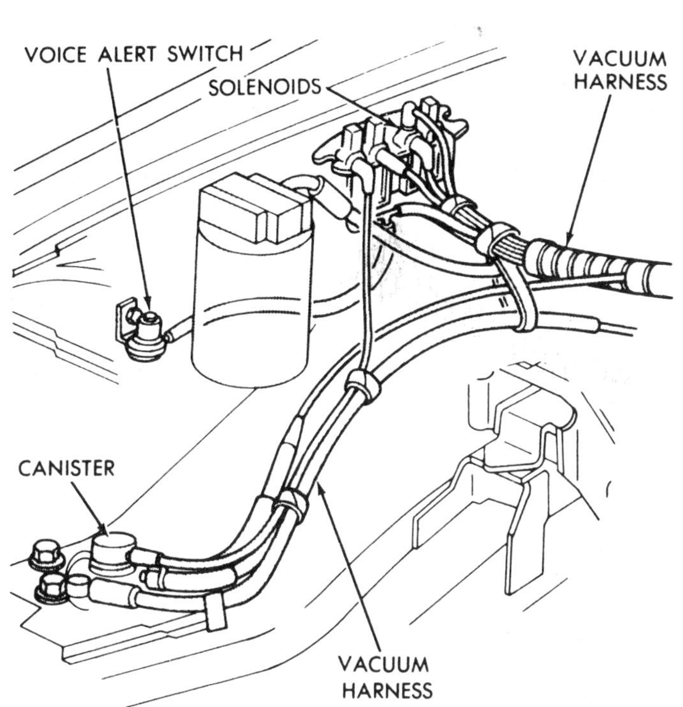

3.13 On some EFI models the canister purge and EGR solenoid are located on the same bracket

3.14 On early EFI models, pull straight out to release the solenoid cover

Use only unleaded gasoline
Avoid prolonged idling
Do not run the engine with a nearly empty fuel tank
Do not prolong engine compression checks
Avoid coasting with the ignition turned off
Do not dispose of a used catalytic converter along with oily or gasoline soaked parts

Checking

3 The catalytic converter requires little if any maintenance and servicing at regular intervals. However, the system should be inspected whenever the vehicle is raised on a lift or if the exhaust system is checked or serviced.
4 Check all connections in the exhaust pipe assembly for looseness and damage. Also check all the clamps for damage, cracks and missing fasteners. Check the rubber hangers for cracks.
5 The converter itself should be checked for damage and dents (maximum 3/4-inch deep) which could affect its performance and/or be hazardous to your health. At the same time the converter is inspected, check the heat shields under it, as well as the heat insulator above it, for damage and loose fasteners.

Component replacement

6 Do not attempt to remove the catalytic converter until the complete exhaust system is cool. Raise the vehicle and support it securely on jackstands. Apply some penetrating oil to the clamp bolts and allow it to soak in. Disconnect the oxygen sensor (if equipped) from the converter.
7 Remove the bolts and the rubber hangers, then separate the converter from the exhaust pipe. Remove the old gaskets if they are stuck to the pipes.
8 Installation of the converter is the reverse of removal. Use new exhaust pipe gaskets and tighten the clamp nuts to the specified torque. Connect the oxygen sensor wire (if equipped), start the engine and check carefully for exhaust leaks.

5 Exhaust Gas Recirculation (EGR) system

Refer to illustrations 5.6a, 5.6b, 5.6c, 5.6d, 5.13, 5.27 and 5.40

General description

1 This system recirculates a portion of the exhaust gases into the intake manifold or carburetor in order to reduce the combustion temperatures and decrease the amount of nitrogen oxide (NOx) produced.
2 The main component in the system is the EGR valve. On carburetor equipped models, it operates in conjunction with the Coolant Vacuum Switch Cold Closed (CVSCC) valve on 2.2L engines and the thermo valves on 2.6L engines. On EFI models it works with the backpressure transducer and (on some models) the EGR solenoid.
3 On 2.2L carburetor equipped engines the coolant valve and the EGR valves remain shut at low engine temperatures. At higher engine temperatures the coolant valve opens, allowing vacuum to be applied to the EGR valve so the exhaust gas can recirculate.
4 On 2.6L engines, the flow of recirculated exhaust gas is controlled by sub and dual EGR valves and temperature sensitive thermo valves. The sub EGR valve is operated directly by the throttle linkage, while the dual EGR valve is controlled by carburetor vacuum. The primary valve of the dual EGR valve operates during small openings of the throttle and the secondary valve takes over when the opening is larger. The vacuum which operates the dual EGR valve is supplied by a coolant temperature actuated thermo valve so that EGR function doesn't affect driveability.
5 On EFI models the EGR valve is a backpressure type. The amount of exhaust gas admitted is regulated by engine vacuum and the backpressure transducer in the signal line. This transducer uses exhaust system backpressure to control the EGR valve vacuum, bleeding the vacuum off to the atmosphere whenever the backpressure at the valve itself drops below the calibrated level. The EGR valve and transducer are controlled by the EGR solenoid (operated by the logic module) which controls the vacuum flow to the EGR valve body in accordance with engine temperature and driving conditions. Symptoms of problems associated with the EGR system on EFI models are rough idling or stalling when at idle, rough engine performance during light throttle application and stalling during deceleration.

6

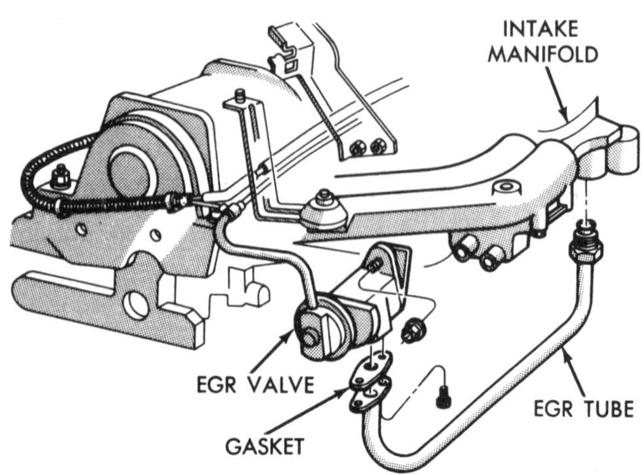

5.6a Typical 2.2L carburetor equipped engine EGR system components — exploded view.

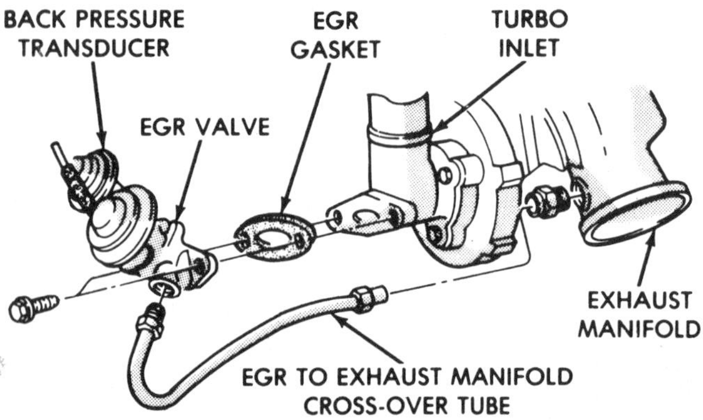

5.6c Turbocharged engine EGR system components

Checking

6 Check all hoses for cracks, kinks, broken sections and proper connection **(see illustrations)**. Inspect all system connections for damage, cracks and leaks.

2.2L carburetor equipped engine

7 To check the EGR valve operation, bring the engine up to operating temperature and, with the transmission in Neutral (tires blocked to prevent movement), allow it to idle for 70 seconds. Open the throttle abruptly so that the engine speed is between 2000 and 3000 rpm and then allow it to close. The EGR valve stem should move if the control system is working properly. The test should be repeated several times. Movement of the stem indicates that the control system is functioning correctly.

8 If the EGR valve stem does not move, check all of the hose connections to make sure they are not leaking or clogged. Disconnect the vacuum hose and apply the specified vacuum with a hand pump. If the stem still does not move, replace the EGR valve with a new one. If the valve does open, measure the valve travel to make sure it is within the specified limit.

9 Apply vacuum with the pump and then clamp the hose shut. The valve should stay open for 30 seconds or longer. If it does not, the diaphragm is leaking and the valve should be replaced with a new one.

10 To check the coolant valve (CVSCC) located in the thermostat housing, bypass it with a length of 3/16-inch hose. If the EGR valve did not operate under the conditions described in Step 7, but does operate properly with the CVSCC bypassed, the CVSCC is defective and should be replaced.

11 If the EGR valve does not operate with the CVSCC bypassed, the carburetor must be removed to check and clean the slotted port in the throttle bore and the vacuum passages and orifices in the throttle body.

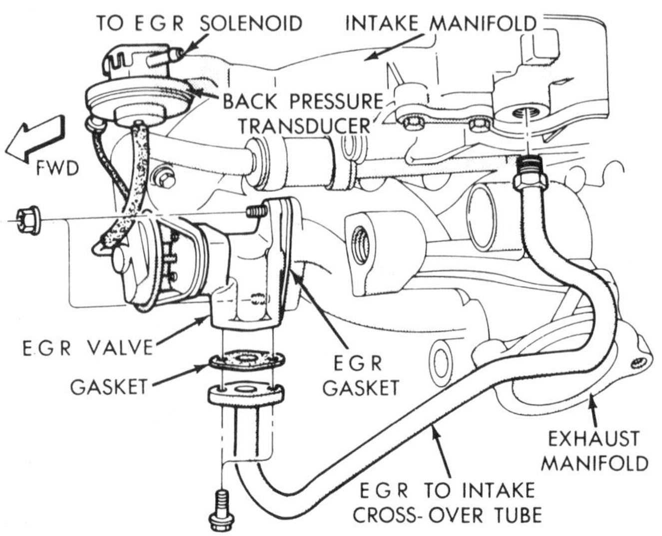

5.6b Non-turbocharged EFI engine EGR system components

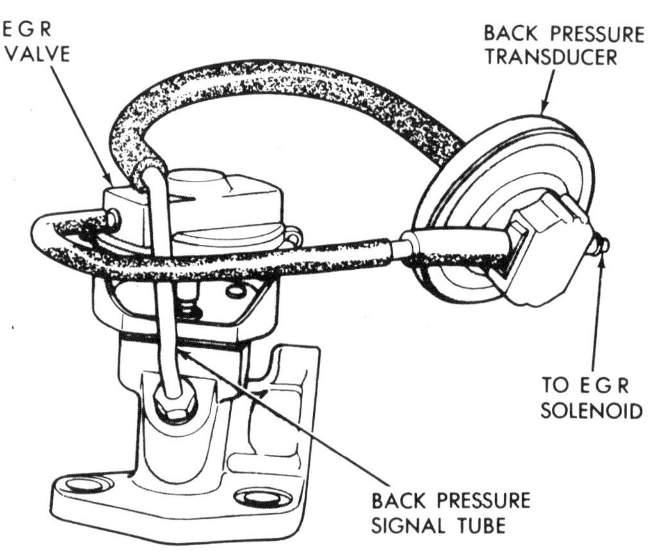

5.6d EFI engine EGR valve and backpressure transducer component layout

Use solvent to remove deposits and check for flow with light air pressure.

12 Remove the EGR valve and inspect the poppet and seat area for deposits. If the deposits are more than a thin film of carbon, the valve should be cleaned. To clean the valve, apply solvent and allow it to penetrate and soften the deposits, making sure that none gets on the valve diaphragm, as it could be damaged. Use a vacuum pump to hold the valve open and carefully scrape the deposits from the seat and poppet area with a tool. Inspect the poppet and stem for wear and replace the valve with a new one if wear is found.

2.6L engine

13 Check all hoses and connections for cracks, kinks, damage and correct installation **(see illustration)**.

14 With the engine cold, start and run it at idle. Block the tires to prevent any movement of the vehicle during testing.

15 Increase the speed to 2500 rpm and check the secondary EGR valve to make sure that it does not operate when the engine is cold. If it does, the thermo valve is faulty and must be replaced with a new one.

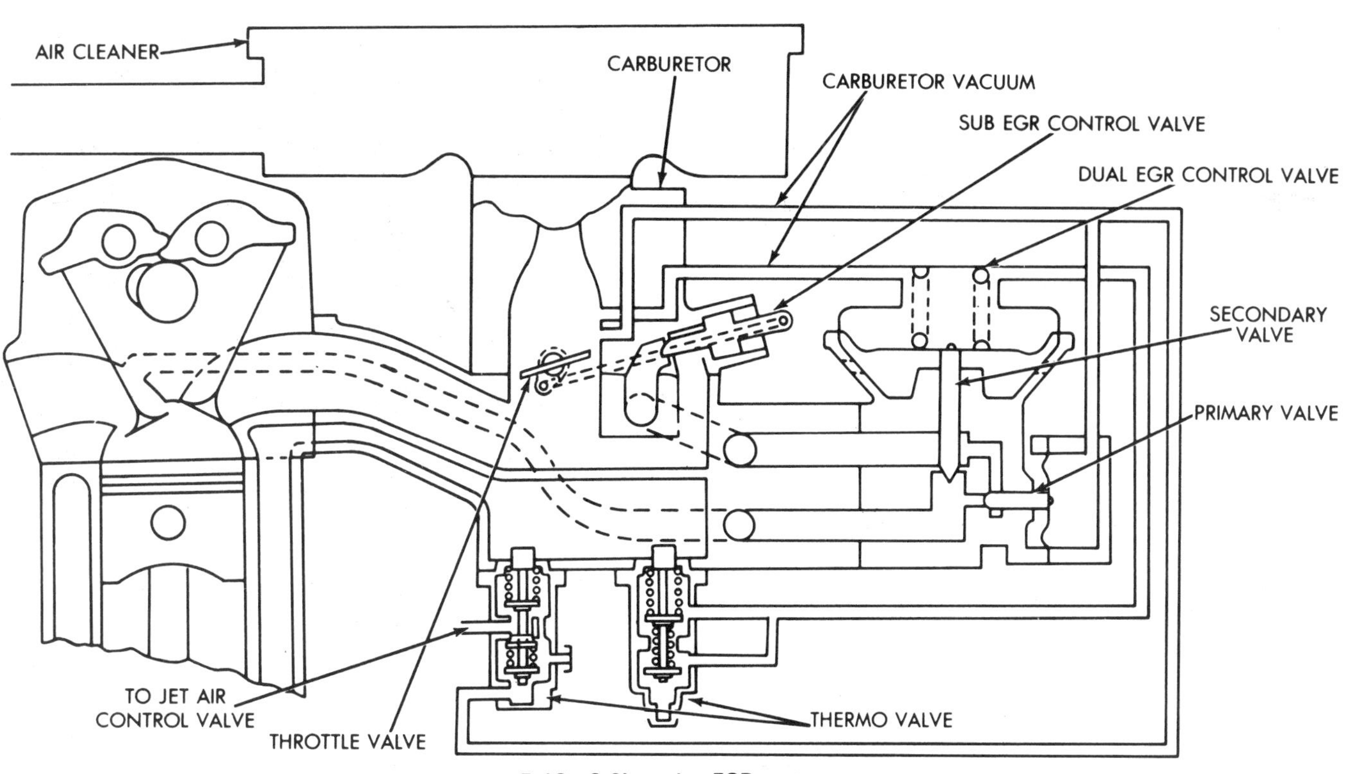

5.13 2.6L engine EGR system

16 Allow the engine to warm up and watch the secondary EGR valve to see that it opens as the temperature rises and the idle speed increases. If it does not open, the secondary EGR valve itself or the thermo valve is faulty.

17 To check the secondary EGR valve and the thermo valve, disconnect the green striped vacuum hose from the carburetor and connect a vacuum pump to the hose. Apply six inches of vacuum with the pump as you open the sub EGR valve.

18 If the engine idle becomes unstable, the secondary valve of the dual EGR is operating properly. If the idle speed is unchanged, the secondary valve or the thermo valve is faulty and must be replaced with a new one.

19 Reconnect the green striped hose and disconnect the yellow striped hose at the carburetor.

20 Connect the hand vacuum pump to the hose and, while opening the sub EGR valve, apply six inches of vacuum.

21 If the idle becomes unstable, the primary EGR valve is operating properly. If the idle is unchanged, the primary EGR valve or the thermo valve is not operating and should be replaced with a new one.

EFI equipped engine (non-turbocharged)

22 To check the EGR valve operation, bring the engine up to operating temperature with the transaxle in Neutral (tires blocked to prevent movement).

23 Disconnect the hose from the transducer and connect a vacuum pump. Start the engine, raise the engine speed to approximately 2000 rpm, hold it there and apply ten inches of vacuum with the pump. The EGR valve stem should move and stay open for at least 30 seconds if the control system is working properly.

24 Measure the valve travel to make sure it is within the specified limit. If the stem moves but will not stay open, the EGR valve/backpressure transducer assembly is faulty and must be replaced with a new one.

25 If the EGR valve stem does not move except when vacuum from the pump is applied, remove the EFI throttle body (Chapter 4) and clean the EGR ports in the throttle bore and body with solvent.

26 If the engine exhibits rough idle, dies when returned to idle or the idle is both rough and slow, the EGR valve is leaking in the closed position. Inspect the EGR tube for leaks at the connection to the manifold. Loosen the tube connection and then tighten it securely. Remove the EGR valve and transducer assembly and inspect the poppet to make sure it is seated. If it is not, replace the EGR valve transducer assembly with a new one; do not attempt to clean the EGR valve.

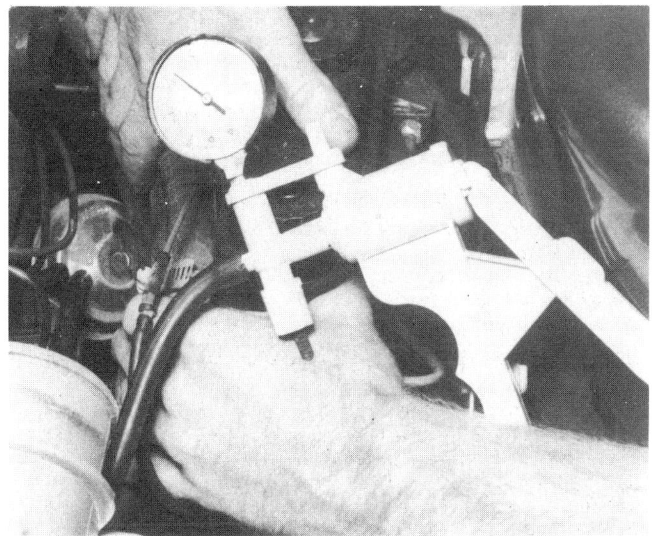

5.27 Check the EGR valve by applying vacuum with a pump (air cleaner partially removed for clarity)

EFI equipped engine (turbocharged)

27 With the engine cold, disconnect the vacuum hose from the EGR valve and connect a vacuum pump, apply vacuum and make sure the valve holds vacuum **(see illustration)**. If the valve does not hold vacuum, replace it with a new one.

28 Disconnect the vacuum pump and connect a vacuum gauge to the EGR valve. Start the engine and verify that the gauge reading is zero, indicating that the EGR valve and transducer are holding vacuum.

29 With the engine still cold, increase the engine speed to approximately 2000 rpm and hold it there. If the gauge shows an unsteady vacuum reading above zero, the EGR solenoid is faulty and should be replaced with a new one.

30 Disconnect the vacuum hose between the EGR backpressure solenoid and the EGR solenoid. Connect the vacuum gauge, start the engine and make sure the reading is at least five inches of vacuum, indicating that the system is working properly and holding vacuum.

6

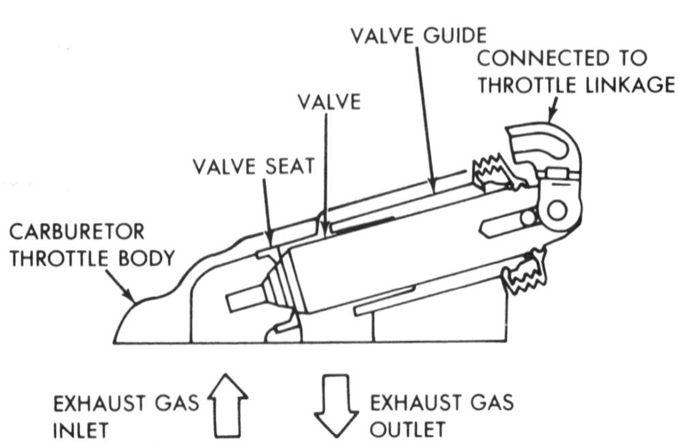

5.40 2.6L engine sub EGR valve layout

31 Warm the engine up to normal operating temperature (the EGR solenoid will now be open), increase the engine speed to approximately 2000 rpm and make sure that the vacuum reading is still at least five inches of vacuum. If the reading is less, there is a vacuum leak between the EGR solenoid and the EFI throttle body.
32 Remove the vacuum gauge and reconnect the vacuum line.
33 Disconnect the EGR valve-to-backpressure transducer vacuum hose and connect the vacuum gauge to the hose. The gauge should still read approximately five inches of vacuum with the engine off. If it does not, replace the EGR valve and backpressure transducer assembly with a new one.
34 Start the engine and raise the engine speed to approximately 2000 rpm. Connect a vacuum pump to the EGR valve vacuum motor and slowly apply vacuum. If the system is operating properly, the engine speed will begin to drop when 2 to 3.5-inches of vacuum is applied.
35 Release the vacuum and allow the engine to slow to idle speed. Apply vacuum with the pump to make sure the engine speed again drops when 2 to 3.5-inches of vacuum is applied. If the speed does not drop, check the EGR supply tube and passages to make sure they are not blocked, clearing them if necessary. If they are open, then the EGR valve/backpressure transducer and tube are faulty and must be replaced with new units.
36 Apply ten inches of vacuum to the EGR valve vacuum motor. The system should hold the vacuum for at least ten seconds if it is operating properly. If it does not hold vacuum, the EGR valve/backpressure transducer assembly is faulty and must be replaced with a new unit.

Component replacement

2.2L carburetor equipped engine

37 The CVSCC can be replaced by removing the vacuum hoses and unscrewing the valve.
38 To replace the EGR valve, remove the air cleaner, air injection pump and shield. Disconnect the metal tube and vacuum hose, remove the two retaining nuts and detach the valve.

2.6L engine

39 The dual EGR valve is located on the lower part of the intake manifold. It is replaced by removing the vacuum hoses and unbolting it. It may be necessary to tap the valve gently with a soft-face hammer to break the gasket seal so it can be removed. Use a new gasket when installing the valve and check the vacuum hoses for proper routing.
40 The sub EGR valve is located on the base of the carburetor and is connected by a linkage. Pry off the spring clip and remove the pin attaching the plunger to the linkage. Hold the end of the linkage up and remove the spring and the steel ball from the end of the plunger **(see illustration)**.
41 Slip the rubber boot off and slide the plunger out of the carburetor throttle body. Before installing the plunger, lubricate it with a small amount of light oil. Install the steel ball and spring, hold the linkage in place and insert the pin. Carefully slide the spring clip into place, then check for smooth operation of the valve plunger.
42 The thermal valves are threaded into the intake manifold. Drain some coolant (Chapter 1), then pull off the vacuum hose and unscrew the valve from the housing.

6.2 The oxygen sensor (arrow) is screwed into the exhaust manifold; on some models it is accessible only from below

EFI equipped engine

43 To remove the EGR valve/backpressure transducer, disconnect the vacuum hose from the backpressure transducer assembly, then pull the assembly from the mounting clip.
44 Remove the bolts or unscrew the tube nut and disconnect the cross-over tube from the EGR valve.
45 Remove the EGR valve retaining bolts and detach the EGR valve/ backpressure transducer assembly from the engine.
46 The EGR solenoid is located under a cover at the right front corner of the engine compartment, adjacent to the EVAP purge solenoid. The cover is held in place by clips on 1984 models and by the solenoid bracket retaining nut on later models.
47 Refer to Section 3 for the solenoid replacement procedure.

6 Oxygen sensor replacement

Refer to illustration 6.2

1 The oxygen sensor must be replaced at the specified interval (Chapter 1). The sensor is threaded into the exhaust manifold. On some models it may be necessary to raise the front of the vehicle and support it securely on jackstands for access to the underside of the engine compartment.
2 Disconnect the oxygen sensor wire by unplugging the connector **(see illustration)**.
3 Use a wrench to unscrew the sensor.
4 Use a tap to clean the threads in the exhaust manifold.
5 If a new sensor is to be installed, apply anti-seize compound to the threads. New sensors will already have the anti-seize compound on their threads.
6 Install the sensor, tighten it to the specified torque and plug in the connector.

7 Heated inlet air system

Refer to illustrations 7.1a, 7.1b, 7.11 and 7.19

General description

1 This system, used on carburetor equipped and non-turbocharged EFI engines, is designed to improve driveability, reduce emissions and prevent carburetor icing in cold weather by directing hot air from around the exhaust manifold to the air cleaner intake (see illustrations).
2 On 2.2L/2.5L engines the system is made up of two circuits. When

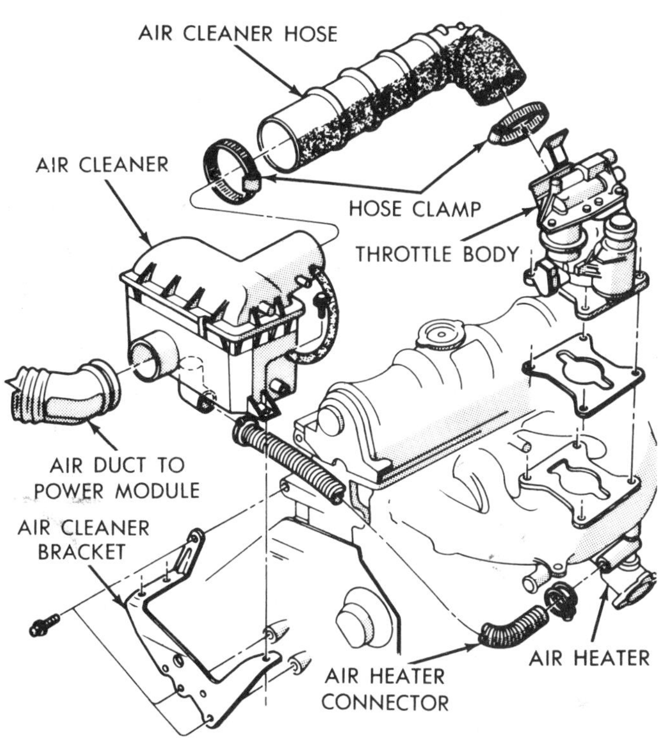

7.1a Heated inlet air system components (2.2L/2.5L EFI engine shown) — exploded view

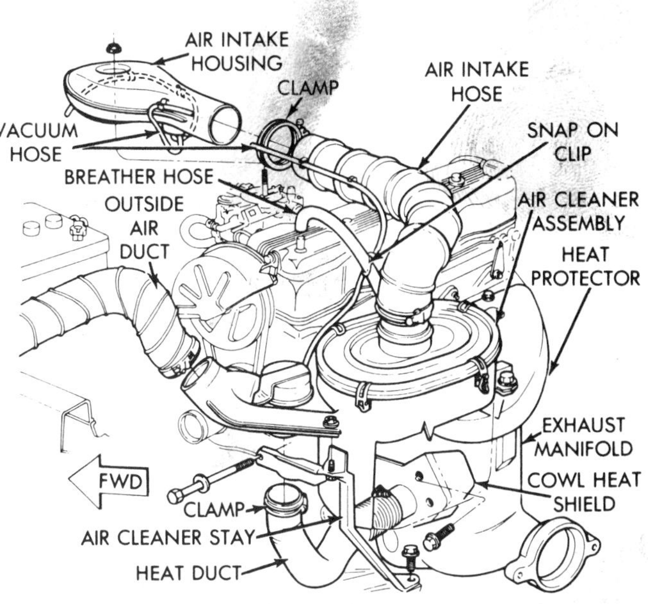

7.1b 2.6L engine heated inlet air system components — exploded view

the outside air temperature is below 65°F (19°C) on carburetor equipped engines or 115°F (46°C) on EFI engines, the intake air flows through the flexible connector, up through the air cleaner and into the carburetor or throttle body.
3 When the air temperature is above 90°F (32°C) on carburetor equipped engines or 115°F (46°F) on EFI engines, air enters the air cleaner through the outside air duct.
4 On 2.6L engines, the door in the air cleaner assembly is controlled by a vacuum motor which is acutated by a bi-metal temperature sensor. The sensor reacts to both intake manifold vacuum and the air temperature inside the air cleaner itself.
5 When the air temperature inside the air horn is 85°F (30°C) or below, the air bleed valve in the sensor remains closed and intake manifold vacuum opens the air control door to direct heated air to the carburetor.
6 When the air temperature inside the air cleaner is 113°F (45°C) or above, the sensor air bleed valve opens the air control door, allowing outside air directly into the carburetor. At temperatures between the two extremes, the sensor provides a blend of outside and heated air to the carburetor.

Checking

General

7 Refer to Chapter 1 for the general checking procedure. If the system is not operating properly, check the individual components as follows.
8 Check all vacuum hoses for cracks, kinks, proper routing and broken sections. Make sure the shrouds and ducts are in good condition as well.

2.2L/2.5L engine

9 Remove the air cleaner assembly from the engine and allow it to cool to 65°F (19°C) (carburetor equipped engine) or 115°F (46°C) (EFI engine). Apply 20-inches of vacuum to the sensor with a hand vacuum pump.
10 The door should be in the up (heat on) position with the vacuum applied. If it is not, check the vacuum diaphragm.
11 To check the diaphragm, slowly apply vacuum with the hand pump while watching the door **(see illustration)**.
12 The door should not begin to open at less than two inches and should be fully open at four inches or less. With 20-inches applied, the diaphragm should not bleed down more than ten inches in five minutes.

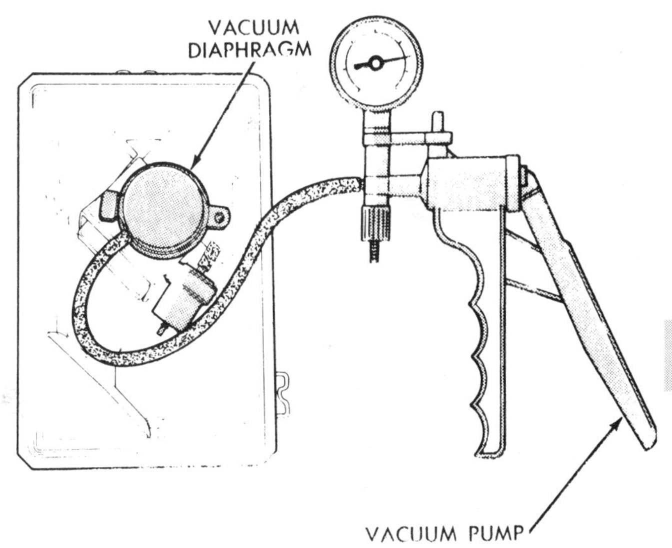

7.11 Checking the inlet air vacuum diaphragm

13 Replace the sensor and/or vacuum diaphragm with new units if they fail any of the tests. Test the new unit(s) as described before reinstalling the air cleaner assembly.

2.6L engine

14 With the engine cold and the air temperature less than 85°F (30°C), see if the air control door is in the up (heat on) position.
15 Warm up the engine to operating temperature. With the air temperature at the entrance to the snorkel at 113°F (45°C), the door should be in the down (heat off) position.
16 Remove the air cleaner assembly from the engine and allow it to cool to 85°F (30°C). Connect a hand vacuum pump to the sensor.
17 Apply 15-inches of vacuum to the sensor and see if the door is now in the up (heat on) position. If it is not, check the vacuum motor.
18 Apply ten inches of vacuum to the motor with the vacuum pump and see if the valve is in the up position. If it is not, replace the motor with a new one. On these vehicles the vacuum motor is an integral part of the air cleaner body and the entire assembly must be replaced.

6

Component replacement

Vacuum diaphragm

19 With the air cleaner removed, disconnect the vacuum hose and drill out the rivet **(see illustration)**.

20 Disengage the diaphragm by tipping it forward slightly while turning it counterclockwise. Once disengaged, the unit can be removed by moving it to one side, disconnecting the rod from the control door and detaching it from the air cleaner assembly.

21 Check the control door for free travel by raising it to the full up position and allowing it to fall closed. If it does not close easily, free it up. Check the hinge pin for free movement also, using compressed air or spray cleaner to remove any foreign matter.

22 To install the diaphragm, insert the rod end into the control door and position the diaphragm tang in the slot, turning the diaphragm clockwise until it engages. Rivet the tab in place.

23 Connect the vacuum hose.

Sensor

24 Disconnect the vacuum hoses and use a screwdriver to pry the retaining clips off. Detach the sensor from the housing.

25 To install the sensor, place the gasket on it and insert it into the housing.

26 Hold the sensor in place so that the gasket is compressed to form a good seal and install the new retaining clips.

27 Connect the vacuum hoses.

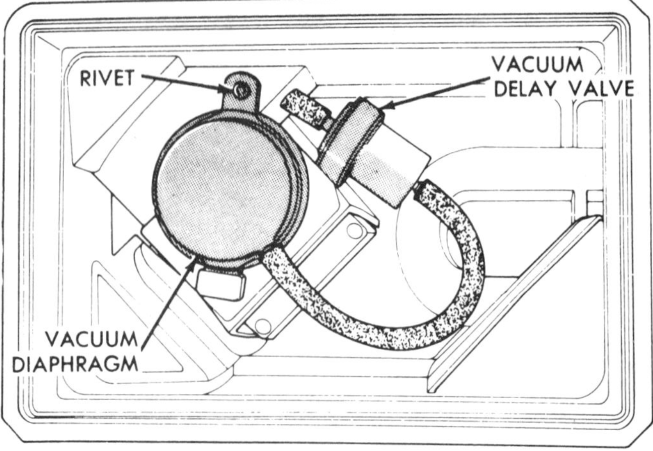

7.19 Remove the rivet to replace the vacuum diaphragm (2.2L engine)

8 Jet air system (2.6L engine)

The jet air system utilizes additional intake valves (jet valves) which provide for air, or a super lean mixture, to be drawn from the air intake into the cylinders. The jet valves are operated by the same cams as the intake valves. They use a common rocker arm so the jet valves and the intake valves open and close simultaneously.

On the intake stroke of the engine, fuel/air mixture flows through the intake ports into the combustion chambers. At the same time, jet air is forced into each combustion chamber because of the pressure difference between the jet intake in the throttle bore and the jet valve in each cylinder as the piston moves down. At small throttle openings, there is a large pressure difference, giving the jet air a high velocity. This scavenges the residual gases around the spark plug and creates good ignition conditions. It also produces a strong swirl in the combustion chamber, which lasts throughout the compression stroke and improves flame propagation after ignition, assuring high combustion efficiency and lowering exhaust emissions. As the throttle opening is increased, less jet air is forced in and jet swirl diminishes, but the increased flow through the intake valve ensures satisfactory combustion.

A thermo valve which works in conjunction with the EGR system controls the air flow to the jet valves.

Maintenance consists of adjusting the jet valve clearances at the same time the intake and exhaust valves are adjusted, as described in Chapter 1.

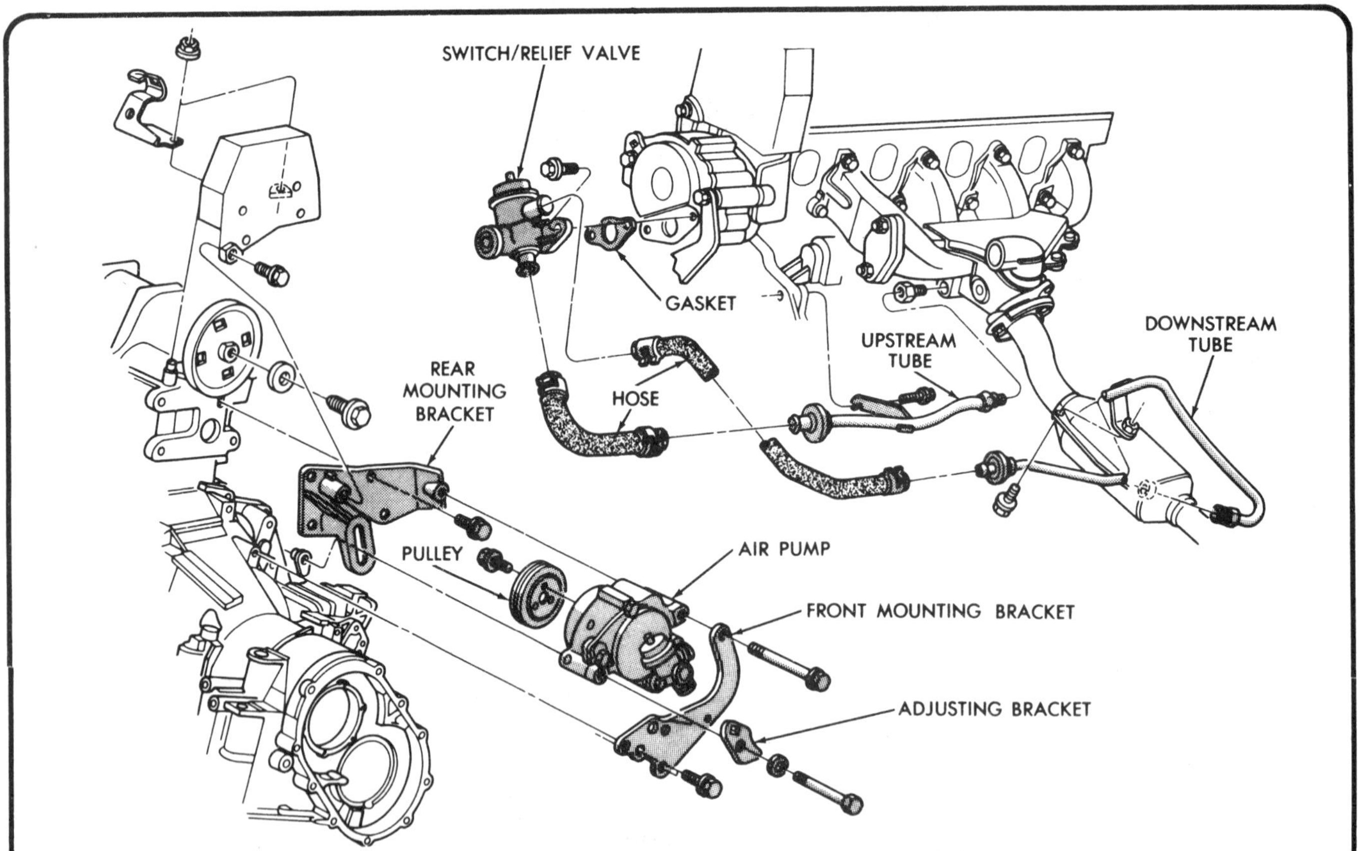

SWITCH/RELIEF VALVE
GASKET
UPSTREAM TUBE
DOWNSTREAM TUBE
REAR MOUNTING BRACKET
HOSE
PULLEY
AIR PUMP
FRONT MOUNTING BRACKET
ADJUSTING BRACKET

9.2 Typical air injection system components — exploded view (2.2L Calif. model shown)

9 Air Injection (AI) system (2.2L carburetor equipped engine)

Refer to illustrations 9.2, 9.9, 9.10 and 9.16

General description

1 This system supplies air under pressure to the exhaust ports to promote the combustion of unburned hydrocarbons and carbon monoxide before they are allowed to exit the exhaust.

2 The AI system consists of an air pump driven by a belt from the rear of the camshaft, a relief valve and associated hoses and check valves, which protect the system from hot exhaust gases **(see illustration)**.

Checking

General

3 Visually check the hoses, tubes and connections for cracks, loose fittings and separated parts. Use soapy water to isolate a suspected leak.

4 Check the drivebelt condition and tension (Chapter 1).

9.9 Removing the air pump drivebelt shield mounting bolts

9.10 Loosening the air pump pivot bolt

Air pump

5 The air pump can only be checked using special equipment. Noise from the pump can be due to improper drivebelt tension, faulty relief or check valves, loose mounting bolts and leaking hoses or connections. If these conditions have been corrected and the pump still makes excessive noise, there is a good chance that it is faulty.

Relief valve

6 If air can be heard escaping from the relief valve with the engine at idle, the valve is faulty and must be replaced with a new one.

Check valve

7 Remove the hose from the inlet tube. If exhaust gas escapes past the inlet tube, the check valve is faulty and must be replaced.

Component replacement

Air pump

Caution: *Do not rotate the camshaft with the air pump removed.*

8 Remove the air hoses from the air pump and the relief valve.

9 Remove the air pump drivebelt pulley shield (see illustration).

10 Loosen the pump pivot and adjustment bolts and remove the drivebelt **(see illustration)**.

11 Remove the bolts and detach the pump from the engine.

12 Remove the relief valve from the pump and clean all gasket material from the valve mating surface.

13 Attach the relief valve to the new air pump, using a new gasket. Transfer the pulley from the old pump to the new one.

14 With the drivebelt over the air pump pulley, place the pump in position and loosely install the bolts.

15 Loosen the rear air pump bracket-to-transaxle housing bolts.

16 Place the drivebelt on the camshaft pulley, use a breaker bar to exert pressure on the bracket (not the pump housing) and adjust the belt until the tension is correct (Chapter 1). Tighten the locking bolt, followed by the pivot bolt **(see illustration)**.

17 Tighten the air pump bracket bolt to the specified torque, install the pulley shield and reconnect the hoses to the pump and relief valve.

Relief valve

18 Disconnect the hoses from the relief valve, remove the two bolts and detach the valve from the pump. Carefully remove any gasket material from the valve and pump mating surfaces.

19 Place a new gasket in position and install the valve, tightening the bolts to the specified torque. Reconnect the hoses.

Check valve

20 Disconnect the hose from the valve inlet and remove the nut securing the tube to the exhaust manifold or converter. Loosen the starter motor bolt and remove the check valve from the engine.

21 Attach the new valve to the exhaust manifold or converter, tighten the starter motor bolt and connect the air hose.

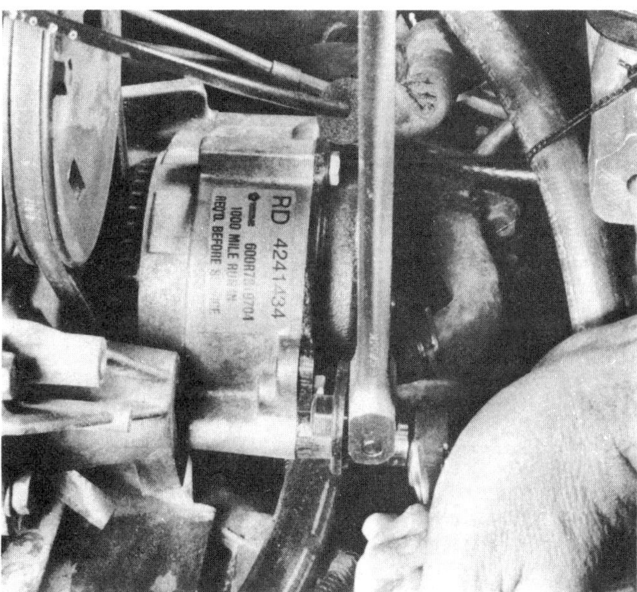

9.16 Use a breaker bar to apply leverage to the air pump bracket as the bolts are tightened

10 Pulse Air Feeder (PAF) system (2.6L engine)

Refer to illustration 10.2

General description

1 The PAF system injects air into the exhaust system between the front and rear catalytic converters, using the engine power pulsations. This injected air increases the efficiency of the rear converter and reduces emissions.

2 The pulse air feeder consists of a main reed valve, sub reed valve and associated hoses. Air is drawn from the air cleaner into the main reed valve which is acutated by the pressure pulsations from within the crankcase. The air passes to the sub reed valve, which is actuated by the exhaust system pulsations, to the exhaust system and then the rear converter **(see illustration)**.

Checking

3 Disconnect the hose from the air cleaner and, with the engine running, place your hand over the end. If no vacuum is felt, check the hoses for leaks. If the hoses are alright, replace the PAF assembly with a new one.

Component replacement

4 Remove the air deflector duct from the right side of the radiator. Remove the carburetor shield, the oil dipstick and the dipstick tube. Remove the PAF mounting bolts.

5 Raise the vehicle and support it securely.

6 Disconnect the hoses and remove the PAF assembly from the vehicle.

7 Place the new pulse air feeder assembly in position and connect the hoses.

8 Lower the vehicle and install the mounting bolts. Check the dipstick O-ring to make sure it is in good condition and install the dipstick and tube. Install the carburetor shield and radiator air deflector.

11 Electronic feedback carburetor (2.2L engine)

Refer to illustrations 11.7, 11.11, 11.14, 11.16 and 11.20

General description

1 The electronic feedback carburetor emission system relies on an electronic signal, which is generated by an exhaust gas sensor, to control a variety of devices and keep emissions within limits. The system works in conjunction with a three-way catalyst to control the levels of carbon monoxide, hydrocarbons and oxides of nitrogen.

2 The system operates in two modes: open loop and closed loop. When the engine is cold, the fuel/air mixture is controlled by the computer in accordance with a program designed in at the time of production. The fuel/air mixture during this time will be richer to allow for proper engine warm-up. When the engine is at operating temperature, the system operates at closed loop and the fuel/air mixture is varied depending on the information supplied by the exhaust gas sensor.

3 The system consists of the carburetor, computer, air switching valve, coolant control engine vacuum switch, catalytic converters and oxygen sensor.

Checking

4 Prior to checking the system, check the computer for proper operation as described in Chapter 5. Also, make sure that all vacuum hoses and electrical wires are properly routed and securely connected.

5 Apply 16-inches of vacuum to the computer with a vacuum pump. Disconnect the hose from the air switching valve and connect a vacuum gauge to the hose (see Step 6 below). Start the engine and allow it to warm up to operating temperature. Run the engine at approximately 2000 rpm for two minutes and make sure the carburetor switch is not grounded.

Air switching system

6 Right after starting the engine, there should be a vacuum reading which will slowly drop to zero as the engine warms up.

7 If there is no vacuum, check the coolant controlled engine vacuum switch (CCEVS) for continuity. If there is no continuity, correct the fault or replace the switch **(see illustration)**.

8 With the engine at operating temperature, shut it off, remove the vacuum hose from the valve and then connect a hand vacuum pump to the valve. Start the engine and make sure air blows out of the side port. Apply vacuum to the valve. Air should now blow out of the bottom port of the valve.

9 Before proceeding, check the engine temperature sensor as described in Chapter 5.

Carburetor regulator

10 Remove the computer vacuum hose and plug it. Connect a vacuum pump to the carburetor and apply 14-inches of vacuum. With the engine at 2000 rpm, disconnect the regulator solenoid connector at the solenoid. On non-air conditioned models, only the green wire should be disconnected. The engine speed should increase at least 50 rpm. Reconnect the solenoid wire(s) and make sure that the engine speed slowly returns to normal.

11 Unplug the six pin connector from the combustion control com-

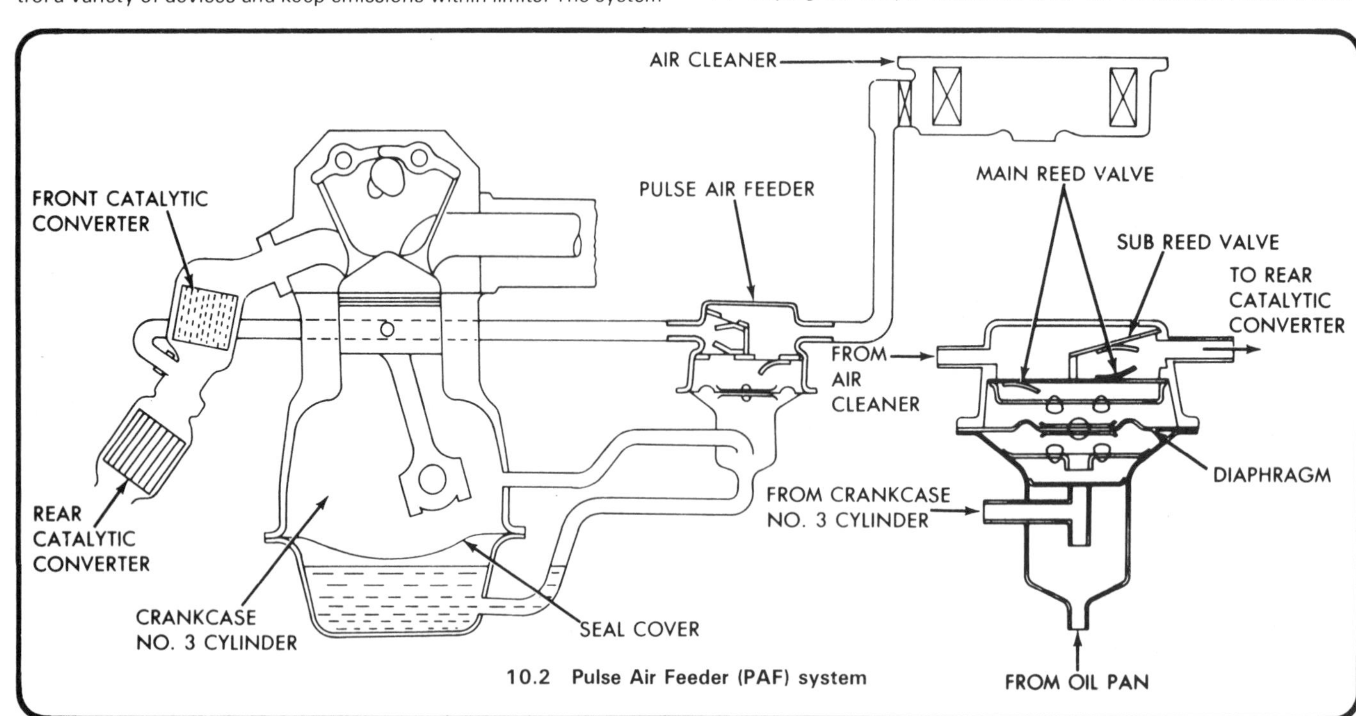

10.2 Pulse Air Feeder (PAF) system

puter and momentarily connect a ground to connector pin 15 **(see illustration)**.

12 Engine speed should decrease at least 50 rpm. If it does not, check the carburetor for air leaks.

Electronic fuel control computer

13 With the engine at normal operating temperature and the carburetor switch not grounded, connect a tachometer.

14 Start the engine and maintain an idle of 2000 rpm. Connect a voltmeter to the green solenoid output wire which leads to the carburetor. Disconnect the electrical harness at the oxygen sensor and connect a jumper wire between the harness connector and the negative battery terminal **(see illustration)**.

15 The engine speed should increase at least 50 rpm and the voltmeter should read at least ten volts. With the wire held in one hand, touch the battery positive terminal with your other hand. The engine speed should drop by at least 50 rpm and the voltmeter reading should be five volts or less. Replace the computer with a new one if it fails both tests.

Oxygen sensor

16 Connect the voltmeter to the solenoid output wire, reconnect the oxygen sensor and make sure the carburetor switch is not grounded. Start the engine, run it at 2000 rpm and hold the choke plates closed **(see illustration)**. This simulates a full rich condition and within ten seconds the voltage should drop to five volts or less. If it does not, disconnect the PCV hose. This simulates a full lean condition and the voltage should increase to ten volts or more. *Do not take more than 90 seconds to complete these tests.* If the sensor fails both tests, replace it with a new one.

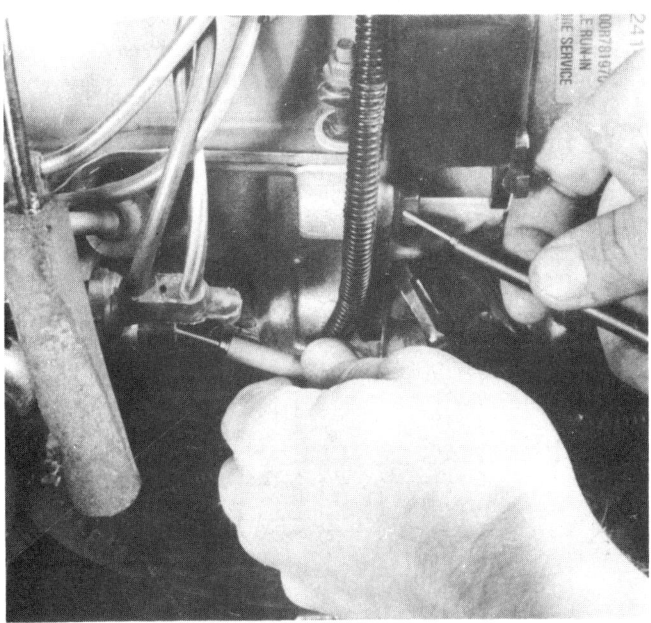

11.7 Checking the vacuum switch for continuity

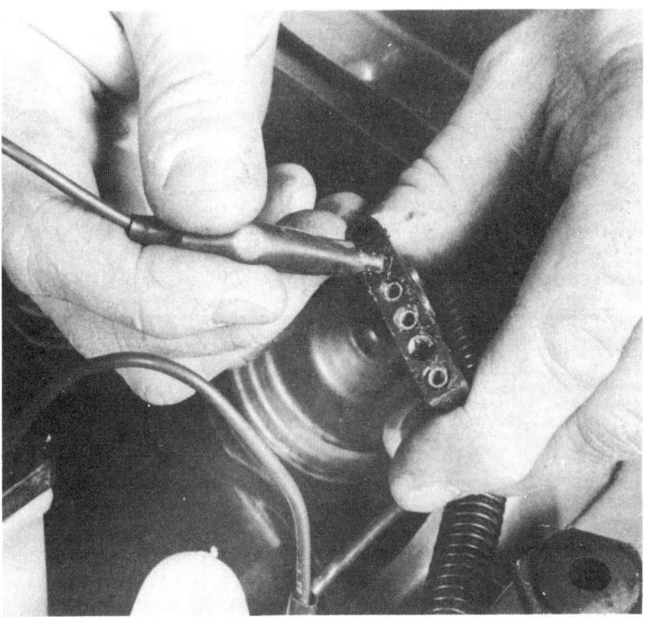

11.11 Grounding pin 15 of the six pin connector

6

11.14 Grounding the oxygen sensor wire to the negative battery post

11.16 Holding the choke closed while testing the oxygen sensor

Component replacement

17 Replacement of the ignition computer is covered in Chapter 5.
18 Mark the hose locations on the air switching valve, remove the hoses and disconnect the valve.
19 The CCEVS is replaced by removing the vacuum hoses and unscrewing the valve. Coat the threads of the new valve with gasket sealant prior to installation.
20 To replace the carburetor solenoid, unplug the electrical connector and remove the two retaining screws. Detach the solenoid from the carburetor **(see illustration)**.
21 Refer to Section 6 for oxygen sensor replacement.

12 Mikuni carburetor systems (2.6L engine)

Refer to illustrations 12.5, 12.7a, 12.7b, 12.8 and 12.9

General description

1 The Mikuni carburetor on 2.6L engines is equipped with a variety of devices which reduce emissions while maintaining driveability.
2 The system consists of a Coasting Air Valve (CAV), Air Switching Valve (ASV), Deceleration Spark Advance System (DSAS), High Altitude Compensation (HAC) (on some models), Jet Air Control Valve (JACV) and a throttle opener.
3 The CAV, ASV and DSAS reduce hydrocarbon emissions while maintaining driveability and fuel economy by shutting off fuel flow and advancing the spark during deceleration.
4 The HAC maintains the proper fuel/air mixture during high altitude driving by means of an atmospheric pressure sensitive bellows.
5 The JACV helps decrease HC and CO emissions, while the choke is operating, by opening to allow additional jet air flow and eliminating an over rich condition **(see illustration)**.
6 The throttle opener controls the engine idle speed during operation of the air conditioner.

Checking

ASV and CAV

7 With the engine at idle, unplug the solenoid valve electrical connector. If the idle speed drops or the engine stalls, the ASV and CAV are operating properly. With the engine again at idle, check the solenoid connector with a voltmeter. If no voltage is present, the wiring or speed sensor is faulty. Check the solenoid connector with the engine at 2500 rpm to make sure there is voltage. If there is no voltage, there is a fault in the speed sensor and it must be replaced with a new one **(see illustrations)**.

DSAS

8 Connect a timing light and allow the engine to run at idle. With the timing light on the timing marks, disconnect the electrical connector from the solenoid valve. If the timing does not advance, the solenoid valve and/or advance mechanism are faulty **(see illustration)**.

HAC

9 Since special equipment is required to test the HAC, checking is confined to making sure associated hoses and connections are secure **(see illustration)**.

Throttle opener

10 With the engine idling, turn on the air conditioner. If the idle speed does not increase, there is a fault in the speed sensor or wiring.

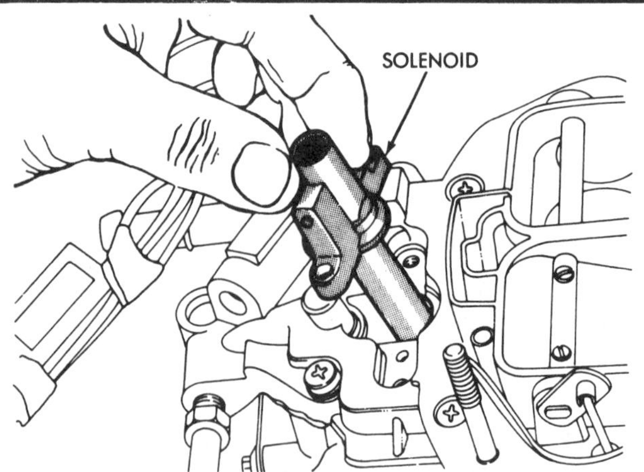

11.20 The carburetor solenoid is attached to the top of the carburetor with two screws

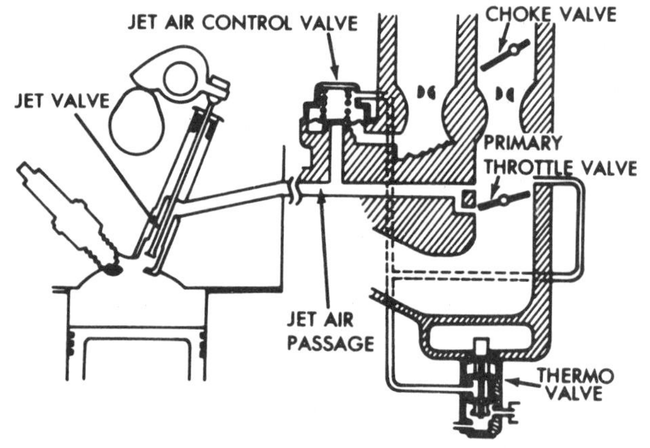

12.5 Jet Air Control Valve (JACV) system (2.6L engine)

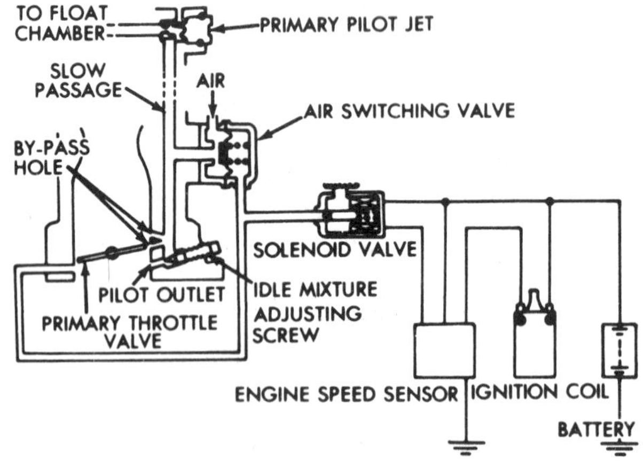

12.7a Air Switching Valve (ASV) system (2.6L engine)

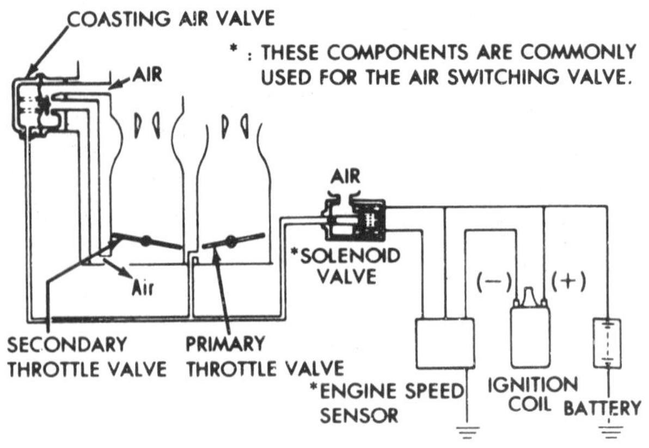

12.7b Coasting Air Valve (CAV) system (2.6L engine)

Component replacement

11 Locate the solenoid valve or speed sensor by tracing the wires or hoses from the component which they control. Disconnect the wires and/or hoses and install a new unit.

13 Automatic choke system

Refer to illustrations 13.3 and 13.4

General description

1 The automatic choke system temporarily supplies a rich fuel/air mixture to the engine by closing the choke plate(s) during cold engine starting.

2 On 2.2L engines, the choke is electrically operated, while 2.6L engines use a sealed wax pellet-type choke system.

3 On 2.2L engines, an electric signal from the oil pressure switch operates the choke control switch and activates the choke heater so that it slowly opens the choke plates as the engine warms up **(see illustration)**. This progressively leans out the mixture until the engine is warmed up.

4 On 2.6L engines, the wax pellet thermo sensing unit opens the choke as the coolant temperature increases. When started from cold, the choke valve is partially opened by a vacuum kicker actuated by manifold vacuum. This prevents an overly rich fuel/air mixture and the resultant increased emissions. The fast idle cam on the choke set lever controls the rate of throttle valve opening. If the vehicle is driven with a wide open throttle setting when cold, the choke is opened by the choke unloader so the mixture will not be overly rich **(see illustration)**.

Checking

5 Refer to Chapter 1 for the automatic choke checking procedure.

14 Air aspirator system

Refer to illustration 14.5

General description

1 The aspirator system uses exhaust pulsations to draw fresh air from the air cleaner into the exhaust system. This reduces carbon

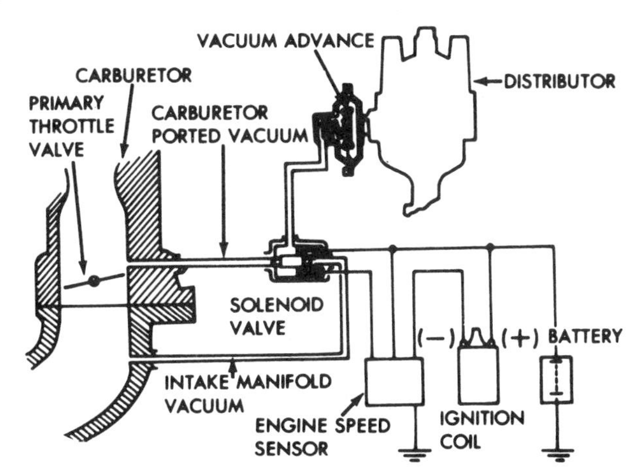

12.8 Deceleration Spark Advance System (DSAS) (2.6L engine)

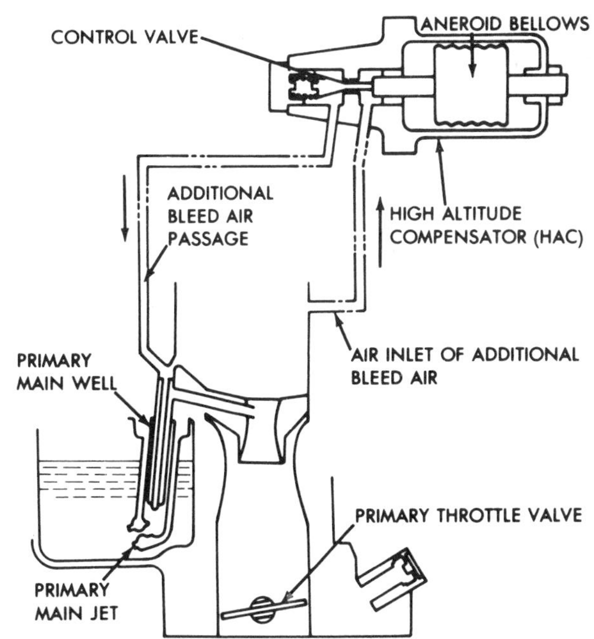

12.9 High Altitude Compensation (HAC) system (2.6L engine)

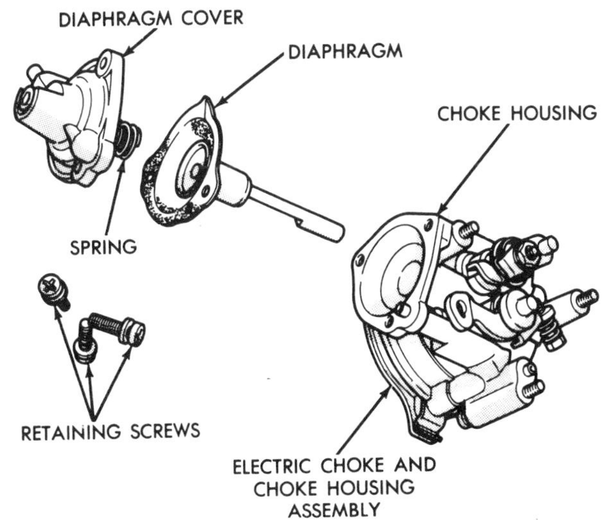

13.3 2.2L engine electric choke components – exploded view

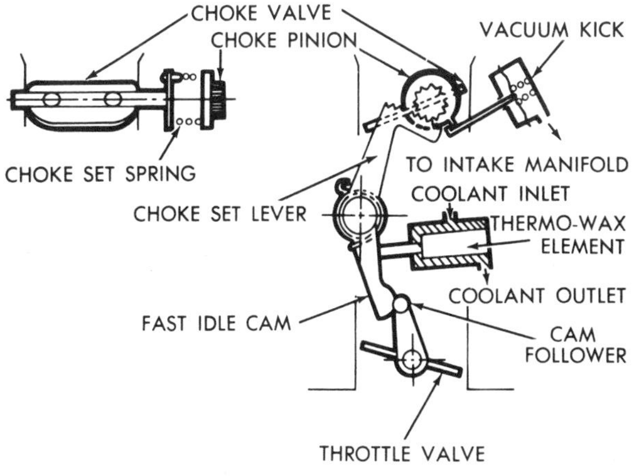

13.4 2.6L engine choke components

6

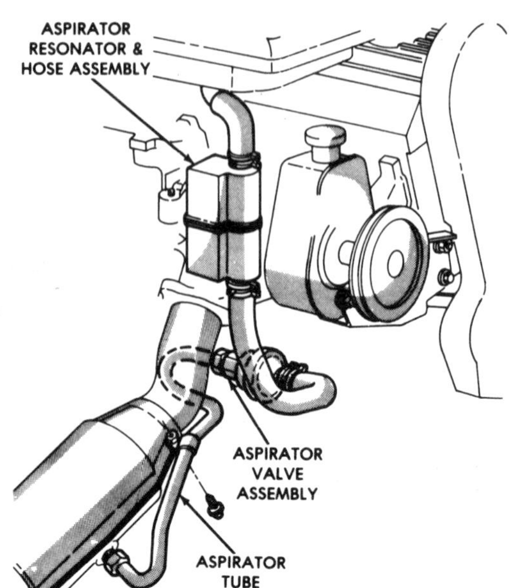

14.5 Typical air aspirator system components

monoxide (CO) and, to a lesser degree, hydrocarbon (HC) emissions.
2 The system is composed of a valve, hoses and tubes between the air cleaner assembly and the exhaust system.

3 The aspirator valve works most efficiently at idle and slightly off idle, where the negative exhaust pulses are strongest. The valve remains closed at higher engine speeds.

Checking

4 Aspirator valve failure results in excessive exhaust system noise from under the hood and hardening of the rubber hose from the valve to the air cleaner.
5 If exhaust noise is excessive, check the aspirator tube-to-exhaust manifold joint and the valve and air cleaner hose connections for leaks **(see illustration)**. If the manifold joint is leaking, retighten the tube fitting. If the hose connections are leaking, install new hose clamps (if the hose has not hardened). If the hose has hardened, replace it with a new one as well.
6 To determine if the valve has failed, disconnect the hose from the inlet. With the engine idling (transmission in Neutral), the exhaust pulses should be felt at the inlet. If a steady stream of exhaust gases is escaping from the inlet, the valve is defective and should be replaced with a new one.

Component replacement

7 The valve can be replaced by removing the hose clamp, detaching the hose and unscrewing the tube fitting.
8 The aspirator tube can be replaced by unscrewing the fittings at the valve and manifold and removing the bracket bolt.

Chapter 7 Part A Manual transaxle

Contents

Specifications

General

Transaxle type	4 or 5-speed, synchronized in all forward gears	
Fluid type and capacity	See Chapter 1	
Torque specifications	**Ft-lbs**	**Nm**
Gearshift housing-to-case bolt	21	28
Gearshift lever nut*		
1982 through 1986	21	28
1987	29	39
1988	27	36
Anti-rotational link (non-turbocharged models)		
Upper bolt and nut	40	54
Lower bolt and nut	40	54
Anti-rotational damper (turbocharged models)		
Upper nut	16	22
Lower bolt and nut	40	54
Anti-rotational link or damper bracket nuts	17	23
Fill plug**	24	33
Transaxle case-to-engine block bolt	70	95
Mount-to-block and case bolt	70	95
Shift linkage adjusting pin	9	12
Speedometer gear bolt	60 in-lb	7
End cover bolt	21	28
Selector cable adjusting screw		
1982 and 1983 models	60 in-lb	7
1984 and later models	55 in-lb	6
Crossover cable adjusting screw		
1982 and 1983 models	60 in-lb	7
1984 and later models	55 in-lb	6
Rod-type gearshift linkage tube clamp bolt	19	25

**This nut must be replaced with a new one each time it is removed*
***Metal plug only — rubber plug is a press fit*

7A

1 General information

The manual transaxle combines the transmission and differential assemblies into one compact unit.

The gearshift features a manual reverse lockout device and synchromesh is used on all forward speeds. Both rod and cable operated shift mechanisms are used on these models.

2 Gearshift linkage — adjustment

Refer to illustrations 2.3a, 2.3b, 2.4, 2.6, 2.7, 2.8 and 2.16

Cable-type linkage

1 In the event of hard shifting, disconnect both cables at the transaxle and then operate the shifter from the driver's seat. If the shift lever

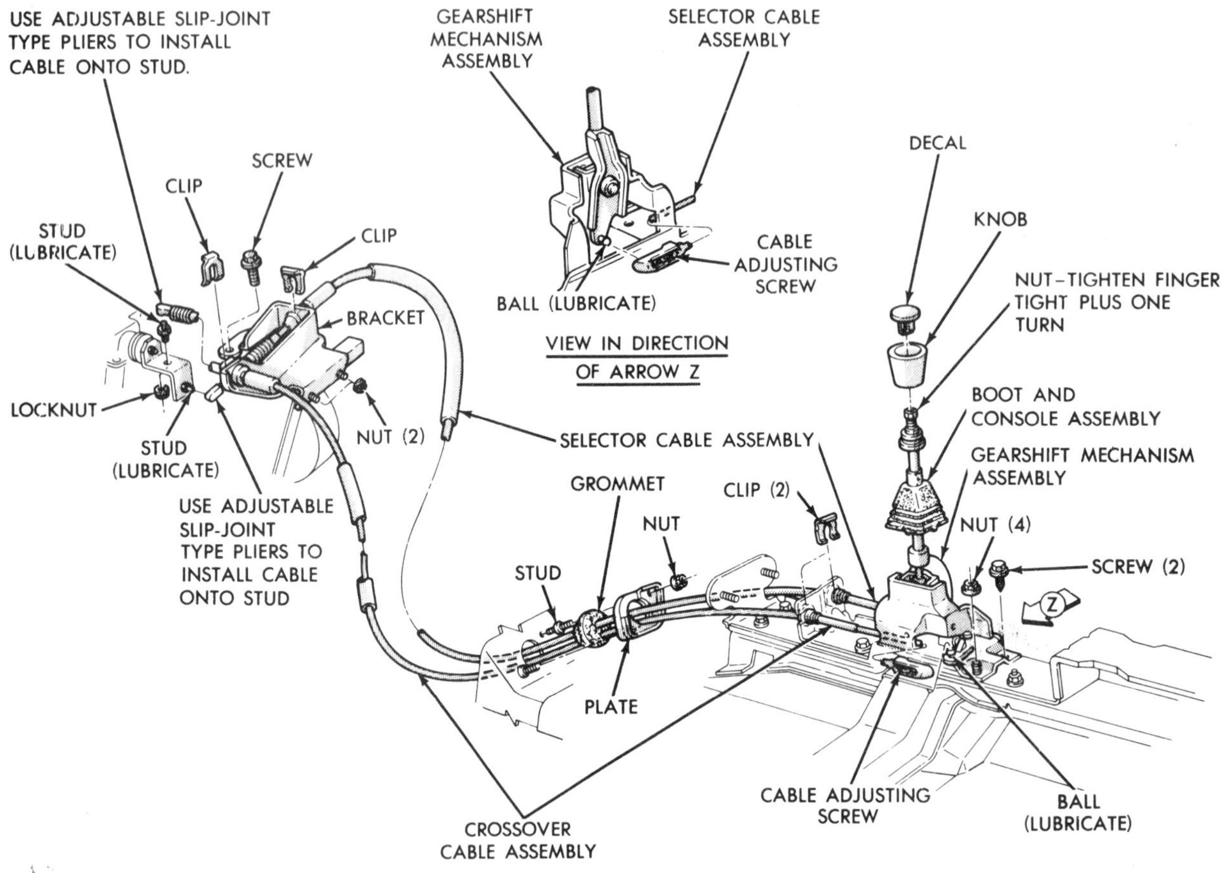

2.3a Typical cable-type shift linkage components — exploded view

moves smoothly through all positions with the cables disconnected, then the cable linkage should be adjusted as follows.

2 Raise the hood and place a pad or blanket over the left fender to protect it.

3 Remove the lock pin from the transaxle selector shaft housing. Reverse the lock pin so the longer end is down, reinstall it in the hole and move the selector shaft in. When the lock pin aligns with the hole in the selector shaft, thread it into place so the shaft is locked in the 1st/2nd Neutral position **(see illustrations)**.

4 Pry the shift pattern decal out with a small screwdriver and unscrew the gearshift knob. Remove the Reverse lockout pull-up ring retaining nut and lift off the pull-up ring **(see illustration)**. Remove the rubber boot and the console (Chapter 11).

5 Fabricate two five-inch long adjusting pins from 5/16-inch wire. Bend one end of each pin at a right angle so the pins are easy to grasp.

6 Insert one adjusting pin into the crossover cable hole in the shift mechanism and the other into the selector cable hole **(see illustration)**.

7 Use an in-lb torque wrench to tighten the selector cable adjusting screw to the specified torque **(see illustration)**.

8 Use the in-lb torque wrench to tighten the crossover cable adjusting screw as well **(see illustration)**.

9 Remove the adjusting pins from the shift mechanism.

10 Install the console, the pull-up ring and nut and the shift knob.

11 Unscrew the lock pin from the selector housing, reinstall it with the longer end up and tighten it to the specified torque.

12 Check the shifter operation in 1st and Reverse and make sure the reverse lockout mechanism works properly.

Rod-type linkage

13 Open the hood and cover the left fender to protect it.

14 Lock the selector shaft in the 1st/2nd Neutral position as described in Step 3 **(see illustration 2.3b)**

15 Raise the vehicle and support it securely on jackstands.

16 Working under the vehicle, loosen the gearshift connector clamp bolt **(see illustration)**. Make sure the connector moves freely within

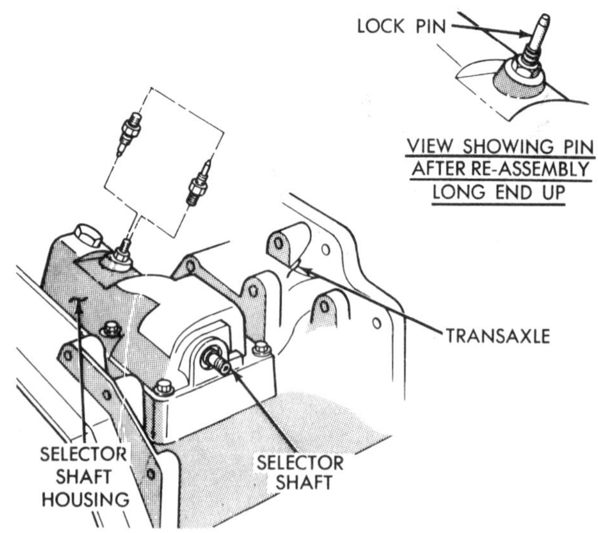

2.3b Use the lock pin to secure the transaxle selector shaft prior to cable linkage adjustment

the gearshift tube.

17 Place the shifter mechanism in position with the isolator contacting the upright flange and the isolator rib aligned with the hole in the lockout bracket. With no pressure on the linkage, tighten the clamp bolt to the specified torque.

18 Lower the vehicle.

19 Remove the lock pin, reverse it so the longer end is upright, screw it into place and then tighten it to the specified torque.

20 Check the shifter operation in 1st and Reverse and make sure the reverse lockout mechanism works properly.

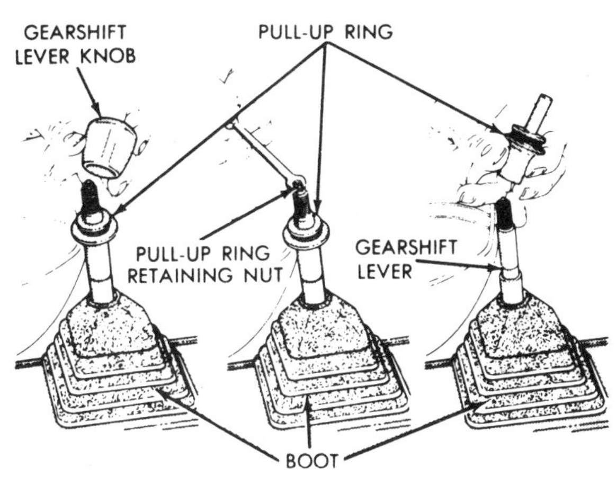

2.4 Shift knob and pull-up ring removal details

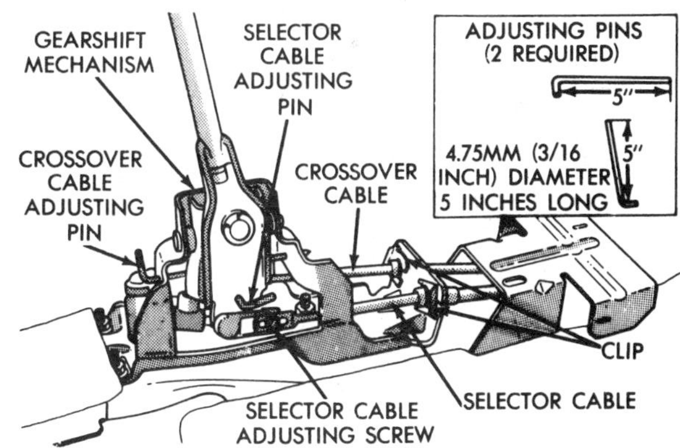

2.6 Fabricate the cable adjusting pins and install them as shown here

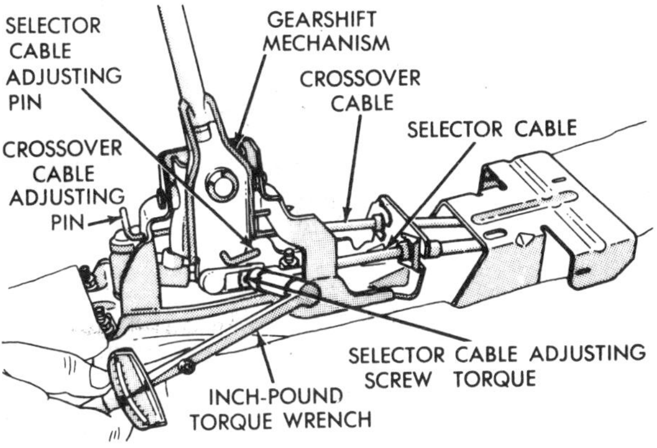

2.7 Adjusting the selector cable with a torque wrench

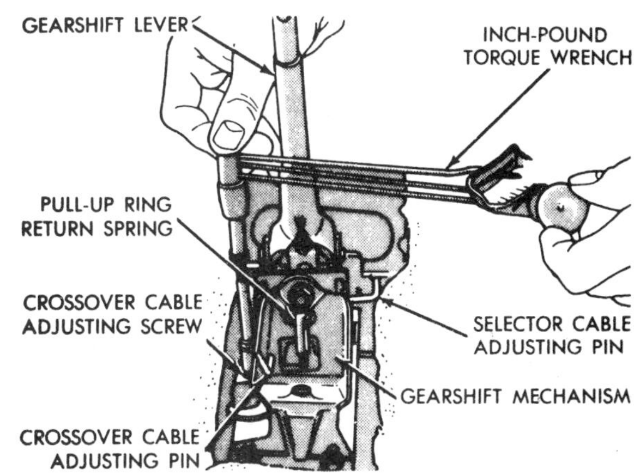

2.8 Adjusting the crossover cable with a torque wrench

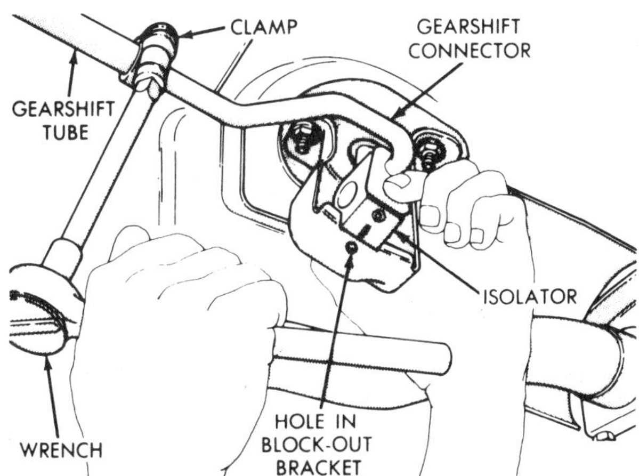

2.16 When adjusting the rod-type shift linkage, make sure the ridge on the isolator is centered in the hole in the block-out bracket before tightening the clamp nut

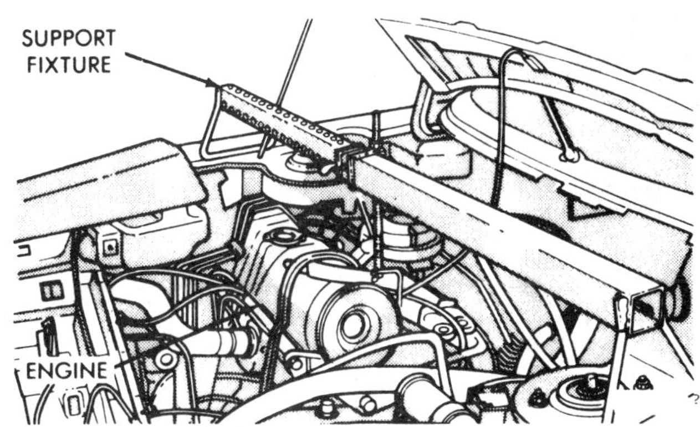

3.3 Support the engine from above with the special fixture as shown here or a with a jack from underneath

3 Manual transaxle – removal and installation

Refer to illustrations 3.3, 3.6, 3.8, 3.10, 3.12 and 3.17

1 Disconnect the negative cable at the battery. Place the cable out of the way so it cannot accidentally come in contact with the negative terminal of the battery, as this would once again allow power into the electrical system of the vehicle.

2 Remove the hood (Chapter 11), raise the front of the vehicle and support it securely on jackstands.

3 Attach a "lifting eye" to the number four cylinder exhaust manifold bolt and support the engine with the special support fixture **(see illustration)**. As an alternative, if care is exercised, a jack can be used to support the engine from below. Be sure to position a block of wood between the jack head and the engine oil pan if a jack is used.

4 Disconnect the gearshift linkage, clutch cable and speedometer drive gear.

5 Remove the front wheels and the left splash shield.

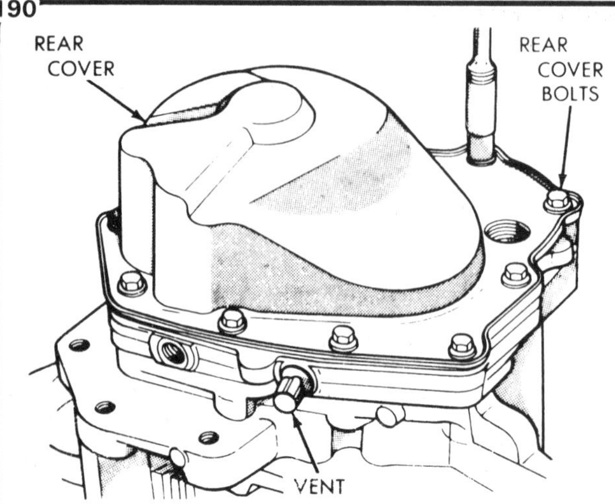

3.6 Loosen the rear end cover bolts in a criss-cross pattern to avoid warping the cover, which could result in oil leaks

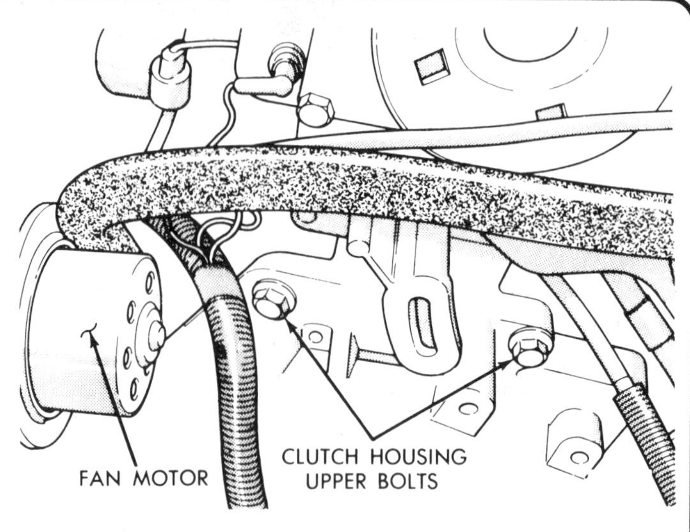

3.8 Upper clutch housing bolt locations

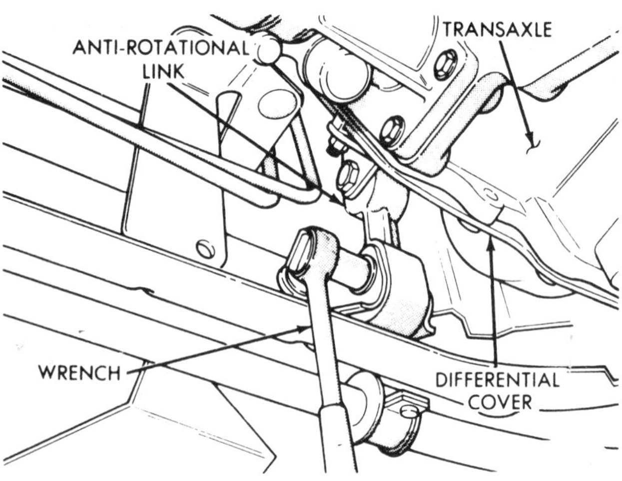

3.10 Removing the anti-rotational link (non-turbocharged models)

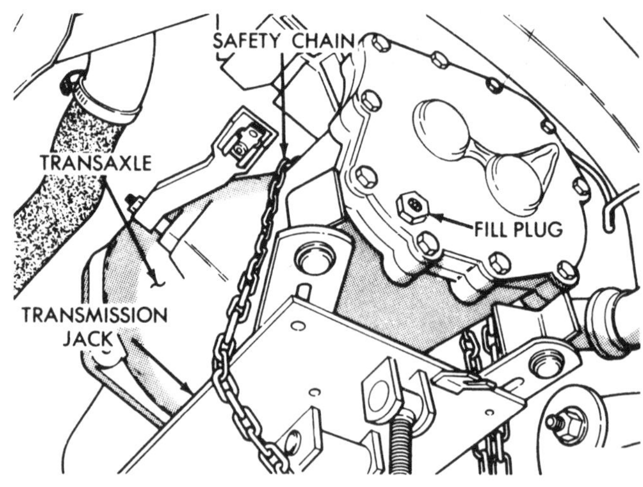

3.12 Support the transaxle with a jack when removing it (note the safety chain)

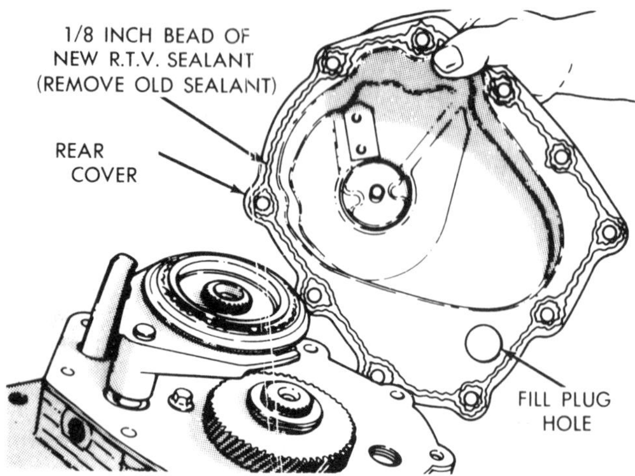

3.17 Apply RTV-type sealant as shown (be sure to go around the bolt holes) when installing the rear end cover

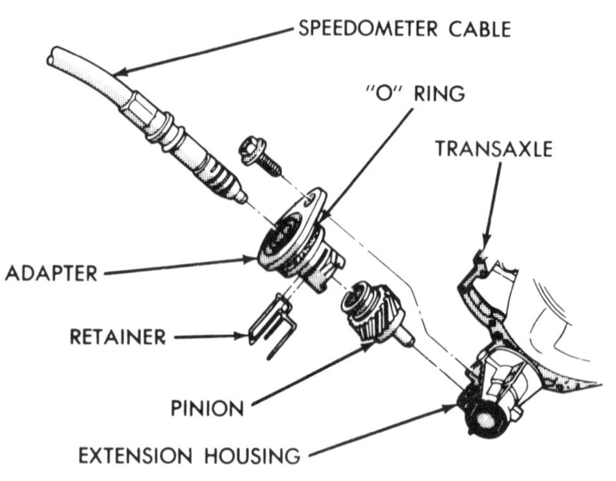

4.1 Speedometer gear assembly components – exploded view

6 Position a large drain pan (at least three quart capacity) under the transaxle and drain the fluid by removing the rear cover **(see illustration)**.
7 Place a jack under the transaxle to support its weight.
8 Remove the clutch housing bolts **(see illustration)**.
9 Remove the left engine mount.
10 Unbolt the anti-rotational link (non-turbocharged engine) or damper (turbocharged engine) between the chassis and transaxle **(see illustration)**.
11 Remove the driveaxles as described in Chapter 8.
12 Carefully pull the transaxle away from the engine and lower it **(see illustration)**.
13 When installing the transaxle, locating pins can be fabricated and used in place of the top two bolts. Cut the heads off two proper size bolts with a hacksaw and remove any burrs from the ends with a file or grinder. Use a hacksaw to cut slots in the ends of the locating pins so they can be unscrewed with a screwdriver and replaced with bolts.
14 Install the driveaxles (Chapter 8).
15 Install the anti-rotational link or damper and tighten the fasteners to the specified torque.
16 Install the left engine mount and tighten the bolts to the specified torque.
17 If the transaxle rear cover has not been installed prior to this point, clean the cover and transaxle mating surfaces thoroughly. Apply a 1/8-inch bead of RTV-type sealant to the cover **(see illustration)** and install the cover and bolts.
18 Fill the transaxle to the bottom of the fill plug hole with the specified lubricant (see Chapter 1).
19 Install the splash shield and the front wheels.
20 Remove the support from the engine and connect the battery cable.
21 Lower the front of the vehicle.
22 Check the gearshift linkage operation to make sure all gears engage smoothly and easily. If they do not, adjust the linkage as described in Section 2.

4 Manual transaxle speedometer gear assembly – removal and installation

Refer to illustration 4.1

1 The speedometer gear assembly is located in the transaxle extension housing **(see illustration)**.
2 Remove the retaining bolt and carefully work the speedometer assembly up and out of the extension housing.
3 Remove the retainer and separate the pinion from the adapter.
4 Check the speedometer cable to make sure that transaxle lubricant has not leaked into it. If there is fluid in the cable, remove the adapter and replace the small O-ring with a new one. Reconnect the cable to the adapter.
5 Install a new O-ring and connect the adapter to the pinion gear, making sure the retainer is securely seated.
6 Make sure the mating surfaces of the adapter and the extension housing are clean, as debris could cause misalignment of the gear.
7 Attach the assembly to the transaxle, install the retaining bolt and tighten it to the specified torque.

5 Manual transaxle service and repair

Because of the special tools and expertise required to disassemble, overhaul and reassemble the transaxle, it is recommended that it be left to a dealer service department or a transmission repair shop.

Chapter 7 Part B Automatic transaxle

Contents

Specifications

General

Transaxle type	3-speed, fully automatic	
Fluid type and capacity	See Chapter 1	
Torque specifications	**Ft-lbs**	**Nm**
Differential cover bolts	14	19
Neutral start and back-up light switch	25	34
Throttle cable adjustment bracket lock screw	9	12
Speedometer gear bolt	5.2	7
Torque converter-to-driveplate bolts		
1982 through 1985	40	54
1986 on	55	74

1 General information

The automatic transaxle combines a 3-speed automatic transmission and differential assembly into one unit. Power from the engine passes through the torque converter and the transmission to the differential assembly and then to the driveaxles.

All models feature a transaxle oil cooler with the oil-to-air cooler element located in the radiator side tank.

2 Gearshift linkage — adjustment

Refer to illustrations 2.2 and 2.4

1 Place the gearshift lever in Park.
2 Working in the engine compartment, loosen the gearshift cable clamp bolt on the transaxle bracket **(see illustration)**.
3 Pull the shift lever all the way to the front detent (Park) position by hand.
4 Keep pressure on the shift lever and tighten the cable clamp bolt **(see illustration)**.
5 Check the shift lever in the Neutral and Drive positions to make sure it is within the confines of the lever stops. The engine should start only when the lever is in the Park or Neutral position.

3 Throttle cable — adjustment

Refer to illustrations 3.3 and 3.6

1 The throttle cable controls a valve in the transaxle which governs shift quality and speed. If shifting is harsh or erratic, the throttle cable should be adjusted.
2 The adjustment must be made with the engine at normal operating temperature (or disconnect the choke to ensure that the carburetor is not on the fast idle cam).

1982 through 1985 models

3 Loosen the adjustment bracket lock screw **(see illustration)**.
4 To ensure proper adjustment, the bracket must be free to slide back-and-forth. If necessary, remove it and clean the slot and sliding surfaces as well as the screw.
5 Slide the bracket to the left (toward the engine) to the limit of its travel. Release the bracket and move the throttle lever all the way to the right, against the internal stop, then tighten the adjustment bracket lock screw to the specified torque.

2.2 Typical automatic transaxle shift linkage components – exploded view

2.4 When tightening the shift cable clamp bolt, maintain pressure with one hand on the shift lever (arrow) as the bolt is tightened

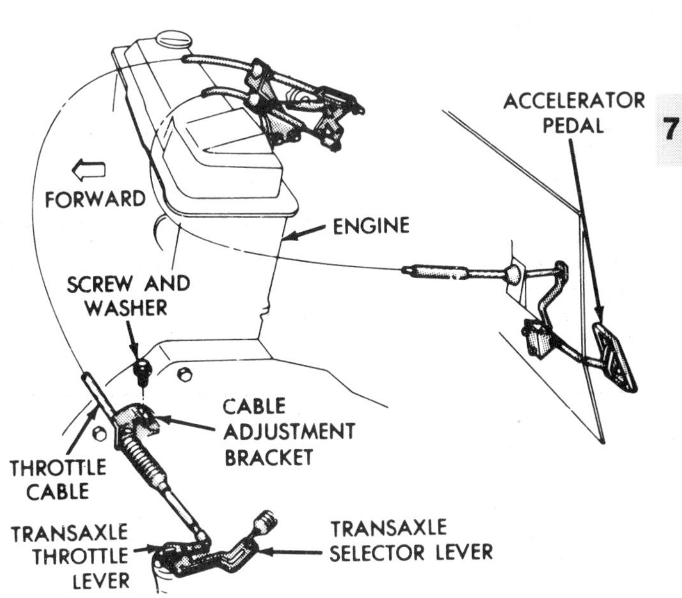

3.3 Throttle cable layout – 1982 through 1985 models

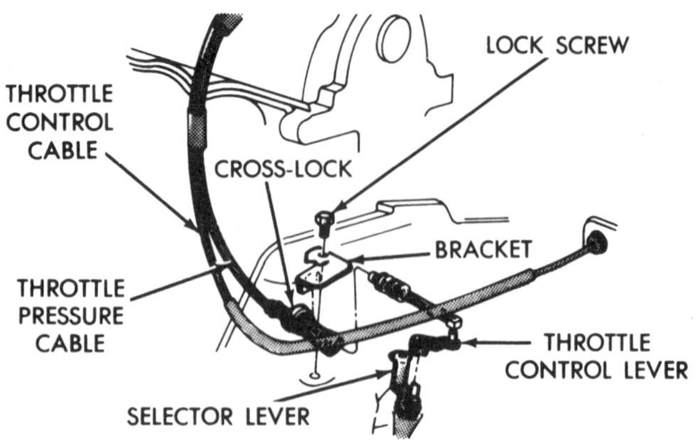

3.6 Throttle cable layout — 1986 and later models

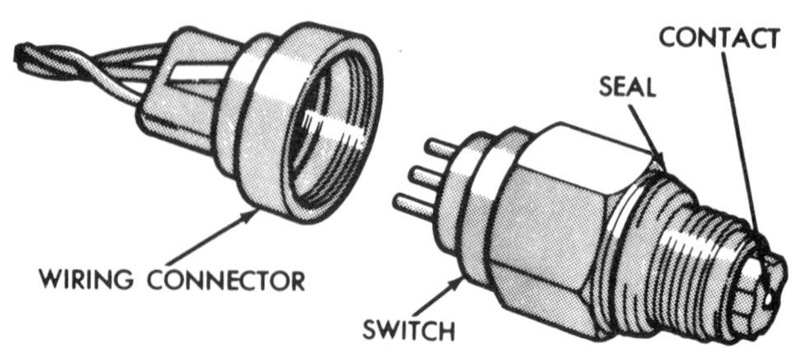

4.6 Neutral start and back-up light switch

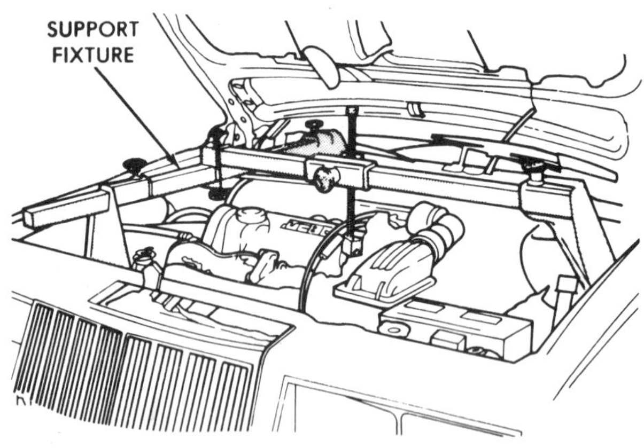

5.7 The weight of the engine must be supported with the special fixture or a jack as the transaxle is removed

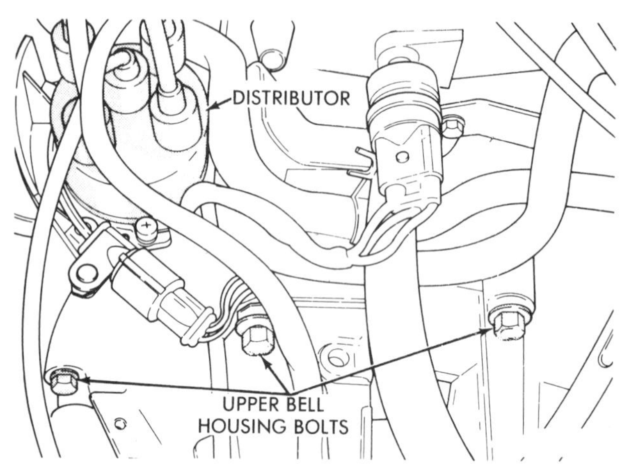

5.8 Upper bellhousing bolt locations

1986 and later models

6 Loosen the cable mounting bracket lock screw and position the bracket so the alignment tabs are in contact with the transaxle casting **(see illustration)**. Tighten the lock screw to the specified torque.
7 Release the cross-lock on the cable assembly by pulling up on it. To ensure proper adjustment, the cable must be free to slide all the way toward the engine, against the stop, after the cross-lock is released.
8 Move the transaxle throttle control lever clockwise as far as possible (against the internal stop) and press the cross-lock down into the locked position.
9 It is a good idea to lubricate the linkage and cable components at this time. Do not lubricate any of the throttle linkage components.

All models

10 Connect the choke (if disconnected) and check the cable action. Move the transaxle throttle cable all the way forward, release it slowly and make sure that it returns completely.

4 Neutral start and back-up light switch — check and replacement

Refer to illustration 4.6

1 The Neutral start and back-up light switch is located at the lower front edge of the transaxle. The switch controls the back-up light and the center terminal of the switch grounds the starter solenoid circuit when the transaxle is in Park or Neutral, allowing the engine to start.
2 Prior to checking the switch, make sure the gearshift linkage is properly adjusted (Section 2).
3 Unplug the connector and use an ohmmeter to check for continuity between the center terminal and the case. Continuity should exist only when the transaxle is in Park or Neutral.
4 Check for continuity between the two outer terminals. Continuity should exist only when the transaxle is in Reverse. No continuity should exist between either outer terminal and the case.
5 If the switch fails any of the tests, replace it with a new one.
6 Position a drain pan under the switch to catch the fluid released when the switch is removed. Unscrew the switch and remove it from the transaxle **(see illustration)**.
7 Move the shift lever from Park to Neutral and check to see if the switch operating fingers are centered in the opening.
8 Install the new switch, tighten it to the specified torque and plug in the connector. Repeat the checks on the new switch.
9 Check the fluid level and add fluid as required (see Chapter 1).

5 Automatic transaxle — removal and installation

Refer to illustrations 5.7, 5.8, 5.12a, 5.12b, 5.13, 5.16, 5.17, 5.19, 5.20, 5.21 and 5.22

Removal

1 Disconnect the negative cable at the battery. Place the cable out of the way so it cannot accidentally come in contact with the negative terminal of the battery, as this would once again allow power into the electrical system of the vehicle.
2 Drain the cooling system (Chapter 1).
3 On 2.2L carburetor equipped engines, remove the air injection pump.
4 Disconnect the heater hoses and move them out of the way.
5 Remove the transaxle shift and throttle position cables and fasten them out of the way.

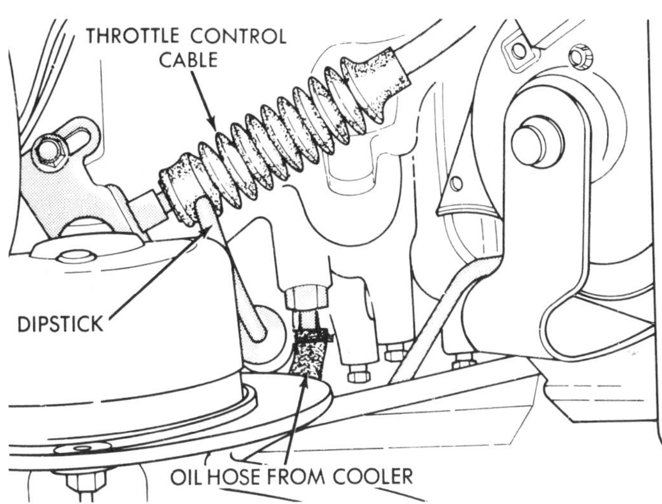

5.12a The transaxle oil cooler return hose . . .

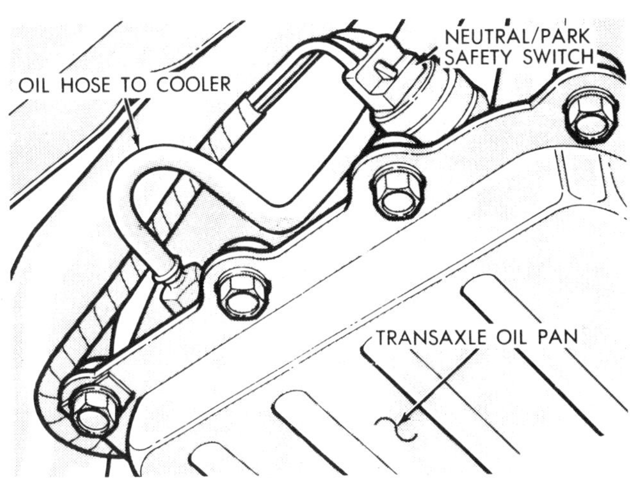

5.12b . . . and supply hose should be detached at the transaxle

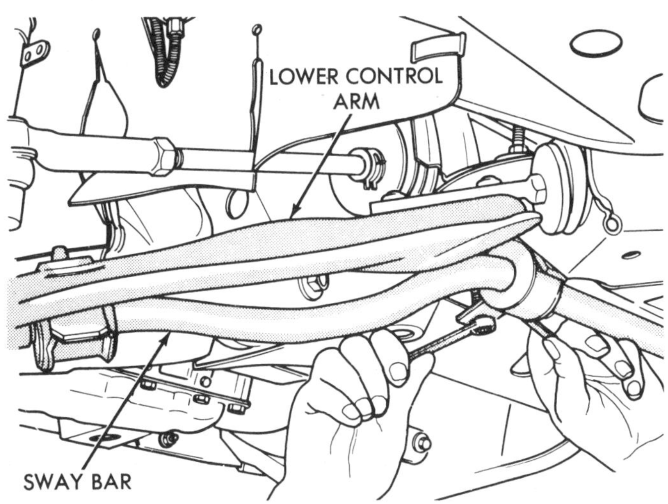

5.13 Removing the sway bar mount bolts

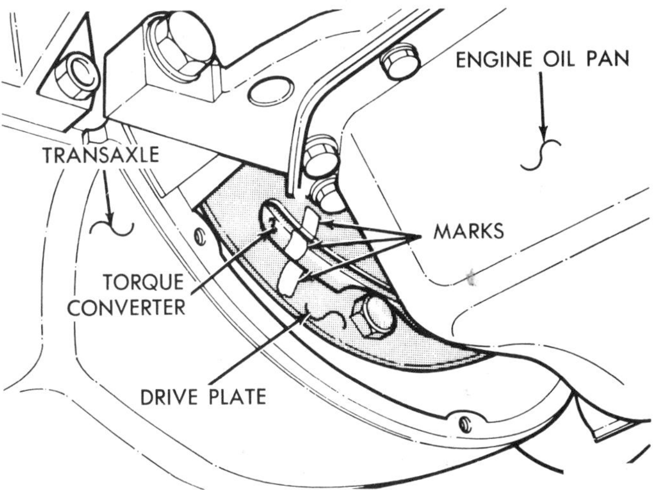

5.16 Be sure to mark the torque converter and driveplate so they can be reinstalled in the same relative position

6 Remove the air cleaner assembly.
7 Support the engine from above with the special fixture **(see illustration)** or from below with a jack (place a block of wood between the jack and the engine oil pan to prevent damage).
8 Remove the upper bellhousing bolts **(see illustration)**.
9 Remove the driveaxle cotter pins and nuts. Raise the vehicle and support it securely. The engine must be supported in the raised position as well.
10 Remove all under vehicle splash shields.
11 Remove the speedometer drive gear and unplug all electrical connectors.
12 Disconnect the fluid cooler lines at the transaxle and plug them **(see illustrations)**.
13 Loosen the sway bar bushing bolts, unbolt the ends from the lower control arms and pull the sway bar down out of the way **(see illustration)**.
14 Remove the driveaxles and (if equipped) the intermediate shaft (Chapter 8).
15 Remove the lower bellhousing cover to provide access to the torque converter.
16 Mark the torque converter-to-driveplate relationship so they will be reinstalled in the same position **(see illustration)**. Remove the torque converter-to-driveplate bolts (turn the crankshaft with a socket and extension on the pulley bolt to gain access to the driveplate bolts).
17 Remove the engine mount bracket from the front crossmember **(see illustration)**.

7B

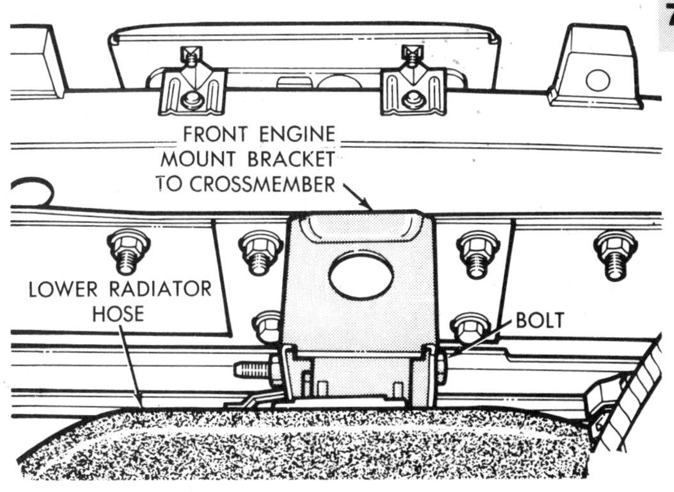

5.17 Engine mount bracket-to-front crossmember location

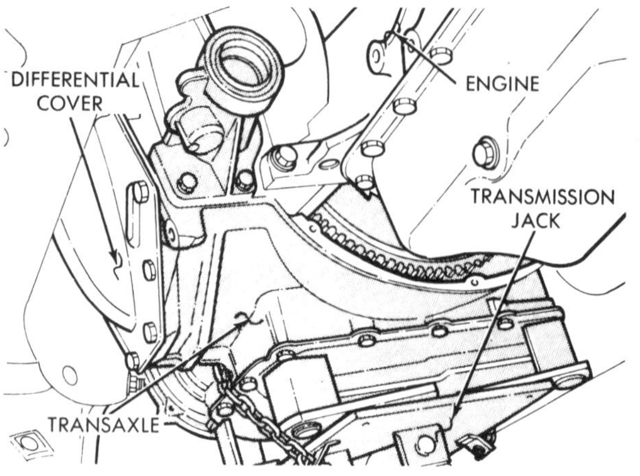

5.19 Support the transaxle with a jack (note the safety chain used to prevent the transaxle from falling off the jack)

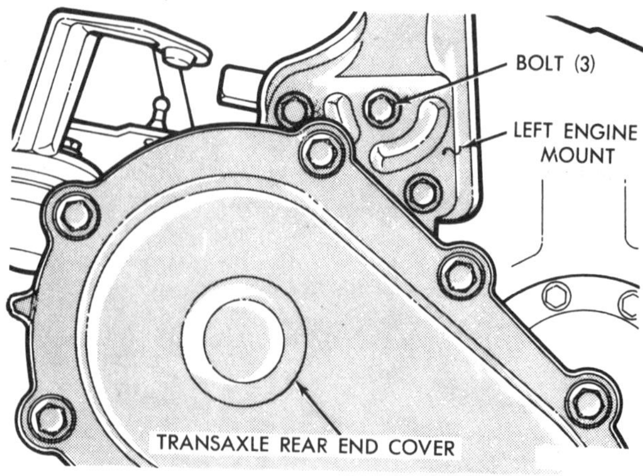

5.20 Left transaxle-to-engine mount bolt locations

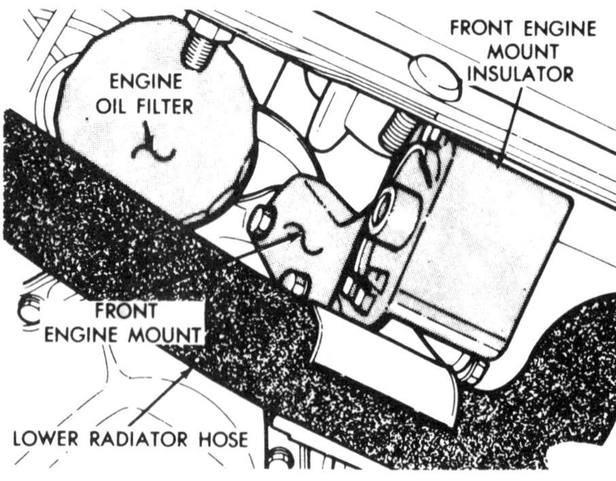

5.21 Front chassis-to-engine mount bolt locations

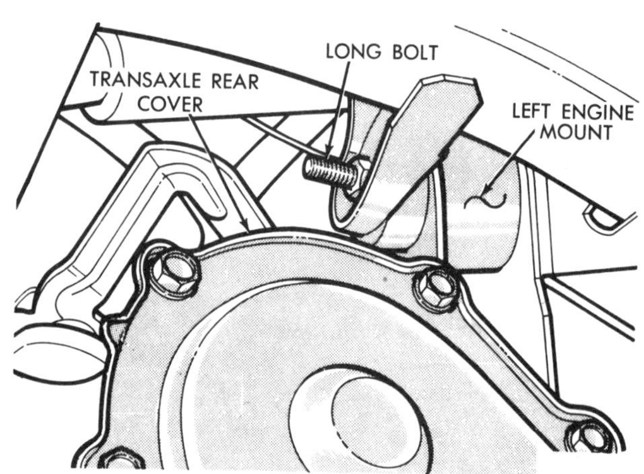

5.22 Left engine mount bolt location

18 Remove the starter and wiring harness assembly (Chapter 5).
19 Support the transaxle with a jack **(see illustration)**.
20 Remove the left transaxle-to-engine mount bolts **(see illustration)**.
21 Remove the front chassis-to-engine mount bolts from the engine and transaxle **(see illustration)**.
22 Remove the left engine mount **(see illustration)**.
23 Carefully pry the transaxle away from the engine.
24 Pull the transaxle away from the engine, making sure the torque converter remains on the input shaft.
25 Move the transaxle away from the engine and lower it from the engine compartment. Be careful not to contact the inner end of the lower suspension arm.

Installation

26 To install the transaxle, raise it into position with the torque converter in place on the input shaft.
27 Move the transaxle into place against the engine, align the bolt holes and install the upper bellhousing bolts.
28 Install the left engine mount.
29 Align the torque converter and driveplate marks made during removal, install the bolts and tighten them to the specified torque.
30 Install the bellhousing cover and the front mount.
31 Install the starter and electrical harness (Chapter 5).
32 Install the driveaxles (Chapter 8).
33 Install the sway bar and tighten the bolts and nuts to the specified torque (Chapter 11).
34 Plug in the transaxle electrical connectors.
35 Install the under vehicle splash shields (if equipped).
36 Install the driveaxle nuts, lower the vehicle and tighten the nuts as described in Chapter 8.
37 Install the air injection pump and bracket (2.2L carburetor equipped engine).
38 Install the air cleaner assembly.
39 Connect the transaxle cooler lines and tighten them securely.
40 Connect the transaxle shift and throttle cables.
41 Connect the heater hoses and refill the cooling system.
42 Refill the transaxle (Chapter 1).
43 Connect the negative battery cable.

6 Automatic transaxle speedometer gear assembly — removal and installation

Refer to Section 4 in Part A. The procedure is the same regardless of the type of transaxle involved.

7 Automatic transaxle service and repair

Because of the special tools, equipment and expertise required to disassemble, overhaul and reassemble the transaxle, it is recommended that it be left to a dealer service department or a transmission repair shop.

Chapter 8 Clutch and driveaxles

Contents

Specifications

Clutch

Flywheel runout limit	0.003 in (0.07 mm)
Clutch lining wear limit	0.015 in (0.38 mm)
Pressure plate warpage limit	0.020 in (0.50 mm)
Clutch cover warpage limit	0.015 in (0.38 mm)

Driveaxle length

1982 and 1983 models	Check with dealer service department
1984 models	
GKN driveaxle	
Right (tan tape)	10.1 to 10.4 in (257 to 265 mm)
Left (silver tape)	10.0 to 10.6 in (254 to 269 mm)
Citroen driveaxle	
Right (red tape)	9.5 to 9.9 in (241 to 251 mm)
Left (yellow tape)	9.4 to 10.0 in (238 to 255 mm)
1985 models	
GKN driveaxle	
Right (tan tape)	10.1 to 10.4 in (257 to 265 mm)
Left (silver tape)	10.0 to 10.6 in (254 to 269 mm)
Right (blue tape)	19.9 to 20.3 in (505 to 515 mm)
Left (blue tape)	10.2 to 10.9 in (259 to 277 mm)
ACI driveaxle	
Right (green tape)	18.8 to 19.1 in (477 to 585 mm)
Left (green tape)	9.0 to 9.6 in (229 to 244 mm)
GKN/ACI driveaxle	
Right (orange tape)	19.4 to 19.7 in (492 to 500 mm)
Left (orange tape)	9.6 to 10.2 in (243 to 258 mm)
Citroen driveaxle	
Right (red tape)	9.5 to 9.9 in (241 to 251 mm)
Left (yellow tape)	9.4 to 10.0 in (238 to 255 mm)
Right (white tape)	18.9 to 19.4 in (480 to 492 mm)
Left (white tape)	9.4 to 10.0 in (238 to 255 mm)
SSG driveaxle	
Right (gold tape)	17.8 to 18.5 in (457 to 469 mm)
Left (gold tape)	8.5 to 9.1 in (216 to 232 mm)
1986 models	
GKN driveaxle	
Right (blue tape)	19.9 to 20.3 in (505 to 515 mm)
Left (blue tape)	10.2 to 10.9 in (259 to 277 mm)
Right (tan tape)	10.1 to 10.4 in (257 to 265 mm)
Left (silver tape)	10.0 to 10.6 in (254 to 269 mm)
ACI driveaxle	
Right (green tape)	18.8 to 19.1 in (477 to 485 mm)
Left (green tape)	9.0 to 9.6 in (229 to 244 mm)
GKN/ACI driveaxle	
Right (orange tape)	19.4 to 19.7 in (492 to 500 mm)
Left (orange tape)	9.6 to 10.2 in (243 to 259 mm)
Citroen driveaxle	
Right (white tape)	18.9 to 19.4 in (480 to 492 mm)
Left (white tape)	9.4 to 10.0 in (238 to 255 mm)
Right (red tape)	9.5 to 9.9 in (241 to 251 mm)
Left (yellow tape)	9.4 to 10.0 in (238 to 255 mm)

Driveaxle length (continued)

1987 (2.2L/2.5L engines)	
GKN driveaxle	
Right	19.9 to 20.3 in (505 to 515 mm)
Left	8.9 to 9.6 in (227 to 245 mm)
ACI driveaxle	
Right	18.8 to 19.1 in (477 to 485 mm)
Left	7.8 to 8.3 in (197 to 212 mm)
GKN/ACI driveaxle	
Right	19.4 to 19.7 in (492 to 500 mm)
Left	8.3 to 8.9 in (211 to 226 mm)
Citroen driveaxle	
Right	18.9 to 19.4 in (480 to 492 mm)
Left	8.1 to 8.8 in (206 to 223 mm)
SSG driveaxle	
Right	17.9 to 18.5 in (457 to 469 mm)
Left	7.2 to 7.9 in (184 to 200 mm)
1987 (2.6L engine)	
GKN driveaxle	
Right	19.7 to 20.1 in (501 to 510 mm)
Left	8.7 to 9.3 in (222 to 237 mm)
Citroen driveaxle	
Right	18.9 to 19.4 in (480 to 492 mm)
Left	8.1 to 8.8 in (206 to 223 mm)
1987 (2.2L turbocharged engine)	
GKN driveaxle	10.1 to 10.4 in (257 to 265 mm)
Citroen driveaxle	9.5 to 9.9 in (241 to 251 mm)
SSG driveaxle	8.6 to 9.0 in (219 to 228 mm)
1988 (2.2L/2.5L engines)	
GKN driveaxle (69-92)	
Right	19.9 to 20.3 in (505 to 515 mm)
Left	8.9 to 9.6 in (227 to 245 mm)
GKN driveaxle (82-98)	
Right	19.3 to 19.6 in (490 to 498 mm)
Left	8.9 to 9.2 in (227 to 234 mm)
ACI driveaxle	
Right	18.8 to 19.1 in (477 to 485 mm)
Left	7.8 to 8.3 in (197 to 212 mm)
SSG driveaxle	
Right	18.0 to 18.5 in (457 to 469 mm)
Left	7.2 to 7.9 in (184 to 200 mm)
1988 (2.2L turbocharged engine)	
SSG driveaxle	7.4 to 7.7 in (187 to 196 mm)
GKN driveaxle	8.9 to 9.2 in (227 to 234 mm)
1988 (3.0L V6 engine) (GKN driveaxle)	
Right	18.9 to 19.2 in (481 to 489 mm)
Left	8.5 to 8.8 in (216 to 224 mm)

Torque specifications	**Ft-lbs**	**Nm**
Flywheel-to-crankshaft bolts		
1982 and 1983	60	81
1984 and 1985	65	88
1986 on	70	95
Pressure plate-to-flywheel bolts	21	28
Clutch cable retainer bolt nut	21	28
Steering knuckle-to-balljoint clamp bolt/nut	70	95
Driveaxle nuts	180	245
Intermediate shaft		
Bracket-to-engine bolt	40	54
Bracket-to-bearing bolt	21	28
Wheel lug nuts	95	129

1 General information

Refer to illustration 1.2

The clutch disc is held in place against the flywheel by the pressure plate springs. During disengagement, such as during gear shifting, the clutch pedal is depressed, which operates a cable, pulling on the release lever so the release bearing pushes on the pressure plate springs, disengaging the clutch.

The clutch pedal incorporates a self-adjusting device which compensates for clutch disc wear **(see illustration)**. A spring in the clutch pedal arm maintains tension on the cable and the adjuster pivot grabs the positioner adjuster when the pedal is depressed and the clutch is released. Consequently the slack is always taken up in the cable, making adjustment unnecessary.

Power from the engine passes though the clutch and transaxle to the front wheels by two driveaxles. On non-turbocharged models the driveaxles are unequal length, while turbocharged models are equipped with equal length driveaxles and feature an intermediate shaft incorporating a Cardan joint. The driveaxles consist of three sections: the inner splined ends whicn are held in the differential by clips or springs, two constant velocity (CV) joints and outer splined ends which are held in the hub by a nut. The CV joints are internally splined and contain ball bearings which allow them to operate at various lengths and angles

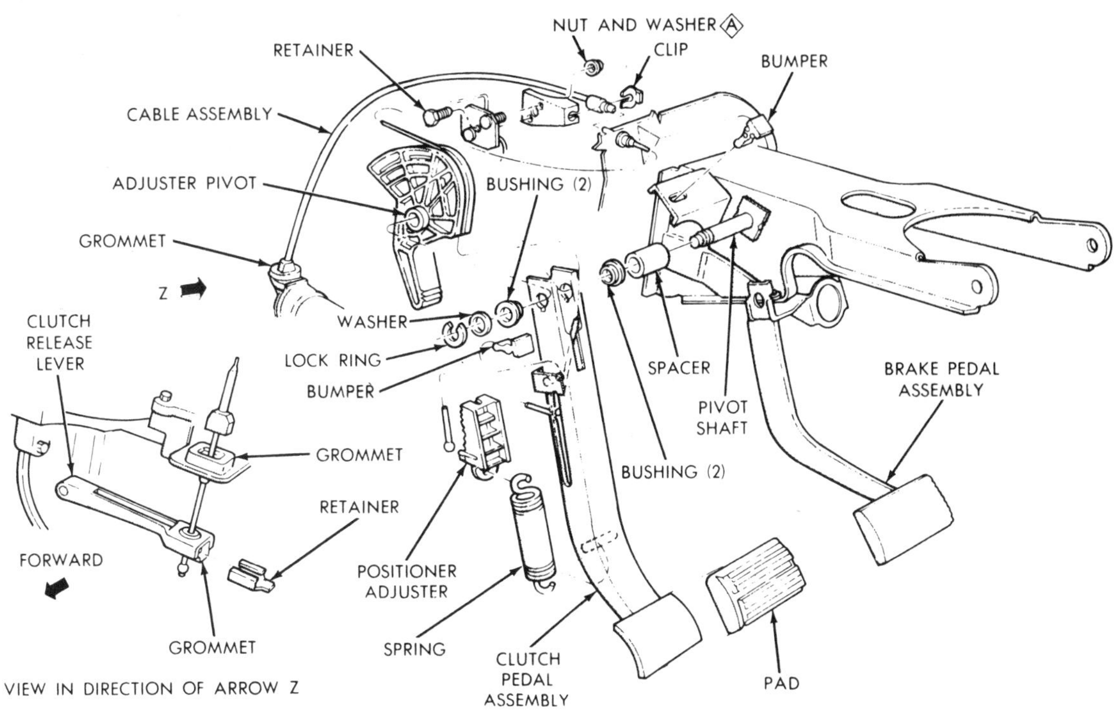

1.2 Self-adjusting clutch linkage components — exploded view

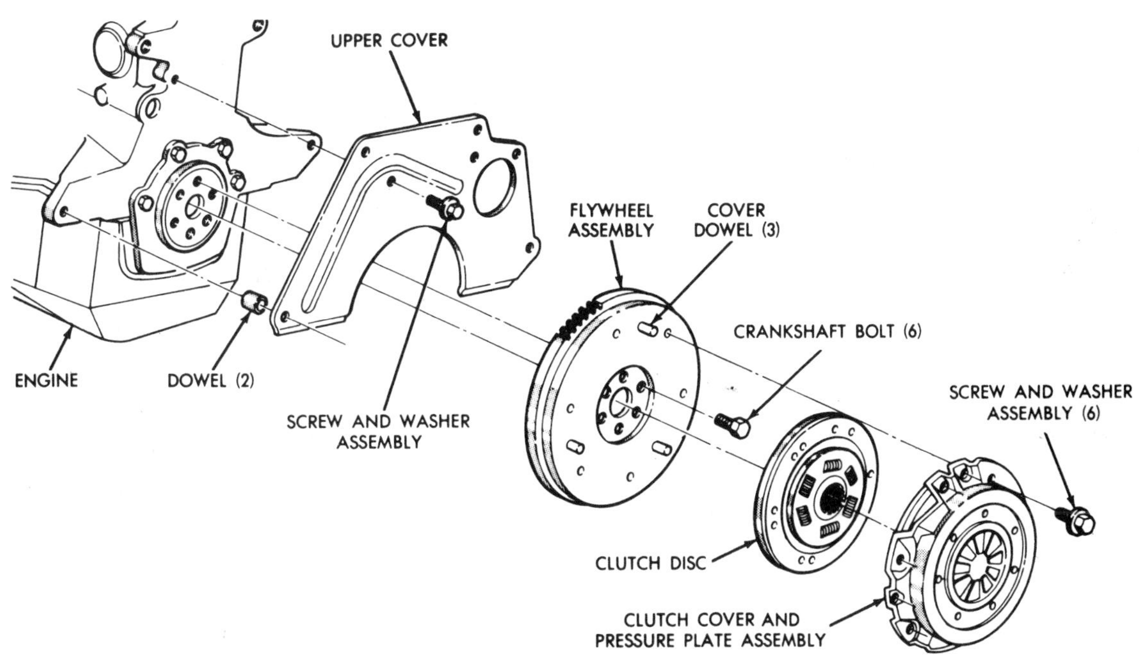

2.4 Clutch components — exploded view

as the driveaxles move through their full range of travel. The CV joints are lubricated with special grease and are protected by rubber boots which must be inspected periodically for cracks, tears and signs of leakage, which could lead to damage of the joints and failure of the driveaxle.

The driveaxles are identified as "GKN", "ACI", "SSG" or "Citroen" assemblies (depending on the manufacturer). Vehicles may be equipped with any of these types. However, they should not be interchanged. The driveaxles on your vehicle can be identified by referring to illustration 6.2.

2 Clutch — removal, inspection and installation

Refer to illustrations 2.4 and 2.16

1 Remove the transaxle (Chapter 7).

2 Mark the position of the pressure plate assembly on the flywheel so it can be installed in the same position.

3 Loosen the pressure plate bolts 1/4-turn at a time, in a criss-cross pattern, to avoid warping the cover.

4 Remove the pressure plate and clutch disc **(see illustration)**.

8

5 Handle the disc carefully, taking care not to touch the lining surface, and set it aside.
6 Remove the clutch release shaft.
7 Slide the clutch release bearing and fork assembly off the input shaft. Remove the fork from the thrust plate. Inspect the bearing for damage, wear and cracks. Hold the center of the bearing and spin the outer race. If the bearing doesn't turn smoothly or if it is noisy, replace it with a new one.
8 Clean the dust out of the clutch housing with a vacuum cleaner or clean cloth. *Do not use compressed air, as the dust probably contains asbestos, which can endanger your health if inhaled.*
9 Inspect the friction surfaces of the clutch disc and flywheel for signs of uneven contact, indicating improper mounting or damaged clutch springs. Check the surfaces for burned areas, grooves, cracks and other signs of wear. It may be necessary to remove a badly grooved flywheel and have it machined to restore the surface. Light glazing of the flywheel surface can be removed with fine sandpaper. Attach a dial indicator to the engine and, with the contact plunger within the wear circle of the flywheel, rotate the crankshaft 180 degrees. The flywheel runout should be within the specified limit. Be sure to push the crankshaft forward so the end play won't be included in the runout measurement.
10 To determine clutch disc lining wear, measure the distance from the rivet head to the lining surface and compare it to the Specifications. Check the lining for contamination by oil or grease and replace the disc with a new one if any is present. Check the center of the disc to make sure it is clean and dry, shows no signs of overheating and that the springs are not broken. Slide the disc onto the input shaft temporarily to make sure the fit is snug and the splines are not burred or worn.
11 Check the flatness of the pressure plate with a straightedge. Look for signs of overheating, cracks, grooves and ridges. The inner end of the release levers should not show any signs of uneven wear. Replace the pressure plate with a new one if its condition is in doubt.
12 Make sure the cover fits snugly on the flywheel dowels. Replace the cover with a new one if it fits loosely on the dowels.
13 Clean the old grease from the release bearing. Fill the cavities and coat the inner liner surfaces with multi-purpose grease.
14 Lubricate the rounded thrust pads and spring clip cavities of the fork with multi-purpose grease. Make sure the spring clips on the bearing are not distorted and then attach the fork to the bearing by sliding the thrust pads under the spring clips.
15 Position the clutch disc on the flywheel, centering it with an alignment tool.
16 With the disc held in place by the alignment tool, place the pressure plate assembly in position on the flywheel dowels, aligning it with the marks made at the time of removal **(see illustration)**.
17 Install the bolts and tighten them in a criss-cross pattern, one or two turns at a time, until they are at the specified torque.
18 Slide the fork and bearing assembly into position on the bearing pilot.
19 Install the release shaft bushings in the housing and slide the shaft into position. Retain the shaft with the clip which fits into the groove near the large bushing.
20 Install the release lever, retaining it to the shaft with the clip.
21 Install the transaxle.

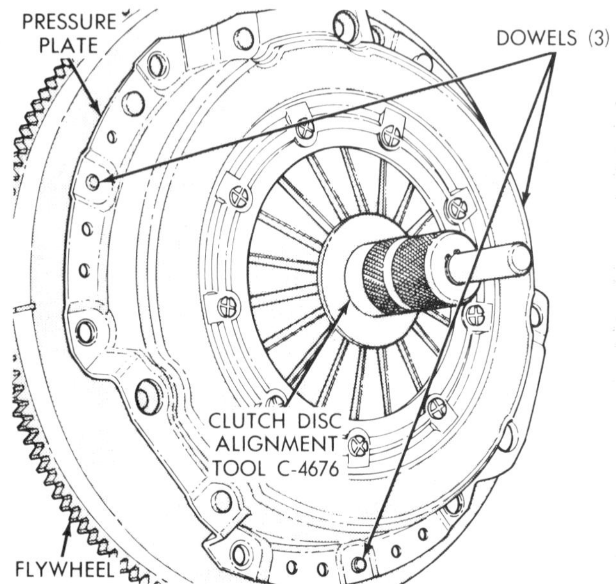

2.16 When installing the clutch disc and pressure plate, a clutch alignment tool must be used to center the disc

4.3 Use a socket to remove the intermediate shaft bearing mount bolts

3 Driveaxles, constant velocity (CV) joints and boots – check

Refer to illustration 3.1

1 The driveaxles, CV joints and boots **(see illustration)** should be inspected periodically and whenever the vehicle is raised, such as during chassis lubrication. The most common symptom of driveaxle or CV joint failure is knocking or clicking noises when turning.
2 Raise the vehicle and support it securely on jackstands.
3 Inspect the CV joint boots for cracks, leaks and broken retaining bands. If lubricant leaks out through a hole or crack in a boot, the CV joint will wear prematurely and require replacement. Replace any damaged boots immediately (Section 6).
4 Inspect the entire length of each axle for cracks, dents and signs of twisting and bending.
5 Grasp each axle, rotate it in both directions and move it in and out to check for excessive movement, indicating worn splines or loose CV joints.

4 Intermediate shaft (turbocharged models) – removal and installation

Refer to illustrations 4.3 and 4.6

Removal

1 Remove the right driveaxle (Section 5).
2 Remove the retaining bolt and push up on the speedometer cable to disengage the gear from the transaxle.
3 Remove the bearing mount assembly bolts **(see illustration)**.
4 Grasp the intermediate shaft/bearing assembly securely with both hands and withdraw it from the transaxle.
5 Have an assistant with a drain pan ready to catch the fluid which will pour from the transaxle with considerable force when the shaft is withdrawn.

3.1 Driveaxle and CV joint components

1 Right outer CV joint boot
2 Right inner CV joint boot
3 Intermediate shaft bearing mount
4 Intermediate shaft cardan joint
5 Transaxle extension
6 Transaxle
7 Left inner CV joint boot
8 Left outer CV joint boot

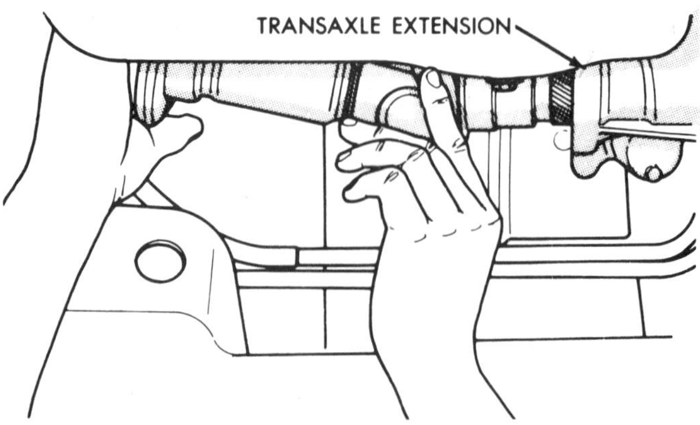

4.6 Support the intermediate shaft while inserting the splines into the transaxle extension

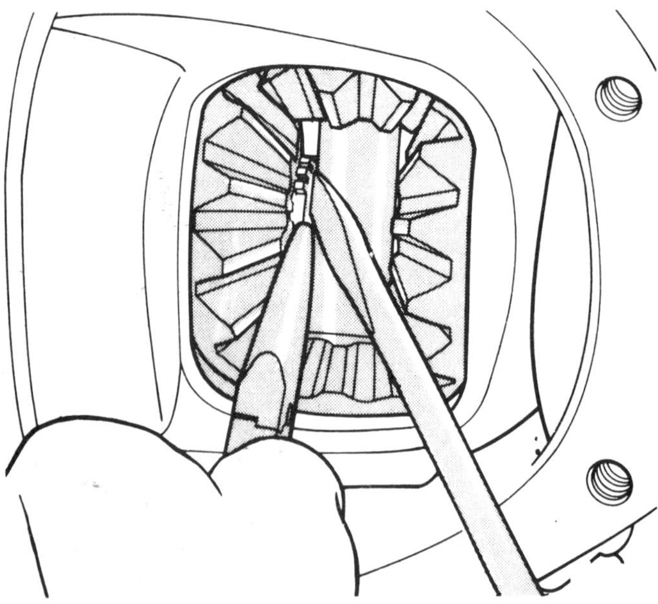

5.3b Compress the circlip tangs while pushing the shaft into the differential side gear

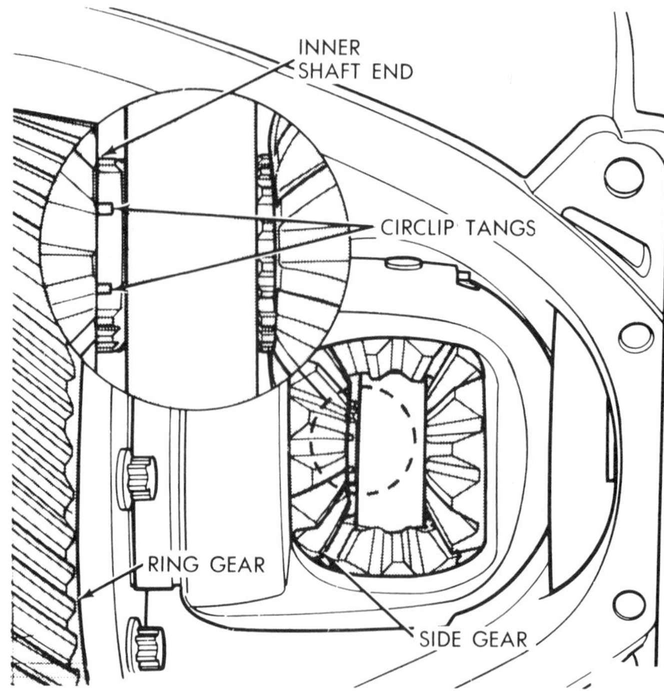

5.3a The driveaxle retaining circlips (arrows) are difficult to see and may be hard to reach with a pair of pliers

5.5 Remove the suspension arm-to-steering knuckle clamp bolt nut (arrow)

Installation

6 Place the intermediate shaft and bearing assembly in position and carefully insert the splined stub yoke into the transaxle extension housing **(see illustration)**.

7 Place the bearing mount in position and install the retaining bolts. Tighten the mount-to-engine bolts to the specified torque.

8 Lubricate the inside splines and the pilot bore of the intermediate shaft with a liberal coat of multi-purpose grease.

9 Install the right driveaxle.

5 Driveaxles – removal and installation

Refer to illustrations 5.3a, 5.3b, 5.5, 5.7, 5.8 and 5.22

Removal

1 Remove the front hub bearing cap, cotter pin, nut lock and wave washer. With the weight of the vehicle on the wheels and an assistant applying the brakes, loosen the axle nut.

2 Raise the vehicle, support it securely and remove the front wheel, axle nut and washer.

3 On some 1982 automatic transaxle equipped models the driveaxle inner ends are retained in the differential side gears by circlips which must be released prior to driveaxle removal. Remove the differential cover (Chapter 7) and rotate the driveaxle to expose the circlip tangs **(see illustration)**. Compress the circlip tangs with a pair of needle-nose pliers and use a screwdriver to push the axleshaft into the splined cavity of the side gear **(see illustration)**. Pull the axle out slightly.

4 On all models, remove the speedometer gear prior to removing the right axle.

5.7 Grasp the outer CV joint and pull the steering knuckle out to separate it from the driveaxle

5.8 Support both CV joints as the driveaxle is removed and do not pull on the shaft

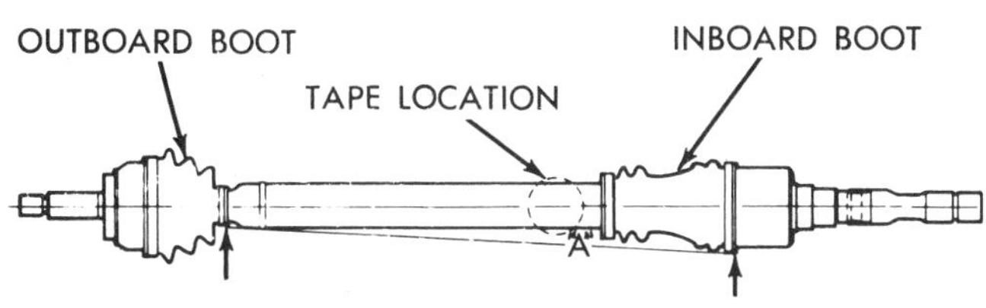

5.22 Measure each driveaxle between the points indicated by the arrows to verify correct length (A)

5 Remove the steering knuckle-to-balljoint clamp bolt **(see illustration)**.
6 Pry the lower balljoint stud out of the steering knuckle. **Note:** *the sway bar must be disconnected from the suspension arm to allow enough movement to separate the balljoint.*
7 Grasp the outer CV joint and the steering knuckle and pull the steering knuckle out to separate the driveaxle from the hub **(see illustration)**. Be careful not to damage the CV joint boot. **Caution:** *Do not pry on or damage the wear sleeve on the CV joint when separating it from the hub.*
8 Grasp the CV joints so they will be supported during removal and withdraw the driveaxle from the differential. **Caution:** *Do not pull on the shaft – pull only on the inner CV joint* **(see illustration)**.
9 The driveaxles, when in place, secure the hub bearing assemblies. If the vehicle is to be supported or moved on wheels while the driveaxles are removed, install a bolt through each hub and thread nuts onto them to keep the bearings from loosening.

Installation

10 Prior to installation, clean the wear sleeve on the driveaxle outer CV joint and the seal in the hub. Lubricate the entire circumference of the seal lip and fill the seal cavity with grease. Apply a 1/4-inch bead of grease to the wear sleeve seal contact area as well.
11 On circlip equipped driveaxles, install new circlips in the inner CV joint shaft grooves.
12 Apply a small amount of multi-purpose grease to the splines at each end of the driveaxle. Place the driveaxle in position and carefully insert the inner end of the shaft into the transaxle.
13 Push the steering knuckle out and insert the outer splined shaft of the CV joint into the hub.
14 Rejoin the balljoint stud to the steering knuckle, install the clamp bolt and tighten it to the specified torque.
15 Install the sway bar ends, if removed (see Chapter 10).
16 On circlip equipped driveaxle models, install the differential cover (Chapter 7).
17 Install the speedometer gear.
18 Install the wheels, the washers and the axle nuts.
19 Tighten the driveaxle nuts to the specified torque and install the wave washers, the nut locks and **new** cotter pins.

Driveaxle position check

20 These vehicles have engine mounts with slotted holes which allow for side-to-side positioning of the engine. If the vertical bolts on the right or left upper engine mounts have been loosened for any reason, or if the vehicle has been damaged structurally at the front end, driveaxle length must be checked/corrected. A driveaxle that is shorter than required will result in objectionable noise, while a driveaxle that is longer than necessary may result in damage.
21 The vehicle must be completely assembled, the front wheels must be properly aligned and pointing straight ahead and the weight of the vehicle must be on all four wheels.
22 Using a tape measure, check the distance from the inner edge of the outboard boot to the inner edge of the inboard boot on both driveaxles. Take the measurement at the lower edge of the driveaxles (six o'clock position) **(see illustration)**. Note that the required dimension varies with engine type, transaxle type and driveaxle manufacturer.
23 If the dimensions are not as specified, the engine mount bolts can be loosened and the engine repositioned to obtain the specified driveaxle lengths. If the engine cannot be moved enough within the range of the slotted engine mounts, check for damaged or distorted support brackets and side rails.
24 If the engine is moved, refer to Chapter 7 and adjust the shift linkage.

6 Constant velocity (CV) joints – disassembly, inspection and reassembly

Refer to illustrations 6.2, 6.4, 6.6, 6.7, 6.8, 6.9a, 6.9b, 6.11a, 6.11b, 6.15, 6.16a, 6.16b, 6.16c, 6.18, 6.19, 6.23, 6.25a, 6.25b, 6.25c, 6.26a, 6.26b, 6.31a, 6.31b, 6.31c, 6.35, 6.36, 6.37, 6.38, 6.41, 6.43, 6.44, 6.45a, 6.45b, 6.45c, 6.45d and 6.49

1 Obtain a CV joint rebuild or replacement kit.

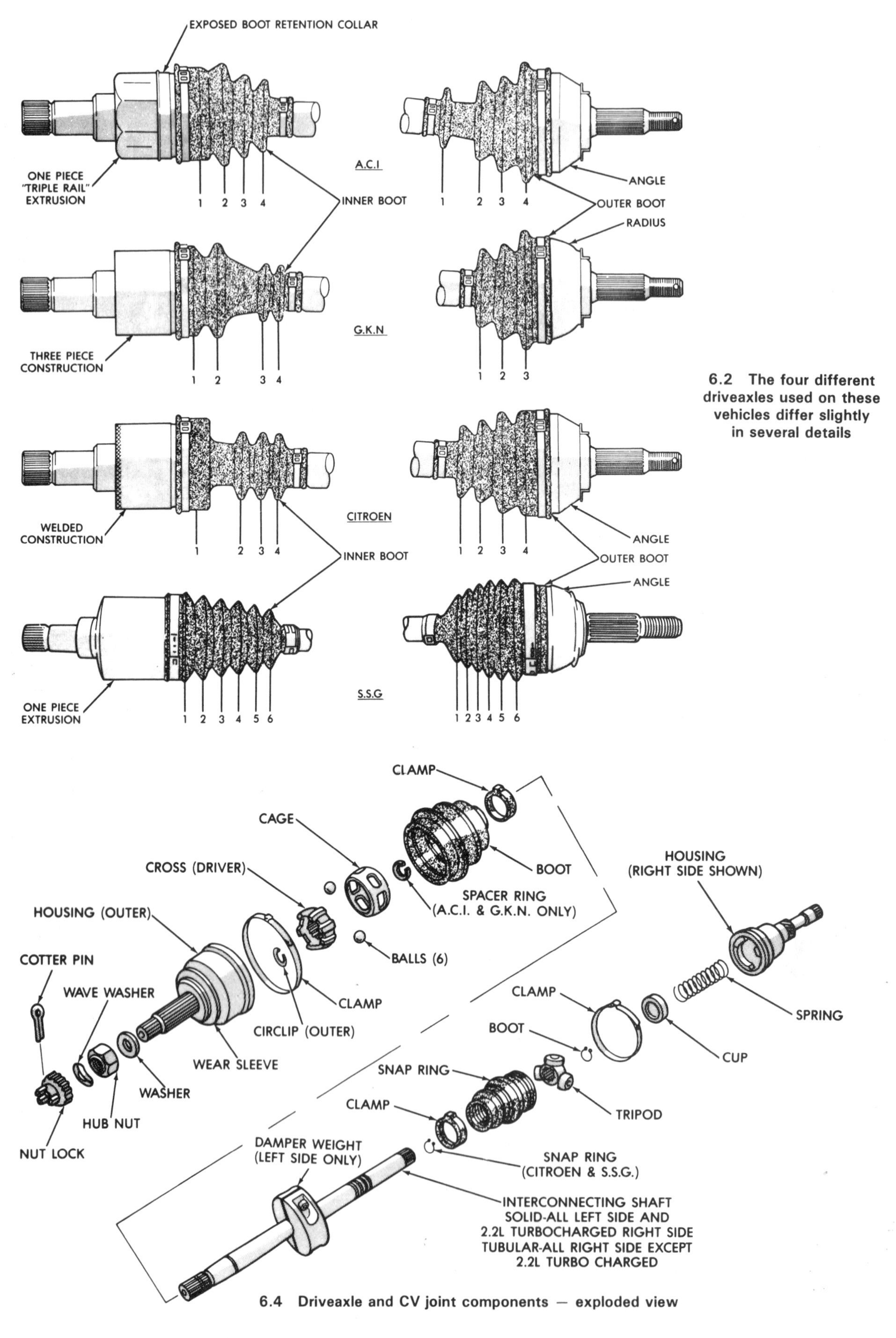

6.2 The four different driveaxles used on these vehicles differ slightly in several details

6.4 Driveaxle and CV joint components — exploded view

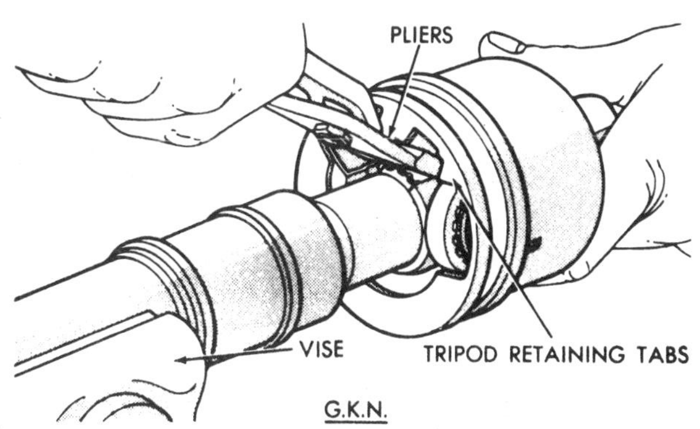

6.6 To separate the inner joint tripod from the housing on GKN driveaxles, the retaining tabs must be bent up with a pair of pliers

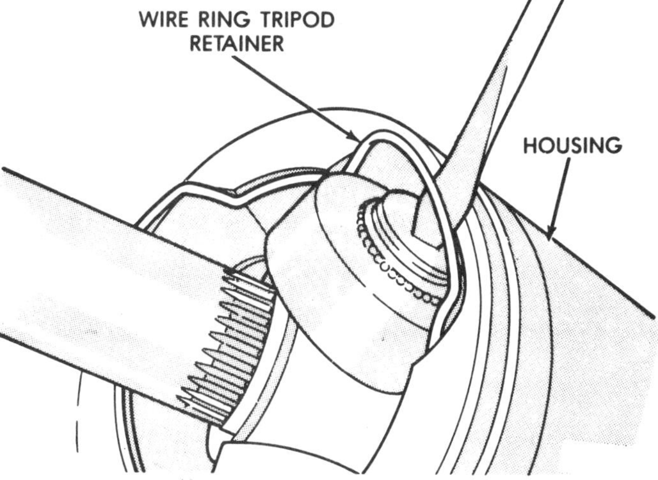

6.8 Use a screwdriver to pry the SSG driveaxle CV joint tripod wire retaining ring out of the housing

6.7 Carefully pry up on the retainer ring at each bearing roller to disassemble Citroen driveaxle inner CV joints

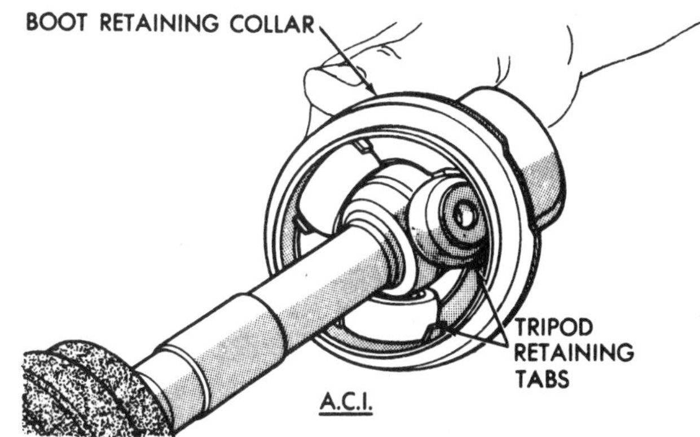

6.9a On 1984 ACI driveaxles, align the rollers with the tabs and snap them out, one at a time

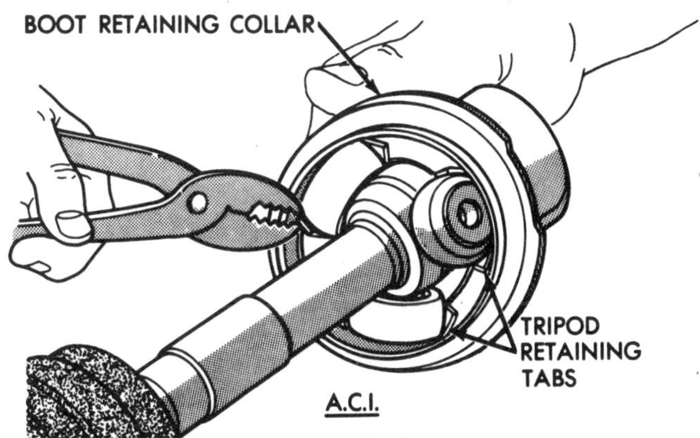

6.9b On 1985 and later model ACI driveaxles, compress the spring and bend each tab back with a pair of pliers to remove the tripod

2 Remove the driveaxles (Section 5) and identify which type they are **(see Section 1 and the accompanying illustration)**.

3 Place one of the driveaxles in a vise, using wood blocks to protect it from the vise jaws, so the CV joint can be easily worked on. If the CV joint has been operating properly with no noise or vibration, replace the boot as described in Section 7. If the CV joint is badly worn or has run for some time with no lubricant due to a damaged boot, it should be disassembled and inspected.

Inner CV joint

4 Remove the clamps and slide the boot back to gain access to the tripod retention system **(see illustration)**.

5 Depending on the type of CV joint assembly, separate the tripod from the housing as follows.

6 On GKN driveaxles, the retaining tabs are an integral part of the housing cover. Hold the housing and lightly compress the retention spring while bending the tabs back with a pair of pliers **(see illustration)**. Support the housing as the retention spring pushes it from the tripod. This will prevent the housing from reaching an unacceptable angle and keep the tripod rollers from being pulled from the tripod studs.

7 Citroen driveaxles utilize a tripod retainer ring which is rolled into a groove in the housing. Slightly deform the retainer ring at each roller with a screwdriver **(see illustration)**. The retention spring will push the housing from the tripod. The retainer ring can also be cut carefully from the housing. New rings are included in the rebuild kit and can be installed by rolling the edge into the machined groove in the housing with a hammer and punch.

8 On SSG driveaxles the tripod is retained in the housing by a wire ring. Pry the ring out of the groove with a screwdriver and slide the tripod from the housing **(see illustration)**.

9 On ACI driveaxles, the tripod retaining pads are part of the boot retaining collar which is staked in place. On 1984 models, place the housing in position so that the three rollers are flush with the retaining tabs. Pull the housing while angling the joint slightly so that the rollers can be snapped through the tabs, one at a time. Be careful not to angle the joint too far as this could cause the tripod rollers to be pulled from the studs. On 1985 and later models, compress the retaining spring lightly while bending the tabs back with a pair of pliers **(see illustrations)**. Be sure to support the housing as the spring pushes it from the tripod.

10 When removing the housing from the tripod, hold the rollers in place on the studs to prevent the rollers and needle bearings from falling. After the tripod is out of the housing, secure the rollers in place with tape.

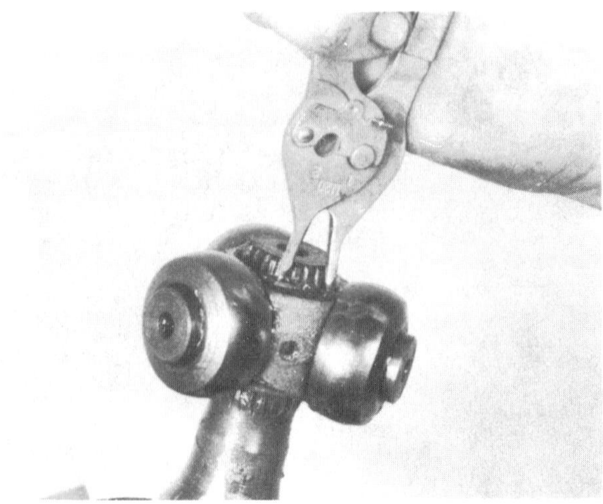
6.11a The tripod is held on the shaft with a snap-ring

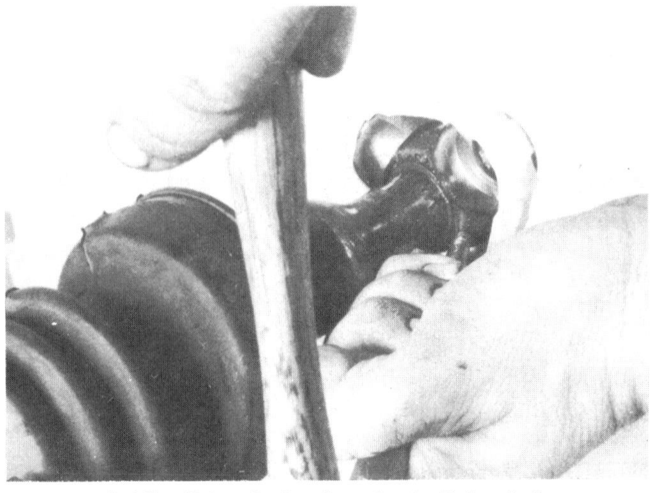
6.11b Drive the bearing tripod off the shaft (note the tape retaining the bearings)

6.15 Detach the Citroen driveaxle retainer ring with a pair of pliers

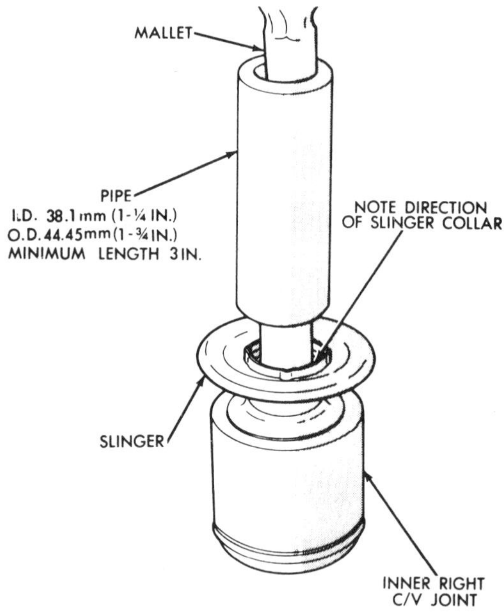

6.16a 1984 turbocharged model inner right CV joint slinger collar installation

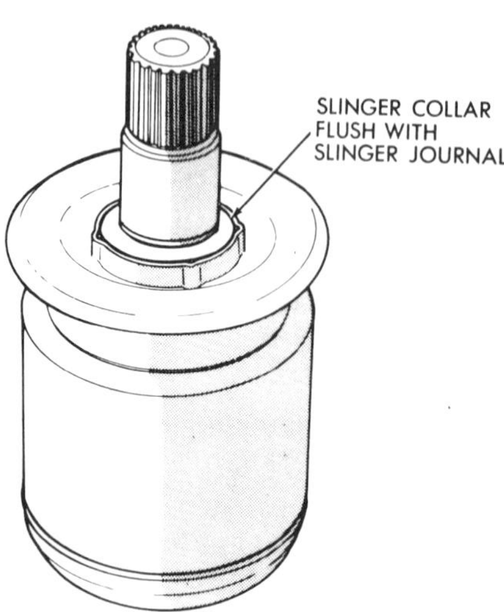

6.16b Proper installation of the 1984 turbocharged model right inner slinger

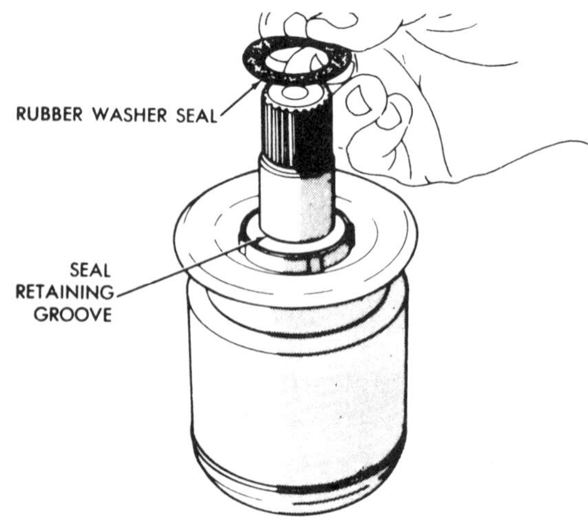

6.16c Install the rubber seal washer over the splines and into the retaining groove (1984 turbocharged models)

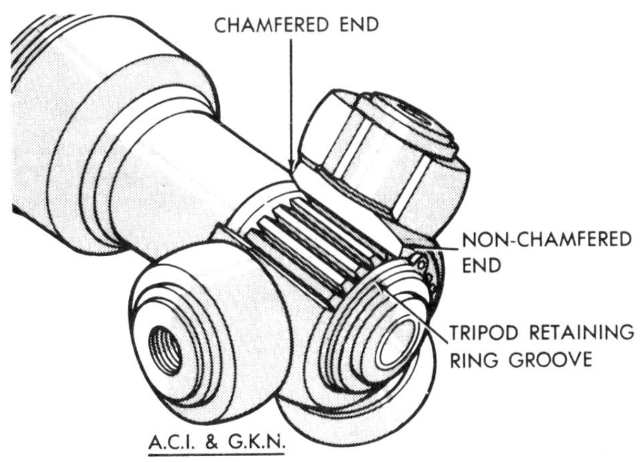

6.18 On GKN and ACI driveaxles, the non-chamfered end of the tripod must face OUT when it is installed on the shaft

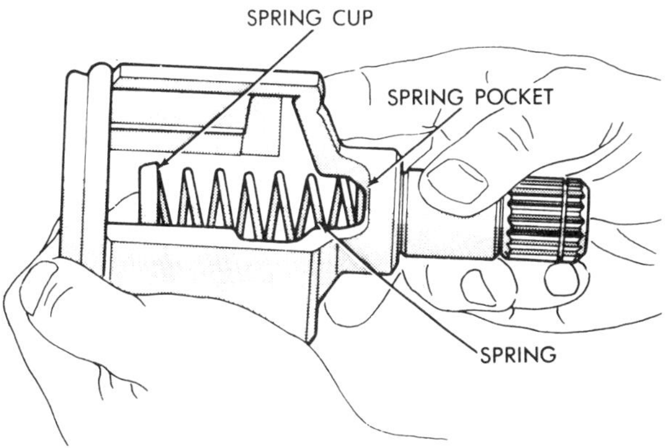

6.23 When assembling the inner CV joint, make sure the spring is seated in the housing pocket and position the cup with the concave side OUT

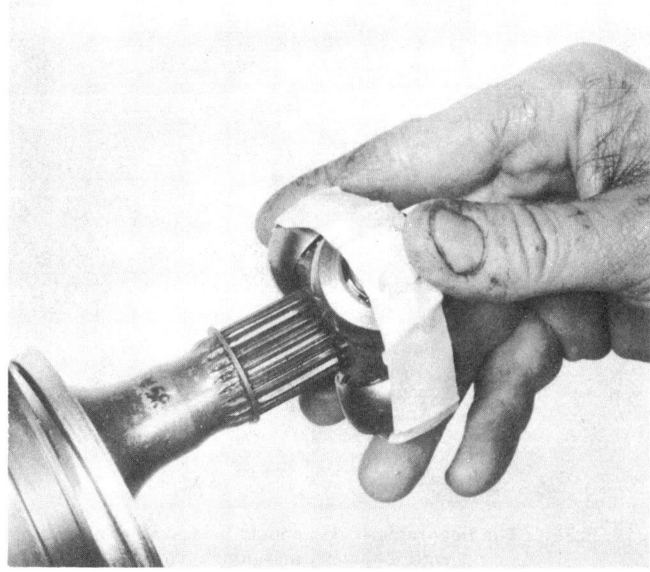

6.19 On GKN driveaxles, make sure the tripod assembly is installed correctly (Citroen and SSG driveaxles are equipped with tripods that can be installed either way)

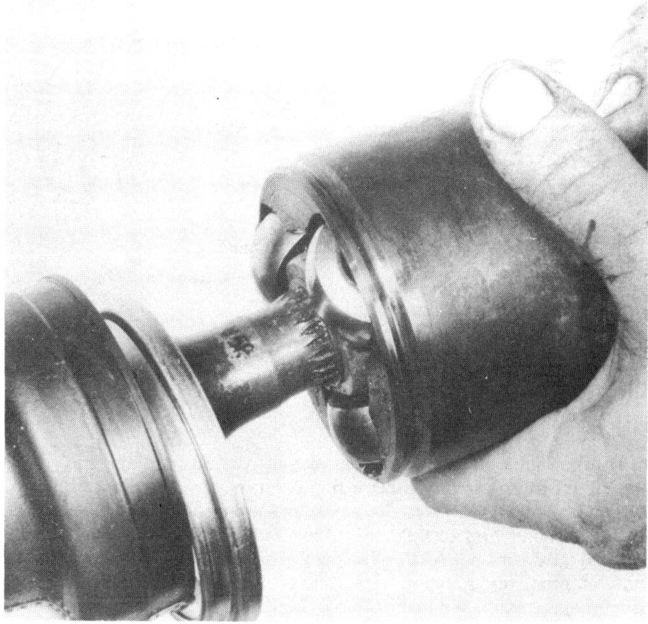

6.25a Make sure the bearing grooves in the housing have been greased, then slide the housing over the tripod until it bottoms

11 Remove the snap-ring **(see illustration)** and use a brass drift to drive the bearing and tripod assembly from the splined shaft **(see illustration)**.
12 Clean the grease from the tripod assembly. Check for scoring, wear, corrosion and excessive play and replace any damaged or worn components with new ones.
13 Inspect the inner splined area of the bearing tripod for wear and damage, replacing parts as necessary.
14 Remove all of the old grease from the housing. Inspect the housing splines, ball raceways, spring, spring cup and the spherical end of the shaft for wear, damage, nicks and corrosion, replacing parts as necessary.
15 Place the housing in a vise and remove the retainer ring with a pair of pliers **(see illustration)**.
16 On 1984 turbocharged models, install a new slinger on the right inner housing **(see illustrations)**.
17 Install the new boot on the axle.
18 On GKN and ACI driveaxles, slide the tripod onto the shaft with the non-chamfered end facing out (next to the snap-ring groove) **(see illustration)**.
19 Citroen and SSG driveaxles are equipped with tripods that can be installed with either end out (both ends are the same) **(see illustration)**. Be sure to first install the wire ring tripod retainer on the interconnecting shaft before sliding the tripod onto the shaft.
20 If necessary, use a section of pipe or a socket and a hammer to carefully tap the tripod onto the shaft until it just clears the snap-ring groove.
21 Install a new snap-ring and make sure it is seated in the groove.
22 On GKN driveaxles, distribute two of the three packets of grease supplied with the kit in the boot and the remaining packet in the housing. On ACI driveaxles, distribute one of the two supplied packs of grease in the boot and the remaining pack in the housing. On SSG driveaxles, distribute one half pack in the housing and the rest in the boot. On Citroen driveaxles, distribute two-thirds of the grease in the packet in the boot and the remaining amount in the housing. Make sure the grease is applied to the bearing grooves in the housing.
23 Position the spring in the housing spring pocket with the cup attached to the exposed end of the spring **(see illustration)**. Apply a small amount of grease to the concave surface of the spring cup.
24 On GKN driveaxles, slip the tripod into the housing and bend the retaining ring tabs down to their original positions. Make sure the tabs can hold the tripod in the housing.
25 On Citroen driveaxles slide the housing over the tripod until it bottoms **(see illustration)**. Install a new retainer ring by rolling the edge

6.25b The new retainer ring should be staked in place with a hammer and punch

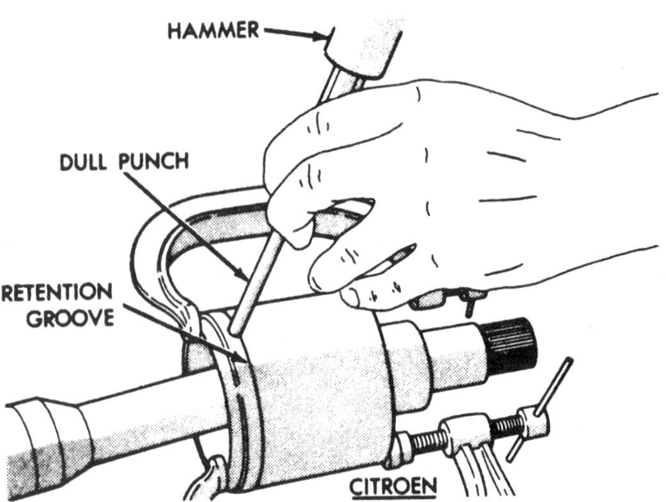

6.25c If the retainer ring is difficult to hold in place while staking it into the groove, use C-clamps to steady it

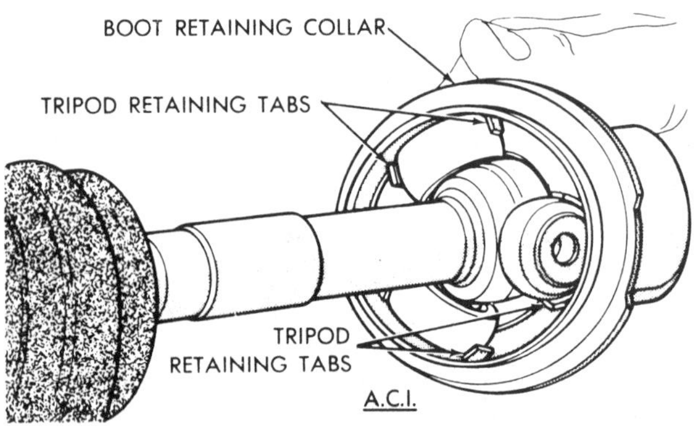

6.26a On 1984 model ACI driveaxles, snap each roller into place, one at time

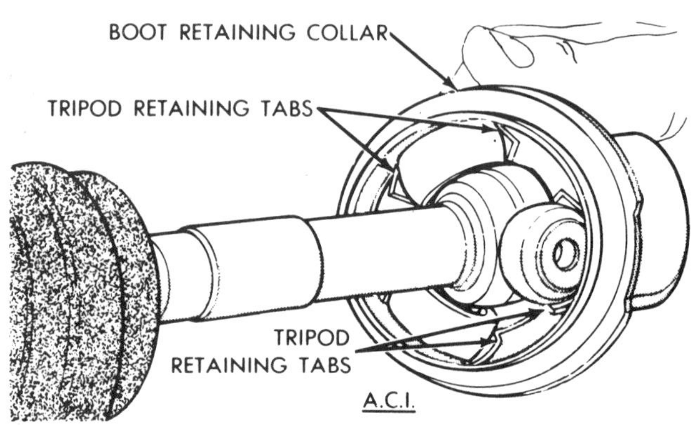

6.26b On 1985 and later ACI driveaxles, press the housing onto the tripod

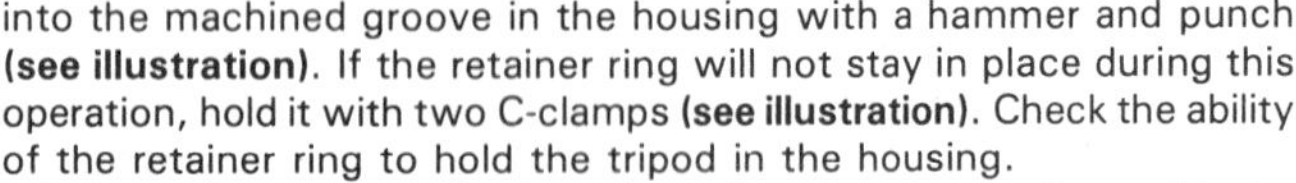

into the machined groove in the housing with a hammer and punch **(see illustration)**. If the retainer ring will not stay in place during this operation, hold it with two C-clamps **(see illustration)**. Check the ability of the retainer ring to hold the tripod in the housing.

26 On 1984 model ACI driveaxles, align the tripod rollers with the retaining tabs and housing tracks and snap one roller at a time through the retaining tabs **(see illustrations)**. Make sure the retaining tab holds the tripod securely in the housing. On 1985 and later model ACI driveaxles, slip the tripod into the housing but do not bend the retaining tabs back to their original positions. Reattach the boot instead, which will hold the housing on the shaft. When the driveaxle is reinstalled on the vehicle, make sure the tripod is re-engaged in the housing.

27 On SSG driveaxles, slip the tripod into the housing and install the wire retaining ring. Check to make sure the ring holds the tripod securely in the housing.

28 Make sure the retention spring is centered in the housing spring pocket when the tripod is installed and seated in the spring cup.

29 Install the boot and retaining clamp (Section 7).

Outer CV joint

30 Mount the axleshaft in a vise with wood blocks to protect it, remove the boot clamps and push the boot back.

31 Wipe the grease from the joint. On GKN, ACI and Citroen driveaxles, use a soft-face hammer to drive the housing from the axle **(see illustrations)**. Support the CV joint as this is done and rap the housing sharply on the outer edge to dislodge it from the internal circlip installed on the shaft. On SSG driveaxles a circlip located in a groove in the cross locks the outer joint to the shaft **(see illustration)**. Loosen the damper weight bolts, mark its position and slide the weight and the boot toward the inner joint. Remove the circlip with snap-ring pliers and slide the inner joint off the axle.

32 Slide the boot off the driveaxle. If the CV joint was operating properly and the grease does not appear to be contaminated, just replace the boot (Section 7). Bypass the following disassembly procedure. If the CV joint was noisy, proceed with the disassembly procedure to determine if it should be replaced with a new one.

33 Remove the circlip from the driveaxle groove and discard it (the rebuild kit will include a new circlip). GKN and ACI driveaxles are equipped with a large spacer ring, which must not be removed unless the driveaxle is being replaced with a new one.

34 Clean the axle spline area and inspect for wear, damage, corrosion and broken splines.

35 Clean the outer CV joint bearing assembly with a clean cloth to remove excess grease. Mark the relative position of the bearing cage, cross and housing **(see illustration)**.

36 Grip the housing shaft securely in the wood blocks in the vise. Push down one side of the cage and remove the ball bearing from the opposite side. Repeat the procedure in a criss-cross pattern until all of the balls are removed **(see illustration)**. If the joint is tight, tap on the cross (not the cage) with a hammer and brass drift.

37 Remove the bearing assembly from the housing by tilting it vertically and aligning two opposing elongated cage windows in the area between the ball grooves **(see illustration)**.

38 Turn the cross 90 degrees to the cage and align one of the spherical

6.31a On ACI, GKN and Citroen driveaxles, the outer joint housing can be dislodged from the shaft circlip with a soft-face hammer . . .

6.31b . . . and removed by hand

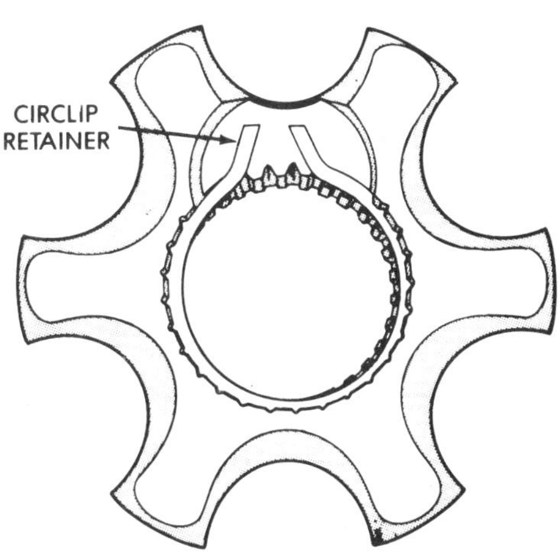

6.31c The SSG driveaxle outer joint is retained by a circlip

6.35 Mark the bearing cage, cross and housing relationship after removing the grease

6.36 With the cage and cross tilted, the balls can be removed one at a time

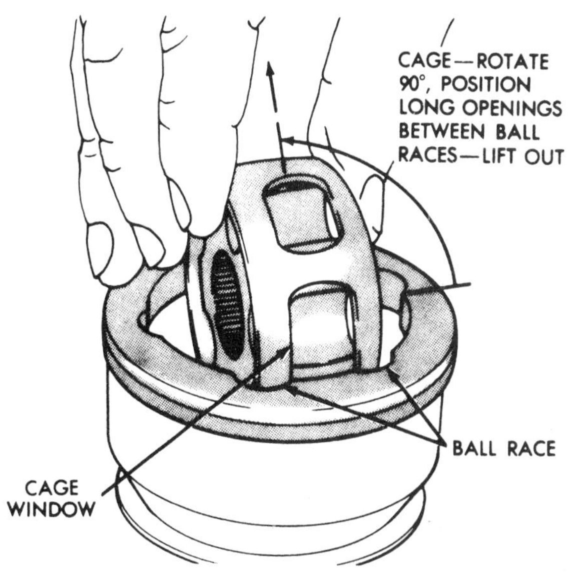

6.37 Bearing cage and cross removal details (outer CV joint)

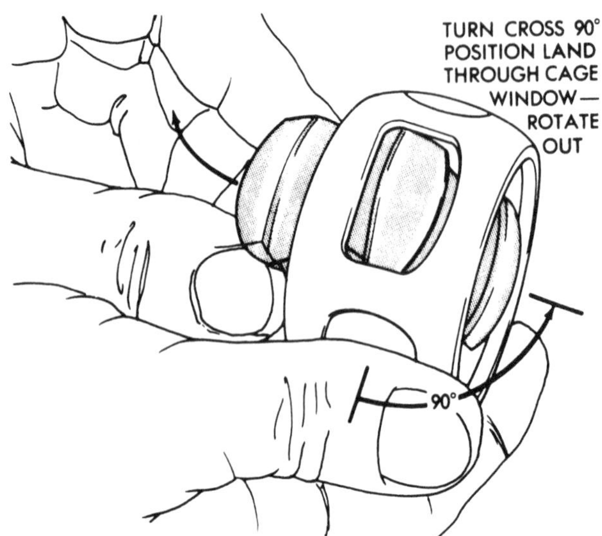

6.38 Bearing cross removal details (outer CV joint)

6.41 The wear sleeve can be pried off the housing with a large screwdriver if replacement is necessary

6.43 The bearing cross will slide into the cage by aligning one of the lands with the elongated window in the cage

6.44 Lower the cage and cross assembly into the housing with the elongated window aligned with the race

lands with an elongated cage window. Raise the land into the window and swivel the cross out of the cage **(see illustration)**.

39 Clean all of the parts with solvent and dry them with compressed air (if available).

40 Inspect the housing, splines, balls and races for damage, corrosion, wear and cracks. Check the bearing cross for wear and scoring in the races. If any of the components are not serviceable, the entire CV joint assembly must be replaced with a new one.

41 Check the outer housing wear sleeve for damage and distortion. If it is damaged or worn, pry the sleeve from the housing **(see illustration)** and replace it with a new one. A special tool is made for this purpose, but a large section of pipe will work if care is exercised (do not nick or gouge the seal mating surface).

42 Apply a thin coat of oil to all CV joint components before beginning reassembly.

43 Align the marks and install the cross in the cage so one of the cross lands fits into the elongated window **(see illustration)**.

44 Rotate the cross into position in the cage and install the assembly in the CV joint housing, again using the elongated window for clearance **(see illustration)**.

45 Rotate the cage into position in the housing. On GKN and ACI driveaxles, the large cross counterbore must face out **(see illustration)**. On Citroen driveaxles, the cage and cross chamfers must face out **(see illustration)**. On SSG driveaxles,the circlip in the cross must face out **(see illustration)**. The marks made during disassembly should face out and be aligned **(see illustration)**.

46 Pack the lubricant from the kit into the ball races and grooves.

47 Install the balls into the elongated holes, one at a time, until they are all in position.

48 Place the driveaxle in the vise and slide the boot over it. On ACI, GKN and Citroen driveaxles, install a new circlip in the axle groove, taking care not to twist it. SSG driveaxles have a reuseable circlip which is part of the driver assembly.

49 Place the CV joint housing in position on the axle, align the splines and rap it sharply with a soft-face hammer **(see illustration)**. Make sure it is seated on the circlip by attempting to pull it from the shaft.

50 Install the boot (Section 7).

51 Install the driveaxle (Section 5).

JOINT HOUSING
BOOT RETAINING GROOVE-A.C.I.
CROSS-LARGE COUNTERBORE OUT
WEAR SLEEVE
CROSS-SMALL COUNTERBORE INWARD
BOOT RETAINING SHOULDER-G.K.N.

6.45a On GKN and ACI driveaxles, make sure the large cross counterbore faces OUT when the CV joint is reassembled

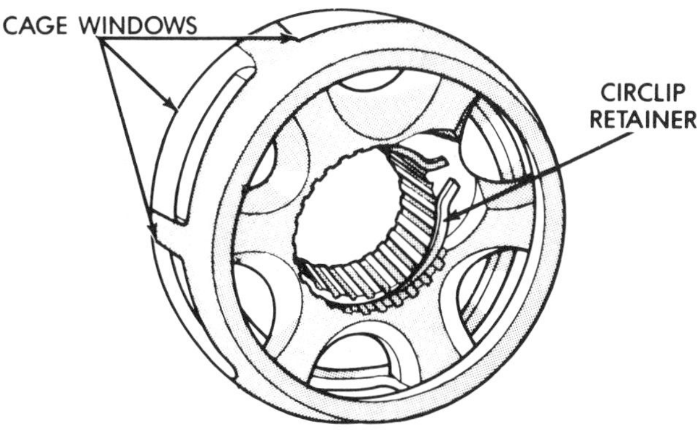

6.45c On SSG driveaxles, the circlip in the cross must face OUT

7 Constant velocity (CV) joint boots — removal and installation

Refer to illustrations 7.9, 7.11, 7.12, 7.18, 7.19, 7.21a, 7.21b, 7.22, 7.23a, 7.23b and 7.23c

Note: *If the instructions supplied with the replacement boot kit differ from the instructions here, follow the ones with the new boots. A special tool is required to install the factory-supplied boot clamps, so it may be a good idea to leave the entire procedure to a dealer service department. Do-it-yourself kits which offer greatly simplified installation may be available for your vehicle. Consult your auto parts counterman or your local dealer for more information on these kits.*

1 If the boot is cut, torn or leaking, it must be replaced and the CV joint inspected as soon as possible. Even a small amount of dirt in the joint can cause premature wear and failure. Obtain a replacement boot kit before beginning this procedure.
2 Remove the driveaxle (Section 4).
3 Disassemble the CV joint and remove the boot as described in Section 6.
4 Inspect the CV joint to determine if it has been damaged by contamination or running with too little lubricant. If you have any doubts about the condition of the joint components, perform the inspection procedures described in Section 5.

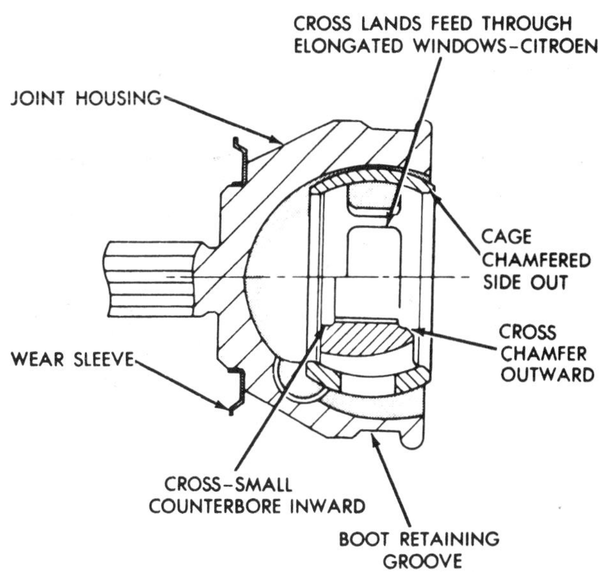

6.45b On Citroen driveaxles, make sure the cross and cage chamfers face OUT when the CV joint is reassembled

6.45d Make sure the marks are aligned properly and that the bearing cross is installed with the correct side out (see text for details)

6.49 Strike the end of the housing shaft with a soft-face hammer to engage it with the shaft circlip

5 Clean the old lubricant from the CV joint and repack it with the lubricant supplied with the kit.
6 Pack the interior of the new boot with the remaining lubricant.
7 Install the boot and clamps as follows.

GKN, SSG and ACI driveaxles

8 GKN units generally are equipped with metal ladder-type clamps. However, two alternate clamps are also used. They include a small rubber clamp at the shaft end of the inner CV joint and a large spring-type clamp on the housing.
9 If so equipped, slide the small rubber clamp over the shaft. Slide the small end of the boot over the shaft and position it as follows: On right inner joints, the small end of the boot lip must be aligned with the mark on the shaft. On left inner and all outer joints, position the small end of the boot in the groove in the shaft **(see illustration)**.
10 Place the rubber clamp in the boot groove (if so equipped) or install the metal clamp.
11 Make sure the boot is properly located on the shaft, then locate the metal clamp tangs in the slots, making the clamp as tight as possible by hand **(see illustration)**.
12 Squeeze the clamp bridge with tool number C-4124 to complete the tightening procedure **(see illustration)**. Do not cut through the clamp bridge or damage the rubber boot.
13 Reassemble the CV joints and driveaxle components (Section 6).
14 Locate the large end of the boot over the shoulder or in the groove in the housing (make sure the boot is not twisted).
15 Install the spring-type clamp or ladder-type clamp. If a ladder-type clamp is used, repeat the tightening procedure described in Steps 11 and 12.

Citroen driveaxles

16 Slide the boot over the shaft. If installing an outer CV joint boot, position the vent sleeve under the boot clamp groove.
17 On right inner joints, align the boot lip face with the inboard edge of the part number label. If the label is missing, use the mark left by the original boot. On left inner and all outer joints, position the boot between the locating shoulders and align the edge of the lip with the mark made by the original boot. **Note:** *Clamping procedures are identical for attaching the boot to the shaft and the CV joint housing.*

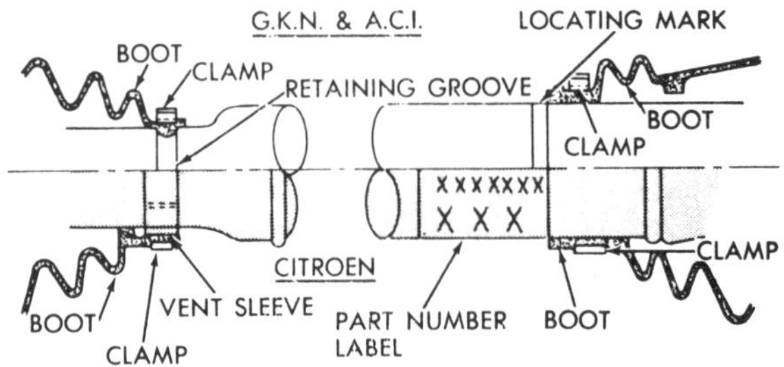

7.9 CV joint rubber boot installation details

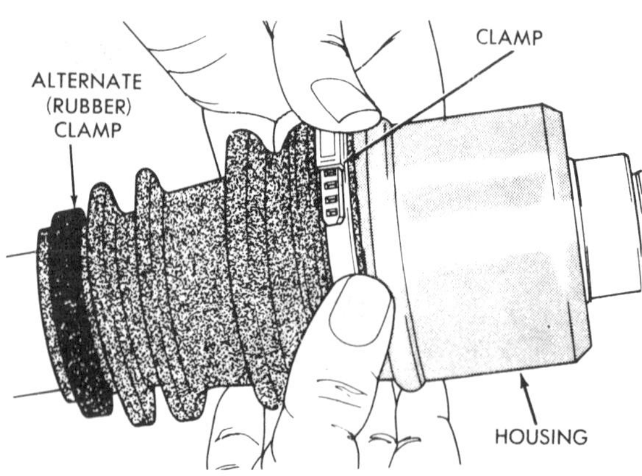

7.11 Installing a ladder-type boot clamp by hand (GKN driveaxles) (note the rubber clamp installed on the small end of the boot)

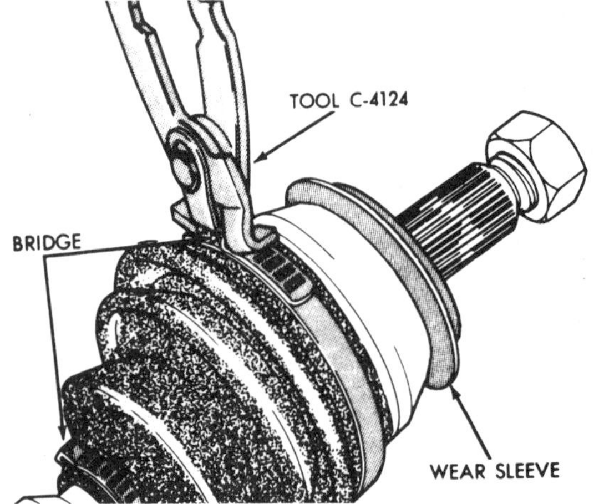

7.12 Squeezing the ladder-type boot clamp bridge with the special tool

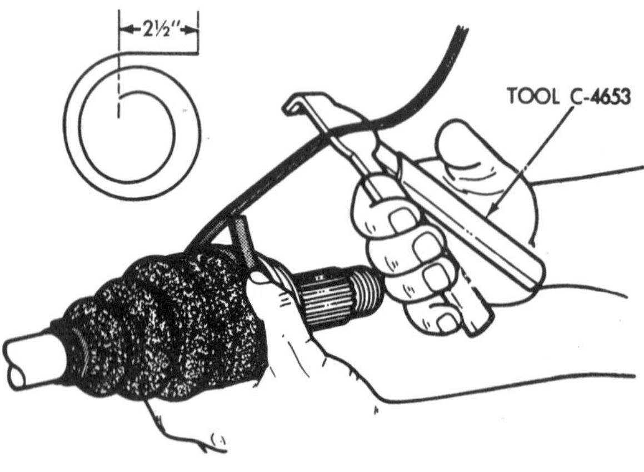

7.18 Wrap the clamp around the boot twice, leaving 2-1/2 inches of extra material, then cut it off

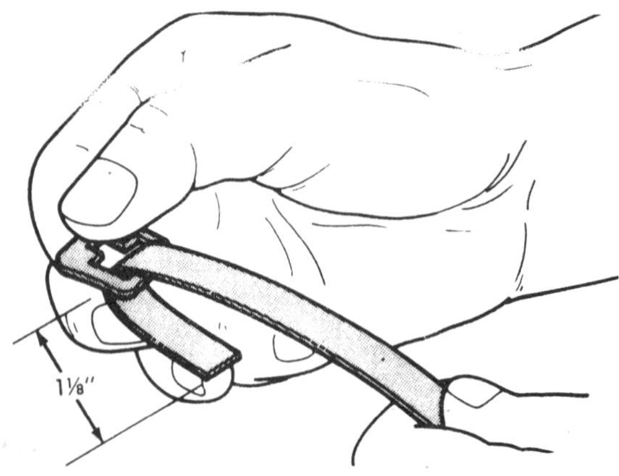

7.19 Pass the strap through the buckle and fold it back about 1-1/8 inch on the inside of the buckle

18 Wrap the clamping strap around the boot twice, plus 2-1/2 inches, and cut it off **(see illustration)**.

19 Pass the end of the strap through the buckle opening and fold it back about 1-1/8 inch on the inside of the buckle **(see illustration)**.

20 Position the clamping strap around the boot, on the clamping surface, with the eye of the buckle toward you. Wrap the strap around the boot once and pass it through the buckle, then wrap it around a second time and pass it through the buckle again.

21 Fold the strap back slightly to prevent it from unwinding itself **(see illustration)**, then open the special tool (C-4653) and place the strap in the narrow slot, about 1/2-inch from the buckle **(see illustration)**.

22 Hold the strap with one hand and push the tool forward and up slightly, then fit the tool hook into the buckle eye **(see illustration)**.

23 Tighten the strap by closing the tool handles **(see illustration)**, then rotate the tool down slowly while releasing the pressure on the handles **(see illustration)**. Allow the handles to open progressively, then open the tool all the way and slide it sideways off the strap. **Caution:** *Never fold the strap back or rotate the tool down while squeezing the handles together (if this is done, the strap will be broken)* **(see illustration)**.

24 If the strap is not tight enough, repeat the procedure. Always engage the tool about 1/2-inch from the buckle. Make sure the strap moves smoothly as tightening force is applied and do not allow the buckle to fold over as the strap passes through it.

25 When the strap is tight, cut it off 1/8-inch above the buckle and fold it back neatly. It must not overlap the edge of the buckle.

26 Repeat the procedure for the remaining boot clamps.

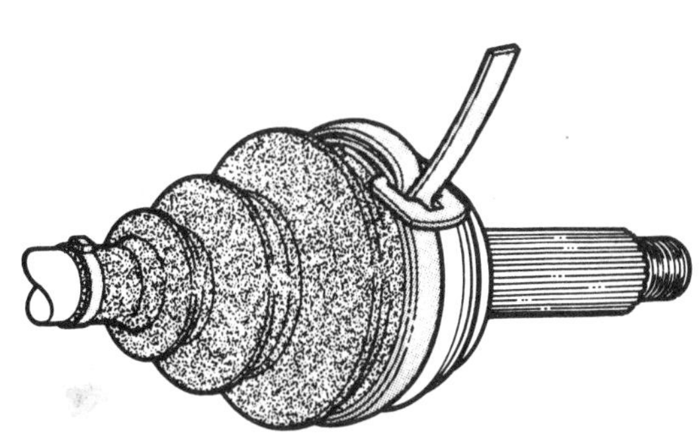

7.21a After installing it on the boot, bend the strap back so it doesn't unwind

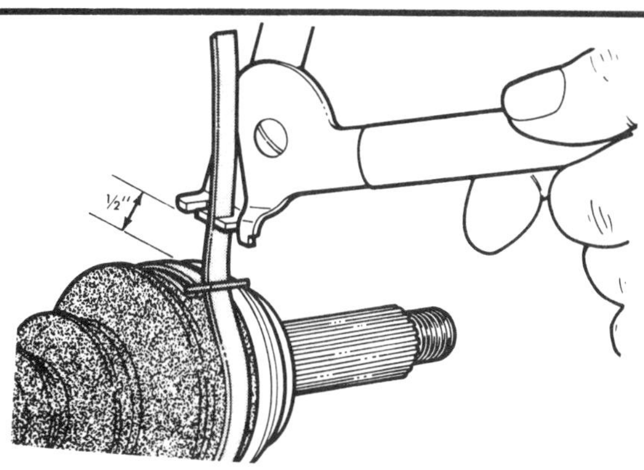

7.21b Attach the special tool about 1/2-inch from the buckle, . . .

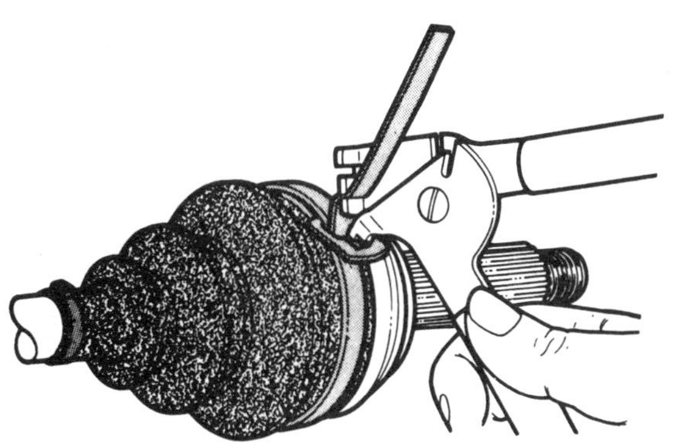

7.22 . . . then push the tool forward and up and engage the hook in the buckle eye

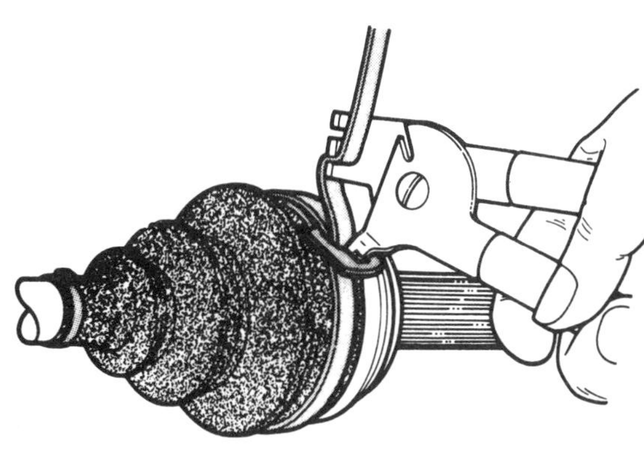

7.23a Close the tool handles slowly to tighten the clamp strap, . . .

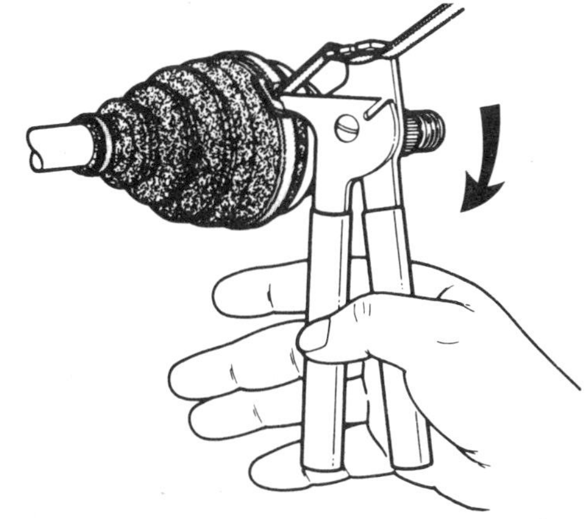

7.23b . . . then rotate the tool down while releasing the pressure on the handles (allow the handles to open)

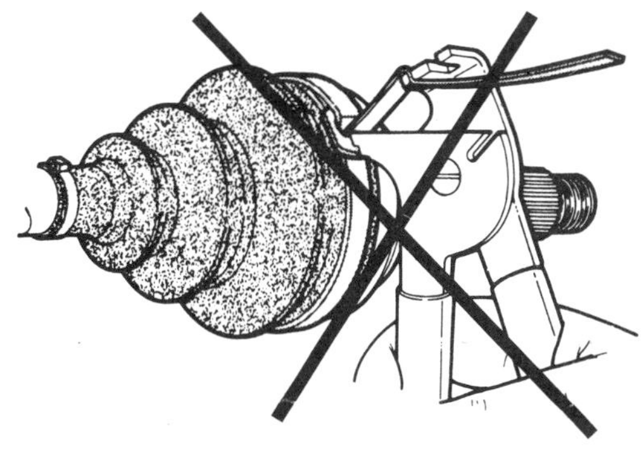

7.23c DO NOT rotate the tool down while applying pressure to the handles

8

Chapter 9 Brakes

Contents

Specifications

General

Brake fluid type	See Chapter 1

Drum brakes

Standard drum diameter	
1982 and 1983	
Standard	7.87 in (200 mm)
Heavy duty	8.66 in (220 mm)
1984 on	8.66 in (220 mm)
Minimum drum diameter	See marks on drum
Out-of-round limit	0.002 in (0.05 mm)
Runout limit	0.006 in (0.15 mm)
Brake lining thickness limit	See Chapter 1
Wheel cylinder bore diameter	
Standard	0.625 in (15.9 mm)
Heavy duty	0.563 in (14.3 mm)

Disc brakes

Pad thickness limit	See Chapter 1
Brake disc thickness	
Standard	0.930 to 0.940 in (23.87 to 24.13 mm)
Minimum	0.882 in (22.4 mm)*
Brake disc thickness variation limit (1-inch from edge)	0.0005 in (0.013 mm)
Brake disc runout limit (1-inch from edge)	0.005 in (0.13 mm)
Hub runout limit	0.003 in (0.08 mm)
Caliper bore honing limit	0.001 in (0.0254 mm)

** See marks on disc (they supersede information printed here)*

Torque specifications	Ft-lbs	Nm
Master cylinder-to-booster nuts	17 to 25	23 to 34
Power brake booster nuts	17 to 25	23 to 34
Wheel cylinder bolts	75 in-lbs	8
Backing plate-to-rear axle bolts	35 to 55	47 to 75
Disc brake caliper adapter bolts		
1982 and 1983	70 to 100	85 to 136
1984 on	130 to 190	176 to 258
Disc brake caliper guide pins		
ATE	18 to 26	25 to 35
Kelsey Hayes	25 to 35	34 to 47
Bearing retainer mounting bolt	17 to 25	23 to 34
Parking brake pedal assembly-to-cowl bolts	17 to 25	23 to 34

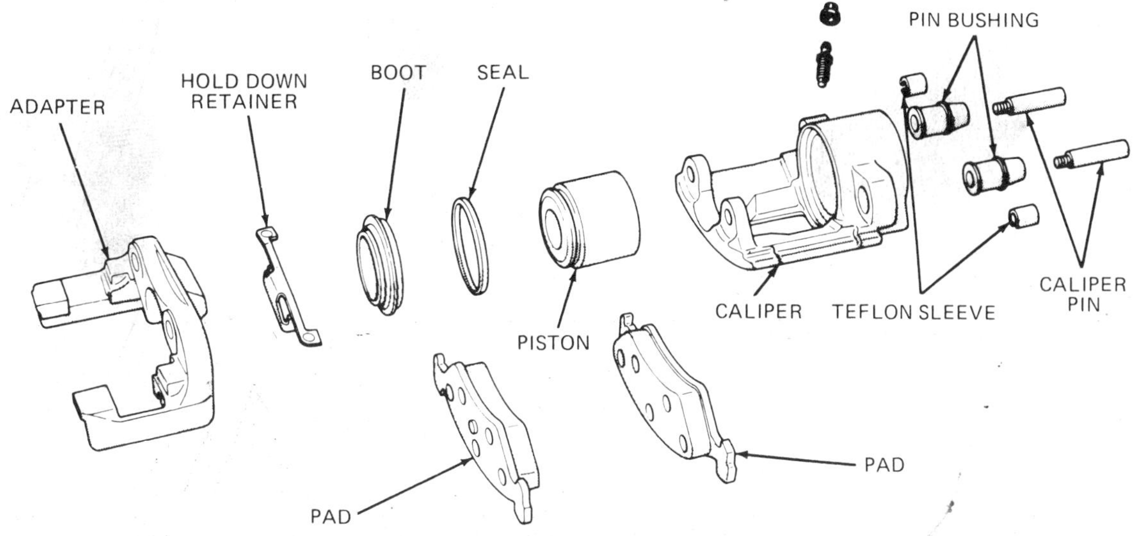

2.2a Kelsey Hayes disc brake caliper components — exploded view

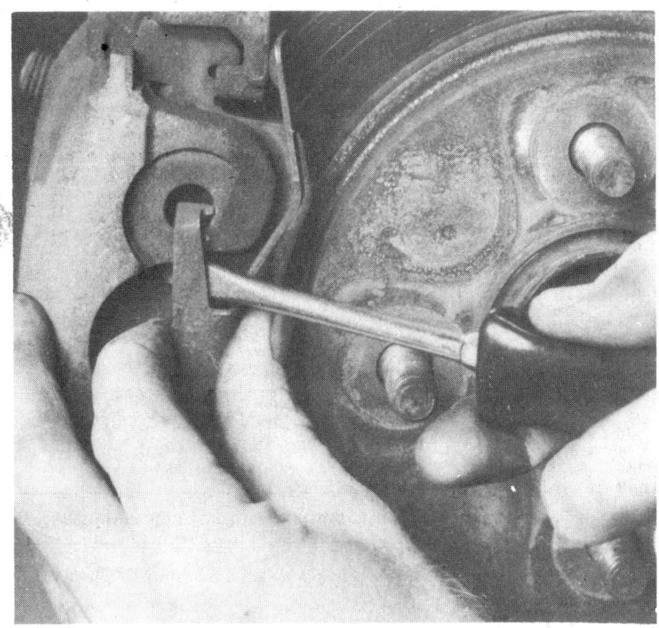

2.2b Push in on the hold down spring retainer and pry it out of the caliper

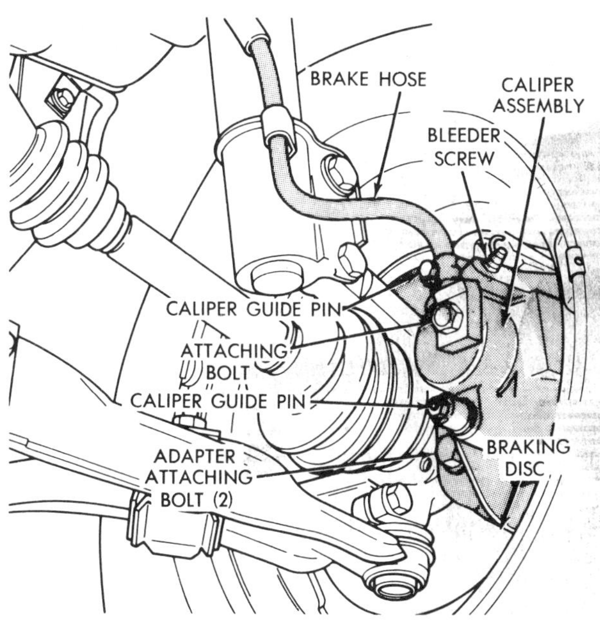

2.3 Loosen only the caliper guide pins, not the adapter attaching bolts

1 General information

All models are equipped with disc-type front and drum-type rear brakes which are hydraulically-operated and vacuum-assisted.

The front brakes feature a single piston, floating caliper design. Disc brake calipers from two different manufacturers are used on these models: ATE and Kelsey Hayes. The brakes differ in design and parts are not interchangeable.

The rear drum brakes are leading/trailing shoe type with a single pivot. Early model rear drum brakes (1982 only) require adjustment at specified intervals. Later models feature automatic adjustment.

Front drive vehicles tend to wear the front brake pads at a faster rate than rear drive vehicles. Consequently it is important to inspect the brake pads frequently to make sure they have not worn to the point where the disc itself is scored or damaged. Note that the pad thickness limit on these models includes the metal portion of the brake pad, not just the lining material (see Chapter 1).

All models are equipped with a cable-actuated parking brake which operates the rear brakes.

The hydraulic system is a dual line type with a dual master cylinder and separate systems for the front and rear brakes. In the event of brake line or seal failure, half the brake system will still operate.

9

2 Disc brake pads (Kelsey Hayes) — replacement

Refer to illustrations 2.2a, 2.2b, 2.3, 2.5, 2.6 and 2.7

Caution: *Disc brake pads must be replaced on both front wheels at the same time — never replace the pads on only one wheel. Disassemble one brake at a time so the remaining brake can be used as a guide if difficulties are encountered during reassembly.*

1 Raise the front of the vehicle and support it securely on jackstands. Block the rear wheels and set the parking brake, then remove the front wheels.

2 Remove the hold down retainer by pushing down at the center and prying it out with a screwdriver **(see illustrations)**.

3 Loosen the caliper guide pins enough to allow the caliper to be removed **(see illustration)**.

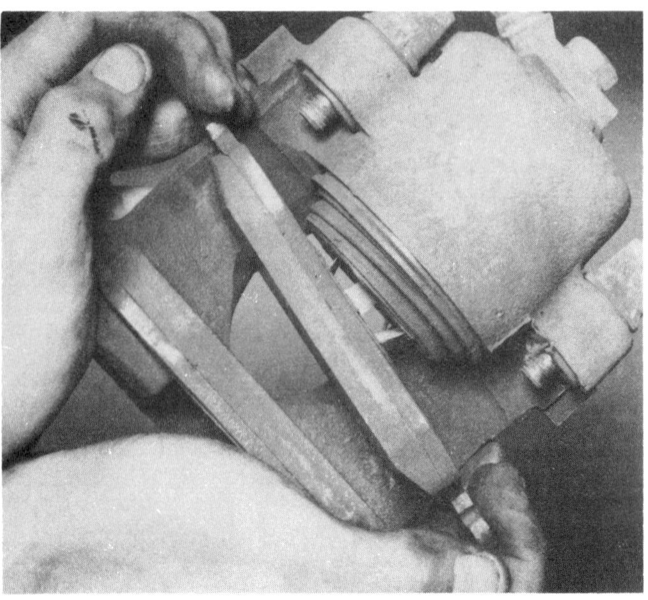

2.5 Remove the inner pad by pulling the retainer out of the piston

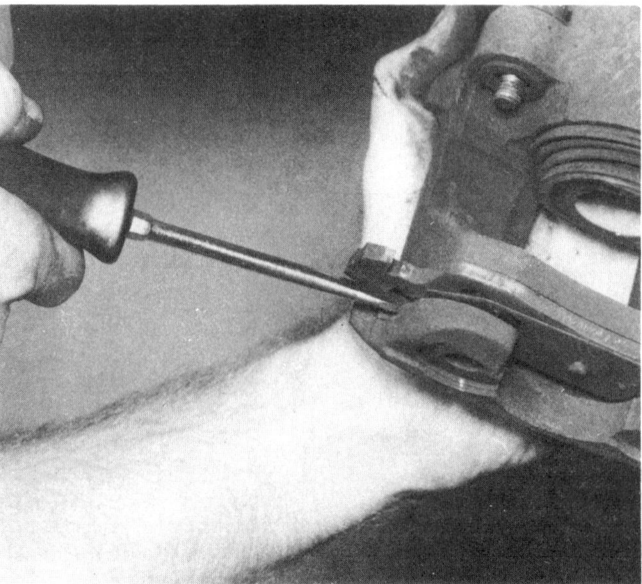

2.6 Pry the outer pad off the caliper if it is stuck

4 Move the caliper forward and off the adapter and brake disc. The inner pad will remain with the caliper.
5 Remove the inner pad by unsnapping the retainer from the piston **(see illustration)**.
6 Remove the outer pad from the adaptor. If the noise suppression gasket causes the pad to adhere to the caliper, pry it loose with a screwdriver **(see illustration)**.
7 Support the caliper out of the way with a wire hanger **(see illustration)**. **Warning:** *Do not allow the caliper to hang by the brake hose.*
8 Refer to Chapter 1 and compare the measured lining/backing material thickness to the Specifications there.
9 Inspect the caliper and adapter for wear, damage, rust and fluid leaks. If the caliper-to-adapter mating surfaces are rusty, clean them thoroughly with a wire brush (the caliper must be free to move as the brakes are applied).
10 Apply Mopar lubricant (no. 2932524) or high-temperature brake grease to the adapter-to-brake pad and caliper mating surfaces. Remove the protective paper from the noise suppression gasket on both pads. Install the inner brake pad by pressing the retainer into the piston recess. **Caution:** *Do not get any grease on the pad lining material, gasket surface or brake disc.*
11 Place the outer pad in position in the caliper.
12 Install the caliper over the brake disc and adapter.
13 Install the guide pins by hand, taking care not to cross-thread them. Tighten the guide pins to the specified torque.
14 Install the pad retainer.
15 Repeat the procedure for the remaining caliper.
16 The remaining steps are the reverse of disassembly. When installing the wheels and tires, tighten the lug nuts in a criss-cross pattern and work up to the specified torque in two steps (see Chapter 1 for torque recommendations). The first step should be equal to one-half the specified torque.
17 Drive the vehicle and make several stops to wear off any foreign material on the pads and seat them on the disc.

3 Disc brake pads (ATE) – replacement

Refer to illustrations 3.2a, 3.2b, 3.2c, 3.4 and 3.6

Caution: *Disc brake pads must be replaced on both front wheels at the same time – never replace the pads on only one wheel. Disassemble one brake at a time so the remaining brake can be used as a guide if difficulties are encountered during reassembly.*

1 Raise the front of the vehicle and support it securely on jackstands. Block the rear wheels and set the parking brake, then remove the front wheels.

2.7 Hang the caliper out of the way on a piece of wire so the hose is not damaged

2 Remove the caliper guide pin and slide the caliper off the adapter and brake pads. It may be necessary to carefully pry the caliper up with a screwdriver or pry bar **(see illustrations)**.
3 Support the caliper out of the way with a wire hanger. **Warning:** *Do not allow the caliper to hang by the brake hose.*
4 Disengage the anti-rattle spring clip and detach the outer brake pad from the adapter **(see illustration)**.
5 Remove the brake disc (Section 4).
6 Disengage the anti-rattle clip and remove the inner brake pad **(see illustration)**.
7 Refer to Chapter 1 and compare the measured lining/backing material thickness to the Specifications there.
8 Inspect the caliper and adapter for wear, damage, rust and fluid leaks. If the caliper-to-adapter mating surfaces are rusty, clean them thoroughly with a wire brush (the caliper must be free to move as the brakes are applied).
9 Apply Mopar lubricant (no. 2932524) or high-temperature brake grease to the adapter-to-brake pad and caliper mating surfaces. Remove the protective paper from the noise suppression gasket on both pads. Install the inner brake pad, making sure the anti-rattle spring clip is

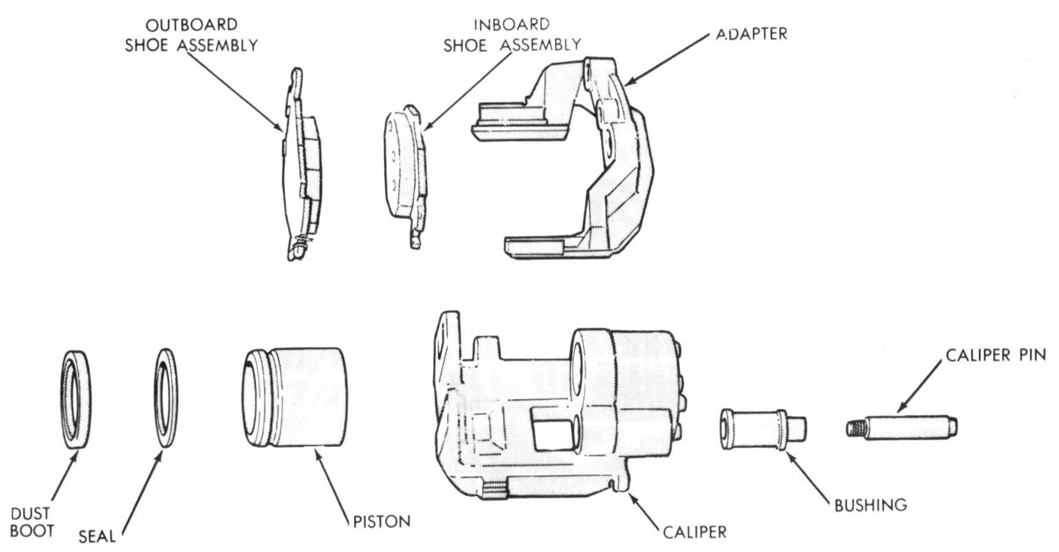

3.2a ATE disc brake components — exploded view

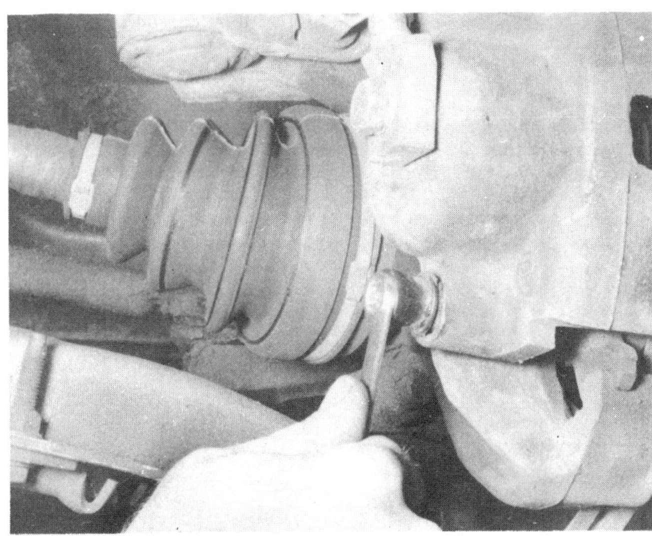

3.2b Remove the caliper guide pin with a wrench

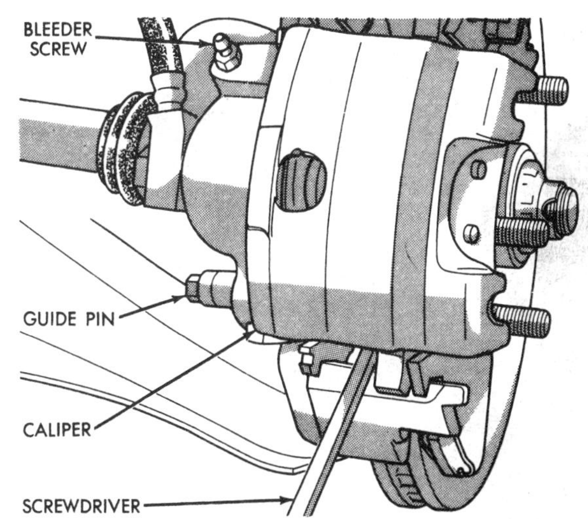

3.2c The caliper may be stuck and require gentle prying to detach it from the adapter and pads

3.4 After the caliper is detached, remove the outer brake pad and anti-rattle clip

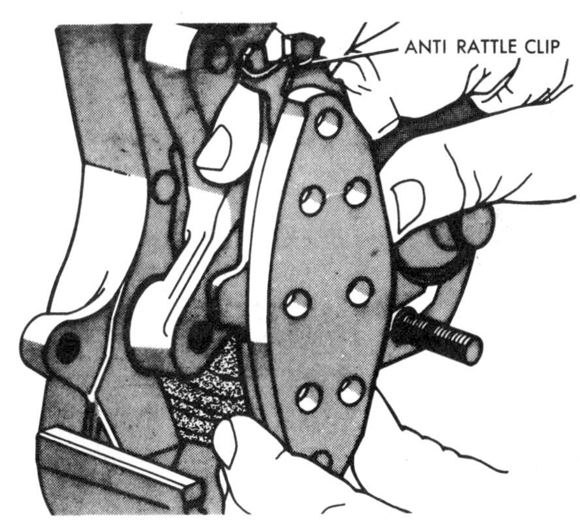

3.6 Removing the inner pad (note how the anti-rattle clips are positioned as the pads are removed)

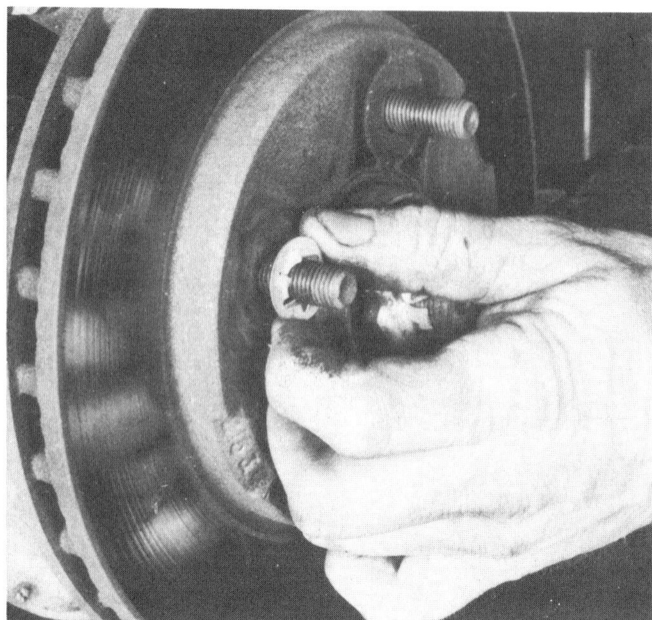

4.3a The disc retainer must be unscrewed to detach the disc

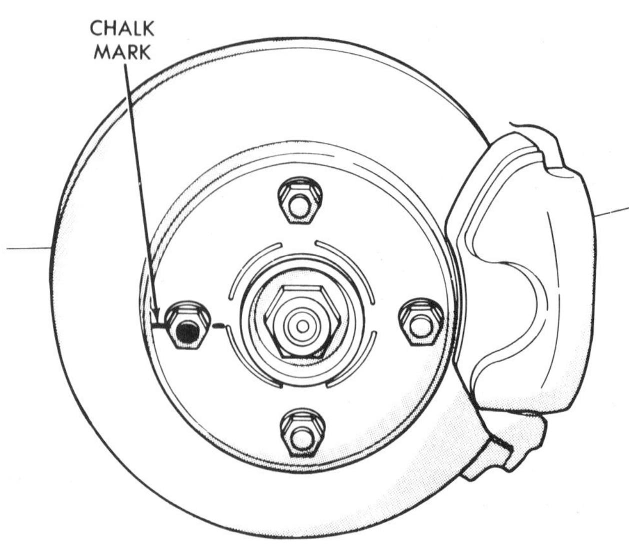

4.3b Mark the disc and the hub so they can be rejoined in the same relative position

4.4 Checking hub runout with a dial indicator

4.6 Checking disc runout with a dial indicator (make sure the lug nuts are in place and tightened evenly)

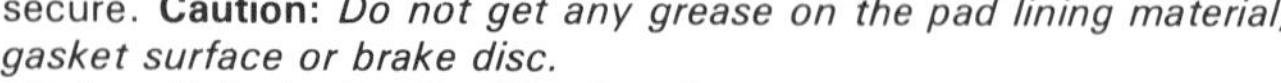

secure. **Caution:** *Do not get any grease on the pad lining material, gasket surface or brake disc.*

10 Install the brake disc (Section 4).

11 Place the outer pad in position in the adapter.

12 Slide the caliper into position over the pad and disc assembly.

13 Install the guide pin and tighten it to the specified torque. Do not cross-thread the guide pin as it is installed.

14 Repeat the procedure for the remaining caliper.

15 The remaining steps are the reverse of disassembly. When installing the wheels and tires, tighten the lug nuts in a criss-cross pattern and work up to the specified torque in two steps (see Chapter 1 for torque recommendations). The first step should be equal to one-half the specified torque.

16 Drive the vehicle and make several stops to wear off any foreign material on the pads and seat them on the disc.

4 Brake disc – removal, inspection and installation

Refer to illustrations 4.3a, 4.3b, 4.4, 4.6, 4.8a and 4.8b

1 Raise the front of the vehicle and support it securely on jackstands. Block the rear wheels and set the parking brake, then remove the front wheels.

2 Remove the caliper and pads (Section 2 or 3).

3 Unscrew the disc retainer **(see illustration)**. Mark one wheel stud and the disc so that it can be reinstalled in the same relative position **(see illustration)**, then slide the disc off the hub.

4 Use a dial indicator to check the hub runout **(see illustration)**. Replace the hub (Chapter 10) if the runout is beyond the specified limit.

5 Inspect the disc for cracks, score marks, rust, deep grooves, burned areas and distortion. If damage goes so deep into the friction surface

4.8a Measure the disc thickness with a micrometer at several points around its circumference (1-inch from the edge)

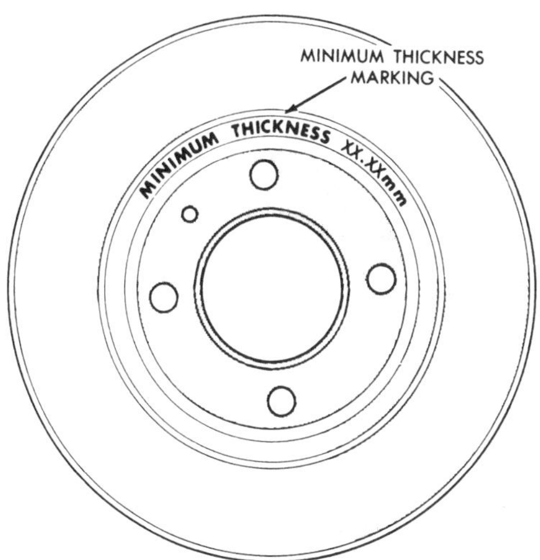

4.8b The disc can be resurfaced if the machining operation will not result in a disc thickness less than the minimum stamped on it

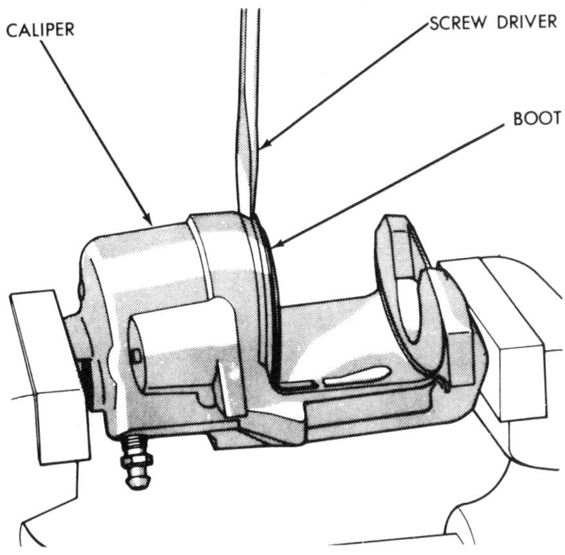

5.7 Prying the dust boot out of the caliper bore

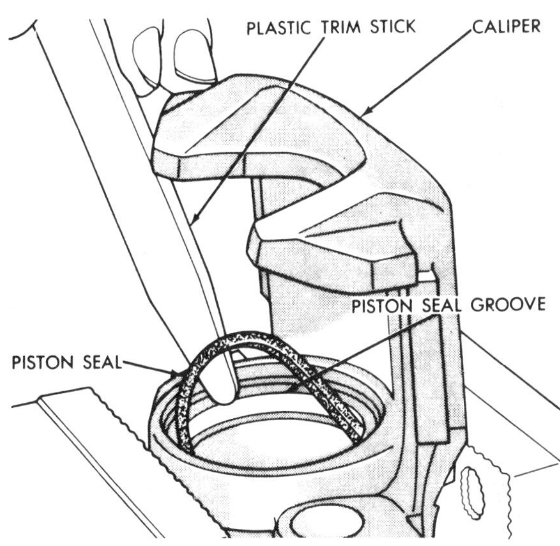

5.8 The piston seal must be removed with a plastic or wooden tool to avoid damage to the bore and seal groove

that the disc cannot be refinished and still maintain the minimum thickness, it must be replaced with a new one.

6 Reinstall the disc in the marked position and install the wheel lug nuts. Check the disc for runout with a dial indicator **(see illustration)**.

7 If the runout is beyond the specified limit, remove the disc and reinstall it 180 degrees from the original position. Recheck the runout. If it is still excessive, either have the disc resurfaced or replace it with a new one.

8 With the disc in its original position, check the thickness at 12 equally spaced points around the circumference **(see illustration)**. Replace the disc with a new one if the thickness varies more than the specified limit (or have it resurfaced if it can be done without reducing the thickness beyond the minimum) **(see illustration)**.

9 Install the caliper and pads.

10 Install the front wheels and lower the vehicle.

5 Disc brake caliper — removal, overhaul and installation

Refer to illustrations 5.7, 5.8, 5.9, 5.13 and 5.15

Removal

1 Raise the front of the vehicle and support it securely on jackstands. Block the rear wheels and set the parking brake, then remove the front wheels.

2 Remove the caliper (Section 2 or 3).

3 Have an assistant push on the brake pedal very slowly until the piston moves out of the caliper. Do not remove the piston at this time as it will be followed by a stream of brake fluid. The piston should extend from the caliper enough to be easily removed but be retained by the boot. Prop the brake pedal in any position below the first inch of travel to prevent loss of brake fluid. **Warning:** *Do not allow your fingers to come between the piston and the caliper, as serious injury could result.*

4 If both calipers are being serviced, disconnect the flexible brake hose at the frame bracket and plug the metal line so the remaining caliper piston can be forced out of the caliper by hydraulic pressure.

5 Remove the bolt and detach the caliper from the brake hose.

6 Place the caliper on a workbench which has been covered with several layers of newspaper (to absorb the brake fluid), then remove the piston.

Overhaul

7 Mount the caliper in a vise, pry the dust boot from the bore and discard it **(see illustration)**.

8 Carefully remove the piston seal from the bore using a wooden or plastic tool **(see illustration)**. **Warning:** *Do not use a metal tool of any kind to remove the seal as damage to the caliper bore will result.*

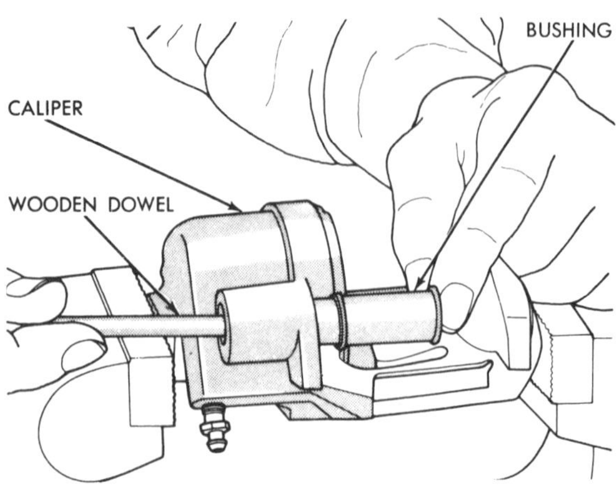

5.9 Removing the guide pin bushing

9 Remove the guide pin bushing by pushing it out of the bore with a wooden dowel, then discard it **(see illustration)**.

10 Clean the components with brake system solvent or denatured alcohol and blow them dry with compressed air, if possible. **Warning:** *Do not, under any circumstances, use petroleum-based solvents or gasoline to clean brake parts.*

11 Check the caliper bore for scratches and corrosion. Light scratches or imperfections in the bore can be removed with fine crocus cloth. If deeper sratches are present, they can be removed with a honing tool if the bore is not enlarged more than the specified amount. Replace the caliper with a new one if the bore is badly scored. Inspect the piston for damage and wear. Replace it with a new one if it is badly worn or scratched or if the caliper bore has been honed.

12 Insert the new guide pin bushing. Compress the bushing flanges with your fingers and work them into position by pushing in on the bushing with your fingertips or a plastic tool until they are seated.

13 Lubricate the new piston seal with brake assembly lubricant or clean brake fluid and install it in the bore groove. Start the seal into the groove and carefully press it into place by working around the circumference with your fingers **(see illustration)**.

14 Coat the inside of the new dust boot with clean brake fluid and attach it to the piston.

15 Insert the piston into the bore and push it in until it bottoms **(see illustration)**.

16 Press the new dust boot into the counterbore with a large socket or section of pipe.

17 Repeat the procedure for the remaining caliper.

Installation

18 Install the caliper(s) (Section 2 or 3).

19 Attach the brake hose to the caliper, using **new** sealing washers, and tighten the bolt securely.

20 Bleed the brakes as described in Section 13.

21 Check the operation of the brakes very carefully before putting the vehicle into normal service.

6 Rear brake shoes — adjustment (1982 only)

1 The rear drum brakes on these models should be periodically adjusted to compensate for wear of the brake shoe linings.

2 Raise the vehicle and support it securely on jackstands.

3 Remove the rubber plug from the adjustment access hole in the backing plate **(see illustration 8.27)**.

4 Release the parking brake and, if necessary, back off the cable adjustment so the cable is slack.

5 Remove the rubber adjusting hole plug from the backing plate .

6 Insert a narrow screwdriver through the hole in the backing plate and turn the star wheel until the brake drags slightly as the tire is turned **(see illustration 8.28)**.

7 Back off the star wheel until the tire turns freely.

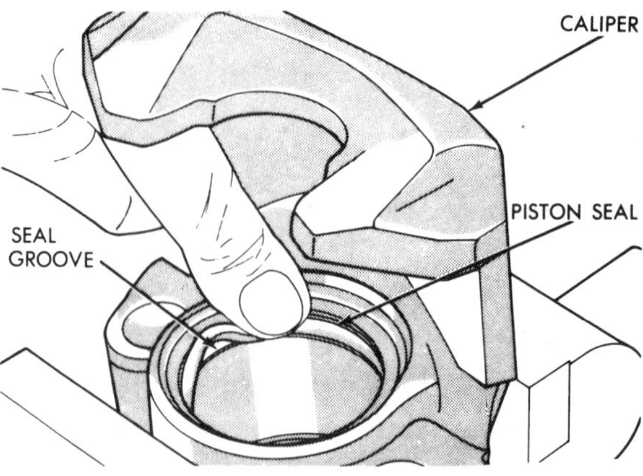

5.13 Start the new seal in the groove and push it in with your fingers (make sure it is not twisted)

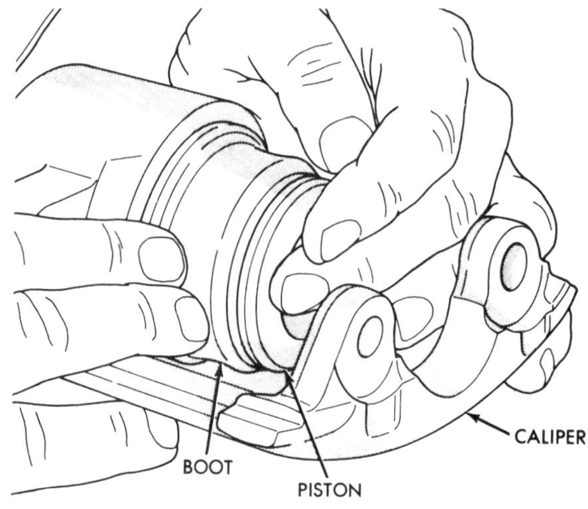

5.15 Install the piston and boot by hand only

8 Repeat the adjustment on the opposite wheel.

9 Install the plugs in the backing plate access holes.

10 Adjust the parking brake.

11 Lower the vehicle and check the brake operation very carefully before placing the vehicle into normal service.

7 Rear brake shoes — replacement (1982 only)

Refer to illustrations 7.3, 7.4, 7.5, 7.6, 7.7a, 7.7b, 7.8, 7.15, 7.17 and 7.21

Caution: *Always replace the brake shoes on both wheels at the same time — never replace just one set. Disassemble one brake at a time so the remaining brake can be used as a guide if difficulties are encountered during reassembly.*

1 Raise the rear of the vehicle, support it securely on jackstands and block the front wheels. Remove the rear wheels.

2 Remove the hub/brake drum assembly as described in Chapter 10.

3 Use brake system solvent to remove dust and brake fluid from the shoe assembly components **(see illustration)**. **Warning:** *Brake dust contains asbestos, which is harmful to your health. Do not blow it out of the brake shoe assembly with compressed air and do not inhale any of it.*

4 Disconnect the parking brake cable from the lever **(see illustration)**.

5 Remove the two lower brake shoe-to-anchor springs **(see illustration)**.

6 Remove the shoe hold down springs by depressing them and sliding them off the pins **(see illustration)**.

7 Back off the adjuster screw assembly and remove it **(see illustrations)**.

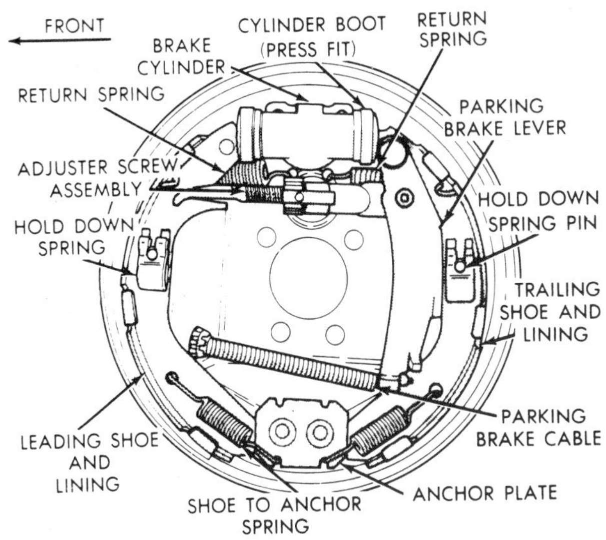

7.3 Rear drum brake components — left side shown (1982 only)

7.4 Pull the parking brake cable to the rear to disengage it from the lever

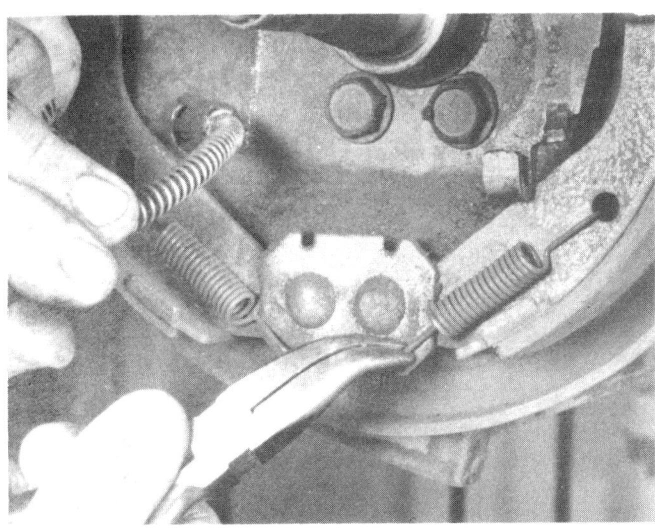

7.5 Hold the parking brake cable out of the way while disconnecting the shoe-to-anchor springs

7.6 Compress the hold down springs and slide them off the pins

7.7a Use a pair of pliers to hold the adjuster clip out of the way while backing off the adjuster screw, then . . .

7.7b . . . disengage the adjuster clevis from the front shoe

7.8 **Rotate the rear shoe and parking brake lever assembly forward to remove it from the backing plate**

7.15 **Lubricate all of the shoe pivot and backing plate contact points with high-temperature grease**

7.17 **Rotate the rear shoe and parking brake lever assembly into position in the wheel cylinder piston**

7.21 **Pull back the spring cover and attach the end of the cable to the lever**

8 Rotate the rear shoe forward and remove it, followed by the leading shoe **(see illustration)**.

9 Check the shoe linings to make sure they indicate full contact with the drum.

10 Check the drum for cracks, score marks and signs of overheating. Measure the inside diameter of the drum and compare it to the size stamped on the drum **(see illustration 8.13)**. Minor imperfections in the drum surface can be removed with fine emery paper. Deep score marks can be removed by having the drum turned by an automotive machine shop (as long as the maximum diameter is not exceeded). Check the drum for runout. Replace the brake drum with a new one if it is not usable.

11 Check the brake springs for signs of discolored paint, indicating overheating, and distorted end coils. Replace them with new ones if necessary.

12 Check the adjuster screw assembly and threads for bent, corroded and damaged components. Replace the assembly if the screw threads are damaged or rusted. Clean the threads and lubricate them with white lithium-based grease.

13 Check the wheel cylinder boots for damage and signs of leakage.

14 Rebuild or replace the wheel cylinder if there is any sign of leakage around the boots **(see illustration 8.16)**.

15 Check for rough or rusted shoe contact areas on the backing plate, then lubricate the contact points with high-temperature grease **(see illustration)**.

16 Insert the upper return spring into the backing plate and install the leading shoe. Be sure to seat the ends securely in the wheel cylinder piston and anchor pivot.

17 Install the trailing shoe return spring and then rotate the shoe and parking brake lever assembly to the rear, into position **(see illustration)**. Seat the shoe ends in the anchor pivot and wheel cylinder.

18 Insert the adjuster screw assembly into the shoe notch, making sure the forward facing clevis of the screw is pointed down. Turn the adjusting star wheel until the screw is secure in the support.

19 Lightly lubricate the hold down springs with high-temperature grease and install them.

20 Install the shoe-to-anchor springs.

21 Pull the parking brake cable housing spring back to expose the cable and attach it to to the lever **(see illustration)**.

22 Install the hub/drum assembly and the wheel. Repeat the procedure

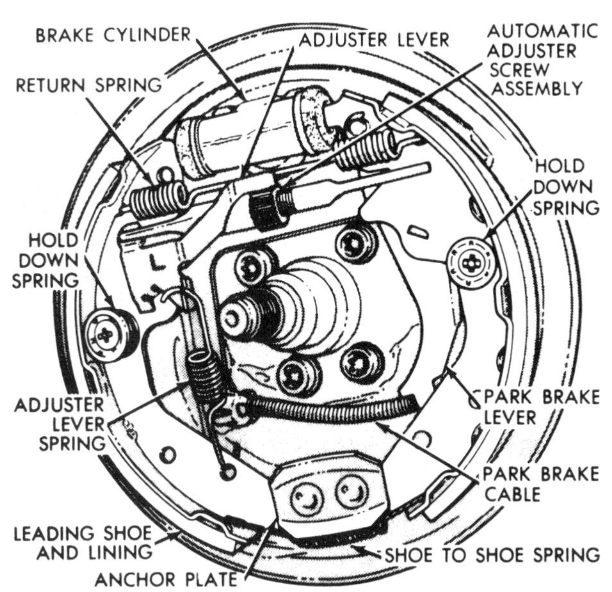

8.3 Rear drum brake components — left side shown (1983 on)

8.4a Use a pair of pliers to undo the adjuster lever spring . . .

8.4b . . . and detach the adjuster lever

8.5 Back off the adjuster star wheel

for the other wheel.
23 Adjust the brakes (Section 6).
24 Lower the vehicle and check the brake operation very carefully before placing the vehicle into normal service.

8 Rear brake shoes — replacement (1983 on)

Refer to illustrations 8.3, 8.4a, 8.4b, 8.5, 8.6, 8.7, 8.8a, 8.8b, 8.9a, 8.9b, 8.10, 8.11, 8.13, 8.15, 8.16, 8.18, 8.19, 8.20, 8.27 and 8.28

1 Raise the rear of the vehicle, support it securely on jackstands and block the front wheels. Remove the rear wheels.
2 Remove the hub/brake drum assembly as described in Chapter 10.
3 Use brake system cleaner to remove dust and brake fluid from the shoe assembly components **(see illustration)**. **Warning:** *Brake dust contains asbestos, which is harmful to your health. Do not blow it out of the brake shoe assembly with compressed air and do not inhale any of it.*
4 Remove the adjuster lever spring and adjuster lever **(see illustrations)**.
5 Back off the adjuster screw assembly star wheel **(see illustration)**.
6 Disconnect the parking brake cable from the trailing shoe with a pair of pliers **(see illustration)**.

8.6 Use a pair of pliers to pull the cable from the parking brake lever

8.7 Use a brake hold down spring tool or a pair of pliers to depress the hold down spring and turn the retainer

8.8a Pull the brake shoe assembly out of the wheel cylinder, . . .

8.8b . . . then disengage the bottoms of the shoes from the anchor plate

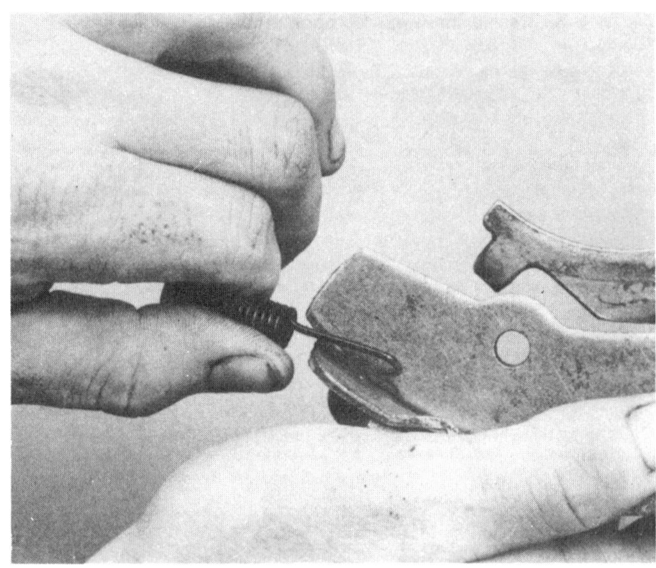

8.9a Unhook the lower spring . . .

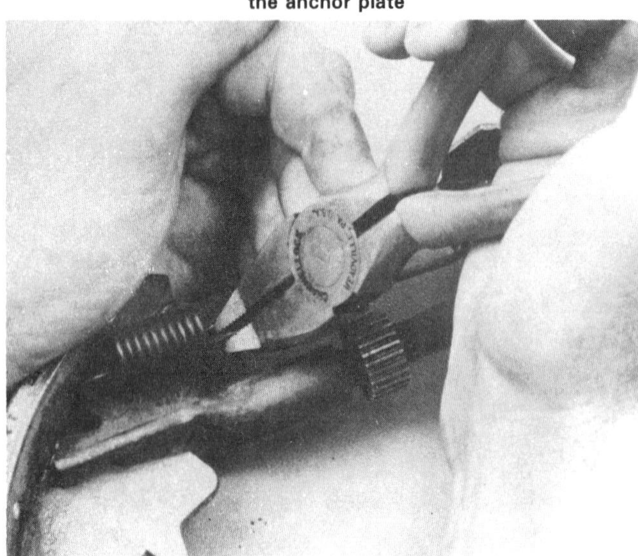

8.9b . . . and use a pair of pliers to disengage the upper spring and shoes

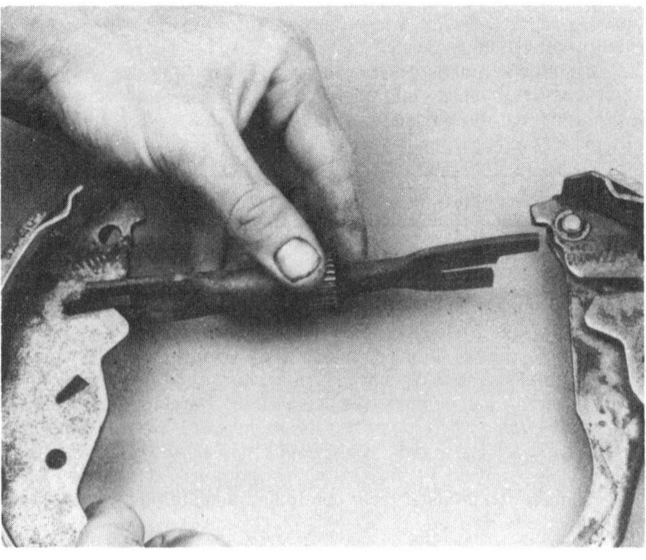

8.10 Detach the adjuster from the shoes

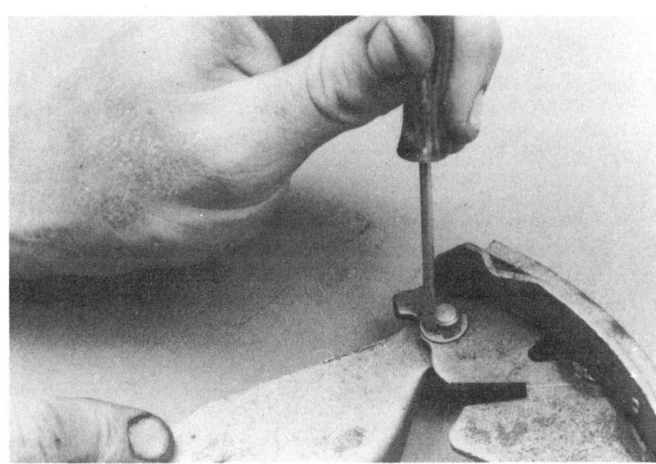

8.11 Use a small screwdriver to pry the parking brake lever clip off the post

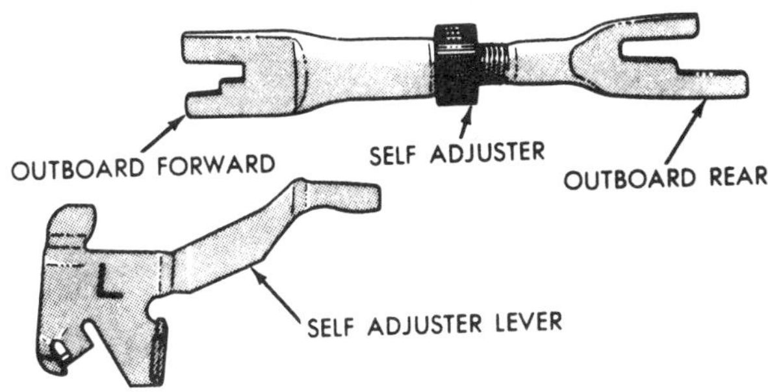

8.15 Adjuster components – exploded view

7 Remove the hold down springs by depressing them with a pair of pliers or a special tool and turning the retainer until the slot aligns with the flattened end of the pin, allowing removal **(see illustration)**.
8 Disengage the brake shoe assembly from the wheel cylinder at the top and the anchor plate at the bottom and remove it from the backing plate **(see illustrations)**.
9 Place the assembly on a work surface and remove the springs **(see illustrations)**.
10 Separate the shoes from the adjuster **(see illustration)**.
11 Remove the parking brake lever retainer clip with a small screwdriver and transfer the lever to the new shoe **(see illustration)**.
12 Check the shoe linings to make sure they indicate full contact with the drum.
13 Check the drum for cracks, score marks and signs of overheating. Measure the inside diameter of the drum and compare it to the size stamped on the drum **(see illustration)**. Minor imperfections in the drum surface can be removed with fine emery paper. Deeper score marks can be removed by having the drum turned by an automotive machine shop (as long as the maximum diameter is not exceeded). Check the drum for runout. Replace the brake drum with a new one if it is not usable.
14 Check the brake springs for signs of discolored paint, indicating overheating, and distorted end coils. Replace them with new ones if necessary.
15 Check the adjuster screw assembly and threads for bent, corroded and damaged components. Replace the assembly if the screw threads are damaged or rusted. Clean the threads and lubricate them with white lithium-based grease **(see illustration)**.
16 Check the wheel cylinder boots for damage and signs of leakage **(see illustration)**.
17 Rebuild or replace the wheel cylinder if there is any sign of leakage around the boots.
18 Check for rough or rusted shoe contact areas on the backing plate, then lubricate the contact points with high-temperature grease **(see illustration)**.

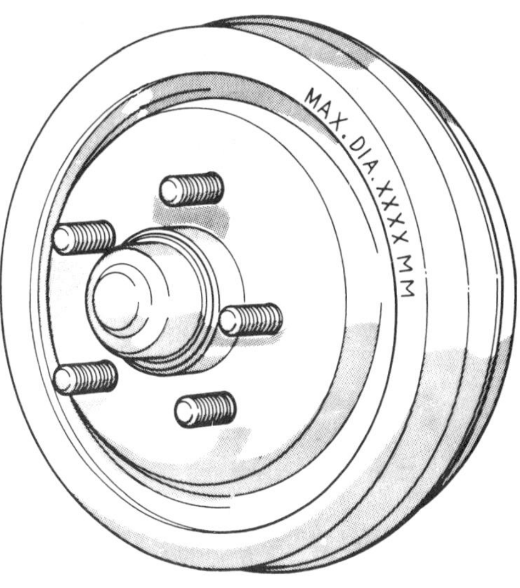

8.13 The maximum allowable inside diameter of the drum is stamped on it

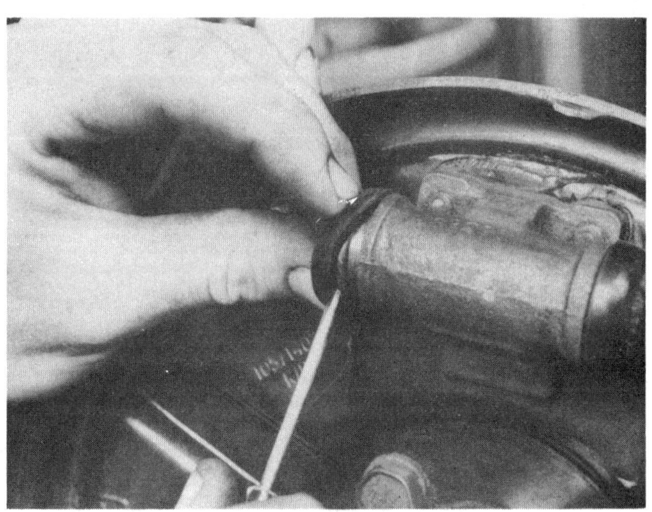

8.16 Carefully peel back the wheel cylinder boots to check for brake fluid leakage

8.18 The shoe contact areas on the backing plate must be smooth and lubricated with high-temperature grease

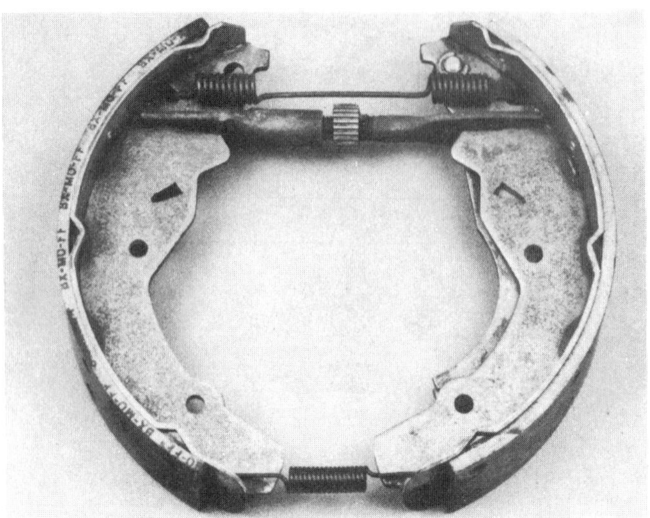

8.19 Assemble the shoes, adjuster and springs prior to installation on the backing plate

8.20 Use a pair of pliers to insert the parking brake cable into the lever

8.27 Pry the rubber plug out of the adjusting hole with a screwdriver

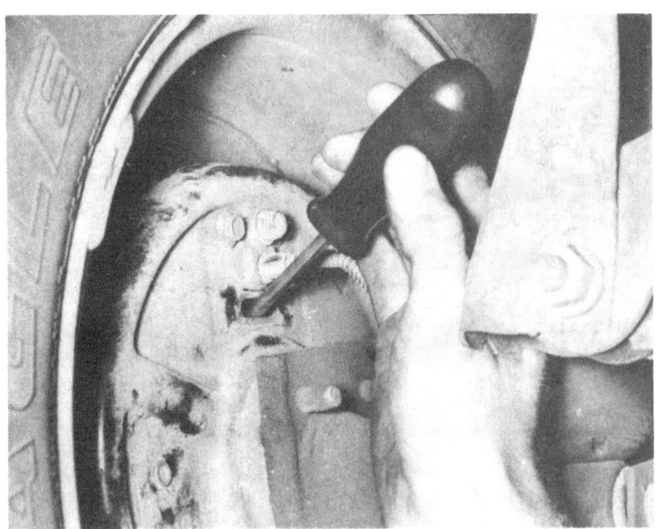

8.28 Insert the screwdriver into the hole and turn the star wheel

19 Assemble the shoes over the adjuster and connect the return springs **(see illustration)**.
20 Place the assembly in position on the backing plate and insert the parking brake cable into the parking brake lever **(see illustration)**
21 Spread the bottom spring enough to allow the lower ends of the shoes to be seated in the anchor plate.
22 Spread the top spring and seat the shoes in the wheel cylinder pistons.
23 Insert the pins through the backing plate from the rear and hold them in place while installing the hold down springs and retainers.
24 Install the adjuster lever and connect the spring to it.
25 Turn the adjuster until the shoes are retracted enough to allow the drum to be reinstalled.
26 Install hub/drum assembly and the wheel. Repeat the procedure for the other wheel.
27 Remove the rubber plug from the hole in the backing plate **(see illustration)**.
28 Insert a narrow screwdriver through the hole in the backing plate and turn the star wheel until the brake drags slightly as the tire is turned **(see illustration)**.
29 Back off the star wheel until the tire turns freely.
30 Repeat the adjustment on the opposite wheel.
31 Install the plugs in the backing plate access holes.
32 Adjust the parking brake.
33 Lower the vehicle and check the brake operation very carefully before placing the vehicle into normal service.

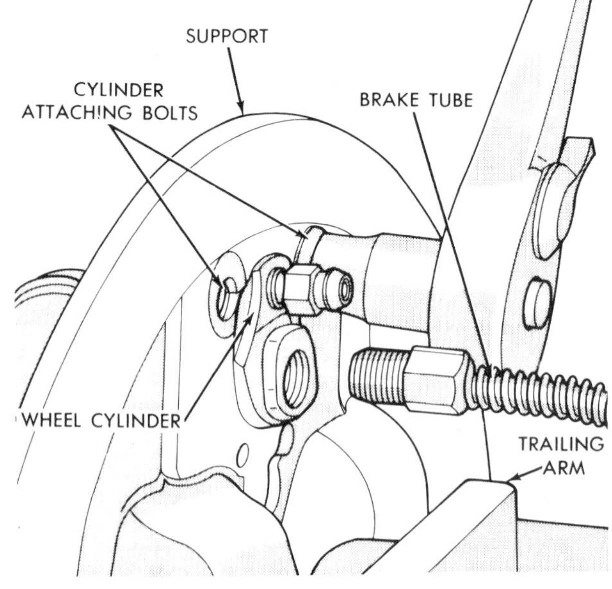

9.4 Removing the wheel cylinder mounting bolts

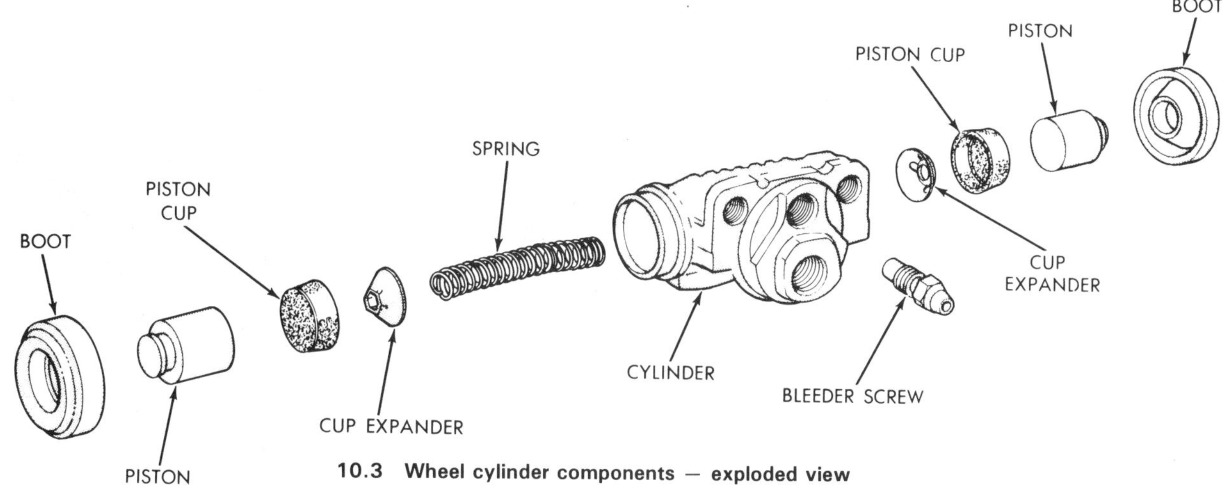

10.3 Wheel cylinder components — exploded view

11.2 Loosen the brake line fittings with a flare nut wrench if one is available (otherwise, be careful not to round off the fitting hex)

9 Rear wheel cylinder — removal and installation

Refer to illustration 9.4

1 Raise the rear of the vehicle and support it securely on jackstands, then block the front wheels. Remove the rear wheels.
2 Remove the rear hub/drum (Chapter 10) and brake shoes (Section 7 or 8).
3 Disconnect the brake line from the back of the wheel cylinder and plug it.
4 Unbolt the wheel cylinder and remove it from the backing plate **(see illustration)**. Clean the backing plate and wheel cylinder mating surfaces.
5 Apply RTV-type sealant to the wheel cylinder mating surface of the backing plate.
6 To install the wheel cylinder, hold it in position, install the mounting bolts and tighten them to the specified torque.
7 Unplug the brake line, insert it into the wheel cylinder fitting and carefully thread the flare nut into place. Once the nut is properly started, tighten it securely with a wrench (use a flare nut wrench if available).
8 Install the brake shoes and the hub/drum.
9 Bleed the brakes.
10 Install the wheels and lower the vehicle. Check the brake operation very carefully before placing the vehicle into normal service.

10 Rear wheel cylinder — overhaul

Refer to illustration 10.3

1 You must have a clean place to work, clean rags, some newspapers, a wheel cylinder rebuild kit, a container of brake fluid and some denatured alcohol to perform a wheel cylinder overhaul.
2 Remove the wheel cylinder as described in Section 9.
3 Remove the bleeder screw **(see illustration)** and check to make sure it is not obstructed.
4 Carefully pry the boots from the wheel cylinder and remove them.
5 Push in on one piston and force out the opposite piston, cups and spring with the cup expanders from the bore.
6 Clean the wheel cylinder, pistons and spring with clean brake fluid, denatured alcohol or brake system solvent and dry them with compressed air. **Warning:** *Do not, under any circumstances, use petroleum-based solvents or gasoline to clean brake parts.*
7 Check the cylinder bore and pistons for score marks and corrosion (pitting). Slight imperfections in the bore can be removed with fine crocus cloth (use a circular motion). Black stains on the cylinder walls are caused by the cups and will not impair brake operation. If the pistons or wheel cylinder bore are badly scored or pitted, replace the wheel cylinder.
8 Lubricate the components with clean brake fluid or brake assembly lubricant prior to installation.
9 With the cylinder bore coated with clean brake fluid or brake assembly lube, install the spring and cup expanders. Install the cups in each end of the cylinder. Make sure the open ends of the cups are facing each other.
10 Engage the boot on the piston and slide the assembly into the bore. Carefully press the boot over the cylinder end until it is seated. Repeat the procedure for the remaining boot and piston.
11 Install the bleeder screw.
12 Attach the wheel cylinder to the backing plate by referring to Section 9.

11 Master cylinder — removal and installation

Refer to illustration 11.2

1 Place several layers of newspaper under the master cylinder to catch spilled brake fluid.
2 Unscrew the steel line flare nuts **(see illustration)**, remove the lines and cap them. Allow the fluid in the master cylinder to drain into a container.
3 Remove the mounting nuts and detach the master cylinder from the booster.
4 Every time the master cylinder is removed, the complete hydraulic system must be bled. The time required to bleed the system can be reduced if the master cylinder is filled with fluid and *bench bled* before the master cylinder is installed on the vehicle.
5 Insert threaded plugs of the correct size into the cylinder outlet holes and fill both reservoirs with brake fluid. The master cylinder should be supported in a level manner so that brake fluid will not spill during the bench bleeding procedure.

be supported in a level manner so that brake fluid will not spill during the bench bleeding procedure.
6 Loosen one plug at a time and push the piston assembly into the bore to force air from the master cylinder. To prevent air from being drawn back into the cylinder, the plug must be tightened before allowing the piston to return to its original position.
7 Since high pressure is not involved in the bench bleeding procedure, an alternative to the removal and replacement of the plug with each stroke of the piston assembly is available. Before pushing in on the piston assembly, remove the plug, then depress the piston as described above. Before releasing the piston, however, instead of replacing the plug, simply put your finger tightly over the hole to keep air from being drawn back into the master cylinder. Wait several seconds for brake fluid to be drawn from the reservoir into the piston bore, then depress the piston again, removing your finger as the brake fluid is expelled. Be sure to put your finger back over the hole each time before releasing the piston When the bleeding procedure is complete for that port, replace the plug and tighten it snugly before going on to the other port to repeat the procedure.
8 Stroke the piston three or four times for each outlet to ensure that all air has been expelled.
9 Refill the master cylinder reservoirs and install the cover assembly. **Note:** *The reservoirs should only be filled to the top of the reservoir divider to prevent overflowing when the cover is installed.*
10 To install the master cylinder, hold it in position, align the pushrod and master cylinder piston and install the mounting nuts. Tighten the nuts to the specified torque.
11 Install the lines and carefully start the flare nuts, taking care not to cross-thread them. After they have been started by hand, tighten them securely with a flare nut wrench.
12 Fill the master cylinder reservoir and bleed the brakes.

12 Master cylinder — overhaul

The master cylinder installed on these vehicles cannot be rebuilt. If problems are encountered, replace it with a new unit.

13 Brake hydraulic system — bleeding

Refer to illustration 13.7

1 If the brake system has air in it, operation of the brake pedal will be spongy and imprecise. Air can enter the brake system whenever any part of the system is dismantled or if the fluid level in the master cylinder reservoir runs low. Air can also get into the system though a hole too small to allow fluid to leak out.
2 To bleed the brakes, you will need an assistant to pump the brake pedal, a supply of new brake fluid, a plastic container, a clear plastic or vinyl tube, which will fit over the bleeder screw fitting, and a wrench for the bleeder screw.
3 There are four locations at which the brake system is bled: both front brake caliper assemblies and the rear brake wheel cylinders.
4 Check the fluid level in the master cylinder reservoir. Add fluid if necessary to bring it up to the correct level (see Chapter 1). Use only the recommended brake fluid and do not mix different types. Never use fluid from a container that has been standing uncapped. You will have to check the fluid level in the master cylinder reservoir often during the bleeding procedure. If the level drops too far, air will enter the system though the master cylinder.
5 Raise the vehicle and support it securely on jackstands.
6 Remove the bleeder screw cap from the wheel cylinder or caliper assembly that is being bled. If more that one wheel must be bled, start with the one farthest from the master cylinder.
7 Attach one end of the clear plastic or vinyl tube to the bleeder screw fitting and place the other end in the plastic container, submerged in a small amount of clean brake fluid **(see illustration)**.
8 Loosen the bleeder screw slightly, then tighten it to the point where it is snug yet easily loosened.
9 Have your assistant pump the brake pedal several times and hold it in the fully depressed position.
10 With pressure on the brake pedal, open the bleeder screw approximately 1/4-turn. As the brake fluid flows through the tube and into the container, tighten the bleeder screw. Again, pump the brake pedal,

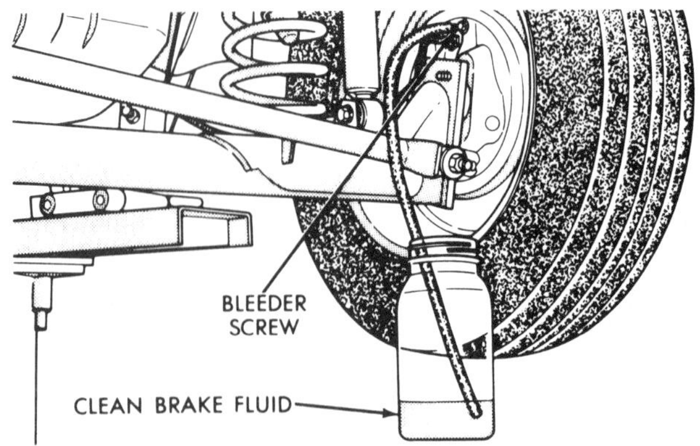

13.7 Brake bleeding equipment setup

hold it in the fully depressed position and loosen the bleeder screw momentarily. Do not allow the brake pedal to be released with the bleeder screw in the open position.
11 Repeat the procedure until no air bubbles are visible in the brake fluid flowing through the tube. Be sure to check the brake fluid level in the master cylinder reservoir while performing the bleeding operation.
12 Completely tighten the bleeder screw, remove the plastic or vinyl tube and install the cap.
13 Follow the same procedure to bleed the other wheel cylinder or caliper assemblies.
14 Check the brake fluid level in the master cylinder to make sure it is adequate, then test drive the vehicle and check for proper brake operation.

14 Parking brake — adjustment

Refer to illustrations 14.3 and 14.6

1 The rear drum brakes must be in proper working order before adjusting the parking brake (see Sections 6 and 7).
2 Block the front wheels to prevent any movement, raise the vehicle and support it securely with jackstands. Release the parking brake lever.
3 Clean the threads of the cable adjusting hook **(see illustration)** with a wire brush and lubricate them with multi-purpose grease.
4 Loosen the adjusting nut until there is slack in the cable.
5 Have an assistant rotate the rear wheels to make sure they turn easily.
6 Tighten the parking brake cable adjusting nut **(see illustration)** until a slight drag can be felt when the rear wheels are rotated.
7 Loosen the nut until the rear wheels turn freely, then back it off an additional two full turns.
8 Apply and release the parking brake several times to make sure it operates properly. It must lock the rear wheels when applied and the wheels must turn easily, without dragging, when it is released.
9 Lower the vehicle.

15 Parking brake cables — removal and installation

Refer to illustration 15.15

1 Raise the vehicle and support it securely on jackstands.

Front cable

2 Working underneath the vehicle, loosen the adjusting nut and disengage the cable from the connectors (see illustration 14.3).
3 Inside the vehicle, lift the floor mat or carpeting and remove the floor pan seal panel.
4 Pull the cable forward to disconnect it from the clevis.
5 Remove the cable assembly through the hole.
6 To install the cable, insert the cable housing retainers into the rail bracket hole and the parking brake pedal assembly. Feed the end of the cable through the holes in the pan and the rail bracket.
7 Install the floor seal.

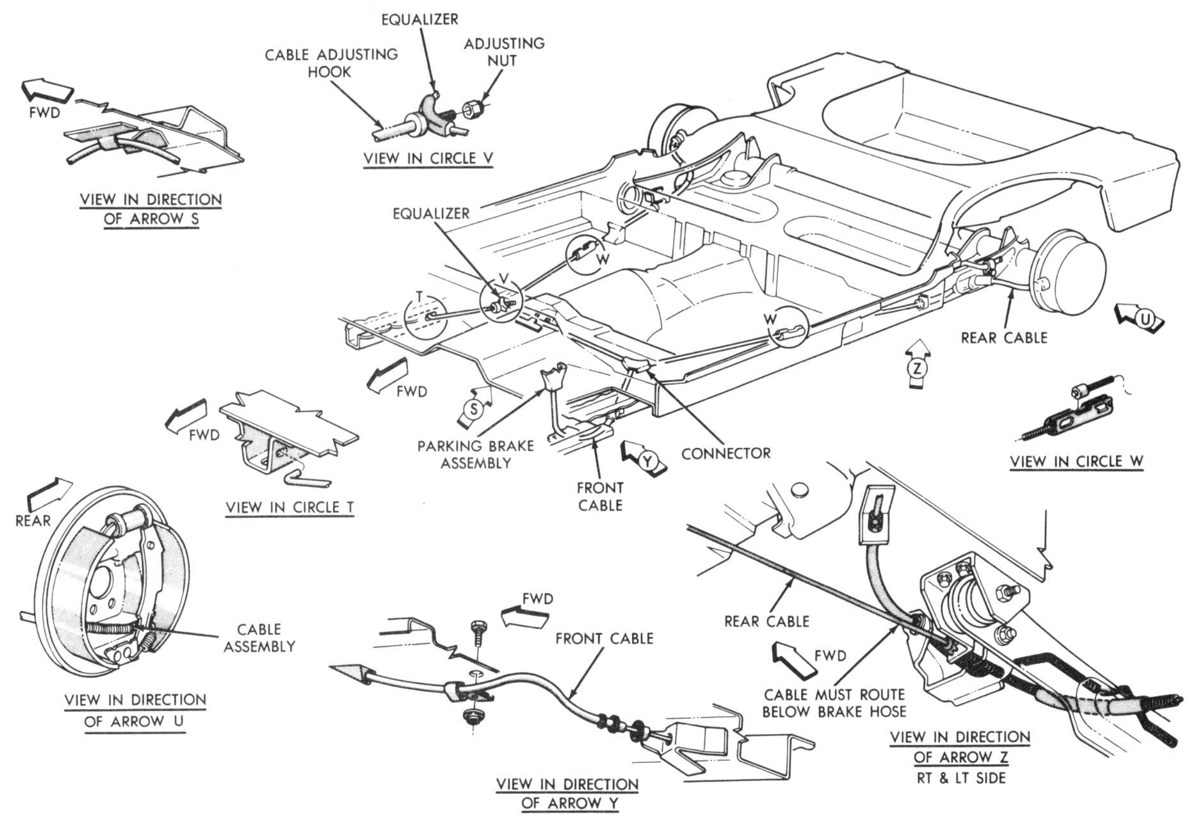

14.3 Parking brake cable layout

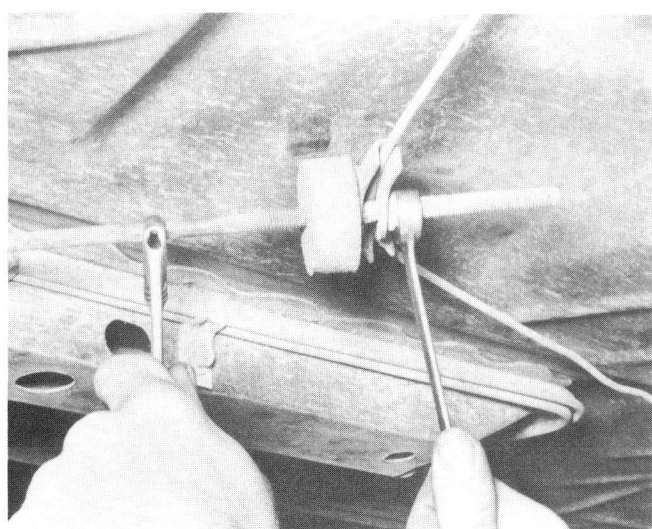

14.6 Tighten the parking brake cable adjusting nut until the brakes drag slightly as the tire is rotated

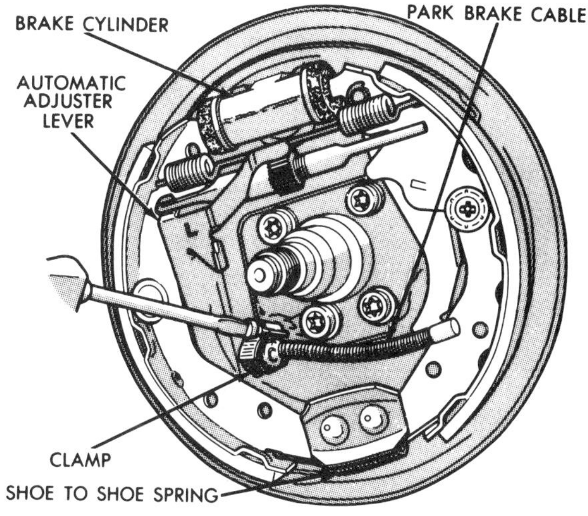

15.15 Removing the rear parking brake cable housing from the backing plate

8 Engage the end of the cable in the lever clevis and seat the cable ends in the parking brake assembly and the rail bracket.
9 Install the floor mat.
10 Engage the rear cable in the equalizer bracket, then adjust it as described in Section 14.

Rear cables

11 Remove the rear wheels and the hub/drum assemblies.
12 Back off the adjusting nut until the cable is slack.
13 Disconnect the rear brake cable from the connector.
14 Disconnect the cable at the brake shoe lever.
15 Use a screw-type hose clamp to compress the retainers so the cable can be removed from the brake backing plate **(see illustration)**. Remove the clamp when the cable is free.
16 Pull the cable from the backing plate and rear axle.
17 To install the cable, insert the cable and the inner housing end through the suspension arm holes and the crossmember cable bracket.
18 Connect the chassis fitting to the bracket.
19 Insert the outer cable end through the support brace hole and snap the retainer into place.
20 Attach the cable to the lever in the brake shoe assembly, making sure the washer is between the cable spring and parking brake lever.
21 Insert the cable inner end into the connector.
22 Install the hub/drum assemblies.
23 Attach the cable to the connector, then adjust the parking brake (Section 14).

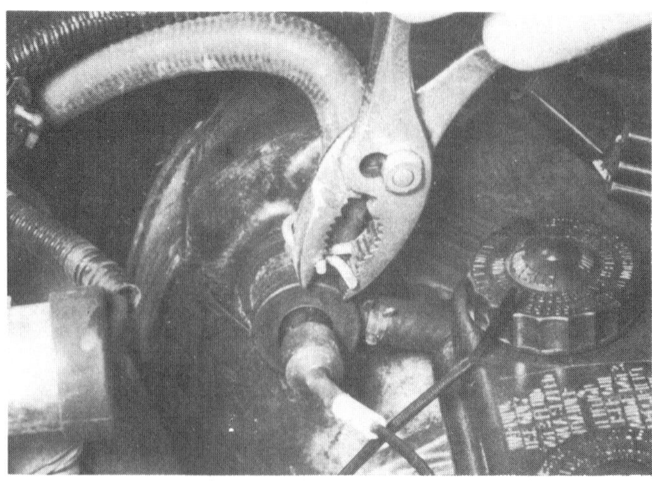
16.3 Use a pair of pliers to loosen and remove the vacuum hose clamp

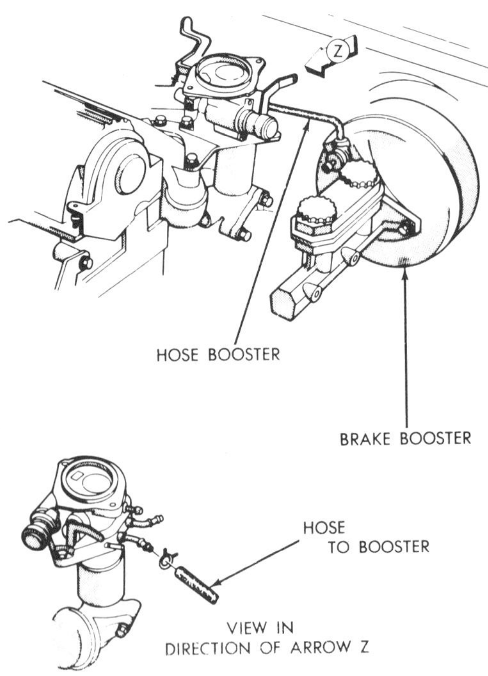

17.6b Brake booster vacuum hose layout – EFI non-turbocharged engine

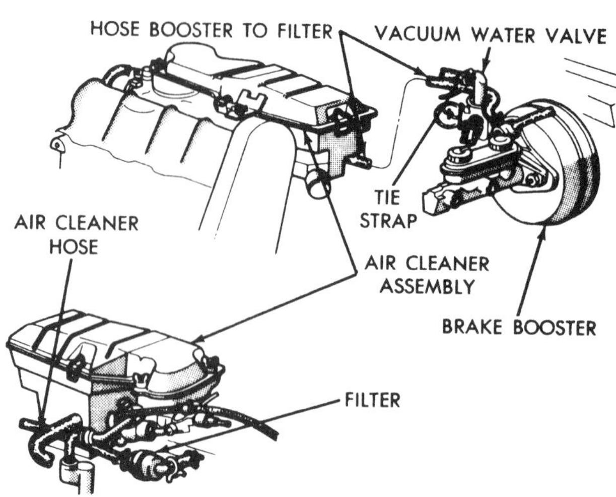

17.6a Typical carburetor equipped engine brake booster vacuum hose layout

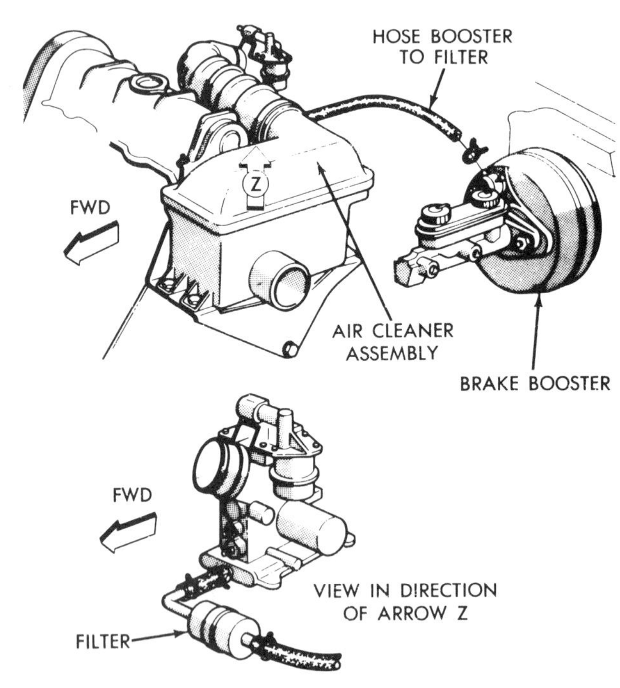

17.6c Brake booster vacuum hose layout – turbocharged engine

16 Power brake booster – removal and installation

Refer to illustration 16.3

1 Remove the master cylinder (Section 11).
2 On manual transaxle equipped vehicles, unfasten the clutch cable bracket and pull the wiring harness up away from the strut tower.
3 Disconnect the vacuum hose at the booster **(see illustration)**.
4 Working underneath the dash inside the vehicle, use a small screwdriver to remove the brake pedal-to-booster retainer clip and pin.
5 Remove the brake light switch and plate assembly.
6 Remove the four retaining nuts and lift the booster from the engine compartment.
7 Installation is the reverse of removal. Lubricate the surface of the brake pedal pin with white lithium-based grease and connect the pedal pin to the pushrod with a **new** retainer clip. Check the operation of the brake light switch and adjust if necessary (Section 18).
8 Check the booster for proper operation (Section 17).

17 Power brake booster – check and overhaul

Refer to illustrations 17.6a, 17.6b and 17.6c

1 Symptoms of brake booster problems include low pedal and excessive braking effort and the brake pedal dropping after the initial application.
2 With the engine off, depress and release the brake pedal several times to bleed any vacuum from the booster.
3 Depress the pedal and hold it with light pressure (between I5 and 25 lbs). Start the engine.
4 If the system is operating properly, the pedal should drop slightly

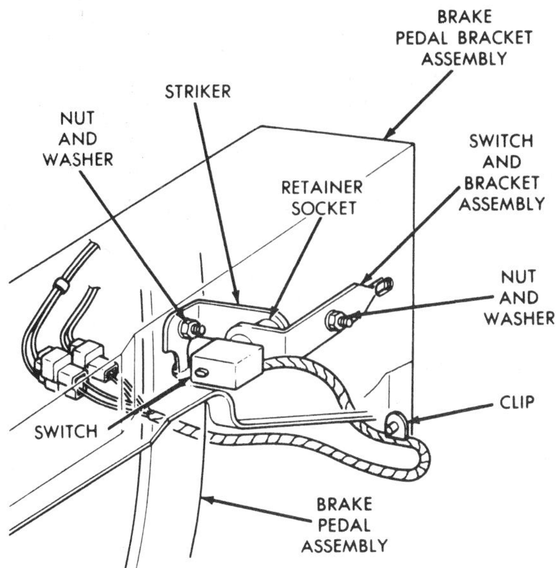

18.1 Brake light switch mounting details

and then stop. Subsequent applications will require less pressure.

5 If the booster fails this check, or if the pedal drops after the initial applicaton, check the vacuum supply.

6 Inspect the vacuum hose for cracks and trace it to the manifold or carburetor. Check the connections, check valve and filter (if equipped) for cracks and leaks, replacing any faulty components **(see illustrations)**.

7 If no defects are found, have the booster operation checked by a dealer service department.

8 The brake booster must not be disassembled for any reason. If the booster is not operating properly, obtain a new or rebuilt unit and install it in the vehicle by referring to Section 16.

18 Brake light switch – removal, installation and adjustment

Refer to illustration 18.1

1 Unplug the wire connectors, grasp the switch and pull it out of the retainer **(see illustration)**.

2 Press the new switch into the retainer and push the switch forward as far as possible. The brake pedal will move forward slightly.

3 Gently pull the pedal back as far as it will go, causing the switch to ratchet back to the correct position. Very little movement is required and no further adjustment is necessary.

19 Brake pedal – removal and installation

Note: *Refer to Chapter 8 for an exploded view illustration of the brake pedal components mentioned in this procedure.*

1 Disconnect the power brake pushrod from the brake pedal.

2 On manual transaxle equipped models, remove the lock ring from the pivot shaft and carefully withdraw the shaft. Remove the clutch pedal assembly, followed by the brake pedal.

3 On automatic transaxle equipped vehicles, remove the pivot shaft nut, withdraw the shaft and remove the brake pedal.

4 To install the pedal, place it in position and insert the pivot shaft.

5 On manual transaxle models, install the clutch pedal assembly and lock ring.

6 On automatic transaxle models, install the pivot shaft nut and tighten it securely.

9

Chapter 10 Steering and suspension systems

Contents

Specifications

Torque specifications

Front suspension	**Ft-lbs**	**Nm**
Strut-to-steering knuckle bolts		
1982 and 1983	45*	61*
1984 through 1986	75*	100*
Strut-to-tower nuts	20	27
Lower control arm balljoint clamp bolt nut		
1982 and 1983	50	68
1984 through 1986	70	95
Lower control arm pivot bolt		
1982 through 1985	105	142
1986	95	129
Lower control arm stub strut nut	70	94
Sway bar bushing retainer nuts	25	34
Hub nut	180	245
Rear suspension		
Trailing arm-to-hanger bracket mounting nuts	40	55
Track bar mounting bolts	65	88
Track bar mounting bracket-to-frame bolt	40	55
Track bar brace/body stud	40	55
Track bar brace-to-stud nut	55	75
Shock absorber mounting bolts	40	55
Brake backing plate-to-stub axle bolts	45	60
Rear hub nut		
Step 1	tighten to 20 to 25 ft-lbs	
Step 2	loosen 1/4-turn	
Step 3	tighten finger-tight	
Steering system		
Steering gear mounting bolts	21	28
Tie-rod end nut	35	47
Tie-rod jam nut	55	75
Crossmember mounting bolts	90	122
Steering wheel nut	45	61
Column clamp stud	20 in-lb	2
Column clamp stud nut and bolt	105 in-lb	12
Power steering pump bracket mounting bolts/nuts		
M-10 stud	35	48
M-10 bolt/nut	30	40
M-8 bolt	21	28
Wheel lug nuts		
1982 and 1983	80	108
1984 through 1986	95	129

** Plus 1/4-turn*

1.1 Front suspension components

1 Tie-rods
2 Sway bar bolts
3 Lower control arm
4 MacPherson struts
5 Sway bar
6 Power steering fluid lines

1.2 Rear suspension components

1 Coil spring
2 Track bar
3 Axle assembly
4 Trailing arm

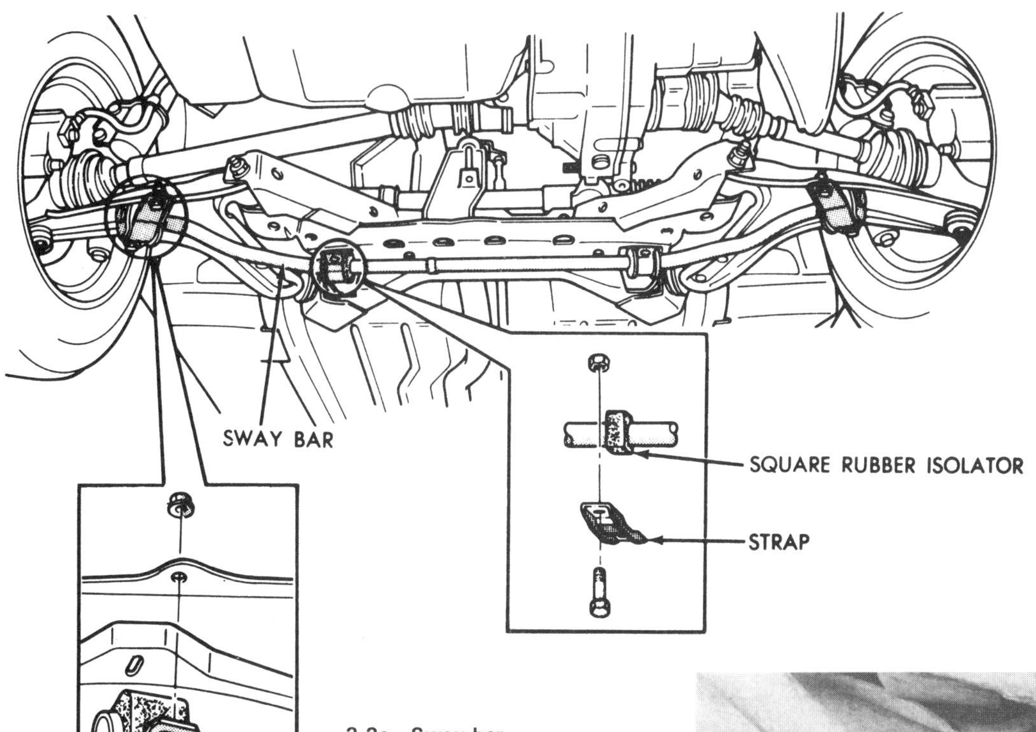

2.2a Sway bar mounting details

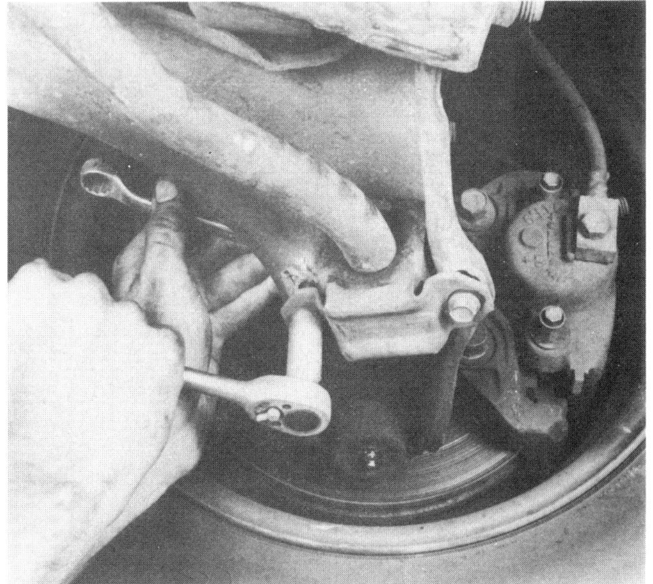

2.2b Use a wrench to hold the nut when removing the sway bar bolts

1 General information

Refer to illustrations 1.1 and 1.2

Front suspension is by MacPherson struts. The steering knuckle is located by a lower control arm and both front control arms are connected by a sway bar **(see illustration)**.

The rear suspension features a beam-type axle with coil springs, located by trailing arms and a track bar **(see illustration)**. Damping is handled by vertically-mounted shock absorbers located between the axle and the chassis.

The rack-and-pinion steering gear is located behind the engine and actuates the steering arms which are integral with the steering knuckles. Power assist is optional and the steering column is designed to collapse in the event of an accident.

Note: *These vehicles use a combination of standard and metric fasteners on the various suspension and steering components, so it would be a good idea to have both types of tools available when beginning work.*

2 Sway bar – removal and installation

Refer to illustrations 2.2a and 2.2b

1 Raise the front of the vehicle, support it securely on jackstands and remove the front wheels.

2 Remove the sway bar nuts, bolts, and retainers at the control arms **(see illustrations)**.

3 Unbolt the clamps at the crossmember and remove the sway bar from the vehicle.

4 Check the bar for damage, corrosion and signs of twisting.

5 Check the clamps, bushings and retainers for distortion, damage and wear. Replace the inner bushings by prying them open at the split and removing them. Install the new bushings with the curved surface up and the split facing toward the front of the vehicle. The outer bushing can be removed by cutting it off or hammering it from the bar. Force the new bushing onto the end of the bar until 1/2-inch of the bar is protruding.

6 Place the upper bushing retainers in position on the crossmember bushings, attach the bar to the crossmember and then install the lower clamps, bolts and nuts.

7 Install the bushing retainers, nuts and bolts at the lower control arm.

8 Raise the lower control arms to normal ride height and tighten the nuts to the specified torque.

9 Install the wheels and lower the vehicle.

3 Lower control arm – removal, inspection and installation

Refer to illustrations 3.2a, 3.2b, 3.4 and 3.5

1 Raise the front of the vehicle, support it securely on jackstands and remove the front wheels. Detach the sway bar (Section 2).

2 Remove the pivot bolt and nut from the control arm **(see illustrations)**.
3 Remove the rear stub strut nut, retainer and bushing.
4 Remove the balljoint clamp bolt and nut from the steering knuckle **(see illustration)**.
5 Disconnect the balljoint stud from the steering knuckle. Be careful not to separate the inner CV joint **(see illustration)**.
6 Remove the sway bar nuts, separate the control arm and remove it from the vehicle.
7 Remove the rear stub strut bushing and sleeve assembly.
8 Inspect the lower control arm for distortion and the bushings for wear, damage and deterioration. Replace a damaged or bent control arm with a new one. If the inner pivot bushing or the balljoint are worn, take the control arm assembly to a dealer service department or a repair shop, as special tools are required to replace them. The strut bushings can be replaced by sliding them off the strut.
9 Assemble the retainer, bushing and sleeve on the stub strut.
10 Place the control arm in position over the sway bar and attach the stub strut and front pivot to the crossmember.
11 Install the pivot bolt and stub strut assembly in the crossmember, with the nuts finger tight.
12 Attach the balljoint stud to the steering knuckle and tighten the clamp bolt to the specified torque.
13 Attach the sway bar end to the control arm and tighten the clamp

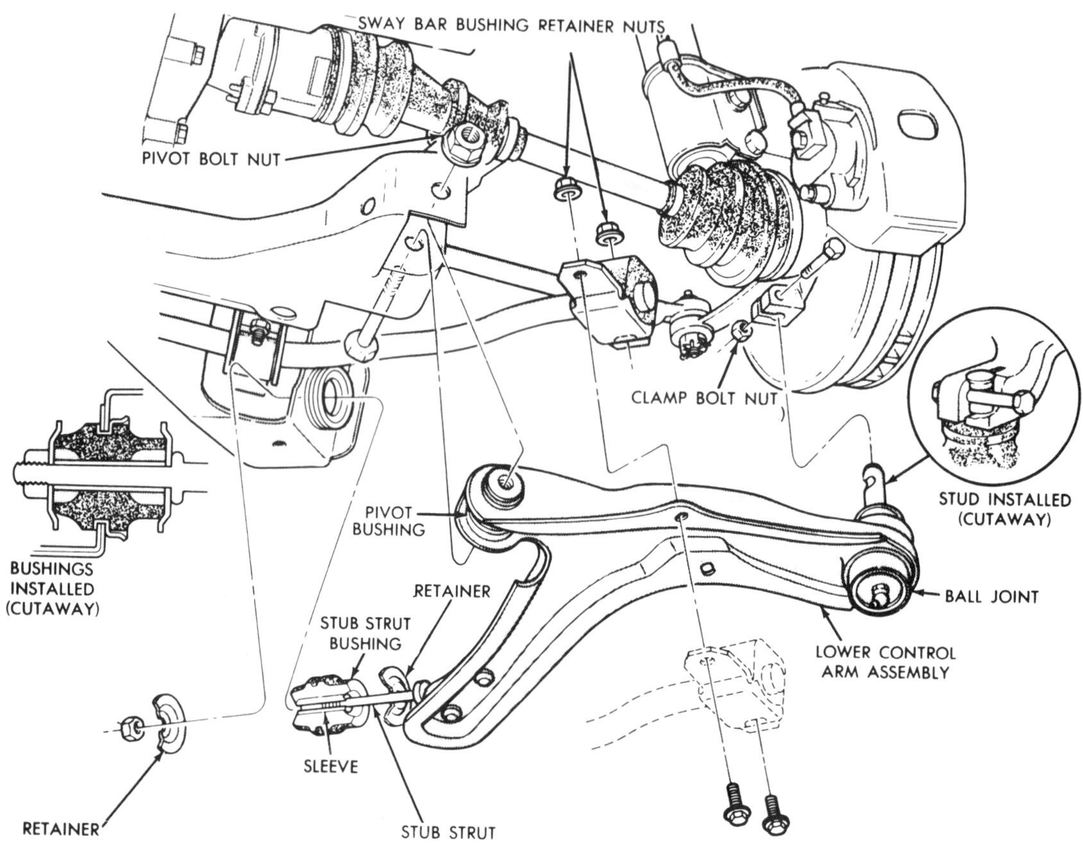

3.2a Lower control arm components — exploded view

3.2b Removing the lower control arm pivot bolt nut

3.4 Removing the balljoint clamp bolt and nut to release the control arm

bolt to the specified torque.
14 Install the wheels and lower the vehicle. With the vehicle weight on the suspension, tighten the pivot bolt and stub strut nuts to the specified torque.

4 Balljoints — check

Refer to illustration 4.2

1 The suspension balljoints are designed to operate without free play.
2 To check for wear, grasp the grease fitting and attempt to move it with the vehicle weight resting on the front suspension **(see illustration)**.
3 If there is any movement, the balljoint is worn and must be replaced with a new one (if the balljoint is worn the grease fitting will move easily). Since special equipment is required to press the balljoint from the control arm, it is recommended that the job be left to a dealer service department or a repair shop.

5 Steering knuckle and hub — removal, inspection and installation

Refer to illustrations 5.1, 5.4, 5.9, 5.11a, 5.11b, 5.13, 5.14 and 5.18

Removal

1 With the vehicle weight resting on the front suspension, remove the hub cap, cotter pin, nut lock and spring washer. Loosen, but do not remove, the front hub (axle) nut and wheel nuts **(see illustration)**.
2 Raise the front of the vehicle, support it securely on jackstands and remove the front wheels.

3.5 Pull down sharply to disengage the balljoint stud from the steering knuckle (a pry bar may be required)

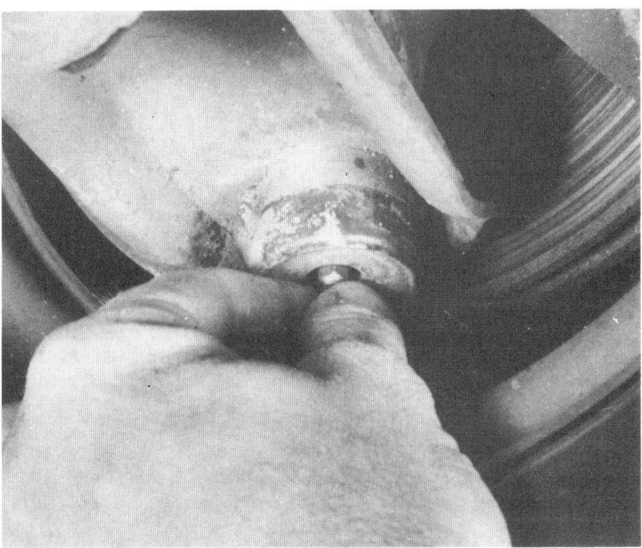

4.2 Each balljoint can be checked for wear by attempting to move the grease fitting

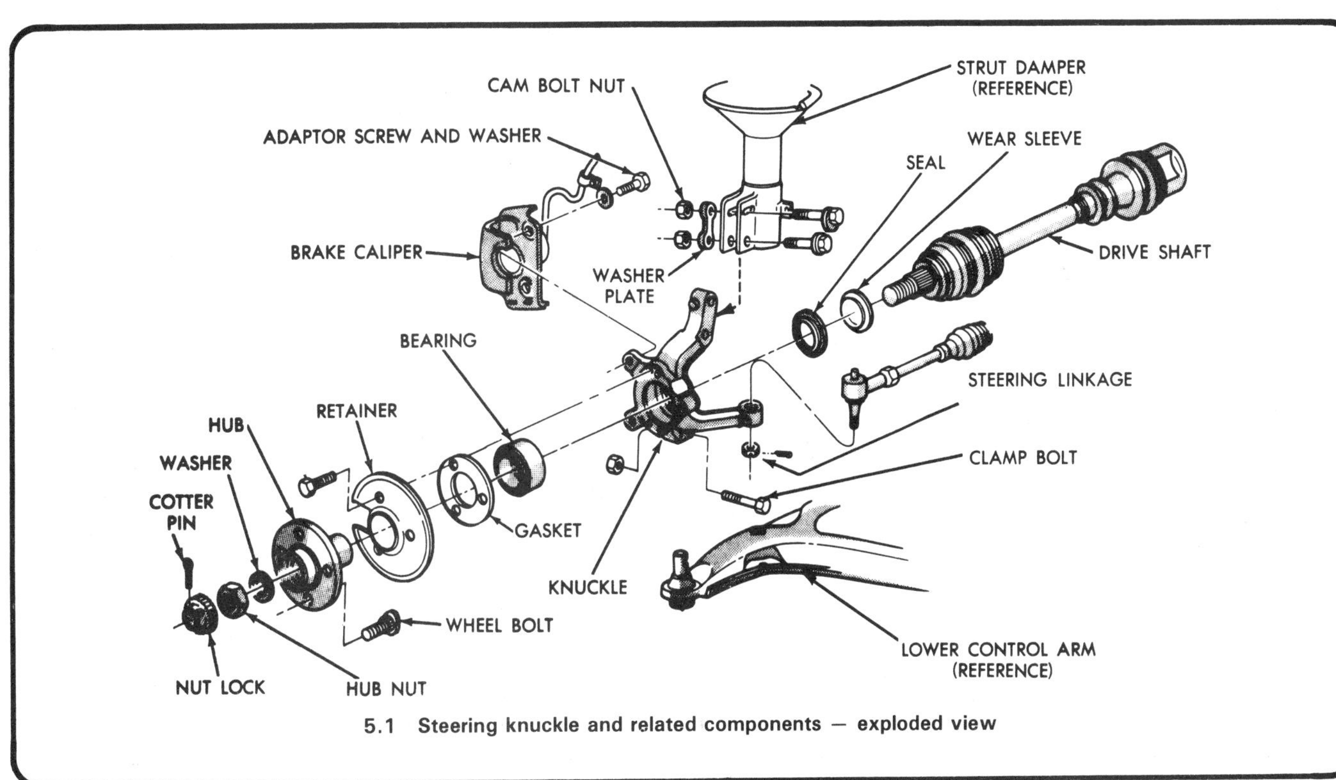

5.1 Steering knuckle and related components — exploded view

10

5.4 Push in on the driveaxle while supporting the outer CV joint

5.9 With the bushing mounting bolts loose, the sway bar can be pulled down and out of the way

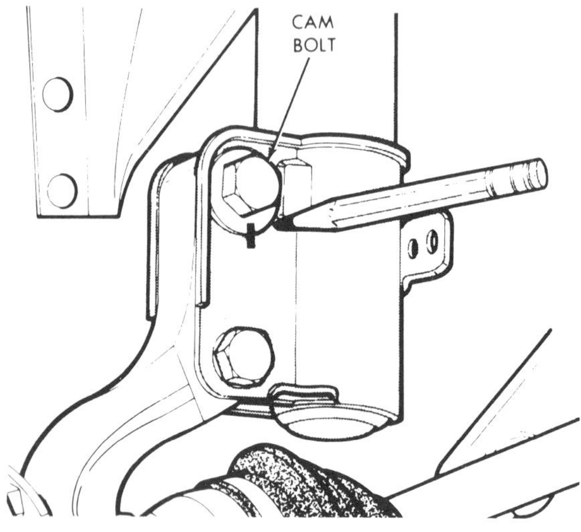

5.11a Mark the location of the upper (1982 and 1983 models) . . .

5.11b . . . or lower (1984 and later models) cam bolt head before removing the bolts and separating the strut from the steering knuckle

3 Remove the hub nut and washer.

4 Push the driveaxle in until it is free of the hub **(see illustration)**. It may be necessary to tap on the axle end with a brass drift punch and hammer to dislodge the driveaxle from the hub.

5 Remove the cotter pin and nut and use a puller to disconnect the steering tie-rod from the hub (Section 22).

6 Move the tie-rod out of the way and secure it with a piece of wire.

7 Disconnect the brake hose from the shock strut by removing the bolt and retainer.

8 Remove the caliper and brake pads (Chapter 9), then remove the adapter from the steering knuckle. Taking care not to twist the brake hose, hang the caliper out of the way in the wheel well with a piece of wire.

9 Loosen the sway bar bushing bolts, unbolt the ends from the control arm and pull the sway bar down and out of the way **(see illustration)**.

10 Remove the retainer from the wheel stud and pull the brake disc off.

11 Mark the cam bolt and washer location prior to removal. The cam bolt is the upper bolt on early (1982 and 1983) models and the lower bolt on later (1984 and later) models **(see illustrations)**.

12 Remove the balljoint pinch bolt and nut and disengage the balljoint from the hub.

13 Remove the steering knuckle-to-strut bolts and nuts **(see illustration)**.

14 With the knuckle and hub assembly in the straight-ahead position, grasp it securely and pull it directly out and off the driveaxle splines **(see illustration)**.

Inspection

15 Place the assembly on a clean work surface and wipe it off with a lint-free cloth. Inspect the knuckle for rust, damage and cracks. Check the bearings by rotating them to make sure they move freely. The bearings should be packed with an adequate supply of clean grease. If there is too little grease, or if the grease is contaminated with dirt, clean the bearings and inspect them for wear, scoring and looseness. Repack the bearings with the specified lubricant. Inspect the grease seals to make sure they are not torn or leaking. Further disassembly will have to be left to your dealer service department or a repair shop because of the special tools required.

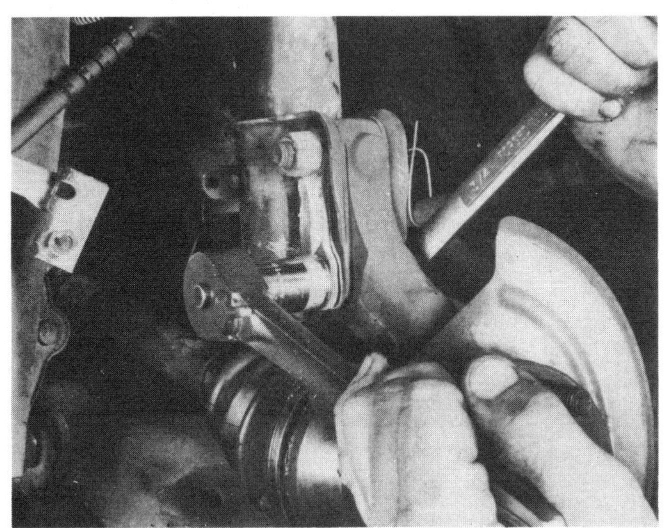

5.13 Removing the steering knuckle-to-strut bolts and nuts

5.14 Pull the steering knuckle out and off the driveaxle splines

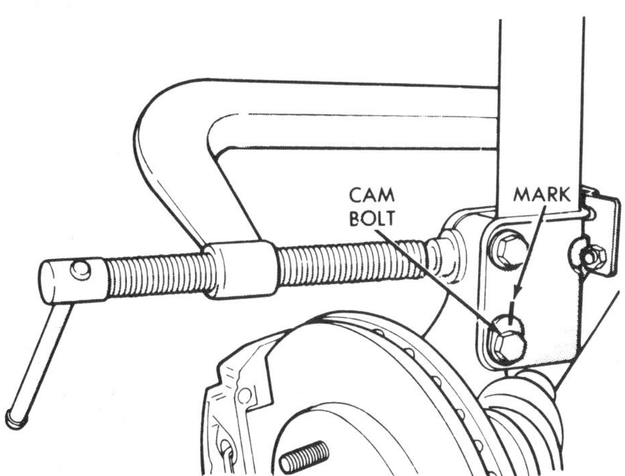

5.18 Use a C-clamp to pull the strut and steering knuckle into alignment (1984 and later model shown)

Installation

16 Prior to installation, clean the CV joint seal and the hub grease seal with solvent (don't get any solvent on the CV joint boot). Lubricate the entire circumference of the CV joint wear sleeve and seal contact surface with multi-purpose grease (refer to Chapter 8 if necessary).
17 Carefully place the knuckle and hub assembly in position. Align the splines of the axle and the hub and slide the hub into place.
18 Install the knuckle-to-strut bolts and nuts, followed by the balljoint pinch bolt and nut. Adjust the knuckle so that the mark made during removal is aligned with the cam bolt and washer. It may be necessary to use a large C-clamp to pull the steering knuckle and strut together and line up the marks **(see illustration)**. Install the washer plate and nuts and tighten the nuts to the specified torque.
19 Install the tie-rod end, tighten the nut and install the cotter pin.
20 Install the brake disc, pads and caliper/adapter assembly.
21 Connect the brake hose to the shock strut.
22 Attach the sway bar ends to the control arm and tighten the fasteners to the specified torque.
23 Push the CV joint completely into the hub to make sure it is seated and install the washer and hub nut finger tight.
24 Install the wheels and lower the vehicle.
25 With an assistant applying the brakes, tighten the hub nut to the specified torque. Install the spring washer, nut lock and a **new** cotter pin.
26 With the weight of the vehicle on the suspension, check the steering knuckle and balljoint nuts to make sure they are tightened properly.
27 Have the vehicle front end alignment checked.

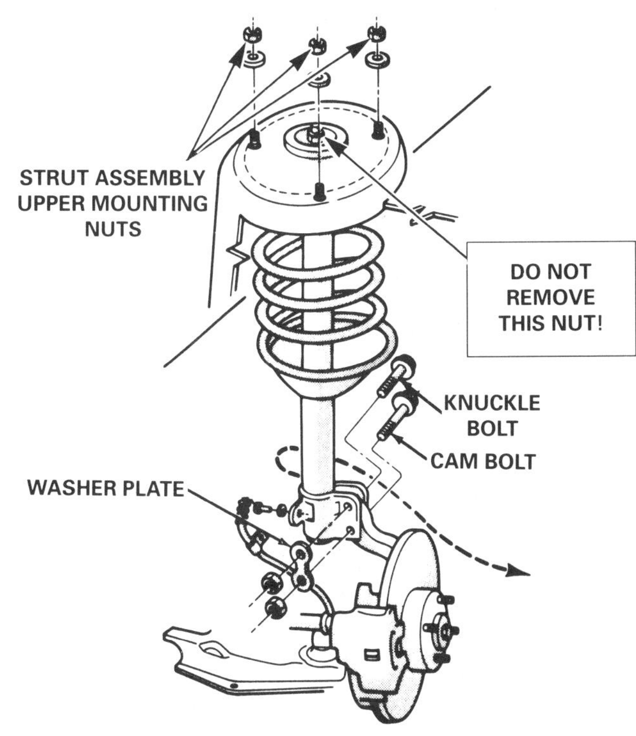

6.6 Shock absorber strut and spring assembly removal details

6 Front shock absorber strut and spring assembly – removal, inspection and installation

10

Refer to illustration 6.6

1 Loosen the front wheel nuts.
2 Raise the vehicle and support it securely on jackstands. Remove the front wheels.
3 Mark the location of the cam bolt and washer as described in Step 11 of the previous Section.
4 Remove the strut-to-steering knuckle nuts, bolts and washer plate.
5 Disconnect the brake hose from the strut.
6 Remove the upper mounting nuts, disengage the strut from the steering knuckle and detach it from the vehicle **(see illustration)**.

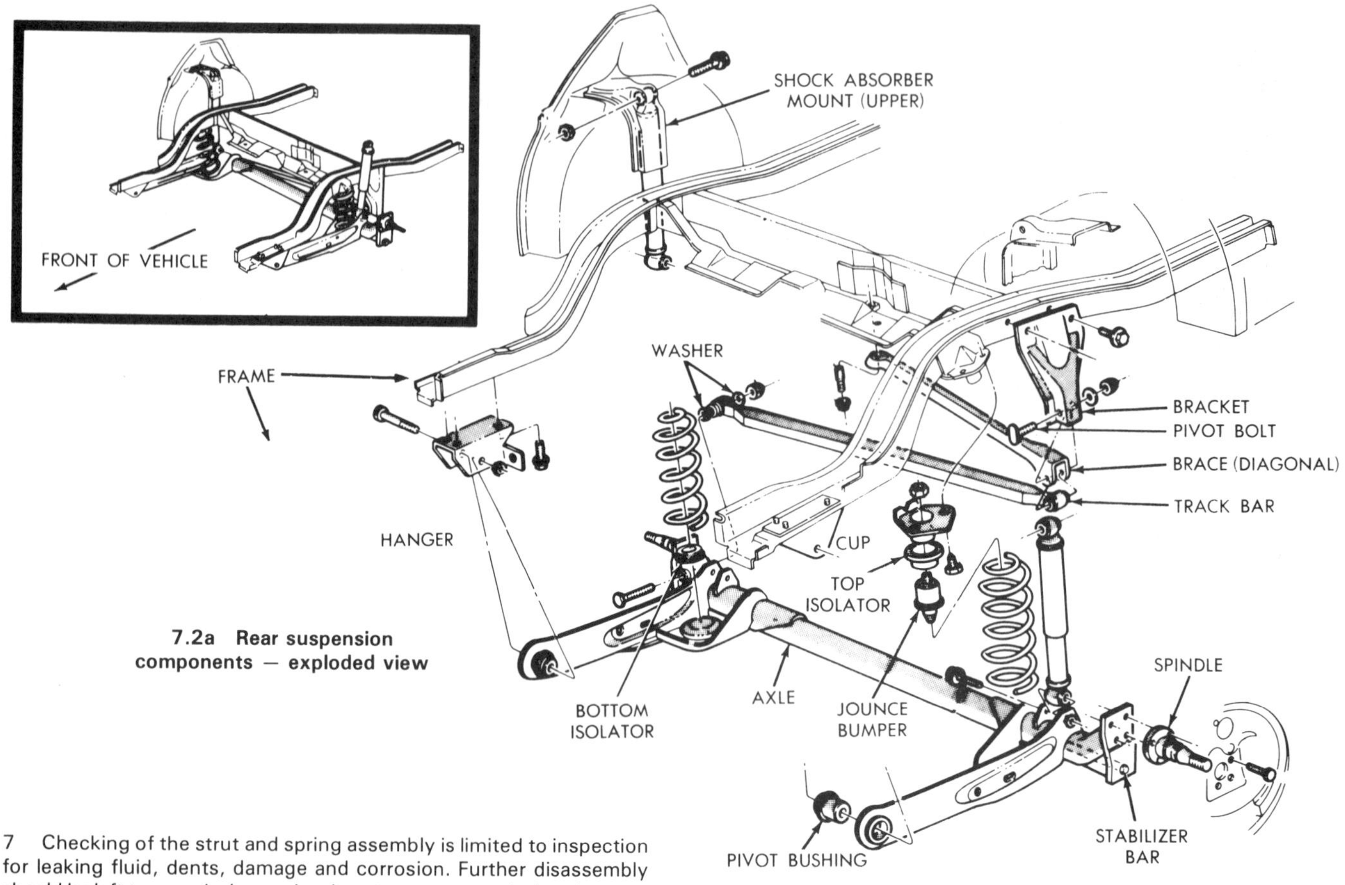

7.2a Rear suspension components — exploded view

7 Checking of the strut and spring assembly is limited to inspection for leaking fluid, dents, damage and corrosion. Further disassembly should be left to your dealer service department or a repair shop because of the special tools and expertise required.

8 To install the strut, place it in position with the studs extending up through the shock tower. Install the nuts and tighten them to the specified torque.

9 Attach the strut to the steering knuckle, then insert the mounting bolts and washer plate.

10 Use a large C-clamp to align the knuckle and strut so the cam bolt marks line up. Install the nuts on the cam and knuckle bolts and tighten them to the specified torque, plus 1/4-turn. Remove the clamp.

11 Attach the brake hose to the strut.

12 Install the wheels and lower the vehicle.

7.2b Support the rear axle with a jack before removing the shock absorber mounting bolts

7 Rear shock absorber — removal, inspection and installation

Refer to illustrations 7.2a, 7.2b, 7.3a and 7.3b

1 Raise the rear of the vehicle and support it securely on jackstands.

2 Support the axle with a jack and remove the rear wheels **(see illustrations)**.

3 Remove the lower and upper shock mounting bolts **(see illustrations)** and detach the shock absorber.

4 Grasp the shock at each end and pump it in and out several times. The action should be smooth, with no binding or dead spots. Check for fluid leakage. Replace the shock with a new one if it is leaking or if the action is rough. Always replace the shocks in pairs.

5 Hold the shock in position and install the bolts. Tighten the upper bolt to the specified torque. Lower the vehicle and tighten the lower bolt to the specfied torque.

8 Rear Hub/drum assembly — removal and installation

Refer to illustrations 8.2, 8.3, 8.7 and 8.8

Removal

1 Block the front wheels, raise the rear of the vehicle, support it securely on jackstands and remove the rear wheels. Make sure the parking brake is released and that the hub turns freely. It may be necessary to back off the brake adjuster (Chapter 9).

2 Remove the grease cap, cotter pin, nut lock and brake drum retaining nut **(see illustration)**.

3 Grasp the brake drum and pull it out enough to dislodge the outer wheel bearing and washer **(see illustration)**.

4 Remove the bearing.

5 Withdraw the hub/drum from the axle.

Installation

6 Place the hub in position on the axle, install the outer wheel bearing and washer and push the assembly into place.

7 Install the retaining nut and the wheel. Rotate the tire while tightening the nut to the specified torque **(see illustration)**. Stop rotating the tire and back off the nut 1/4-turn, then tighten it finger tight only while rotating the tire.

8 Install the nut lock, cotter pin and grease cap **(see illustration)**.

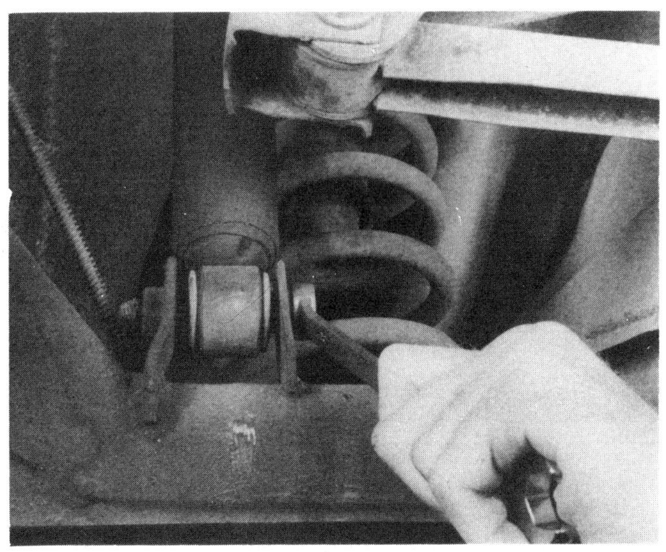
7.3a Each rear shock is held in place by one lower . . .

7.3b . . . and one upper bolt

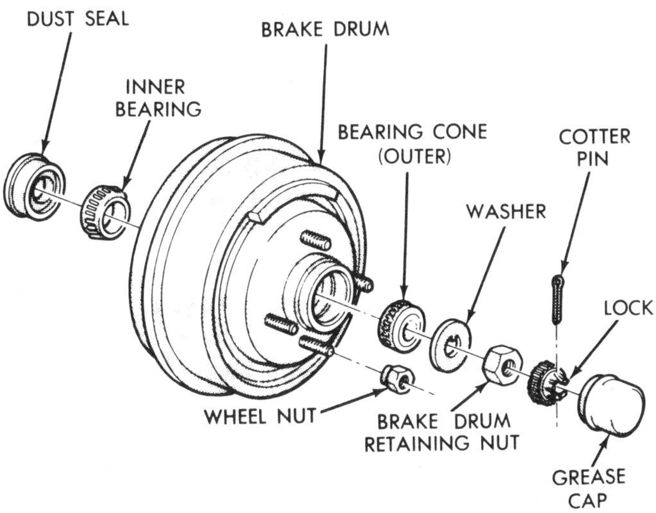

8.2 Rear hub and bearings — exploded view

8.3 Pull out on the brake drum to dislodge the outer bearing while holding it so it doesn't fall

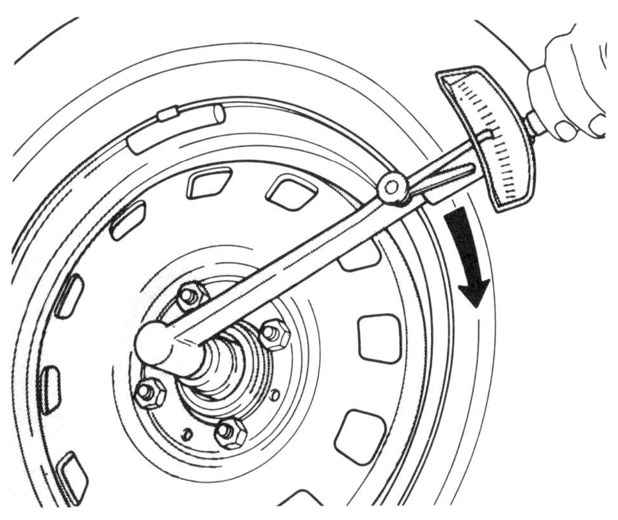
8.7 Rotate the tire as the hub nut is tightened to the specified torque

8.8 Tap the grease cap evenly into place with a hammer

10

9.7 The bearing races can be driven out with a hammer and drift punch (work carefully and do not damage the hub)

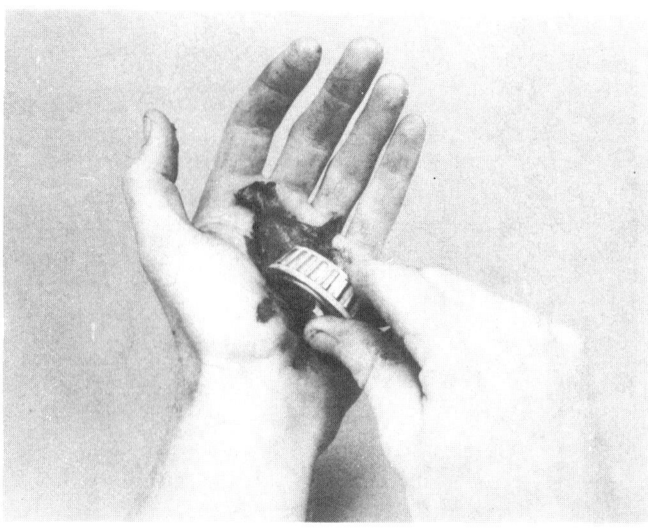

9.9 Work the grease into the rollers from the rear of the bearing race

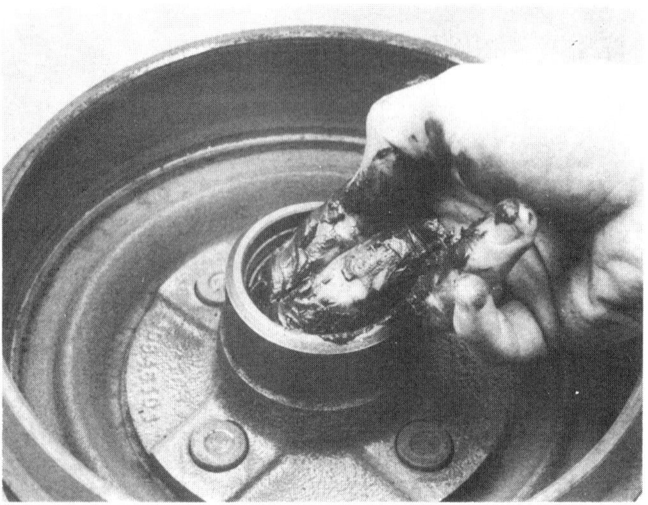

9.10a Put a small amount of grease in the hub cavity . . .

9.10b . . . and on the center of the spindle

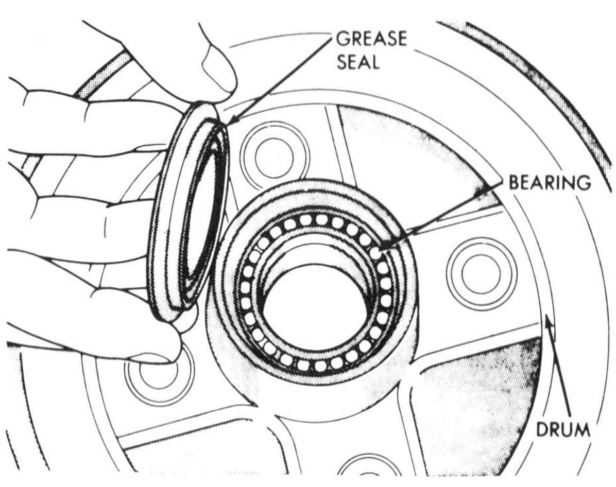

9.11a Make sure the bearing is in place in the hub before installing the grease seal

9.11b Tap the seal into place with a hammer and a wood block

Pull out on the drum; the end play in the hub should not exceed 0.001 to 0.003-inch (0.025 to 0.076 mm).
9 Lower the vehicle and tighten the wheel lug nuts.

9 Rear hub and bearings – inspection and lubrication

Refer to illustrations 9.7, 9.9, 9.10a, 9.10b, 9.11a and 9.11b

1 Remove the hub from the vehicle (Section 8).
2 Inspect the bearings for proper lubrication and signs that the grease has been contaminated by dirt (grease will be gritty) or water (grease will have milky-white appearance).
3 Use a hammer and a 3/4-inch diameter wood dowel to drive the inner bearing and seal out of the hub (discard the seal).
4 Clean the bearings with solvent and dry them with compressed air.
5 Check the bearings for wear, pitting and scoring of the roller and cage. Light discoloration of the bearing surfaces is normal, but if the surfaces are badly worn or damaged, replace the bearings with new ones.
6 Clean the hub with solvent and remove the old grease from the hub cavity. **Warning:** *Do not immerse the hub/drum assembly in solvent and do not get any solvent on the brake drum lining contact surface.*
7 Inspect the bearing races for wear, signs of overheating, pitting and corrosion. If the races are worn or damaged, drive them out with a hammer and a drift punch **(see illustration)**.
8 Drive the new races in with a section of pipe and a hammer, but be very careful not to damage them or get them cocked in the bore.
9 Pack the bearings with high-temperature, multi-purpose EP grease prior to installation. Work generous amounts of grease in from the back of the cage so the grease is forced up through the rollers **(see illustration)**.
10 Add a small amount of grease to the hub cavity and to the center of the spindle **(see illustrations)**.
11 Lubricate the outer edge of the new grease seal, insert the bearing and press the seal into position with the lip facing in **(see illustration)**. Make sure the seal is seated completely in the hub by tapping it evenly into place with a hammer and block of wood **(see illustration)**. Apply grease to the seal cavity and lip and the polished sections of the spindle.
12 Install the hub and drum assembly as described in Section 8.

10 Rear spindle – inspection, removal and installation

Removal

1 Remove the rear hub/drum (Section 8).
2 Clean the axle and inspect the bearing contact surfaces for wear and damage.
3 The axle should be replaced with a new one if it is bent, damaged or worn.
4 Disconnect the parking brake cable.
5 Disconnect and plug the rear brake line at the wheel cylinder (see Chapter 9 if necessary).
6 Remove the four backing plate mounting bolts and detach the brake assembly and spindle. The bolts may have Torx-type heads, which require a special tool for removal. Be sure to mark the location of any spindle shims.

Installation

7 Place the shim(s) (if equipped), spindle and brake assembly in position, install the bolts and tighten them to the specified torque in a criss-cross pattern.
8 Connect the brake line and parking brake cable.
9 Install the hub/drum (Section 8), bleed the brakes and adjust the parking brake (Chapter 9).

11 Steering system – general information

All models are equipped with rack-and-pinion steering. The steering gear is bolted to the chassis directly behind the engine and operates the steering arms through tie-rods. The inner ends of the tie-rods are protected by rubber boots which should be inspected periodically for secure attachment, tears and leaking lubricant.

As an option, some models are equipped with power assisted steering. The power assist system consists of a belt-driven pump and associated lines and hoses. The power steering system fluid level should be checked periodically (Chapter1).

The steering wheel operates the steering shaft which actuates the steering gear through a universal joint. Looseness in the steering can be caused by wear in the steering shaft universal joint, the steering gear, the tie-rod ends and loose retaining bolts. Inadequate lubrication of the steering shaft seal can cause binding of the steering; the seal should be lubricated periodically (Chapter 1).

12 Steering wheel – removal and installation

Refer to illustrations 12.4 and 12.5

1 Disconnect the negative cable at the battery. Place the cable out of the way so it cannot accidentally come in contact with the negative terminal of the battery, as this would once again allow power into the electrical system of the vehicle.
2 Remove the center pad assembly by grasping it securely and pulling straight out, releasing the clips.
3 Unplug the connector and remove the horn switch.
4 Remove the steering wheel retaining nut **(see illustration)** and mark the relationship of the steering shaft and hub to simplify installation.
5 Use a puller to remove the steering wheel **(see illustration)**. **Caution:** *Do not hammer on the shaft to remove the steering wheel.*

12.4 Removing the steering wheel retaining nut with a breaker bar

12.5 Use a puller to remove the steering wheel – DO NOT hammer on the shaft!

10

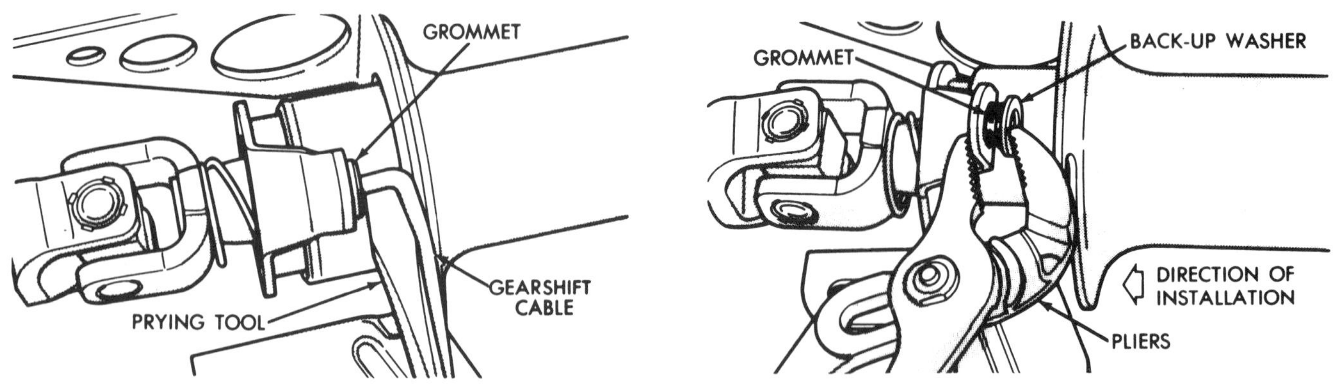

13.2 Prying the shift cable rod out of the grommet

13.10 Installing the new shift cable rod grommet

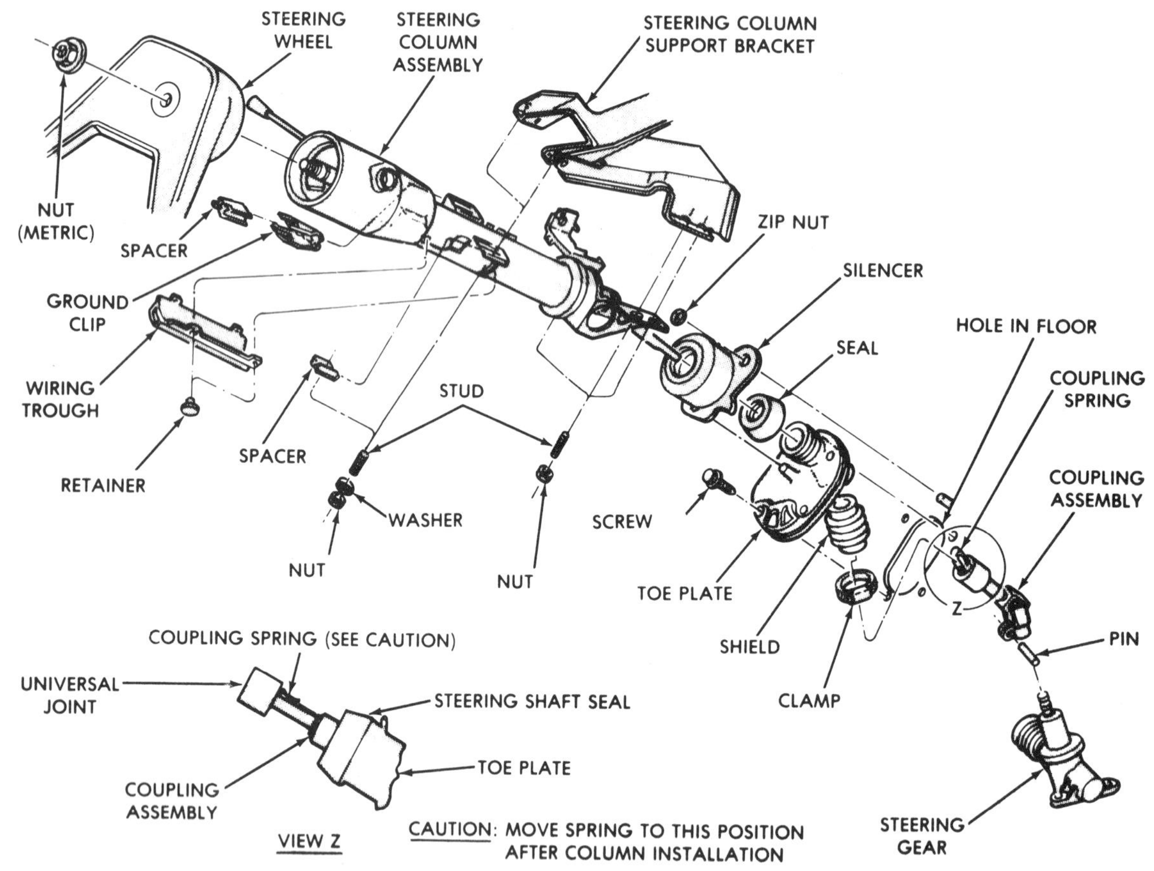

14.2a Typical fixed steering column components – exploded view

6 To install the wheel, align the mark on the steering wheel hub with the mark made on the shaft during removal and slip the wheel onto the shaft. Install the hub nut (and damper if removed) and tighten it to the specified torque.
7 Install the horn switch and button.
8 Install the center pad assembly.
9 Connect the negative battery cable.

13 Steering column – removal and installation

Refer to illustrations 13.2 and 13.10

Removal

1 Disconnect the negative cable at the battery. Place the cable out of the way so it cannot accidentally come in contact with the negative terminal of the battery, as this would once again allow power into the electrical system of the vehicle.
2 On column shift models, pry the gearshift cable rod from the grommet in the shift lever. Remove the cable from the lower bracket **(see illustration)**.
3 Unplug the steering column wiring connectors at the column jacket.
4 Remove the steering wheel (Section 12).
5 Remove the instrument panel column cover and the lower reinforcement, then disconnect the bezel (Chapter 11).
6 On *1982 through 1984 models*, remove the shift indicator set screw and pointer. On *1985 and later models*, remove the shift indicator cable from the slot in the shift housing.
7 Remove the steering column-to-instrument panel and lower panel bracket retaining nuts. *Do not remove the roll pin.*
8 Grasp the steering column assembly firmly and pull it toward the rear so the lower stub shaft is disconnected from the steering gear coupling. On *1985 and later models*, reinstall the anti-rattle coupling

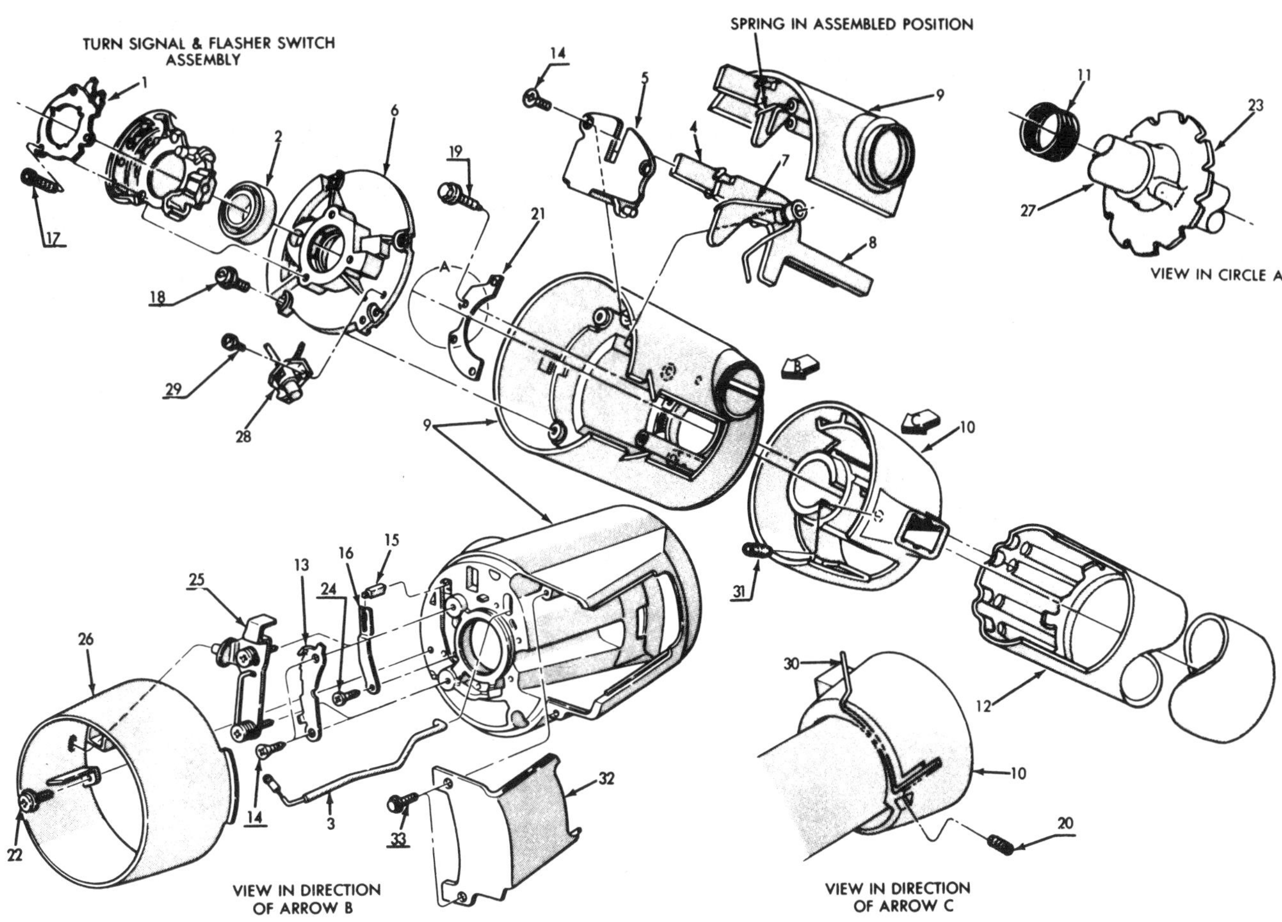

14.2b Upper steering column components (1982 through 1985 models) — exploded view

1 *Plate*
2 *Upper bearing*
3 *Ignition switch rod*
4 *Lever*
5 *Bellcrank*
6 *Upper bearing housing*
7 *Spring*
8 *Lever*
9 *Lock housing*
10 *Gearshift housing*
11 *Lock plate spring*
12 *Jacket*
13 *Gearshift lever gate*
14 *Screw*
15 *Plunger*
16 *Spring*
17 *Screw*
18 *Screw*
19 *Screw and washer*
20 *Set screw*
21 *Plate*
22 *Screw*
23 *Lock plate*
24 *Screw*
25 *Lock inhibitor (floor shift)*
26 *Plastic shroud (floor shift)*
27 *Steering shaft*
28 *Key light*
29 *Screw*
30 *Pointer/indicator*
31 *Set screw*
32 *Lock cover*
33 *Cover screw*

spring all the way into the lower coupling tube. Be sure it snaps into the slot in the coupling.

9 Remove the assembly carefully from the vehicle. **Note:** *On vehicles equipped with a speed control and manual transaxle, be careful not to damage the clutch pedal speed control switch.*

Installation

10 Prior to installation, install a new grommet in the shift lever (from the rod side), using a pair of pliers and a back-up washer so it will snap into place **(see illustration)**. Use multi-purpose grease to lubricate the grommet.

11 Place the steering column in position with the stub shaft aligned with the lower coupling and insert the shaft into the coupling.

12 Install the retaining nuts (use washers on the breakaway capsules) and pull the column to the rear while tightening the nuts.

13 Using a pair of needle-nose pliers, pull the coupling spring up until it touches the spacer on the stub shaft **(see illustration 14.2a)**.

14 Using a pair of pliers, snap the gearshift cable rod into the grommet. Check and adjust the linkage (Chapter 7).

15 Install the steering wheel.

16 Plug in the wiring connectors.

17 Install the shift indicator pointer or the indicator cable.

18 Install the panel column cover, lower reinforcement and bezel.

19 Slowly move the shift lever through all positions to make sure the indicator needle is aligned properly; adjust it as necessary (later models are automatically adjusted as the shift lever is moved).

20 Connect the negative battery cable and check the operation of the horn and lights.

14 Steering column (fixed) (1982 and later column shift models) — disassembly, inspection and reassembly

Refer to illustrations 14.2a, 14.2b, 14.8, 14.9, 14.15 and 14.25

10

Note: *The fixed steering column used on 1982 and later column shift and 1982 through 1985 floor shift models is of the same design. The 1986 and later floor shift model columns are different (Section 15). The steering column used on some models may differ slightly in appearance and details from the one shown in the illustrations, but the procedure is essentially the same. The steering column used on 1982 through 1985 floor shift models is also slightly different than the column shift and may require the procedure to be modified slightly.*

1 Remove the breakaway capsules and clamp the bracket in a vise, using blocks of wood to protect the bracket.

2 Pry the wiring trough retainers loose and remove the trough **(see illustrations)**.

14.8 Removing the upper steering column bearing housing snap-ring

14.9 Lifting out the bearing housing

14.15 Apply grease to the lower bearing outer edge and contact surface

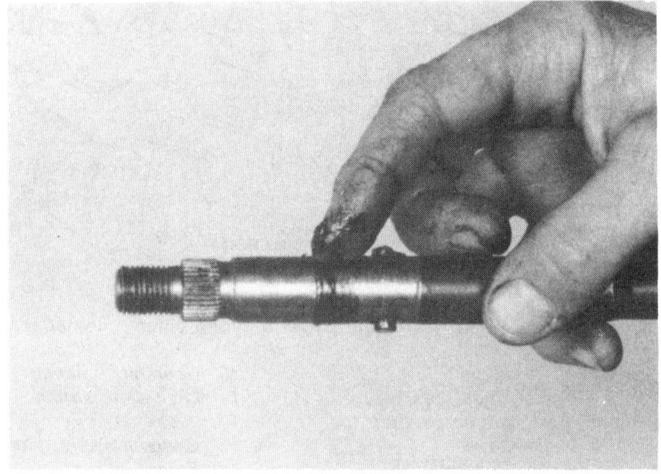

14.25 Cover the O-ring and surrounding shaft area with grease

3 Remove the shift lever by driving out the roll pin with a small punch and a hammer. Protect the steering column surface with masking tape and back up the opposite side of the lever base with a deep socket while driving the pin out.
4 Remove the screws, detach the turn signal lever cover and remove the washer/wiper switch assembly.
5 Pull the hider up the control stalk and remove the two screws that hold the control stalk sleeve to the washer/wiper switch. Rotate the control stalk to the full clockwise position and remove the shaft from the switch by pulling it straight out.
6 Remove the screws and detach the turn signal/flasher switch (lift it up to remove it).
7 Disconnect the horn and key light ground wires and remove the ignition key light.
8 Remove the shaft upper bearing retaining screws, then remove the shaft snap-ring **(see illustration)**. *Do not allow the steering shaft to slide out of the jacket.*
9 Slide the bearing housing, lock plate and spring from the shaft **(see illustration)**. Remove the shaft through the lower end of the column.
10 Remove the screw and lift out the key buzzer assembly.
11 Remove the ignition switch mounting screws, then rotate the switch 90 degrees on the rod and slide it off.
12 Remove the two screws and disengage the dimmer switch from the actuator rod.
13 Remove the mounting screws and slide the bellcrank up in the lock housing until it can be disconnected from the ignition switch actuator rod.
14 Place the cylinder in the Lock position and remove the key. Insert two small screwdrivers into the lock cylinder release holes and push in to release the retainers (the lower release hole is just above the buzzer switch screw hole). At the same time, pull the lock cylinder out of the housing bore. Remove the screws and detach the lock housing and plate.
15 Inspect the steering shaft bearings for wear, looseness and signs of binding. The bearings should be replaced with new ones if there is appreciable wear or rough action. Lubricate the bearing with multi-purpose grease prior to installation **(see illustration)**.
16 Lubricate the end of the shift lever, install the spring in the housing, position the lever and tap the roll pin into place. Assemble the key cylinder plunger spring and attach the assembly to the lock housing.
17 Install the shift lever gate on the lock housing.
18 With the shift lever in the middle position, attach the lock housing plate to the column jacket and install the screws. Make sure the keyway on the housing is inserted into the slot in the jacket before tightening the screws (tighten them a little at a time, following a criss-cross pattern).
19 Install the dimmer switch (Chapter 12).
20 Lubricate the lock lever assembly and install it in the lock housing.

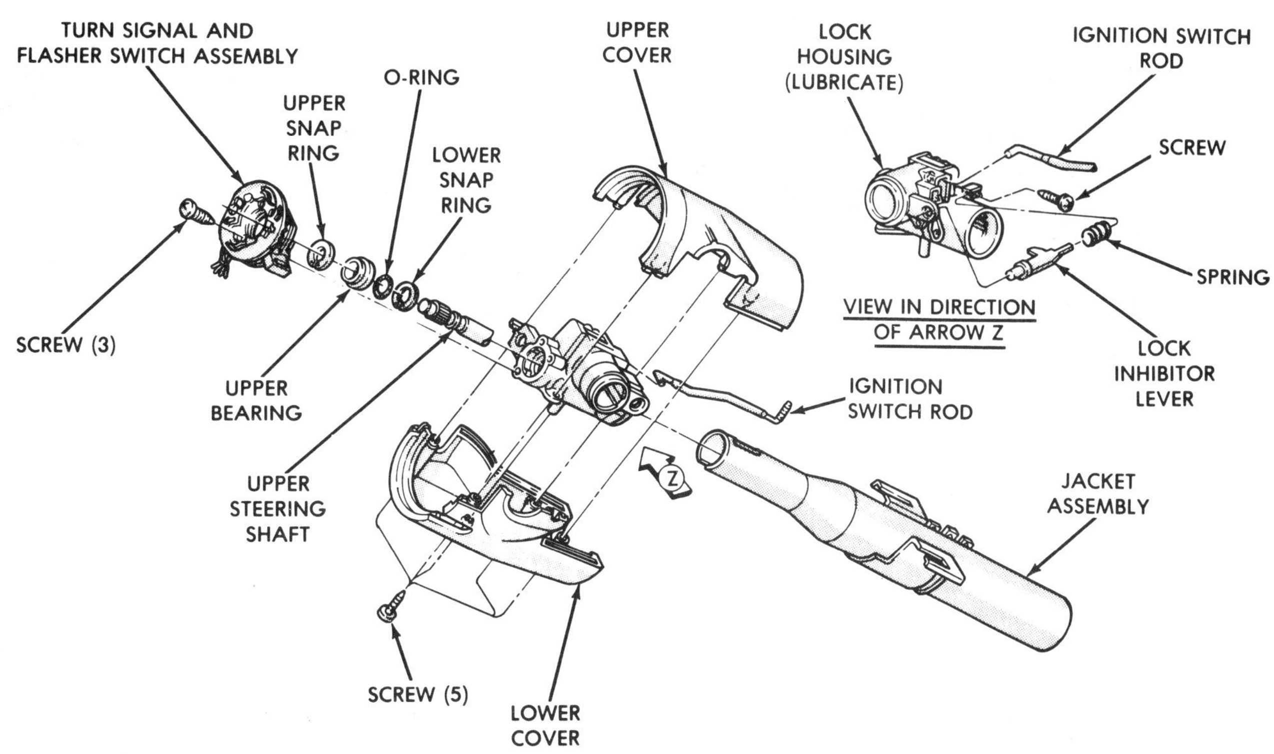

15.1a 1986 and later floor shift model upper steering column components — exploded view

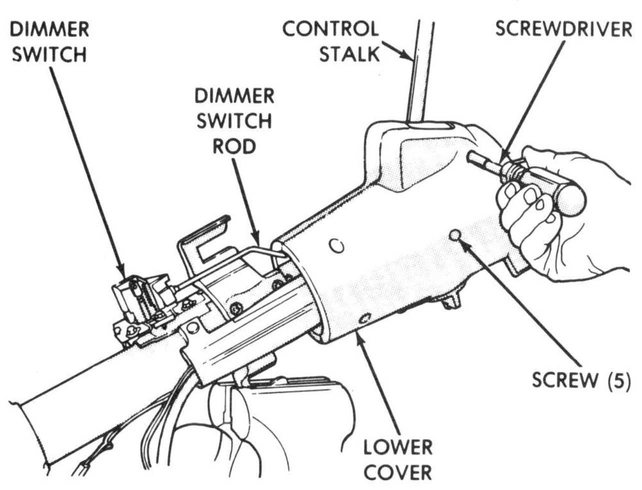

15.1b Removing the column cover (1986 and later floor shift models)

Seat the pin in the bottom of the slots and make sure the lock lever spring leg is in place in the casting notch.

21 Install the ignition switch actuator rod up from the bottom of the lock housing and connect the bellcrank. Position the bellcrank assembly in the lock housing while pulling the switch rod down the column, then attach the bellcrank (the shift lever should be in Park).

22 Attach the ignition switch to the rod and rotate it 90 degrees so the rod will lock in position.

23 Install the ignition lock, turn the key to the Lock position and remove it, which will cause the buzzer actuating lever to retract. Insert the key again, push in and turn the cylinder until the retainers align and the cylinder snaps into place. Make sure the key cylinder and the ignition switch are in the Lock position and tighten the mounting screws.

24 Push the wires leading from the key buzzer switch down the column through the space between the housing and the jacket. Remove the key and tighten the switch screws.

25 Install the bearing and spring onto the steering shaft. Install the O-ring on the shaft and lubricate it **(see illustration)**.

26 Insert the steering shaft into the column and press the bearing into place in the housing. Push up on the steering shaft so the spring will be compressed and install the snap-ring.

27 Install the lock plate, anti-rattle spring and bearing and housing assembly, retaining it with the snap-ring.

28 Install the bearing housing retaining screws.

29 Install the key light assembly, followed by the turn signal switch. Feed the wires down the steering column through the opening between the bearing and lock housing.

30 Install the retainer plate and screws and connect the ground wires.

31 Assemble the wiper switch, shaft, cover, or speed control switch, hider and knob.

32 Place the washer/wiper switch assembly in the lock housing and feed the wires through the lock and shift housings. Connect the wires to the turn signal switch.

33 Insert the dimmer switch actuating rod up through the housing and connect it to the washer/wiper switch.

34 Adjust the dimmer switch as described in Chapter 12.

35 Install the turn signal lever cover and the breakaway capsules.

36 Install the wiring trough, being careful not to pinch the wires, and install new retainers if needed.

10

15 Steering column (fixed) (1986 and later floor shift models) — disassembly, inspection and reassembly

Refer to illustrations 15.1a, 15.1b, 15.2, 15.3, 15.4, 15.5, 15.6, 15.7, 15.8, 15.9, 15.10 and 15.11

1 Clamp the bracket in a vise and remove the upper and lower covers **(see illustrations)**.

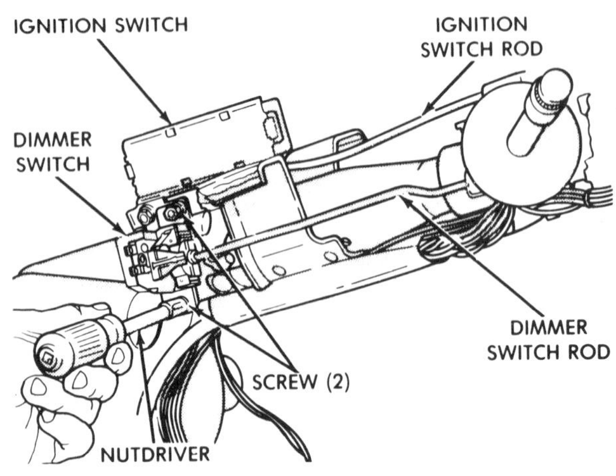

15.2 Dimmer switch removal and installation details (1986 and later floor shift models)

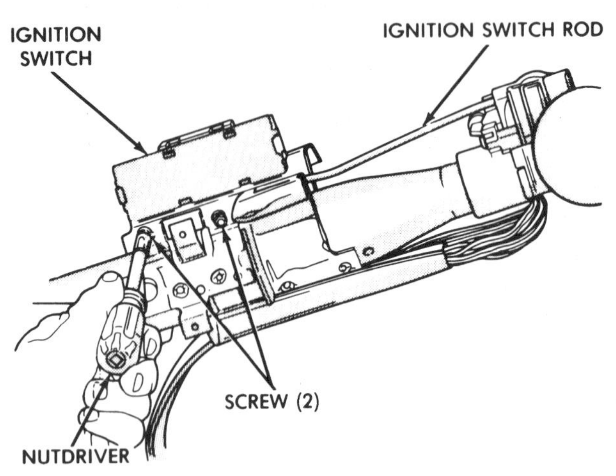

15.3 Ignition switch removal and installation details (1986 and later floor shift models)

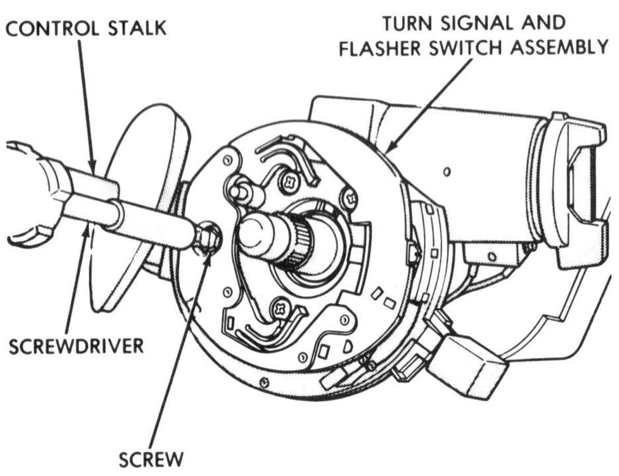

15.4 Washer/wiper switch removal and installation details (1986 and later floor shift models)

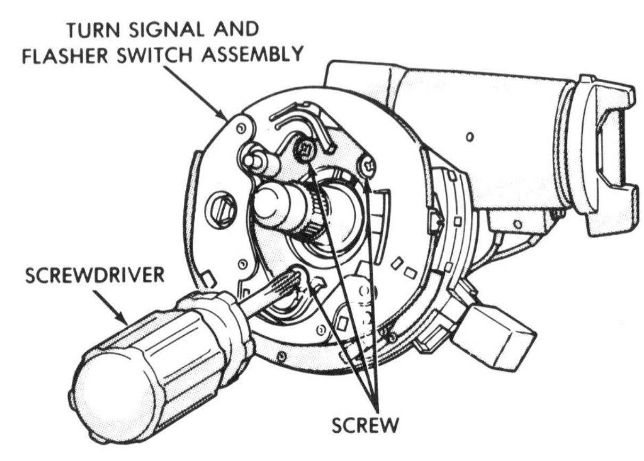

15.5 Turn signal and flasher switch removal and installation details (1986 and later floor shift models)

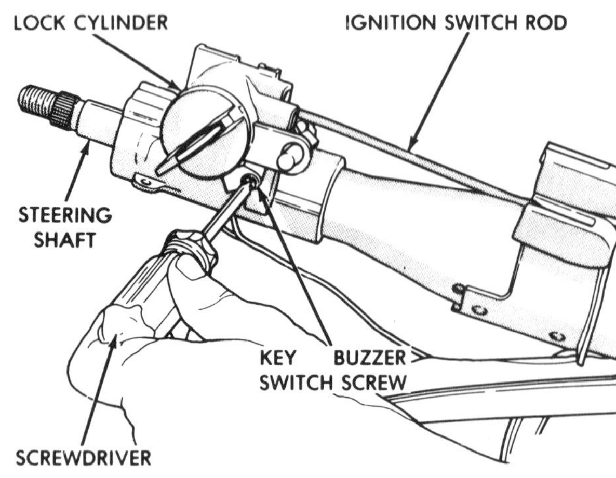

15.6 Key buzzer removal and installation details (1986 and later floor shift models)

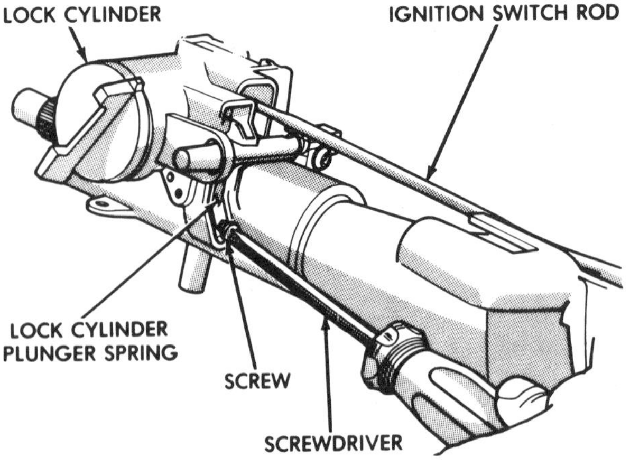

15.7 Lock cylinder plunger removal and installation details (1986 and later floor shift models)

2 Remove the retaining screws, disengage the switch rod and remove the dimmer switch **(see illustration)**.
3 Remove the two retaining screws, disengage the rod and lift the ignition switch off **(see illustration)**.
4 Remove the retaining screw and lift off the washer/wiper switch **(see illustration)**.
5 Remove the three screws and detach the turn signal and flasher switch **(see illustration)**.
6 Remove the key buzzer switch retaining screws and detach the switch **(see illustration)**.
7 Remove the retaining screw and release the lock cylinder plunger **(see illustration)**.
8 Insert a small screwdriver into the release hole and with the key removed, pull the lock cylinder out of the housing **(see illustration)**.
9 Remove the screw, disengage the rod and remove the lock lever inhibitor assembly **(see illustration)**.
10 Use snap-ring pliers to remove the upper bearing snap-ring, then slide the bearing from the shaft **(see illustration)**.
11 Remove the steering shaft through the lower end of the column jacket **(see illustration)**.
12 Reassembly is the reverse of the disassembly procedure.

16 Steering column (tilt-wheel) – disassembly, inspection and reassembly

Other than removal and installation of the steering wheel and column assemblies, procedures for the tilt-wheel column vary considerably from those for the fixed column. Because of the special tools and expertise required, work on the tilt-wheel steering column assembly should be referred to your dealer service department or a repair shop.

17 Steering gear – removal and installation

Refer to illustration 17.4

1 Raise the vehicle, support it securely on jackstands and remove the front wheels. Remove the steering column assembly (Section 13), leaving the lower universal joint with the steering gear.
2 Disconnect the tie-rod ends from the steering knuckles (Section 22).
3 Remove the anti-rotational link or damper from the crossmember.

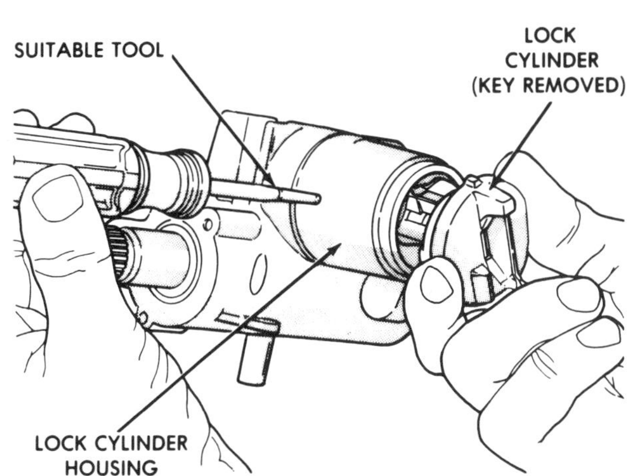

15.8 Lock cylinder removal (1986 and later floor shift models)

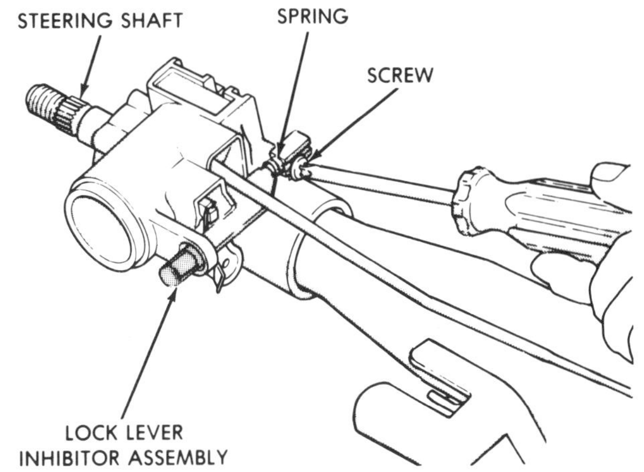

15.9 Lock lever inhibitor assembly details (1986 and later floor shift models)

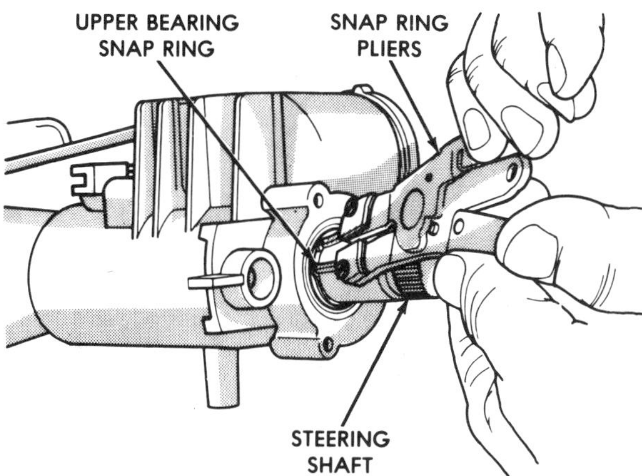

15.10 Removing the upper bearing snap-ring (1986 and later floor shift models)

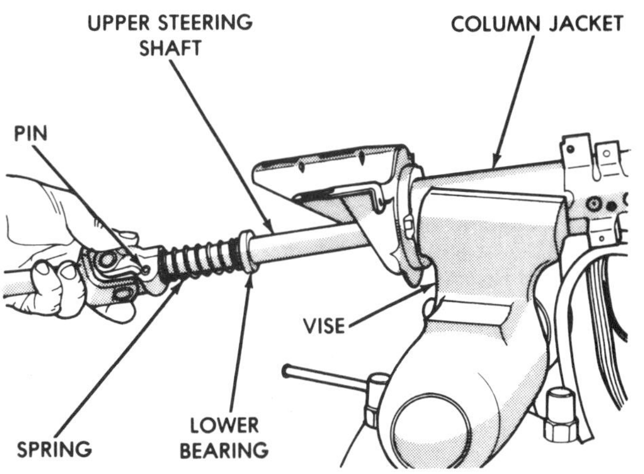

15.11 Slide the steering shaft out of the lower end of the column jacket (1986 and later floor shift models)

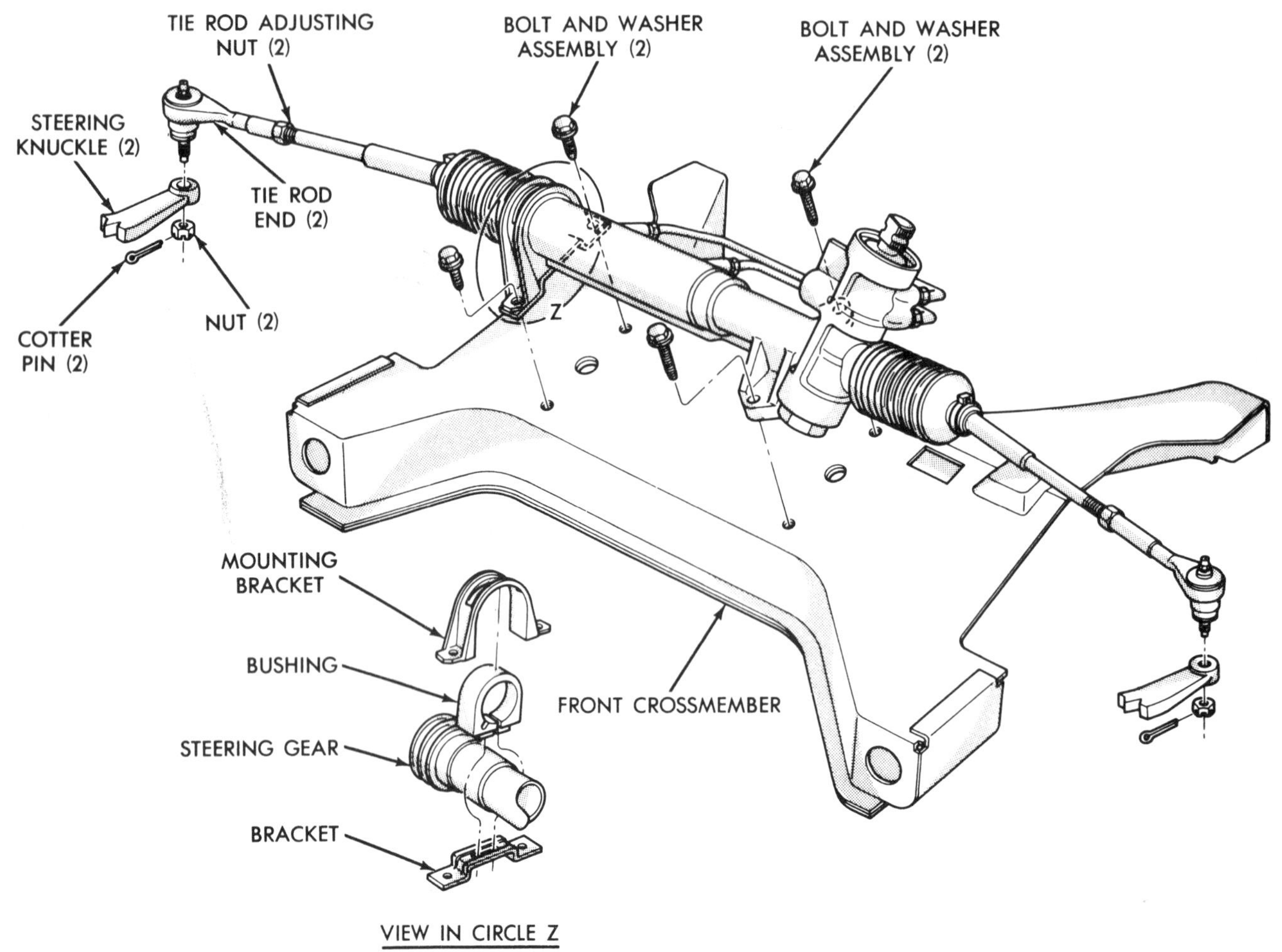

17.4 Steering gear mounting details

4 Support the front crossmember with a jack, then remove the four crossmember bolts **(see illustration)**.
5 Lower the crossmember with the jack to gain access to the steering gear.
6 Remove the boot seal and splash shields from the crossmember.
7 On power steering equipped models, disconnect the hoses and drain the fluid into a container.
8 Remove the steering gear mounting bolts and separate it from the crossmember by withdrawing it to the left side of the vehicle.
9 To install the steering gear, position it in the crossmember, install the bolts and tighten them securely.
10 Attach the tie-rod ends to the steering knuckles.
11 On power steering equipped models, reconnect the hoses (use new O-rings).
12 On manual steering equipped models, check to make sure the master serrations on the steering gear shaft are properly aligned so the steering shaft will be installed in the straight-ahead position.
13 Install the boot seal and splash shields.
14 Raise the crossmember and steering gear into position with the jack, install the four crossmember bolts and tighten them securely (the right rear bolt is a pilot bolt and must be tightened first).
15 Install the steering column assembly.
16 Install the front wheels and lower the vehicle.
17 On power steering equipped models, start the engine and bleed the steering system (Section 20). While the engine is running, check for leaks at the hose connections.
18 Have the front end alignment checked by a dealer service department or an alignment shop.

18 Power steering pump (2.2L/2.5L engine) – removal and installation

Note: *All fasteners used on the power steering pump mounting brackets are metric.*

1 Open the hood and disconnect the two wires from the air conditioner clutch switch (if equipped).
2 Remove the drivebelt adjustment locking bolt from the front of the pump and (if equipped) the nut from the end hose bracket.
3 Raise the vehicle and support it securely on jackstands.
4 Remove the pump pressure hose locating bracket at the crossmember, disconnect the hose from the steering gear and drain the fluid through the hose into a container.
5 While the fluid is draining, remove the right side splash shield to expose the drivebelts.
6 Disconnect the hoses from the pump and plug all openings so that dirt cannot enter.
7 Remove the lower stud nut and pivot bolt from the pump, then lower the vehicle.
8 Remove the drivebelt from the pulley, then move the pump to the rear and remove the adjustment bracket.
9 Turn the pump around so the pulley is facing toward the rear of the vehicle and lift it up and out of the engine compartment.
10 Install the adjustment bracket on the pump. Make sure the tab is in the lower left front mounting hole.
11 Lower the pump into position in the engine compartment.
12 Raise the vehicle and support it securely.

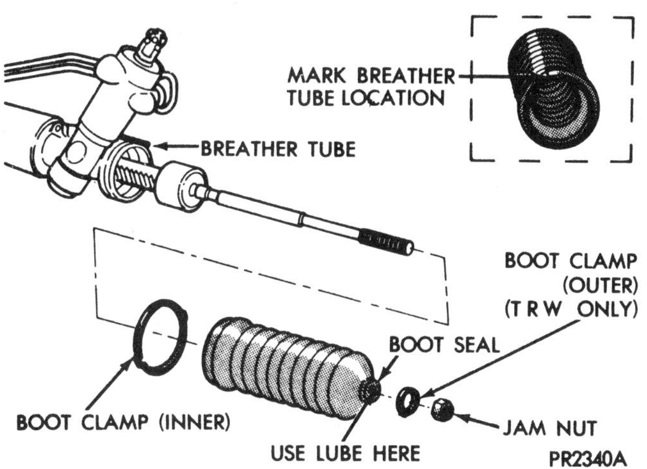

21.4 Steering gear boot replacement details

13 Install the lower pump bolt and stud nut finger tight.
14 Using new O-rings, attach the hoses to the pump.
15 Place the drivebelt on the pulley, then lower the vehicle.
16 Install the adjustment bolt and nut, adjust the belt to the proper tension (Chapter l) and tighten the nut.
17 Raise the vehicle, tighten the lower stud nut and pivot bolt and install the splash shield.
18 Lower the vehicle and connect the air conditioner switch wires.
19 Fill the pump to the top of the filler neck with the specified fluid.
20 Start the engine, bleed the air from the system (Section 20) and check the fluid level.

19 Power steering pump (2.6L engine) – removal and installation

1 Disconnect and plug the power steering pump hoses. Plug the pump ports.
2 Remove the pump pivot and adjustment bolts and detach the drivebelt.
3 Lift the pump and bracket from the engine compartment.
4 Place the pump in position and install the pivot and adjustment bolts and nuts finger tight.
5 Attach the hoses to the pump and tighten the tube nuts.
6 Install the drivebelt, adjust it to the proper tension (Chapter 1) and tighten the bolts/nuts.
7 Fill the pump to the top of the filler neck with the specified fluid, bleed the system and check the fluid level.

20 Power steering system – bleeding

1 The power steering system must be bled whenever a line is disconnected.
2 Check the fluid level in the reservoir; add the specified fluid to bring it up to the proper level (see Chapter 1 if necessary).
3 Start the engine and slowly turn the steering wheel several times from left-to-right and back again. Do not turn the wheel fully from lock-to-lock. Check the fluid level, topping it up as necessary until it remains steady and no more bubbles appear in the reservoir.

21 Steering gear boots – replacement

Refer to illustration 21.4

1 Raise the vehicle and support it securely on jackstands.
2 Remove the tie-rod end (Section 22).
3 Remove the boot clamp(s). Only TRW model steering gears have

22.2 Use a puller to separate the tie-rod ends from the steering knuckles

an outer boot clamp.
4 Mark the location of the breather tube, use a small screwdriver to lift the boot out of the groove in the steering gear and remove the boot **(see illustration)**.
5 Prior to installation, lubricate the boot groove in the steering tie-rod with silicone-type grease.
6 Slide the new boot into position on the steering gear until it seats in the groove and install a new inner clamp. Make sure the breather tube fits securely in the boot.
7 Install the clamp(s).
8 Install the tie-rod end.
9 Lower the vehicle.
10 Have the front end alignment checked by a dealer service department or an alignment shop.

22 Tie-rod ends – removal and installation

Refer to illustration 22.2

1 Raise the front of the vehicle, support it securely on jackstands, block the rear wheels and set the parking brake. Remove the front wheels.
2 Disconnect the tie-rod from the steering knuckle with a puller **(see illustration)**.
3 Mark the location of the jam nut, then loosen it enough to allow the rod end to be unscrewed and removed from the tie-rod.
4 Thread the tie-rod end onto the rod to the marked position and tighten the jam nut securely.
5 Connect the tie-rod end to the steering knuckle, install the nut and tighten it to the specified torque. Install a **new** cotter pin.
6 If a new tie-rod end has been installed, have the front end alignment checked by a dealer service department or an alignment shop.

23 Steering angles and wheel alignment – general information

Proper wheel alignment is essential to proper steering and even tire wear. Symptoms of alignment problems include pulling to one side or the other and uneven tire wear.

If these symptoms are present, check for the following before having the alignment adjusted:

Loose steering gear mounting bolts
Damaged or worn steering gear mounts
Improperly adjusted wheel bearings

Bent tie-rods
Worn balljoints
Insufficient steering gear lubricant
Improper tire pressure
Mixing tires of different construction

Alignment problems in the rear suspension are manifested in uneven tire wear or uneven tracking of the rear wheels. This can be easily checked by driving the vehicle straight across a puddle of water onto a dry patch of pavement. If the rear wheels do not follow the front wheels exactly, the alignment should be adjusted.

Front or rear wheel alignment should be left to a dealer service department or an alignment shop.

24 Wheels and tires — general check

1 Check the tire pressures (cold) weekly.
2 Inspect the sidewalls and treads periodically for damage and signs of abnormal or uneven wear.
3 Make sure the wheel lug nuts are properly tightened.
4 Do not mix tires of dissimilar construction or tread pattern on the same axle.
5 Never include the temporary spare in the tire rotation pattern as it is designed for use only until a damaged tire is repaired or replaced.
6 Periodically inspect the wheels for elongated or damaged lug holes, distortion and nicks in the rim. Replace damaged wheels.
7 Clean each wheel inside and out and check for rust and corrosion, which could lead to wheel failure.
8 If the wheels are balanced on the vehicle, one wheel stud and lug hole should be marked whenever a wheel is removed so that it can be reinstalled in the original position. Wheels should not be moved to a different axle position.

25 Wheels and tires — removal and installation

1 With the vehicle on a level surface, the parking brake engaged and the transaxle in Neutral (manual) or Park (automatic), remove the hub cap (if equipped) and loosen, but do not remove the wheel lug nuts.
2 Using a jack positioned in the proper location (see *Jacking and Towing* at the beginning of this manual), raise the vehicle so the tire clears the ground.
3 Remove the lug nuts.
4 Remove the wheel and tire.
5 If a flat tire is being replaced, make sure there is adequate clearance for the new inflated tire, then mount the wheel and tire on the wheel studs.
6 Apply a light coat of spray lubricant or light oil to the wheel stud threads and install the lug nuts snugly with the cone-shaped end facing the wheel.
7 Lower the vehicle until the tire contacts the ground and the wheel studs are centered in the wheel holes.
8 Tighten the nuts evenly in a criss-cross pattern.
9 Lower the vehicle and remove the jack.
10 Install the hub cap.

Chapter 11 Body

Contents

Specifications

Torque specifications	Ft-lbs	Nm
Hood-to-hinge bolts	9.5	12
Hood latch bolts	9.5	12
Energy absorbing unit-to-body bolt	20 to 25	28 to 34
Fender mounting bolts	9.5	12
Front seat bolts	20	28
Liftgate hinge bolts	9.5	12
Deck lid hinge bolts	9.5	12

1 General information

These models are of unitized construction. The body is designed to provide vehicle rigidity so that a separate frame is not necessary. Front and rear frame side rails integral with the body support the front end sheet metal, front and rear suspension systems and other mechanical components. Due to this type of construction, it is very important that, in the event of collision damage, the underbody be thoroughly checked by a facility with the proper equipment.

Component replacement and repairs possible for the home mechanic are included in this Chapter.

Although all models are very similar, some procedures may differ somewhat from one body design to another. The body designations are as follows:

C/V body — Chrysler LeBaron, Town and Country, Dodge 400
E body — Chrysler E Class, New Yorker, Dodge 600, Plymouth Caravelle
H body — Chrysler LeBaron GTS and Dodge Lancer

2 Maintenance — body and frame

1 The condition of your vehicle's body is very important, because it is on this that the second hand value will mainly depend. It is much more difficult to repair a neglected or damaged body than it is to repair mechanical components. The hidden areas of the body, such as the fender wells, the frame, and the engine compartment, are equally important, although obviously do not require as frequent attention as the rest of the body.

2 Once a year, or every 12,000 miles, it is a good idea to have the underside of the body and the frame steam cleaned. All traces of dirt and oil will be removed and the underside can then be inspected carefully for rust, damaged brake lines, frayed electrical wiring, damaged cables, and other problems. The front suspension components should be greased after completion of this job.

3 At the same time, clean the engine and the engine compartment using either a steam cleaner or a water soluble degreaser.

4 The fender wells should be given particular attention, as undercoating can peel away and stones and dirt thrown up by the tires can cause the paint to chip and flake, allowing rust to set in. If rust is found, clean down to the bare metal and apply an anti-rust paint.

5 The body should be washed once a week (or when dirty). Wet the vehicle thoroughly to soften the dirt, then wash it down with a soft sponge and plenty of clean soapy water. If the surplus dirt is not washed off very carefully, it will in time wear down the paint.

6 Spots of tar or asphalt coating thrown up from the road should be removed with a cloth soaked in solvent.

7 Once every six months, give the body and chrome trim a thorough waxing. If a chrome cleaner is used to remove rust from any of the vehicle's plated parts, remember that the cleaner also removes part of the chrome, so use it sparingly.

This photo sequence illustrates the repair of a dent and damaged paintwork. The procedure for the repair of a hole is similar. Refer to the text for more complete instructions

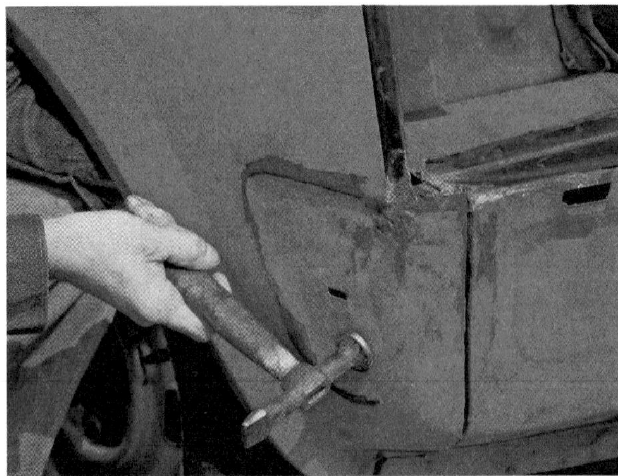

After removing any adjacent body trim, hammer the dent out. The damaged area should then be made slightly concave

Use coarse sandpaper or a sanding disc on a drill motor to remove all paint from the damaged area. Feather the sanded area into the edges of the surrounding paint, using progressively finer grades of sandpaper

The damaged area should be treated with rust remover prior to application of the body filler. In the case of a rust hole, all rusted sheet metal should be cut away

Carefully follow manufacturer's instructions when mixing the body filler so as to have the longest possible working time during application. Rust holes should be covered with fiberglass screen held in place with dabs of body filler prior to repair

Apply the filler with a flexible applicator in thin layers at 20 minute intervals. Use an applicator such as a wood spatula for confined areas. The filler should protrude slightly above the surrounding area

Shape the filler with a surform-type plane. Then, use water and progressively finer grades of sandpaper and a sanding block to wet-sand the area until it is smooth. Feather the edges of the repair area into the surrounding paint.

Use spray or brush applied primer to cover the entire repair area so that slight imperfections in the surface will be filled in. Prime at least one inch into the area surrounding the repair. Be careful of over-spray when using spray-type primer

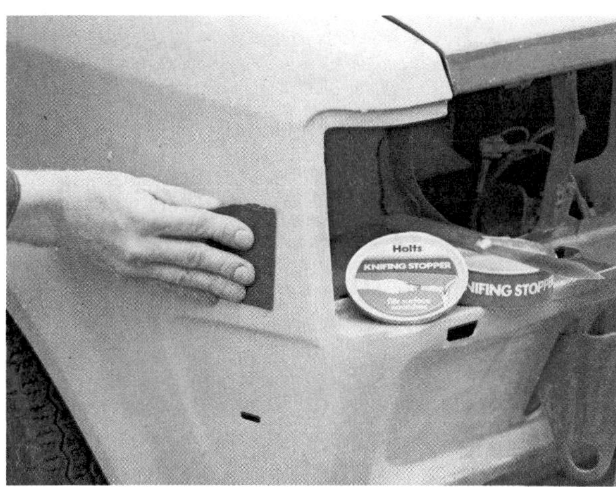

Wet-sand the primer with fine (approximately 400 grade) sandpaper until the area is smooth to the touch and blended into the surrounding paint. Use filler paste on minor imperfections

After the filler paste has dried, use rubbing compound to ensure that the surface of the primer is smooth. Prior to painting, the surface should be wiped down with a tack rag or lint-free cloth soaked in lacquer thinner

Choose a dry, warm, breeze-free area in which to paint and make sure that adjacent areas are protected from over-spray. Shake the spray paint can thoroughly and apply the top coat to the repair area, building it up by applying several coats, working from the center

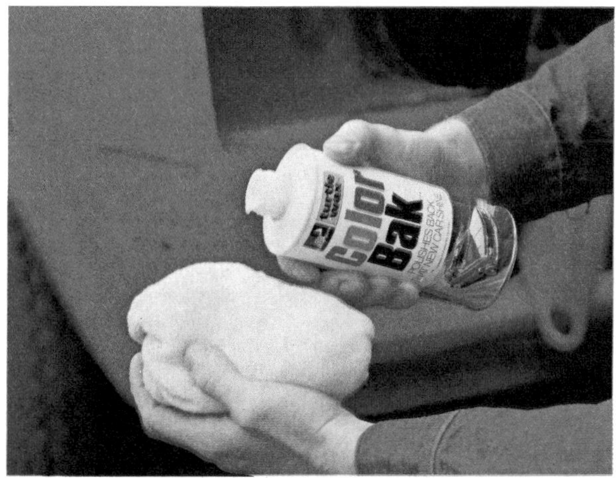

After allowing at least two weeks for the paint to harden, use fine rubbing compound to blend the area into the original paint. Wax can now be applied

3 Maintenance – upholstery and carpets

1 Every three months remove the carpets or mats and clean the interior of the vehicle (more frequently if necessary). Vacuum the upholstery and carpets to remove loose dirt and dust.
2 If the upholstery is soiled, apply upholstery cleaner with a damp sponge and wipe it off with a clean, dry cloth.

4 Body repair – minor damage

See color photo sequence "Repair of minor scratches"

1 If the scratch is superficial and does not penetrate to the metal of the body, repair is very simple. Lightly rub the scratched area with a fine rubbing compound to remove loose paint and built up wax. Rinse the area with clean water.
2 Apply touch-up paint to the scratch, using a small brush. Continue to apply thin layers of paint until the surface of the paint in the scratch is level with the surrounding paint. Allow the new paint at least two weeks to harden, then blend it into the surrounding paint by rubbing with a very fine rubbing compound. Finally, apply a coat of wax to the scratch area.
3 If the scratch has penetrated the paint and exposed the metal of the body, causing the metal to rust, a different repair technique is required. Remove all loose rust from the bottom of the scratch with a pocket knife, then apply rust inhibiting paint to prevent the formation of rust in the future. Using a rubber or nylon applicator, coat the scratched area with glaze-type filler. If required, the filler can be mixed with thinner to provide a very thin paste, which is ideal for filling narrow scratches. Before the glaze filler in the scratch hardens, wrap a piece of smooth cotton cloth around the tip of a finger. Dip the cloth in thinner and then quickly wipe it along the surface of the scratch. This will ensure that the surface of the filler is slightly hollow. The scratch can now be painted over as described earlier in this section.

Repair of dents

4 When repairing dents, the first job is to pull the dent out until the affected area is as close as possible to its original shape. There is no point in trying to restore the original shape completely as the metal in the damaged area will have stretched on impact and cannot be restored to its original contours. It is better to bring the level of the dent up to a point which is about 1/8-inch below the level of the surrounding metal. In cases where the dent is very shallow, it is not worth trying to pull it out at all.
5 If the back side of the dent is accessible, it can be hammered out gently from behind using a soft-face hammer. While doing this, hold a block of wood firmly against the opposite side of the metal to absorb the hammer blows and prevent the metal from being stretched.
6 If the dent is in a section of the body which has double layers, or some other factor makes it inaccessible from behind, a different technique is required. Drill several small holes through the metal inside the damaged area, particularly in the deeper sections. Screw long, self tapping screws into the holes just enough for them to get a good grip in the metal. Now the dent can be pulled out by pulling on the protruding heads of the screws with locking pliers.
7 The next stage of repair is the removal of paint from the damaged area and from an inch or so of the surrounding metal. This is easily done with a wire brush or sanding disk in a drill motor, although it can be done just as effectively by hand with sandpaper. To complete the preparation for filling, score the surface of the bare metal with a screwdriver or the tang of a file or drill small holes in the affected area. This will provide a good grip for the filler material. To complete the repair, see the Section on filling and painting.

Repair of rust holes or gashes

8 Remove all paint from the affected area and from an inch or so of the surrounding metal using a sanding disk or wire brush mounted in a drill motor. If these are not available, a few sheets of sandpaper will do the job just as effectively.
9 With the paint removed, you will be able to determine the severity of the corrosion and decide whether to replace the whole panel, if possible, or repair the affected area. New body panels are not as expensive as most people think and it is often quicker to install a new panel than to repair large areas of rust.
10 Remove all trim pieces from the affected area except those which will act as a guide to the original shape of the damaged body, such as headlight shells, etc. Using metal snips or a hacksaw blade, remove all loose metal and any other metal that is badly affected by rust. Hammer the edges of the hole inward to create a slight depression for the filler material.
11 Wire brush the affected area to remove the powdery rust from the surface of the metal. If the back of the rusted area is accessible, treat it with rust-inhibiting paint.
12 Before filling is done, block the hole in some way. This can be done with sheet metal riveted or screwed into place, or by stuffing the hole with wire mesh.
13 Once the hole is blocked off, the affected area can be filled and painted. See the following sub-section on filling and painting.

Filling and painting

14 Many types of body fillers are available, but generally speaking, body repair kits which contain filler paste and a tube of resin hardener are best for this type of repair work. A wide, flexible plastic or nylon applicator will be necessary for imparting a smooth and contoured finish to the surface of the filler material. Mix up a small amount of filler on a clean piece of wood or cardboard (use the hardener sparingly). Follow the manufacturer's instructions on the package, otherwise the filler will set incorrectly.
15 Using the applicator, apply the filler paste to the prepared area. Draw the applicator across the surface of the filler to achieve the desired contour and to level the filler surface. As soon as a contour that approximates the original one is achieved, stop working the paste. If you continue, the paste will begin to stick to the applicator. Continue to add thin layers of paste at 20-minute intervals until the level of the filler is just above the surrounding metal.
16 Once the filler has hardened, the excess can be removed with a body file. From then on, progressively finer grades of sandpaper should be used, starting with a 180-grit paper and finishing with 600-grit wet-or-dry paper. Always wrap the sandpaper around a flat rubber or wooden block, otherwise the surface of the filler will not be completely flat. During the sanding of the filler surface, the wet-or-dry paper should be periodically rinsed in water. This will ensure that a very smooth finish is produced in the final stage.
17 At this point, the repair area should be surrounded by a ring of bare metal, which in turn should be encircled by the finely feathered edge of good paint. Rinse the repair area with clean water until all of the dust produced by the sanding operation is gone.
18 Spray the entire area with a light coat of primer. This will reveal any imperfections in the surface of the filler. Repair the imperfections with fresh filler paste or glaze filler and once more smooth the surface with sandpaper. Repeat this spray-and-repair procedure until you are satisfied that the surface of the filler and the feathered edge of the paint are perfect. Rinse the area with clean water and allow it to dry completely.
19 The repair area is now ready for painting. Spray painting must be carried out in a warm, dry, windless and dust free atmosphere. These conditions can be created if you have access to a large indoor work area, but if you are forced to work in the open, you will have to pick the day very carefully. If you are working indoors, dousing the floor in the work area with water will help settle the dust which would otherwise be in the air. If the repair area is confined to one body panel, mask off the surrounding panels. This will help minimize the effects of a slight mismatch in paint color. Trim pieces such as chrome strips, door handles, etc., will also need to be masked off or removed. Use masking tape and several thicknesses of newspaper for the masking operations.
20 Before spraying, shake the paint can thoroughly, then spray a test area until the spray painting technique is mastered. Cover the repair area with a thick coat of primer. The thickness should be built up using several thin layers of primer rather than one thick one. Using 600-grit wet-or-dry sandpaper, rub down the surface of the primer until it is very smooth. While doing this, the work area should be thoroughly rinsed with water and the wet-or-dry sandpaper periodically rinsed as well. Allow the primer to dry before spraying additional coats.
21 Spray on the top coat, again building up the thickness by using several thin layers of paint. Begin spraying in the center of the repair area and then, using a circular motion, work out until the whole repair area and about two inches of the surrounding original paint is covered. Remove all masking material 10 to 15 minutes after spraying on the final coat of paint. Allow the new paint at least two weeks to harden,

then use a very fine rubbing compound to blend the edges of the new paint into the existing paint. Finally, apply a coat of wax.

5 Body repair — major damage

1 Major damage must be repaired by an auto body shop specifically equipped to perform unibody repairs. These shops have the specialized equipment required to do the job properly.
2 If the damage is extensive, the underbody must be checked for proper alignment or the vehicle's handling characteristics may be adversely affected and other components may wear at an accelerated rate.
3 Due to the fact that all of the major body components (hood, fenders, etc.) are separate and replaceable units, any seriously damaged components should be replaced rather than repaired. Sometimes these components can be found in a wrecking yard that specializes in used vehicle components, often at considerable savings over the cost of new parts.

6 Maintenance — hinges and locks

Once every 3000 miles, or every three months, the door and hood hinges and locks should be given a few drops of light oil or lock lubricant. The door striker plates can be given a thin coat of grease to reduce wear and ensure free movement.

7 Windshield and stationary glass — replacement

The windshield and stationary window glass on all models is sealed in place with a special butyl compound, which makes glass replacement a complex job. Removal of the existing sealant requires the use of an electric knife specially made for the operation.

In view of this, it is not recommended that stationary glass removal be attempted by the home mechanic. If replacement is necessary due to breakage or leakage, the work should be referred to your dealer service department or a qualified glass or body shop.

8 Weatherstripping — maintenance and replacement

1 The weatherstripping should be kept clean and free of contaminants such as gasoline and oil. Spray the weatherstripping periodically with silicone lubricant to reduce abrasion, wear and cracking.
2 The weatherstripping is retained to the doors by adhesive above the vehicle beltline and by clips below it.
3 To remove the weatherstripping, release the plastic clip at the bottom of the door. Work your way around the outer edge of the door and carefully pull the weatherstripping free.
4 Clean the channel to remove residual adhesive and weatherstripping which would interfere with the installation of the new weatherstripping.
5 Apply a thin coat of adhesive to the upper portion of the door and install the new weatherstripping. Be sure to push it completely into the channel and secure the clips.

9 Door trim panel — removal and installation

Refer to illustrations 9.1 and 9.13

C/V and E body

1 Remove the armrest, door latch remote control bezel and pull strap bezels **(see illustration)**.
2 Insert a screwdriver or pry bar between the door and trim panel, adjacent to each retaining clip, and disengage each clip in turn until the panel can be removed.
3 Lift the panel up and slide it to the rear to remove it.
4 If access to the door is required, carefully peel off the plastic water shield and sound deadener. When reinstalling the panel, it may be necessary to use adhesive to hold the shield and sound deadener to the door.
5 Place the trim panel in position and insert the upper edge into the glass opening.
6 Align the retaining clips with the holes in the door and push them into place, starting at the rear.
7 The remainder of installation is the reverse of removal.

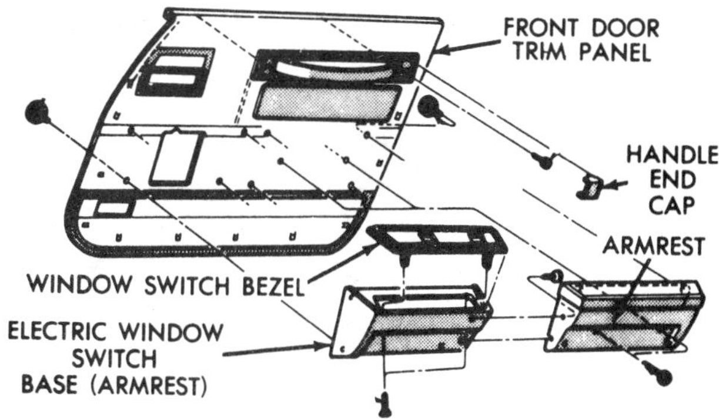

9.1 C/V and E body door trim panel details

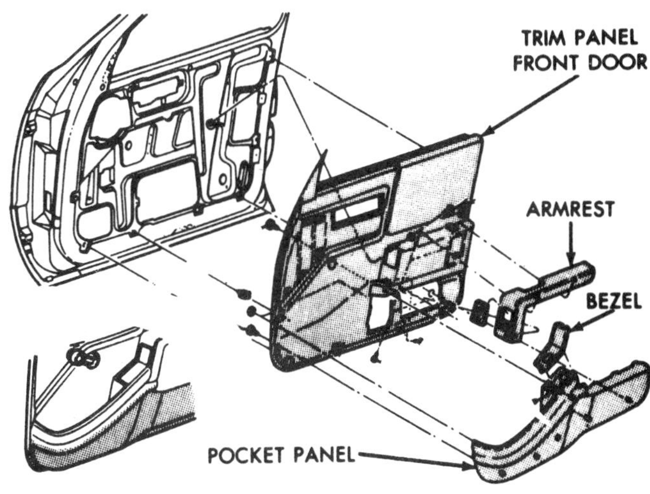

9.13 H Body door trim panel details

H body

8 Lower the window glass.
9 On power window equipped models, disconnect the negative cable at the battery. Place the cable out of the way so it cannot accidentally come in contact with the negative terminal of the battery, as this would once again allow power into the electrical system of the vehicle. Remove the screw at the forward edge of the switch plate, lift the plate and unplug the connector.
10 On manual window models, remove the screw and pull the window crank off.
11 On all models, pry off the outside mirror remote control bezel (if equipped), remove the two screws and remove the control by sliding it to the rear.
12 Remove the screw in the armrest pull cup area.
13 Disengage the eight clips around the edges of the panel using a screwdriver. Flex the forward upper corner of the panel to disengage the remaining two clips and lift off the trim panel **(see illustration)**.
14 Disconnect the door courtesy light wires (if equipped).
15 If access to the door is required, carefully peel off the plastic water shield and the sound deadener. When reinstalling the panel, it may be necessary to use adhesive to hold the shield and sound deadener to the door.
16 Installation is the reverse of removal.

11

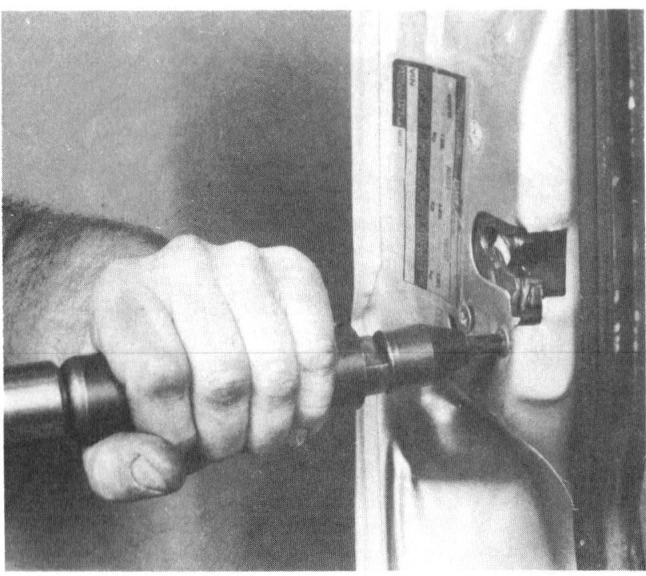
10.4 An impact screwdriver makes the job of loosening the door latch screws easier

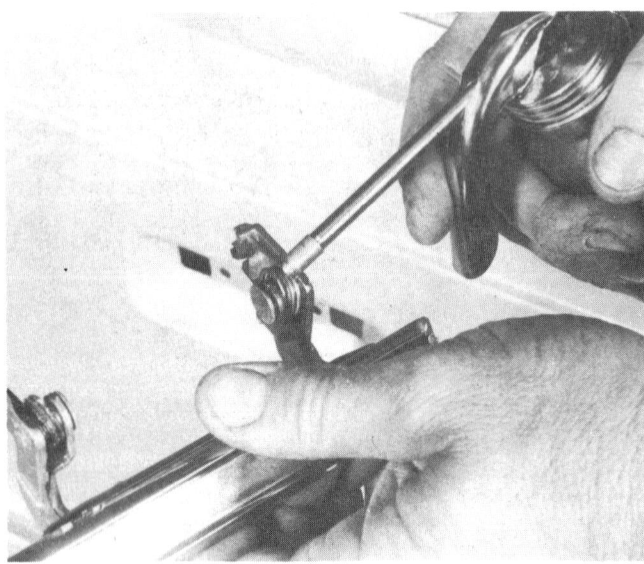
11.3 Lubricate the door handle mechanism by squirting oil into the hinge pivot areas

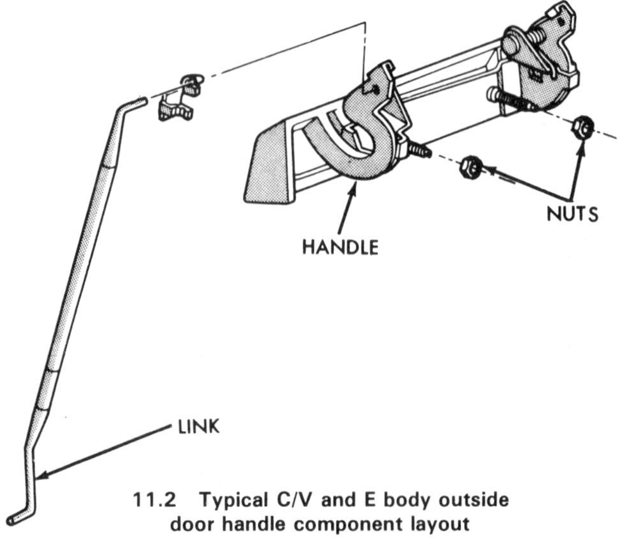

11.2 Typical C/V and E body outside door handle component layout

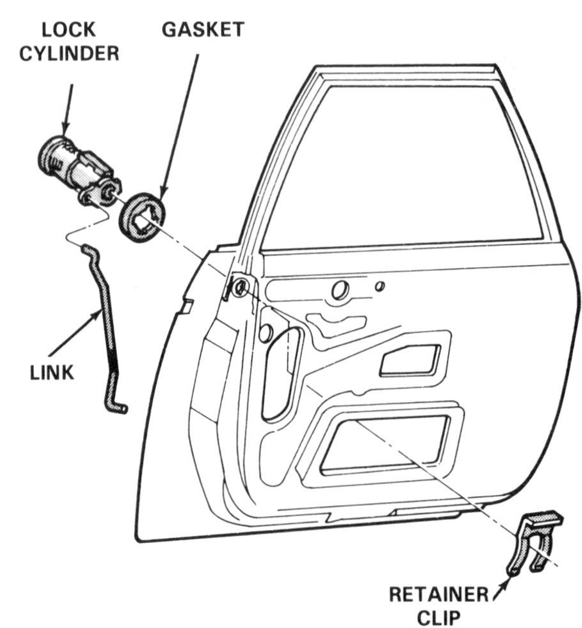

11.5 Typical C/V and E body lock cylinder installation details

10 Door latch assembly – removal and installation

Refer to illustration 10.4

1 Remove the trim panel, water shield and sound deadener (Section 9).

2 Disconnect the links from the outside handle, key lock cylinder, remote control, latch lock and electric motor (if equipped).

3 On H body models, remove the door glass, rear glass run channel, outer weather strip and outside mirror.

4 Remove the three latch mounting screws. It may be necessary to use an impact-type screwdriver to loosen the screws **(see illustration)**. The screws on later models are Torx-type, requiring the use of a special tool.

5 Lubricate all sliding surfaces of the latch assembly with white lithium base grease prior to installation.

6 Place the latch in position and install the screws loosely. Tighten the screws evenly in a criss-cross pattern so the latch is drawn up to the desired centered position.

7 Connect the links which were disconnected during removal and install the door panel.

8 Adjust the latch (C/V, E body) (Section 19).

11 Door outside handle and lock cylinder – removal and installation

Refer to illustrations 11.2, 11.3, 11.5, 11.10a, 11.10b and 11.12

C/V and E body

1 Raise the glass to the full up position and remove the door trim panel.

2 Disconnect the handle link from the latch, remove the mounting nuts and detach the handle from the door **(see illustration)**.

3 Prior to installation, lubricate the door handle hinge pivot areas with clean engine oil **(see illustration)**.

4 To install the handle, place it in position, attach the link and install the nuts.

5 To remove the lock cylinder, disconnect the link from the cylinder latch and slide the cylinder retainer clip off **(see illustration)**.

6 Installation is the reverse of removal.

H body

7 Lower the window and disconnect the negative cable from the battery.

USE BRASS OR ALUMINUM .125 IN. 3.175 mm
.375 IN. 9.525 mm
BEVEL WITH NUMBER 3 DRILL
7.25 IN. 184.15 mm

11.10a H body illuminated entry switch tool details

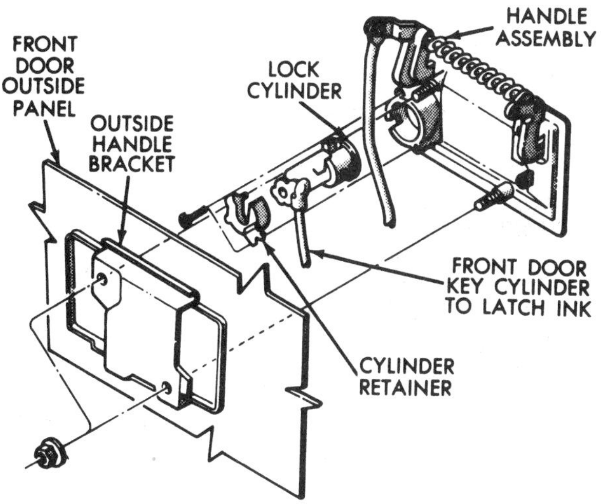

11.12 Outside door handle and lock cylinder details (H body)

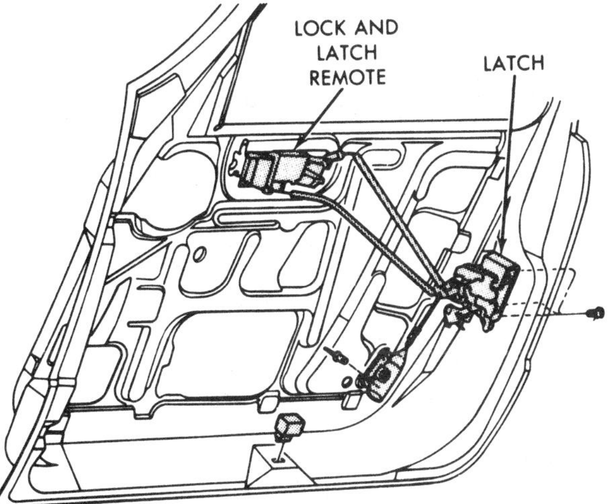

12.5 H body inside (remote control) door handle details

8 Refer to Section 9 and remove the door trim panel. Peel back the liner to expose the rear of the major access hole.
9 Remove the glass, rear glass run channel, outer belt weatherstripping and the outside mirror.
10 Remove the illuminated entry switch (if equipped) with a fabricated tool **(see illustrations)**.
11 Disconnect the handle links from the latch and the lock.
12 Remove the two mounting nuts, pull the handle out and remove the lock cylinder from the handle **(see illustration)**.

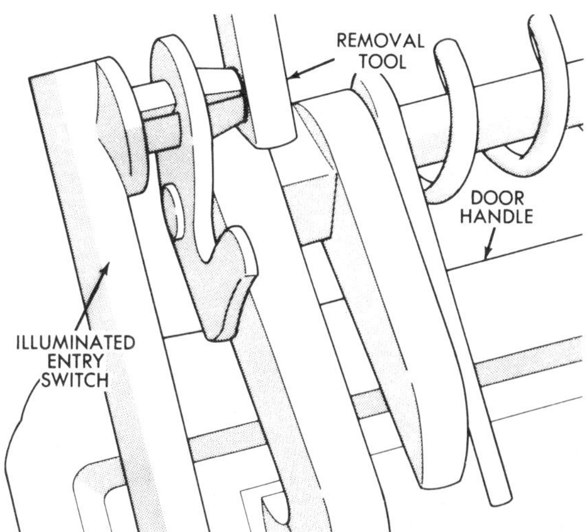

11.10b Removing the illuminated entry switch (H body)

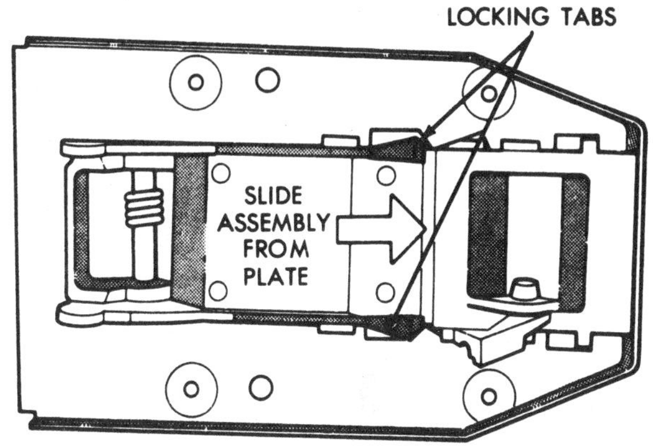

12.4 Depress the locking tabs to release the door handle assembly from the mounting plate (C/V and E body)

13 Place the lock cylinder in the handle, install the retainer and tighten the screws securely.
14 Install the handle in the door and tighten the nuts securely.
15 Connect the links to the handle and the lock.
16 Install the illuminated entry switch.
17 Install the door trim panel.

12 Door inside handle – removal and installation

Refer to illustrations 12.4 and 12.5

1 The door inside handle is often called the remote control handle.
2 Raise the glass all the way (fully closed position).
3 Refer to Section 9 and remove the door trim panel and liner.

C/V and E body

4 Disconnect the links, remove the mounting screws and detach the control assembly and mounting plate. Squeeze the two locking tabs together and slide the assembly from the plate **(see illustration)**.

11

H body

5 On front doors, remove the outside mirror mounting nut and disconnect the two links from the latch. Remove the three inside handle mounting screws and detach the handle with the links attached **(see illustration)**.
6 On rear doors, drill out the handle retaining rivet.
7 Installation is the reverse of removal.

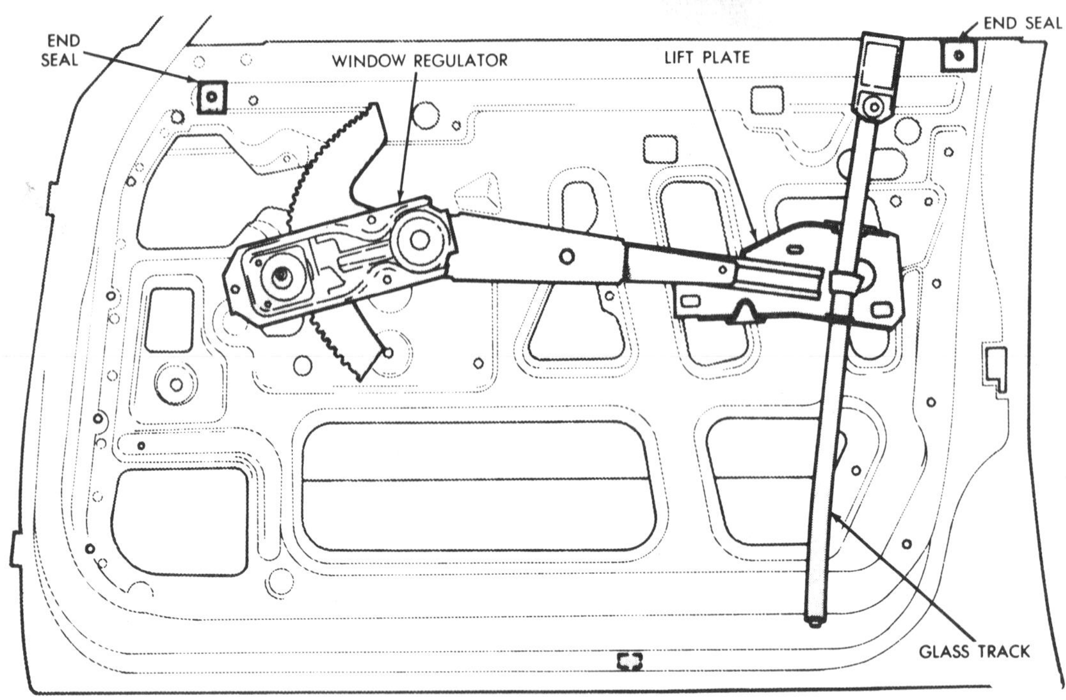

13.4 Gear drive-type regulator component layout (C/V and E body)

13 Gear drive-type window regulator — removal and installation

Refer to illustrations 13.4 and 13.8

1 Refer to Section 9, remove the door trim panel and peel back the watershield.

C/V and E body

2 Prop the glass securely in the full up position.
3 Drive out the center of the regulator retaining rivets and drill out the remainder with a 1/4-inch drill bit.
4 Disconnect the regulator arm and remove the regulator assembly from the door **(see illustration)**.
5 To install the regulator, place it in position and connect the arm to the lift plate. Use 1/4–20 screws with nuts in place of the rivets and secure the regulator to the door. Tighten the screws and nuts securely.

H body

6 Prop the glass 1/4-inch from the full up position.
7 On power window models, disconnect the negative cable at the battery. Place the cable out of the way so it cannot accidentally come in contact with the negative terminal of the battery, as this would once again allow power into the electrical system of the vehicle. Remove the regulator-to-arm bolt and unplug the motor harness connector. Drill out the rivets attaching the regulator to the door and remove the regulator.
8 On manual regulator models, drill out the three mounting rivets, slide the regulator off the glass lift channel and remove it **(see illustration)**.
9 Installation is the reverse of removal. Use short 1/4–20 screws and nuts to secure the regulator. Tighten the nuts and screws securely.
10 Install the door trim panel.

14 Flex drive-type window regulator — removal and installation

Refer to illustrations 14.5, 14.7a and 14.7b

1 Remove the door trim panel (Section 9).

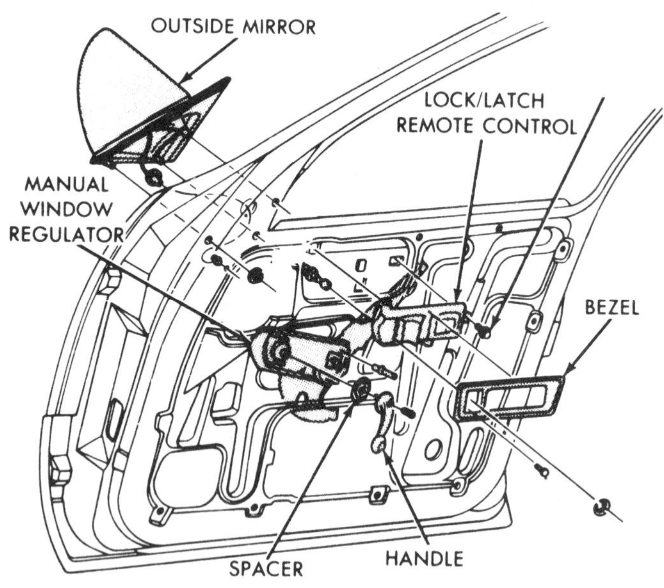

13.8 H body gear drive-type regulator details

2 Disconnect the negative cable at the battery. Place the cable out of the way so it cannot accidentally come in contact with the negative terminal of the battery, as this would once again allow power into the electrical system of the vehicle.
3 On C/V and E body models, move the glass attachment to the door access hole and remove the glass-to-drive arm bolt.
4 On H body models, prop the glass one inch from the full up position.
5 Use an electric drill and an appropriate size bit to drill out the regulator mounting rivet heads **(see illustration)**.
6 Rotate the regulator and flex drive assembly and withdraw it through the major access hole. On electrical regulator models, disconnect the wiring harness.

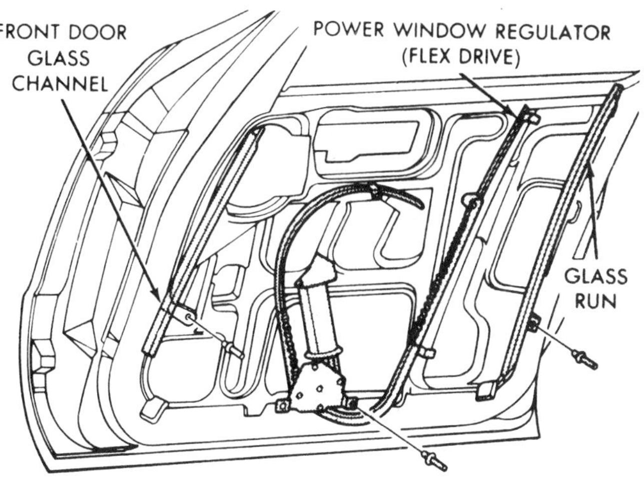

14.5 Typical H body flex drive-type regulator details

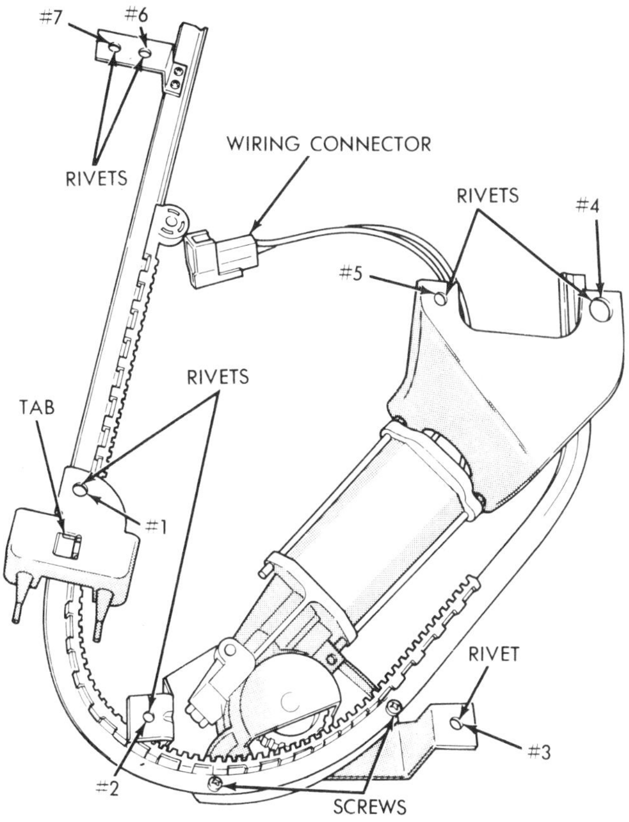

14.7b Electrical flex drive-type regulator mount points and tightening sequence (C/V and E body)

7 Installation is the reverse of removal. Make sure the flex drive is clean and well lubricated before installation. Use 1/4–20 x 1/2-inch screws and nuts in place of the rivets. Tighten them securely. On C/V and E body models, the nuts and screws must be tightened in sequence to prevent the possibility of binding **(see illustrations)**.

15 Front door glass – removal and installation

Refer to illustrations 15.5, 15.6 and 15.7

1 Remove the door trim panel (Section 9).

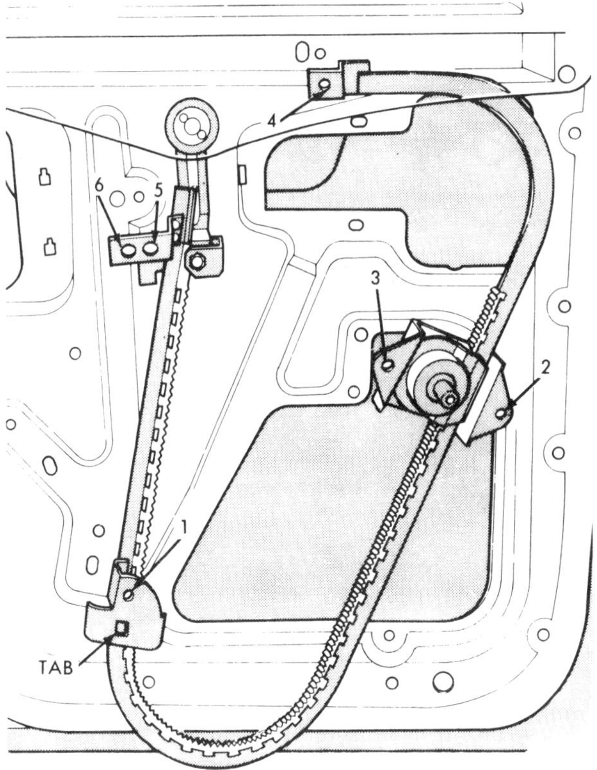

14.7a Manual flex drive-type regulator mounting bolt location and tightening sequence (C/V and E body)

15.5 Grasp the weatherstrip firmly and pull up and to the rear to detach it

C/V and E body

2 Lower the glass sufficiently to provide access to the mounting nuts and bolts.

3 Remove the nuts and bolts.

4 Lower the window mechanism completely and disengage the glass.

5 Remove the outer glass weatherstrip from the door by pushing it up from underneath and disengaging the clips **(see illustration)**.

15.6 Tilt the glass toward the outside of the door and lift up to remove it

15.7 Use your finger to apply white multi-purpose grease to lubricate the window glass track

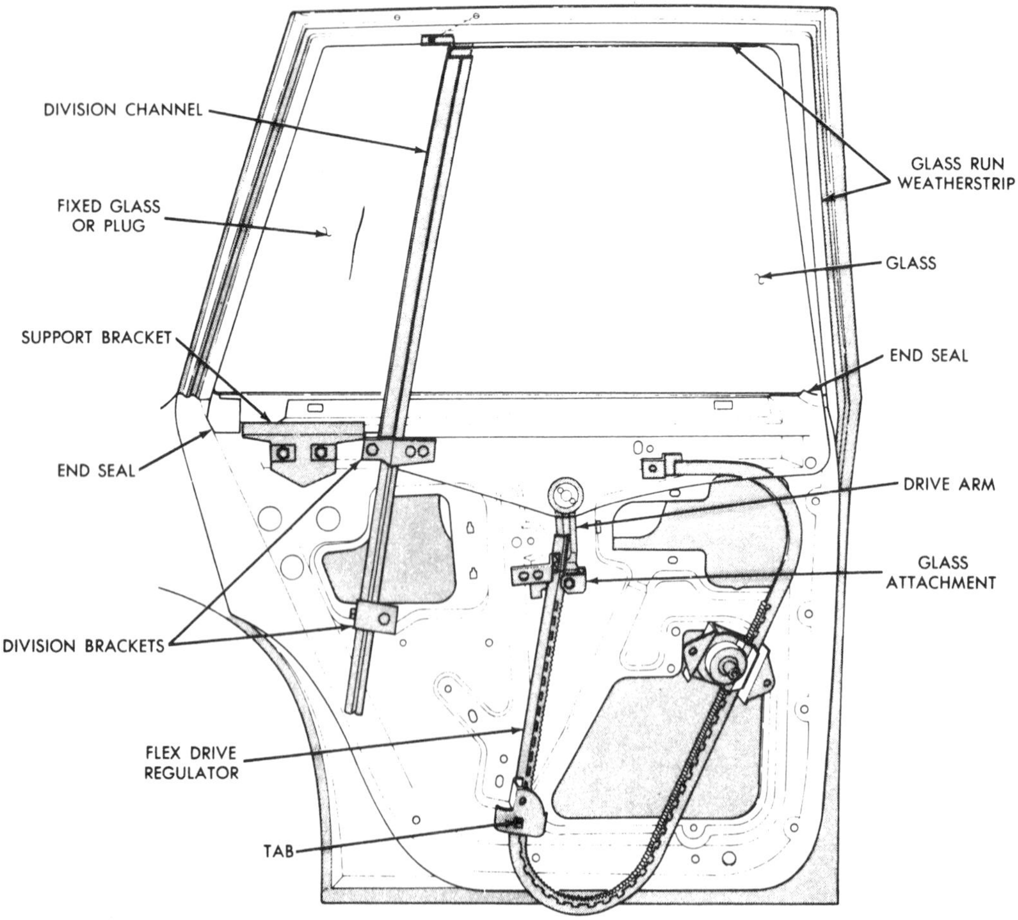

16.3 C/V and E body rear door glass component details

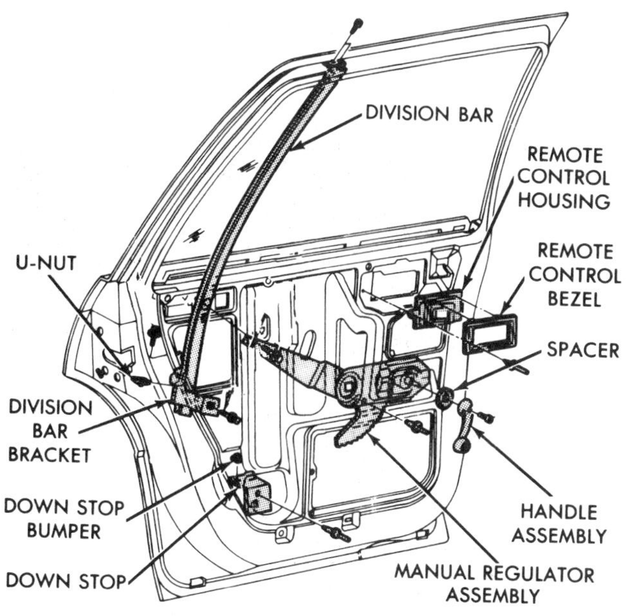

16.22 Rear door glass details (H body)

6 Lift the glass up and out toward the outside of the window opening **(see illustration)**.
7 While the glass is out, it is a good idea to lubricate the window mechanism with white lithium base grease **(see illustration)**.
8 To install the glass, lower it into the door and seat it in the mechanism.
9 Install the nuts and bolts finger tight.
10 Raise the glass completely until it seats in the channel at the top of the opening and tighten the nuts and bolts securely.
11 Lower the glass.
12 Lower the weatherstripping into position, align the clips and then press it into place. Install the door trim panel.

H body

13 Lower the glass enough to provide access to the sliders and rear glass guide.
14 Use Miller Tool No. C-4867 or equivalent to disengage the glass sliders from the rear glass slide. **Note:** *Failure to use this tool could cause damage to the rear glass run guide.*
15 Rotate the glass up 45 degrees and remove it from the door.
16 Installation is the reverse of removal.
17 Install the door trim panel.

16 Rear door glass – removal and installation

Refer to illustrations 16.3 and 16.22

1 Remove the door trim panel (Section 9).

C/V and E body

2 Remove the end seals from the front and rear of the door.
3 Remove the fixed vent window support bracket and detach the division channel-to-door inner panel brackets **(see illustration)**.
4 Remove the door glass run weatherstrip.
5 Remove the screw from the top of the division channel and remove the fixed glass.
6 Detach the clips and remove the outside weatherstripping.
7 Raise the division channel, door glass and drive arm assembly, rotate it 90 degrees and lift it out through the glass opening.
8 To install it, lower the division channel, door glass and drive assembly into the window opening. Make sure the lower bracket is parallel to the opening and lower the assembly until the upper division channel is near the opening. Rotate the assembly 90 degrees and lower

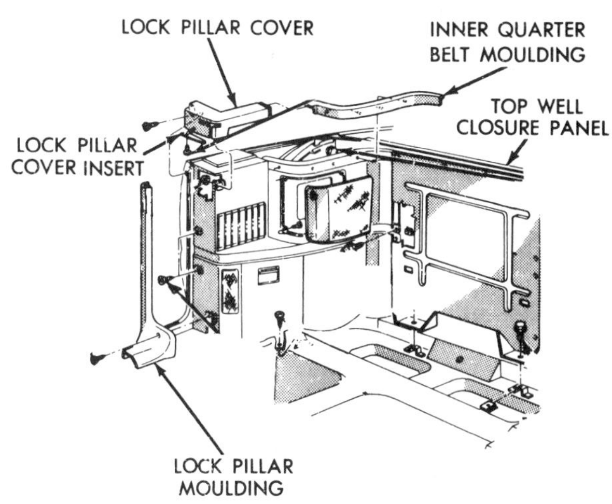

17.1 Convertible model rear quarter panel installation details

the channel to the bottom of the door.
9 Lift the glass and place the drive arm in position on the flex drive arm, attaching it with the shoulder bolt.
10 Install the outside weatherstripping and place the fixed glass bracket in position.
11 Use a rocking motion to position the glass in the door so that it rests loosely on the bracket.
12 Attach the rear edge of the division channel to the fixed glass.
13 Install the door glass run weatherstrip.
14 Install the upper and lower division channel brackets.
15 Push the fixed glass bracket up and secure it.
16 Install the end seals and the door trim panel.

H body

17 Brace the glass 1/4-inch from the full up position.
18 On manual regulator models, drill out the three rivets attaching the regulator and slide the roller out of the lift channel.
19 On electrical regulator models, remove the regulator arm bolt.
20 Insert Miller Tool No. C–4867 or equivalent into the division bar channel and pry the glass out of the glass run.
21 Lower the glass down into the door.
22 Remove the two mounting screws on the division bar and detach the lower bracket **(see illustration)**.
23 Remove the beltline screw through the access hole in the inner panel.
24 Remove the two screws attaching the division bar to the top of the door and detach the division bar.
25 Lift the glass up and remove it from the door.
26 To install the glass, lower it into the door and position the division bar.
27 Install the two screws at the top of the door, the beltline screw and the lower bracket screws. Tighten the screws securely.
28 Raise the glass and snap the glass guides into the channel glass run.
29 On manual regulator models, prop up the glass and insert the roller into the glass lift channel. Attach the regulator to the door panel with rivets or short 1/4–20 screws and nuts. Tighten the nuts and screws securely.
30 On electrical regulator models, connect the regulator to the regulator arm bolt. Tighten the bolt securely.
31 Install the door panel.

17 Rear quarter window regulator and glass (convertible models) – removal and installation

Refer to illustrations 17.1 and 17.3

1 Remove the rear quarter trim panel by first removing the rear seat, unbolting the front seat belt and removing the trim panel-to-floor bolt. Remove the quarter panel retaining bolts and screws and the seat belt retractor and lift the quarter panel out **(see illustration)**.

2 Lower the glass.
3 Remove the stabilizer, unbolt the glass from the lift plate and the regulator from the mounting plate **(see illustration)**. Remove the floor pan-to-regulator mounting plate brace and unbolt the mounting plate. Remove the regulator from the mounting plate.
4 Installation is the reverse of removal.

18 Door latch striker (C/V and E body) – adjustment

Refer to illustration 18.1

1 Loosen the latch striker **(see illustration)**.
2 Move the striker to approximately the center of its travel.
3 Close the door slowly and check to make sure that it does not move up or down excessively as it contacts the striker.
4 If necessary, loosen the striker, adjust the position and retighten it.
5 Readjust as necessary until the door closes smoothly and the weatherstripping around the door compresses evenly all the way around.

19 Door latch (C/V and E body) – adjustment

Refer to illustration 19.1

1 Loosen the door latch adjusting screw with a 5/32-inch Allen wrench inserted through the access hole in the door face **(see illustration)**.
2 Adjust the latch by moving the Allen wrench and screw up in the slot and tightening the screw securely.
3 Check the door handle position to make sure it is flush with the door surface.
4 Check the latch and door for proper operation.
5 Readjust as necessary to obtain smooth closing with the door handle flush with the surface.

20 Deck lid or liftgate latch, striker and lock cylinder – removal and installation

Refer to illustrations 20.1 and 20.3

Latch

1 Open the deck lid, mark the location of the latch and remove the bolts, latch and link assembly **(see illustration)**.
2 To install the latch, place it in the marked position and install the bolts. Tighten the bolts securely.

Striker

3 Remove the mounting bolts and lift the striker away from the sheet metal **(see illustration)**.
4 Installation is the reverse of removal.

Lock cylinder

5 Remove the retaining nut and withdraw the cylinder from the body. On later models you must drill out the rivets and remove the pentastar medallion along with the cylinder **(see illustration 20.1)**.
6 To install the lock cylinder, insert it into position and install the nut. On later models, install the medallion using 5/32-inch rivets.

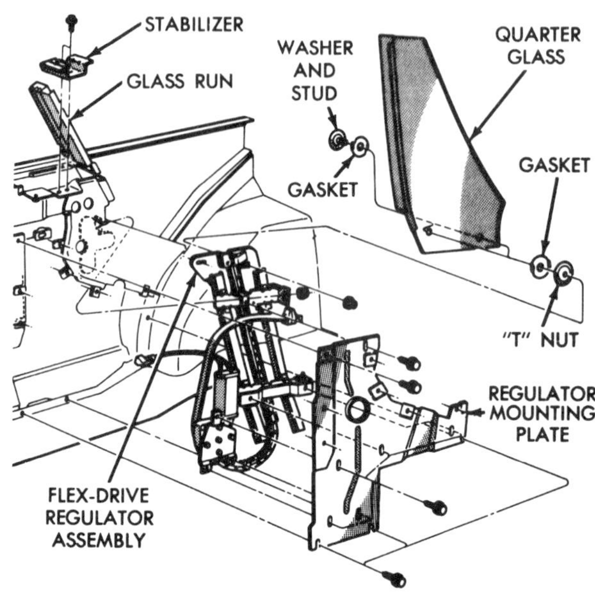

17.3 Convertible model rear quarter window regulator and glass details

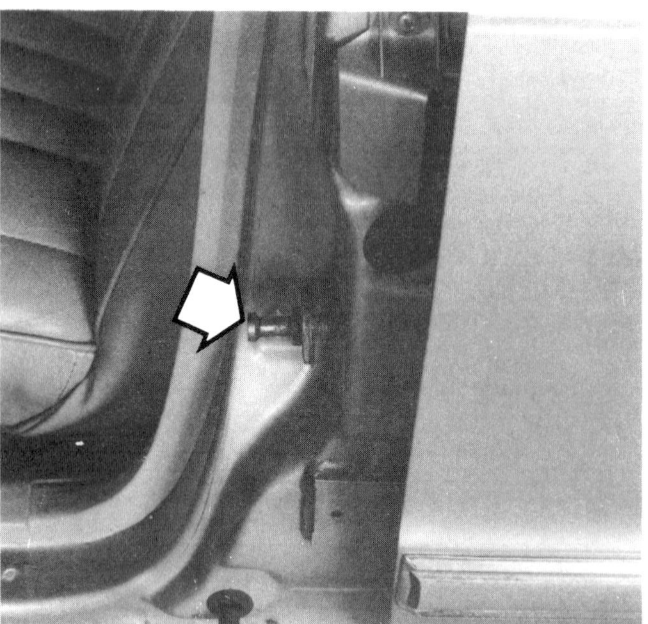

18.1 Unscrew the door latch striker (arrow) and then screw it in finger tight before adjusting it

19.1 Insert the Allen wrench through the access hole in the door to adjust the door latch

21 Deck lid torsion bar – adjustment

Refer to illustration 21.1

1 The closing tension of the deck lid can be adjusted by moving the right torsion bar to the number one slot and the left bar to the number two slot **(see illustration)**.

2 After adjustment, close the deck lid and check that the latch action is smooth and the lid is flush with the body. Repeat the adjustment procedure until the deck lid closes easily without excessive force.

22 Liftgate prop – removal and installation

Refer to illustration 22.2

1 Open the liftgate and support it on the side on which the prop is to be replaced.

2 Remove the mounting fasteners and detach the prop **(see illustration)**. The lower end of the prop is held in place with pins that are retained by clips.

3 Installation is the reverse of removal.

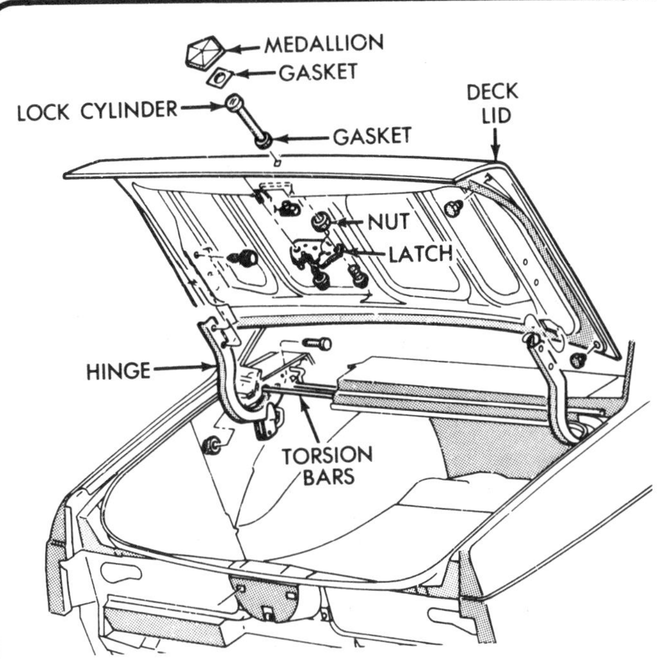

20.1 Later model trunk lid latch details

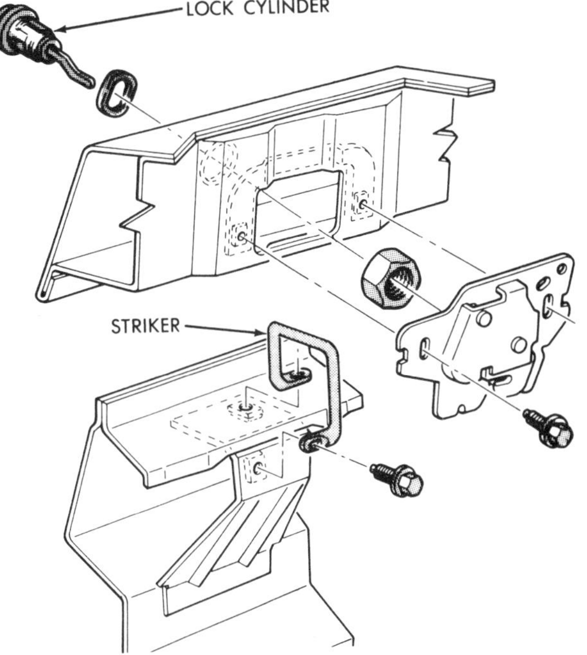

20.3 Typical early model trunk lid latch and striker component layout

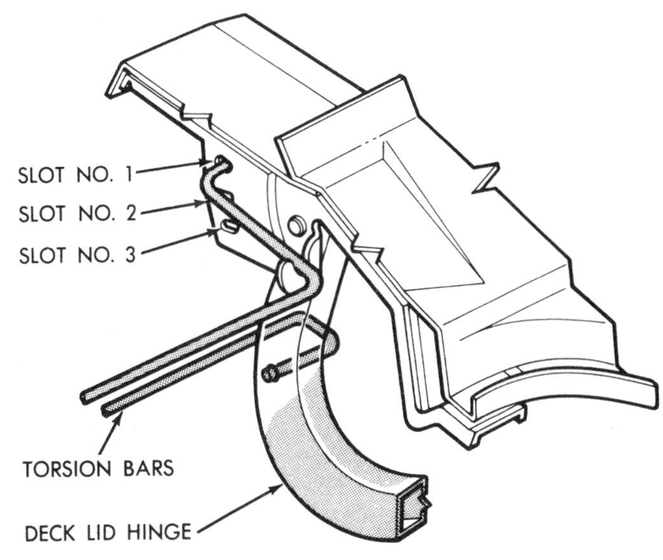

21.1 Deck lid torsion bar adjustment details

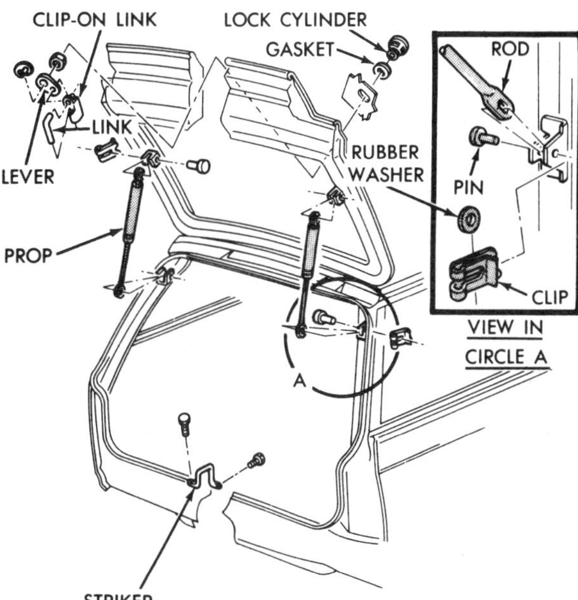

22.2 Liftgate prop mounting details

11

23 Outside rear view mirror – removal and installation

Refer to illustrations 23.1, 23.7 and 23.8

C/V and E body

1 Remove the bezel mounting screw and disengage the bezel from the channel bracket (manual models) or loosen the bezel set screw (remote control models) to release the cable control **(see illustration)**.
2 Remove the door trim panel.
3 Remove the mounting screws and disengage the mirror and seal from the door.
4 Installation is the reverse of removal.

H body

5 Remove the door trim panel.
6 On electric mirror models, unplug the wiring connector.
7 Pry out the rubber plugs and remove the mirror mounting nuts **(see illustration)**.
8 Use a screwdriver to pry the rubber grommet out of the door and remove the mirror from the vehicle **(see illustration)**.
9 Installation is the reverse of removal.

24 Hood – removal and installation

1 Outline the hinges on the hood to simplify reinstallation and alignment.
2 Place a protective covering (an old blanket should work fine) over the windshield area and make sure it extends down over the ends of both fenders.
3 Place a block of wood between the hood and windshield to prevent sudden rearward movement of the hood.
4 Have an assistant support one side of the hood as the bolts are removed, then remove the remaining bolts and detach the hood. Store it where it will not be damaged.
5 Installation is the reverse of removal. Be sure to align the hinges inside the marks made during removal before tightening the bolts.

25 Hood latch and cable – removal and installation

Refer to illustrations 25.1 and 25.6

Cable

1 Release the cable from the hood latch by pulling the cable toward the latch and lifting the ball end from the slot **(see illustration)**.
2 In the passenger compartment, disconnect the cable at the hood latch lever. Connect a piece of string or thin wire to the cable.
3 Pull the cable through the firewall into the engine compartment.
4 Connect the string or wire to the new cable and pull it through the firewall into the passenger compartment.
5 Connect the cable at the latch lever and the hood latch.

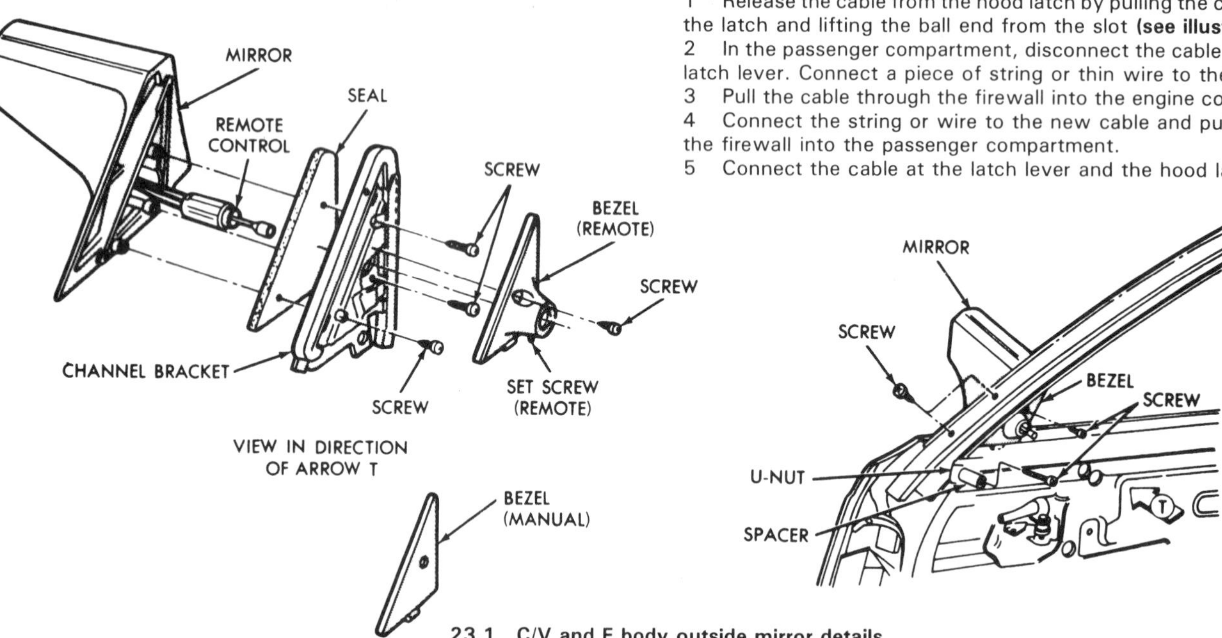

23.1 C/V and E body outside mirror details

23.7 Use a socket and extension to remove the mirror mounting nuts

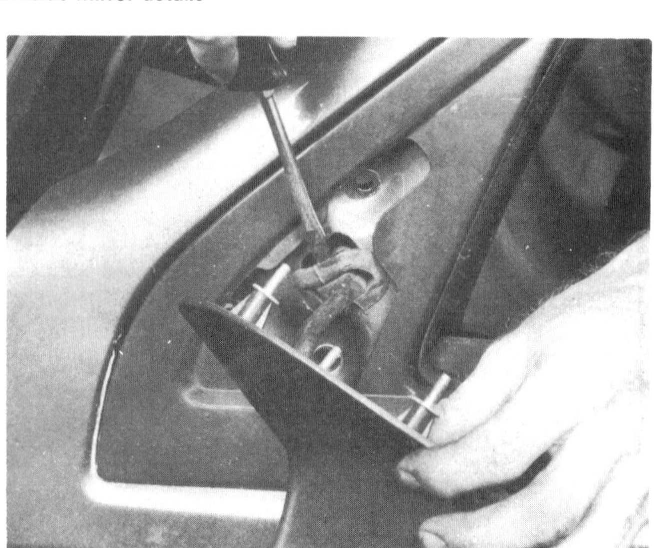

23.8 Pry the wiring grommet out of the door opening with a screwdriver

Latch

6 Disconnect the release cable from the latch, mark the mounting bolt location, remove the bolts and lift the latch away from the radiator brace **(see illustration)**.

7 To install the latch, place it in position and install the bolts in the marked locations. Connect the release cable.

26 Bumpers – removal and installation

Refer to illustrations 26.4a, 26.4b, 26.8a and 26.8b

1 Raise the vehicle and support it securely on jackstands.

2 It is a good idea to place supports such as jacks or jackstands under the bumpers before removal.

Front bumper

3 Remove the turn signal lights.

4 Remove the mounting nuts and bolts and lower the bumper/fascia assembly from the vehicle **(see illustrations)**.

5 Remove the energy absorber-to-body bolts and withdraw the units from the body.

6 Installation is the reverse of removal. Be sure to tighten the energy absorber unit bolts to the specified torque.

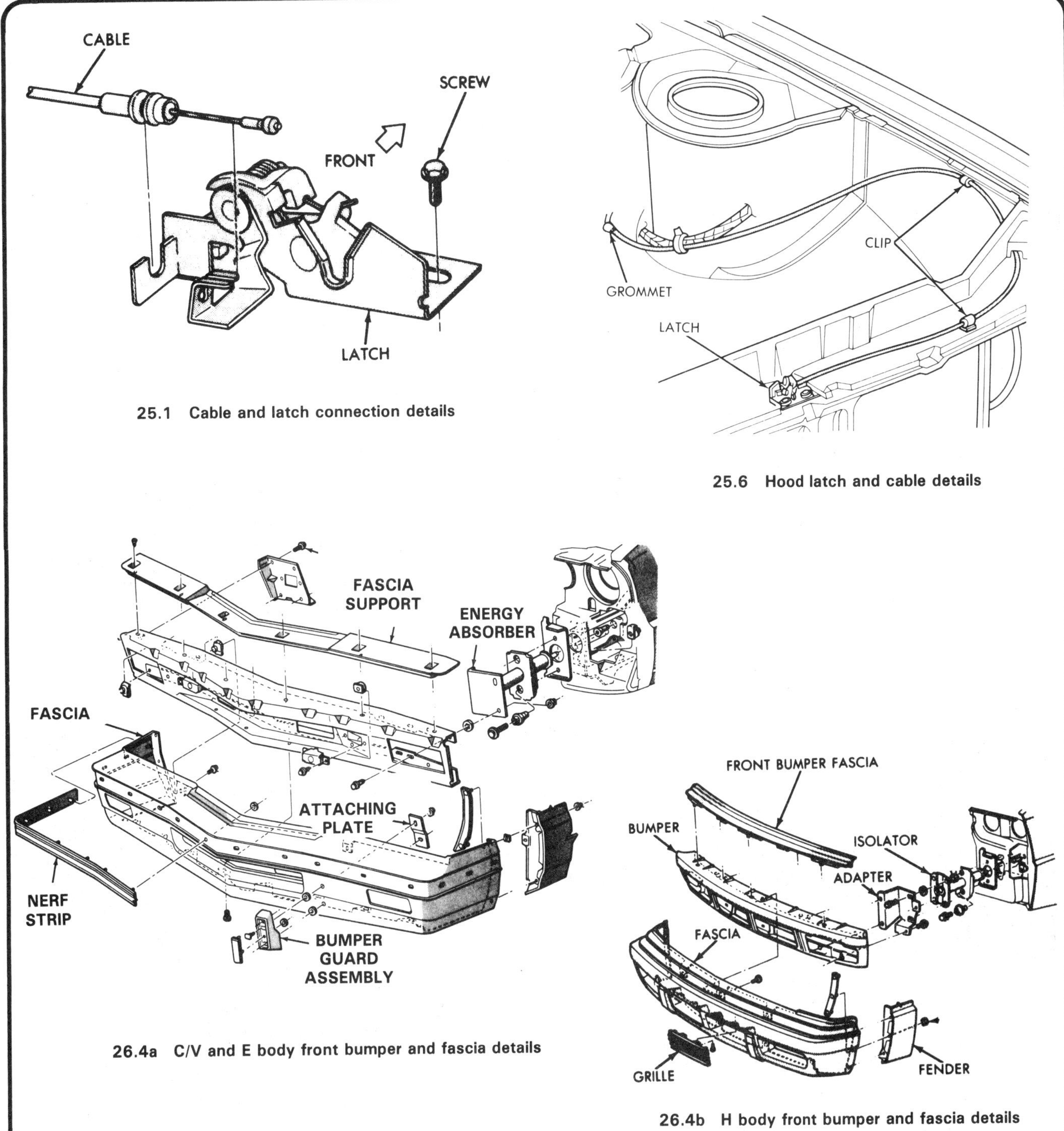

25.1 Cable and latch connection details

25.6 Hood latch and cable details

26.4a C/V and E body front bumper and fascia details

26.4b H body front bumper and fascia details

11

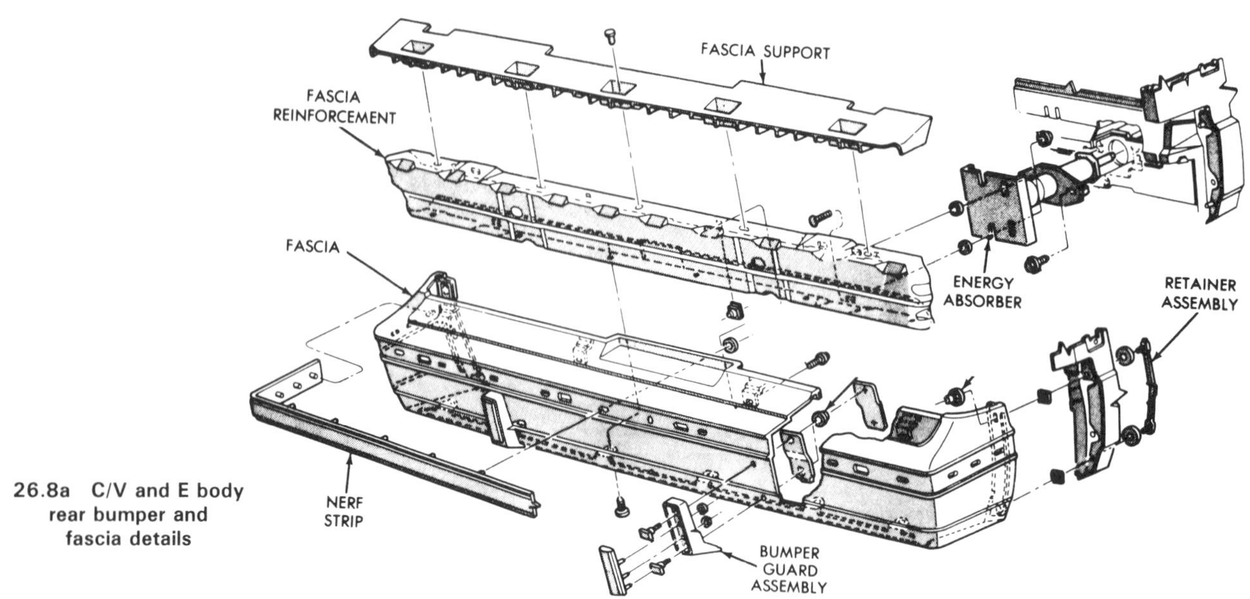

26.8a C/V and E body rear bumper and fascia details

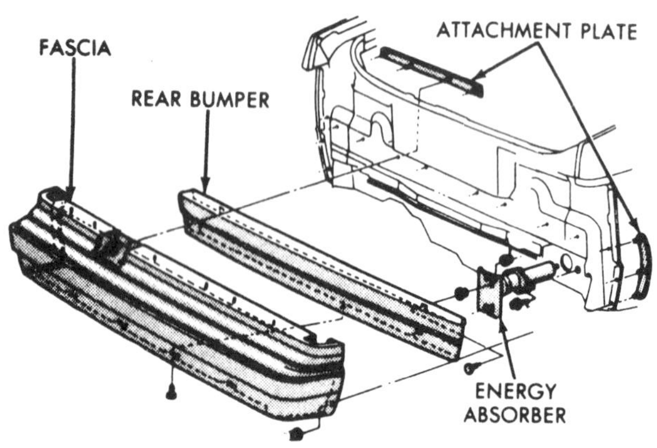

26.8b H body rear bumper and fascia details

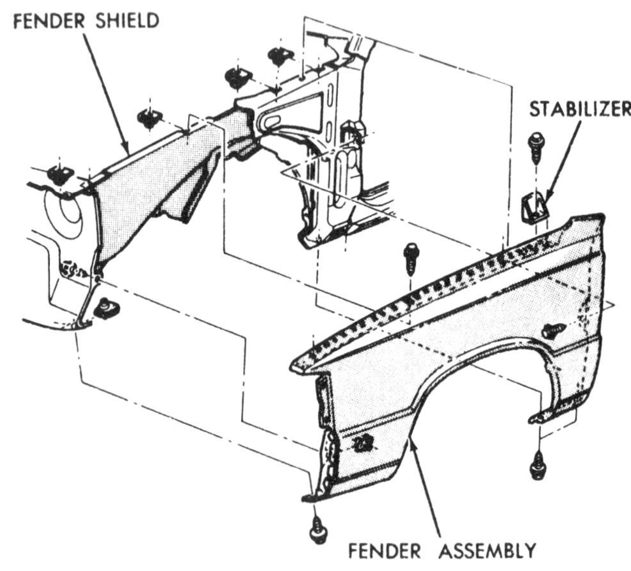

27.6 Typical front fender installation details

Rear bumper

7 Support the fascia with a jack.
8 Remove the bumper/fascia assembly-to-energy absorber unit nuts and lower the bumper/fascia assembly from the vehicle **(see illustrations)**.
9 Remove the energy absorber-to-body bolts and withdraw the unit from the body.
10 Installation is the reverse of removal. Be sure to tighten the energy absorber unit bolts to the specified torque.

27 Front fender – removal and installation

Refer to illustration 27.6

1 Unplug the park, turn signal and headlight wiring.
2 Cover the forward edge of the door so that it will not be damaged during fender removal.
3 Pry out the non-reuseable plastic fasteners retaining the splash shield to the fender.
4 Remove the fascia-to-fender retaining nuts.
5 Raise the hood and secure it in the open position.
6 Remove the fasteners and detach the fender from the vehicle **(see illustration)**.
7 Installation is the reverse of removal. Use new splash shield fasteners. The gaps at the cowl, door front edge and door top edge should be equal.

28 Glove box – removal and installation

See illustrations 28.2a and 28.2b

1 Disconnect the retainer strap (if equipped) by pushing the center pin out of the fastener.
2 Remove the retaining screws, lower the glove box assembly and unplug the electrical connector (if equipped). Remove the glove box from the instrument panel **(see illustrations)**.
3 Installation is the reverse of removal.

29 Console – removal and installation

Refer to illustrations 29.3 and 29.18

1 Disconnect the negative cable at the battery. Place the cable out of the way so it cannot accidentally come in contact with the negative terminal of the battery, as this would once again allow power into the electrical system of the vehicle.

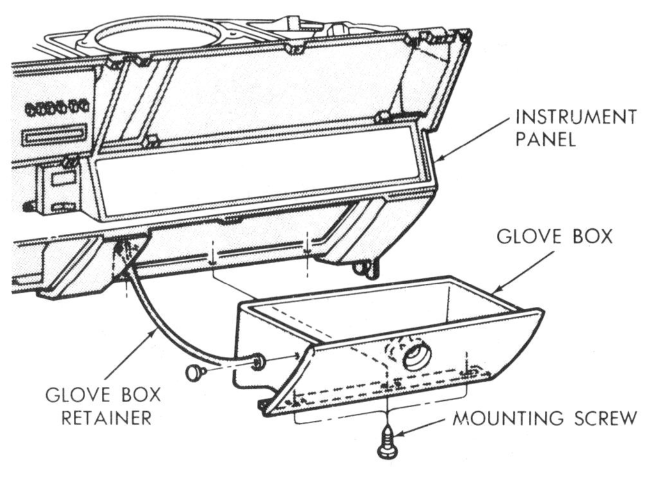

28.2a C/V and E body glove box details

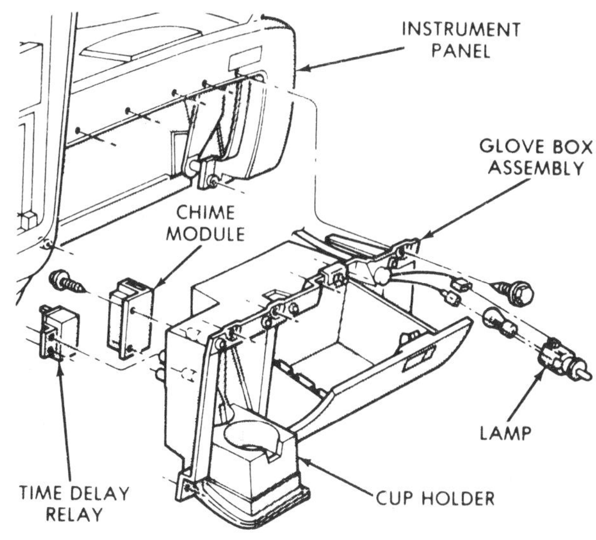

28.2b H body glove box details

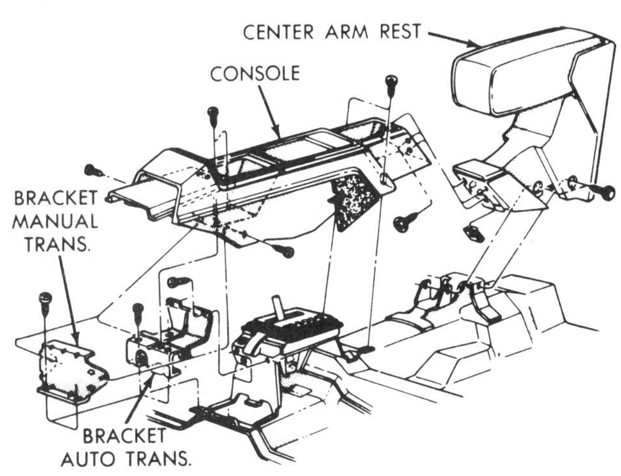

29.3 C/V and E body console details

29.18 H body console details

C/V and E body

2 Pry out the retainers and remove the carpet from both sides of the console (if equipped).
3 Remove the mounting screws **(see illustration)**.
4 Lift the console sufficiently for access to the wiring and unplug the connectors.
5 On manual transaxle models, unscrew the shift knob.
6 On automatic transaxle models it may be necessary to disconnect the shifter cable.
7 Remove the console from the vehicle.
8 Installation is the reverse of removal. Adjust the automatic transaxle shift cable if necessary so that the engine starts only in Park or Neutral (Chapter 7).

H body

9 Place the shift lever in Neutral.
10 Remove the carpet panels from both sides of the console.
11 Pry out the two screw cover plates from the rear of the console.
12 To remove the cubby box, open the door, remove the four mounting screws and detach the box from the console.
13 To remove the navigator housing, remove two Torx-head mounting screws, pull the housing out, unplug the electrical connector and detach the housing.
14 The cassette storage unit is removed by simply pulling it out.
15 Remove the automatic transaxle bezel as follows. Remove the two screws, lift up and remove the shifter knob. Loosen the hex head bolt on the right side of the shifter, slide the selector off the bracket and remove the cable. Remove the two mounting screws, lift the bezel up from the front, unplug the wiring harness and remove the bezel from the console.
16 Remove the manual transaxle bezel as follows. Unscrew the shifter knob and remove the nut and ring. Lift up the front of the bezel, unplug the electrical connector and lift the bezel off.
17 Unplug the rear console electrical connector.
18 Remove the console mounting nuts and bolts **(see illustration)**, slide the console to the rear to unlatch it from the intrument panel and lift it off.
19 Remove the three screws from the underside of the front console and lift off the rear console.
20 Installation is the reverse of removal. Adjust the shift mechanism as necessary (Chapter 7).

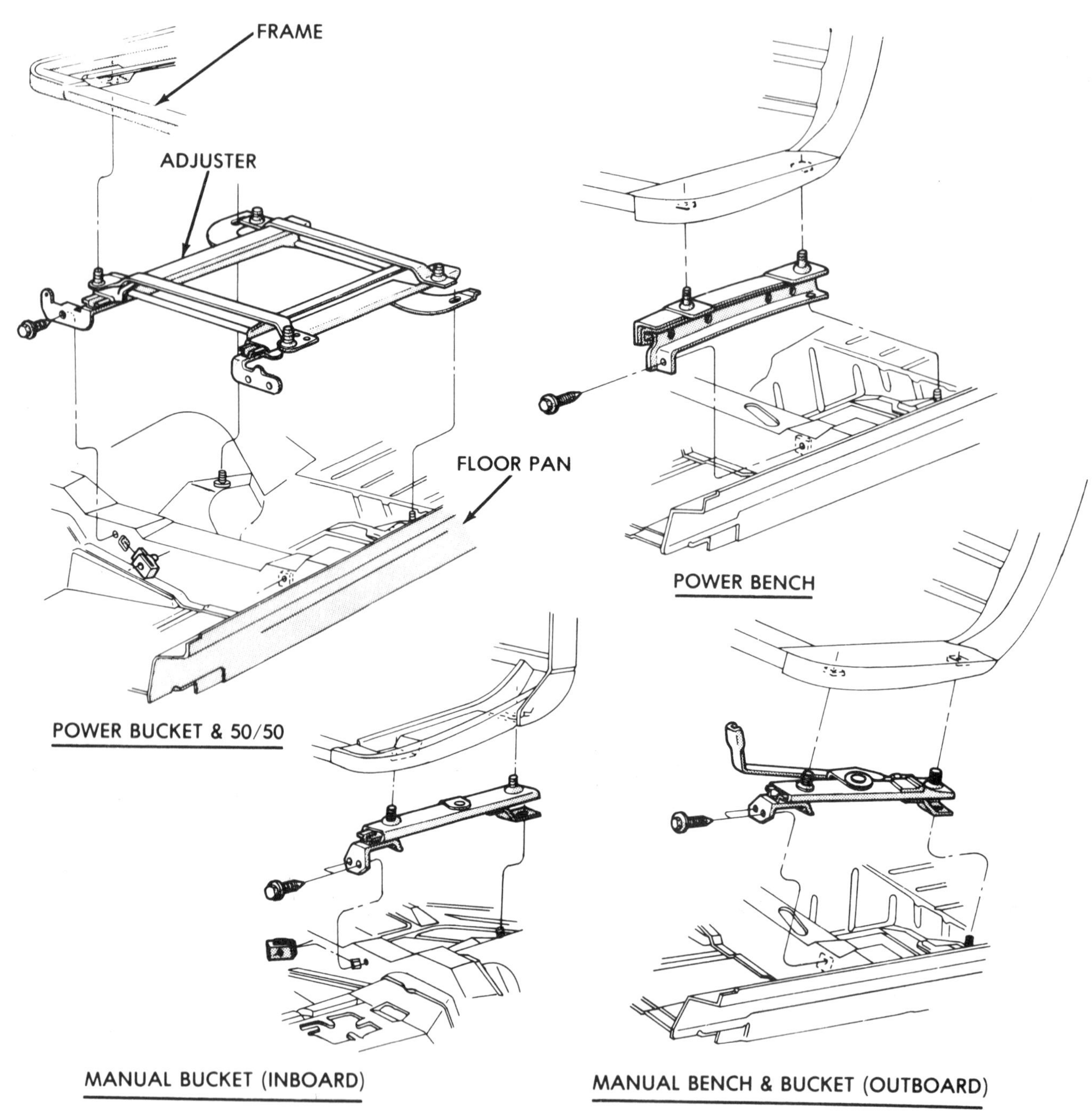

30.2 Typical C/V and E body front seat installation details

30 Seats – removal and installation

Refer to illustrations 30.2, 30.3a, 30.3b, 30.6, 30.8, 30.13, 30.15 and 30.17

1 When doing extensive work in the interior of the vehicle, it is a good idea to remove the seats.

Front seat

C/V and E body

2 Remove the mounting bolts and nuts and lift the seat from the vehicle **(see illustration)**.

3 To remove the recliner mechanism, remove the seat back trim panel and then remove enough of the hog rings to allow access to the mechanism. **Caution:** *The seat recliner return spring is under tension when the seat back is in the upright position. The seat back must be folded forward prior to removal of the seat back or recliner mechanism. Refer to the* ***accompanying illustrations*** for recliner removal and installation.

4 To install the seat, place it in position and tighten the nuts and bolts securely.

H body

5 Move the seat to the forward position.

6 Remove the nuts retaining the rear of the seat to the floor, then move the seat to the rear and remove the front seat mounting bolts **(see illustration)**.

7 Remove the seat.

8 To remove the recliner, remove the seat cushion shield, seat back shield and recliner mechanism from the seat **(see illustration)**. **Caution:** *The seat recliner return spring is under tension when the seat back*

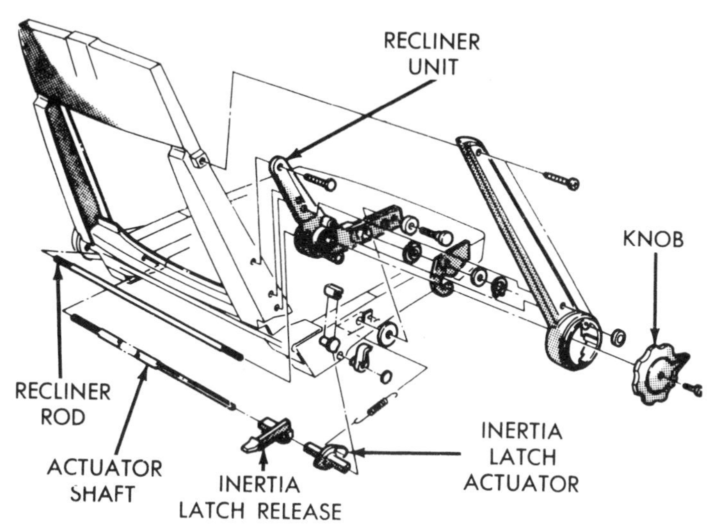

30.3a C/V and E body standard seat recliner details

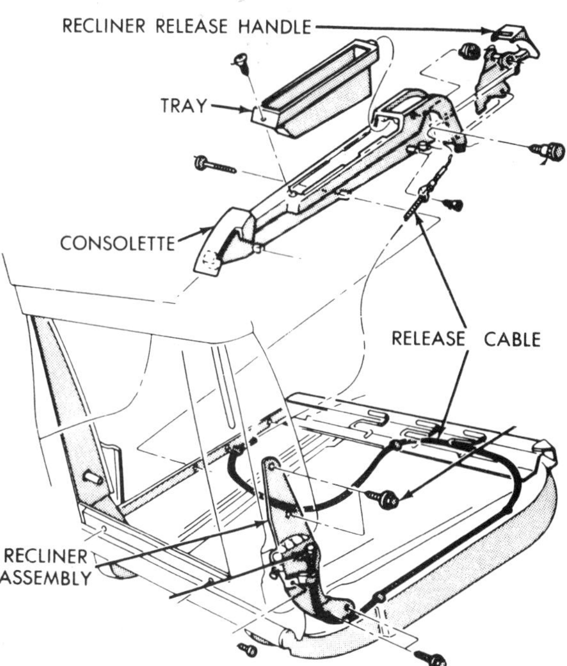

30.3b C/V and E body 50/50-type seat recliner details

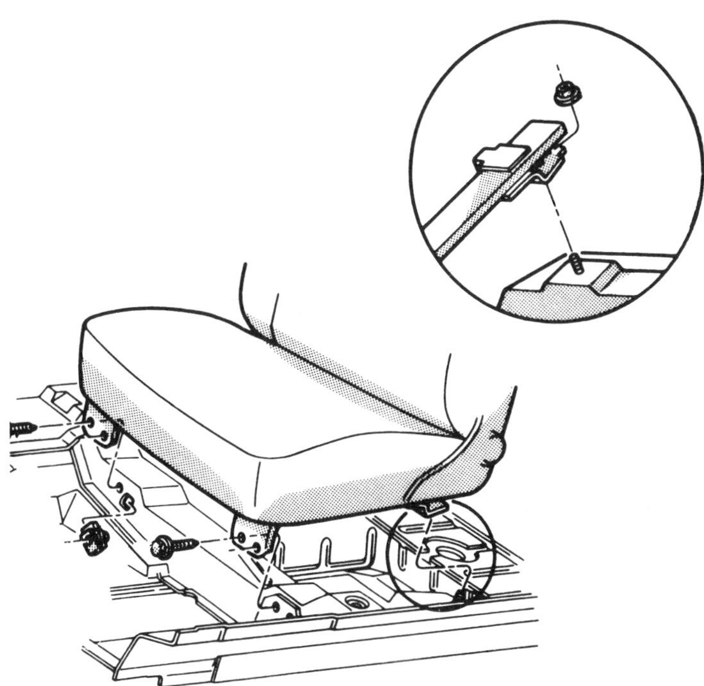

30.6 H body front bucket seat installation details

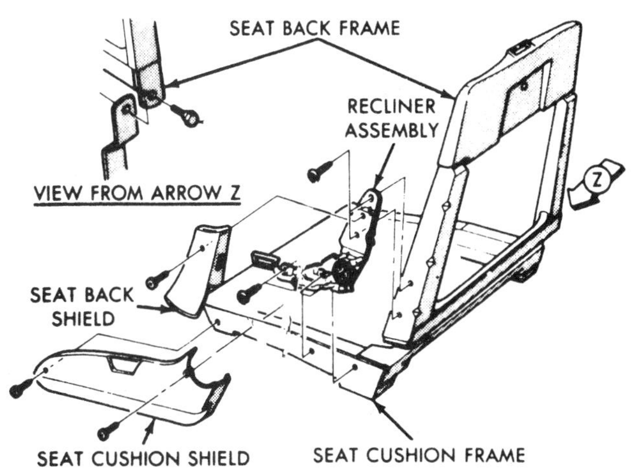

30.8 H body seat recliner details

is in the upright position. The seat back must be folded forward prior to removal of the seat back or recliner mechanism.

9 Seat and recliner installation is the reverse of removal.

Rear seat back

C/V and E body – sedan

10 Remove the two bolts from the bottom of the rear seat back and lift the seat assembly from the vehicle.

11 To remove the rear seat back, unsnap the seat belt retainers and lift the seat back up to disengage the wires from the support pocket.

12 Installation is the reverse of removal.

C/V and E body – convertible

13 Remove the two mounting bolts at the front face of the floor pan tunnel and pull forward and up to remove the cushion **(see illustration)**.

14 Installation is the reverse of removal.

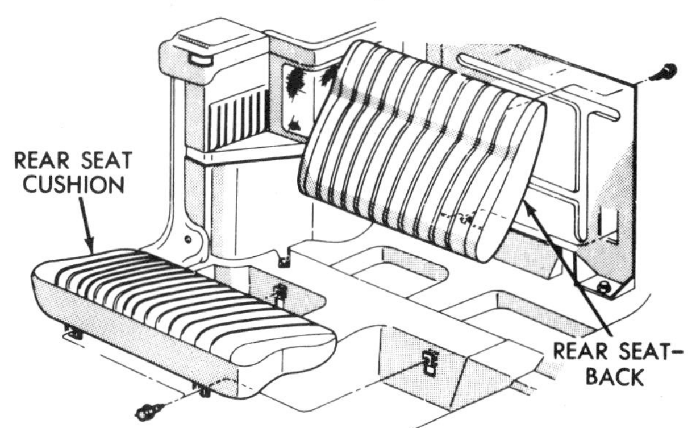

30.13 Convertible rear seat details

11

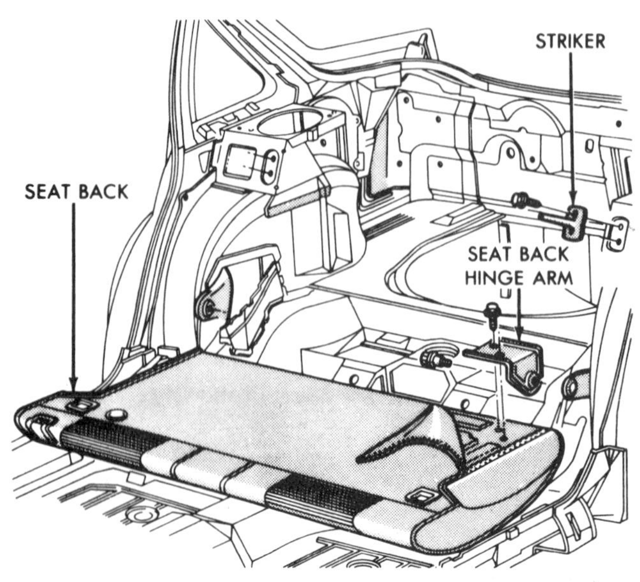

30.15 Fold down bench-type seat details

H body — bench-type seat back

15 Peel the corner of the rear seat carpet back from the velcro fastener, remove the seat back-to-hinge screws and detach the seat back from the vehicle **(see illustration)**.

16 Installation is the reverse of removal.

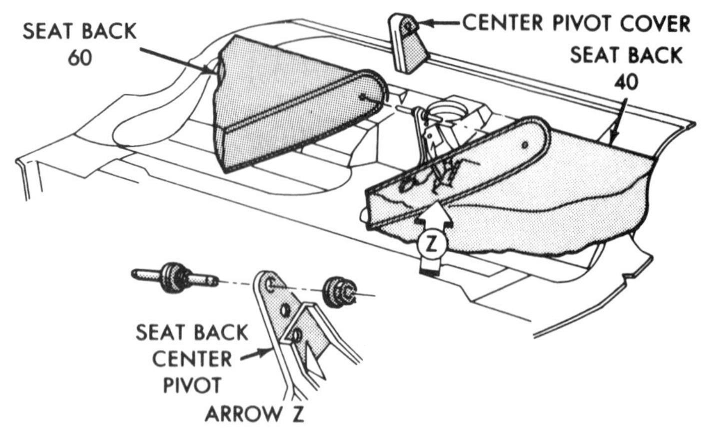

30.17 60/40 seat back details

H body — 60/40-type seat back

17 Remove the seat back-to-hinge screws and detach the seat back **(see illustration)**.

Rear seat cushion

18 Remove the bolts attaching the seat cushion to the floor and detach the seat cushion.

19 Installation is the reverse of removal.

Chapter 12 Chassis electrical system

Contents

Specifications

Bulb application

	Number
Headlights	
High beam	PH4651
High and low beam	PH4656
Front parking and turn signal lights	2057
Center high-mounted brake light	921
Rear stop and turn signal lights	2057
Rear license and side marker lights	168
Back-up lights	1156

Fusible link wire color code

	Wire gauge
Black	12
Red	14
Dark blue	16
Gray	18
Orange	20

1 General information

This Chapter covers repair and service procedures for the various lighting and electrical components not associated with the engine. Information on the battery, alternator, voltage regulator, ignition and starting systems can be found in Chapter 5.

The electrical system is a 12-volt negative ground type. Power for the electrical system and accessories is supplied by a lead/acid type battery which is charged by the alternator. The circuits are protected from overload by a system of fuses and fusible links. **Caution:** *Whenever the electrical system is worked on, the negative battery cable should be disconnected to prevent electrical shorts and/or fires.*

Although all models are very similar, some procedures may differ somewhat from one body designation to another. Where there are differences, references to the body designation will be made in the text. The body designations are as follows:

C/V body — Chrysler LeBaron, Town and Country, Dodge 400
E body — Chrysler E Class, New Yorker, Dodge 600, Plymouth Caravelle
H body — Chrysler LeBaron GTS and Dodge Lancer

2 Electrical troubleshooting – general information

A typical electrical circuit consists of an electrical component, any switches, relays, motors, etc. related to that component and the wiring and connectors that connect the component to both the battery and the chassis. To aid in locating a problem in the most common electrical circuits, several wiring diagrams are included at the end of this manual.

Before tackling any troublesome electrical circuit, first study the appropriate diagrams to get a complete understanding of what makes up that individual circuit. Trouble spots, for instance, can often be narrowed down by noting if other components related to that circuit are operating properly or not. If several components or circuits fail at one time, chances are the problem lies in the fuse or ground connection, as several circuits often are routed through the same fuse and ground connections.

Electrical problems often stem from simple causes, such as loose or corroded connections, a blown fuse or melted fusible link. Prior to any electrical troubleshooting, always visually check the condition of the fuse, wires and connections in the problem circuit.

If testing instruments are going to be utilized, use the diagrams to plan ahead of time where you will make the necessary connections in order to accurately pinpoint the trouble spot.

The basic tools needed for electrical troubleshooting include a circuit tester or voltmeter (a 12-volt bulb with a set of test leads can also be used), a continuity tester, which includes a bulb, battery and set of test leads, and a jumper wire, preferably with a circuit breaker incorporated, which can be used to bypass electrical components.

Voltage checks should be performed if a circuit is not functioning properly.

Connect one lead of a circuit tester to either the negative battery terminal or a known good ground. Connect the other lead to a connector in the circuit being tested, preferably nearest to the battery or fuse. If the bulb of the tester lights, voltage is reaching that point, which means the part of the circuit between that connector and the battery is problem free. Continue checking along the entire circuit in the same fashion. When you reach a point where no voltage is present, the problem lies between there and the last good test point. Most of the time the problem is due to a loose connection. **Note:** *Keep in mind that some circuits receive voltage only when the ignition key is in the Accessory or Run position.*

A method of finding shorts in a circuit is to remove the fuse and connect a test light or voltmeter in its place to the fuse terminals. There should be no load in the circuit. Move the wiring harness from side-to-side while watching the test light. If the bulb lights, there is a short to ground somewhere in that area, probably where insulation has rubbed off of a wire. The same test can be performed on other components of the circuit, including the switch.

A ground check should be done to see if a component is grounded properly. Disconnect the battery and connect one lead of a self-powered test light, such as a continuity tester, to a known good ground. Connect the other lead to the wire or ground connection being tested. If the bulb lights, the ground is good. If the bulb does not light the ground is not good.

A continuity check is performed to see if a circuit, section of circuit or individual component is passing electricity properly. Disconnect the battery and connect the leads of a self-powered test light, such as a continuity tester, to the circuit. If the bulb lights, there is continuity, which means the circuit is passing electricity properly. Switches can be checked in the same way.

Remember that all electrical circuits are composed basically of electricity running from the battery, through the wires, switches, relays, etc. to the electrical component (light bulb, motor, etc.). From there it is run to the body (ground), where it is passed back to the battery. Any electrical problem is basically an interruption in the flow of electricity to and from the battery.

3 Fuses and fusible links – replacement

Refer to illustrations 3.2 and 3.6

Caution: *Do not bypass a fuse with pieces of metal or aluminum foil as serious damage to the electrical system could result.*

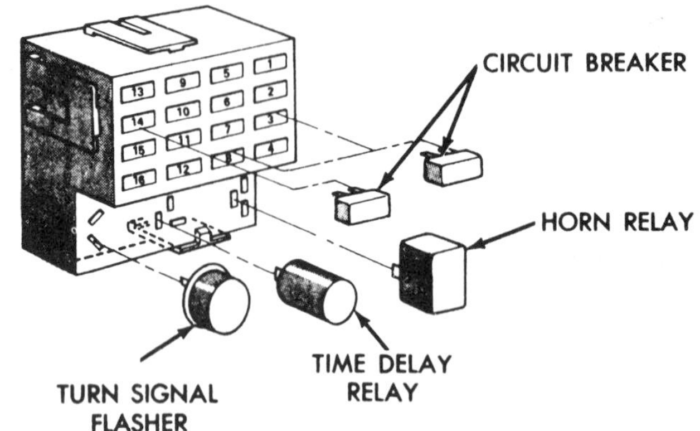

3.2 Typical fuse block component layout

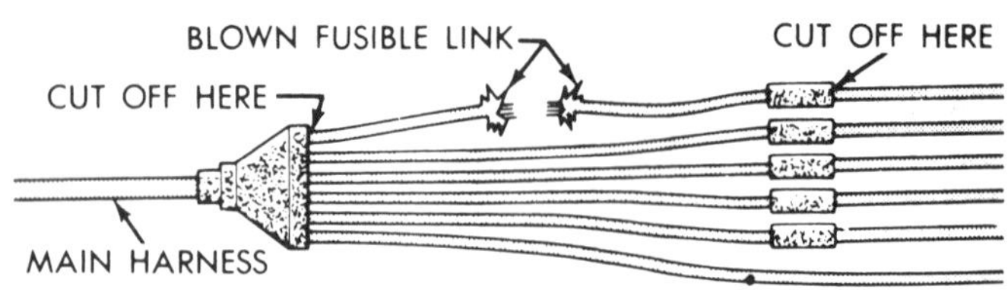

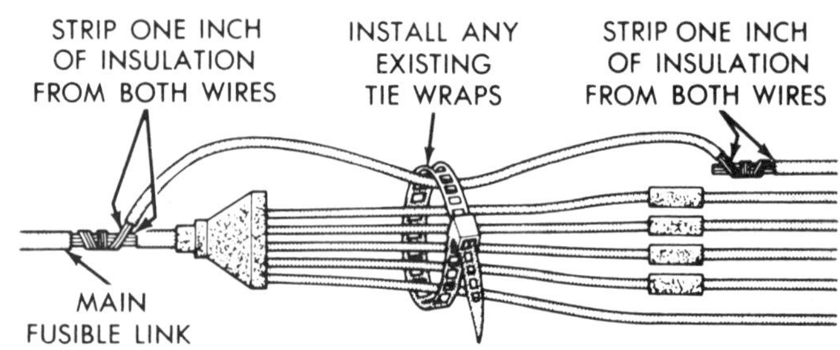

3.6 Multiple fusible link repair details

1 The fuse block is located below the dash, adjacent to the steering column or in the glove box behind a panel. Put your finger in the notch at the bottom of the panel and pull it back sharply to remove and expose the fuse block.

2 With the ignition switch off, remove each fuse in turn by grasping it and pulling it from the block **(see illustration)**. Replace the blown fuse with a new one of the same value by pushing it into place. Install the cover panel.

3 If the fuses in the fuse block are not blown and the headlights or other components are inoperable, check the fusible links, located in the wiring harness adjacent to the left suspension strut tower. Before replacing a fusible link, determine the reason that it burned out. Replacing the link without finding and correcting the cause for the failure could lead to serious damage to the electrical system.

4 Determine the proper gauge for the replacement link by referring to the Specifications. Obtain the new link or link wire from your dealer.

5 Disconnect the negative batery cable and cut off all of the remaining burned out fusible link.

6 Strip off one inch of insulation from both ends of the new fusible link and the main harness wire **(see illustration)**.

7 Install the new fusible link by twisting the ends securely around the main link wire. On multiple links, the replacement wire must be

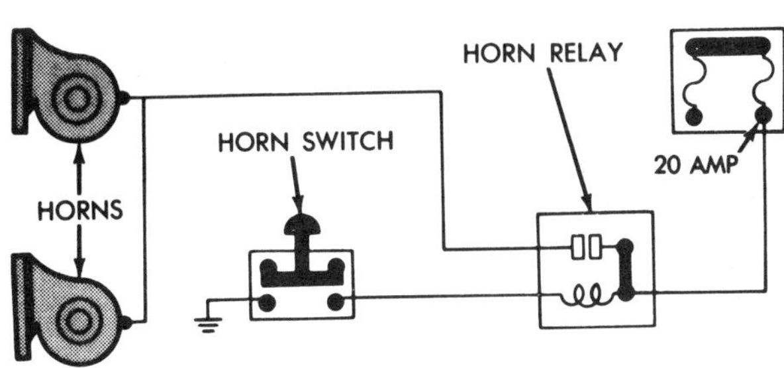

4.2 Horn wiring diagram

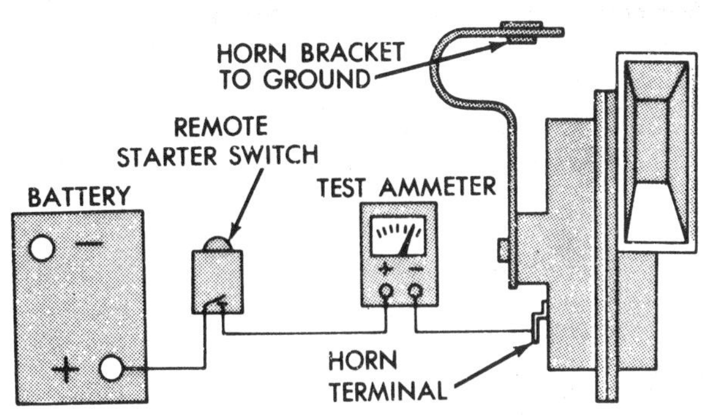

4.6 Horn adjustment ammeter hook-up

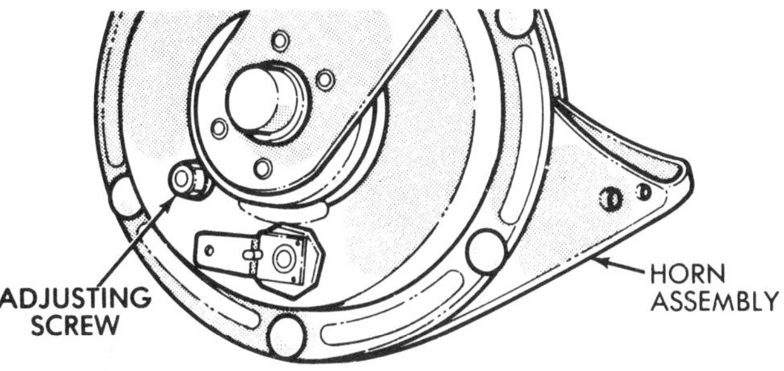

4.7 Horn adjusting screw location

connected to the main wires beyond the connector insulators of the old link.

8 Solder the wires together with non-acid core solder. After the connection has cooled, wrap the splice with at least three layers of electrical tape.

4 Horn – check and adjustment

Refer to illustrations 4.2, 4.6 and 4.7

1 On 1982 models, if the horn will not sound, release the parking brake, place the transaxle selector lever in Park or Neutral and watch the brake light on the dash as you start the engine. If the light does not come on, the steering column is not properly grounded to the instrument panel so the horn switch is not grounded.

2 On all models, if the brake light works but the horn does not sound, check for a blown fuse **(see illustration)**. If the new fuse blows when the horn button is pushed, there is a short in the horn assembly itself or between the fuse terminal and the horn.

3 If the fuse is good and the horn still does not sound, unplug the connector at the horn and insert a test light lead. Ground the other test lead and note whether the light comes on. If it does, the horn is faulty or improperly grounded. Check the horn for proper grounding by connecting a wire between the negative battery cable and the horn bracket; be sure to scratch through the paint. If the horn does not sound, replace the horn relay, located on the fuse block, with a new one.

4 If the horn sounds continuously, replace the horn relay with a known good one. If the horn still sounds, pull off the horn button and make sure that the horn contact wire is not shorting out against the hub.

5 To adjust the horn loudness and tone, first determine which horn is in need of adjustment. Disconnect the horn which is not being adjusted.

6 Connect the horn to the positive terminal of the battery with a remote starter switch and an ammeter in series **(see illustration)**.

7 With the remote starter switch depressed, the ammeter should read between 4.5 and 5.5 amps. To adjust, turn the adjusting screw clockwise to decrease or counterclockwise to increase the current **(see illustration)**. Check the horn for satisfactory tone and current draw after each adjustment.

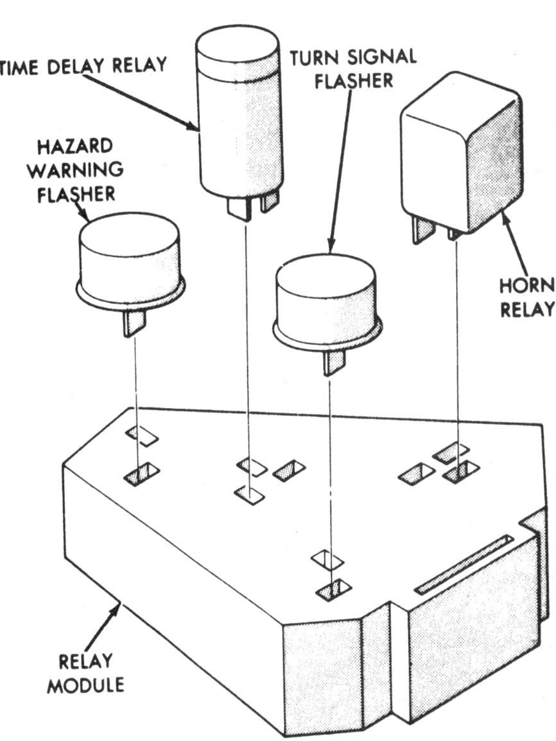

5.5 On H body models, the turn signal and hazard flashers are located on the relay module

5 Flasher units – replacement

Refer to illustration 5.5

1 The hazard and turn signal flasher units are located on or adjacent to the fuse block.

2 On 1982 models, the turn signal flasher and hazard flasher units are located on the lower left corner of the fuse block and can be replaced easily **(see illustration 3.2)**.

3 On 1983 and 1984 models, the turn signal flasher is located on the fuse block and the hazard flasher is taped to the main wiring harness.

4 On 1985 and later C/V and E body models, the turn signal flasher is on the fuse block and the hazard flasher is clipped to the instrument panel below the fuse block.

5 On 1985 and later H body models, the turn signal and hazard warning flasher units are located on the relay module under the instrument panel **(see illustration)**.

6 Headlights – removal and installation

Refer to illustrations 6.1, 6.2 and 6.4

1 Remove the headlight bezel **(see illustration)**.
2 Remove the retainer screws, taking care not to disturb the adjuster screws **(see illustration)**.
3 Pull the headlight out far enough to gain access to the connector.
4 Unplug the connector and remove the headlight **(see illustration)**.
5 To install a headlight, plug in the wire connector, position the light and install the retainer and screws.
6 Install the headlight bezel.

7 Headlight adjuster screw – replacement

Refer to illustrations 7.2, 7.3, 7.4 and 7.5

1 Remove the headlight (Section 6).
2 Use a pair of pliers to remove the retaining spring **(see illustration)**.
3 Loosen the adjuster screw enough to allow removal of the headlight bucket **(see illustration)**.
4 Use a small screwdriver to push back the locking tabs and rock the adjuster screw back and forth while pulling on it **(see illustration)**.
5 To install the new screw, push it securely into place **(see illustration)**.
6 Installation of the related components is the reverse of removal. Adjust the headlights as described in Section 8.

8 Headlights – alignment

1 It is always best to have the headlights aligned with the proper equipment, but the following procedure may be used for temporary adjustment.
2 Position the vehicle on level ground ten feet in front of a dark wall. The wall must be at right angles to the centerline of the vehicle.
3 Draw a vertical line on the wall corresponding to the centerline of the vehicle.
4 Rock the vehicle on the suspension to ensure that it settles at the proper level and check the tires to make sure that they are at the proper pressure. Measure the height between the ground and the center of the headlights.
5 Draw a horizontal line across the wall at this measured height. Mark a cross on the horizontal line on either side of the vertical centerline equal to the distance between the center of each light and the centerline of the vehicle.

6.1 Headlight bezel mounting screws (arrows)

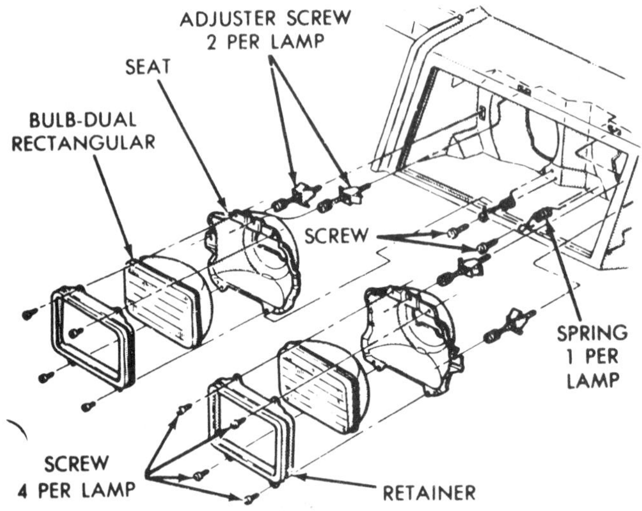

6.2 Be sure to remove only the retaining screws – not the adjuster screws

6.4 Hold on to the headlight securely when detaching the wiring connector from the terminals at the rear

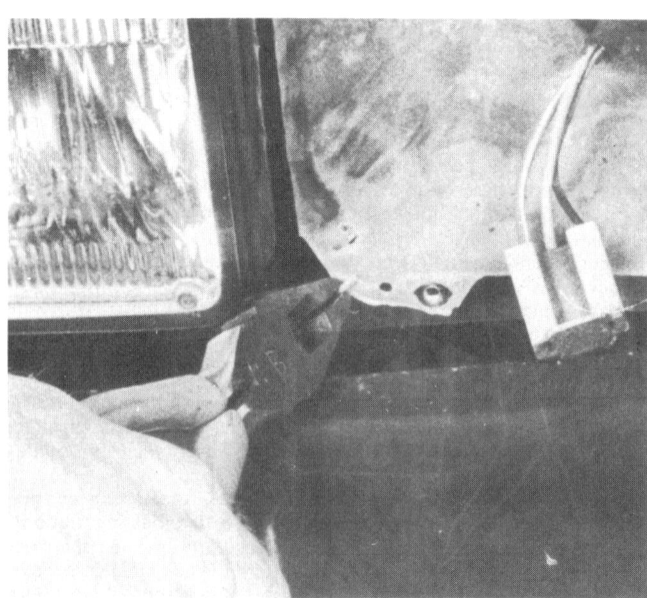

7.2 Pull the headlight bucket spring out to detach it

6 Turn the headlights on and switch them to High beam.
7 Use the adjuster screws to align the center of each beam with the crosses which were marked on the horizontal line.
8 Rock the vehicle again to make sure the beams return to the same position. Check the operation of the dimmer switch.
9 The headlights should be adjusted with the proper equipment at the earliest opportunity.

9 Front exterior bulbs — replacement

Refer to illustrations 9.1a, 9.1b, 9.5 and 9.8

Note: *Prior to installation it is a good idea to lubricate the metal terminal area of a new bulb with light grease or petroleum jelly.*

Turn signal and parking lights

Bumper mounted light

1 From under the front of the vehicle, grasp the bulb socket, push in and rotate it in a counterclockwise direction to remove it from the housing **(see illustrations)**.
2 Push the bulb in, turn it counterclockwise and withdraw it from the socket.

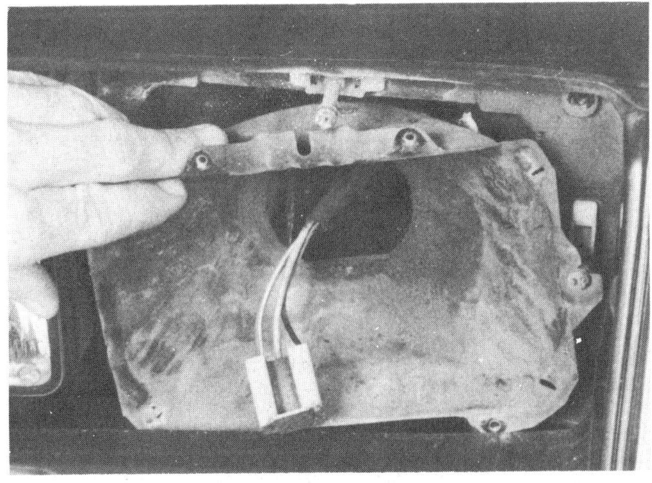

7.3 Loosen the adjuster screw enough to allow the headlight bucket to be removed from the opening

7.4 Use a screwdriver to release the adjuster screw locking tabs

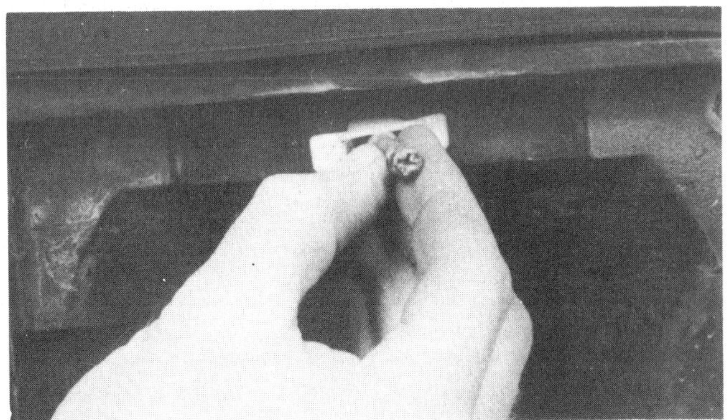

7.5 Press the new adjuster screw in until it locks into place

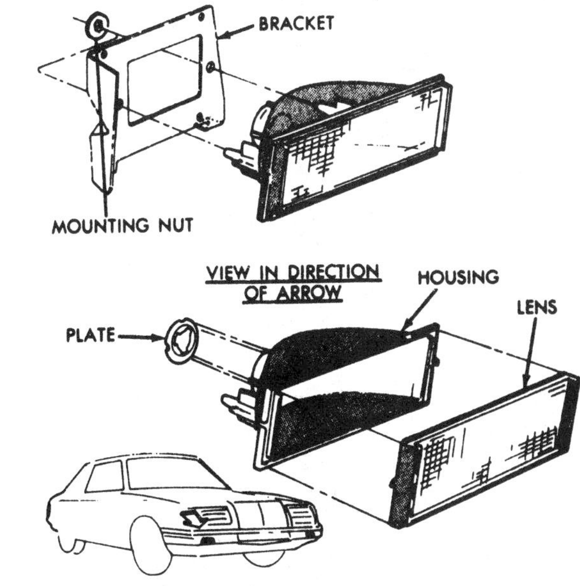

9.1a Front parking and turn signal light details (1982 through 1985 C/V and E body)

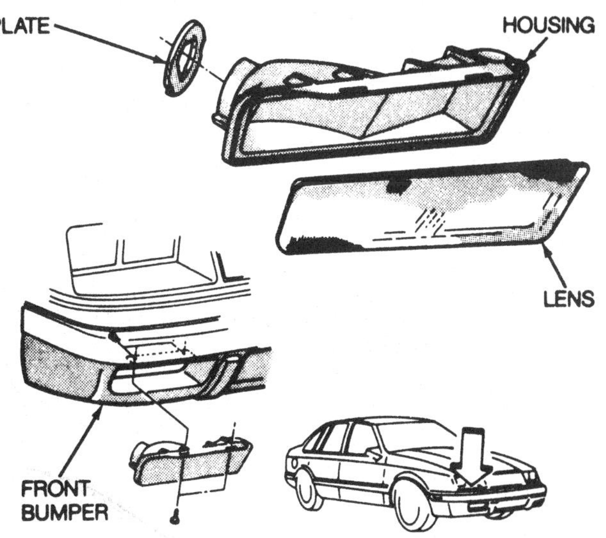

9.1b H body front parking and turn signal light details

12

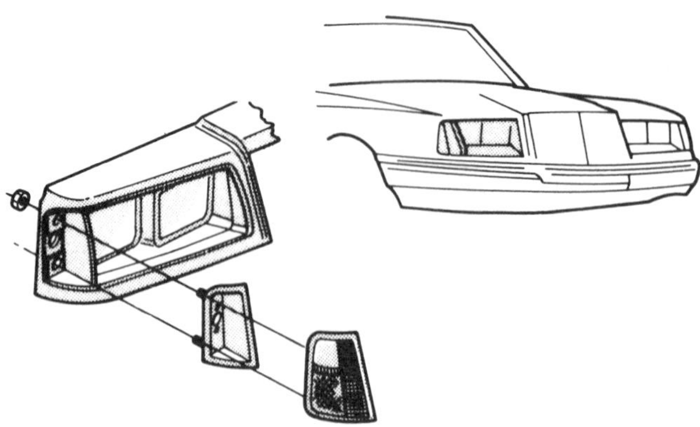

9.5 The park and turn signal light bulbs are reached after removing the bezel

3 Place the socket in position with the tabs aligned with those in the housing, press in and turn it clockwise.
4 To replace the lense, remove the two nuts or screws.

Headlight bezel mounted light

5 Remove the retaining screws and detach the bezel **(see illustration)**.
6 Rotate the bulbs counterclockwise and withdraw them from the housing.
7 To replace the bezel housing, remove the two mounting screws.

Front side marker lights

8 From underneath, rotate the bulb holder counterclockwise and withdraw it from the housing **(see illustration)**.
9 Remove the bulb from the holder.

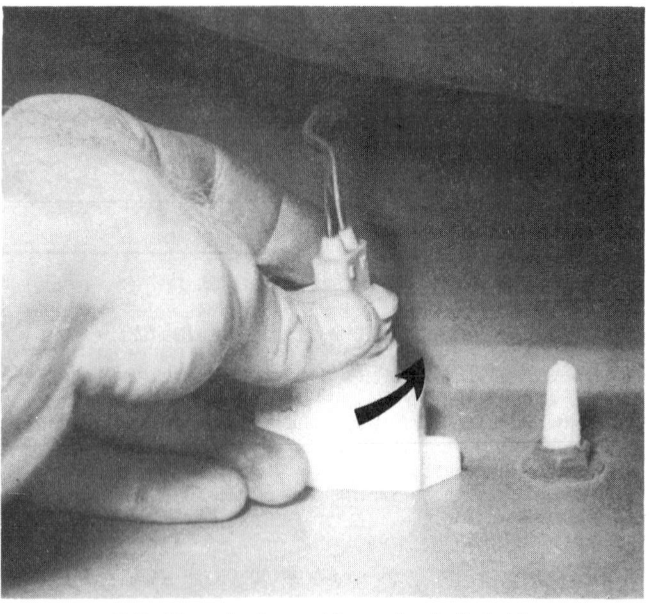

9.8 Turn the front side marker bulb holder counterclockwise to remove it

10 Rear exterior bulbs — replacement

Refer to illustrations 10.2, 10.8, 10.13, 10.15, 10.17, 10.19, 10.21, 10.22a and 10.22b

Tail, stop, turn signal and back-up lights

1 Open the trunk or liftgate.

Station wagon models

2 Remove the housing mounting nuts **(see illustration)**.
3 Pull the bulb sockets out of the housing, disconnect the ground wire and set the housing aside.
4 Replace the bulbs, plug the sockets into the housing and connect the ground wire. Install the housing and mounting nuts.

C/V and E body sedan and coupe

5 Remove the appropriate socket by rotating it counterclockwise and withdrawing it from the housing. Push the bulb in and turn it counterclockwise to remove it from the socket.
6 Installation is the reverse of removal.

H body sedan

7 Pull the trim cover (held in place with velcro fasteners) away from the housing.
8 Remove the four plastic wingnuts and pull the housing away from the rear quarter panel **(see illustration)**.
9 Remove the appropriate socket by rotating it counterclockwise and withdrawing it from the housing.
10 Remove the bulb from the socket.
11 Install the new bulb by pressing in and rotating it clockwise.
12 Install the socket by aligning the tabs, pushing in and turning it clockwise.

Center high-mounted brake light

Station wagon

13 Remove the liftgate inner trim panel to expose the bulb **(see illustration)** .
14 Rotate the bulb counterclockwise to remove it.

Convertible

15 Remove the two screws and pull the light from the cover **(see illustration)**.
16 Remove the bulb by pushing in and turning it.

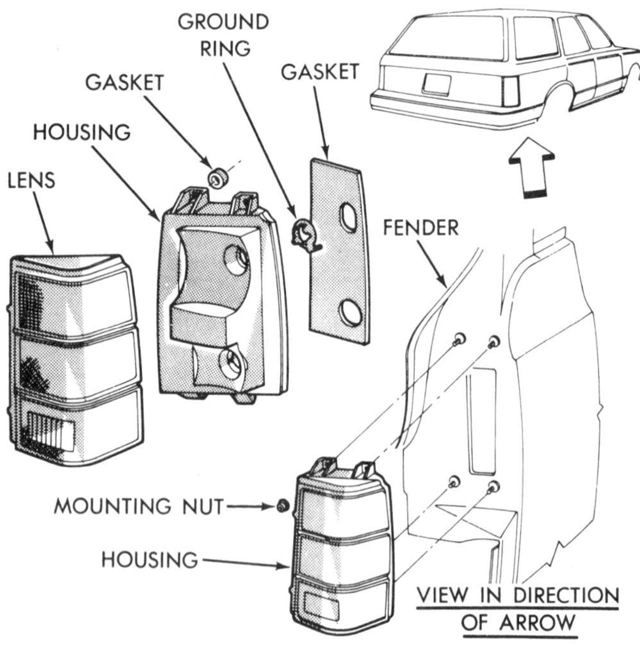

10.2 Station wagon rear bulb replacement details

C/V body

17 Pull the cover from the light, remove the two mounting screws and pull the light from the adapter **(see illustration)**.
18 Remove the bulb by pushing in and turning it.

E body

19 Pull the cover off the light and adapter, remove the two screws and detach the adapter **(see illustration)**.
20 Remove the bulb by pushing in and turning it.

H body

21 Remove the two light mounting screws for access to the bulb **(see illustration)**.

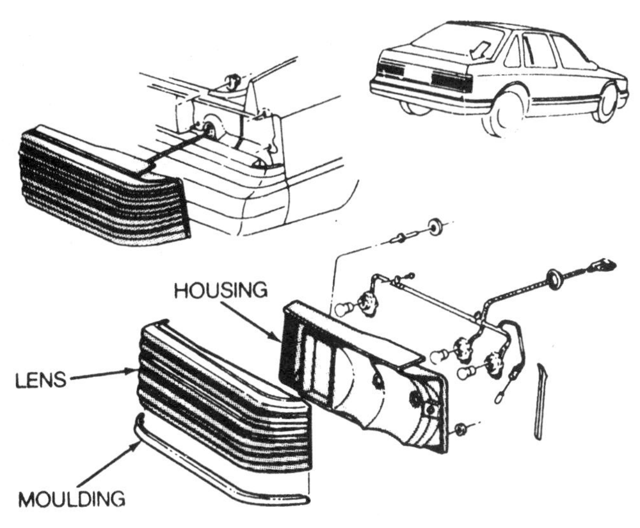

10.8 H body rear bulb replacement details

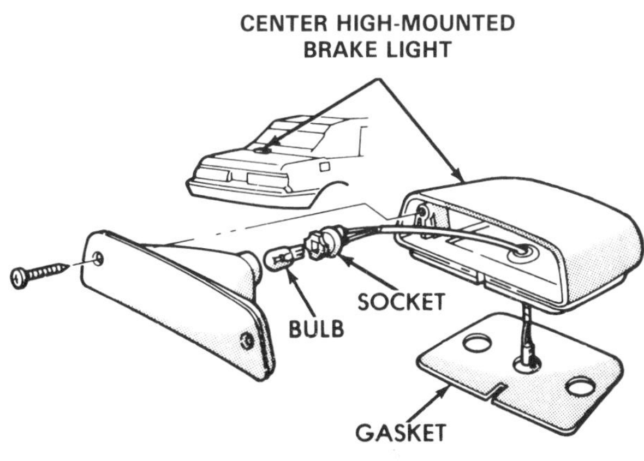

10.15 Convertible model center high-mounted brake light details

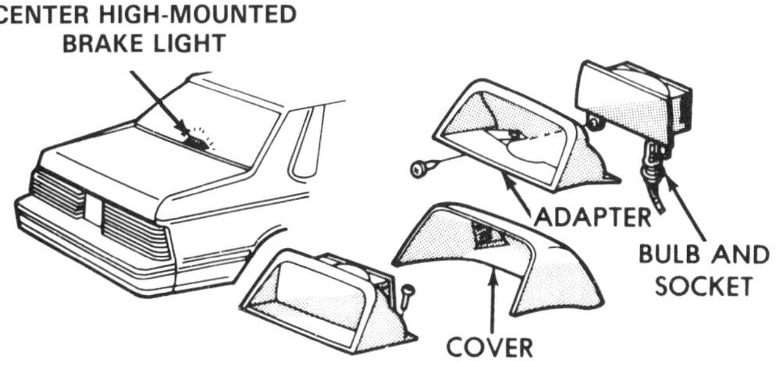

10.19 E body center high-mounted brake light details

CENTER HIGH-MOUNTED
BRAKE LIGHT
BULB
SOCKET

10.13 Station wagon center high-mounted brake light details

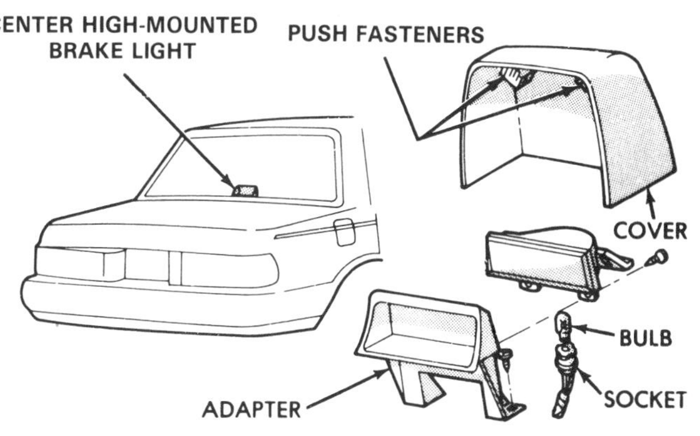

10.17 C/V body center high-mounted brake light details

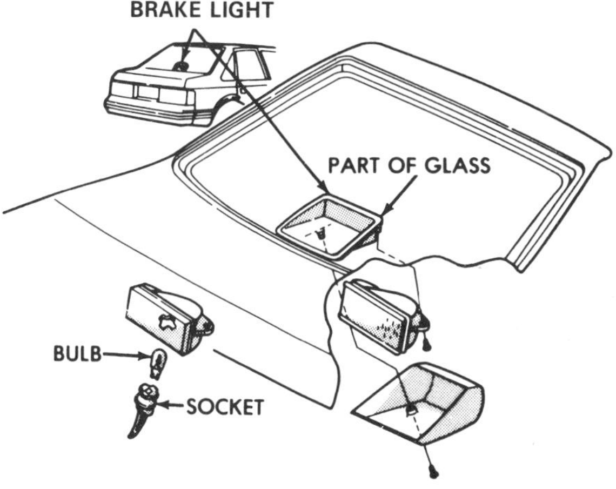

10.21 H body center high-mounted brake light details

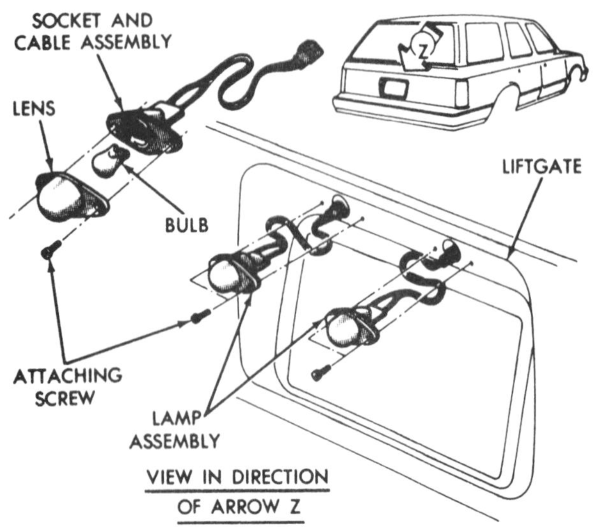

10.22a Station wagon license plate light details

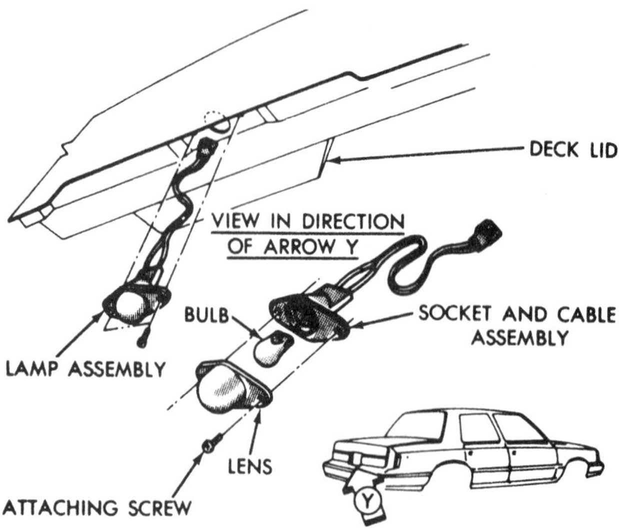

10.22b Typical sedan license plate light details

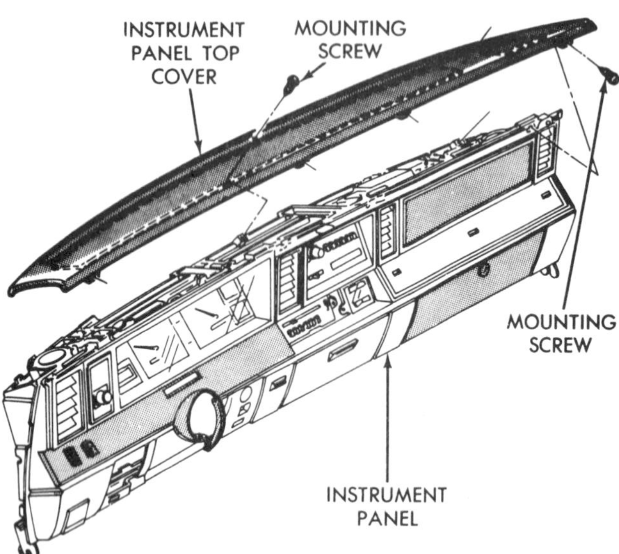

11.3a On C/V and E body models equipped with monaural radios, remove the instrument panel cover, . . .

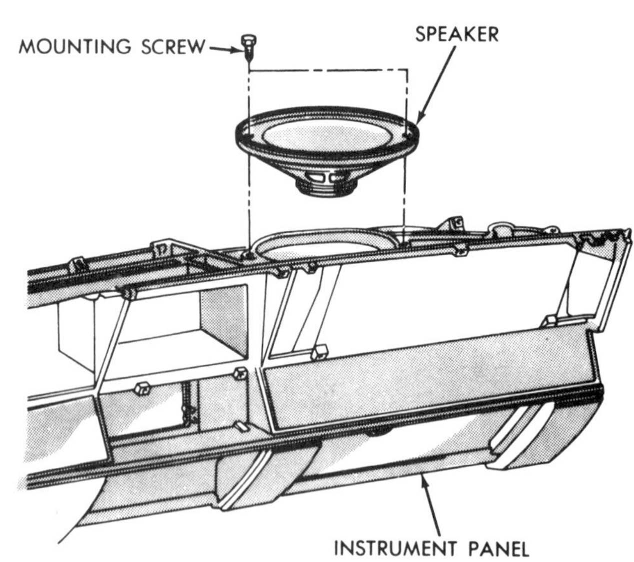

11.3b . . . followed by the speaker

License plate light

22 Remove the screws and detach the cover **(see illustrations)**.
23 Grasp the bulb securely and pull it from the socket.
24 Insert the new bulb and install the cover and screws.

11 Radio – removal and installation

Refer to illustrations 11.3a, 11.3b, 11.4 and 11.11

1 Disconnect the negative cable at the battery. Place the cable out of the way so it cannot accidentally come in contact with the negative terminal of the battery, as this would once again allow power into the electrical system of the vehicle.

C/V and E body

Standard models

2 Remove the left instrument panel bezel.
3 On monaural models, remove the instrument panel top cover **(see illustration)**. Remove the mounting screws, unplug the connector and remove the speaker **(see illustration)**.
4 Remove the mounting screws, pull the radio out sufficiently to allow the connectors to be unplugged and remove the radio from the dash **(see illustration)**.
5 Installation is the reverse of removal.

Console equipped models

6 Remove thee two screws from the bottom of the console trim bezel and detach the bezel from the console.
7 Remove the two mounting screws and pull the radio out sufficiently to unplug the connectors and disconnect the ground cable and antenna.
8 Remove the radio.
9 Installation is the reverse of removal.

H body

10 Remove the instrument cluster bezel (Section 21).
11 Remove the two mounting screws, pull the radio out and disconnect the wiring **(see illustration)**.
12 Disconnect the ground strap and detach the radio.
13 Installation is the reverse of removal.

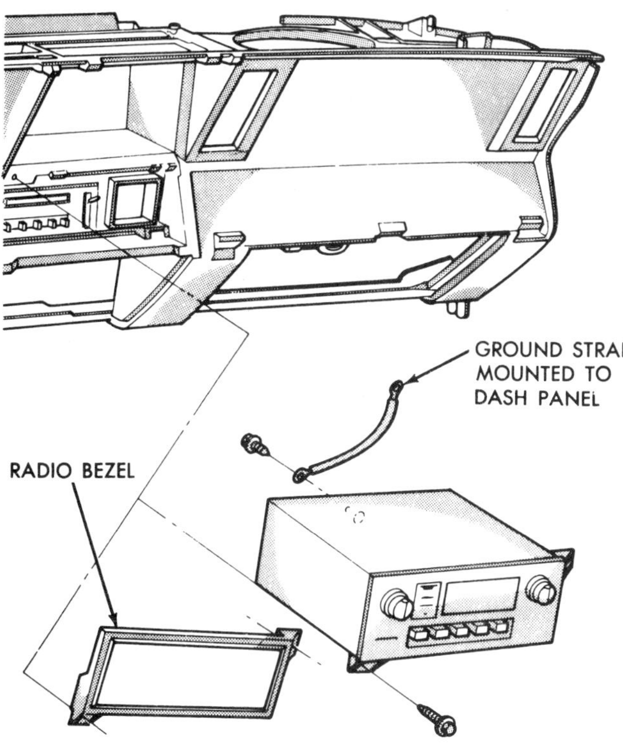

11.4 C/V and E body radio mounting details

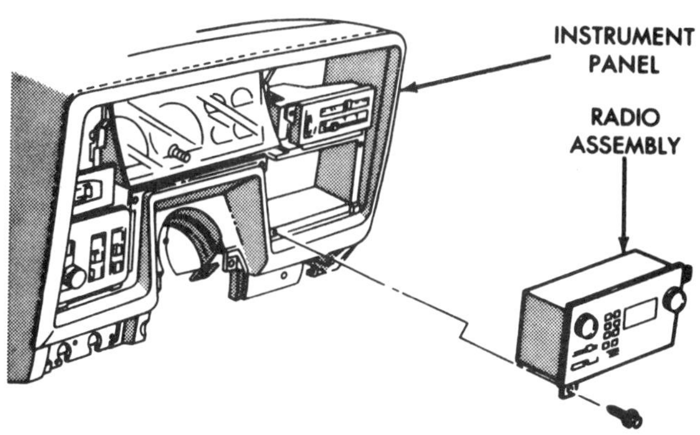

11.11 H body radio mounting details

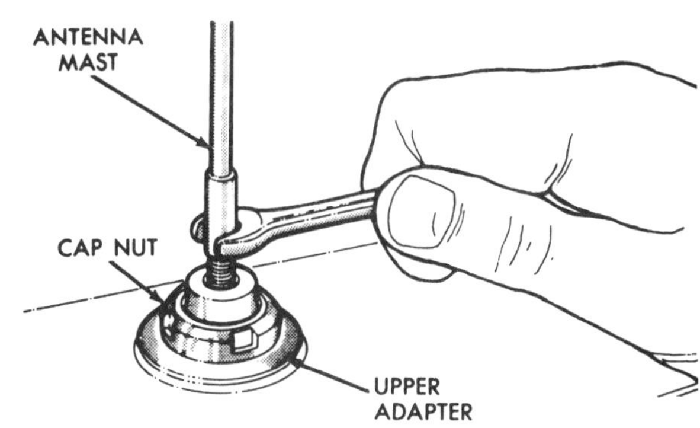

12.3 Removing the radio antenna mast

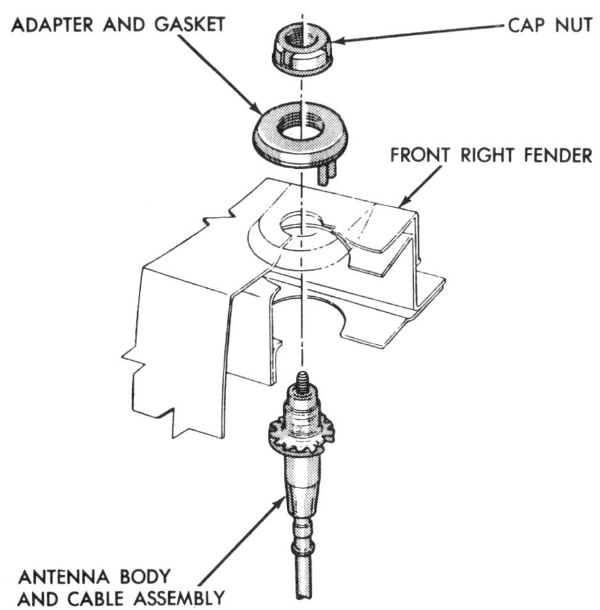

12.4 The antenna lead and body are accessible from inside the fender

12 Antenna – removal and installation

Refer to illustrations 12.3 and 12.4

1 Disconnect the negative cable at the battery. Place the cable out of the way so it cannot accidentally come in contact with the negative terminal of the battery, as this would once again allow power into the electrical system of the vehicle.

2 Remove the radio (Section 11).

3 Use a wrench to unscrew the antenna mast from the cap nut **(see illustration)**.

4 Use a pair of needle-nose pliers to unscrew and remove the cap nut and adapter (remove the gasket with the adapter) **(see illustration)**.

5 From under the fender, remove the three inner fender shield-to-fender screws, pull the shield back for access and remove the antenna body and lead assembly.

6 To install the antenna, insert the body and lead assembly into the fender and install the adapter, gasket and cap nut.

7 Install the antenna mast.

8 Install the fender shield screws.

9 Install the radio and connect the negative battery cable. Don't forget to hook the antenna lead to the radio.

13 Ignition switch – removal and installation

Refer to illustration 13.6

1 Disconnect the negative cable at the battery. Place the cable out of the way so it cannot accidentally come in contact with the negative terminal of the battery, as this would once again allow power into the electrical system of the vehicle.

2 On early models, remove the under dash sound deadener panel.

3 Remove the cruise control clutch speed switch (if equipped).

4 Remove the steering column cover (see Chapter 11 for more information on the steering column, if necessary).

5 Remove the steering column-to-support bracket nuts, then carefully lower the column until the ignition switch is exposed (it is mounted on top of the steering column).

12

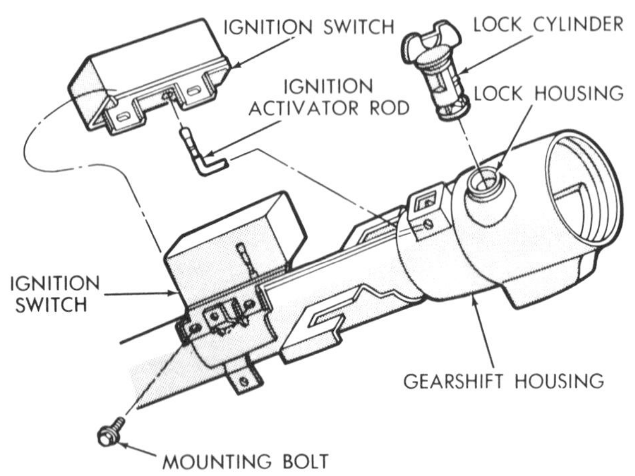

13.6 Ignition switch mounting details

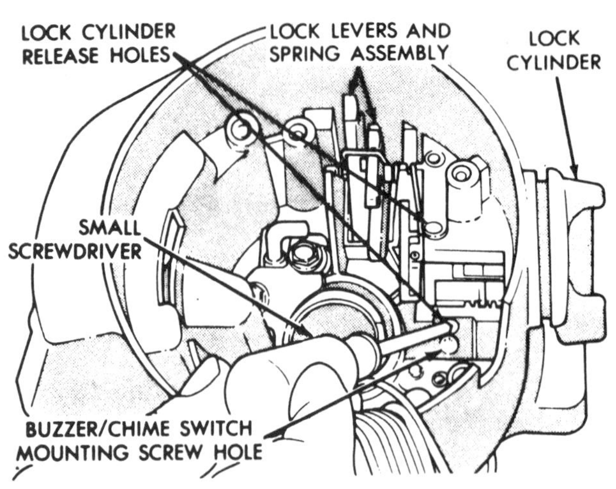

14.9 Ignition lock cylinder removal details (except 1986 and later floor shift models)

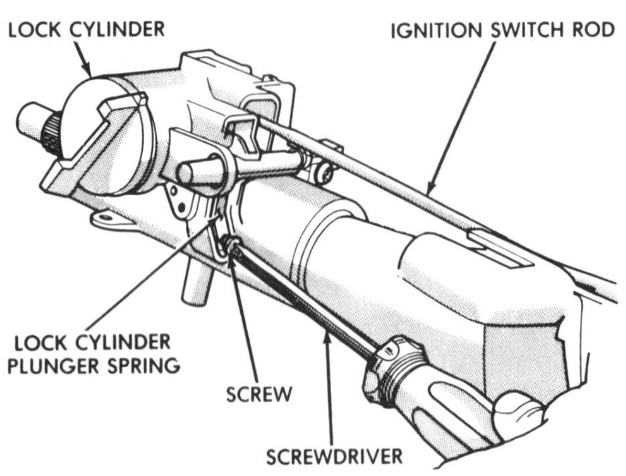

14.19 Use a screwdriver to remove the lock cylinder plunger (1986 and later floor shift models)

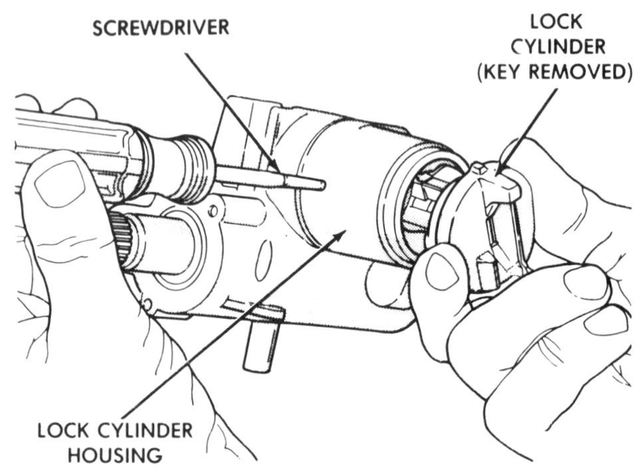

14.20 Lock cylinder removal details (1986 and later floor shift models)

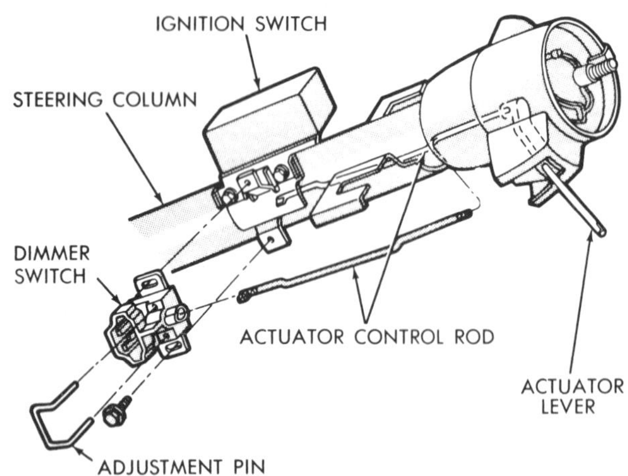

15.4 Dimmer switch installation and adjustment details (except 1986 and later floor shift models)

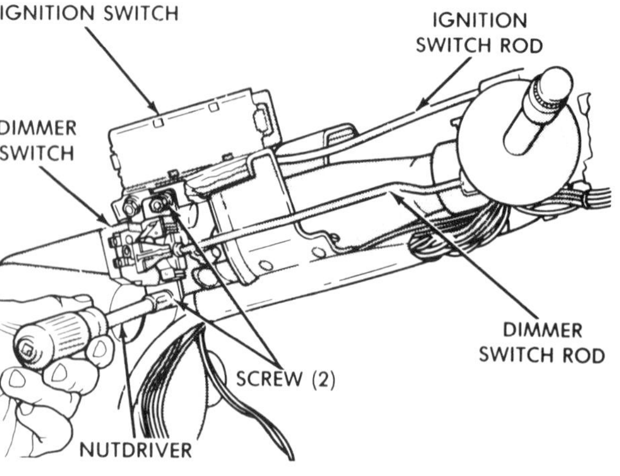

15.5 1986 and later floor shift model dimmer switch installation details

6 Remove the two mounting bolts, rotate the switch 90 degrees and detach it from the ignition activator rod **(see illustration)**.
7 To install the switch, support the rod and rotate the switch 90 degrees until it snaps into place on the rod. Plug in the electrical connector. Install the mounting bolts loosely.
8 With the key removed and the lock cylinder in the Lock position, adjust the switch by moving it up (toward the steering wheel) to take up the slack in the rod, then tighten the bolts securely.
9 The remainder of installation is the reverse of removal.

14 Ignition lock cylinder (fixed column) – removal and installation

Refer to illustrations 14.9, 14.19 and 14.20

1 Disconnect the negative cable at the battery. Place the cable out of the way so it cannot accidentally come in contact with the negative terminal of the battery, as this would once again allow power into the electrical system of the vehicle.

All except 1986 and later floor shift models

2 Remove the steering wheel (Chapter 10).
3 Remove the turn signal and hazard warning switches.
4 Remove the four screws and the snap-ring and detach the upper shaft bearing and housing.
5 Remove the lock plate and spring.
6 Separate the ignition key buzzer switch wiring connector.
7 Remove the screws from the steering lock bellcrank mechanism.
8 Place the lock cylinder in the Lock position and pull the key out.
9 Insert a small screwdriver into each release hole while pulling out on the lock cylinder to remove it **(see illustration)**.
10 To install the lock cylinder, insert it and seat the lock lever spring leg securely in the bottom of the notch in the lock casting.
11 Connect the actuator rod to the lock housing and attach the bellcrank. Install the screws.
12 Turn the key to the Lock position and remove it.
13 Push the lock cylinder housing in far enough to contact the switch actuator, insert the key, press it in and rotate the cylinder. When the inner parts of the mechanism are in alignment, the cylinder will move in, the spring loaded retainers will snap into place and the cylinder will be locked into the housing.
14 Plug in the key buzzer connector and install the lock plate and spring
15 Install the upper bearing housing, screws and snap-ring.
16 Install the turn signal and hazard warning switches.
17 Install the steering wheel and reconnect the battery cable.

1986 and later floor shift models

18 Remove the upper and lower steering column covers.
19 Remove the lock cylinder plunger **(see illustration)**.
20 With the key removed, insert a small screwdriver into the release hole and withdraw the lock cylinder **(see illustration)**.
21 To install the lock cylinder, insert it until it locks into the housing and then install the lock cylinder plunger.
22 Connect the negative battery cable.

15 Dimmer switch – removal, adjustment and installation

Refer to illustrations 15.4 and 15.5

1 Disconnect the negative cable at the battery. Place the cable out of the way so it cannot accidentally come in contact with the negative terminal of the battery, as this would once again allow power into the electrical system of the vehicle.
2 Remove the steering column cover.
3 Unplug the connector, remove the mounting screws and detach the switch from the steering column.
4 On all except 1986 and later floor shift models, position the switch, insert the control rod, install the screws finger tight and plug in the connector **(see illustration)**.
5 On 1986 and later floor shift models, place the switch in position, insert the control rod and install the screws. Tighten the screws securely and plug in the connector **(see illustration)**.
6 On all except 1986 and later floor shift models, fabricate an adjustment pin from a piece of wire and insert the pin ends into the switch. Adjust the switch by pushing it gently to the rear to take up the slack in the control rod and tighten the mounting screws.
7 Remove the adjustment pin.
8 Install the steering column cover and connect the negative battery cable.

16 Washer/wiper switch (fixed column) – removal and installation

Refer to illustrations 16.3a and 16.3b

1 Disconnect the negative cable at the battery. Place the cable out of the way so it cannot accidentally come in contact with the negative terminal of the battery, as this would once again allow power into the electrical system of the vehicle.
2 Remove the steering wheel (Chapter 10) and on 1986 and later floor shift models, the column covers.
3 Remove the screw which retains the turn signal switch to the wiper/washer switch or the column **(see illustrations)**.
4 Pull the hider up the control stalk. Remove the screws and detach the control stalk.

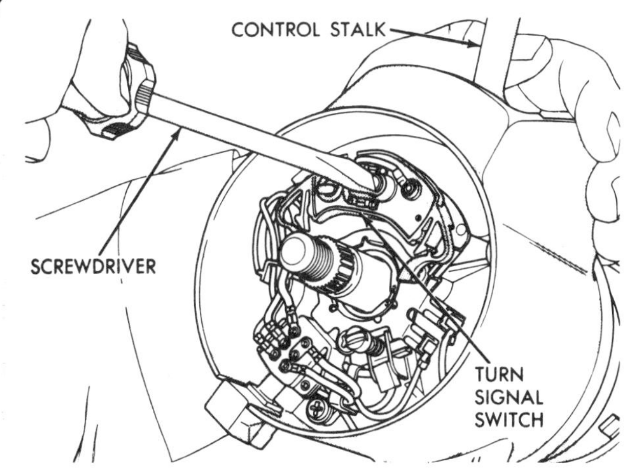

16.3a The turn signal switch screw must be removed to detach the wiper/washer switch (except 1986 and later floor shift models)

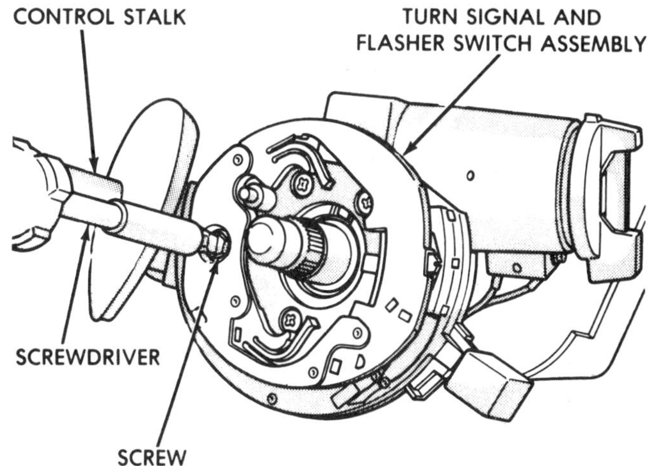

16.3b 1986 and later floor shift model wiper/washer switch details

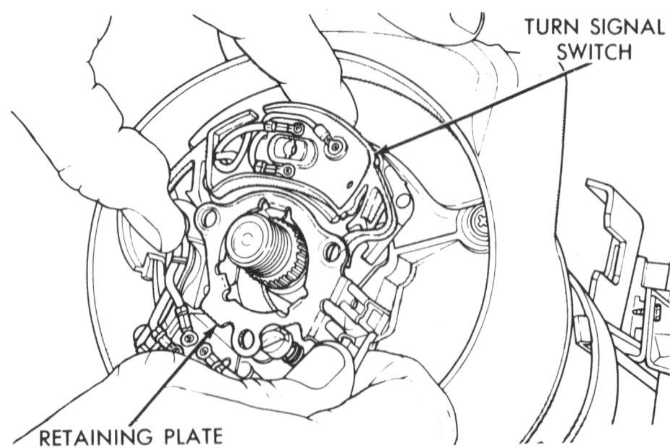

17.7 The turn signal switch can be lifted out after removing the upper bearing retainer screws (except 1986 and later floor shift models)

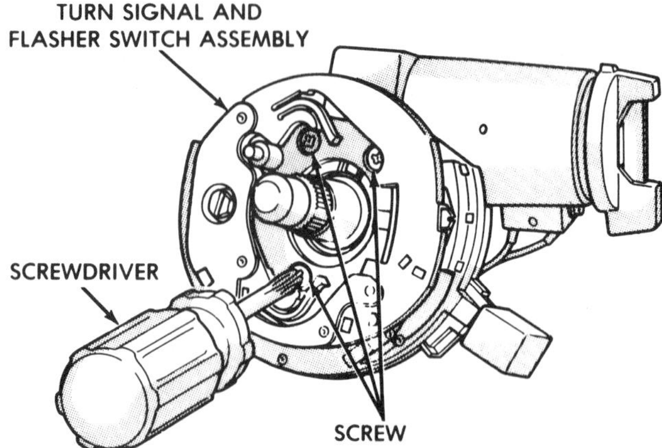

17.8 1986 and later floor shift model turn signal switch screw locations

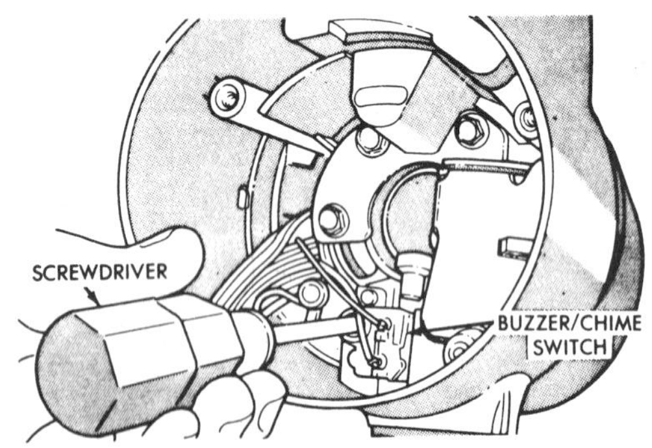

18.5a Key buzzer switch removal and installation details (except 1986 and later floor shift models)

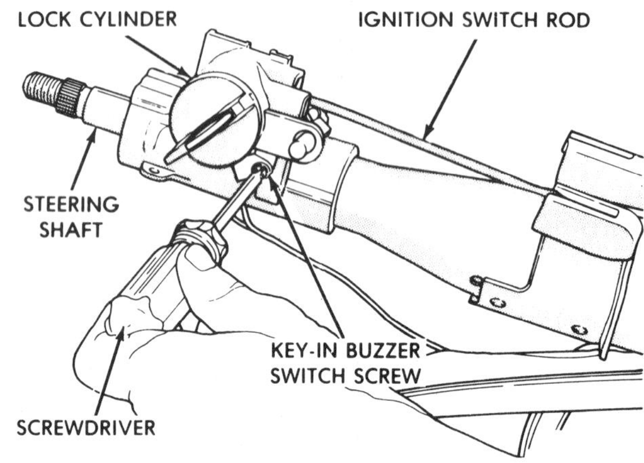

18.5b 1986 and later floor shift model key buzzer installation details

5 Remove the wiring trough cover and unplug the switch connector.
6 Remove the switch and carefully pull the wiring out of the steering column.
7 To install the switch, insert the wiring harness into the column and thread it down the column and into position. Plug in the connector.
8 Place the wiper/washer switch in position, making sure the dimmer switch actuating rod is securely seated. Install the mounting screw.
9 Install the steering wheel.
10 Attach the stalk and hider
11 Install the wiring trough cover and column covers.
12 Connect the negative battery cable.

17 Turn signal/hazard warning switch (fixed column) – removal and installation

Refer to illustrations 17.7 and 17.8

1 Disconnect the negative cable at the battery. Place the cable out of the way so it cannot accidentally come in contact with the negative terminal of the battery, as this would once again allow power into the electrical system of the vehicle.
2 Remove the steering wheel (Chapter 10) and on 1986 and later models, the column covers.
3 Remove the wiring trough cover.
4 Remove the lower instrument panel cover from the base of the steering column.
5 Separate the wiring connector.
6 Remove the screw which retains the turn signal switch and washer/wiper switch. Disengage the washer/wiper switch from the column and allow it to hang by the wires.
7 Except on 1986 and later floor shift models, remove the screws retaining the turn signal/hazard warning switch and the upper bearing retainer, then detach the assembly from the column **(see illustration)**.
8 On 1986 and later floor shift models, remove the turn signal and hazard warning switch mounting screws **(see illustration)**.
9 Carefully pull the wiring harness up through the column.
10 Prior to installation, lubricate the full circumference of the turn signal switch pivot with light grease.
11 Insert the wiring harness through the hub (all except 1986 and later floor shift models) and down the steering column (all models).
12 On all except 1986 and later floor shift models, place the switch assembly and bearing retainer in position and install the screws.
13 On 1986 and later floor shift models, place the switch assembly in position and install the mounting screws.
14 With the washer/wiper switch in position, install the turn signal switch mounting screw.
15 Plug in the connector and install the wiring trough cover.
16 Install the lower instrument panel cover and steering column panel.
17 Install the steering wheel.
18 Connect the negative battery cable.

18 Key buzzer/chime switch (fixed column) – removal and installation

Refer to illustrations 18.5a and 18.5b

1 Disconnect the negative cable at the battery. Place the cable out of the way so it cannot accidentally come in contact with the negative terminal of the battery, as this would once again allow power into the electrical system of the vehicle.
2 Remove the steering wheel (Chapter 10) and on 1986 and later models, the column covers.
3 On all except 1986 and later floor shift models, remove the turn

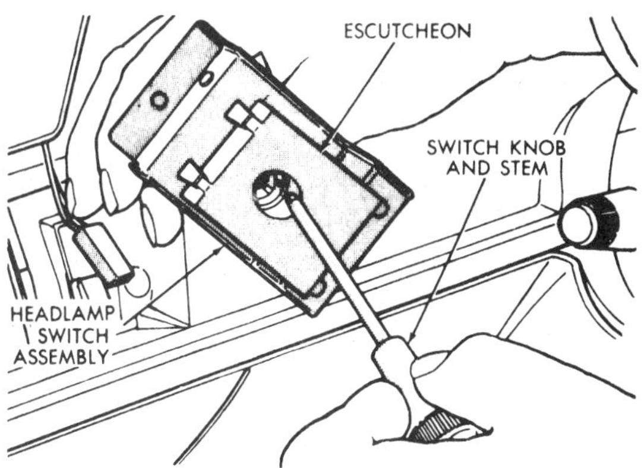

19.5 Depress the headlight switch button with a screwdriver to release the knob (C/V and E body)

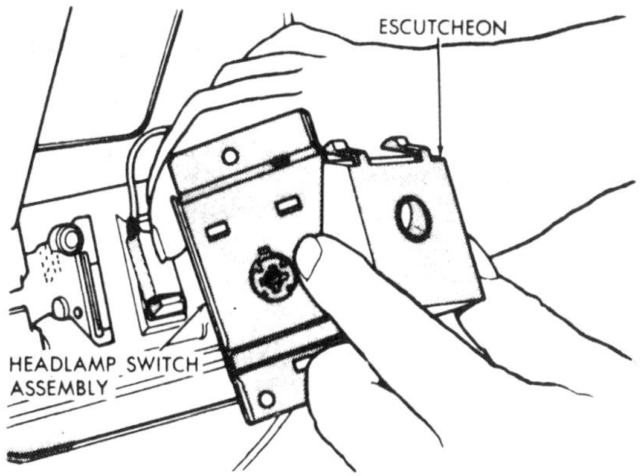

19.6 Grasp the escutcheon securely and unsnap it from the switch (C/V and E body)

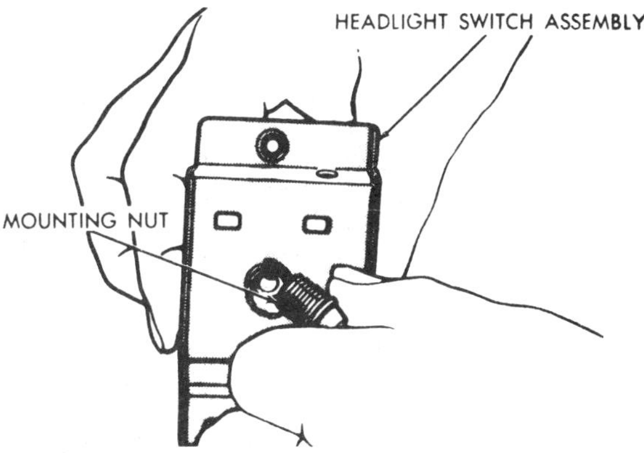

19.7 Unscrew the mounting nut to remove the headlight switch (C/V and E body)

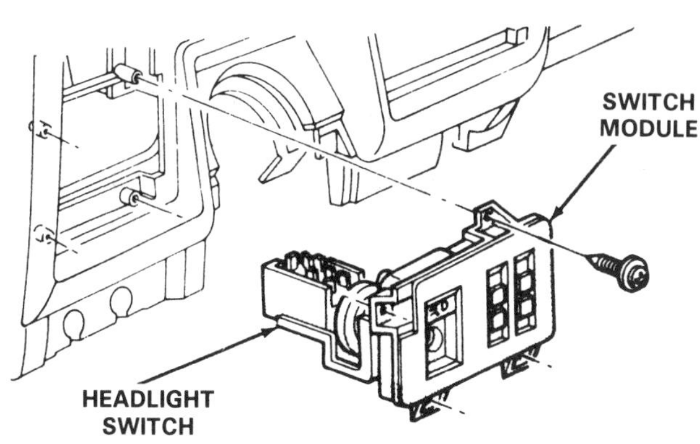

19.9 H body headlight switch module details

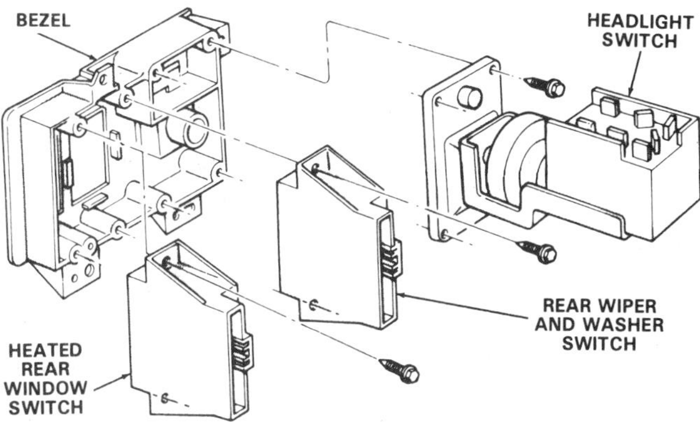

19.11 H body headlight switch component layout

signal/hazard warning switch, the upper bearing housing and the lock plate and spring.

4 Remove the cable trough cover and disconnect the switch connector.

5 Remove the mounting screw and detach the switch and wire from the steering column **(see illustrations)**.

6 To install the switch, insert the wire down through the hub and column, place the switch in position and install the mounting screw.

7 On all except 1986 and later floor shift models, install the lock plate and spring, the upper bearing housing and the turn signal/hazard warning switch.

8 On 1986 and later floor shift models, place the switch in position and install the mounting screw.

9 Plug in the connector and install the wiring trough cover.

10 Install the steering wheel and column covers.

11 Connect the negative battery cable.

19 Headlight switch – removal and installation

Refer to illustrations 19.5, 19.6, 19.7, 19.9 and 19.11

1 Disconnect the negative cable at the battery. Place the cable out of the way so it cannot accidentally come in contact with the negative terminal of the battery, as this would once again allow power into the electrical system of the vehicle.

C/V and E body

2 Remove the switch assembly trim bezel.

3 Remove the three screws and detach the switch assembly plate from the dash panel.

4 Carefully pull the assembly out and disconnect the wires.

5 Remove the headlight switch knob and stem by depressing the button on the switch **(see illustration)**.

6 Unsnap the headlight switch escutcheon **(see illustration)**.

7 Remove the nut attaching the switch to the mounting plate **(see illustration)**.

8 Installation is the reverse of removal.

H body

9 Remove the headlight and accessory switch module **(see illustration)**.

10 Press the button located on the bottom of the switch and remove the knob and shaft by pulling it out.

11 Remove the screws and detach the headlight switch from the module **(see illustration)**.

12 Remove the retaining nut and detach the mounting plate from the switch.

13 Installation is the reverse of removal.

20 Speedometer (conventional instrument panel) – removal and installation

1 Disconnect the negative cable at the battery. Place the cable out of the way so it cannot accidentally come in contact with the negative terminal of the battery, as this would once again allow power into the electrical system of the vehicle.
2 Remove the screws and detach the instrument cluster bezel and mask.
3 Remove the speedometer mounting screws.
4 Disconnect the cable in the engine compartment, pull the speedometer out slightly, detach the cable and remove the speedometer.
5 On cruise control equipped vehicles it will also be necessary to disconnect the speedometer cable from the servo unit located in the engine compartment.
6 To install the speedometer, place it in position and press it into the cable assembly until it locks in place. Connect the cable in the engine compartment.
7 Install the mounting screws and the cluster mask and bezel assembly.
8 Connect the cruise control servo to the cable (if equipped).
9 Connect the negative battery cable.

21 Instrument cluster bezel and mask (conventional instrument panel) – removal and installation

Refer to illustrations 21.4a, 21.4b, 21.5, 21.6 and 21.10

1 Disconnect the negative cable at the battery. Place the cable out of the way so it cannot accidentally come in contact with the negative terminal of the battery, as this would once again allow power into the electrical system of the vehicle.

C/V and E body

2 On column shift models, place the selector in the 1st gear position.
3 On 1984 and later models, remove the radio knobs.
4 Remove the bezel mounting screws **(see illustrations)**.
5 Grasp the bezel securely and pull it to the rear to remove it **(see illustration)**.
6 Remove the cluster mask by unsnapping the retaining clips **(see illustration)**.
7 To install the mask, place it over the clips and press in on it.
8 To install the bezel, place it in position and install the mounting screws.

H body

9 On column shift models, place the gear selector in Low.
10 Remove the eleven Torx-head retaining screws and detach the bezel from the instrument panel **(see illustration)**.
11 Unscrew the trip odometer reset knob, remove the two screws and press-in retainers and lift off the mask and lens assembly.
12 Installation is the reverse of removal.

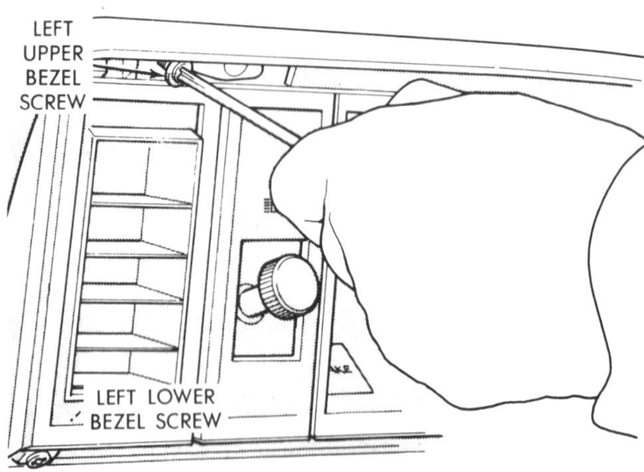

21.4a Left instrument cluster bezel screw locations (1982 and 1983 C/V and E body)

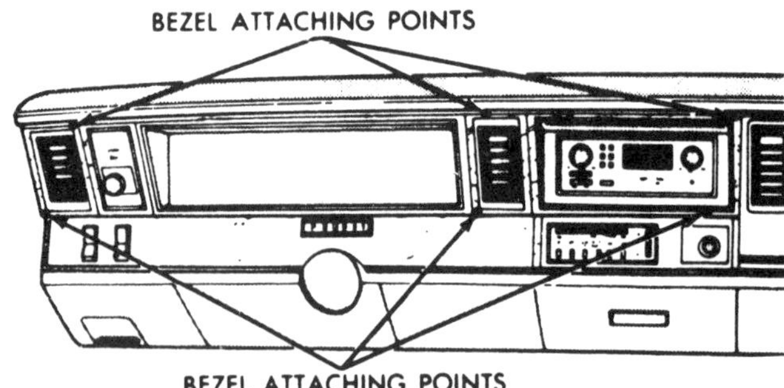

21.4b 1984 and later instrument cluster bezel screw locations (C/V and E body)

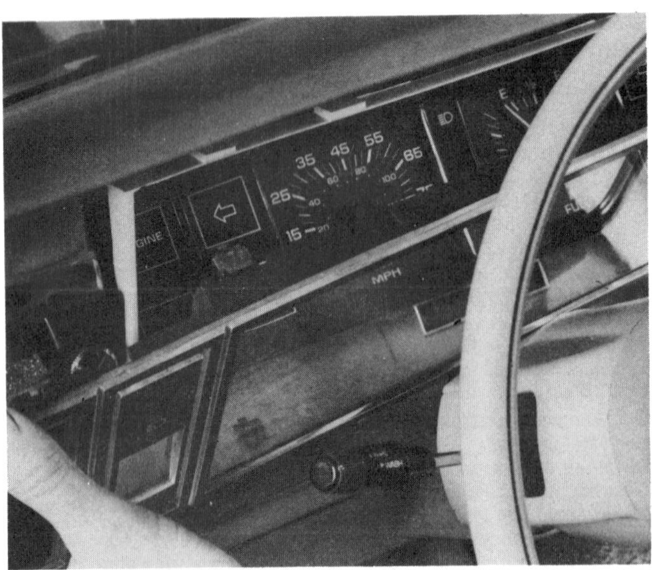

21.5 After removing the screws, pull the instrument cluster bezel away from the mask

21.6 Pull back sharply on the mask to unsnap it from the clips

22 Instrument cluster (conventional instrument panel) – removal and installation

Refer to illustrations 22.5 and 22.12

1 Disconnect the negative cable at the battery. Place the cable out of the way so it cannot accidentally come in contact with the negative terminal of the battery, as this would once again allow power into the electrical system of the vehicle.

C/V and E body

2 Remove the instrument cluster bezel and mask (Section 21).
3 On 1982 and 1983 models, remove the right hand upper trim bezel.
4 Remove the forward (nearest the windshield) instrument panel pad screws, lift the rear edge and remove the remaining screws.
5 Remove the two mounting screws, then carefully pull the cluster out just enough to detach the speedometer cable and wiring connectors at the rear **(see illustration)**.
6 Remove the cluster to the right of the steering column.
7 Installation is the reverse of removal.

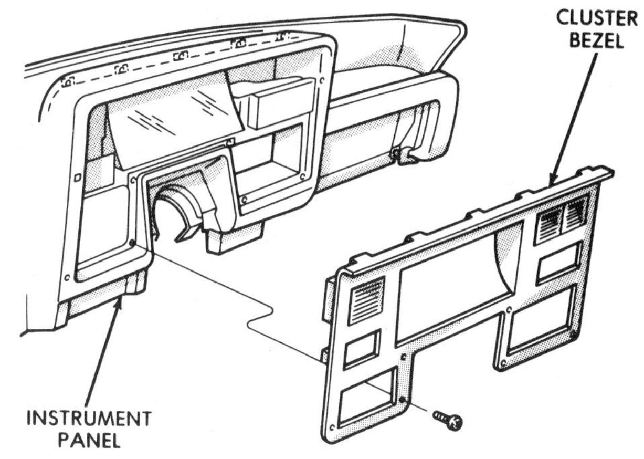

21.10 H body instrument cluster bezel and mask details

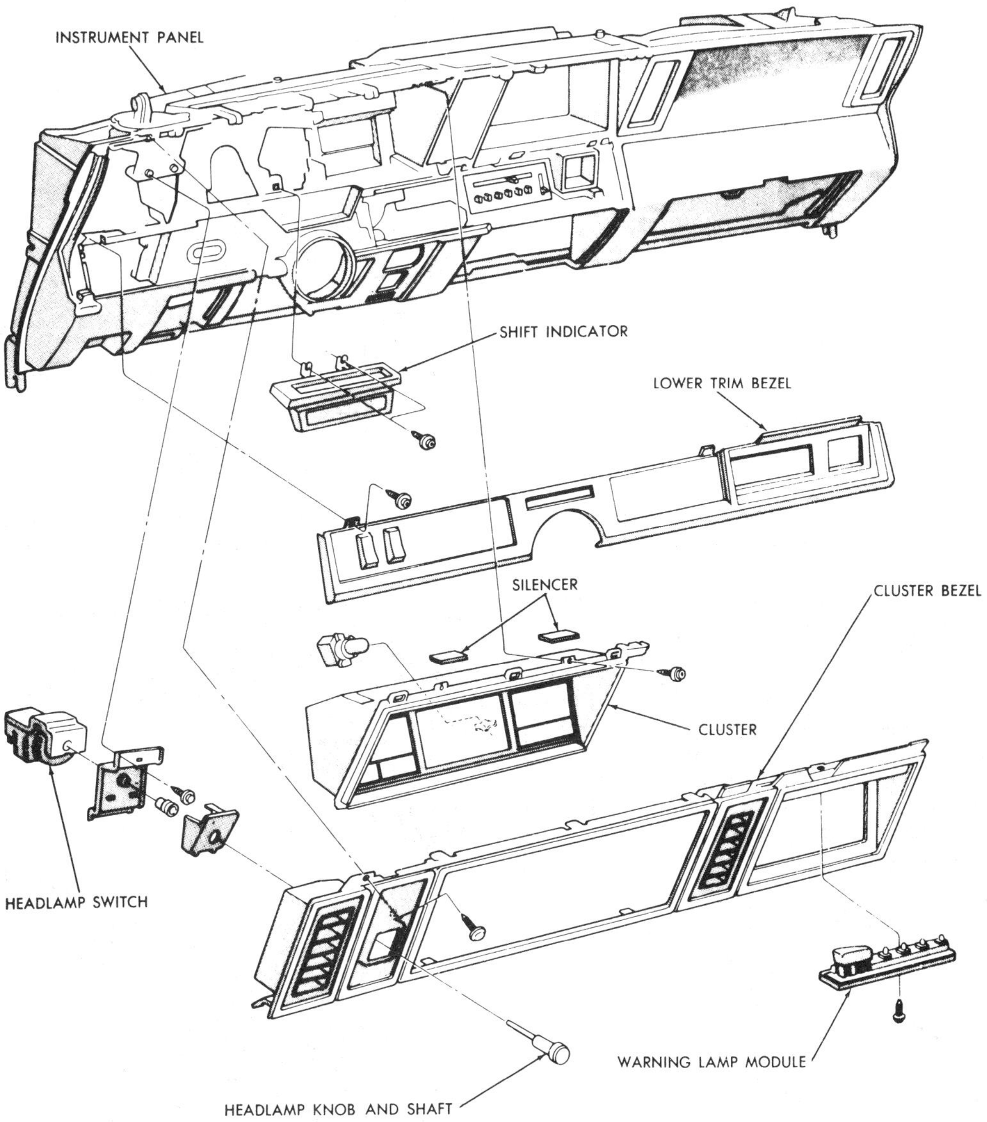

22.5 C/V and E body instrument cluster details

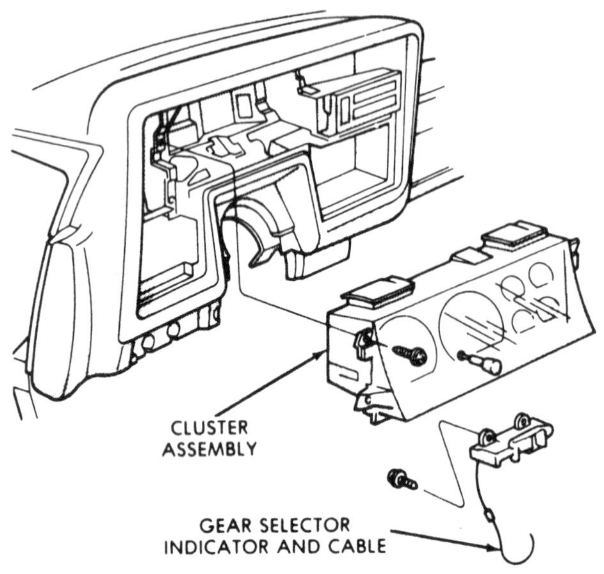

22.12 H body instrument cluster details

H body

8 Remove the cluster bezel.
9 Remove the lower steering column cover and disconnect the gear selector cable.
10 Remove the mask and lens.
11 Remove the speedometer and disconnect the cable.
12 Detach the cluster and withdraw the assembly from the instrument panel **(see illustration)**.
13 Installation is the reverse of removal.

23 Instrument cluster printed circuit board (conventional instrument panel) — removal and installation

1 Refer to Section 22 and remove the instrument cluster.
2 Remove the light bulb sockets from the rear of the cluster.
3 Remove the screws and detach the printed circuit board.
4 Installation is the reverse of removal.

24 Instrument cluster bulbs (conventional instrument panel) — replacement

1 Remove the instrument cluster (Section 22).
2 Remove the light bulbs from the rear of the cluster by turning the bulbs counterclockwise to release them .

25 Electronic instrument cluster — general information

The electronic instrument cluster is removed in the same way as the conventional cluster except that it is not necessary to disconnect the speedometer. Due to the special tools and techniques required, all work on the electronic instrument cluster must be left to a dealer service department or a repair shop.

26 Windshield wiper motor — removal and installation

Refer to illustrations 26.3, 26.4, 26.5, 26.6, 26.7a, and 26.7b

Removal

1 Open the hood.
2 Disconnect the negative cable at the battery. Place the cable out of the way so it cannot accidentally come in contact with the negative terminal of the battery, as this would once again allow power into the electrical system of the vehicle.

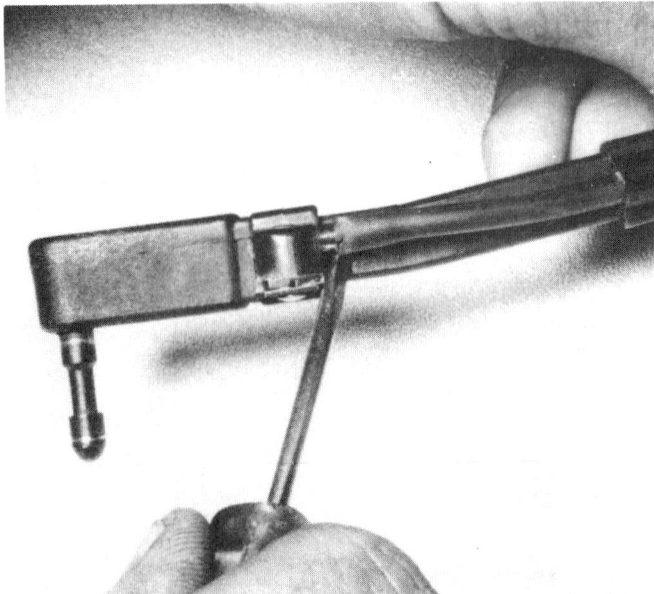

26.3 Push the washer hose off the wiper arm with a small screwdriver

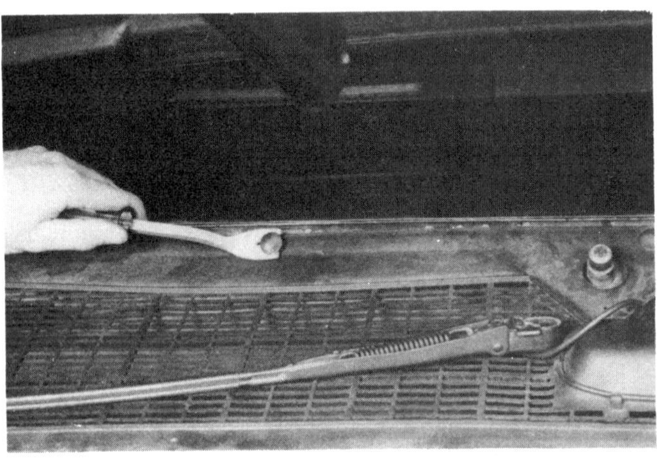

26.4 A forked tool such as the one shown here makes prying the cowl water deflector clips out an easier job

3 Remove the wiper arms and disconnect the washer hoses **(see illustration)**.
4 Pry out the clips and remove the cowl plenum water deflector **(see illustration)**.
5 Remove the cover (2 bolts) from the wiper motor and unplug the electrical connectors **(see illustration)**.
6 Remove the perforated grill **(see illustration)**
7 Remove the wiper pivot mounting bolts, the three motor mounting nuts and unplug the motor and relay electrical connectors **(see illustrations)**.
8 Remove the motor, wiper arms and pivot assembly.
9 To remove the wiper arm from the motor, mark the relative position of the arm and motor, support the arm securely in a vise and remove the retaining nut **(see illustrations 26.7a and 26.7b)**.
10 Detach the arm from the motor.

Installation

11 Install the arm on the motor and tighten the nut securely.
12 Insert the wiper assembly into place, extend the arms until the pivots can be pulled into place and install bolts.

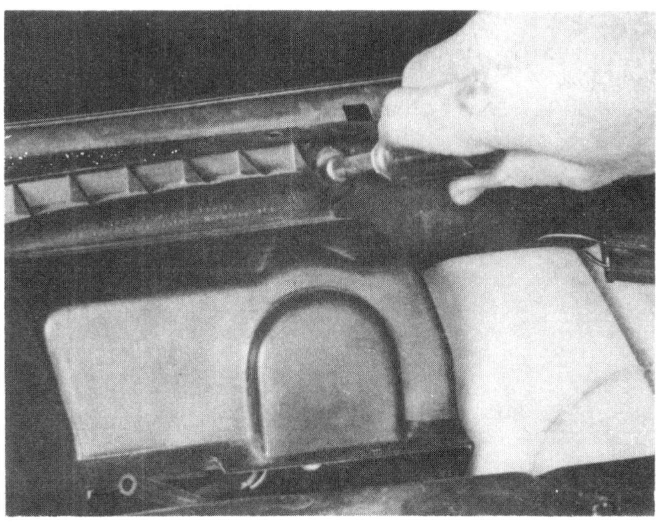

26.5 A nut driver can be used to remove the wiper cover bolts

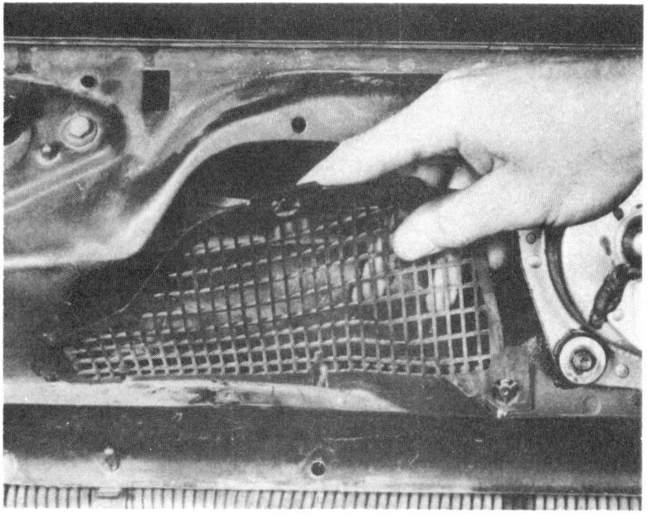

26.6 Remove the perforated grille by pulling it from the access hole

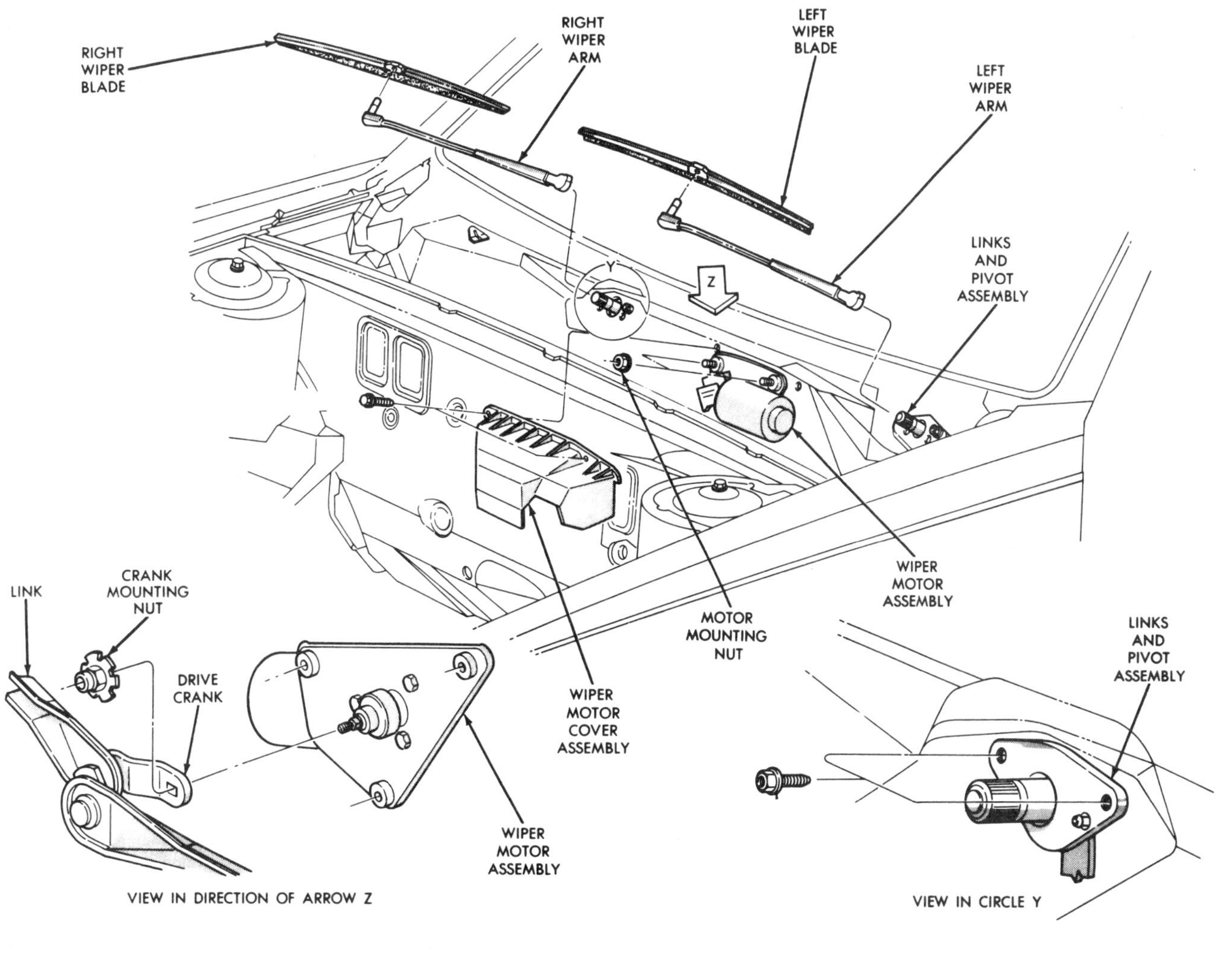

26.7a C/V and E body windshield wiper motor installation details

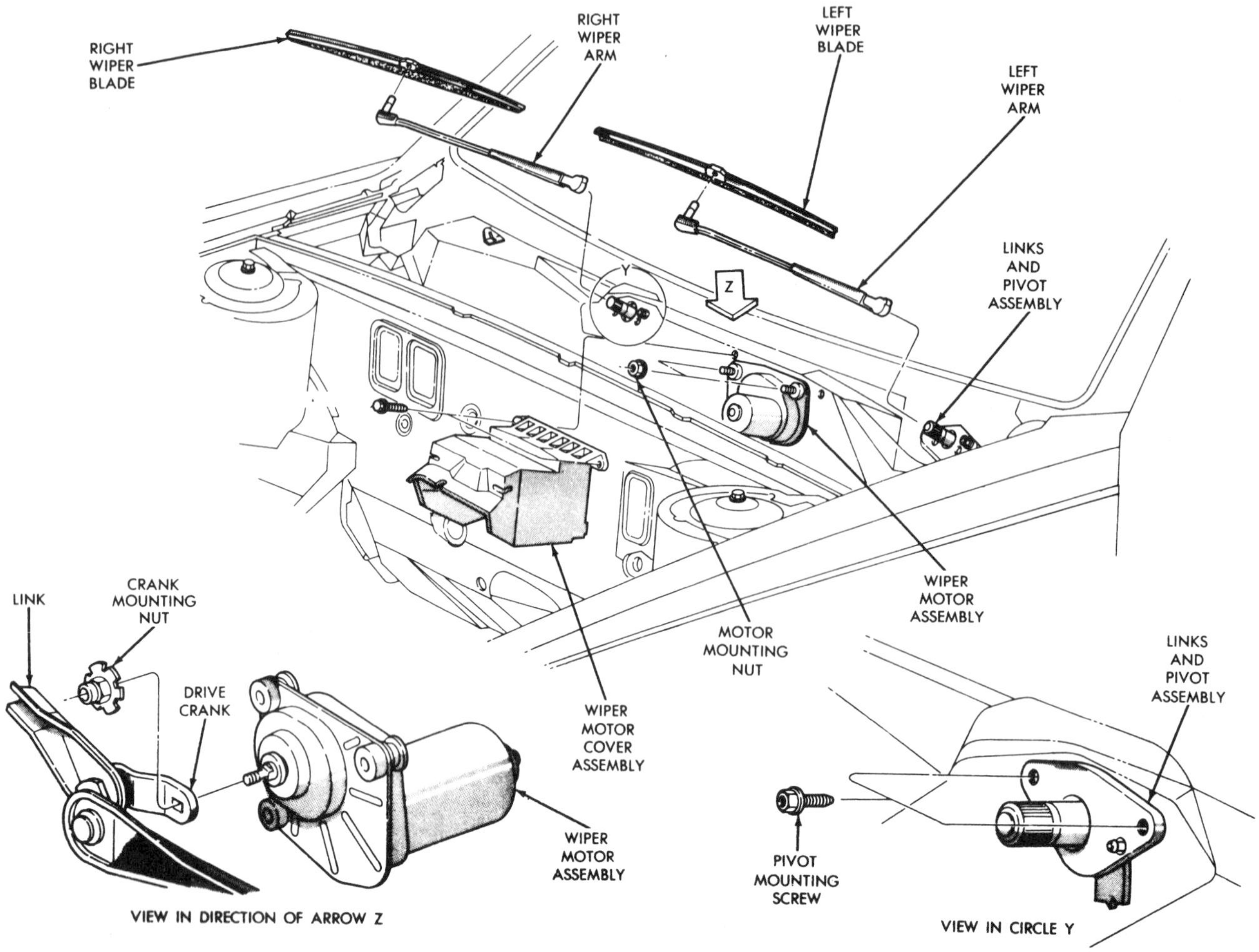

26.7b H body windshield wiper motor installation details

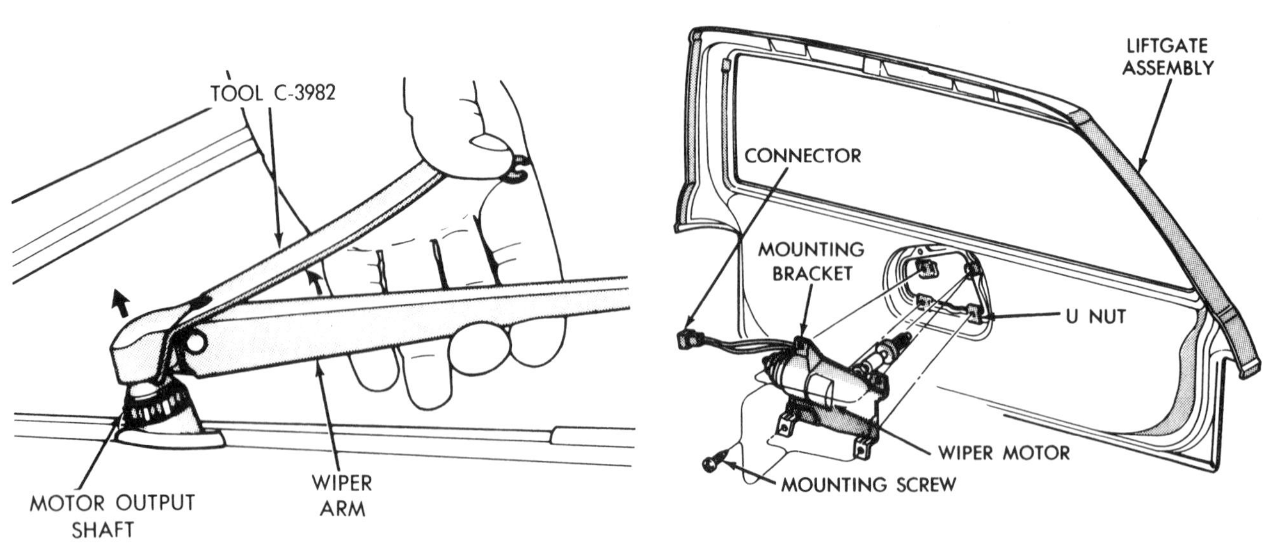

27.2 Remove the rear liftgate wiper arm with the special tool

27.5a Station wagon rear liftgate wiper details

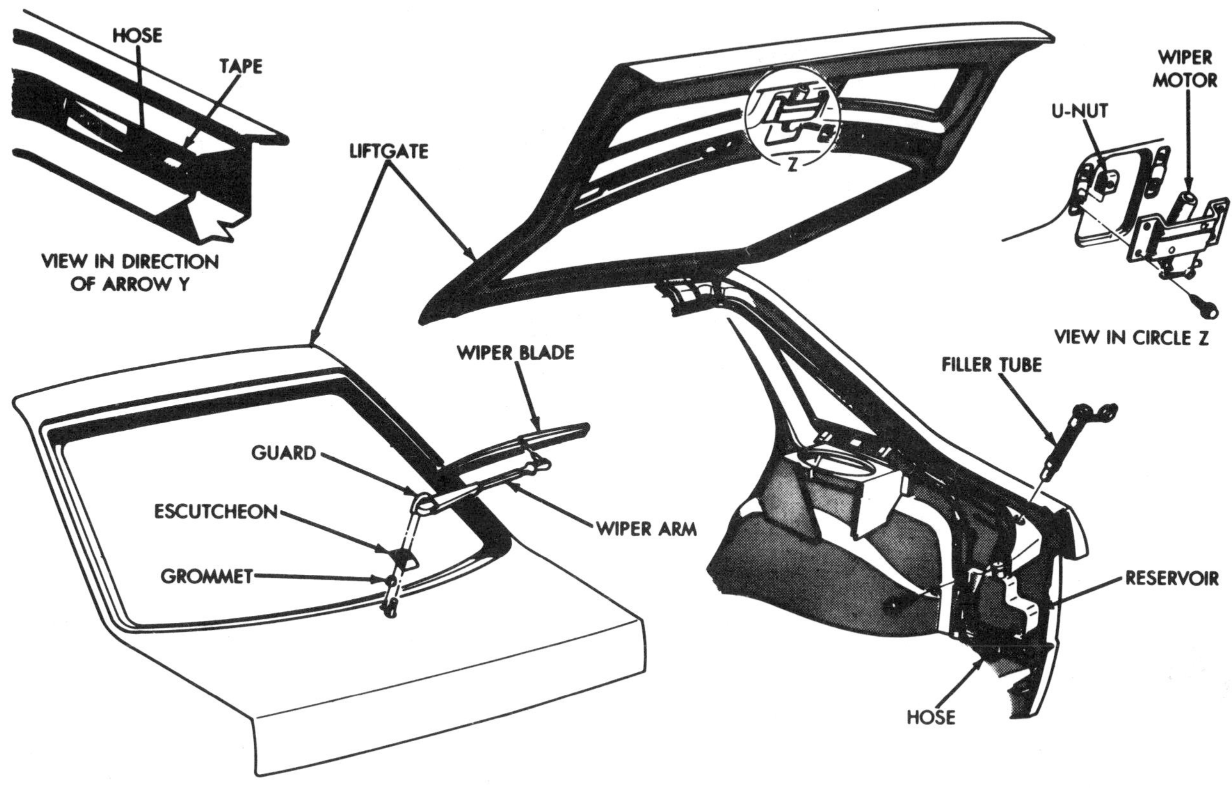

27.5b Sedan rear liftgate wiper details

13 Install the motor and relay and install the nuts. Tighten the nuts securely.
14 Plug in the connectors and install the grille and water deflector.
15 Install the wiper arms and washer hoses.
16 Connect the battery.

27 Liftgate wiper motor – removal and installation

Refer to illustrations 27.2, 27.5a and 27.5b

Removal

1 Disconnect the negative cable at the battery. Place the cable out of the way so it cannot accidentally come in contact with the negative terminal of the battery, as this would once again allow power into the electrical system of the vehicle.

2 Remove the wiper arm with special tool C–3982 or equivalent **(see illustration)**. **Note:** *Using a screwdriver to pry the arm off could damage it and allow the arm to eventually fall off the pivot.*

3 Remove the trim panel.

4 Unplug the connector.

5 Remove the four wiper motor mounting screws and detach the motor and bracket assembly from the liftgate **(see illustrations)**

6 Unbolt the motor from the mounting plate and transfer the plate to the new motor.

Installation

7 Place the motor in position and install the screws. Tighten the screws securely and plug in the connector.

8 After installation, place the trim panel in place and push the retaining pin into the hole at one end. Use the palm of your hand to seat it and work along the entire length to seat them all. Install any plastic clips and screws.

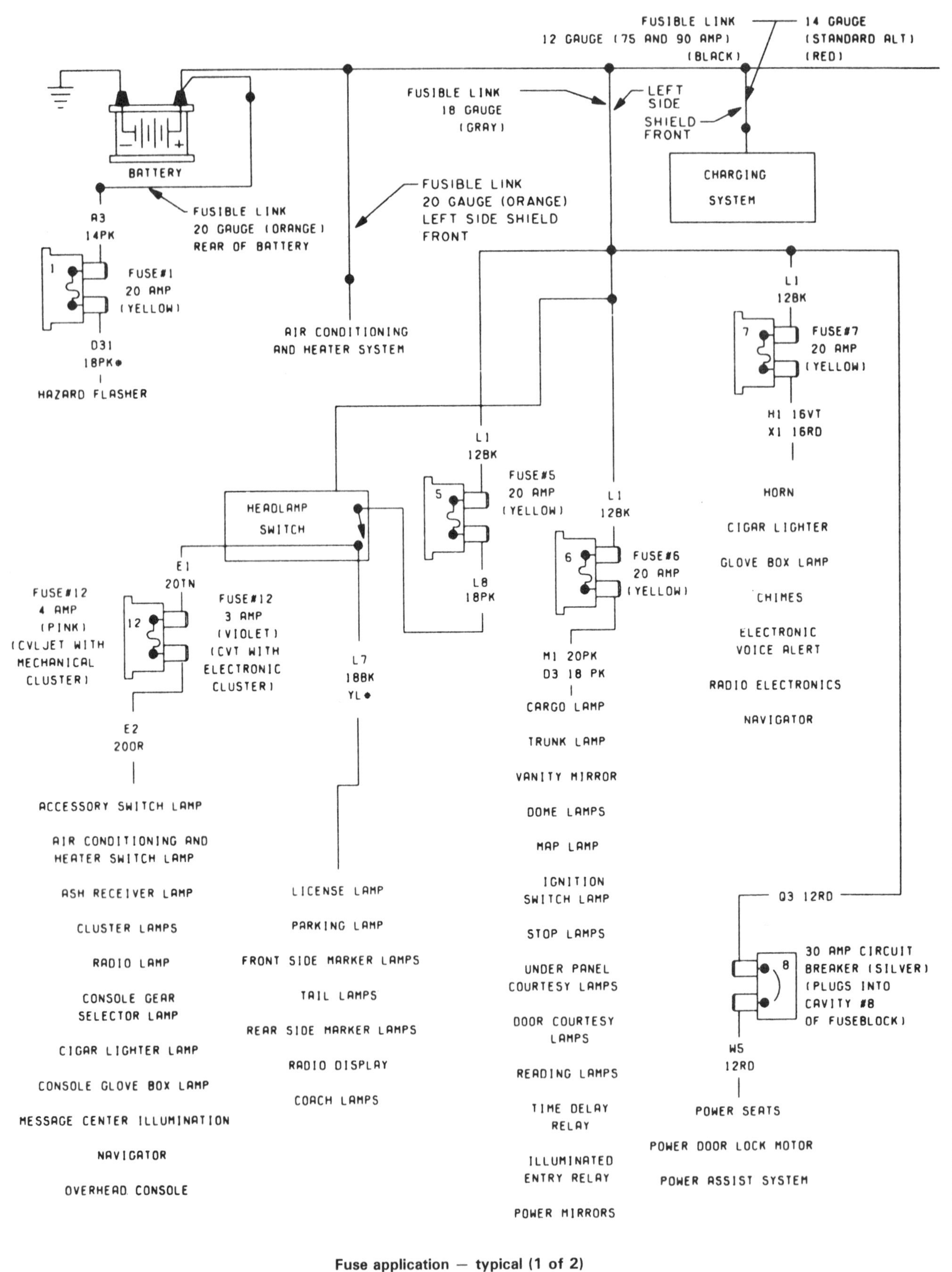

Fuse application — typical (1 of 2)

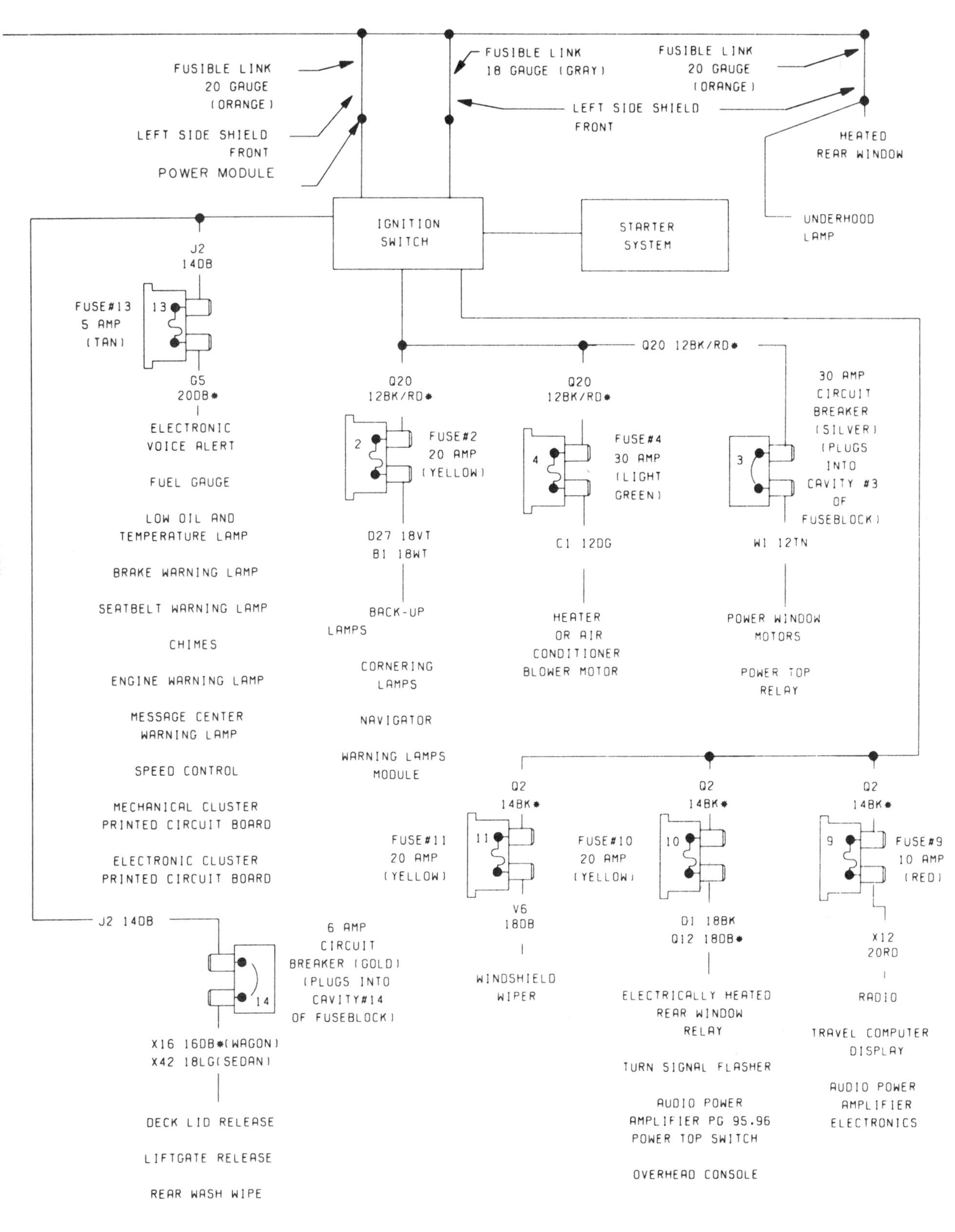

Fuse application — typical (2 of 2)

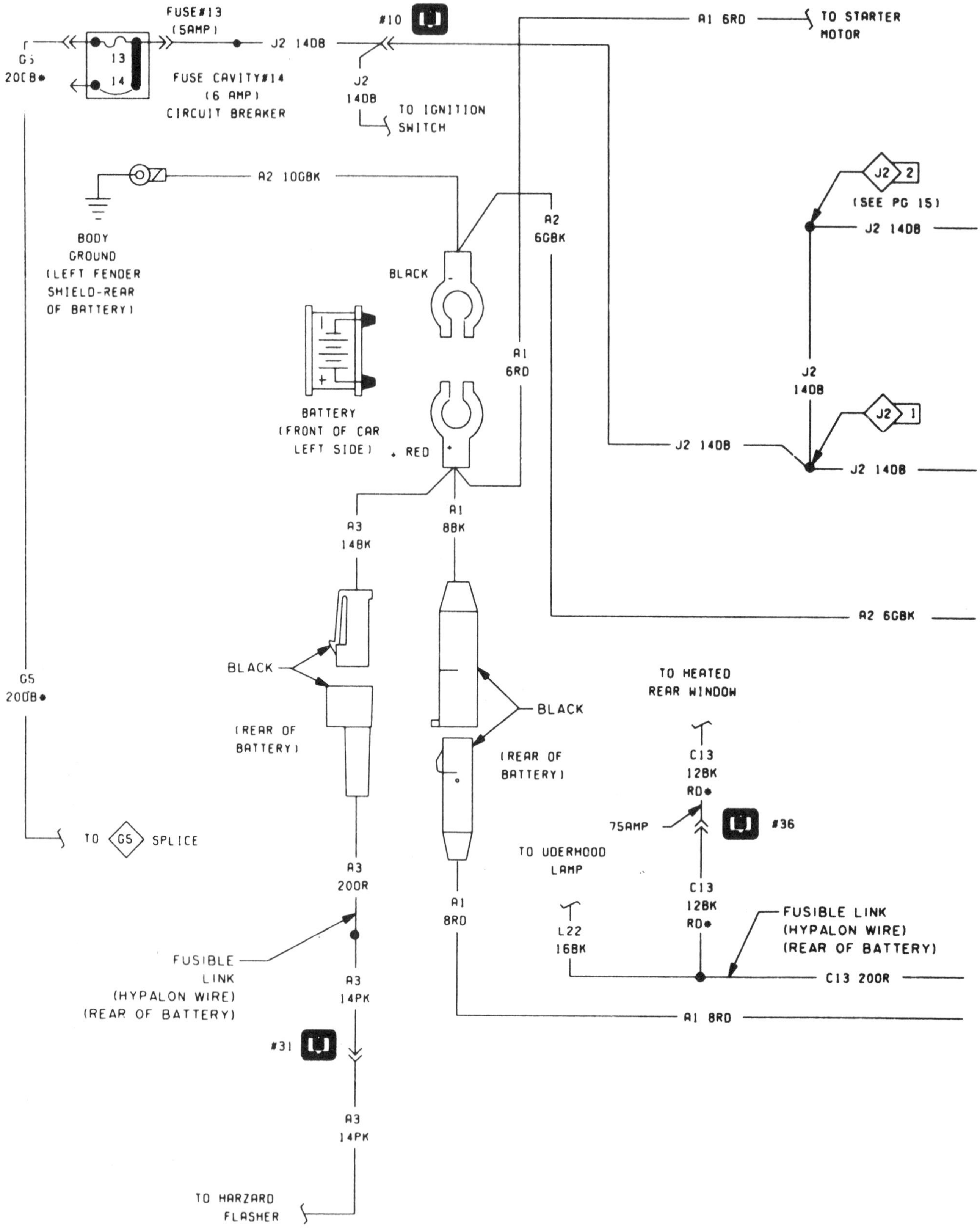

FUSE#13 (5AMP)
G5 20DB●
13
14
J2 14DB
FUSE CAVITY#14 (6 AMP) CIRCUIT BREAKER
#10
J2 14DB
TO IGNITION SWITCH
A1 6RD
TO STARTER MOTOR
A2 10GBK
BODY GROUND (LEFT FENDER SHIELD-REAR OF BATTERY)
A2 6GBK
BLACK
J2 2
(SEE PG 15)
J2 14DB
BATTERY (FRONT OF CAR LEFT SIDE)
A1 6RD
+ RED
J2 14DB
J2 1
J2 14DB
J2 14DB
A3 14BK
A1 8BK
A2 6GBK
BLACK
BLACK
G5 20DB●
(REAR OF BATTERY)
(REAR OF BATTERY)
TO HEATED REAR WINDOW
C13 12BK RD●
75AMP
#36
TO GS SPLICE
TO UDERHOOD LAMP
A3 20OR
A1 8RD
C13 12BK RD●
L22 16BK
FUSIBLE LINK (HYPALON WIRE) (REAR OF BATTERY)
FUSIBLE LINK (HYPALON WIRE) (REAR OF BATTERY)
A3 14PK
C13 20OR
A1 8RD
#31
A3 14PK
TO HARZARD FLASHER

Typical charging system wiring diagram (1 of 2)

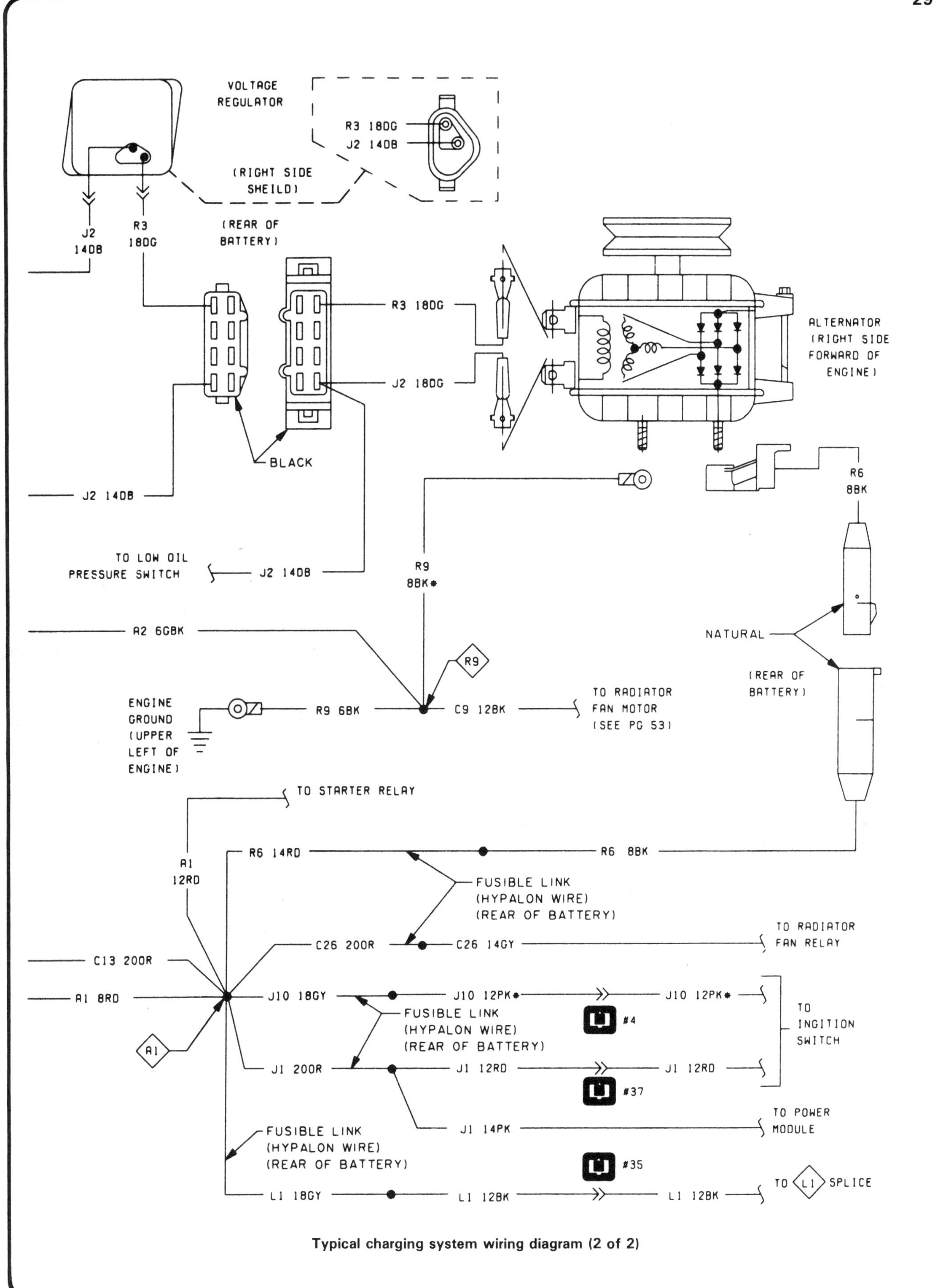

Typical charging system wiring diagram (2 of 2)

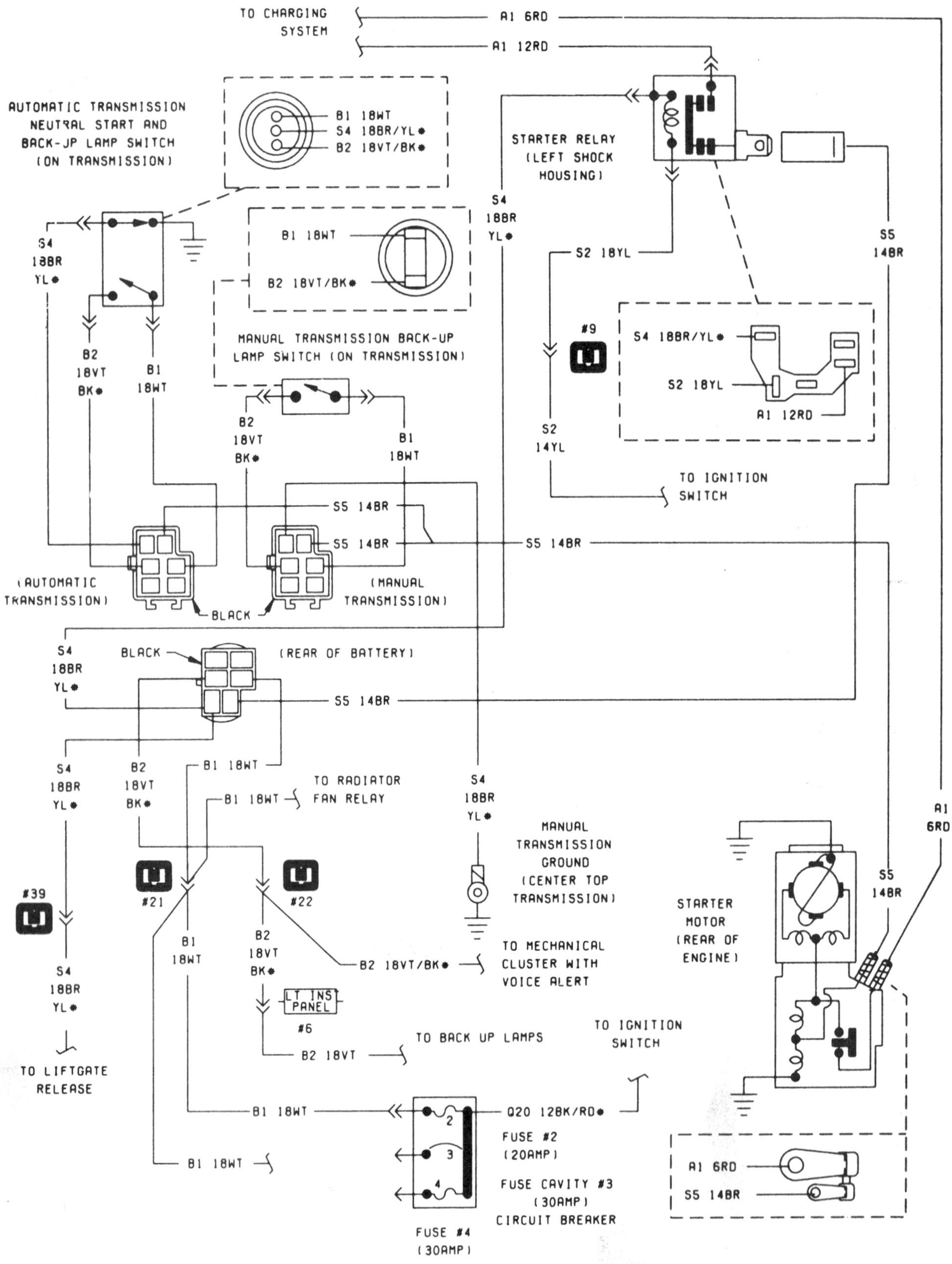

Typical starting system wiring diagram

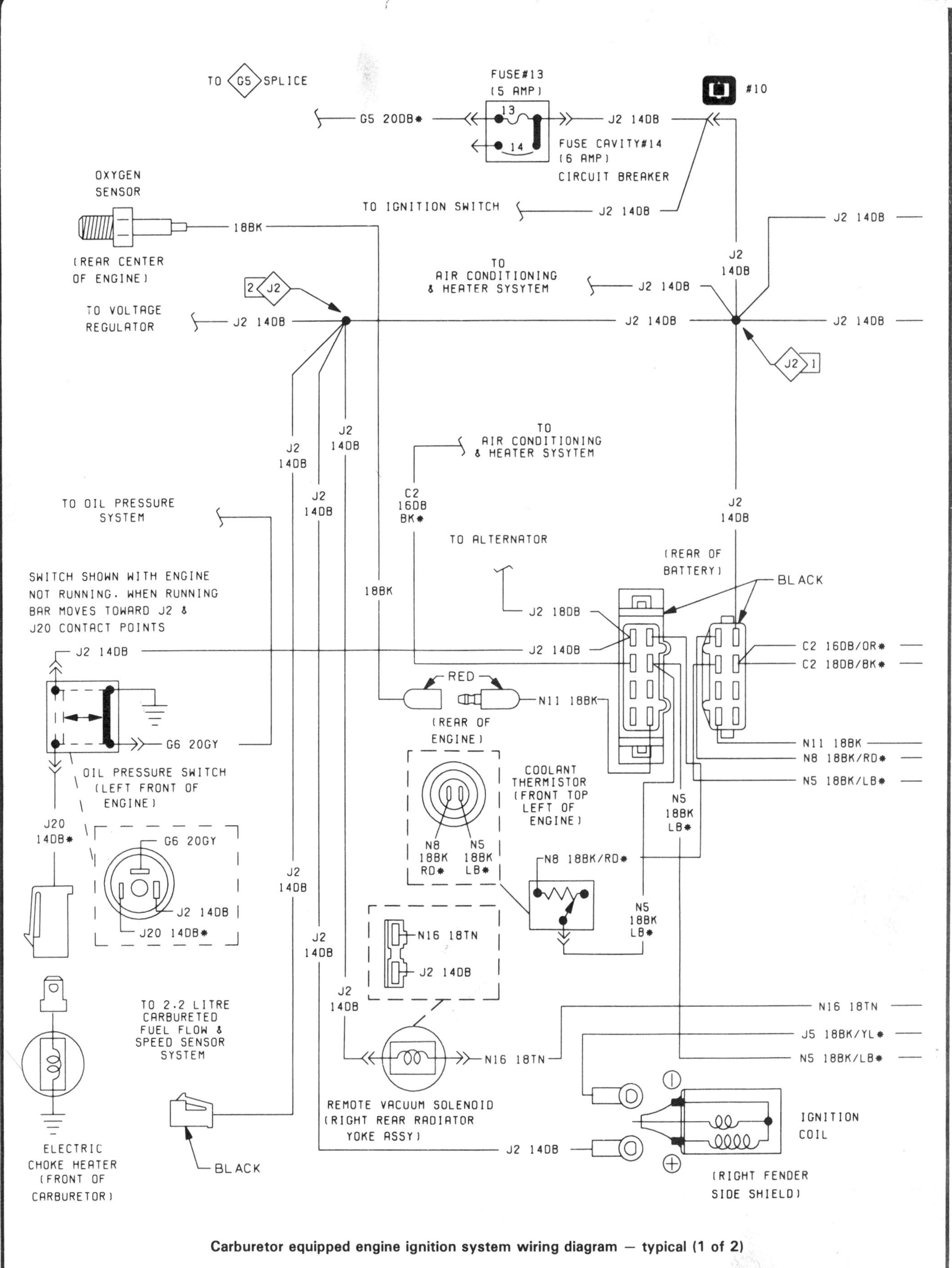

Carburetor equipped engine ignition system wiring diagram — typical (1 of 2)

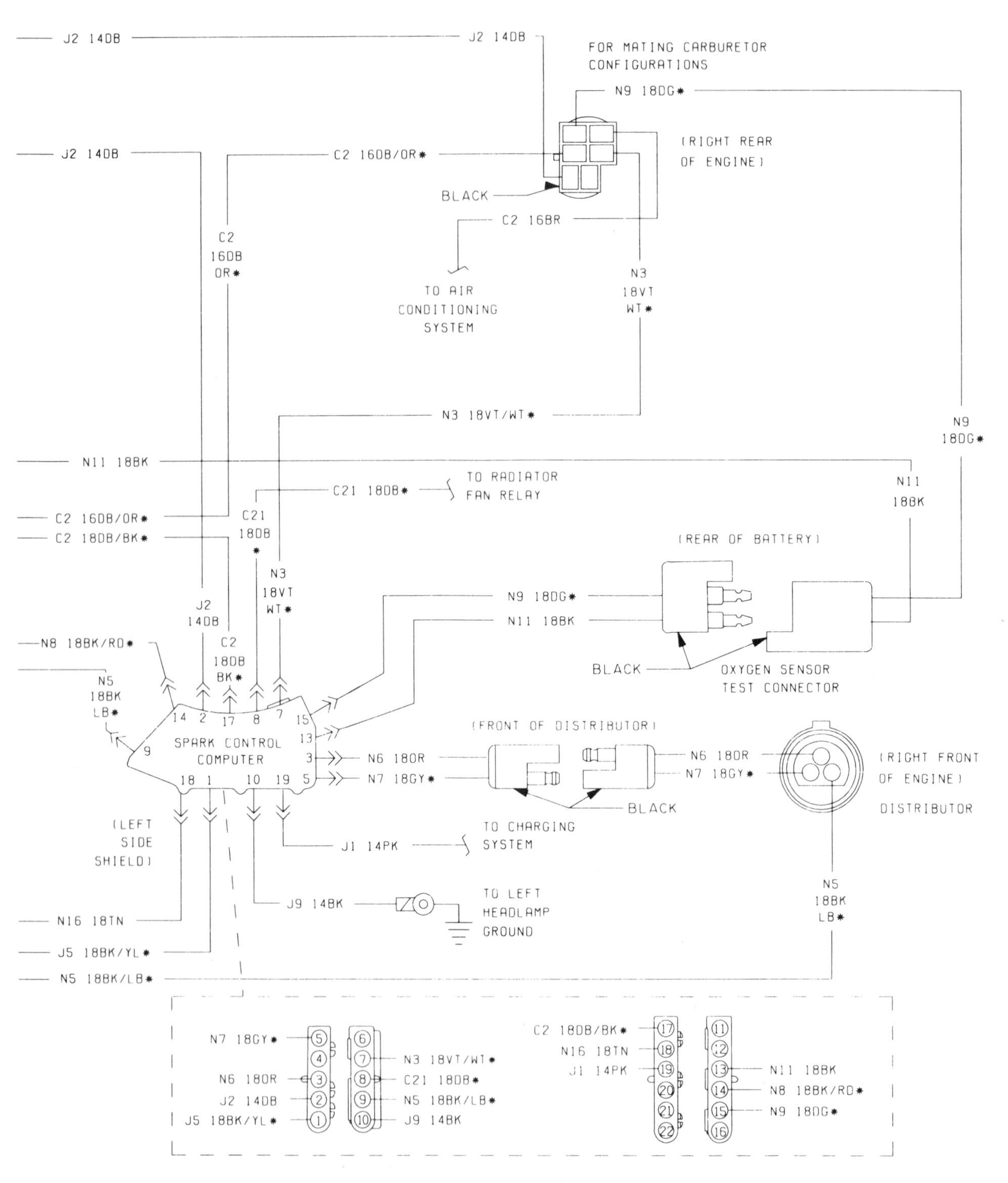

Carburetor equipped engine ignition system wiring diagram — typical (2 of 2)

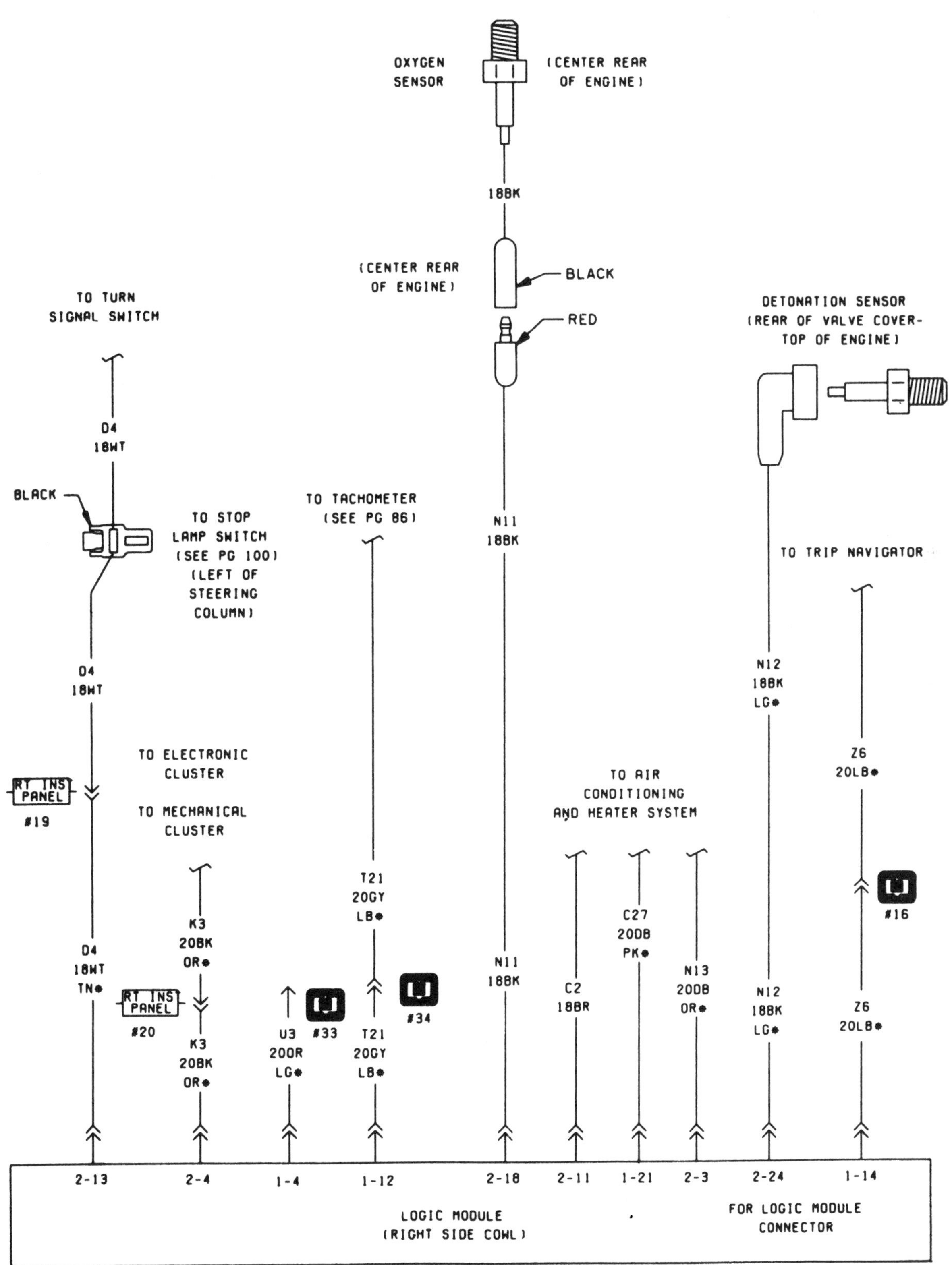

Turbocharged engine ignition system wiring diagram — typical (1 of 5)

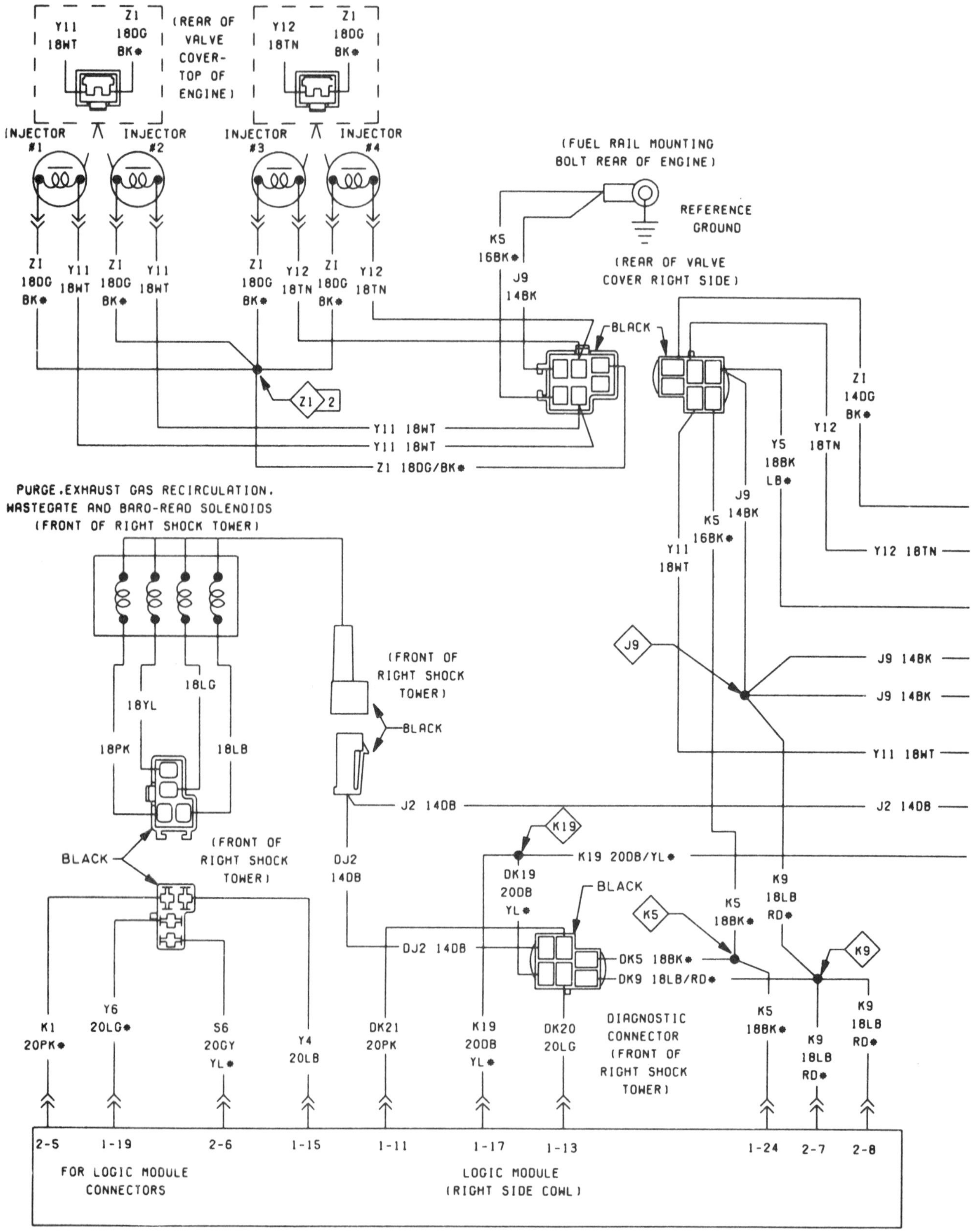

Y11 18WT
Z1 18DG BK*
(REAR OF VALVE COVER-TOP OF ENGINE)
Y12 18TN
Z1 18DG BK*
INJECTOR #1
INJECTOR #2
INJECTOR #3
INJECTOR #4
Z1 18DG BK*
Y11 18WT
Z1 18DG BK*
Y11 18WT
Z1 18DG BK*
Y12 18TN
Z1 18DG BK*
Y12 18TN
Z1 2
Y11 18WT
Y11 18WT
Z1 18DG/BK*
(FUEL RAIL MOUNTING BOLT REAR OF ENGINE)
REFERENCE GROUND
K5 16BK*
J9 14BK
(REAR OF VALVE COVER RIGHT SIDE)
BLACK
Z1 14DG BK*
Y12 18TN
Y5 18BK LB*
J9 14BK
K5 16BK*
Y11 18WT
Y12 18TN
J9
J9 14BK
J9 14BK
Y11 18WT
J2 14DB
J2 14DB

PURGE, EXHAUST GAS RECIRCULATION, WASTEGATE AND BARO-READ SOLENOIDS (FRONT OF RIGHT SHOCK TOWER)
18LG
18YL
18PK
18LB
(FRONT OF RIGHT SHOCK TOWER)
BLACK
BLACK
(FRONT OF RIGHT SHOCK TOWER)
DJ2 14DB
K19
K19 20DB/YL*
DK19 20DB YL*
BLACK
DJ2 14DB
DK5 18BK*
DK9 18LB/RD*
K5
K5 18BK*
K9 18LB RD*
K9
K1 20PK*
Y6 20LG*
S6 20GY YL*
Y4 20LB
DK21 20PK
K19 20DB YL*
DK20 20LG
DIAGNOSTIC CONNECTOR (FRONT OF RIGHT SHOCK TOWER)
K5 18BK*
K9 18LB RD*
K9 18LB RD*
2-5
1-19
2-6
1-15
1-11
1-17
1-13
1-24
2-7
2-8
FOR LOGIC MODULE CONNECTORS
LOGIC MODULE (RIGHT SIDE COWL)

Turbocharged engine ignition system wiring diagram – typical (2 of 5)

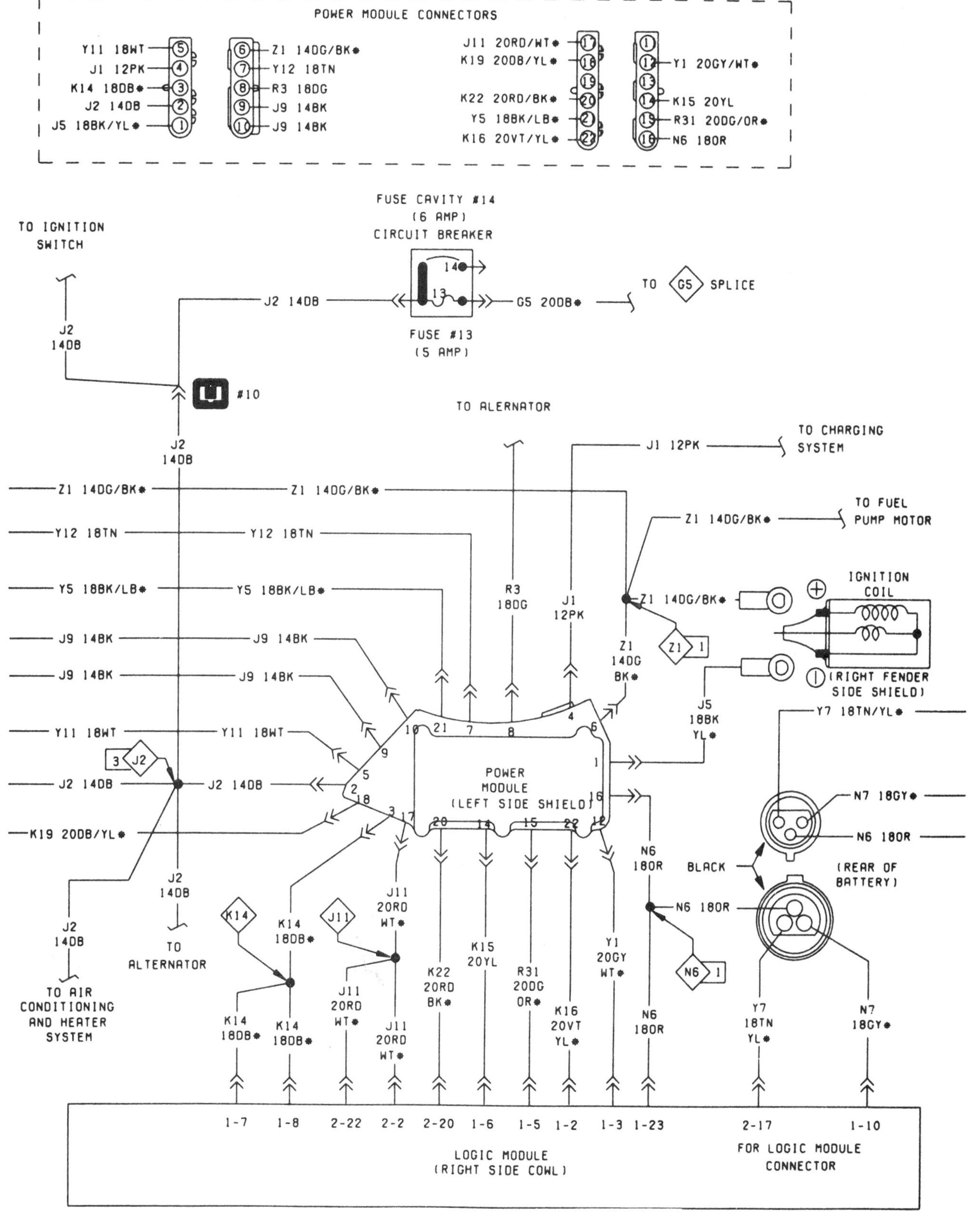

Turbocharged engine ignition system wiring diagram — typical (3 of 5)

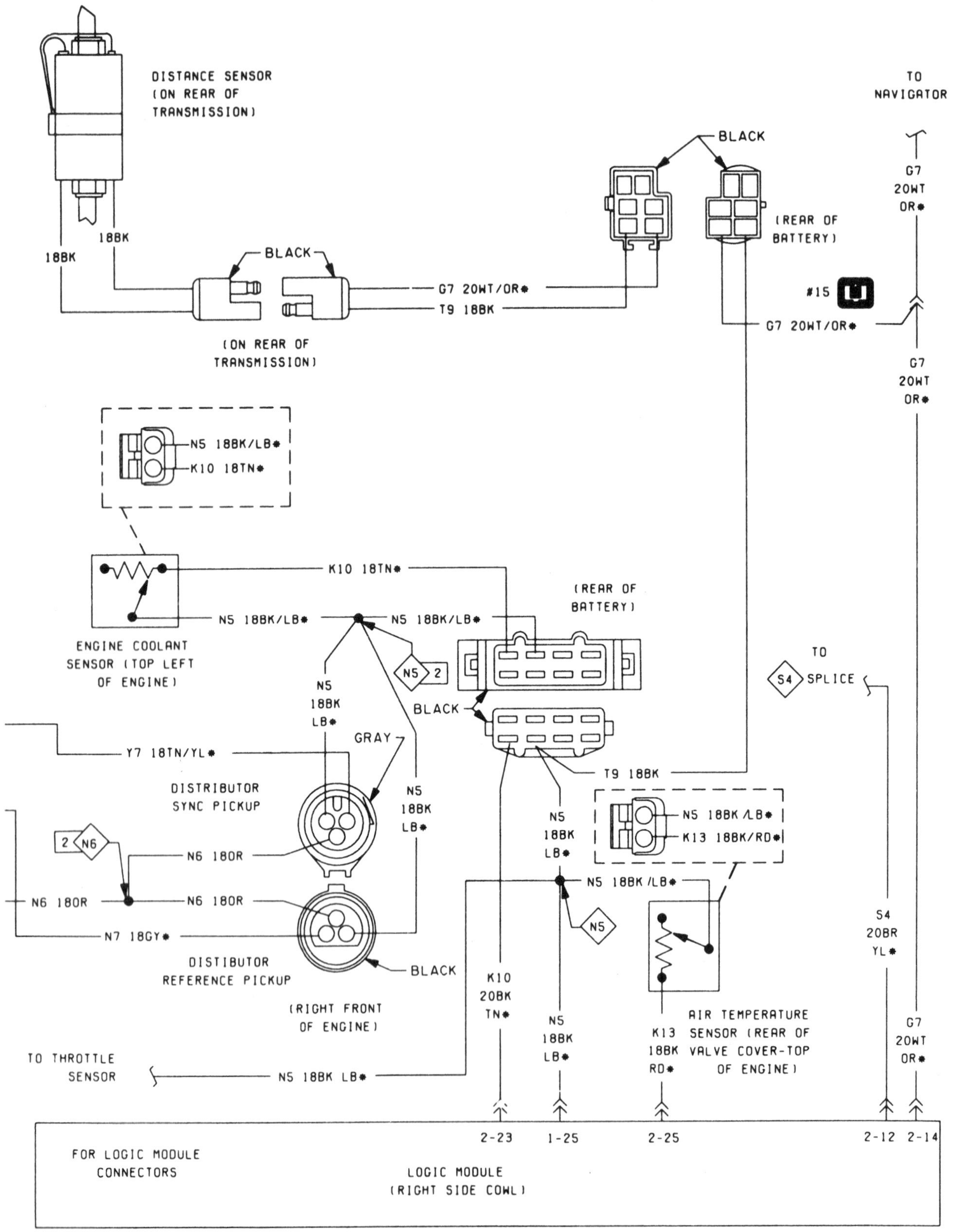

DISTANCE SENSOR (ON REAR OF TRANSMISSION)

18BK
18BK
BLACK
(ON REAR OF TRANSMISSION)
G7 20WT/OR*
T9 18BK
BLACK
(REAR OF BATTERY)
TO NAVIGATOR
G7 20WT OR*
#15
G7 20WT/OR*
G7 20WT OR*

N5 18BK/LB*
K10 18TN*
K10 18TN*
N5 18BK/LB*
N5 18BK/LB*
ENGINE COOLANT SENSOR (TOP LEFT OF ENGINE)
(REAR OF BATTERY)
N5 2
N5 18BK LB*
BLACK
GRAY
Y7 18TN/YL*
DISTRIBUTOR SYNC PICKUP
N5 18BK LB*
T9 18BK
N5 18BK LB*
N5 18BK/LB*
K13 18BK/RD*
TO
S4 SPLICE
2 N6
N6 18OR
N6 18OR
N6 18OR
N7 18GY*
N5 18BK/LB*
N5
DISTIBUTOR REFERENCE PICKUP
BLACK
(RIGHT FRONT OF ENGINE)
K10 20BK TN*
N5 18BK LB*
K13 18BK RD*
AIR TEMPERATURE SENSOR (REAR OF VALVE COVER-TOP OF ENGINE)
S4 20BR YL*
G7 20WT OR*
TO THROTTLE SENSOR
N5 18BK LB*
2-23
1-25
2-25
2-12
2-14
FOR LOGIC MODULE CONNECTORS
LOGIC MODULE (RIGHT SIDE COWL)

Turbocharged engine ignition system wiring diagram — typical (4 of 5)

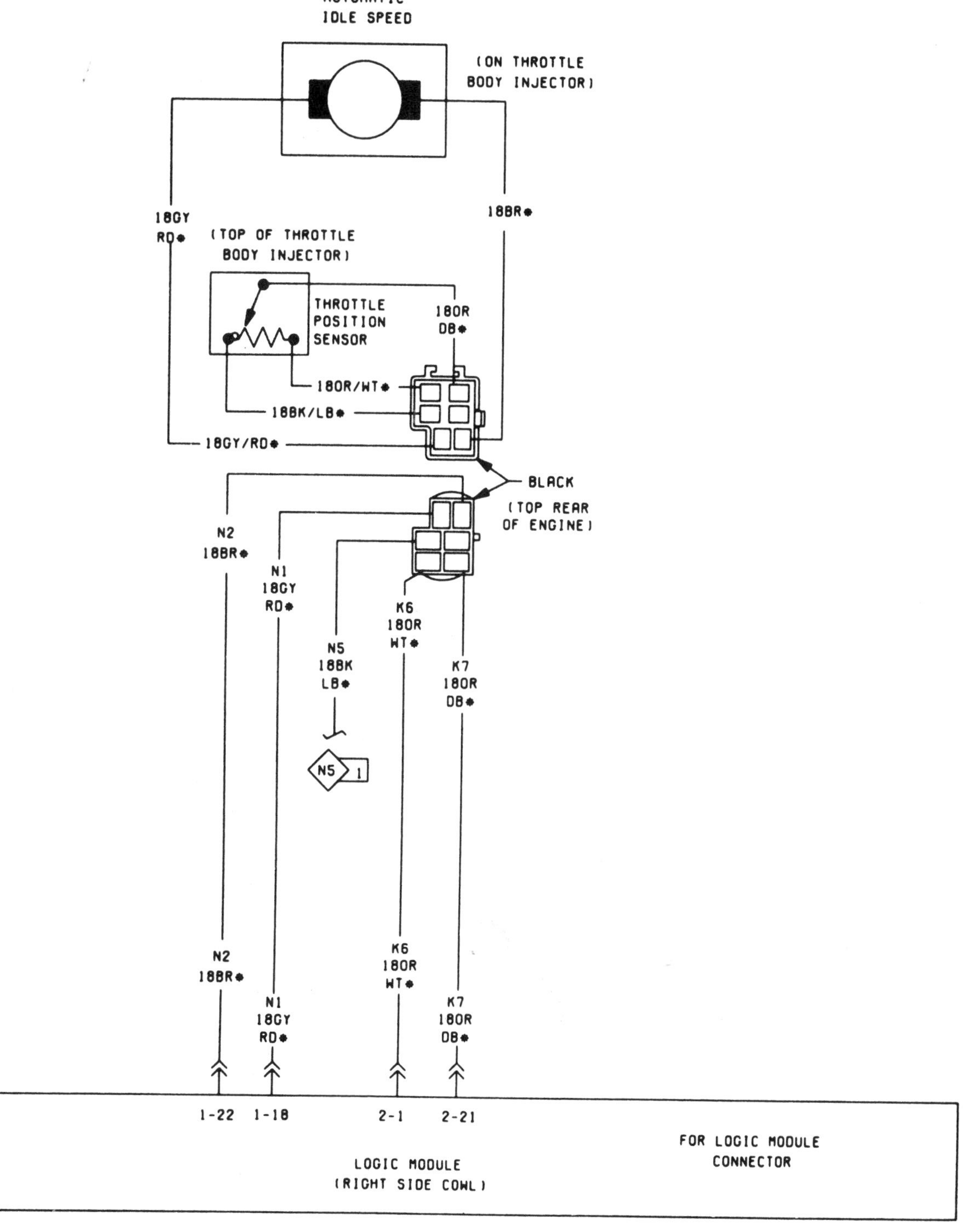

Turbocharged engine ignition system wiring diagram — typical (5 of 5)

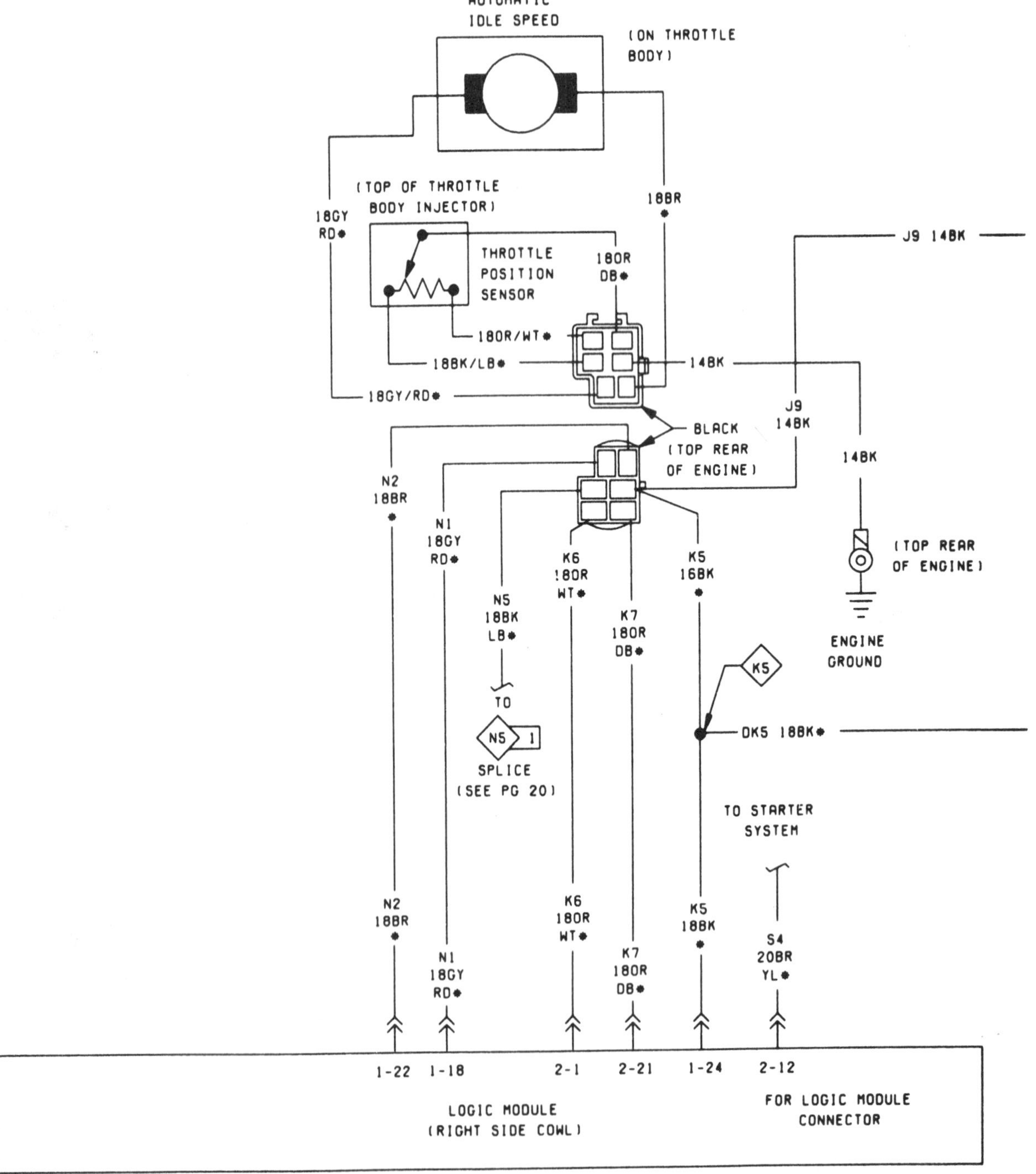

EFI equipped non-turbocharged engine ignition system wiring diagram — typical (1 of 4)

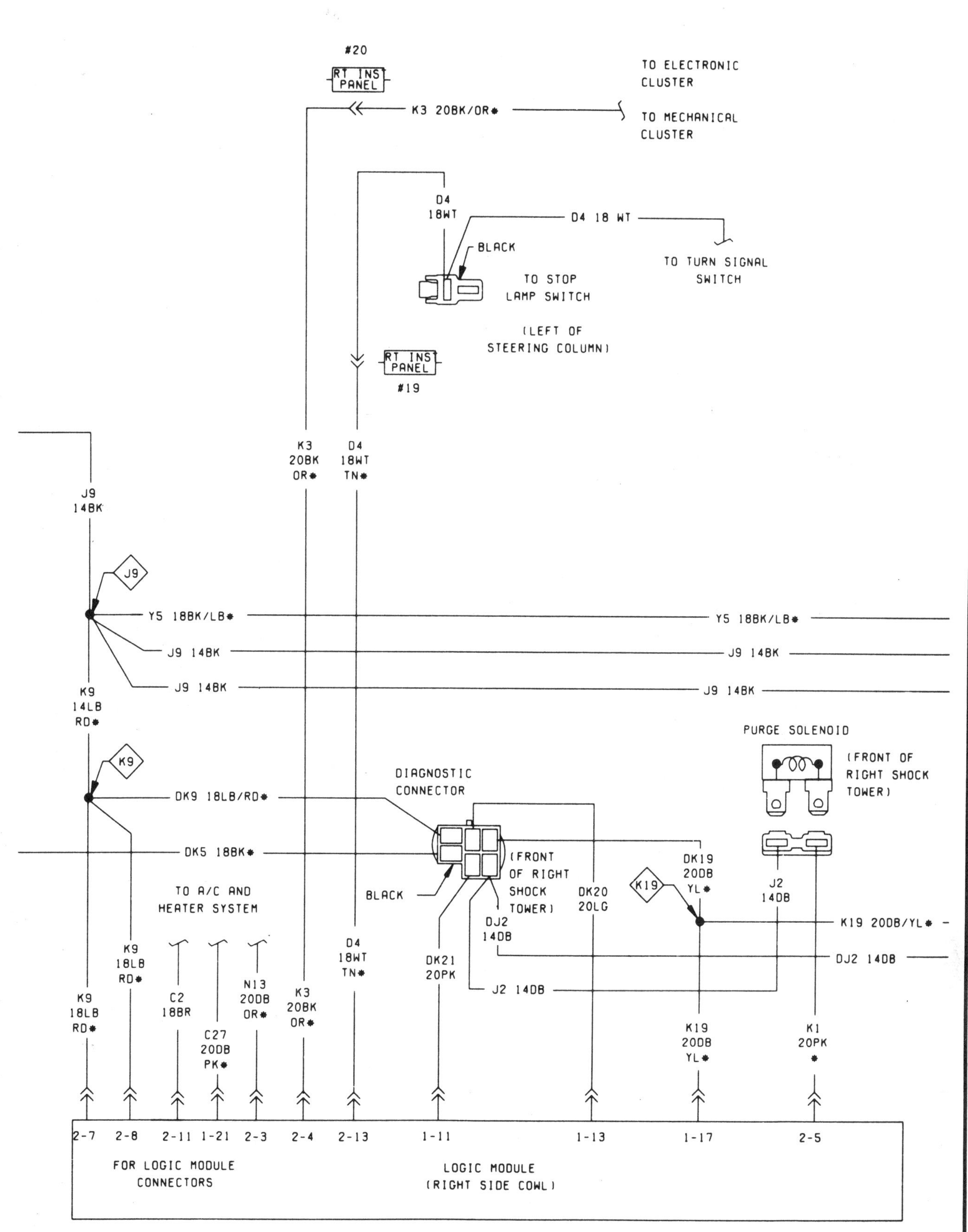

EFI equipped non-turbocharged engine ignition system wiring diagram — typical (2 of 4)

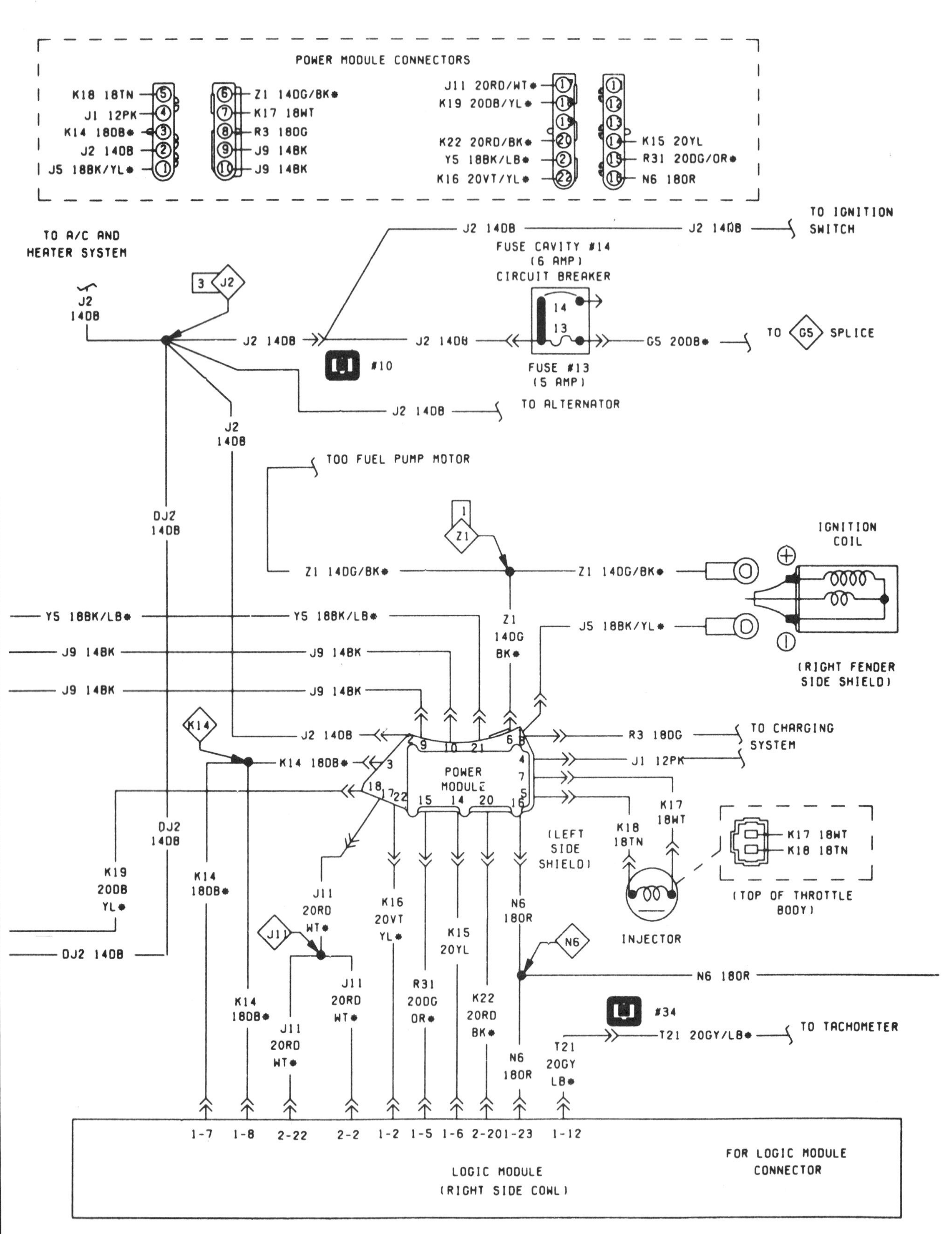

EFI equipped non-turbocharged engine ignition system wiring diagram – typical (3 of 4)

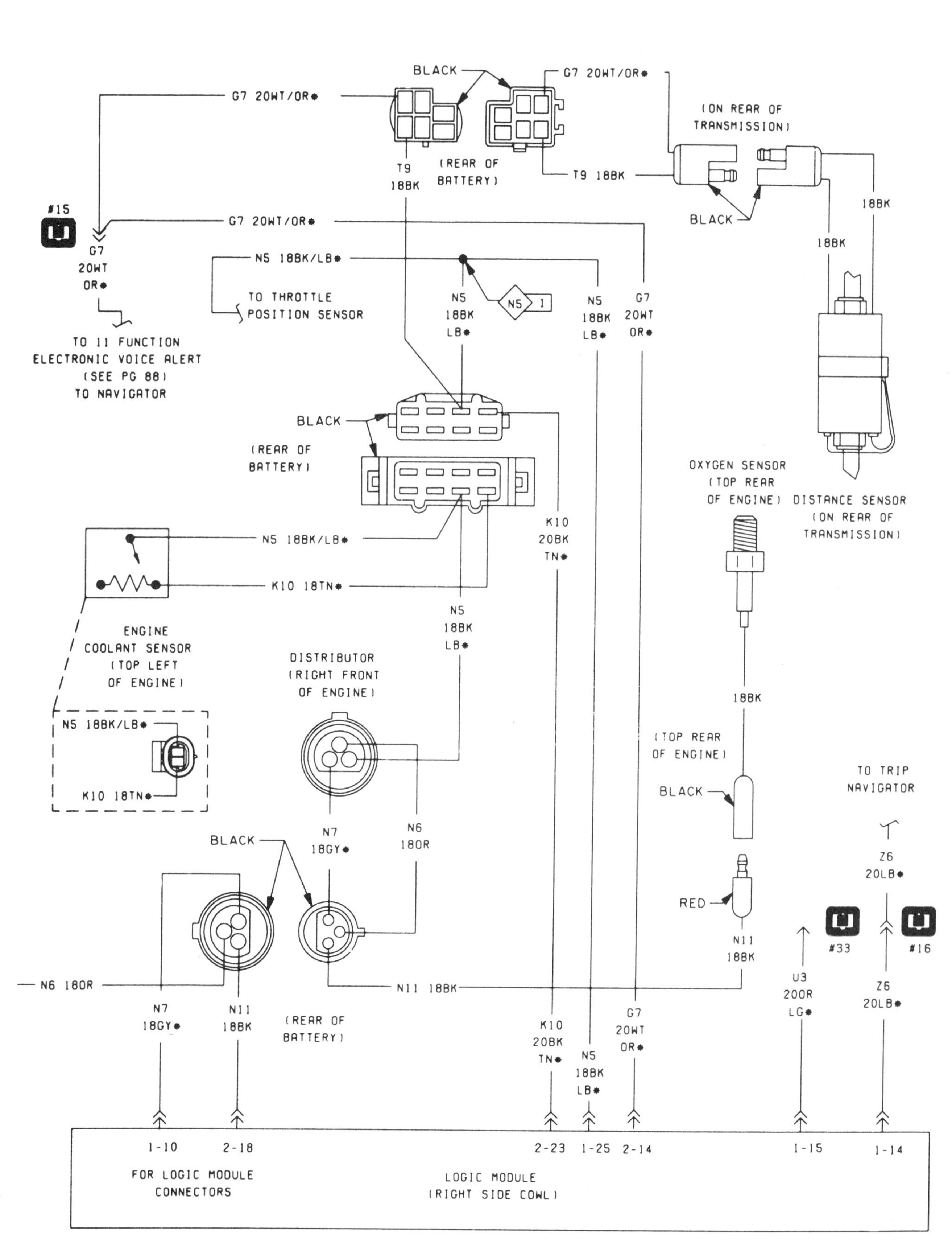

EFI equipped non-turbocharged engine ignition system wiring diagram — typical (4 of 4)

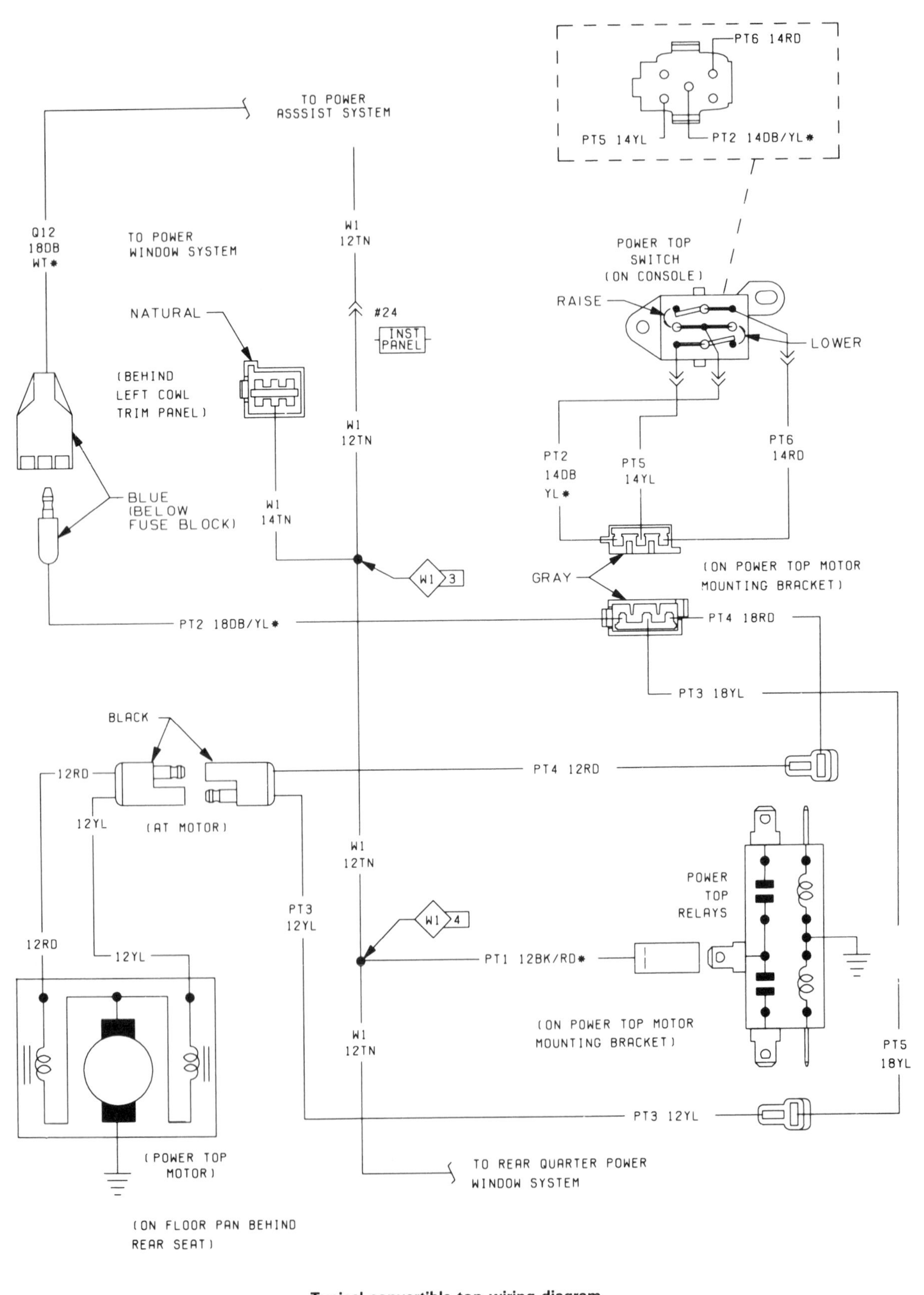

Typical convertible top wiring diagram

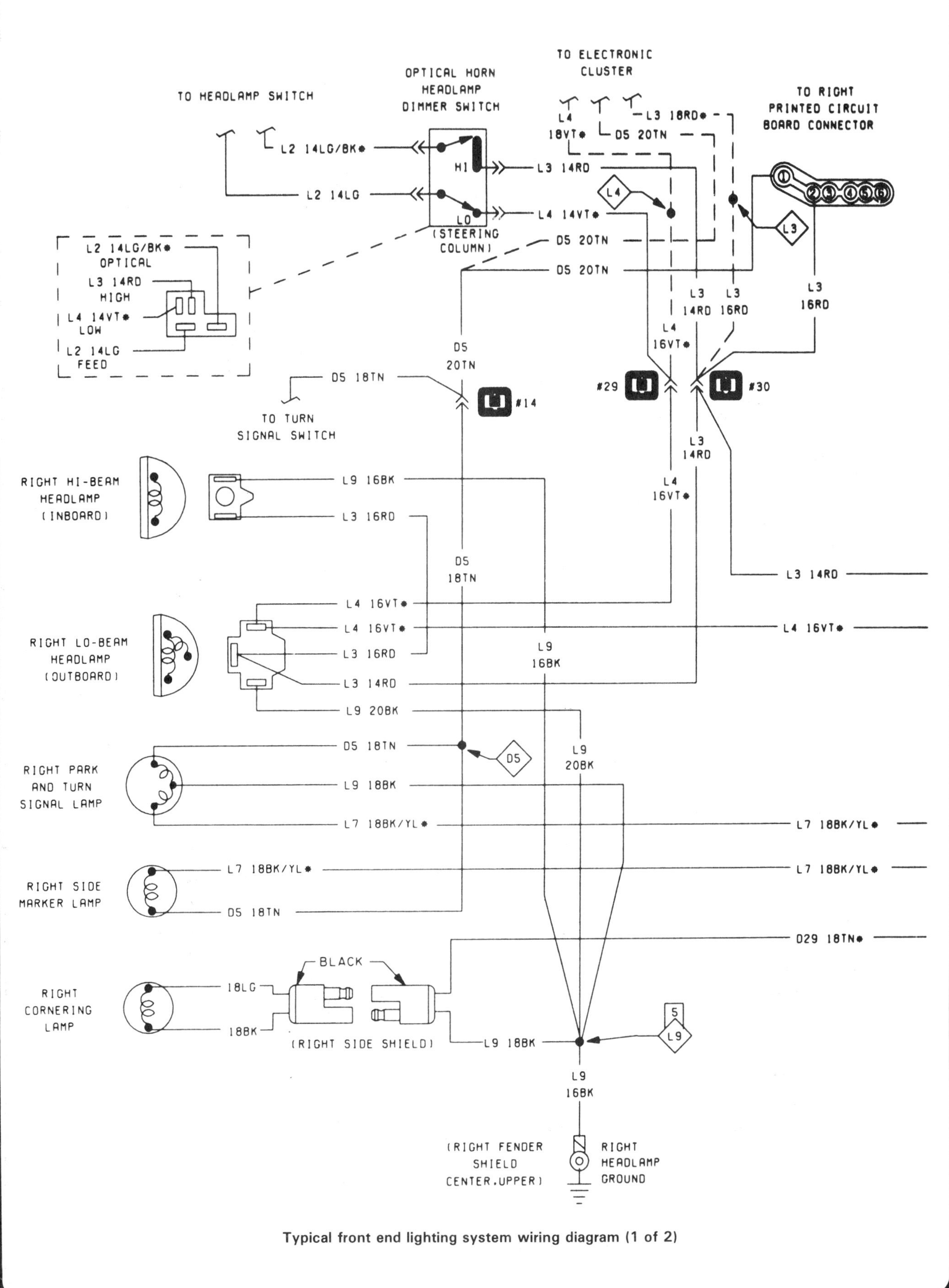

Typical front end lighting system wiring diagram (1 of 2)

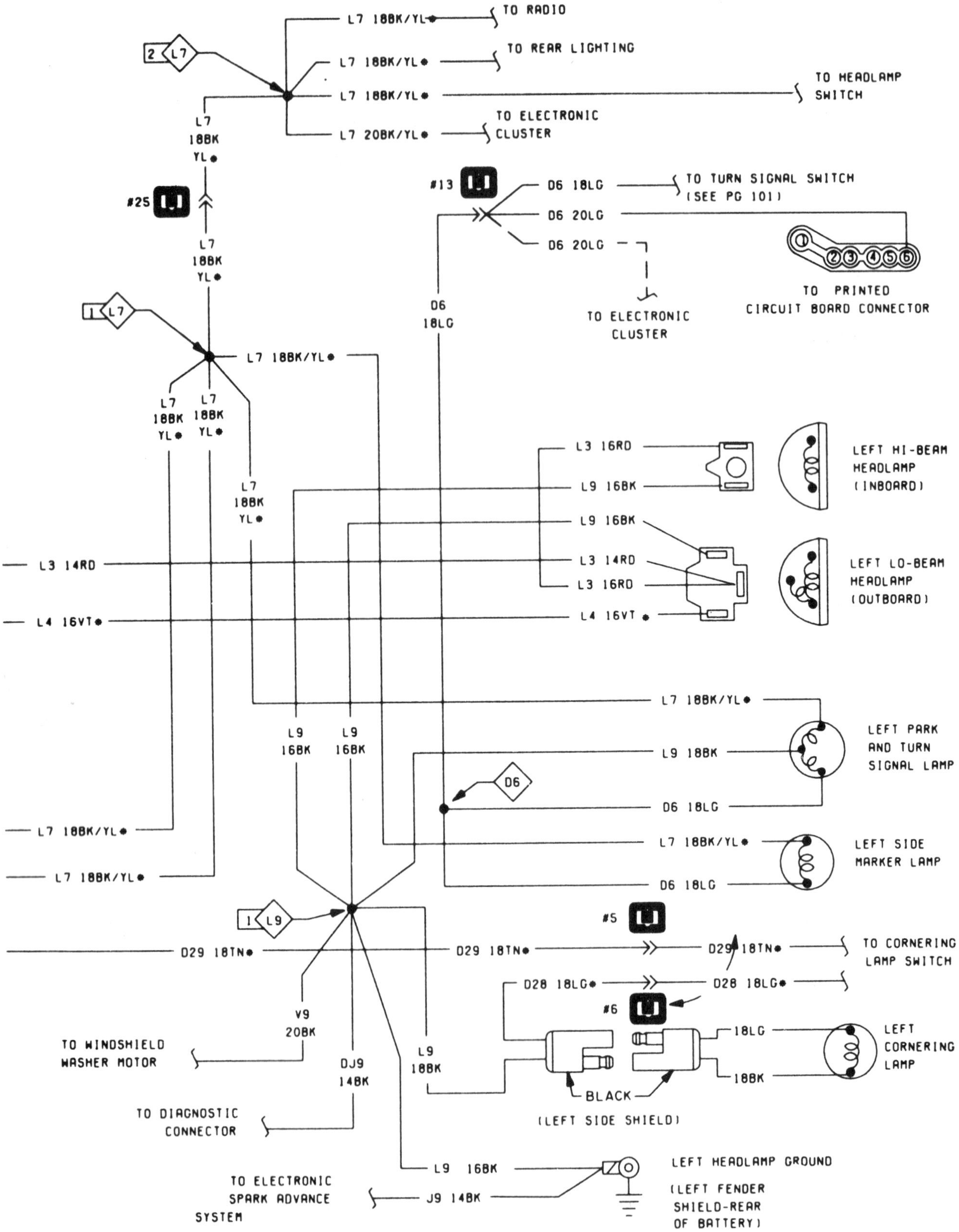

2 L7

L7 18BK/YL TO RADIO

L7 18BK/YL TO REAR LIGHTING

L7 18BK/YL TO HEADLAMP SWITCH

L7 20BK/YL TO ELECTRONIC CLUSTER

L7 18BK YL

#25

L7 18BK YL

#13

D6 18LG TO TURN SIGNAL SWITCH (SEE PG 101)

D6 20LG

D6 20LG

TO ELECTRONIC CLUSTER

1 2 3 4 5 6

TO PRINTED CIRCUIT BOARD CONNECTOR

D6 18LG

1 L7

L7 18BK/YL

L7 18BK YL

L7 18BK YL

L7 18BK YL

L3 16RD

L9 16BK

LEFT HI-BEAM HEADLAMP (INBOARD)

L9 16BK

L3 14RD

L3 14RD

L3 16RD

LEFT LO-BEAM HEADLAMP (OUTBOARD)

L4 16VT

L4 16VT

L7 18BK/YL

L9 16BK

L9 16BK

L9 18BK

LEFT PARK AND TURN SIGNAL LAMP

D6

D6 18LG

L7 18BK/YL

L7 18BK/YL

LEFT SIDE MARKER LAMP

L7 18BK/YL

D6 18LG

1 L9

#5

D29 18TN

D29 18TN

D29 18TN TO CORNERING LAMP SWITCH

D28 18LG

D28 18LG

#6

V9 20BK

TO WINDSHIELD WASHER MOTOR

DJ9 14BK

L9 18BK

18LG

18BK

LEFT CORNERING LAMP

BLACK

(LEFT SIDE SHIELD)

TO DIAGNOSTIC CONNECTOR

L9 16BK

LEFT HEADLAMP GROUND (LEFT FENDER SHIELD-REAR OF BATTERY)

TO ELECTRONIC SPARK ADVANCE SYSTEM

J9 14BK

Typical front end lighting system wiring diagram (2 of 2)

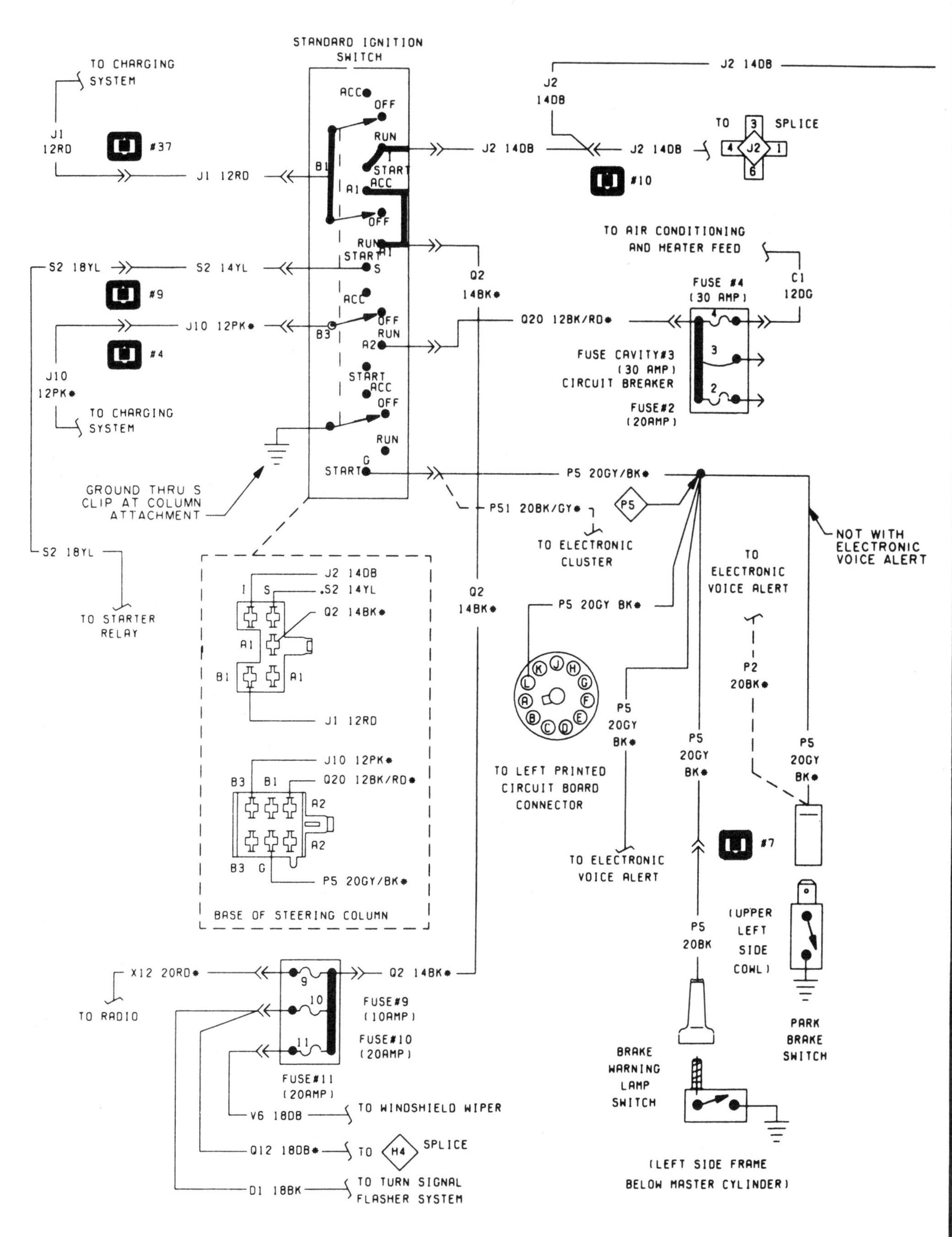

Typical ignition switch wiring diagram

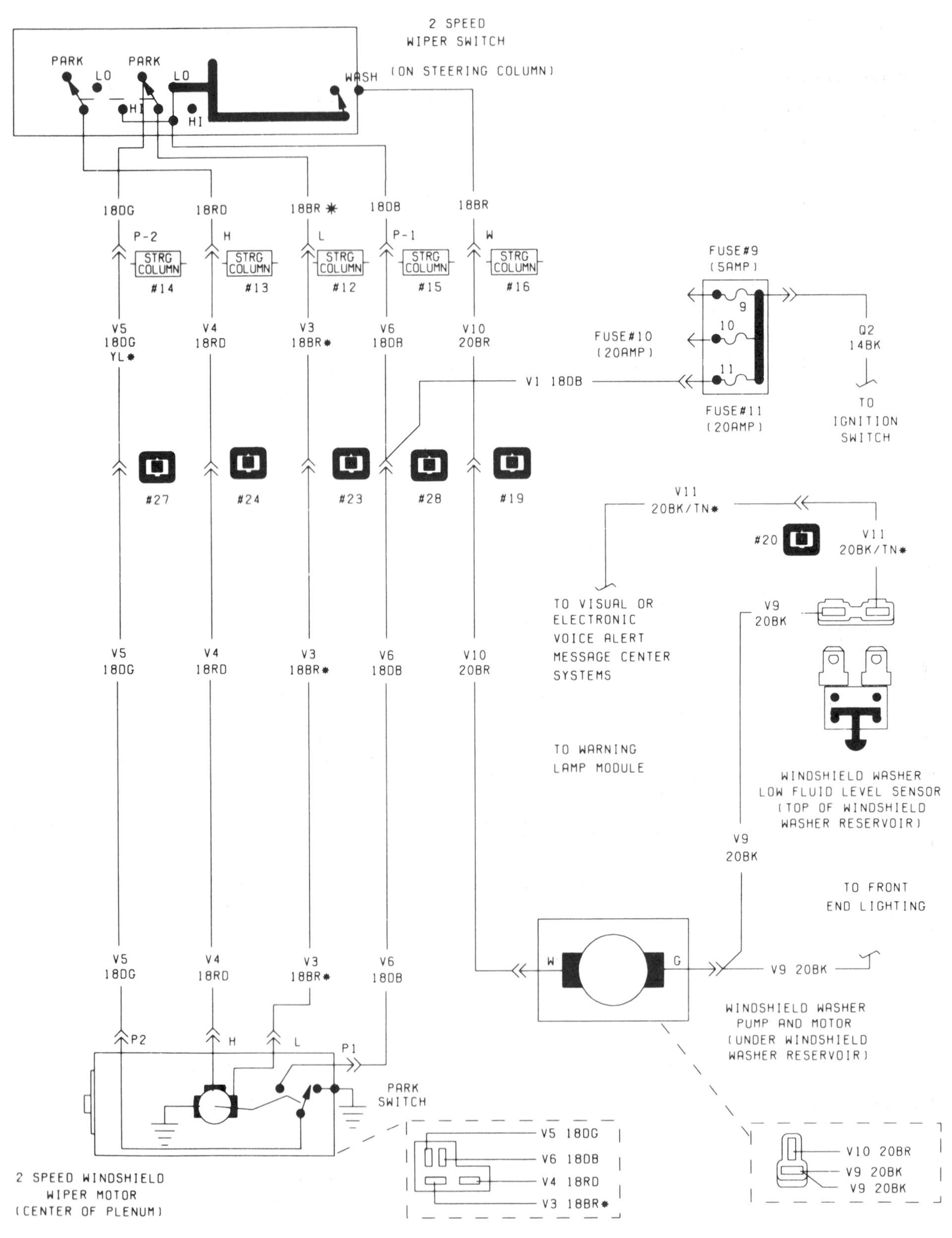

Typical wiper system wiring diagram

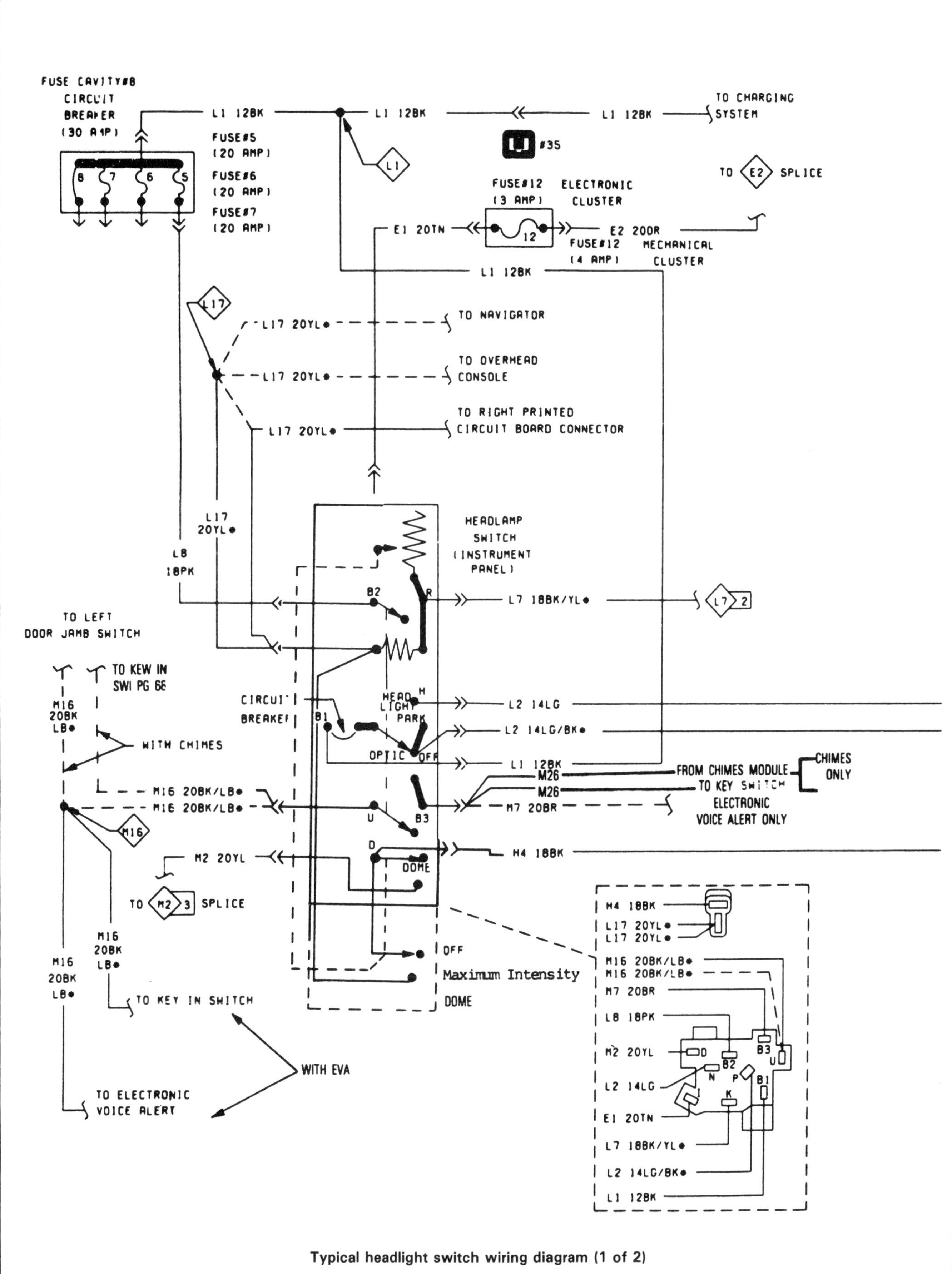

Typical headlight switch wiring diagram (1 of 2)

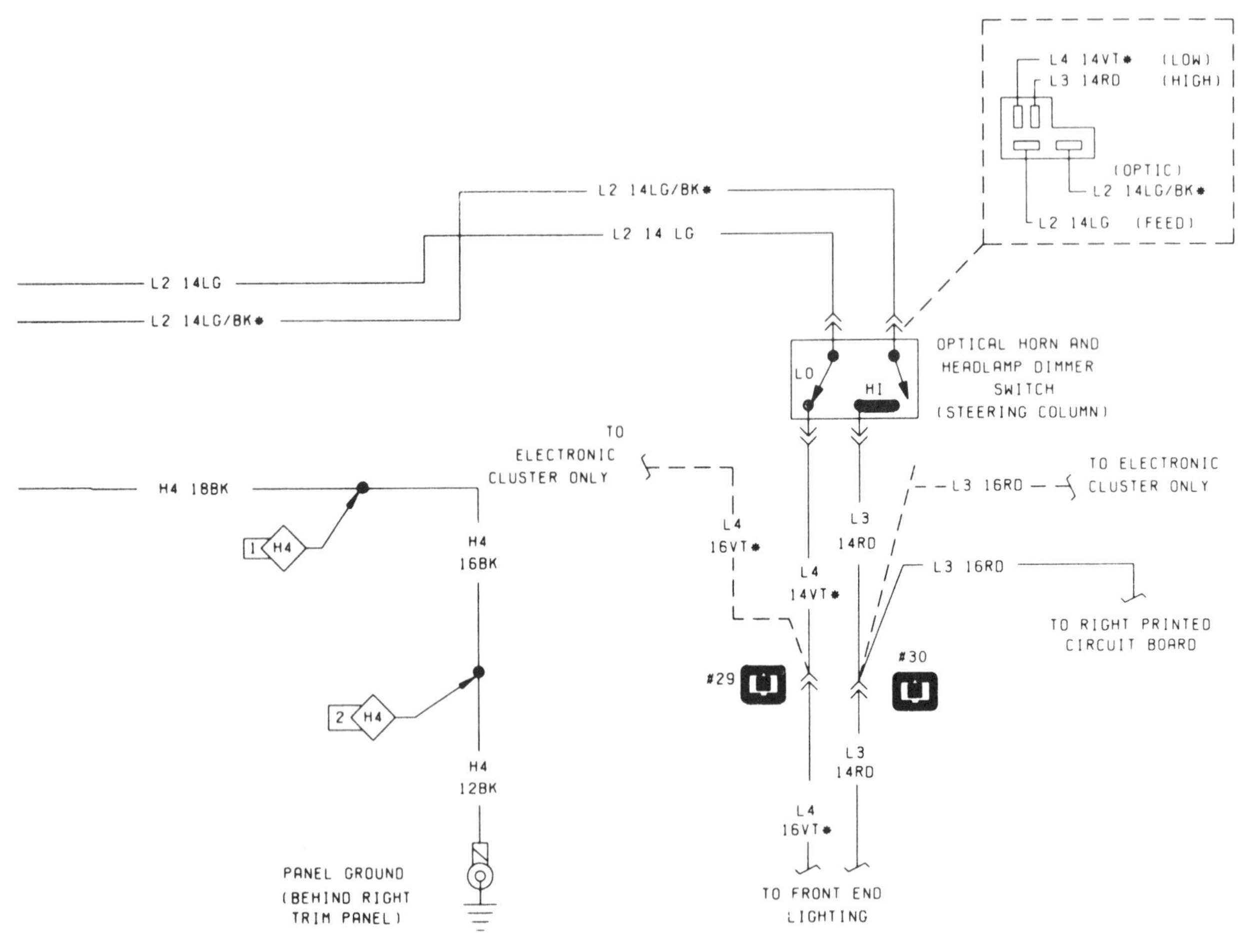

Typical headlight switch wiring diagram (2 of 2)

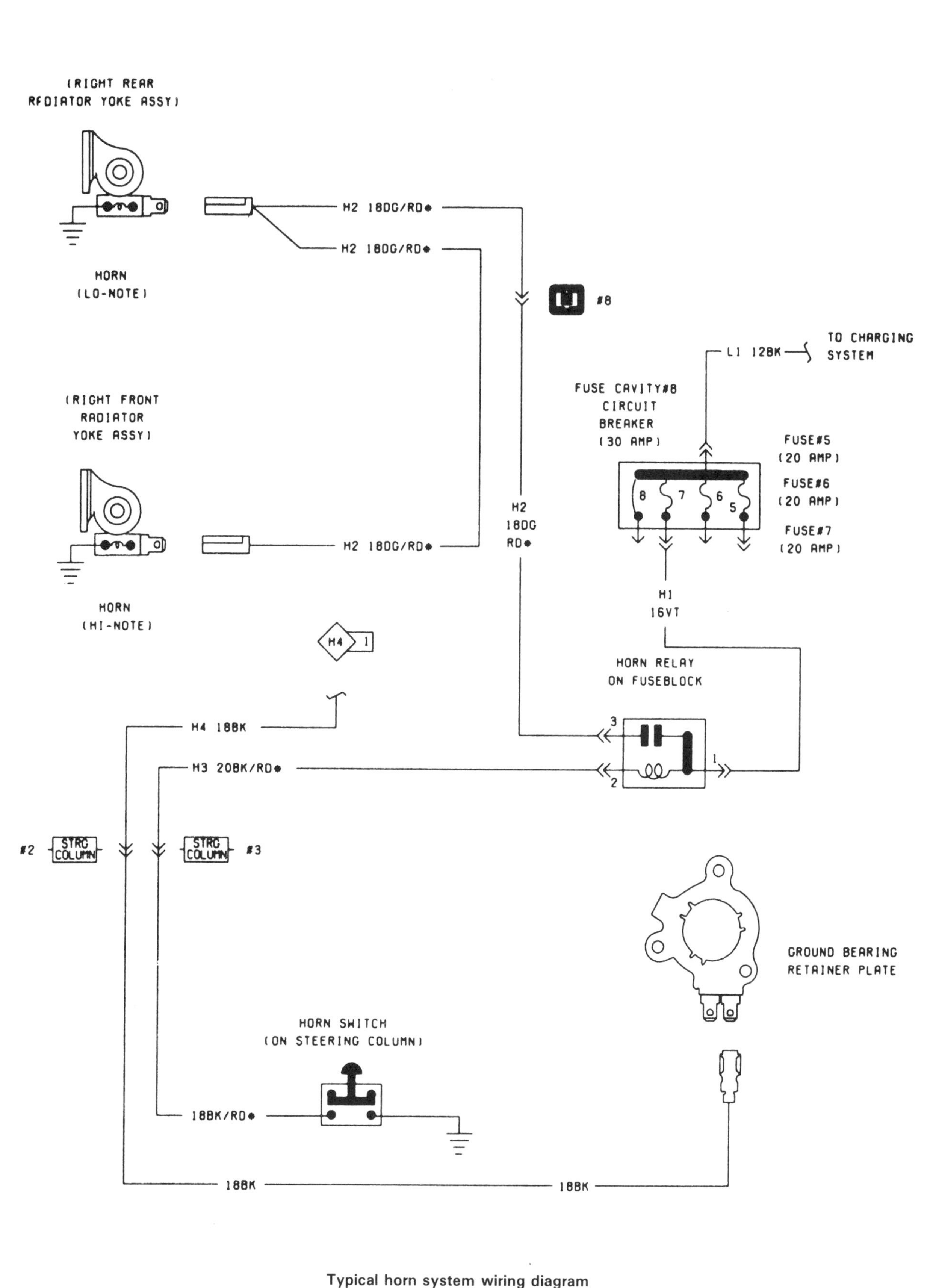

Typical horn system wiring diagram

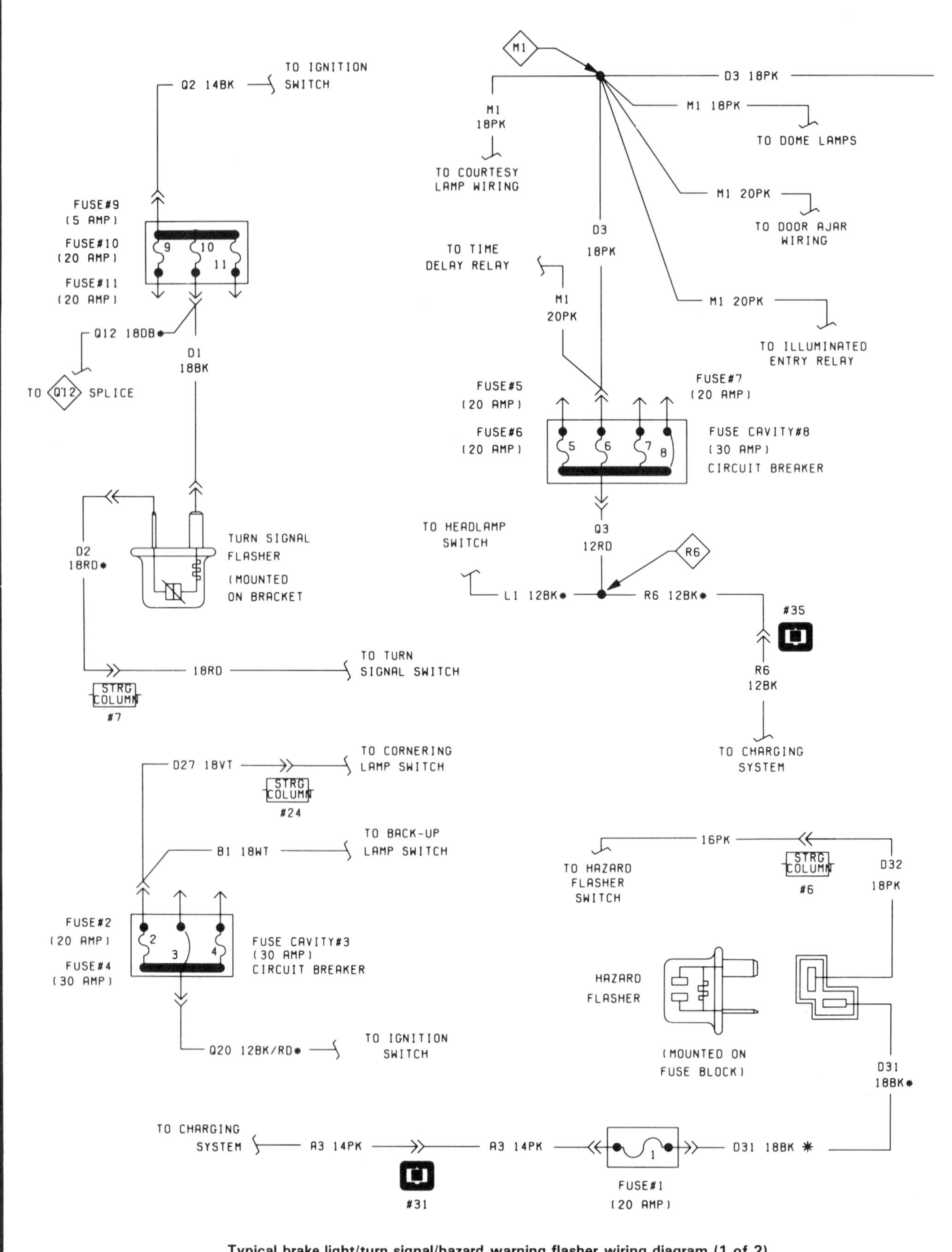

Typical brake light/turn signal/hazard warning flasher wiring diagram (1 of 2)

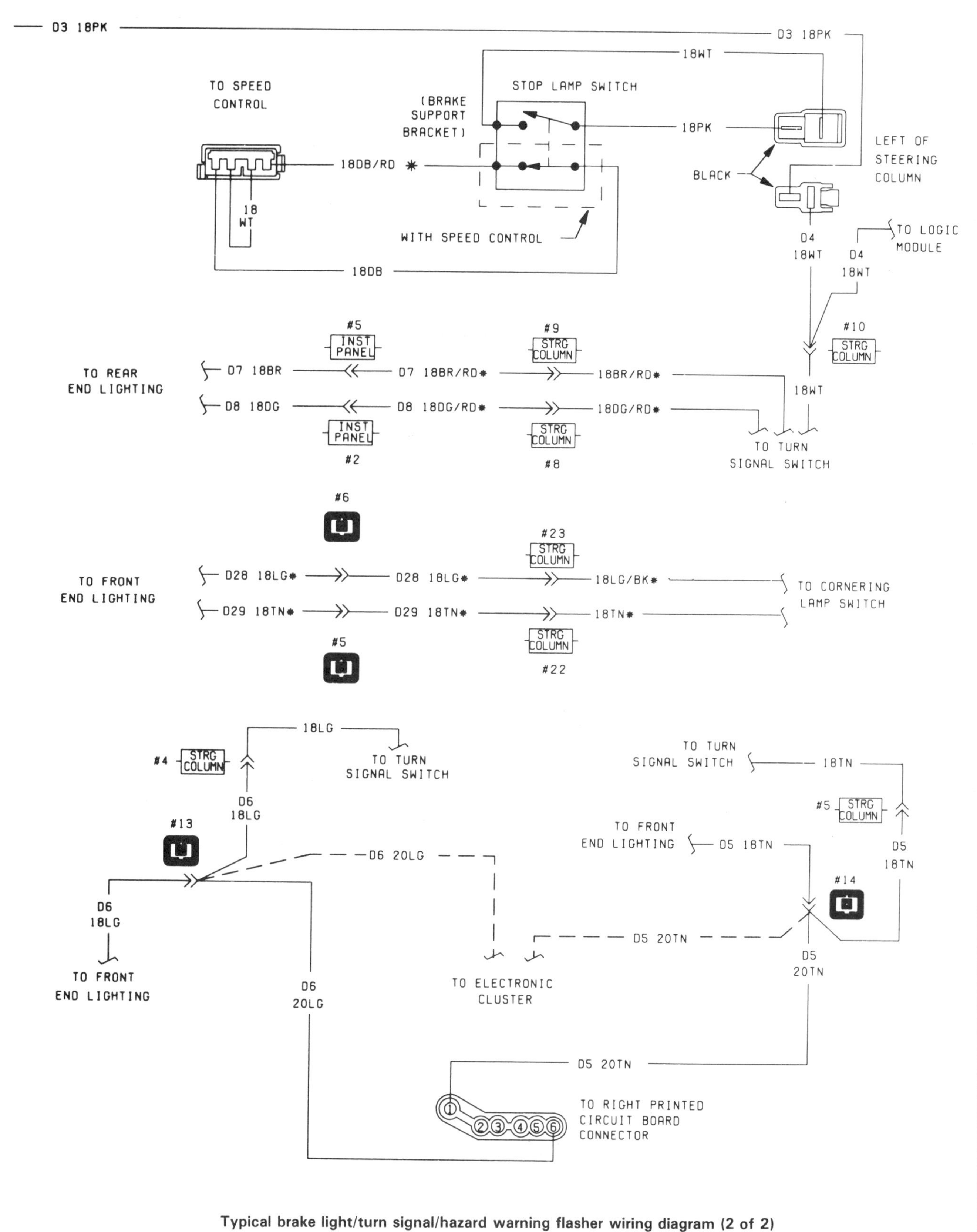

Typical brake light/turn signal/hazard warning flasher wiring diagram (2 of 2)

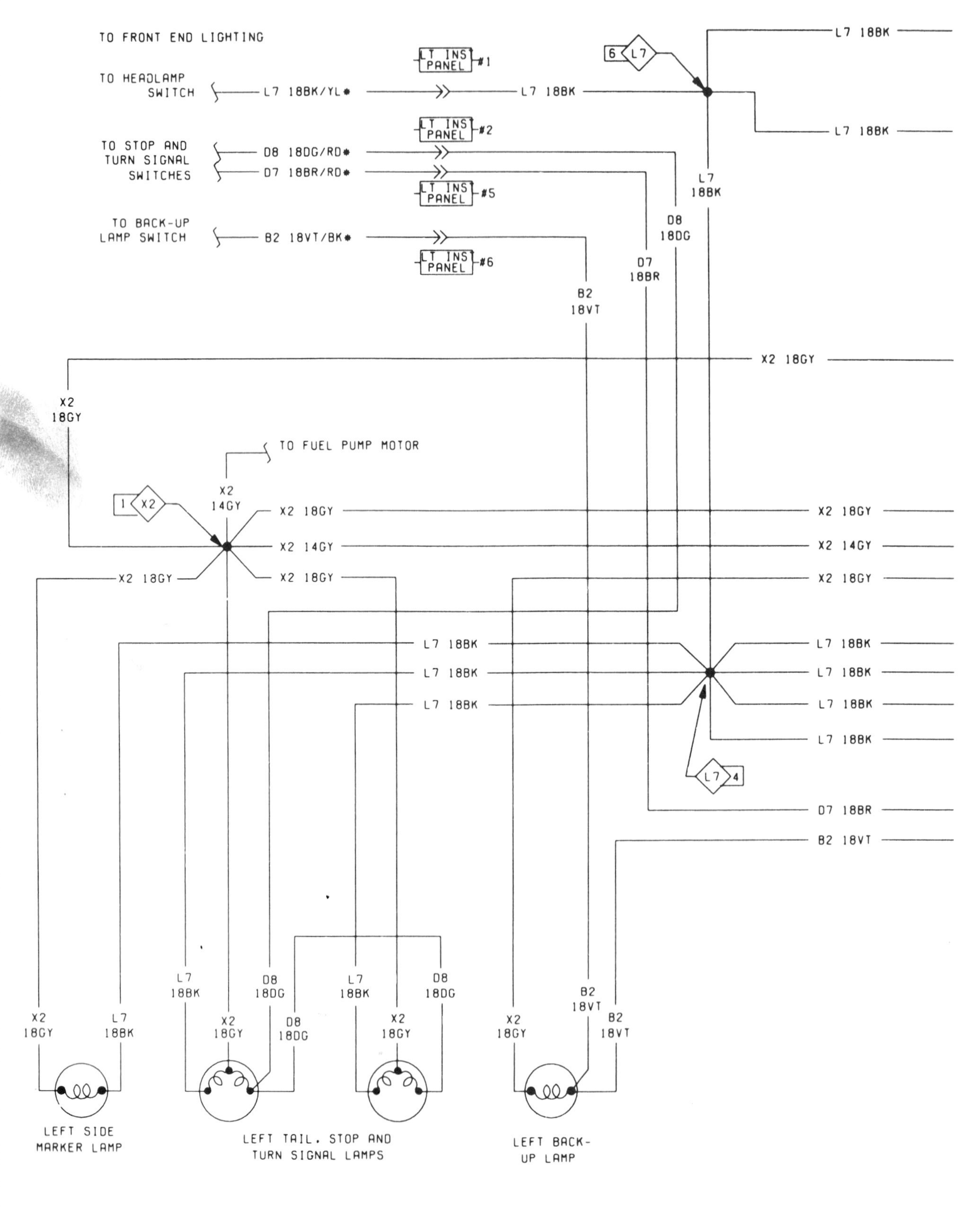

Typical rear end lighting system wiring diagram

Index

F

G

H

I

J

L

M

O

HAYNES AUTOMOTIVE MANUALS

NOTE: New manuals are added to this list on a periodic basis. If you do not see a listing for your vehicle, consult your local Haynes dealer for the latest product information.

ALFA-ROMEO

531 **Alfa Romeo Sedan & Coupe** '73 thru '80

AMC

Jeep CJ – *see JEEP (412)*
694 **Mid-size models,** Concord, Hornet, Gremlin & Spirit '70 thru '83
934 **(Renault) Alliance & Encore** all models '83 thru '87

AUDI

615 **4000** all models '80 thru '87
428 **5000** all models '77 thru '83
1117 **5000** all models '84 thru '88
207 **Fox** all models '73 thru '79

AUSTIN

049 **Healey 100/6 & 3000** Roadster '56 thru '68
Healey Sprite – *see MG Midget Roadster (265)*

BLMC

260 **1100, 1300 & Austin America** '62 thru '74
527 **Mini** all models '59 thru '69
*646 **Mini** all models '69 thru '88

BMW

276 **320i** all 4 cyl models '75 thru '83
632 **528i & 530i** all models '75 thru '80
240 **1500 thru 2002** all models except Turbo '59 thru '77
348 **2500, 2800, 3.0 & Bavaria** '69 thru '76

BUICK

Century (front wheel drive) – *see GENERAL MOTORS A-Cars (829)*
*1627 **Buick, Oldsmobile & Pontiac Full-size (Front wheel drive)** all models '85 thru '90 **Buick** Electra, LeSabre and Park Avenue; **Oldsmobile** Delta 88 Royale, Ninety Eight and Regency; **Pontiac** Bonneville
*1551 **Buick Oldsmobile & Pontiac Full-size (Rear wheel drive)** **Buick** Electra '70 thru '84, Estate '70 thru '90, LeSabre '70 thru '79 **Oldsmobile** Custom Cruiser '70 thru '90, Delta 88 '70 thru '85, Ninety-eight '70 thru '84 **Pontiac** Bonneville '70 thru '86, Catalina '70 thru '81, Grandville '70 thru '75, Parisienne '84 thu '86
627 **Mid-size** all rear-drive **Regal & Century** models with V6, V8 and Turbo '74 thru '87
Regal – *see GENERAL MOTORS (1671)*
Skyhawk – *see GENERAL MOTORS J-Cars (766)*
552 **Skylark** all X-car models '80 thru '85

CADILLAC

*751 **Cadillac Rear Wheel Drive** all gasoline models '70 thru '90
Cimarron – *see GENERAL MOTORS J-Cars (766)*

CAPRI

296 **2000 MK I Coupe** all models '71 thru '75
283 **2300 MK II Coupe** all models '74 thru '78
205 **2600 & 2800** V6 Coupe '71 thru '75
375 **2800 Mk II** V6 Coupe '75 thru '78
Mercury Capri – *see FORD Mustang (654)*

CHEVROLET

*1477 **Astro & GMC Safari Mini-vans** all models '85 thru '90
554 **Camaro** V8 all models '70 thru '81
*866 **Camaro** all models '82 thru '90
Cavalier – *see GENERAL MOTORS J-Cars (766)*
Celebrity – *see GENERAL MOTORS A-Cars (829)*
625 **Chevelle, Malibu & El Camino** all V6 & V8 models '69 thru '87
449 **Chevette & Pontiac T1000** all models '76 thru '87
550 **Citation** all models '80 thru '85
*1628 **Corsica/Beretta** all models '87 thru '90
274 **Corvette** all V8 models '68 thru '82
*1336 **Corvette** all models '84 thru '89
704 **Full-size Sedans** Caprice, Impala, Biscayne, Bel Air & Wagons, all V6 & V8 models '69 thru '90
Lumina – *see GENERAL MOTORS (1671)*
319 **Luv Pick-up** all 2WD & 4WD models '72 thru '82
626 **Monte Carlo** all V6, V8 & Turbo models '70 thru '88
241 **Nova** all V8 models '69 thru '79
*1642 **Nova and Geo Prizm** all front wheel drive models, '85 thru '90
*420 **Pick-ups '67 thru '87 – Chevrolet & GMC,** all V8 & in-line 6 cyl 2WD & 4WD models '67 thru '87
*1664 **Pick-ups '88 thru '90 – Chevrolet & GMC** all full-size (C and K) models, '88 thru '90
*1727 **Sprint & Geo Metro** '85 thru '91
*831 **S-10 & GMC S-15 Pick-ups** all models '82 thru '90
*345 **Vans – Chevrolet & GMC,** V8 & in-line 6 cyl models '68 thru '89
208 **Vega** all models except Cosworth '70 thru '77

CHRYSLER

*1337 **Chrysler & Plymouth Mid-size** front wheel drive '82 thru '89
K-Cars – *see DODGE Aries (723)*
Laser – *see DODGE Daytona (1140)*

DATSUN

402 **200SX** all models '77 thru '79
647 **200SX** all models '80 thru '83
228 **B-210** all models '73 thru '78
525 **210** all models '78 thru '82
206 **240Z, 260Z & 280Z** Coupe & 2+2 '70 thru '78
563 **280ZX** Coupe & 2+2 '79 thru '83
300ZX – *see NISSAN (1137)*
679 **310** all models '78 thru '82
123 **510 & PL521 Pick-up** '68 thru '73
430 **510** all models '78 thru '81
372 **610** all models '72 thru '76
277 **620 Series Pick-up** all models '73 thru '79
720 Series Pick-up – *see NISSAN Pick-ups (771)*
376 **810/Maxima** all gasoline models '77 thru '84
124 **1200** all models '70 thru '73
368 **F10** all models '76 thru '79
Pulsar – *see NISSAN (876)*
Sentra – *see NISSAN (982)*
Stanza – *see NISSAN (981)*

DODGE

*723 **Aries & Plymouth Reliant** all models '81 thru '89
*1231 **Caravan & Plymouth Voyager Mini-Vans** all models '84 thru '89
699 **Challenger & Plymouth Saporro** all models '78 thru '83
236 **Colt** all models '71 thru '77
419 **Colt (rear wheel drive)** all models '77 thru '80
610 **Colt & Plymouth Champ (front wheel drive)** all models '78 thru '87
*556 **D50 & Plymouth Arrow Pick-ups** '79 thru '88
*1668 **Dakota Pick-up** all models '87 thru '90
234 **Dart & Plymouth Valiant** all 6 cyl models '67 thru '76
*1140 **Daytona & Chrysler Laser** all models '84 thru '89
*545 **Omni & Plymouth Horizon** all models '78 thru '90
*912 **Pick-ups** all full-size models '74 thru '90
*349 **Vans – Dodge & Plymouth** V8 & 6 cyl models '71 thru '89

FIAT

080 **124 Sedan & Wagon** all ohv & dohc models '66 thru '75
094 **124 Sport Coupe & Spider** '68 thru '78
310 **131 & Brava** all models '75 thru '81
479 **Strada** all models '79 thru '82
273 **X1/9** all models '74 thru '80

FORD

*1476 **Aerostar Mini-vans** all models '86 thru '90
788 **Bronco and Pick-ups** '73 thru '79
*880 **Bronco and Pick-ups** '80 thru '90
014 **Cortina MK II** all models except Lotus '66 thru '70
295 **Cortina MK III** 1600 & 2000 ohc '70 thru '76
268 **Courier Pick-up** all models '72 thru '82
789 **Escort & Mercury Lynx** all models '81 thru '90
560 **Fairmont & Mercury Zephyr** all in-line & V8 models '78 thru '83
334 **Fiesta** all models '77 thru '80
754 **Ford & Mercury Full-size,** Ford LTD & Mercury Marquis ('75 thru '82); Ford Custom 500, Country Squire, Crown Victoria & Mercury Colony Park ('75 thru '87); Ford LTD Crown Victoria & Mercury Gran Marquis ('83 thru '87)
359 **Granada & Mercury Monarch** all in-line, 6 cyl & V8 models '75 thru '80
773 **Ford & Mercury Mid-size,** Ford Thunderbird & Mercury Cougar ('75 thru '82); Ford LTD & Mercury Marquis ('83 thru '86); Ford Torino, Gran Torino, Elite, Ranchero pick-up, LTD II, Mercury Montego, Comet, XR-7 & Lincoln Versailles ('75 thru '86)
*654 **Mustang & Mercury Capri** all models including Turbo '79 thru '90
357 **Mustang V8** all models '64-1/2 thru '73
231 **Mustang II** all 4 cyl, V6 & V8 models '74 thru '78
204 **Pinto** all models '70 thru '74
649 **Pinto & Mercury Bobcat** all models '75 thru '80
*1026 **Ranger & Bronco II** all gasoline models '83 thru '89
*1421 **Taurus & Mercury Sable** '86 thru '90
*1418 **Tempo & Mercury Topaz** all gasoline models '84 thru '89
1338 **Thunderbird & Mercury Cougar/XR7** '83 thru '88
*1725 **Thunderbird & Mercury Cougar** '89 and '90
*344 **Vans** all V8 Econoline models '69 thru '90

GENERAL MOTORS

*829 **A-Cars** – Chevrolet Celebrity, Buick Century, Pontiac 6000 & Oldsmobile Cutlass Ciera all models '82 thru '89
*766 **J-Cars** – Chevrolet Cavalier, Pontiac J-2000, Oldsmobile Firenza, Buick Skyhawk & Cadillac Cimarron all models '82 thru '90
*1420 **N-Cars** – Buick Somerset '85 thru '87; Pontiac Grand Am and Oldsmobile Calais '85 thru '90; Buick Skylark '86 thru '90
*1671 **GM: Buick** Regal, **Chevrolet** Lumina, **Oldsmobile** Cutlass Supreme, **Pontiac** Grand Prix, all front wheel drive models '88 thru '90

GEO

Metro – *see CHEVROLET Sprint (1727)*
Tracker – *see SUZUKI Samurai (1626)*
Prizm – *see CHEVROLET Nova (1642)*

GMC

Safari – *see CHEVROLET ASTRO (1477)*
Vans & Pick-ups – *see CHEVROLET (420, 831, 345, 1664)*

(continued on next page)

** Listings shown with an asterisk (*) indicate model coverage as of this printing. These titles will be periodically updated to include later model years — consult your Haynes dealer for more information.*

Haynes North America, Inc., P.O. Box 978, Newbury Park, CA 91320 • (818) 889-5400 • (805) 498-6703

HAYNES AUTOMOTIVE MANUALS

(continued from previous page)

NOTE: New manuals are added to this list on a periodic basis. If you do not see a listing for your vehicle, consult your local Haynes dealer for the latest product information.

HONDA
138 **360, 600 & Z** Coupe all models '67 thru '75
351 **Accord CVCC** all models '76 thru '83
*1221 **Accord** all models '84 thru '89
160 **Civic 1200** all models '73 thru '79
633 **Civic 1300 & 1500 CVCC** all models '80 thru '83
297 **Civic 1500 CVCC** all models '75 thru '79
*1227 **Civic** all models '84 thru '90
*601 **Prelude CVCC** all models '79 thru '89

HYUNDAI
*1552 **Excel** all models '86 thru '89

ISUZU
*1641 **Trooper & Pick-up**, all gasoline models '81 thru '90

JAGUAR
098 **MK I & II**, 240 & 340 Sedans '55 thru '69
*242 **XJ6** all 6 cyl models '68 thru '86
*478 **XJ12 & XJS** all 12 cyl models '72 thru '85
140 **XK-E** 3.8 & 4.2 all 6 cyl models '61 thru '72

JEEP
*1553 **Cherokee, Comanche & Wagoneer Limited** all models '84 thru '89
412 **CJ** all models '49 thru '86

LADA
*413 **1200, 1300. 1500 & 1600** all models including Riva '74 thru '86

LAND ROVER
314 **Series II, IIA, & III** all 4 cyl gasoline models '58 thru '86
529 **Diesel** all models '58 thru '80

MAZDA
648 **626** Sedan & Coupe (rear wheel drive) all models '79 thru '82
*1082 **626 & MX-6 (front wheel drive)** all models '83 thru '90
*267 **B1600, B1800 & B2000 Pick-ups** '72 thru '90
370 **GLC Hatchback (rear wheel drive)** all models '77 thru '83
757 **GLC (front wheel drive)** all models '81 thru '86
109 **RX2** all models '71 thru '75
096 **RX3** all models '72 thru '76
460 **RX-7** all models '79 thru '85
*1419 **RX-7** all models '86 thru '89

MERCEDES-BENZ
*1643 **190 Series** all four-cylinder gasoline models, '84 thru '88
346 **230, 250 & 280** Sedan, Coupe & Roadster all 6 cyl sohc models '68 thru '72
983 **280 123 Series** all gasoline models '77 thru '81
698 **350 & 450** Sedan, Coupe & Roadster all models '71 thru '80
697 **Diesel 123 Series** 200D, 220D, 240D, 240TD, 300D, 300CD, 300TD, 4- & 5-cyl incl. Turbo '76 thru '85

MERCURY
See FORD Listing

MG
475 **MGA** all models '56 thru '62
111 **MGB** Roadster & GT Coupe all models '62 thru '80
265 **MG Midget & Austin Healey Sprite Roadster** '58 thru '80

MITSUBISHI
*1669 **Cordia, Tredia, Galant, Precis & Mirage** '83 thru '90
Pick-up – *see Dodge D-50 (556)*

MORRIS
074 **(Austin) Marina 1.8** all models '71 thru '80
024 **Minor 1000** sedan & wagon '56 thru '71

NISSAN
1137 **300ZX** all Turbo & non-Turbo models '84 thru '89
*1341 **Maxima** all models '85 thru '89
*771 **Pick-ups/Pathfinder** gas models '80 thru '88
*876 **Pulsar** all models '83 thru '86
*982 **Sentra** all models '82 thru '90
*981 **Stanza** all models '82 thru '90

OLDSMOBILE
Custom Cruiser – *see BUICK Full-size (1551)*
658 **Cutlass** all standard gasoline V6 & V8 models '74 thru '88
Cutlass Ciera – *see GENERAL MOTORS A-Cars (829)*
Cutlass Supreme – *see GENERAL MOTORS (1671)*
Firenza – *see GENERAL MOTORS J-Cars (766)*
Ninety-eight – *see BUICK Full-size (1551)*
Omega – *see PONTIAC Phoenix & Omega (551)*

PEUGEOT
161 **504** all gasoline models '68 thru '79
663 **504** all diesel models '74 thru '83

PLYMOUTH
425 **Arrow** all models '76 thru '80
For all other PLYMOUTH titles, see DODGE listing.

PONTIAC
T1000 – *see CHEVROLET Chevette (449)*
J-2000 – *see GENERAL MOTORS J-Cars (766)*
6000 – *see GENERAL MOTORS A-Cars (829)*
1232 **Fiero** all models '84 thru '88
555 **Firebird** all V8 models except Turbo '70 thru '81
*867 **Firebird** all models '82 thru '89
Full-size Rear Wheel Drive – *see Buick, Oldsmobile, Pontiac Full-size (1551)*
Grand Prix – *see GENERAL MOTORS (1671)*
551 **Phoenix & Oldsmobile Omega** all X-car models '80 thru '84

PORSCHE
*264 **911** all Coupe & Targa models except Turbo & Carrera 4 '65 thru '89
239 **914** all 4 cyl models '69 thru '76
397 **924** all models including Turbo '76 thru '82
*1027 **944** all models including Turbo '83 thru '89

RENAULT
141 **5 Le Car** all models '76 thru '83
079 **8 & 10** all models with 58.4 cu in engines '62 thru '72
097 **12 Saloon & Estate** all models 1289 cc engines '70 thru '80
768 **15 & 17** all models '73 thru '79
081 **16** all models 89.7 cu in & 95.5 cu in engines '65 thru '72
598 **18i & Sportwagon** all models '81 thru '86
Alliance & Encore – *see AMC (934)*
984 **Fuego** all models '82 thru '85

ROVER
085 **3500 & 3500S Sedan** 215 cu in engines '68 thru '76
*365 **3500 SDI V8** all models '76 thru '85

SAAB
198 **95 & 96** V4 all models '66 thru '75
247 **99** all models including Turbo '69 thru '80
*980 **900** all models including Turbo '79 thru '88

SUBARU
237 **1100, 1300, 1400 & 1600** all models '71 thru '79
*681 **1600 & 1800** 2WD & 4WD all models '80 thru '89

SUZUKI
*1626 **Samurai/Sidekick and Geo Tracker** all models '86 thru '89

TOYOTA
*1023 **Camry** all models '83 thru '90
150 **Carina Sedan** all models '71 thru '74
229 **Celica ST, GT & liftback** all models '71 thru '77
437 **Celica** all models '78 thru '81
*935 **Celica** all models except front-wheel drive and Supra '82 thru '85
680 **Celica Supra** all models '79 thru '81
1139 **Celica Supra** all in-line 6-cylinder models '82 thru '86
361 **Corolla** all models '75 thru '79
961 **Corolla** all models (rear wheel drive) '80 thru '87
*1025 **Corolla** all models (front wheel drive) '84 thru '91
*636 **Corolla Tercel** all models '80 thru '82
230 **Corona & MK II** all 4 cyl sohc models '69 thru '74
360 **Corona** all models '74 thru '82
*532 **Cressida** all models '78 thru '82
313 **Land Cruiser** all models '68 thru '82
200 **MK II** all 6 cyl models '72 thru '76
*1339 **MR2** all models '85 thru '87
304 **Pick-up** all models '69 thru '78
*656 **Pick-up** all models '79 thru '90

TRIUMPH
112 **GT6 & Vitesse** all models '62 thru '74
113 **Spitfire** all models '62 thru '81
028 **TR2, 3, 3A, & 4A** Roadsters '52 thru '67
031 **TR250 & 6** Roadsters '67 thru '76
322 **TR7** all models '75 thru '81

VW
091 **411 & 412** all 103 cu in models '68 thru '73
159 **Beetle & Karmann Ghia** all models '54 thru '79
238 **Dasher** all gasoline models '74 thru '81
*884 **Rabbit, Jetta, Scirocco, & Pick-up** all gasoline models '74 thru '89 & **Convertible** '80 thru '89
451 **Rabbit, Jetta & Pick-up** all diesel models '77 thru '84
082 **Transporter 1600** all models '68 thru '79
226 **Transporter 1700, 1800 & 2000** all models '72 thru '79
084 **Type 3 1500 & 1600** all models '63 thru '73
1029 **Vanagon** all air-cooled models '80 thru '83

VOLVO
203 **120, 130 Series & 1800 Sports** '61 thru '73
129 **140 Series** all models '66 thru '74
244 **164** all models '68 thru '75
*270 **240 Series** all models '74 thru '90
400 **260 Series** all models '75 thru '82
*1550 **740 & 760 Series** all models '82 thru '88

SPECIAL MANUALS
1479 **Automotive Body Repair & Painting Manual**
1654 **Automotive Electrical Manual**
1480 **Automotive Heating & Air Conditioning Manual**
1763 **Ford Engine Overhaul Manual**
482 **Fuel Injection Manual**
1666 **Small Engine Repair Manual**
299 **SU Carburetors** thru '88
393 **Weber Carburetors** thru '79
300 **Zenith/Stromberg CD Carburetors** thru '76

See your dealer for other available titles

4-1-91

Over 100 Haynes motorcycle manuals also available

** Listings shown with an asterisk (*) indicate model coverage as of this printing. These titles will be periodically updated to include later model years — consult your Haynes dealer for more information.*

Haynes North America, Inc., P.O. Box 978, Newbury Park, CA 91320 • (818) 889-5400 • (805) 498-6703